FASHION MERCHANDISING

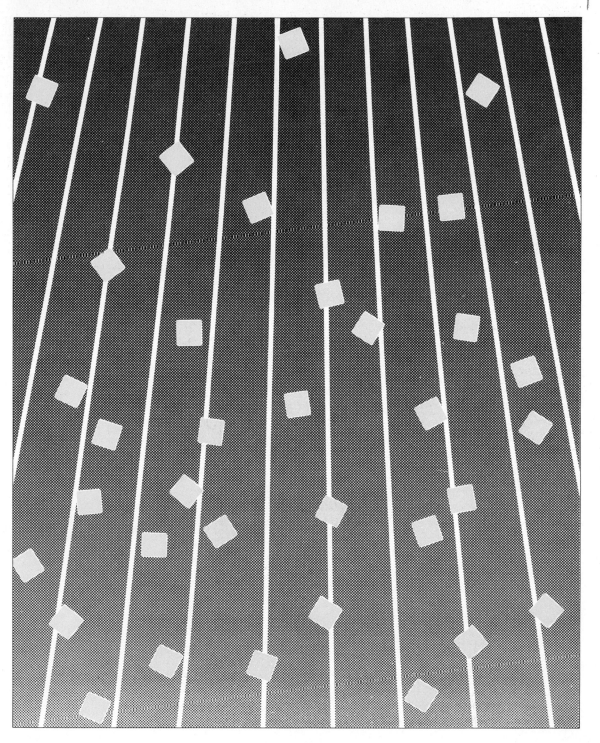

The Gregg/McGraw-Hill Marketing Series

Burke *Advertising in the Marketplace,* Second Edition

Corbman *Textiles: Fiber to Fabric,* Fifth Edition

Gillespie and Hecht *Retail Business Management,* Second Edition

Reece and Manning *Wilson RV An In-Basket Simulation for Management and Supervisory Development*

Troxell and Stone *Fashion Merchandising,* Third Edition

FASHION MERCHANDISING
THIRD EDITION

Mary D. Troxell

Consultant
Fashion Merchandising
Training Programs
Sarasota, Florida

Elaine Stone

Assistant Professor
Fashion Institute of Technology
New York, New York

Gregg Division
McGraw-Hill Book Company

New York   Atlanta   Dallas   St. Louis   San Francisco
Auckland   Bogotá   Guatemala   Hamburg   Johannesburg   Lisbon
London   Madrid   Mexico   Montreal   New Delhi   Panamá   Paris
San Juan   São Paulo   Singapore   Sydney   Tokyo   Toronto

Sponsoring Editor/Mary Alice McGarry
Editing Supervisor/Mitsy Kovacs
Design Supervisor/Caryl Spinka
Production Supervisor/Priscilla Taguer
Photo Editor/Mary Ann Drury

Cover Designer/Tom Christopher
Text Illustrator/Barbara Maslen

Photo Credits/Library of Congress Collections: p. 2; Marimekko:
p. 17; Bergdorf Goodman: p. 37; Metropolitan Museum of Art:
p. 52; Fashion Institute of Technology/John Senzer; p. 74; American Fur
Industry/Leber Katz Agency: p. 97; Karen Zebulon: p. 115; Ken
Karp: pp. 147, 225,278, 296; Courtesy of F.W. Woolworth Company: p. 171; Bloomingdale's: p. 200; Kip Peticolas/Fundamental
Photographs: p. 260; National Cash Register: p. 314; Sears, Roebuck
and Co.: p. 334; Cotton, Inc.: p. 355; Mimi Forsyth/Monkmeyer:
p. 378; Teuscher: p. 400; Courtesy of Fashion Institute of Technology:
p. 417; Rhoda Galyn: p. 433.

Library of Congress Cataloging in Publication Data

Troxell, Mary D
    Fashion merchandising.

    Bibliography: p.
    Includes index.
    1.   Clothing trade—United States.   2.   Fashion.
I.   Stone, Elaine, joint author.   II.   Title.
HD9940.U4T74   1981   687'.068'8   80-25077
ISBN 0-07-065280-5

  2 3 4 5 6 7 8 9 0 DODO 8 9 8 7 6 5 4 3 2 1

ISBN 0-07-065280-5

Fashion merchandising operates at all levels of the fashion business. Because all of the industries that constitute the fashion merchandising business are continuously involved in new developments, technologies, theories, and trends, fashion merchandising as an area of study is dynamic, exciting, and always changing.

The third edition of *Fashion Merchandising* is the result of the authors' eagerness to help students recognize the changes occurring throughout the fashion industry and understand the implications these changes have for the merchandising of fashion products at both the production and the retail levels. While it is important to note that the basic activities of fashion merchandising have changed very little, so that the original concept of *Fashion Merchandising* remains valid, the third edition of this textbook updates, expands, and strengthens all the areas that relate to the application of those basic activities. Further, this edition reflects the authors' efforts to transmit to students the excitement of the fashion business. The number of illustrations has been increased; a livelier writing style has been employed; and activities to involve the students personally have been devised.

Fashion Merchandising, Third Edition, differs from other textbooks on the subject in two very important ways. First, since fashion merchandising is practiced at all levels of the fashion business, this textbook covers all the marketing levels involved in successful fashion merchandising. It demonstrates for students the complete interrelationships of all the industries that make up the fashion business, from the industries that furnish raw materials to those that provide the finished products. The textbook then takes the students through the disciplines of planning, promoting, and selling the finished product through various types of distribution channels.

Fashion merchandising is practiced in many types of businesses. Some are large and some are small. Some are located in large urban metropolitan areas; some, in small suburban areas. *Fashion Merchandising* performs the important role of helping students gain a greater awareness of available fashion-related careers. With background knowledge obtained from the text and the end-of-chapter and end-of-unit activities, students should be able to select the specific industries in which they have a personal interest, as well as the kinds of working environments and geographical locations in which they are most comfortable.

ORGANIZATION OF THE TEXT

Fashion Merchandising, Third Edition, prepares students for a wide range of entry-level jobs available throughout the vast fashion business. The text treats the subject matter largely in terms of men's, women's, and children's apparel and accessories. However, the concepts it develops are equally applicable to the merchandising of other fashion-influenced goods, such as home furnishings, household linens, and so on.

The third edition of *Fashion Merchandising* uses the classroom-tested organization of the second edition. It is structured according to the following sequential learning order: Unit 1, The Dynamics of Fashion; Unit 2, Marketers of Fashion; and Unit 3, Retail Merchandising of Fashion.

Unit 1: The Dynamics of Fashion

The first four chapters acquaint the student with the fundamentals of fashion and the basic principles that govern all fashion movement and change. This unit provides many new examples and features a number of new illustrations.

Chapter 1, "The Nature of Fashion," introduces fashion terminology, examines the components of fashion, and explains why fashion is always subject to change. Chapter 2 explores the manner in which economic, sociological, and psychological factors influence fashion demand. Chapter 3 discusses the rhythmic changes in the silhouette, the cyclical movement of fashion, and how to predict fashion trends with relative accuracy. Chapter 4 explains how fashions start; the roles and responsibilities of designers, manufacturers, and retailers; the major theories relating to fashion adoption and dissemination; and why most people follow rather than lead fashion change.

Unit 2: Marketers of Fashion

The next six chapters of the text trace the history and development, organization and operation, merchandising activities, and marketing trends of industries engaged in producing and distributing fashion. All six chapters have been carefully revised and updated.

Chapter 5 discusses textile fibers and fabrics. Chapter 6 explains the renewed vigor of the fur industry and the widespread appeal of leather apparel and accessories. Chapter 7 has been augmented to cover manufacturers of children's, as well as women's, apparel. Similarly, Chapter 8 now discusses manufacturers of boyswear as well as menswear. Chapter 9, which has been greatly expanded, details the operations of those firms that produce fashion accessories. An updated and expanded Chapter 10 explores the major foreign sources of fashion inspiration and fashion goods. Finally, Chapter 11 examines the major types of retail organizations that operate as distributors of fashion goods to the consumer.

Unit 3: Retail Merchandising of Fashion

The remaining 10 chapters examine in detail each of the merchandising activities a buyer of fashion goods might be expected to perform at the retail level. Chapter 12 shows how consumer demand can be analyzed and forecast. Chapters 13 and 14 explain how budgets and plans are prepared to meet anticipated demand. Chapters 15 and 16 describe the various types of forms and reports that retail management uses to evaluate merchandising operations. The activities involved in preparing for and actually making the buying trip to the market are outlined in Chapter 17. Chapters 18 and 19 examine methods of promoting and selling fashion merchandise. Chapter 20 describes the teamwork necessary to coordinate the promotional activities of related fashion departments of a store. The last chapter, Chapter 21, shows how various types of stores create and maintain their unique fashion personalities.

Appendix: Career Opportunities in Fashion

The appendix offers some guidelines and sugges-

tions to those who are looking for specific ways to channel career goals. Whether a student's interests are in design, manufacturing, small-business ownership or management, or in some phase of a related service-oriented business, this section of the text describes each of the possible fields and helps the student identify specific jobs of interest in the fashion industry. It ensures that students understand the specific skills, training, and experience required for entry into each job.

Glossary and Bibliography

The third edition of *Fashion Merchandising* provides a glossary of over 250 frequently used terms. Most of these terms are defined in the text, but the glossary also introduces and defines other terms commonly used in fashion merchandising. The comprehensive, updated bibliography contains complete information on references cited in the text and also lists other works of major importance to the fashion merchandising student.

End-of-Chapter Activities

Each of the 21 chapters in the text concludes with three or four kinds of student-oriented activities designed to enrich and reinforce the instructional material. A "Merchandising Vocabulary" section in each chapter explains fashion and merchandising terms introduced for the first time in that chapter. The student will recognize these terms when they appear in subsequent chapters.

"Merchandising Review" asks questions about the key concepts of each chapter. These questions provoke thought, encourage classroom discussion, and develop recall of the material presented in the text.

The section called "Merchandising Digest" consists primarily of an excerpt from the text. It asks the student to explain the significance of the excerpt and to support the explanation with specific illustrations. This activity affords the student an opportunity to apply theory to actual situations and to draw on his or her own background and experiences.

In a few instances where the chapter material lends itself to such treatment, a brief "Case Study" or "Merchandising Assignment" is provided for the students to solve. This educational activity helps students apply newly acquired knowledge in a practical, self-instructional way.

End-of-Unit Activities

A new feature of this edition is the "Fashion Project," drawn from authentic merchandising situations, which ends each unit. These fashion projects emphasize and reinforce the instructional elements brought out in each unit. The projects enrich instruction and suggest to students that fashion merchandising is a dynamic and exciting field.

INSTRUCTOR'S MANUAL AND KEY

An instructor's manual and key is available to adopters at no cost. It includes a number of options for organizing the fashion merchandising curriculum, contains general suggestions for teaching the course, and provides an annotated bibliography of books, trade journals, and trade associations. The key to the text includes answers to all end-of-chapter and end-of-unit exercises.

A new feature of this edition is a test bank of six tests containing test material for the units, a mid-term test, and a final examination. The tests are composed of 500 objective questions and are ready to duplicate.

ACKNOWLEDGMENTS

The authors are grateful to the many educators and business people who have given them encourage-ment, information, and helpful suggestions for this new edition.

Dr. Mary Anderton, of Memphis State University, made suggestions for updating and improving the second edition. Sylvia Sheppard, the Fashion Institute of Design of Los Angeles; Jean McKinney Lang, St. Petersburg Junior College; Karen K. Heuer, Des Moines Area Community College; and Jacqueline Murphy-Zolno, Temple University; read the manuscript of this edition and offered us excellent ideas and advice. We also extend our thanks to the following fashion industry personnel who shared their expertise with us: William Rapp, the Tanner's Council of America; Jess Chernak, the American Fur Industry; Nina McLemore, May Department Stores International; Philip Coward, The Mister Shop; Bonnie Michaels, Maas Brothers, Inc.; and Beth Philips, the French Apparel Center; and to those individuals and business firms who provided new and excellent illustration material.

But it is to our senior editor, Mary Alice McGarry, that we are especially grateful. Without her invaluable support and encouragement this edition would never have been possible.

We regret that space does not permit us to personally thank each of our many friends in all segments of the fashion business who supplied, throughout the development of this edition, their encouragement as well as significant amounts of current and trend trade information.

Mary D. Troxell
Elaine Stone

CONTENTS

1

THE DYNAMICS
OF FASHION

The term **dynamics** refers to any basic forces and the laws relating to them that explain the patterns of change or growth of these forces. Unit 1 of this book focuses on the dynamics of fashion. Fashion is one of the strongest forces in our lives today. It determines trends in our use of goods and services. Fashion is of utmost importance to the consumer who follows it, to the designer and manufacturer who cater to it, and to the retailer who distributes it.

The study of fashion begins, naturally enough, with the fundamentals. These fundamentals involve many bodies of knowledge, including psychology, economics, sociology, art, history, and religion.

The four chapters in Unit 1 discuss the fundamentals of fashion and the relationships between fashion and other existing forces. Discussed are:

- The basic vocabulary of fashion; the components of fashion; the

intangible elements of fashion; and the basic principles relating to fashion and its movement

- The environmental factors—economic, sociological, and psychological—that have an influence on both current fashion interest and demand
- The movement of fashion; how fashions change; and how an understanding of this movement can be used to analyze and predict fashion trends
- The leaders and followers of fashion; the role of designers, producers, and retailers; how fashions disseminate

Fashion is a science; it involves known facts and the prediction of actions and reactions based on those facts. Unit 1 presents an in-depth discussion of the nature of fashion and how it works. This information is essential for those interested in merchandising fashion goods at either the wholesale or the retail level.

1

THE NATURE OF FASHION

Vital, challenging, forceful, individual, changing. Fashion is all these, and an influence in our lives that is constantly growing. Fashion influences what we wear, what we eat, where we live, how we travel, and how we amuse ourselves. It also encourages the world marketplace to expand, manufacturers to produce, marketers to sell, and consumers to buy. Fashion touches the daily lives of nearly everyone, and we all reveal our personality and individuality in the ways that we use fashion.

Fashion today is big business; thousands of people are employed in either "the fashion industries" or the "fashion business." The "fashion industries" are considered to be those engaged in producing the materials used in the production of apparel and accessories for men, women, and children, including the merchandise categories known as "boys" and "girls." Throughout this book, any reference to "fashion industries" means these, unless others are specifically mentioned. The term "fashion business" includes all industries and services connected with fashion: manufacturing, distribution, advertising, publishing, and consulting—any business concerned with goods or services in which fashion is a factor.

As the power of fashion to influence our lives grows, several misconceptions about it continue to be widely held. The first and most common misconception is that designers and retailers dictate what the fashion will be and then force it upon helpless consumers. In reality it is consumers themselves who decide what the fashion will be by their acceptance or rejection of the styles that are offered.

The second misconception is that fashion acts as an influence on women only. Men today are as influenced by and responsive to

fashion as women. Fashion is the force that causes women to raise or lower skirt lengths, straighten or frizz their hair, and change from sportswear to dressy clothes. Fashion is also the force that influences men to grow or shave off mustaches and beards, choose wide or narrow ties and lapels, and change from casual jeans into three-piece suits.

The third misconception is that fashion is a mysterious and unpredictable force. Actually, its direction can be determined and its changes predicted with remarkable accuracy by those who study and understand the fundamentals of fashion. Fashion was once considered an art form controlled by designers who dictated its content. But it has now evolved into a science that can be measured and evaluated. The merchandising of fashion, or **fashion merchandising,** refers to the planning required to have the right fashion-oriented merchandise at the right time, in the right place, in the right quantities, and at the right prices.

THE TERMINOLOGY OF FASHION

Fashion is a complex subject—a subject that intrigues and fascinates and has been studied throughout history. In the study of fashion today, certain words and phrases are used over and over again: "high fashion," "mass fashion," "style," "design," "apparel," "taste," "classic," and "fad." The exact meanings of these terms must be understood so that concepts can be discussed without confusion. One of the major pioneers in the field of fashion merchandising was Dr. Paul H. Nystrom. The definitions used in this section are his and are generally accepted in the academic study of fashion.[1]

Fashion

A style that is accepted and used by the majority of a group at any one time is a **fashion.** Short skirts, pointed-toe shoes, long hair, beards and mustaches, and natural makeup have all been fashions. And no doubt each will again be accepted by the majority in a group of people with similar interests or characteristics —college students, for example, or young career-oriented men and women.

Fashions can be categorized according to the group to which they appeal. **High fashion** refers to those styles or designs accepted by a limited group of fashion leaders—the elite among consumers—who are first to accept fashion change. High-fashion styles or designs are generally introduced, produced, and sold in small quantities and at relatively high prices to socialites, entertainers, and fashion innovators. **Mass fashion,** or **volume fashion,** refers to those styles or designs that are widely accepted. These fashions are usually produced and sold in large quantities at moderate to low prices and appeal to the greatest majority of fashion-conscious consumers.

Style

A "style" is a characteristic or distinctive mode of presentation or conceptualization in a particular field. There are styles in writing, speak-ing, home decorating, and table manners. In apparel, **style** is the characteristic or distinctive appearance of a garment—the combination of features that makes it different from other garments. For example, skirts are one style of women's apparel, and pants are another. Men's tailored jackets are one style, while sport jackets are another.

Although styles come and go in terms of acceptance, a specific style always remains a style, whether it is currently in fashion or not. Also, several styles may be in fashion at one time. Pantsuits and dresses, for example, are completely different styles, but may both be fashionable at the same time for many of the same occasions.

Some styles are named for the period of history in which they originated—Grecian, Roman, Renaissance, and Empire, for example. When such styles return to fashion, their basic elements remain the same. Minor details are altered to reflect the taste or needs of the era in which they reappear. For example, the Empire style of the early nineteenth century featured a waistline cinched high up under the bust. That style can still be bought today, but with modifications for current fashion acceptance.

Design

A **design** is a specific version of a style. The skirt, for example, is a style in women's apparel. The many variations in which it is available are the designs—gored, A-line, box-pleated, and knife-pleated, to name a few. A coat is a style. The variations in body length and width and in neckline and sleeve treatment constitute the various designs of that style. Manufacturers usually produce several designs or variations of a popular style. A cardigan sweater, for example, will be offered in variations of texture, color, and decoration.

In everyday usage, however, fashion manufacturers and retailers refer to a design as a "style," a "style number," or simply a "number." When a buyer says he or she is going to reorder a style or mark down a number, chances are the buyer is probably talking about a specific design.

Bathing suits in 1900, 1930, and 1980. Tastes change as drastically as styles do.

Taste

The Latin proverb *"De gustibus non est disputandum"* means "There can be no disputing taste." According to another well-known proverb, "There is no accounting for taste." "Taste" can be defined as the ability to discern and appreciate that which makes for excellence at a particular time in a particular circumstance. In other words, **taste** refers to an individual's opinion of what is and what is not attractive and appropriate.

Good taste in fashion, therefore, means sensitivity not only to what is artistic but also to what is appropriate for a given occasion. A style may be beautiful. But if inappropriate to the particular circumstances, it may not be considered in good taste. Even in the liberated atmosphere of the 1970s when so many dress codes disappeared, certain standards of good taste still prevailed. One might have dared to wear a see-through blouse to the office, for example, but it would not have been considered in good taste.

Dr. Nystrom described the relationship between taste and fashion this way: "Good taste essentially is making the most artistic use of current fashion . . . bridging the gap between good art and common usage."[2]

Timing, too, plays a part in what is considered good or bad taste. British costume authority, James Laver, saw the relationship between taste and fashion in terms of its acceptance level. A style, he said, is thought to be:[3]

"indecent"	10 years before its time
"shameless"	5 years before its time
"outré"	1 year before its time
"smart"	in its time
"dowdy"	1 year after its time
"hideous"	10 years after its time
"ridiculous"	20 years after its time

While the time an individual fashion takes to complete this course may vary depending on the style, the concept of the course being cyclical in nature is a valid one. (See Chapter 3.) A new style is often considered daring and in dubious taste. It is then gradually accepted, then widely accepted, and finally gradually discarded.

Although we often assume that fashions are unique to our times, our parents, grandparents, and even our more distant ancestors lived through the same fashion cycles. The troubled world scene and the electronic explosion of the last decades, however, have brought about a major change in timetables of fashion cycles. Cycles are not only shorter but repeat themselves within a shorter space of time. Thus, young people in the 1970s looked back with nostalgia to the life and styles of the 1950s as presented to them in such television programs as "Happy Days," and "Laverne and Shirley." Yet, despite the momentary fads and the fact that expansion and contraction of the time periods for different styles may occur, Laver's cycle is a valid one.

A Classic

Some styles or designs continue to be considered in good taste over a long period—exceptions in the usual rapid movement of styles through their fashion life cycles. A **classic** is a style or design that satisfies a basic need and remains in general fashion acceptance for an extended period of time.

Almost every wardrobe has some classics in it, and some wardrobes are mostly classics. A classic is characterized by simplicity of design as well as length of time in fashion. The shirtwaist dress has been a classic for many years. So have the simple pump and the cardigan sweater.

A Fad

Fashions that suddenly sweep into popularity and then quickly disappear are called "fads." These enthusiasms appear quickly, are exaggerated in design, and are soon quickly gone from the scene. One has only to recall the body painting of the early 1970s as an example. In the world of apparel, a short-lived fashion that affects relatively few people within the total population is called a **fad**. Fads follow the same cycle as fashions do, but their rise in popularity is much faster, their acceptance much shorter, and their decline to obsolescence much more rapid than that of true fashions. Because they can come and go in a single season, fads have been called "miniature fashions."

Fake flowers to be worn with all types of clothing made their appearance in 1977, were briefly seen everywhere, and then were gone. The extremely high platform shoe of 1976 is another example of a recent fad. While adults are not immune to fads, teenagers are especially susceptible. They have experimented with micromini skirts, gaudily decorated jeans and T-shirts, and unisex wooden-soled clogs.

Sometimes what appears to be a fad lives on to become a classic. Gold chain jewelry is an example. Although wearing thin chains of gold began as a fad, the skyrocketing value of gold has elevated gold chains to the status of fashion classic. The cowboy boot is another fad which is on its way to becoming a classic.

Fads come and go. The Davy Crockett cap was a popular children's fad in the 1950s.

John Dominis, Life Magazine © Time, Inc.

The chemise, or sack dress, is probably the outstanding example of this phenomenon. After an instant rise to popularity in the late 1950s, it quickly passed from the fashion scene. A few years later, the chemise reappeared as the shift. In 1974, the chemise again appeared in the Paris collections, modified to eliminate its former disadvantages. American manufacturers quickly reproduced it in several versions and in a wide price range. The appearance of the chemise again in the 1980s shows that only time will tell whether that design is a fad or a fashion classic.

COMPONENTS OF FASHION

Fashion design does not just happen, nor is there a magic wand a designer can wave to create a new design. Fashion design involves the combination of four basic elements or components—silhouette, detail, texture, and color. It is only through a change in one or more of these basic components that a new fashion evolves. This is true of any fashion-influenced product, from kitchen appliances to automobiles, apartment houses to office buildings, and from accessories to apparel.

Silhouette

The **silhouette** of a costume is its overall outline or contour. It is also frequently referred to as "shape" or "form."

It may appear to the casual observer that women have worn countless silhouettes throughout the centuries. Research shows, however, that there are actually only three basic forms—straight or tubular, bell-shaped or bouffant, and the bustle or back-fullness—with many variations.[4]

The same research also shows that since the mid-eighteenth century, these three basic silhouettes have consistently come into fashion in the same sequence, each recurring approximately once every 100 years and lasting for about 35 years. For example, the triangle shape (a variation of the straight, or tubular, silhouette) of the 1930s and 1940s reoccurred in the wide-shoulder, narrow-hip silhouette of

Details

The individual elements that give a silhouette its form or shape are called **details.** These include trimmings, skirt and pant length and width, and shoulder, waist, and sleeve treatment.

Silhouettes evolve gradually from one to another through changes in detail. When the trend in a detail reaches an extreme, a reversal of the trend takes place. For example, skirts became extremely short in the late 1960s. The reversal began to show itself in the increasing number of longer-length styles available in the 1970s, and by the early 1980s, skirts again began to inch upward to shorter lengths. Men's ties grew narrower during the 1960s, widened again in the 1970s, and predictably narrowed in the early 1980s. Another interesting example is the width of jeans. By the late 1970s, jeans had become so narrow and skintight that sitting or bending in them was a feat. The baggy jean of the early 1980s was the beginning of the reversal trend to a wider, more comfortable version.

Variations in detail allow both designer and consumer to freely express their individuality within the framework of the currently accepted silhouette. To emphasize a natural-waistline silhouette, for example, a slender woman might choose a simple, wide belt, a heavily decorated belt, or a belt in a contrasting color to suit her personality and the occasion. To express his individuality, a man might emphasize the wide-shoulder look with epaulets or heavy shoulder pads.

Texture

One of the most significant components of fashion is texture. **Texture** is the look and feel of material, woven or nonwoven.

Texture can affect the appearance of the silhouette, giving it a bulky or slender look depending on the roughness or smoothness of the materials. A woman dressed in a rough tweed dress and a bulky knit sweater is likely to look larger and squarer than she does in the same dress executed in a smooth jersey and wearing a cashmere sweater. When the bulky

The detail of skirt length can affect its silhouette. But according to the ad shown here, this classic style will look good in any length. Do you agree?

the late 1970s. The widespread sociological change and rapid technological developments of recent decades, however, may have altered both the traditional life span and sequence of these silhouettes.

look is fashionable, popular textures include shaggy tweeds, mohairs, cable-stitched and other heavily ribbed knit fabrics, and rough-textured knit and woven materials. When sleek lines are the fashion, rough textures yield to smooth surfaces and simple flat weaves and knits.

Texture influences the drape of a garment. Chiffon clings and flows, making it a good choice for soft, feminine styles, while corduroy has the firmness and bulk suitable for more casual garments.

Texture affects the color of a fabric by causing the surface to either reflect or absorb light. Rough textures absorb light, causing the colors to appear flat; smooth textures reflect light, causing colors to appear brighter. Anyone who has tried to match colors soon discovers that a color which appears extremely bright in a shiny vinyl, satin, or high-gloss enamel paint seems subdued in a rough wool, a suede, or a stucco wall finish. Because pile surfaces such as velvet both reflect and absorb light, their colors look richer and deeper than they would on flat, smooth surfaces.

Color

Color has always been a major consideration in women's clothing. Especially since World War II, color in men's clothing has been regaining the importance it had in previous centuries. Today color is a key factor in apparel selection for both sexes. It is important in advertising, packaging, and store decor as well.

Historically, colors have been used to denote rank and profession. Purple, for instance, was associated with royalty and in some periods could be worn only by those of noble birth. Black became customary for the apparel of the clergy and for members of the judiciary.

Color symbolism often varies with geographical location. White, for example, is the Western world's symbol of purity, worn by brides and used in communion dresses; in India, white is the color of mourning.

Color has been importantly affected by developments in technology. Better ways of tanning leather and dyeing and finishing fabrics have produced a wider variety of colors and color combinations than ever before for fashion designers to work with. Colors today are also more permanent, more resistant to fading or changing, and thus more acceptable to consumers.

Today a fashion designer's color palette changes with consumers' preferences. In some seasons, all is brightness and sharp contrast, and no color is too powerful to be worn. In other seasons, only subdued colors appeal. Fashion merchants soon develop an eye for color—not only for the specific hues and values popular in a given season, but also for indications of possible trends in consumer preference.

THE INTANGIBLES OF FASHION

A style is tangible, made up of a definite silhouette and details of design. But fashion is shaped by such intangibles as group acceptance, change, the forces at work during a specific era, and people's desire to relate to certain lifestyles.

Acceptance

Group acceptance or approval is implied in any discussion of fashion. An article of clothing may be breathtakingly innovative and aesthetically flawless, yet it is not a fashion until it has been accepted and used by a substantial number of people.

Acceptance need not be universal, however. A style may be adopted by one group while other segments of the population ignore it. The fashions shaped by big-city lifestyles are rarely popular with the suburban crowd, and the carefree, nonconformist fashions on college campuses bear little or no relationship to those accepted by the business crowd.

A style may also be accepted and become a fashion in one part of the world while it is ignored or rejected elsewhere. The igloo of the Eskimos, the thatched hut of the African tribespeople, and the ranch house of the American suburbanites—each is considered fashionable by its own inhabitants. In the same way, many ethnic and religious groups have unique clothing fashions. In this country, the Amish and

In the United States today, some religious groups wear unique apparel.

Ken Karp

the Mennonites can be recognized by their apparel, as can male Hassidic Jews, female Black Muslims, and both male and female members of the Hare Krishna sect.

Acceptance also means that a fashion is considered appropriate to the occasion for which it is worn. Clothes considered appropriate for big-business boardrooms would not be acceptable for casual weekends or outdoor living. Certain extreme styles accepted by college students for campus wear would not be considered appropriate for job interviews.

The group that adopts and rejects a specific style influences and changes what is considered acceptable. For example, the accepted style for women working in the business world was once a dark tailored suit or dress. Today casual separates are widely accepted.

Men's fashions also provide examples. When the term "white-collar class" was born, the collar that gave it its name was high and stiffly starched, and a man never removed his coat or tie in company. Today, fashions for men are much more relaxed, even in office wear. The stiff collar is gone. The dark, tailored suit jacket has given way to a patterned, more casual sport jacket. The white shirt is often replaced by colored or patterned shirts, sometimes worn without a tie.

Regardless of practicality, a style is considered a fashion if it is accepted by the majority of a specific group at a given time and place for a specific occasion. Many fashions can and do exist side by side at any one time because of the varied preferences and activities of different consumer groups.

Change

It is true that we are living in a time of constant and rapid change, but change is not unique to our time. More than 2,500 years ago a Greek philosopher said, "The only external truth in the history of the universe is change."

Fashion especially is subject to never-ending change—sometimes rapid, sometimes gradual. Women's apparel has always showed the most rapid rate of change. Until recently, men's fashions changed more slowly. Fashion in home furnishings changes even more slowly, and architectural fashions more slowly still. Some people constantly seek the new and different, and when a fashion is fully accepted, it has already become too ordinary for them.

The rate of fashion change in women's clothing has greatly accelerated over the last century, and in men's clothing over the last 40 years. Much of this has resulted from the invention of the sewing machine and the development of man-made fibers. These have given designers and manufacturers a faster means of producing garments and a much greater variety of materials to work with. New technology is constantly producing new fibers and blends of fibers. Each seems to offer more than the one before and encourages the discarding of the old. Also, the consumer finds the moderately priced, "off the rack" dress easier to discard than the more expensive hand-sewn or hand-knitted creation.

Modern communications play a major role in today's accelerated rate of fashion change. The mass media spread fashion news across the face of the globe in hours, sometimes seconds. Live television coverage of events around the world not only enables us to see what people are doing but also what they are wearing. Our morning newspapers show us what fashion leaders wore to a party the night before. Even slight fashion changes are given faster and wider publicity than ever before. Consumers who like these changes demand them from merchants, who in turn demand them from manufacturers.

THE FUTILITY
OF FORCING CHANGE. Since fashion changes are outgrowths of changes in consumers' needs, it is seldom possible to force them or hold them back. Efforts have been made from time to time to alter the course of fashion, but they usually fail. Fashion is a potent force which by definition requires support by the majority.

As an example, in the late 1960s, designers and retailers decided that skirts had reached their limit in shortness and that women would soon be seeking change. So the designers designed and the retailers stocked and promoted the midi, a skirt midcalf in length. The design-

The tailored, severe look of the early 1940's was followed by Christian Dior's revolutionary "New Look" which emphasized feminine, flowing lines.

ers and retailers were right in theory but wrong in timing and choice of skirt length. Consumers found the midi too sudden and radical a change and did not accept or buy the style in sufficient numbers to make it a fashion.

Occasionally, necessity and government regulation can interrupt the course of a fash-

ion. During World War II, the United States government controlled the type and quantity of fabric used in consumer goods. One regulation, for instance, prohibited anything but slit pockets on women's garments to avoid using the extra material that patch pockets require. Skirts were short and silhouettes narrow, reflecting the scarcity of material.

MEETING THE DEMAND FOR CHANGE. After the war, a reaction to these designs was to be expected. A new French designer, Christian Dior, caught and expressed the desire for a freer line and a more feminine garment in his first collection, which achieved instant fashion success. Using fabric with a lavishness that had been impossible in Europe or America during the war years, he created his New Look, with long, full skirts, fitted waistlines, and feminine curves.

Dior did not change the course of fashion. He simply recognized and interpreted the need of women at that time to get out of stiff, narrow, unfeminine clothes and into soft, free, feminine ones. Consumers wanted the change, and the lifting of wartime restrictions made it possible to meet their demand.

Another example of a consumer demand for change occurred in menswear just before World War II. Year after year, manufacturers had been turning out versions of a style that had long been popular in England—a padded-shoulder, draped suit. A number of young men from very influential families, who were attending well-known Northeastern colleges, became tired of that look. They wanted a change. They took their objections to New Haven clothing manufacturers, and the result was the natural-shoulder Ivy League suit that achieved widespread popularity for the next 15 to 20 years.

A Mirror of the Times

Fashions have always mirrored the times in which they occur. Because fashions are shaped by the forces of an era, they in turn reflect the way we think and live. The individualistic fashions of the 1980s are a true reflection of the new freedom of lifestyle and expression. The extreme modesty of the Victorian era was reflected in bulky and concealing fashions. The sexual emancipation of the flappers in the 1920s was expressed in their flattened figures, short skirts, and short hair.

Fashions also mirror the times by reflecting the values of each level of society in a given era. The peasant worker in Europe once thought it necessary to have a strong, sturdy wife to help out with work in the fields. Such women were both needed and admired. The common fashions at that time combined puffy sleeves, laced bodices, and full skirts—details which made even slender women look plump and sturdy. While European peasant women wore this costume, the women of the wealthy classes were emphasizing their desired and admired delicacy with entirely different fashions.

Fashions mirror the times by reflecting the degree of rigidity in the class structure of an era. Although it is difficult to imagine today, throughout much of history certain fashions were restricted to the members of certain rigidly defined social classes. In some early eras, royal edicts regulated both the type of apparel that could be worn by each group of citizens and how ornate it could be. Class distinctions were thus emphasized. Certain fashions have also been used to indicate high social standing and material success. During the nineteenth century, the constricted waists of Western women and the bound feet of high-caste Chinese women were silent but obvious evidence that the male head of the household was wealthy and esteemed.

Fashions also mirror the times by reflecting the activities in which the people of an era participate. The importance of court-centered social activities in seventeenth- and eighteenth-century Europe was evidenced in men's and women's ornately styled apparel. Men's fashions became less colorful and more functional only when a new working class was created by the industrial revolution in the late eighteenth and early nineteenth centuries.

Now, in the late twentieth century, social classes are far more fluid and mobile. Many fashions exist simultaneously, and we are all free to adopt the fashions of any social group. Only our incomes restrict us. If we do not wish to join others in their fashion choices, we can create our own modes and standards of dress. The beatniks and hippies of the 1960s had their typical fashions, as did the bohemians of the 1920s and the liberated groups of the 1970s.

The Bettmann Archive, Inc.

In the Middle Ages, wealthy men maintained their wives in leisure. Medieval tapestries emphasize the delicacy of the women's faces, hands, and figures. Slenderness and delicacy were further emphasized by the fashion of the day, with tight-fitting bodices and heavy skirts that artfully concealed any hint of bulk.

Today we are also free to choose fashions that relate to the wide variety of activities in our lives. Wardrobes vary from lifestyle to lifestyle. If a businessman plays tennis each morning before going to the office, his closet probably contains fashions for both the business world and the tennis court, as well as leisure and formal attire. A working woman who also manages a home and family must see that her wardrobe contains fashions suitable for business as well as family-based activities.

PRINCIPLES OF FASHION

While the intangibles of fashion can be vague and difficult to chart, the five fundamental principles of fashion are tangible and precise. From season to season, year to year, these principles do not change. They provide a solid foundation for fashion identification and forecasting. As valid for today's fashion as for yesterday's, they will continue to apply for decades to come.

These five principles are the foundations upon which the study of fashion is based, whether that study concerns the history of fashion, the dissemination of fashion, or the techniques relating to fashion merchandising. References will be made to these principles throughout this book and some of them have already been mentioned. They are as follows:

1. *Consumers establish fashions by their acceptance or rejection of the styles offered.*
Contrary to what some believe, fashions are not created by designers, producers, or retailers. Consumers—customers—create fashion. They decide when a style no longer appeals, and they choose what new style will be favored.

Designers create hundreds of new styles each season, based on what they think may attract customers. From among those many styles, manufacturers choose what they think will be successful, rejecting many more than they select. Retailers choose from the manufacturers' offerings those styles they believe their customers will want. Consumers then make the vital choice. By accepting one style and rejecting another, they—and only they—dictate what styles will become fashions.

2. *Fashions are not based on price.*
The price tag on an item of apparel or an accessory does not indicate whether the item is currently in fashion. Although new styles that may eventually become fashionable are often introduced at high prices, this is less often the case than it once was. One new style may originate in the high-priced salon of a name designer, such as the "Gold Rush" of Calvin Klein in 1979. But another may come into fashion from a chain-store catalog or Army-Navy store stock, as blue jeans did.

Also, items that originally carry high price tags are quickly made available in a variety of price lines if they appear to have considerable customer appeal. A Paris dress style, for instance, may be introduced at a price over $6,000 for a custom-made, hand-sewn copy. A few weeks later, stores may offer ready-to-wear copies of that style in a wide range of prices, including budget prices. The fabric, trimmings, and workmanship will be different, but the style will appear essentially the same.

3. *Fashions are evolutionary in nature; they are rarely revolutionary.*
Throughout history there have probably been only two real revolutions in fashion styles. One of these occurred during the twentieth century: the Dior New Look of 1947. Fashions usually evolve gradually from one style to another. Skirt lengths go up or down an inch at a time, season after season. Suit lapels narrow or widen gradually, not suddenly.

Fashion designers both understand and accept this principle. When developing new design ideas, they always keep the current fashion in mind. They know that few people could or would buy a whole new wardrobe every season, and that the success of their designs ultimately depends on sales. Consumers today buy apparel and accessories to supplement and update the wardrobe they already own, some of which was purchased last year, some the year before, some the year before that, and so on. In most cases, consumers will buy only if the purchase complements their existing wardrobe and does not depart too radically from last year's purchases.

4. *No amount of sales promotion can change the direction in which fashions are moving.*

Promotional efforts on the part of producers or retailers cannot dictate what consumers will buy. The few times that fashion merchants have tried to promote a radical change in fashion, they have not been successful.

In the late 1970s and early 1980s, for example, a strong promotional effort was made to interest young men and women in wearing hats again, as young people had done in the forties and fifties. Although the fashions of the forties and fifties were adopted and adapted by these consumers, no amount of promotion by either the millinery industry or the retailers was able to make these consumers accept hats as an integral part of their fashion wardrobe.

In the same way, promotional effort cannot renew the life of a fading fashion unless the extent of change gives the fashion an altogether new appeal. This is why stores have special-price sales. When the sales of a particular style start slumping, stores know they must clear out as much of that stock as possible, even at much lower prices, to make room for newer styles in which consumers have indicated interest.

5. *All fashions end in excess.*

This saying is sometimes attributed to Paul Poiret, a top Paris designer of the 1920s. There are many examples of its truth. Eighteenth-century hoopskirts ballooned out to 8 feet in diameter, which made moving even from room to room a complicated maneuver. Similarly, miniskirts of the 1960s finally became so short that the slightest movement caused a major problem in modesty.

Once the extreme in styling has been reached, a fashion is nearing its end. The attraction of the fashion wanes and people begin to seek a different look—a new fashion.

MERCHANDISING VOCABULARY

Define or briefly explain the following terms:

Classic	**High fashion**
Design	**Mass or volume fashion**
Details	**Silhouette**
Fad	**Style**
Fashion	**Taste**
Fashion merchandising	**Texture**

MERCHANDISING REVIEW

1. What are the three most common misconceptions about fashion? Do you agree or disagree?
2. Describe several apparel styles that are named for the period of history in which they originated.
3. Describe several apparel styles (for men, women, or chil-

dren) which are in fashion today and can be considered classics.

4. Distinguish between (a) style and fashion, (b) style and design, and (c) classic and fad.
5. What are the four components of all fashions? Briefly explain their interrelationships.
6. Is it possible to force an unwanted fashion on consumers? Defend your answer.
7. What factors have contributed to the acceleration of fashion apparel change during the last 100 years? In your opinion, which factors have had the greatest impact, and why?
8. In what respects do fashions mirror the times? Give examples to illustrate your answer.
9. What are the five basic principles relating to fashion? Discuss the implications of any two of these principles for fashion merchants.
10. Name at least three types of consumer products, other than apparel or accessories, in which you believe fashion plays a dominant role today. What fashion elements or components are featured in each?

MERCHANDISING DIGEST

The following are statements from the text. Discuss the significance of each, citing specific examples to illustrate how each applies to the merchandising of fashion goods.

1. "Acceptance . . . means that a fashion is considered appropriate to the occasion for which it is worn."
2. "Today color is a key factor in apparel selection for both sexes."
3. Today "many fashions exist simultaneously."
4. "Sometimes what appears to be a fad lives on to become a classic."

REFERENCES

[1] Nystrom, *Economics of Fashion*, pp. 3–7; and *Fashion Merchandising*, pp. 33–34.
[2] Nystrom, *Economics of Fashion*, p. 7.
[3] Laver, *Taste and Fashion*, p. 202.
[4] Young, *Recurring Cycles of Fashion*, p. 30.

2

ENVIRONMENTAL INFLUENCES ON FASHION INTEREST AND DEMAND

We all know that the conditions under which we live affect our lives and influence our actions. These conditions make up what is called the **environment.** Just as the environment in one neighborhood differs from that of another, so does it differ among nations and societies.

One aspect of our lives that is influenced by the environment is fashion. This relationship between the environment and fashion interest and demand is influenced by:

- The degree of economic development of a country or society
- The sociological characteristics of the class structure, such as the degree of mobility and the size of the middle class
- The psychological attitudes of consumers

Fashion interest and demand are far greater in some environments than others. Fashion demand flourishes in societies with a high level of physical, economic, and social mobility. When a society or country is traditional and slow changing, there is little demand for fashion and its growth is minimal.

ECONOMIC FACTORS

In the last few years we have all become more familiar with such terms as "emerging nations" and "developing countries." These are terms used to describe countries that are less economically developed than such highly industrialized countries as the United States or Japan. The growth of fashion demand depends on a high level of economic development, which helps to explain the differences in dress between the people of these emerging nations and the people of countries that are highly industrialized.

In his book *On Human Finery,*[1] Quentin Bell underscored the relationship between economics and fashion. He showed that most economically sophisticated countries discard their national costumes long before other nations begin to abandon theirs. England, for example, which led the Western world into the industrial revolution, was the first country to stop wearing traditional national dress. Bell pointed out that Greece, Poland, and Spain, with little in common except for being in similar stages of economic development, retained a national costume when countries with more industrialized economies—Germany, Belgium, Denmark, and Japan—were abandoning theirs.

The twentieth century has provided two

remarkable examples of how countries moving swiftly in economic development also move ahead in fashion. A third example shows how extreme political upheavals can cause a country to change the direction of its economic development, including its attitudes toward fashion.

In the Soviet Union after the 1917 revolution and in China after the communist takeover, clothing, by decree, was both plain and utilitarian. For many years, the people in both countries had no opportunities for fashion expression in their daily lives. In the mid-fifties, however, the Soviet economy had progressed somewhat. Attention then turned to consumer goods, and interest in fashion markedly increased. While they still do not have the many choices available in Western countries, the Soviet people today have a wider selection of fashion apparel than in earlier years. Able to accept or reject offered styles, they are now in a position to create and discard fashions.

Having closed its borders to Western influences for 30 years, the People's Republic of China reemerged in the world economic picture in the late 1970s. As a result, the familiar, drab, workers' uniform—the only dress worn by both males and females—is slowly being replaced by individualized attire. In 1979 the Chinese government underscored its new fashion policy by inviting the great French designer Pierre Cardin to bring the first new apparel fashions to mainland China in three decades.

In 1979 Iran, which had been the most Westernized of the Middle Eastern nations, turned away from Western values as a result of revolution and religious upheaval and returned to the styles of an earlier era in its history. All twentieth-century apparel fashions, particularly those worn by women, were harshly condemned in favor of a national style which had its origins in the eleventh century. Whether this extreme reversal of lifestyle will prevail remains to be seen. Meanwhile, other emerging nations, particularly in the Mideast and Africa, where economic growth is ensured by oil or mineral resources, are turning from traditional, national dress to a more fashion-conscious, Western style.

Consumer Income

Consumers living in highly industrialized economies like that of the United States may choose from a wide variety of goods. Most consumers in such economies also have the money with which to buy those goods.

Consumer income can be measured in terms of personal income, disposable income, and discretionary income. Measurements have shown sharp increases in each of these categories in recent years. Their relative importance, however, depends in part on the purchasing power of a dollar in any given period.

PERSONAL INCOME. The total or gross income received by the population as a whole is called **personal income.** It consists of wages, salaries, interest, and all other income for everyone in the country. Divide personal income by the number of people in the population and the result is per capita personal income.

As Table 2-1 shows, over the years there has been a steady increase in personal income on an average per capita basis. For instance, the average income in the United States in 1950 was about $1,500. In 1978, it was $7,815 or more than five times as much.

DISPOSABLE INCOME. The amount a person has left to spend or save after paying taxes is called **disposable personal income.** It is roughly equivalent to what an employee calls "take-home pay" and provides an approximation of the purchasing power of each consumer during any given year. Table 2-1 indicates that disposable personal income in the United States has risen steadily, but not as rapidly as personal income. This was because taxes took a larger percentage out of the total personal income each year. In 1950, the average amount of disposable income—the income left after taxes—was 91 percent of personal income. In 1978, the average amount of disposable income was 85 percent of personal income.

DISCRETIONARY INCOME. The money that an individual or family can spend or save after

TABLE 2-1
Personal Income and Disposable Personal Income

YEAR	PERSONAL INCOME	DISPOSABLE PERSONAL INCOME	DISPOSABLE INCOME AS PERCENTAGE OF PERSONAL INCOME
1950	$1,491	$1,355	91
1955	1,868	1,654	89
1960	2,212	1,934	87
1965	3,764	2,430	88
1970	3,911	3,348	86
1975	5,879	5,088	87
1978	7,815	6,643	85

Source: Statistical Abstract of the United States, 100th Edition, U.S. Bureau of the Census, p. 438

buying necessities such as food, clothing, shelter, and basic transportation is called **discretionary income.** Of course, the distinction between "necessities" and "luxuries" or between "needs" and "wants" is a subjective one.

PURCHASING POWER
OF A DOLLAR. While Table 2-1 shows that income has gone up each year, it does not mean that people have had an equivalent increase in purchasing power each year. Purchasing power has increased, but not nearly so much as the table might suggest. That is because the value of a dollar—its **purchasing power** or what it will buy—has steadily declined in recent years.

A decline in the purchasing power of money is caused by inflation. **Inflation** is defined as "an increase in the volume of money and credit relative to (the) availability of goods, resulting in a substantial and continuing rise in the general price level."[2] Inflation, therefore, represents an economic situation in which demand exceeds supply. Scarcity of goods and services, in relation to demand, results in ever-increasing prices. Thus in an inflationary period people may earn considerably more money. However, because of the higher taxes on this increased income, plus the spiraling prices of all goods and services, less disposable income and little or no discretionary income remain.

Table 2–2 shows how inflation may affect the price of various products. Note, however, that there is no uniformity among price changes for the various items listed.

EFFECT ON
FASHION MARKETING. Both economic inflation and recession affect consumers' buying patterns. Fashion merchants in particular must have a thorough understanding of the implications of both when planning their inventory assortments and promotional activities.

In a recession, which represents a low point in a business cycle, money and credit become scarce, or "tight." Interest rates are high, production is down, and the rate of unemployment is up. People in the low- and fixed-income group are the hardest hit; those with high incomes are the least affected. Yet these groups are small when compared with the middle-income group. It is the reaction of these middle-income people to any economic squeeze that is the greatest concern of the fashion merchant. For not only is the middle-income group the largest, it is also the most important market for fashion merchandise.

When money is tight, and the economic outlook uncertain, middle-income consumers react in different ways. Some immediately retrench and buy less. A woman who had planned to buy a new winter coat as well as an all-weather coat may decide to purchase the latter and make her current winter coat do for

Courtesy of the H.W. Gossard Co.

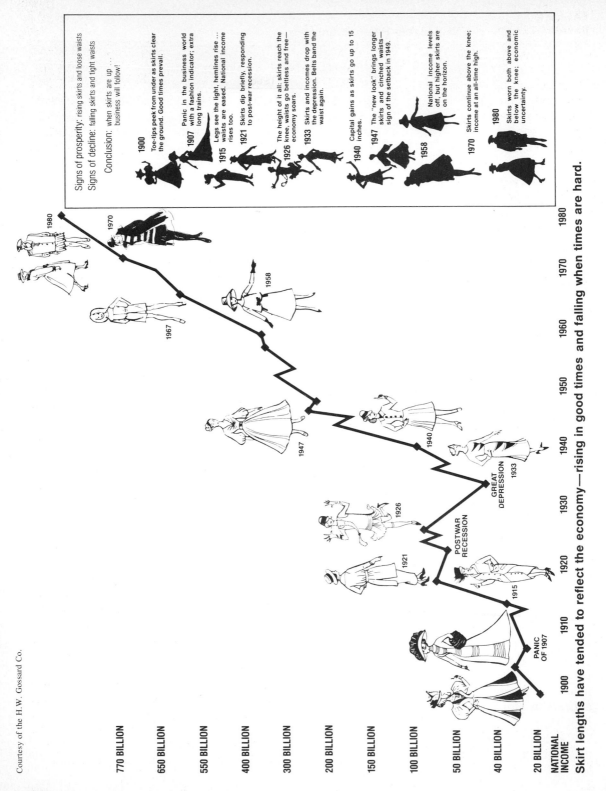

Signs of prosperity: rising skirts and loose waists
Signs of decline: falling skirts and tight waists

Conclusion: when skirts are up ...
business will follow!

1900 Toe-tips peek from under as skirts clear the ground. Good times prevail.

1907 Panic in the business world with a fashion indicator; extra long trains.

1915 Legs see the light, hemlines rise ... waists are eased. National income rises too.

1921 Skirts dip briefly, responding to post-war recession.

1926 The height of it all: skirts reach the knee, waists go beltless and free—economy soars.

1933 Skirts and incomes drop with the depression. Belts band the waist again.

1940 Capital gains as skirts go up to 15 inches.

1947 The "new look" brings longer skirts and cinched waists—sign of the setback in 1949.

1958 National income levels off, but higher skirts are on the horizon.

1970 Skirts continue above the knee; income at an all-time high.

1980 Skirts worn both above and below the knee; economic uncertainty.

770 BILLION
650 BILLION
550 BILLION
400 BILLION
300 BILLION
200 BILLION
150 BILLION
100 BILLION
50 BILLION
40 BILLION
20 BILLION
NATIONAL INCOME

1900 1910 1920 1930 1940 1950 1960 1970 1980

PANIC OF 1907

POSTWAR RECESSION

GREAT DEPRESSION

1900 1915 1921 1926 1933 1940 1947 1958 1967 1970 1980

Skirt lengths have tended to reflect the economy—rising in good times and falling when times are hard.

TABLE 2-2
Purchasing Power: Prices and Income, 1948–1979

ITEM	PRICE IN 1948	PRICE IN 1958	PRICE IN 1968	PRICE IN 1974	PRICE IN 1979	PERCENT CHANGE 1948–1979
Ranch mink coat	$4,200	$4,000	$4,200	$4,500	$6,000	+42.9
Family-sized Chevrolet	$1,255	$2,081	$2,656	$4,119	7,195	+473.3
Pair of blue jeans	$3.95	$3.75	$5.29	$11.25	18.00	+355.7
Gallon of gasoline	25.9¢	30.4¢	33.7¢	55.6¢	1.28	+392.3
Year's tuition at Harvard	$455	$1,250	$2,000	$3,400	$7,985	+1654.9
Hospital cost per in-patient day	$13.09	$28.17	$61.38	$114.90	$233.87	+1686.6
Phone call, New York to Topeka, Kansas	$1.90	$1.80	$1.40	$1.25	$1.31	−31.5
Pound of chicken	61.2¢	46.5¢	39.8¢	55.7¢	.89¢	+45.4
Pound of round steak	90.5¢	$1.04	$1.14	$1.81	$2.49	+175.1
Median family income*	$3,187	$5,087	$8,632	$12,700	$18,966	+495.1

* Half the families in the country earned more, half earned less.
Source: Updated and adapted from a table in *The New York Times*, Aug. 25, 1974.

another season. Some react by choosing more conservative styles. For example, a man who was thinking of buying an expensive new suit for dress occasions may decide that he needs a practical business suit more. Some react by seeking lower prices but without a sacrifice in quality. For example, people who normally do all their purchasing at higher-priced specialty stores may now only patronize them during special sales. These same people will also begin to look for goods of comparable quality at lower prices in department and even discount stores. Merchants recognize the importance of income and price tables as valuable guides to trends in consumer buying patterns. The smart merchant pays attention and adjusts stocks to meet the changing needs and wants of customers. The merchants who choose to ignore these guides may find themselves taking higher markdowns and recording lower profits, inevitable when there is too much stock in relation to sales.

Population

The majority of the population of the United States has some discretionary income and thus can influence the course of fashion. Two factors relating to population, however, have an important bearing on the extent of fashion demand.

The first important factor is the size of the total population and the rate of its growth. The size of the population relates to the extent of current fashion demand, while the rate of its growth suggests what tomorrow's market may become.

The second important factor is the age mix of the population and its projection into the future. These have a bearing on the characteristics of current fashion demand and suggest what they may be in the future.

SIZE OF POPULATION. In 1920 the United States had a population of about 106 million. By 1950 that figure had reached 151 million. And as the 1980 census figures show, the country now records close to 225 million people. This represents a staggering increase of well over 100 million people, or 47 percent, in 60 years.

In 1977 the birthrate of this country showed an upturn, the first reported since 1970. This trend reversed the birthrate drop in the early 1970s. Projections of the population of the United States by the year 2000 range from a high of 270 million to a low of 241 million.

TABLE 2-3

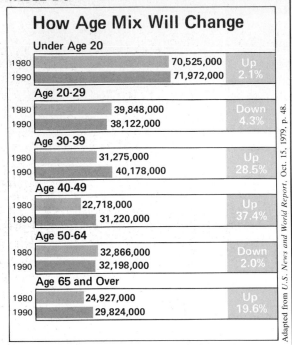

How Age Mix Will Change

Under Age 20

1980	70,525,000	Up 2.1%
1990	71,972,000	

Age 20-29

1980	39,848,000	Down 4.3%
1990	38,122,000	

Age 30-39

1980	31,275,000	Up 28.5%
1990	40,178,000	

Age 40-49

1980	22,718,000	Up 37.4%
1990	31,220,000	

Age 50-64

1980	32,866,000	Down 2.0%
1990	32,198,000	

Age 65 and Over

1980	24,927,000	Up 19.6%
1990	29,824,000	

Adapted from *U.S. News and World Report*, Oct. 15, 1979, p. 48.

The population of the United States continues to grow, but the rate of change is not the same for all age groups. What is the significance of the changes in the 20–29 and 30–39 age groups for the fashion industries?

AGE MIX. While the overall population continues to grow, the growth rate is not the same for all age groups or for both sexes (see Table 2-3). Since each group has its own special fashion interests, needs, and reactions, changes in the age mix both today and tomorrow serve as vital clues to future fashion demand.

Today the largest and fastest-growing age group in the United States is the 24- to 45-year-old group. This is a new factor. The lower birthrate of the early 1970s is now reflected in the 1980 decline in the under-14 group. The resulting decrease in the number of 15- to 24-year-olds will be apparent in 1990. Although the 15- to 24-year-old group is not as large today as other age groups, it will probably continue to be the group most responsive to change and eager for the new. However, since this group will not show an increase until the year 2000, its impact on the current fashion scene is actually reduced.

Because of the longer life span of both men and women, the over-65 group is steadily growing in numbers. This group becomes increasingly important in the fashion world as their earlier retirement, and in some cases increased retirement incomes, allow them to spend many active years wherever and however they choose.

TECHNOLOGICAL ADVANCES

Without competition, we would be clinging to the clumsy and antiquated process of farming and manufacture and the methods of business of long ago, and the twentieth would be no further advanced than the eighteenth century.

So said President William McKinley at the beginning of the twentieth century. In few if any countries has business competition been as keen and fast-growing as in the United States. The competition has fostered many technological advances, many of which have had impact on the fashion field. As technological advances have increased both the variety and availability of new products, the demand for new fashions has increased.

MANUFACTURING
EQUIPMENT AND PROCESSES.

Improved spinning and weaving machines which helped start the industrial revolution were the first major advances in the fashion industry. The mechanical sewing machine was the next advance in the mid-1800s. Today, almost every phase of fabric and apparel manufacture is mechanized, sometimes automated.

Modern sewing machines are powered to operate at high speeds; some specialized machines can produce 5,000 to 6,000 stitches a minute. There are high-speed knitting machines. Embroidery machines can be programmed to stitch different patterns at the turn of a dial and can produce the design on many pieces of cloth at one time. Hems can be power-stitched at high speed or even "welded" by ultrasonic waves. There are bonding machines for welding two thicknesses of cloth. Some can also weld fibers into new types of nonwoven fabrics more supple and delicate than felt, the original nonwoven fabric.

New processes have burgeoned, too. These include ways to make and use a wide variety of man-made fibers, separately or in blends. The industry also is producing blends of man-made and natural fibers for improved quality, appearance, and performance. For example, a new finishing process, called Sanfor-Set, when used on a 100 percent cotton fabric "irons itself in the dryer." The advantages of the natural cotton fiber combined with the Sanfor-Set process make ironing unnecessary.

The development of new methods of treating fabrics has made possible many fashions that could not have been introduced in the past. Bright colors were more readily accepted when they became resistant to fading from sun, rain, and laundry soaps. Pleats became more popular when they were treated to retain their creases through many washings or dry cleanings. Bulky fashions met less resistance when the bulk was achieved without weight.

AGRICULTURE. Agricultural developments have affected the fashion field most strongly in the areas of cotton, wool, fur, and leather. In general, improved agricultural techniques have resulted in more and better-quality products.

Improved seed strains and better control of insect pests and plant diseases have helped increase quality and quantity of cotton grown on an acre. Mechanized equipment helps farmers plant the crop, tend it, and harvest it more efficiently and with less labor. Scientific breeding has produced sheep that yield increasingly better grades of wool. It also has increased the amount of wool that can be clipped from each animal. Improved methods of fur farming and ranching have contributed to better pelts and hides for the fur and leather industries.

COMMUNICATIONS. Not many years ago, news of every sort traveled more slowly. This meant that life moved more slowly and fashions changed more slowly. People in one section of the country learned only after weeks and months what was being worn in other parts of the country. Fashion trends moved as leisurely as the news.

Our electronic age has changed all that. Today we enjoy rapid communication in ever-increasing quantities and infinite varieties. By means of Telstar and almost round-the-clock broadcasting, television brings the world to our homes. Thus it has become a most important medium for transmitting fashion information. Famous designers create special costumes for stars, and we all take note. Changes in the dress and hairstyles of our favorite newscasters, soap opera characters, and talk show personalities have a great impact on us. Examples of this are the fifties craze brought about by Fonzie and the "Happy Days" crowd, and the impact of Farah Fawcett's unique hairstyle on female television viewers. Too, fashion information is transmitted to us through televised fashion shows and commercials.

While television informs us about fashion on a national and international scale, radio also has its valuable place. It is an excellent medium through which local merchants can inform their audiences of special fashion events.

TRANSPORTATION. Improved trucks and super-highways and the growth of the air-freight business all bring the producer of fashion goods and the stores that sell those goods much closer together. Instead of weeks, the transportation of goods from vendor to store now takes days—sometimes only hours if the speed is worth the cost. Consolidated shipping, in which two or more shippers put together a truckload or carload, helps get merchandise to the stores more quickly and at reduced transportation costs.

Developments in transportation have also influenced fashions themselves. The earliest automobiles created a need for dusters, veils, and gauntlets. Today sports cars and motorcycles encourage the wearing of pantsuits, scarfs, and short or divided skirts. Air travel makes any part of the world and any climate accessible in only a matter of hours. It creates a demand for travel and vacation clothes far more varied and versatile than those needed when a vacation meant a trip to a nearby beach or lake. Thus holiday/resort lines are increasingly important in a retailer's merchandise assortment.

SOCIOLOGICAL FACTORS

To understand fashion, it is vital to understand the sociological scene in which fashion trends begin, grow, and fade away. The famous designer Cecil Beaton saw fashion as a social phenomenon which reflects "the same continuum of change that rides through any given age." Changes in fashion, he emphasized, "correspond with the subtle and often hidden network of forces that operate on society. . . . In this sense, fashion is a symbol."[3]

Simply stated, changes in fashion are caused by changes in the attitudes of consumers, which are in turn influenced by changes in the social patterns of the times.

Leisure Time

One of the most important possessions of the average United States citizen today is leisure time—time that can be spent away from the workplace in any way desired. By the end of the 1970s, the number of work hours had shrunk to the point that some companies and government offices now enjoy a four-day workweek. This, in addition to paid holidays, paid vacations, and early retirements, has provided people with an increasing amount of leisure time.

The ways in which people use their leisure time are as varied as people themselves. Some turn to active or spectator sports; others prefer to travel. Many seek outlets for self-improvement, while growing numbers fill their time and enhance their standard of living with a second job. Increased leisure has brought changes to their lives in many ways—in values, standard of living, and scope of activities. As a result, whole new markets have sprung up. There is a demand for larger and

more versatile wardrobes for the many activities these consumers can now explore and enjoy.

CASUAL LIVING. By far the greatest fashion demand resulting from increased leisure time is for casual clothes and sportswear. Casual apparel as it is known today had its initial acceptance in the 1950s, as the middle class began the great trek to the suburbs. A new, more casual kind of clothing was needed by the women who exchanged city sidewalks for lawns and gardens. As the suburbs expanded, casual wear grew in popularity and, in a reversal of the usual pattern, rapidly spread to the cities. Thus it became commonplace rather than shocking to see women wearing slacks on city streets. Today there is general acceptance of appropriate pantsuits or pants as all-occasion wear.

ACTIVE SPORTSWEAR. The sportswear segment of the fashion market has grown to a truly remarkable size in a relatively short time.

Sports clothes have been on the fashion scene since before the turn of the century. But what women wore then for tennis or golf differed little from what was later worn as ordinary streetwear. By the 1920s, however, consumers began demanding apparel that was appropriate for active sports or simply for relaxing in the sunshine.

As a result of the physical fitness and health-related trends of the seventies and eighties, a market called "active sportswear" evolved. With the proliferation of health clubs and exercise classes and clubs, the need for leotards and fashion-related exercise suits grew. The interest in jogging, tennis, skiing, skating, and biking mushroomed, as did the demand for complete wardrobes for each of these active sports.

RETIREMENT LEISURE. Unique to the twentieth century is a special and rapidly growing population segment—retired people. Medical advances, better nutrition, and earlier retirements all have contributed to the growth of this group. It is made up of those who have completed their working careers with plenty of years left for enjoyment of other interests and activities. Through pensions and intelligent planning, many have the means to choose any lifestyle they wish. Instead of spending their retirement years at home or moving in with their children, many are traveling, taking up new studies, involving themselves in civic affairs, and engaging in a wide variety of volunteer activities. Many begin second and even third careers.

Because this group wants apparel that suits their ages, figures, and new interests, they introduce a new element into the leisure fashion market.

Ethnic Influences

In recent years, minority groups in the United States, representing approximately one-eighth of the nation's total population, have experienced some profound sociological changes. Until the late 1950s, the influence of these groups on fashion had been practically nonexistent. The income of more than half of the people in these groups was below that set by the government as the poverty level. Because their purchases were dictated by need, not choice, these people had little influence on fashion.

Since then, however, new laws and the dedicated efforts of many groups and individuals have brought more education, better jobs, and new status to these minority groups. They have increasingly more money to spend and a greater impact on fashion.

Particularly among blacks, fashion reflected these changes. An interest in African culture and civilization grew. For a period of time, Afro hairstyles were widely adopted by men and women. Some men's clothing was influenced by native African dress. And women's fashions were either inspired by African styles or made of African fabrics. Cosmetics designed to emphasize rather than hide the beauty of dark coloring appeared on the market. People of all races found African styles, fabrics, and patterns appealing.

American Indian jewelry and headbands also became popular.

Recently interest has been expressed both in some of the more exotic fashions of the East and in the everyday comfort of the Chinese sandal and quilted jacket. The end of the Viet Nam War and the influx of thousands of refugees from Cambodia and Viet Nam brought

Ethnic influences enrich the fashion scene. Cecily Tyson popularized this African hairstyle in 1972 in the film *Sounder;* in 1979 Bo Derek wore it in the film *10* and gave the style new impetus.

still further traditions and costumes to be shared. Certainly, these are enriching additions to the fashion scene.

Status of Women

In the early 1900s, the American woman was, in many ways, a nonperson. She could not vote, serve on a jury, earn a living at any but a few occupations, own property, or enter public places unescorted. She passed directly from her father's control to her husband's control, without rights or monies. In both households, she dressed to please the man and reflect his status.

Profound changes began to occur, however, during World War I and have accelerated ever since. The most dramatic advances have occurred since the mid-1960s and the advent of the women's movement. Women's demands for equal opportunity, equal pay, and equal rights in every facet of life continue to bring about even more change. These changes have affected not only fashion but the entire field of marketing. A parallel might well be drawn between the goals women have fought to achieve and those sought by other minority groups.

JOBS AND MONEY. In 1976, the Bureau of Labor Statistics projected that 48.4 percent of all women over 16 years of age would be in the work force by 1980. But by September of 1977 that figure had already been reached and surpassed. In just one year, a million women had joined the labor market! Certainly, then, it is not unrealistic to expect that by 1985 half of all American women over 16 will be in the work force.

The dramatic increase in working women has led to a surge in fashion interest, for a woman who works is continuously exposed to fashion. It is everywhere around her as she meets people or shops during her lunch hour or on her way home. As a member of the work force, she now has the incentive, the opportunity, and the means to respond to fashion's appeal.

Finally, women in general today have more money of their own to spend as they see fit. Approximately four women in every six have incomes, earned and unearned, of their own. These women and their acceptance or rejection of offered styles have new importance in the fashion marketplace.

EDUCATION. Often the better educated a woman becomes, the more willing she is to learn new things. She is also more willing to try new fashions, which of course serves to accelerate fashion change. And with more women today receiving more education than ever before, the repercussions on fashion are unmistakable. Today's educated women have had wider exposure than their mothers or grandmothers to other cultures and people of different backgrounds. They are more worldly, more discerning, and more demanding as a result. Their needs speed the fashion tempo.

It is no wonder that Edward Sapir considers education a major factor in fashion change. "Fashion is custom in the guise of departure from custom," says Sapir.[4] To him, fashion is a resolution of the conflict between peoples' revolt against adherence to custom and their reluctance to appear lacking in good taste.

SOCIAL FREEDOM. Perhaps the most marked change in the status of women since the early 1900s is the degree of social freedom they now enjoy. Young women today are free to apply for a job, and to earn, spend, or save their own money. They are free to go unescorted to a restaurant, theater, or other public places. Women travel more frequently than they did in the past. They travel to more distant locations, at a younger age, and often alone. If they can afford it, they may maintain an apartment or share one with others. They are free to come and go, frequently in their own cars.

Short skirts, like those in the 1920s, the early 1940s, and again in the 1960s, are commonly interpreted as a reflection of women's freedom. So, too, is the simplicity of the styles that prevailed in these periods: chemises, sacks, tents, shifts, other variations of loose-hanging dresses, and now slacks and pantsuits.

women mean business

This is the week at Macy's to consider a career that works for you.

Women Mean Business and We Mean You!

A series of seminars designed with you in mind . . . you, the woman of today, who has emerged as a vital force in the world of business. Five days devoted to the possibilities and probabilities confronting you. Five days which could change your life, whether you are starting, re-entering or seeking advancement in today's business world.

Seminars will be conducted by the women who are the movers . . . women in industry, finance, public affairs and the arts. Join them and discover your options and opportunities. Through them, discover yourself!

Mon. March 5th
Beauty Is Their Business
6:00 to 7:30 pm.

You'll find out just how big a business beauty is (and how you can be a part of it) with panelists Diane Young, Manager of National Accounts, Clairol; Adrien Arpel, president of Adrien Arpel

Cosmetics; Carlotta Karlson, Beauty Editor of Harper's Bazaar and Ann C. Sherman, Director of Operations, Retail and Resort Division, Elizabeth Arden.

Tuesday March 6th
Women in the Arts
12:30 to 2:00 pm

Join five lively women from the seven lively arts . . panelists Marilyn Horne, Star of Metropolitan Opera, Liz McCann, Producer of Dracula; Luisa Kreisberg, Director of Public Relations, Museum of Modern Art; Gretchen Cryer, co-author and star of "I'm Getting My Act Together and Taking It On The Road" and Marian Seldes, actress and author of "The Bright Lights, A Theater Life".

Wednesday March 7th
Women in Sales
10:00 to 11:30 pm

Pick up the selling points by these career panelists: David King, Careers for Women, Inc.; Carole Hyatt, author of "The Women's Selling Game: How to Sell Yourself-and Anything Else". Susan Shins, Careers for Women, Inc.; Lou Stanek, Corporate Director of Training, Development and College Relations for Philip Morris.

Women in Media
12:30 to 2:00 pm

Learn all the news from the women who make it with panelists Lynn Caine, author of "Widow" and "Lifelines", Lynn Sherr, ABC Network News Correspondent; Joni Evans, Associate Publisher, Simon & Schuster; Sally Jessy Raphael, WMCA radio personality and Nadine Brozan, reporter for the N.Y. Times.

Thursday March 8th
Finance without Fear
12:30 to 2:00 pm.

Find out about money management and budget planning with panelists Joannine Creen, Executive Vice-President of Catalyst; JoAnn M. Heffernan, Controller, Kenmill Textile Corp. & Treasurer Financial Women's Association of New York, Lynn Jacobs, Project Coordinator, Money-W.I.S.E., Women's Center of Brooklyn College; Debbie Leccese, Director of Administration, Hunter College Center for Lifelong Learning.

Career Life Begins at 35
6 to 7:30 pm.

Learn how to accelerate your game plan with panelists Sue Stricklin, winner of the Atlanta Women's Master's marathon 1978; Helen Ferulli,

Public Education for the Whitney Museum and Dr. Iris Sangiuliano, psychiatrist and author of "In Her Time", Shirley Kanes, facilitator of "Older but Wiser" at Equitable Life Assurance Society.

Friday March 9th
Women Mean Business Anytime, All The Time
10 to 11:30 am

Meet some of the 24-hour women panelists: Isabelle Leeds, Special Assistant to Gov. Carey; Jane Pickens Langley Hoving, actress, singer, philanthropist; Sherrye Henry, WOR radio personality, Elinor Guggenheimer, former Commissioner of Consumer Affairs and President of Women's Forum; and Ronnie Eldridge, Manager of Community Affairs, the Port Authority of N.Y. and N.J.

New Women Network
12:30 to 2:00 pm

Learn how to parlay people into possibilities via panelists Betsy Jaffe, Director of Employer Programs, Catalyst; Alina Novak, Executive Assistant to the President, Equitable Life; Sue Gottesmann, Strategic Planner, the Port Authority of N.Y. & N.J.

How To Register. Co-sponsored with the Hunter College Center for Lifelong Learning, the series will be held in the Special Events Center on 2, Macy's Herald Square.

Costs: $55.00 for the entire series; $15.00 for two morning or evening sessions; $30.00 for four afternoon sessions. Light refreshments will be served. Call (212) 949-4361 to register. (pre-registration is a must.)

Times: Morning Sessions '10-11:30 pm; Afternoon sessions 12:30-2.00 pm; Evening sessions 6-7:30 pm.

All week, rethink the business of fashion for the office: here, the pieces you need. If you plan on going places. Start with a superbly tailored jacket in a nubby oatmeal tweed. Ours is silk/polyester/wool; 205.00. The beige skirt is arrow-narrow slim with an easy side slit; 90.00. Sizes 4-14 by Barry I. Bricken. Under this (and every other tailored thing you own) is a silk suit blouse. White, olive, red, black, violet or mustard, 4-10 by Fenn, Wright & Manson. 50.00. (D.165) Expressions, third floor

macy's

These days, most retailers know that "Women mean business."

There are conflicting theories about these changes, however. One theory is that stiff, unyielding corsets went out with a stiff, unyielding moral code. Another is that they were replaced, with no special significance, by more flexible materials that could mold the figure without discomfort. One can theorize that slacks and pantsuits are expressions of women's freedom—or that these same garments have become fashionable because they are suitable for hopping in and out of the indispensable automobile.

On one point, however, the relationship between fashion and women's lifestyles seems clear: With ever greater activities, women eagerly accept fashions that grant them freedom of movement. Crinolines, hobble skirts, and corsets of the "iron maiden" variety are clearly not compatible with the active lifestyles of modern women. Designers have realized that the hobble skirt of the past would not fit today's lifestyle and have split the slim skirt thigh-high for freedom of movement.

Social Mobility

Almost all societies have classes, and individuals choose either to stand out from or to conform to their actual or aspired-to class. Quentin Bell sees fashion as the process "whereby members of one class imitate those of another, who, in their turn, are driven to ever new expedients of fashionable change."[5]

Bell considers the history of fashion inexplicable without relating it to social classes. He is not alone in his thinking. Other sociologists relate fashion change to changes in social mobility and to the effort to associate with a higher class by imitation.

SOCIAL FLUIDITY.   The United States is sometimes called a classless society, but this is valid only in that there are no hereditary ranks, royalty, or untouchables. Classes do exist, but they are based largely upon occupation, income, education, or avocation, and their boundaries have become increasingly fluid.

Fashion can be a means of crossing class lines. Ski enthusiasts illustrate this point. There are active ski fashions and après-ski clothes within the reach of every income. Once these clothes are donned, only the choice of a ski area is likely to distinguish one class group from another.

MIDDLE-CLASS GROWTH.   Most fashion authorities agree there is a direct relationship between the growth and strength of the middle class and the growth and strength of fashion demand. The middle class has the highest physical, social, and financial mobility. The middle class, because it is the largest class, has the majority vote in the adoption of fashions. Members of the middle class tend to be followers, not leaders, of fashion, but the strength of their following pumps money into the fashion industry. And the persistence of their following often spurs fashion leaders to seek newer and different fashions of their own.

The United States has a very large middle class with both fashion interest and the money to indulge it. It is growing in proportion to the total population thanks to this country's efforts to bring the entire population up to a reasonable standard of living. That growth means a widespread increase in consumer buying power, which in turn generates increased fashion demand.

Physical Mobility

Physical mobility, like social mobility, encourages the demand for and response to fashion. One effect of travel is "cross-pollination" of cultures. After seeing how other people live, travelers bring home a desire to adopt or adapt some of what they observed and make it part of their environment.

Thus Marco Polo brought gunpowder, silks, and spices from the Orient, introducing new products to medieval Europe. Much later, travelers brought touches of Asian and African fashions to Western dress and home furnishings. Later still, Latin American and pre-Columbian influences were introduced into North America, dramatically changing fashion's direction and emphasis in this country.

In the United States, people enjoy physical mobility of several kinds. There is life on wheels, for example—the daily routine for so many people. Both those who drive to work, often in a different city, and those who drive to a shopping center are exposed to a broad range of influences during their daily trips. They have the opportunity to observe the fashions of others and the fashion offerings of retail distributors.

A second form of physical mobility popular among Americans is vacation travel, which takes people to a nearby lake or around the world. Not only does each trip expose travelers to many different fashion influences, but the trip itself demands special fashions. Those who live out of suitcases for a few days or a few months want clothes that are easy to pack, wrinkle-resistant, suitable for a variety of occasions, and easy to keep in order.

A third form of physical mobility is change of residence, which, like travel, exposes an individual to new contacts, new environments, and new fashion influences. According to annual statistics of the Bureau of the Census, about one person out of five changes residence in any given year. This has been the statistical pattern since 1948 when the first such study was made. Among those who move, nearly 20 percent go to a different county within the same state. Another 20 percent move to a different state. These people bring sometimes different fashion ideas to their new residences and adopt or reject some of the new fashions they find in the new locations.

Wars, Disasters, and Crises

Wars, widespread disasters, and crises shake people's lives and focus attention on ideas, events, and places that may be completely new. With these changes, people develop a need for fashions that are compatible with their altered attitudes and environments.

Such changes took place in women's activities and in fashions as a result of the two world wars. World War I brought women into the business world in significant numbers and encouraged their desire for independence and suffrage. It gave them reason to demand styles that allowed freer physical movement. World War II drew women into such traditionally masculine jobs as riveting, for which they previously had not been considered strong enough. It put them in war plants on night shifts. It even brought women other than nurses into the military services for the first time in the country's history. All these changes gave rise to women's fashions previously considered appropriate only for men, such as slacks, sport shirts, and jeans. The Viet Nam War brought more women into the political arena. It set the stage for the equal rights protest movements.

The Depression of the 1930s was a widespread disaster with a different effect on fashions. Because jobs were scarce, considerably fewer were offered to women than had been before. They returned to the home and adopted more feminine clothes. And because money was also scarce during the Depression, wardrobes became skimpier. A single style often served a large number of occasions.

The energy shortage in the late seventies and early eighties brought thermal underwear out of sporting goods catalogs and into department stores. This crisis also brought more sweaters, tights, leg warmers, scarves, boots, mittens, down-filled jackets and vests into the stocks of department and specialty stores. The trend of stocking these goods in fashion outlets was strengthened in the Northeast and West by several severe winters in a row.

PSYCHOLOGICAL FACTORS

Like the ancient song of the sirens, fashion weaves a special magic, enticing consumers to sample its offerings. "Fashion promises many things to many people," says economist Dr. Rachel Dardis. "It can be and is used to attract others, to indicate success, both social and economic, to indicate leadership, and to identify with a particular social group."[6] Fashion interest and demand at any given time relies heavily on the prevailing psychological attitudes.

Basic Psychological Factors

Perhaps the most basic psychological factors that influence fashion demand are boredom, curiosity, reaction to convention, need for self-assurance, and desire for companionship.[7] These factors motivate a large share of people's actions and reactions in general.

BOREDOM. People tend to become bored with fashions too long in use, and boredom leads to restlessness. Garments that have been worn throughout a season finally tire the wearer's eye and sense of touch. The comments heard toward the end of any season illustrate this: "I can't wait to get out of these wools." "I'm tired of that heavy coat." "My clothes simply seem stale."

Boredom and restlessness are particularly noticeable in the case of strong colors, dramatic accessories, and outstanding designs. The color, style, or design begins to grate on both the eyes and the nerves of the wearer. That is why classics—styles that remain popular over a long period of time—are seldom extreme in design or color. Their appeal is pleasant and satisfying but muted and undemanding.

Boredom sets in particularly quickly among people who have a concentrated interest in fashion and fashion-oriented products, whether these are clothes, home furnishings, or other articles. As soon as a product loses its first luster and excitement, or when something newer appears on the market, these people become bored with what they have and restless for something new.

When people experience boredom and restlessness, they seek change. In fashion, the desire for change expresses itself in a demand for something new and satisfyingly different from what one already has. Boredom and restlessness, therefore, feed fashion demand.

CURIOSITY. Curiosity, like boredom, creates restlessness and encourages change for its own sake. Many people like to experiment.

They want to know what is around the next corner and what a garment will look like if its line is changed or certain details added. Curiosity and the need to experiment permeate fashion demand.

Hector Escobosa, former head of the fashionable specialty store I. Magnin's, once described fashion as a "constantly evolving tide, seldom capricious, and generally orderly in its constant evolution." He said that fashion "feeds on new designs, and new designs are created by a dynamic compulsion that keeps creators constantly experimenting, striving for something newer, more exciting, more beautiful."[8]

Curiosity is a desire for new sensations and a spirit of adventure. Curiosity leads to experimentation. It sometimes encourages adoption of fashion styles that conflict with current ideas of beauty and harmony. If the new becomes accepted, it becomes true fashion. If it flames and then dies away, its only significance is as a fad.

Individuals with a highly developed sense of curiosity often find satisfaction in launching new fashions. These are the women and men who are quick to experiment with styles and color combinations in apparel and with new accessories and new ways to wear them.

There is some curiosity in everyone. Some may respond less dramatically than others to its proddings, but curiosity is there, and it keeps fashion demand alive.

REACTION TO CONVENTION. One of the most basic psychological factors influencing fashion demand is the reaction to convention. People's reactions take one of two forms: rebellion against convention, or adherence to it.

Rebellion against convention is characteristic of young people. This involves more than boredom or curiosity; it is a positive rejection of what exists and a search for something new.

Generally, young people from 15 to 24 are the most rebellious, finding adjustment to custom most difficult. One manifestation of youth's rebellion is the rejection of fashions worn by their parents. Clothing styles popular among young people are often radically different from those worn by older groups.

By the age of 25, most people tend to settle down, to accept the responsibilities of family and career, and to make whatever compromises with custom may be necessary. As they mature, those who once rebelled often become adherents to custom and convention.

While rebellion creates new fashions, adherence to convention builds strength in current fashions. For instance, slacks worn by women as ordinary streetwear began to be an accepted fashion by young women in the mid-1960s. At that time, a majority of people did not consider pants proper streetwear for women. Yet their acceptance continued to grow. By the late 1960s and early 1970s, slacks and pantsuits were being worn by women of all ages and classes for many different occasions. They thus became conventional, and their wide acceptance created a stronger demand for the style than the youth market alone could have brought about.

Remember, acceptance by the majority is an important part of the definition of fashion. The majority tend to adhere to convention, either within their own group or class or in general. If a new style adopted by a few does not grow in acceptance, it remains, at best, a fad. And if it wins conventional acceptance for a long enough time, it is on its way to becoming a classic fashion.

Companionship sometimes implies conformity.

SELF-ASSURANCE. The need for self-assurance or confidence is a human characteristic that gives great impetus to fashion demand. Often the need to overcome feelings of inferiority or of disappointment can be satisfied through apparel. People who consider themselves to be well and fashionably dressed have an armor that gives them protection and self-assurance. Those who know that their clothes are dated are at a psychological disadvantage.

Change in dress often helps to create an illusion of change in personality—one way to overcome feelings of inferiority or disappointment. The homemakers or workers who change into after-five apparel put aside their everyday personalities and are transformed in their own eyes into more glamorous people.

Women are believed to have a great need for the reassurance that fashion provides. A marketer of cosmetics credited his spectacular rise to success to his recognition of this element in the feminine character. ''We don't sell cosmetics,'' he said, ''we sell hope.'' And the need for hope, he explained, grows out of woman's perennial need for assurance and recognition. Cosmetics, as this producer advertises them, provide that assurance.

Men, too, have a need for this reassurance and have become more relaxed about admitting this need. In the late seventies and early eighties, cosmetics and fragrances for men became very important. Men all over the world began to enjoy the self-assurance and psychological advantage of such fashion-oriented accessories.

COMPANIONSHIP. The desire for companionship is fundamental in human beings. The instinct for survival of the species drives an individual to seek a mate as one kind of companion. The gregarious nature of humans also encourages them to seek other companions. Fashion plays its part in the human search for all kinds of companionship.

Fashion certainly plays a part when men or women want to attract each other. Women then dress to please and interest a man, and men dress to impress and interest a woman. Both carefully choose fashions that emphasize what they consider their best points and play down what they consider their faults.

Companionship, in its broader sense, however, implies the formation of groups, each of which requires conformity in dress as in other respects. College campuses are a good example. Each campus has its own approved mode of dress for students, usually determined by undergraduate trend-setters. Within the general category of college dress, which is generally quite informal, one campus may favor jeans for women, another shorts, and still another skirts.

In the business world, companionship often expresses itself by the acceptance of a particular style of dress within a particular field of work. In the late 1950s and the very early 1960s, the gray flannel suit was so widely worn by young male executives in advertising and related fields that the phrase "gray flannel suit" identified the young man on his way up in one of these fields. In the mid-1960s, however, nonconformity became an important distinguishing mark for creative people, both in advertising and in other fields. Art directors and copy chiefs of advertising agencies seemed to vie with each other in wearing unusual and colorful working costumes.

Flamboyant or subdued, the mode of dress can be a bid for companionship as well as the symbol of acceptance within a particular group.

The popularity of his and hers sweaters and jeans in the 1970s was another example of the need for companionship. Wearing identical articles of clothing gave couples a feeling of belonging and unity.

General Psychological Attitudes

The general psychological attitudes of consumers also exert an important influence on both fashion interest and fashion demand. When the economy is developing at a rapid rate, with higher incomes, increases in population, and advances in technology accelerating, most consumers are optimistic about the future and tend to spend more freely. They are less concerned about the utilitarian nature of goods and buy more on the basis of "want" than of "need." Thus fashion interest and demand run high, and change accelerates.

In periods of economic uncertainty, however—when taxes and bank interest rates are high, when incomes increase more slowly than do prices, and when unemployment escalates and productivity declines—consumers become pessimistic about the future and tend to spend less freely. Under these conditions, they are more likely to be concerned with the utilitarian or lasting qualities of goods. They buy more on the basis of "need" than of "want." As a result, fashion interest and demand lag, and fashions change at a slower pace.

MERCHANDISING VOCABULARY

Define or briefly explain the following terms:

Discretionary income   **Inflation**

Disposable personal income   **Personal income**

Environment   **Purchasing power**

MERCHANDISING REVIEW

1. What are the three major environmental influences on fashion interest and demand in any era?

2. How does the size and age mix of a population affect fashion demand?
3. How have technological advances in communications affected fashion products?
4. How has the changing status of minority groups affected fashion interest and demand?
5. In what ways does a higher level of education affect fashion interest and demand?
6. What is meant by the term "social mobility"? How does the degree of social mobility affect fashion interest and demand? Give examples to illustrate your answer.
7. Why is it more difficult to identify classes in this country's social structure than it is in many other countries? Upon what factors are classes in the United States largely based?
8. Name three kinds of physical mobility that people in this country enjoy today. How does each influence fashion demand?
9. Name the five basic psychological factors relating to human nature that influence fashion demand. How does each affect fashion interest and demand?
10. How do consumers' psychological attitudes at any particular time influence fashion interest and demand?

MERCHANDISING DIGEST

1. Discuss how technological advances in the following areas have affected interest and the rate of fashion change: (a) manufacturing equipment and processes, (b) transportation.
2. The text states that "changes in fashion are caused by changes in the attitudes of consumers, which are in turn influenced by changes in the social patterns of the times." Discuss how the following have brought about changes in fashion demand: (a) increased leisure time, (b) wars, disasters, and crises.
3. In what ways has the status of women significantly changed in the twentieth century? How has each of these changes affected fashion interest and demand?

REFERENCES

1 Bell, *On Human Finery*, p. 72.
2 *Webster's Seventh New Collegiate Dictionary*, p. 432.
3 Beaton, *The Glass of Fashion*, p. 335 and pp. 379–381.
4 Sapir, *Fashion*, p. 140.
5 Bell, loc. cit.
6 Dardis, "The Power of Fashion," pp. 16–17.
7 Nystrom, *Economics of Fashion*, pp. 66–81.
8 Escobosa, "The Heartbeat of Retailing," *Readings in Modern Retailing*, p. 390.

THE MOVEMENT OF FASHION

Fashion is, in many ways, like a river.

A river is always in motion, continuously flowing—sometimes slowly and gently, at other times rushing and turbulent. It is constantly exciting, never the same. It affects those who ride its currents and those who rest on its shores. Its movements depend on the environment.

All of this is true of fashion, too. The constant movements of fashion depend on an environment made up of social, political, and economic factors. These movements, no matter how obvious or how slight, have both meaning and definite direction. There is a special excitement to interpreting these movements and estimating their speed and direction. And everyone involved in fashion, from the designer to the consumer, is caught up in it.

Textile producers are caught up in it. They must choose their designs, textures, and colors 12 to 18 months before they show their lines to manufacturers. Apparel manufacturers, too, start to work 3 to 9 months before showing a line to buyers, deciding in advance which styles to produce and which fabrics to use in producing them. Retail buyers make their selections from manufacturers' lines 2 to 6 months before the goods will go on the selling floor. Finally, consumers are caught up in choosing a garment that will turn out to be versatile, appropriate, and suitably priced.

How can all these people be sure their choices are based on reliable predictions? Successful ones have a good understanding of certain basic cycles, principles, and patterns that operate in the world of fashion.

THE CYCLING OF FASHION

All fashions move in cycles. The term **fashion cycle** refers to the rise, wide popularity, and then decline in acceptance of a style. The word "cycle" suggests a circle. However, in fashion usage it is represented by a bell-shaped curve (see page 35). Some authorities compare the fashion cycle to a wave, which shows first a slow swell, then a crest, and finally a swift fall. Also like a wave, the movement of a fashion is always forward, never backward.

Unlike waves, however, fashion cycles do not follow each other in regular, measured order. Some take a short time to crest; others, a long time. The length of the cycle from swell to fall may be short or long. And, again unlike waves, fashion cycles overlap.

Stages of the Fashion Cycle

Fashion cycles are best understood by learning to recognize each stage of a style's development. Because there is an orderliness about this development, it may be traced. It may

THE FASHION CYCLE

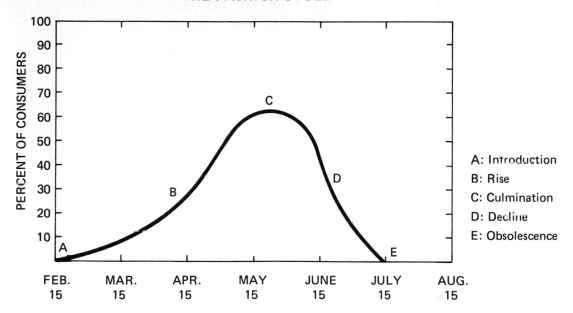

A: Introduction
B: Rise
C: Culmination
D: Decline
E: Obsolescence

even be predicted—on a short-range basis at least—with considerable accuracy. This forward movement of a fashion cycle passes through five stages:

- Introduction
- Rise
- Culmination
- Decline
- Obsolescence

Compare these stages to the timetable suggested by Laver in Chapter 1. A style that Laver would term "shameless" or "outré" would be in the introductory and early rise stages of its cycle. It is considered "smart" when it reaches its culmination. As the fashion declines and nears obsolescence, it passes through the "dowdy," "hideous," and "ridiculous" stages that Laver spoke of.

INTRODUCTION. A producer who offers consumers a new style, color, or texture may be introducing the next new fashion. The new style may be a square toe shoe when pointed toes are popular, or a full skirt when most are

straight. White and black may be offered in the midst of a color craze.

Today most new designs are introduced in higher-priced merchandise. Since they are produced in small quantities, production costs are high. Risks must be considered. Because there is always some possibility of failure when a producer or retailer experiments, prices must be high enough on those styles that sell to cover losses on those that do not. Too, people who like the new often go to only the more expensive stores. They are less likely to seek new fashions in a bargain basement.

RISE. The acceptance of either the original design or its adaptations by an increasing number of consumers is referred to as its **rise.** Prices in this phase are lower generally than at the introductory stage because production is now on a larger scale. This is when exact copies or adaptations of an original style may appear; these are usually made of less expensive materials and produced with less meticulous workmanship.

Many retailers use this stage to merchandise **line-for-line copies** that American manufacturers have duplicated from original couture designer styles. These copies are exactly like the originals except that they have been mass-produced in less expensive fabrics.

Finally, as a new fashion continues to increase in acceptance, **adaptations** appear. Adaptations are designs which have all the dominant features of the style that inspired them but which do not claim to be exact copies. A narrow or padded shoulder, a pleated or A-line skirt, a full or cap sleeve, an abstract or pastel print, a textured or smooth finish to the fabric—such distinguishing features of the original as these may be used in an adaptation.

CULMINATION.   That period when a fashion is at the height of its popularity and use is known as the **culmination,** or plateau, **stage** of the cycle. The fashion then is in such demand that it can be mass-produced, mass-distributed, and sold at prices within the reach of most consumers. This stage may be long or brief, depending on how long the peak in popularity lasts. Remember the cotton velour sweater that was so popular in 1979? It reached its culmination when just about everyone who wanted a velour sweater owned one. The culmination stage of a fashion may be extended in two ways:

1. If a fashion becomes accepted as a classic, it settles into a fairly steady sales pattern.
2. If new details of design, color, or texture are continually introduced, interest in the fashion may be kept alive longer. For example, both sales of and interest in jeans have been maintained by the introduction of the slim leg, the flare leg, the tight fit, and the baggy fit. Variations in weight, construction, and color have also been introduced.

DECLINE.   The decrease in consumer demand because of the boredom that comes from seeing too much of a fashion is referred to as the **decline.** One principle of fashion is that all fashions end in excess. The opposite of this is also true: Excess ends all fashions.

When a fashion's decline sets in, consumers may still be wearing it, but they are no longer willing to buy it at regular prices. They now want newer styles. Leading fashion stores abandon the style; more traditional ones mark down their existing stock to make room for newer styles. Bargain stores offer the style, but at prices well below those that prevailed when the style was in its earlier stages. Production stops immediately or comes slowly to a halt.

There is no predictable timetable for completion of a fashion cycle. Each fashion proceeds at its own speed. One guideline can always be counted on, however. Declines are fast, and a drop to obsolescence is always steeper than the rise to culmination.

OBSOLESCENCE.   When revulsion has set in and a style can no longer be sold at any price, the fashion is in its **obsolescence stage.** As they say in merchandising, "You can't give it away."

Length of Cycles

The cycle of innovation, rise in demand, widespread acceptance, and then rejection occurs with many different kinds of products. It is as true of menswear as of women's apparel. It is also true for refrigerators, automobiles, and architecture. A designer has a new idea. It is introduced as a product. It gathers interest and begins to be accepted. It gains in popularity and is seen everywhere. Then its popularity declines–usually because a newer idea has begun to catch people's attention. All fashions follow this pattern. All that varies is the speed of passing from one stage to the next and the time needed to complete a cycle.

No recent studies have been made of the time it takes for fashion cycles to run their course. Experience, however, indicates that it is steadily decreasing. Among the reasons for this are fast-changing environmental factors, intensified competition among manufacturers and retailers, and consumers' desires for constantly changing assortments from which to select. Too, rapid technological developments tend to make current fashions obsolete more quickly.

Consumers are constantly exposed to a multiplicity of new styles. Some of these win enough acceptance for a cycle to get underway and achieve fashion status. Many are rejected from the start. Each new fashion presses hard at the heels of existing ones. This means that the time required today for a fashion to complete its cycle is noticeably shorter than it was a few decades ago.

Breaks in the Cycle

In fashion, as in everything else, there are always ups and downs, stops and starts. The normal flow of a fashion cycle can be broken or abruptly interrupted by outside influences. The influence can be simply unpredictable weather or a change in group acceptance. Or it can be much more dramatic and far-reaching —war, worldwide economic depression, or a natural disaster, for example.

Although no formal studies have been made of the phenomenon, manufacturers and merchants have a theory about it. They feel that a broken cycle usually picks up where it has stopped once conditions return to normal or once the season that was cut short reopens. Consider the effect that the shortage of petroleum has had on the movement of man-made fibers. Although the success of synthetic fibers—with all their easy-care attributes— was tremendous, their availability was interrupted by petroleum shortages both in 1973 and again in 1979. However, whenever the petroleum supply increased, the level of success of these fibers went back to where it had left off.

Widespread economic depressions and wars also temporarily interrupt the normal progress of a fashion cycle. When there is widespread unemployment, fashion slows its movement tremendously, only resuming its pace with economic recovery and growth.

Wars too affect fashion. They cause shortages which force designers, manufacturers, retailers, and consumers to change fashions less freely. People redirect their interests and fashion takes a backseat. It is true though that after wars and economic depressions have

ended, interest in fashion picks up and it flourishes once again.

Long-Run and Short-Run Fashions

The length of time it takes for individual fashions to complete their cycles varies widely. The terms **long-run** and **short-run** are used to describe fashions that take either more or fewer seasons to complete their cycles than what might be considered average.

Some fashions tend to rise in popular acceptance more slowly than others, thereby prolonging their life. Some stay in popular demand much longer than others do. The decline in popular demand for some fashions may be slower than for others.

Silhouettes, colors, textures, accessories, classics, and fads—the length of time each takes to complete a full demand cycle varies widely with individual characteristics. The level of technological development, existing lifestyles, and psychological reactions to prevailing social and economic conditions also influence these timetables.

SILHOUETTES AND DETAILS. Silhouettes are long-run fashions. They evolve from one to another through a series of changes in detail from one selling season to another. So subtle are some of these changes that last year's garment may not look out of fashion. As a result of a series of almost imperceptible changes over a period of four or five years, however, older apparel may begin to look badly proportioned and out of fashion. In her book, *Recurring Cycles of Fashion*, Agnes Brook Young found that silhouettes changed completely approximately every 35 years.[1]

As a general rule, the more detailed an item of apparel, the sooner it becomes dated. It is interesting to note that many foreign and domestic high-fashion designers express pride in the fact that some of their styles remain fashionably correct for as long as 10 or 15 years.

COLORS AND TEXTURES. Colors and textures were once thought of as secondary and short-run fashions. Color, however, with new scientific studies about its potentially beneficial emotional and psychological effects, has gained importance as an element of fashion. Thus color in fashions of the 1980s has taken on new meaning, and designers and retailers herald new seasons, silhouettes, and details with exciting color stories. The traditional white and pastels for summer and black for winter are limitations of the past.

Textures, too, are less seasonally oriented. Whether a fabric is smooth or nubby, crisp or soft, sheer or opaque, light or heavyweight has more to do with the fashion needs of the customer than of the season. This has become possible with the technological advances in man-made fibers and the new texture finishes for natural fibers.

ACCESSORIES.   For many years, shoes, handbags, jewelry, millinery, gloves, belts, scarfs, and cosmetics were thought of merely as finishing touches for apparel with only seasonal or short-run fashion cycles. Today many accessories are regarded as apparel items and have full-run cycles of fashion acceptance of their own. Handbag and shoe ''wardrobes'' are owned by many consumers and are used to prolong or change the fashion cycles of their basic apparel. Scarfs are also now considered an important fashion accent. They are used as belts or sashes, head coverings, and blouse fill-ins, and in any other exciting or innovative way the customer wishes. The many sizes, lengths, fabrics, and colors of today's scarfs bring variety to their fashion possibilities.

Jewelry moves in both long-run and short-run cycles. Pearls had a long cycle of popularity during the fifties and sixties but declined because of the unstructured and casual look of the seventies. In the eighties, with the return of the look of the fifties and the classic and extravagant look and feel of fashion, pearls have once again begun a fashion cycle.

CLASSICS.   At the long end of the time scale are classics—those fashions that seem permanently arrested in the culmination stage of their cycles. Classics are usually practical and universally appealing. The shirtwaist dress, cardigan sweater, plain pump, neutral hosiery shades for women, and the oxford-type shoe and sport jacket for men are examples.

Classics change, but only superficially. Material, texture, detail, and even silhouette may vary, but the style itself continues in fashion. A woman's pump may be made of any leather, fabric, or plastic. It may have a blunt or a pointed toe and a high or low heel. It may be made in a single color or a combination of colors. Although it changes superficially to relate to current fashions, it remains a pump—not an oxford, a loafer, or a T-strap. Similarly, a shirtwaist dress, whatever its fabric, color, sleeve length, and skirt fullness, remains a shirtwaist.

FADS.   The most transitory and spectacular of short-run fashions are fads. Their rise is meteoric and their decline almost as dramatic. Occasionally, however, fads fool the fashion experts and do not follow the prescribed movements. Some of them start, as usual, with the acceptance of a limited group. Instead of rapidly reaching saturation and abruptly dying, however, they gain general acceptance and become full-fledged fashions. In some cases they even become classics.

Jeans are a perfect example. When college students began to wear jeans to class in the early 1960s, most fashion experts thought of them as a school-crowd fad. However, through the 1960s and 1970s jeans gained greater and greater acceptance, becoming one of the outstanding fashions of the times. Today jeans are considered a classic—and a must for everyone's wardrobe.

Consumer Buying and the Fashion Cycle

Every fashion has both a consumer buying cycle and a consumer use cycle (see page 39). The consumer buying cycle curve rises in direct relation to that of the consumer use cycle. But when the fashion reaches its peak, consumer buying tends to decline more rapidly than consumer use. Different segments of society respond to and tire of a fashion at different times. So different groups continue to wear fashions for varying lengths of time after

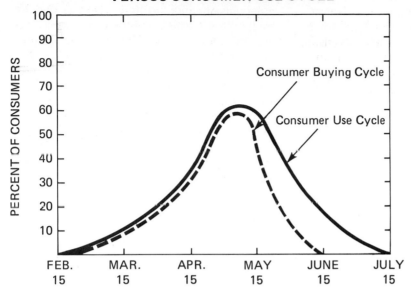

CONSUMER BUYING CYCLE VERSUS CONSUMER USE CYCLE

they have ceased buying them. While each class of consumer is using and enjoying a fashion, the producer and merchant serving that group are already abandoning the style and seeking something newer. Their efforts in this direction are most profitable when they anticipate, rather than follow, the trend of consumer demand.

Consumer buying is often halted prematurely. This happens because producers and sellers no longer wish to risk making and stocking any item they believe will soon decline in popularity. Instead, they concentrate their resources on new items with better prospects of longevity. This procedure is familiar to anyone who has tried to buy summer clothes in late August or skiwear in March.

FACTORS INFLUENCING FASHION MOVEMENT

The fashion cycle has been compared to a force of nature because, in Laver's words, "nothing seems to be able to turn it back until it has spent itself, until it has provoked a reaction by its very excess."[2] Nevertheless, there are factors that can accelerate or retard the

movement of fashion, just as wind can spread a forest fire and rain can slow or stop it.

Accelerating Factors

The influences that exert an accelerating effect on fashion cycles are increasingly widespread buying power, increased leisure, more education, improved status of women, technological advances, sales promotion, and the changes of seasons.

INCREASINGLY
WIDESPREAD BUYING POWER. More widely diffused discretionary income means there are more people with the financial means to respond to a fashion change. The more consumers who flock to a new fashion, the sooner it will reach its culmination. The more widespread the financial ability of consumers to turn to yet a newer fashion, the sooner the current fashion will plunge into obsolescence.

INCREASED LEISURE. Long hours of work and little leisure permitted scant attention to fashion in the past. More leisure time usually means more time to buy and enjoy fashion of many kinds. In the last 20 years, sharp decreases in working hours and increases in paid vacations have encouraged more use of at-home wear, casual clothes, sports apparel, travel clothes, and different types of ordinary business dress. The increased purchases of these types of apparel give impetus to their fashion cycles.

One result of today's increase in leisure time has been the return to catalog buying. Catalog buying originally evolved because people in agrarian societies lived far from stores and had little leisure time for shopping. Today's leisure time has allowed people to add new physical and mental activities to their lives such as sports and hobbies, leaving, once again, little time for shopping. Realizing that their customers are using leisure time in other pursuits, retailers are producing catalogs that come into the consumers' homes and can be read at night or in any spare time. Many department stores employ this technique for special events such as Anniversary Sales, White Sales, Mother's Day, Father's Day, Easter and Christmas.

Many companies with no retail store outlets for shopping have entered the retail business and have been quite successful. The mail-order catalog serves as their only retailing instrument. Some of the more successful catalogs are The Horchow Collection and Consumers Buying Syndicate. Credit card companies have also entered this lucrative field. American Express and Diner's Club catalogs are mailed to every customer that has a credit-card account with them.

The large segment of women entering or reentering the work force has added another impetus to retail business by mail and phone. As advances in cleaning aids have cut house-work time, and with children grown or in school, many women have opted to go to work. Their leisure time thus reduced, these women have stimulated the growth of catalog and direct-mail retailing. They have also forced retailers to offer night, holiday, and Sunday shopping hours, as well as one-stop shopping.

MORE EDUCATION. The increasingly higher level of education in the United States helps to speed up fashion cycles in two ways. First, more people's horizons have been broadened to include new interests and new wants. And second, more people are equipped by education to earn the money to satisfy those wants. These two factors provide significant impetus to the adoption of new fashions.

IMPROVED STATUS OF WOMEN. In a society with few artificial social barriers, women with discretionary income can spend it as they choose. No law or custom prevents any women of means from buying the newest and most prestigious styles in dresses, hats, or shoes. Women thus give impetus to a fashion cycle in its earliest phases. Sex discrimination in the job market has steadily decreased. And social acceptance of women who manage both homes and jobs has steadily increased. As a result, today's women have more discretionary income and are influencing the speed of fashion cycles in the way they use that income.

TECHNOLOGICAL ADVANCES. News, including fashion news, races around the world today. Improved production techniques speed up manufacturing processes. Fast transportation overland, by sea, and by air brings finished goods promptly to retail stores. Little or no time exists between the moment the consumer is psychologically and financially ready to buy and the availability of the goods for purchase. The development of new fibers, finishes, and materials also speeds up cycles. Many of these developments not only improve the wear but also reduce the prices of fashion goods, enabling people of more limited means to buy. The combination of durability and low price encourages those purchases, pushing fashion along in its cycle.

SALES PROMOTION. Consumers cannot be forced to accept a new fashion if they do not want or need it. No amount of publicity, advertising, or promotion can save either a new-born or a fading fashion if the consumer says "no." However, sales promotion can greatly influence how successful a fashion will be. Sales promotion exposure in magazines, newspapers, and TV can help to speed the acceptance of a new fashion or to extend its peak or duration. When short skirts appeared in the 1960s, sales promotion helped women familiarize themselves with this look. Promotion also helped when skirts plummeted to long lengths in the 1970s and again in the early 1980s when shortened lengths returned. Without this assist from sales promotion, the fashion cycle for each look might have taken considerably longer to reach its culmination.

SEASONAL CHANGE. Consumers demand fashion change with the changing calendar. They want to vary the weight and look of their garments according to the seasons. Warm-weather clothes tend to be lighter in both color and weight; cool-weather clothes tend to be darker and heavier. This remains true even though central heating and air conditioning have made the practical need for these changes less real than it was several decades ago.

Increased travel and vacation needs can speed up seasonal change. For instance, when a man intends to travel from New York to Florida for a January vacation, he may decide to buy a new pair of summer slacks for the trip. He may choose from resort assortments, often forerunners of the styles that will be found in the regular seasonal assortments the following spring and summer.

Even in areas where seasonal change does not bring much change in temperature, as in Florida and Hawaii, many people still change their wardrobes with the season. Boredom is a major factor that keeps people from being content with a single, year-round wardrobe.

Retarding Factors

Factors that retard the development of fashion cycles either discourage people from adopting incoming styles or encourage them to continue to use styles that might be considered on the decline. Such factors include the opposites of the accelerating factors as well as habit and custom, religion, sumptuary laws, the nature of the merchandise, and reductions in consumers' buying power.

HABIT AND CUSTOM. By slowing acceptance of new styles and prolonging the life spans of those already accepted, habit and custom exert a braking effect on fashion movement. Habit is at work slowing the adoption of new skirt lengths, silhouettes, necklines, or colors whenever shoppers unconsciously select styles that do not differ perceptibly from those already owned. It is easy for an individual to let habit take over, and some consumers are more susceptible to this tendency than others. Their loyalty to an established style is less a matter of fashion judgment than a natural attraction to the more familiar.

Custom slows progress in the fashion cycle by permitting vestiges of past fashions, status symbols, taboos, or special needs to continue to appear in modern dress. Custom is responsible for such details as buttons on the sleeves of men's suits, vents in their jackets, and the sharp creases down the front of their trousers. Custom usually requires a degree of formality in dress for religious services. The trend toward similarity of dress for men and women in this country has permitted women to wear trousers, but custom still frowns on men in skirts.

A classic example of the influence of custom is the placement of buttons. They are on the right side for men, originating with the need to have the weapon arm available while dressing and undressing. And they are on the left for women, who tend to hold babies on that side and can more conveniently use the right hand for buttons. The stitching on the backs of gloves is another example; it dates back to a time when sizes were adjusted by lacing at these points.

RELIGION. Historically, religious leaders have championed custom and their ceremonial apparel has demonstrated their sanction of the old. They have tended to associate fashion with temptation and have urged their followers to turn their backs on both. Religion today, however, exerts much less of a restraining influence on fashion. Examples of this may be found in the modernization of women's dress in many religious orders and the fact that women no longer consider a hat obligatory when in church.

Recently there has been a countertrend to religion's diminishing impact on fashion. It is particularly evident in the dress adopted by the young followers of Hare Krishna and in the adoption of ancient dress by the followers of the revolution in Iran. In both cases, the religious leaders of these movements have decreed that modern fashions lead to temptation and corruption.

SUMPTUARY LAWS.

Sumptuary laws regulate extravagance and luxury in dress on religious or moral grounds. Height of headdress, length of train, width of sleeve, value and weight of material, and color of dress have all been restricted at times to specific classes by law. Such laws were aimed at keeping each class in its place in a rigidly stratified society.[3]

Other laws, such as those of the Puritans, attempted to keep society's collective mind on a high level, condemning frippery. An order passed in 1638 by the General Court of Massachusetts stated:

No garment shall be made with short sleeves, and such as have garments already made with short sleeves shall not wear same unless they cover the arm to the wrist; and hereafter no person whatever shall make any garment for women with sleeves more than half an ell wide.[4]

And in the eighteenth century, a bill was proposed (but rejected) that stated:

All women of whatever age, rank, profession, or degree, whether virgin, maid, or widow, that shall impose upon, seduce, and betray into matrimony any of His Majesty's subjects by scents, paints, cosmetic washes, artificial teeth, false hair, Spanish wool, iron stays, hoops, high-heeled shoes, or bolstered hips, shall incur the penalty of the law now in force against witchcraft and the like demeanours, and that marriage, upon conviction, shall stand null and void.[5]

People have a way of ignoring local ordinances, however, if they conflict with a fashion cycle that is gathering strength. In New York during the 1930s, fines could be imposed if men or women appeared on the streets in tennis shorts, or if the shoulder straps of bathing suits were not in place on public beaches. What was considered indecent exposure then, shorts for streetwear, for example, is commonplace today.

NATURE OF THE MERCHANDISE.

The nature of the merchandise is sometimes a factor in the rate at which a fashion cycle moves. Silhouettes change more slowly than do colors, textures, and details. Apparel moves in slower cycles than accessories. Men's fashion cycles have traditionally been slower than women's but are gradually speeding up.

REDUCTIONS IN CONSUMERS' BUYING POWER.

Increased spending power can speed up a fashion cycle, as we have seen. And any decrease in spending power—as a result of economic depression, high taxes and interest rates, inflation, strikes, or a high percentage of unemployment—can retard the forward movement of fashion cycles. Similarly, any increase in the number of economically deprived consumers slows down the cycles of fashion. The poor are bystanders in matters of fashion, and bystanders do not keep cycles moving. Laver noted this when he wrote that nothing can make a style permanent except poverty.

RECURRING FASHIONS

In the study of fashion history, we see that styles reoccur, with adaptations dictated by the times in which they reappear. Occasionally an entire "look" is reborn. The elegant, simple look of the late 1940s and early 1950s, for example, was born again for the upbeat generation of the 1980s. Nostalgia influenced choices not only in apparel, but also in hairstyles and makeup.

According to Agnes Brooks Young, there are only three basic silhouettes: (a) bell-shaped, (b) back-fullness, and (c) straight. Moreover, they tend to follow each other historically in regular sequence.

Sometimes a single costume component or a minor detail that earlier exhausted its welcome stages a comeback. At other times, a single article of clothing, like the sandals of the ancient Greeks, returns to popularity.

An outstanding example of recurring men's fashions is the T-shirt. T-shirts originated in France as cotton underwear. They were discovered during World War I by American soldiers who preferred them to their own itchy wool union suits. In the 1940s they reemerged as "tee" shirts for golfing and other active sports. It wasn't until the sixties that they became part of the women's fashion scene as well.

Today it is the T-shirt that has put ego into fashion. T-shirts are bought both for fashion and antifashion reasons, and in both cases they announce to all what the wearer stands for. A T-shirt can project nationality (Je suis Américaine), affiliation (Boys Town), aspiration (Superman), or rock-star preference (the Rolling Stones). T-shirt owners can disclose their identities outright by names, initials, telephone numbers, or even blown-up photographs of themselves transferred onto the T-shirt.[6]

Research indicates that in the past, similar silhouettes and details of design in women's apparel have recurred with remarkable regularity.

In *Recurring Cycles of Fashion,*[7] Young undertook a study of skirt silhouettes and their variations in connection with her interest in theatrical costumes. From data she collected on the 177-year period from 1760 to 1937, she concluded that despite widely held opinions to the contrary, there were actually only three basic silhouettes: the bell-shaped or bouffant, the bustle or back-fullness, and the straight or tubular. Moveover, her data indicated that these three basic silhouettes always followed each other in the same sequence, each recurring about once every 100 years.

Each silhouette with all its variations dominated the fashion scene for a period of approximately 35 years. Having reached an excess in styling, it declined in popularity and yielded to the next silhouette in regular sequence.

A. L. Kroeber, anthropologist, studied

changes in women's apparel over the 330-year period from 1605 to 1936. His conclusions confirm Young's findings that similar silhouettes recur in fashion acceptance approximately once every 100 years. In addition, Kroeber found that similar neck widths recurred every 100 years and similar skirt lengths every 35 years.[8]

PLAYING THE APPAREL FASHION GAME

According to Madge Garland, a well-known English fashion authority, "Every woman is born with a built-in hobby: the adornment of her person. The tricks she can play with it, the shapes she can make of it, the different portions she displays at various times, the coverings she uses or discards . . . " all add up to fashion.[9]

Many clothing authorities read a clear message into the alternate exposure and covering of various parts of the body: sex. Flügel sees sexual attraction as the dominant motive for wearing clothes. Laver suggests that those portions of the body no longer fashionable to expose are "sterilized" and no longer sexually attractive. Those which are newly exposed are **erogenous,** or sexually stimulating. He sees fashion pursuing the ever-shifting erogenous zone, but never quite catching up with it. "If you really catch up," he warns, "you are immediately arrested for indecent exposure. If you almost catch up, you are celebrated as a leader of fashion."[10]

Men's apparel has long played the fashion game, too, but, since the industrial revolution, in a less-dramatic manner than women's. Women's fashions have tended to concentrate mainly on different ways to convey sexual appeal. Men's fashions have been designed to emphasize such attributes as strength, power, bravery, and high social rank. When a male style does emphasize sex, it is intended to project an overall impression of virility.

Pieces of the Game

The pieces with which the women's fashion game is played are the various parts of the female body. Historically, as interest in a part of the anatomy reaches a saturation point, it is withdrawn from the fashion spotlight to be replaced by some other portion.

In the Middle Ages, asceticism was fashionable. Women's clothes were designed to play down, rather than emphasize, femininity. The Renaissance, however, was a period of greater sexual freedom. Women's apparel during this period highlighted the breasts and the abdomen, particularly the latter.

By the eighteenth century, however, the abdomen had lost its appeal. Although the bosom continued to be emphasized, the abdomen was flattened, and heels were raised to facilitate upright carriage. The Empire period, with its high waistline, also stressed the bosom. But the entire body was emphasized with sheer and scanty dresses—some so sheer they could be pulled through a ring. Some advocates of this fashion even wet their apparel so that it would cling to the figure when worn.

During the nineteenth century, fashion interest shifted to the hips, and skirts billowed. Later, the posterior was accented with bustles and trains.

Early in the twentieth century, emphasis switched from the trunk to the limbs, through short skirts and sleeveless or tightsleeved dresses. Flügel interpreted accent on the limbs, together with the suggestion of an underdeveloped torso, as an idealization of youth. He foresaw continued emphasis on youth and boyishness as a result of women's participation in varied activities, the steady march of democracy, and increasing sexual freedom.[11]

THE WAIST. As far back as 3000 B.C., women used corsets in some form to diminish their waist measurements. Accentuation of the waist has taken various forms: cinching, padding above and below, and baring the area, as in modern halter tops and bikinis.

THE SHOULDERS. Baring one or both shoulders in evening wear and on the beach is so commonplace now that it is hard to imagine the furor caused by the strapless gown of the 1930s. Madge Garland points out that the Vic-

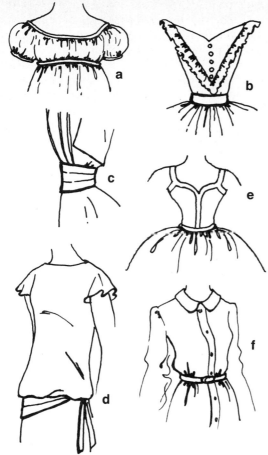

Nearly 200 years of waistlines: (a) 1815, (b) 1850, (c) 1880, (d) 1925, (e) 1950, (f) 1980.

torians exposed shoulders "shamelessly," and Edwardians "covered them hypocritically with wisps of chiffon." [12] In more recent decades, strapless brassieres, or no bra at all, have made it possible for women to expose as much of their shoulders as they choose, particularly in evening and at-home apparel. At the same time, however, fashion emphasis on shoulders was accomplished in street and outerwear through fitted yokes, dropped or extended shoulder lines, and bulky scarfs draped loosely over the shoulders.

THE BOSOM. Ancient Minoan women exposed their breasts, as did Renaissance ladies. In more recent times, women called attention to the bosom with padding, or deep cleavage,

rather than nudity. In mid-century, padded bras added inches to the measurements of young women. Clinging sweaters and plunging necklines heightened the effect. Popular movie actresses posed for publicity photographs that revealed their generous dimensions and increased the popularity of the high-bosomed look.

In the 1960s, fashion interest was focused on short skirts and the legs. As the sixties drew to a close, interest shifted from legs to bosom. By the early 1970s, the natural look of bosoms was "in." Padding and the "push-up" look were gone. The unconstructed, natural look was followed by the "no-bra" look. This reached its culmination and began its decline when bosoms were only slightly concealed beneath see-through fabrics or plunging necklines. As this excess moved to obsolescence, the 1980s ushered in a reemergence of the 1950s bosom. Manufacturers of bras and inner wear are featuring soft-side bras, strapless bras, and molded sports bras to once again give a firmly supported look to the bosom.

THE HIPS. The width and importance of hips follow the movement of skirt silhouettes. Bell-shaped or bouffant, bustle or back-fullness, and straight or tubular—skirt silhouettes dictate the interest in hips. When straight, slim skirts are worn, for example, straight, slim hips are in fashion.

THE DERRIERE. During the nineteenth century, fashion interest shifted to the posterior and was accented with bustles and trains. In the late 1970s and early 1980s, the derriere once again became an important focus of fashion. It became a fashion erogenous zone and helped tight-fitting jeans for men, women, and children become a successful fashion item. Fashion attention was drawn to the derriere, and fashion status was implied by the famous designer label affixed to the seat of the jean.

THE NECKLINE. Early in the twentieth century, the V neck was a daring innovation; women were still accustomed to collars that rose to their ears. As years passed, the V went deeper, at times plunging to the waist. In re-

THE TAFFETA RUFF
*Pure white
moire taffeta
of acetate, by
Premier Etage, $16.*

THE LACE JABOT
*With full lace
collar, in white
or ecru polyester,
by A. Brod, $16.*

THE SILK ASCOT
*Nubbed silk in
off white, red,
black or navy, by
Therese Ahrens, $20.*

THE NET CAPELET
*White French
point d'esprit,
acetate satin trim,
by Premier Etage, $18.*

*Notice the Neck. This year's prettiest focal point. Here we offer the adornments which add charm to fall's classics.
Fashion Accessories, all five BW stores*

BULLOCKS WILSHIRE

LOS ANGELES · PALM SPRINGS · WOODLAND HILLS · NEWPORT BEACH · LA JOLLA

**The neck is often a focal point. This ad reflects some
of the infinite variety of neckwear that is popular today.**

cent years, necklines for daytime wear have shown infinite variety, with scoop necks, backless halter tops, and turtlenecks being worn alongside primly buttoned shirtwaists or wide necklines unfastened to the waist.

THE FEET AND LEGS. For many centuries, legs and ankles were hidden under long skirts. Laced or tied shoes covered the feet and ankles. However, the short skirts and sexy shoes of the Roaring Twenties brought freedom and attention to feet, ankles, and legs. In the forties, beautiful legs reached the peak of their fame, as displayed by the famous pinup picture of Betty Grable. American women were known throughout the world as "long-stemmed American beauties."

Today, interest in feet and legs persists, no matter what the length of skirts and dresses. Interesting textures and colors in hosiery and creative designs in shoes and boots keep the romance and intrigue of legs and feet alive.

THE FIGURE AS A WHOLE. According to Garland, the fashions of the 1950s and 1960s showed off the entire figure:

The modern girl manages at the same time to bare her shoulders, accentuate her bust, pull in her waist, and show her legs to above the knees. It is a triumph of personal publicity over the taboos of the past and the previous limitations of fashion.[13]

This "triumph of personal publicity" in the late 1960s called attention to feet clad only in sandals or low-heeled shoes, to legs sheathed in textured, fishnet, or decorated pantyhose, and to the midthigh where skirts stopped. It ignored the waist much of the time but accentuated it in sportswear with bare midriffs, bikinis, and hip-huggers. Sleeveless dresses, natural-line bras, wide, high cowled collars, drop earrings, wigs, and tinted hair—long and flowing or dramatically cut and arranged—gave the eye much to observe. Areas that were normally covered made their bid for attention, too, with cutouts in dresses and gloves. Previous fashion eras had centered attention on only certain parts of the body. Fashions during the 1960s tended to emphasize all parts.

The general trend in women's fashions for the 1980s again emphasizes the body as a whole, but with softer, less-structured styling. This reflects new attitudes regarding exhibitionism and modesty. Some parts of the body may be exposed and therefore considered erotic. Other parts are equally seductive when covered by fabrics that softly follow their contours without actually revealing them.

Rules of the Game

Laver explains fashion's emphasis in terms of the sexuality of the body. "Fashion really began," he says, "with the discovery in the fifteenth century that clothes could be used as a compromise between exhibitionism and modesty."[14]

The game of emphasizing different areas of the female anatomy at different times has its rules. The first and fundamental rule is that fashion does not flit. It selects one area of the body and stays with that area until every last possibility for excitement has been exhausted. When one part of the body has been overemphasized, fashion concentration shifts to another area. Crinolines and hoops, for example, reached impossible diameters before skirts became narrower. Tight lacing grew so tight that health was endangered before the practice was abandoned.

Garland has suggested a second rule for the fashion game: Only certain parts of the body can be exposed at any given time.[15] Fashion has provided ample illustrations: turtlenecks on sleeveless dresses or sweaters, miniskirted dresses with high necklines and long sleeves, plunging necklines on ankle-length evening gowns.

The third rule of the fashion game is that its movement is always forward, never in reverse. As Robinson has said, "A fashion can never retreat gradually and in good order. Like a dictator it must always expand its aggressions or collapse. Old fashions never fade away; they die suddenly and arbitrarily."[16]

PREDICTING THE MOVEMENT OF FASHION

Producing and selling fashion merchandise to consumers at a profit are what fashion merchandising is all about. The excitement and flair that producers and retailers bring to their segment of merchandising must have a well-defined plan and follow the movement of general fashion preferences.

Fashion moves constantly but at varying speeds toward culmination and inevitable decline. The success of fashion merchandising depends upon the correct prediction of which new styles will be accepted by the majority of consumers. The successful forecaster of fashion must:

1. Distinguish what the current fashions are
2. Estimate how widespread they are
3. Determine at what point in time these fashions will appeal to the firm's target customer groups

With information on these three points, projections—a prime requisite in successful fashion merchandising—become possible.

Identifying Trends

A **fashion trend** is the direction in which fashion is moving. Manufacturers or merchants try to recognize that direction and determine whether it is moving toward or away from maximum acceptance. They can then decide whether to actively promote the fashion, to wait, or to abandon it.

For example, pleated skirts may be a recognized fashion trend. At the introductory and rising stages, retailers will stock and promote an increasingly larger proportion of pleated skirts. When it seems that customers are reaching a point of saturation with this style, retailers will begin introducing slim skirts into their stock in larger and larger numbers. If they have correctly anticipated the downturn in customer demand for pleated skirts, they will have fewer on hand when the downturn occurs. Customers may still be wearing the pleated styles, but they will not be buying them, at least not at regular prices.

Sources of Data

The ability of fashion forecasters to determine the strength and direction of fashion trends among their customers has little to do with clairvoyance. Nor is it a matter of that vague talent called "fashion sense." Good, solid facts about customer acceptance are behind most successful merchandising decisions. Successful merchants collect data by checking their sales records. They also observe what is being worn, both generally and by their own customers. Finally, they determine where each fashion is in its life cycle and when it is likely to be of interest to their customers.

SALES DATA.   Automated methods of collecting sales data, both punch-card and electronic, are a boon to fashion merchants. Some stores have completely automated systems that start right at the cash register. To complete a sale, the salesperson punches into the register not only the price but also several other numbers that appear on the price ticket. These numbers identify the category of merchandise, the style, and perhaps the color, fabric, or size. The information punched into the register is relayed directly to the memory bank of a computer where it is stored and from which it may be recalled in printed summary form as needed. The system can be used to collect information about almost any fashion element that the merchant thinks important to watch.

Automated systems give merchants more accurate details about sales and stock on hand. They also make those figures available for study much more quickly than ever before. This speed is very important in fashion merchandising. It means that results from the testing of new styles and colors are available to the merchant almost immediately. Changes in customers' preferences can be identified quickly, and the rate of sale of affected styles can be charted and evaluated. The speed of automated systems enables buyers to make quick, accurate decisions about reorders.

OBSERVATIONS.   Successful merchants observe what is being generally worn. This adds to what merchants can learn from their own sales experience and from the experience of others. Actual counts may be made at an important charity event, for example, to ascertain which women and how many women are wearing a new style or color.

A fashion merchant's dependence on observation rather than intuition is by no means new. As far back as 1928, Nystrom pointed out:

> *Changes in fashions may be checked and their trends determined by the simple process of making successive periodic counts of the same styles, among the same classes of people, comparing the result from one period to another, and taking note of the change.*[17]

Since fashion is a complex phenomenon involving many elements, observations are most helpful if they are made in terms of each of the four elements of fashion: silhouette, detail, texture, and color. Thus, in a given season, successive observations may show bright colors predominating, but brown on the rise and black making a tentative entry. A series of counts might each time show fewer women wearing the jewel neckline and more wearing turtlenecks and shirt collars.

In addition, observations should take into consideration the characteristics of customers as well as the characteristics of a style. The strength and direction of a trend varies in different age, income, and interest groups, and among groups in different areas. What young suburbanites wear to a club luncheon is not necessarily what urbanites wear to a fashionable restaurant. Successful fashion forecasting requires that merchants first pinpoint what their target groups of customers are wearing today. They can then determine what they are likely to wear tomorrow.

Most merchants do not depend solely on their own observations, however. They consult sources of information about the buying and use habits of customers other than their own. They look at both the local picture and the total picture. They take into account their own sales experience and that of others, their own judgment and that of others. In fashion forecasting, wise merchants draw information from every available source. They then coordinate the data in terms of the fashion preferences of their specific target customers.

Interpreting Influential Factors

To interpret the data they have collected and organized, fashion forecasters, whether merchants, producers, or designers, must put their knowledge of fashion and fashion principles to work. They examine the data and the pattern it shows. They must also take into consideration certain factors which accelerate or retard a fashion cycle among the target group of customers. These factors include current events, the appearance of prophetic styles, sales promotion efforts, and the current canons of taste.

CURRENT EVENTS. Items in the news can influence consumers and affect their response to a fashion. When America and the People's Republic of China resumed diplomatic relations, there was a tremendous revival of Chinese fashions. Both apparel and home furnishings imported from China flooded the stores of America. 1979 became the year of the quilted Chinese jacket.

PROPHETIC STYLES. Good fashion forecasters keep a sharp watch for what they call **prophetic styles.** These are particularly interesting new styles that are still in the introductory phase of their fashion cycle. Taken up enthusiastically by the socially prominent or by the flamboyant young, they may gather momentum very rapidly or they may prove to be nonstarters. Whatever their future course, the degree of acceptance of these very new ideas provides information of interest to experienced observers.

SALES
PROMOTION EFFORTS. Along with the records of past sales, fashion forecasters give thought to the kind and amount of promotion that helps stimulate interest in prophetic styles. They also consider the kind and amount of additional sales promotion they can look forward to. A fiber producer's powerful advertising and publicity efforts may have helped turn slight interest in a product into a much stronger interest during a corresponding period last year. The forecasters' problem is to estimate how far the trend might have developed without those promotional activities. How much momentum remains from last year's push to carry it forward this year, and how much promotional support can be looked for in the future must also be assessed. The promotional effort that the forecaster's own organization plans to expend is only one part of the story; outside efforts, sometimes industrywide, also must be considered in forecasting fashions.

CANONS OF TASTE. In judging the impact of new styles, a forecaster relates them to currently accepted canons of taste and usefulness. In an era of uninhibited exposure of much of the body, one would not expect to sell many high-necked, long-sleeved, demurely styled long dresses. In an era of clear, vibrant color, pastels and misty tones seem to have few advocates. When pastels have their day, bold colors seem crude and inappropriate.

According to Nystrom, fashions that are in accord with currently accepted canons of art, custom, modesty, and utility are most easily accepted. They also go farthest, and last longest.[18]

Importance of Timing

Successful merchants must determine what their particular target group of customers is wearing now and what it is most likely to be wearing a month or three months from now. The data they collect enables them to identify each current fashion, who is wearing it, and what point it has reached in its life cycle.

Since merchants know at what point in a fashion's cycle their customers are most likely to be attracted, they can determine whether a current fashion is one to stock now, or a month from now, or three months from now. For instance, in 1979, baggy jeans and trousers were a new style at the beginning of their cycle. Specialty shops that catered to young fashion leaders rushed to get these new pants into stock. Department stores, whose customers are a little more conservative, took note of this new style and began to add baggies to their inventories in small quantities. They waited until statistics and observations showed that the fashion was building and broadening in appeal. When acceptance was proved, the number and variety of baggies on the selling racks increased.

MERCHANDISING VOCABULARY

Define or briefly explain the following terms:

Adaptations	**Long-run fashion**
Culmination stage	**Obsolescence stage**
Decline stage	**Prophetic styles**
Erogenous	**Rise stage**
Fashion cycle	**Short-run fashion**
Fashion trend	**Sumptuary laws**
Line-for-line copies	

MERCHANDISING REVIEW

1. Name and explain the five phases of a fashion's life cycle.
2. How do adaptations differ from line-for-line copies?
3. What are the two ways in which the culmination stage of a fashion can be extended?
4. What can disrupt the normal progress of a fashion cycle? Once disrupted, can the cycle be resumed? Cite examples to illustrate your answer.
5. Differentiate between long-run and short-run fashions and give examples of each.
6. How does the consumer use cycle differ from the con-

sumer buying cycle? What implications does this have for fashion merchants?

7. What conclusions did Agnes Brooks Young reach in her study of skirt silhouettes from 1760 to 1937?
8. List the "pieces" with which the women's fashion game is played, according to Madge Garland.
9. What are the three basic rules that govern the fashion game, according to leading fashion authorities?
10. How does one predict fashion trends? From what resources can a fashion merchant collect data that will help determine fashion trends?

MERCHANDISING DIGEST

1. Discuss the various factors that tend to accelerate the forward movement of fashions through their cycles, giving at least one example of how each factor has an accelerating effect.
2. Discuss the factors that tend to retard the development of fashion cycles by discouraging the adoption of newly introduced styles. Give at least one example of how each factor exerts a braking influence on fashion development.
3. From your study and appraisal of currently popular styles in women's apparel, do you see any signs which indicate that a new and different silhouette is in the making? If so, what would that silhouette be? Give examples to defend your answer.

REFERENCES

1 Young, *Recurring Cycles of Fashion: 1760–1937*, p. 30.
2 Laver, *Taste and Fashion*, p. 52.
3 Binder, *Muffs and Morals*, pp. 162–164.
4 McClellan, *History of American Costume*, p. 82.
5 Taylor, *It's a Small, Medium, and Outsize World*, p. 39.
6 Pierre, *Looking Good*, p. 149.
7 Young, loc. cit.
8 Kroeber, "On the Principles of Order in Civilizations as Exemplified by Change in Fashion," pp. 235–263.
9 Garland, *Fashion*, p. 11.
10 Laver, op. cit., p. 201.
11 Flügel, *The Psychology of Clothes*, p. 163.
12 Garland, op. cit., p. 18.
13 Ibid., p. 20.
14 Laver, op. cit., p. 200.
15 Garland, op. cit., p. 11.
16 Robinson, "Fashion Theory and Product Design," p. 128.
17 Nystrom, *Fashion Merchandising*, p. 84.
18 Ibid., p. 94.

4

FASHION LEADERS AND FOLLOWERS

In today's world, the old saying is still true—a cat can look at a king. And so can an ordinary person look at a king, or at a wealthy person. And an ordinary person can do even more. Today people of modest means wear the same fashion designs as those worn by royalty and the wealthy. Long gone are the class distinctions that existed throughout history and the dress restrictions that went with them. Today, discretionary income is not only larger but more evenly distributed. This enables more and more people to purchase goods on the basis of fashion rather than utilitarian appeal. Improved technology allows manufacturers to mass-produce and retailers to mass-distribute certain fashion goods profitably. Better education and speedier communications encourage people to want and accept the new much more rapidly than did previous generations. Finally, there exists today in the United States a huge and thriving middle class. It has more leisure time than ever before in which to enjoy fashion, to become bored with what is available, and to seek refreshing new styles.

It is the combination of these factors that has caused fashion during the second half of the twentieth century to move at lightning speed. But how do fashions begin? Who starts them, who sponsors them, and what influences consumers to accept them? Answers to these questions are complex and involve designers, manufacturers, retailers, and most of all, consumers.

The myth that every change in fashion is caused by some Paris designer seeking new ways to make money is, of course, not true. It is consumers who bring about changes in fashion. The needs and wants of consumers change. Their ideas about what is appropriate and acceptable change. And their interests in

life change. These are all reasons for fashion designers and manufacturers to produce new and different styles for consumers' consideration. The charting, forecasting, and satisfaction of consumer demand are the fashion industry's main concerns.

BIRTH OF A FASHION

The current trends in consumers' ideas and attitudes are noted, analyzed, interpreted, and subsequently presented to consumers in the form of new styles. Designers and manufacturers do influence fashion in one important way, however. They provide an unending series of new styles to consumers for their consideration. This allows consumers to choose styles that best express their individual lifestyles.

Many precautions are taken to ensure that designers are presenting what the customer wants. Even so, it is estimated that at least two-thirds of the new designs introduced each season by the fashion industry fail to become fashions. Sometimes designs are introduced too early, before the public is ready to accept them. At other times, their interpretations may be too extreme for consumer acceptance.

Another factor is sometimes overlooked by manufacturers and their designers. A trend may be commonly accepted in many places, yet meet pockets of resistance in certain areas of the country. What is worn in New York today is not necessarily what consumers in less urban areas of the United States are ready to accept. A classic example of this is the case of skirt lengths in the early 1970s. Fashionable women in New York, Chicago, and San Francisco readily accepted the skirt lengths that fell just below the knee or midcalf. Yet women in less cosmopolitan areas continued to wear much shorter skirts. The latter women also considered the pantsuit the most important fashion in the late 1970s, well after the skirt had replaced it in the cities.

The Designer's Role

Another widely held misconception is that designers live and work in "ivory towers," dreamily creating their artistic designs. Nothing could be farther from the truth.

In creating designs that will not only reflect consumer attitudes and needs but also give expression to artistic ideas, fashion designers are continually influenced and limited by many factors. Some of these factors are practical business considerations. The availability of materials and their cost, the particular image that the firm wants to maintain, available production techniques, and labor costs, for exam-

Elyn Zelman

Designers, like Willie Smith shown here, do not live and work in ivory towers. They have to consider the practical—labor matters, production techniques, and availability and costs of materials.

ple, are prime considerations. All designs must be produced at a profit and within the firm's predetermined wholesale price range. In short, there are many practical obstacles for any designer to overcome. Great designers are those who use their creativity to overcome all these limitations and to produce salable, exciting designs.

Designers must continually study the lifestyles of those consumers for whom their designs are intended. Because they work far in advance of the design's final production, they must be able to predict future fashion trends. Finally, the designer must be aware of the effects of current events, socioeconomic conditions, and psychological attitudes relating to fashion interest and demand.

TYPES OF DESIGNERS. Most American designers who are using their artistic and innovative talents to design fashion-oriented merchandise fall into one of three groups: (1) couture, "name," or high-fashion designer, (2) stylist-designer, and (3) free-lance artist-designer.

The couture designer is usually referred to in this country as a "name" designer. Because of the success and originality of their designs, name designers are well known to the fashion-conscious customer. A couture designer is not only responsible for creating the designs but also for the choice of fabric, texture, and color in which each is to be executed. He or she may often be involved in development of the production model, as well as plans for the promotion of the firm's line. A designer may work for a firm, such as Kasper does for Joan Leslie, Gloria Vanderbilt for Murjani, Inc., or Diane Von Furstenberg for Puritan. Other designers may actually own their own firms or be financed by an outside "silent partner."

Until recently, designer names were associated only with original, expensive designs in apparel. Today, many designers, whose names have come to be associated with what is new and original, license their names to manufacturers of accessories, home furnishings, cosmetics, and fragrances.

A second type of designer—the stylist-designer—uses his or her creative talents to adapt or change the successful designs of others. It is important for this designer to understand fabric and style construction as well as the manufacturing process, because designs are usually adapted at lower prices. The stylist-designer usually creates designs at the late-rise or early culmination stage of the fashion cycle. He or she is usually not involved in details relating to either the production of the firm's line or in the planning of its promotional activities.

The third type of designer—the free-lance artist-designer—sells sketches to manufacturers. These sketches may be original designs by the free-lancer or they may be adaptations. They may reflect the free-lancer's own ideas or the manufacturer's specifications. The free-lancer usually works out of a design studio and sells sketches and designs to the general apparel market. With the delivery of a sketch to the manufacturer a free-lancer's job ends.

INSIGHT AND INTUITION. A designer takes a fashion idea and embodies it in new styles. Even the most creative designers, however, frankly disclaim any power to force acceptance of their styles. Few have said so more effectively than Paul Poiret, one of the twentieth century's great Parisian couturiers. He once told an American audience:

I know you think me a king of fashion. . . It is a reception which cannot but flatter me and of which I cannot complain. All the same, I must undeceive you with regard to the powers of a king of fashion. We are not capricious despots such as wake up one fine day, decide upon a change in habits, abolish a neckline, or puff out a sleeve. We are neither arbiters nor dictators. Rather we are to be thought of as the blindly obedient servants of woman, who for her part is always enamoured of change and athirst for novelty. It is our role, and our duty, to be on the watch for the moment at which she becomes bored with what she is wearing, that we may suggest at the right instant something else which will meet her taste and needs. It is there-

fore with a pair of antennae and not a rod of iron that I come before you, and not as a master that I speak, but as a slave . . . who must divine your innermost thoughts.[1]

Insight and intuition, then, play a large part in a designer's success. He or she must constantly experiment with new ideas. When one fashion is reaching that excess which marks its approaching demise, a designer must have new candidates ready and waiting for the public's favor.

On occasion a style or design takes such firm hold on the consumer's affections that it continues to be popular for many seasons. Designers then give it apparent freshness each season by using new details or new materials. For many years the blazer jacket has been widely accepted by both men and women. At many points in fashion history blazers were so widely accepted that they had become almost a uniform. Whenever this happened, designers added variety and a new look through changes in collar treatments, buttons, trims, and new fabrications. In 1980, for example, designers changed from velvet blazers back to the "preppy" look of the grey flannel blazer.

SOURCES OF DESIGN INSPIRATION.

Where does the designer get ideas and inspiration for new fashions? The answer, of course, is everywhere! Through television the designer experiences all the wonders of the entertainment world. In motion picture theaters, the designer is exposed to the influences of all the arts and lifestyles throughout the world.

Sometimes a single entertainment offering can exert remarkable influence on the fashion consciousness of an entire country. Such was the case with the movie *Annie Hall*. Diane Keaton's style of dress had an immediate and powerful impact on younger women. The "Annie Hall look," with its emphasis on liberation, became the fashion costume of the day and then of the year. As each designer made distinctive changes here and there to tailor the look to each special market, what could have been just a fad became a powerful fashion statement. In fact, the arbiters of fashion agree that the Annie Hall look was the "look of the 1970s."

The movie *Annie Hall* is an example, then, of one specific influence on designers. However, most inspiration has a broader base. For example, designers may be influenced by an exotic style from some area of the world that has suddenly become familiar through the news. Such has been the case recently with Africa (which gave us the dashiki) and the oil-rich nations of the Mid-east and Near East (which gave us the galabia). The political nuances of the early and mid-1970s focused attention on the Far East, where designers found endless fashion ideas. Fabrics of pure silk, silk-like materials, and batiks quickly became popular. The slit skirt, the mandarin coat, and the coolie jacket are only a few styles which owe their inspiration to styles from the East.

Entertainment trends probably have one of the most powerful impacts on fashion ideas. The movie *Saturday Night Fever*, for example, introduced an entire nation to the disco scene. As a result, ever-increasing numbers of people demanded disco fashions. As unrestrained, participation entertainment, disco dancing required different styles from those worn by followers of rock, punk rock, or country and western, all of which were largely spectator forms of entertainment. Rock music's performers brought about "mod" fashions and the acceptance of long hair and beards. Country and western music focused designers and consumers on the cowboy hat, boots, and a more clean-cut look. Disco then added the ingredient of glitter and glow. Two decades of rock all but eradicated the music of earlier American popular composers. Disco, however, brought their melodies back with a definite beat, and a whole generation of American youth "discovered" the music of the 1930s and 1940s. Along with the music they became interested in what life was like then and in the way people dressed. On the one hand, then, the disco scene demanded fashions for its throbbing lifestyle. But it also brought a new awareness of and demand for the fashions of the past, giving the fashion designer a multipatterned inspiration.

The Annie Hall look of the 1970s showed the remarkable influence that a single film could have on the fashion consciousness of a whole decade.

Thus, the public is the launcher of new trends. The designer reacts to those trends and creates styles that capture the public's ideas. While ever alert to the new and exciting, fashion designers never lose sight of the recent past. They know that consumers need to anticipate something new each season. But they also recognize that whatever new style is introduced will have to take its place with what consumers already have in their wardrobes. No one starts with all new clothes each season. Rarely does a revolutionary new style succeed. Instead, it is the evolutionary new style that so often becomes the best-selling fashion.

The Manufacturer's Role

Manufacturers would agree with Robinson that "every market into which the consumer's fashion sense has insinuated itself is, by that very token, subject to [the] common, compelling need for unceasing change in the styling of its goods."[2]

Even in such prosaic items as paper napkins, the need for change has produced rainbows of pastels, brilliant deep shades, and whites with dainty prints. Similarly, in basics such as bedsheets or men's dress shirts, the once traditional white has yielded to a variety of colors, stripes, and prints. There is scarcely an industry serving consumers today in which the manufacturer's success does not depend in part upon an ability to attune styling to fashion interest and demand.

TYPES OF MANUFACTURERS. In general, manufacturers of fashion goods can be divided into three groups. One group is made up of firms that produce innovative, high-fashion apparel; it is usually identified as the "better market."

A second group of firms sometimes produces originals. But it usually turns out adaptations of styles which have survived the introductory stage and are in the rise stage of their fashion life cycle. This group of firms is usually identified as the "moderate-priced market." A third group of manufacturers makes no attempt to offer new or unusual styling. Rather, these firms mass-produce close copies or adaptations of styles that have proved their acceptance in higher-priced markets. This group is usually identified as the "budget market."

FASHION INFLUENCE. In the field of women's apparel, manufacturers are committed to producing several new lines a year. A **line** is an assortment of new designs. Some of these may be new in every sense of the word and others merely adaptations of currently popular styles. Producers hope that a few of the designs in a given line will prove "hot"— so precisely in step with demand that their sales will be profitably large.

Occasionally, manufacturers' styles may be too advanced for the fashion tastes of customers. Such producers neither accelerate nor retard fashion; their goods simply do not get wide distribution and have little or no impact upon the public.

For the most part, the fashion industries are made up of manufacturers whose ability to anticipate the public's response to styles is excellent. Those who do badly in this respect, even for a single season, usually reap small sales and large losses. Unless they are unusually well financed, they quickly find themselves out of business. In the fashion industry, the survival of the fittest means the survival of those who give the most able assistance in the birth and growth of fashions that consumers want.

The Retailer's Role

Retailers are in much the same position as producers. They do not create fashion, but they can encourage or retard its progress by the degree of accuracy with which they anticipate the demands of their customers. They seek out in the market styles that they believe are most likely to win acceptance by these target groups.

TYPES OF RETAILERS. There are many ways to classify retail firms. However, when an evaluation is made on the basis of the firms' leadership positions, they tend to fall into three main categories.

First there are firms that are considered fashion leaders. They feature newly introduced styles that have only limited production and distribution. These styles are usually expensive. A second group of retailers—by far the largest in number—features fashions that have captured consumer interest in their introductory stage and are in the late-rise or early-culmination stage of their life cycles. Since these styles are usually widely produced by this time, they are most often offered at moderate prices. A third group of retailers, often called "mass merchants," features widely accepted fashions that are well into the culmination phase of their life cycles. Since fashions at this stage of development are usually mass-produced, mass merchants can and do offer fashions at moderately low to low prices.

FASHION INFLUENCE. Occasionally, retailers are so intuitive or creative that they are a step ahead of their suppliers in anticipating the styles their customers will accept. Such retailers accelerate the introduction and progress of new fashions by persuading manufacturers to produce styles that answer a latent demand.

Normally, however, retailers simply select from what is offered by producers in the market. To do a good job, retailers must carefully shop the markets, selecting styles they feel sure will be of special interest to their customers. They must have the styles in their stores when customers are ready to buy. On the other hand, retailers can hold back good incoming fashions by failing to stock styles that consumers would buy if given the opportunity. Conversely, they can make the mistake of exposing new styles prematurely—that is, before their customers are ready to accept them. No amount of retail effort can make customers buy styles in which they have lost interest or in which they have not yet developed interest. Stocking such merchandise simply means lost sales and probable markdowns.

The more accurately a retailer understands customers' fashion preferences, and the more accurately that understanding is reflected in the assortments purchased, stocked, shown and promoted, the more successful the operation. Also more important is the retailer's fashion role within the community.

THEORIES OF FASHION ADOPTION

Fashions are accepted by a few before they are accepted by the majority. An important step in fashion forecasting is isolating and identifying those few individuals and keeping track of their preferences. Which styles are most likely to succeed as fashions, and how widely and by whom will each be accepted?

Three theories have been advanced to explain the "social contagion" of fashion adoption: the "downward-flow theory," the "horizontal-flow" or mass-market theory, and the "upward-flow theory." Each attempts to explain the course a fashion travels or is likely to travel, and each has its own claim to validity in reference to particular fashions or social environments.

Downward-Flow Theory

The oldest theory of fashion adoption is the **downward-flow theory** (or the "trickle-down theory"). It maintains that in order to be identified as a true fashion, a style must first be adopted by people at the top of the social pyramid. The style then gradually wins acceptance at progressively lower social levels.

Three Theories of Fashion Dissemination

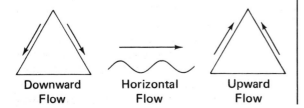

| Downward Flow | Horizontal Flow | Upward Flow |

This theory assumes the existence of a social hierarchy in which lower classes seek identification with levels above them. At the same time, those at the top seek disassociation from those they consider socially inferior. The theory suggests that fashions are accepted by lower classes only if, and after, they are accepted by upper classes and that upper classes will reject a fashion once it has flowed to a lower social level.

Early economists, such as Roe in 1834 and Foley and Veblen at the turn of the twentieth century, were among the first to observe this type of social behavior and its effect upon fashion. In 1903, French sociologist Gabriel Tarde described the spread of fashion in terms of a social water tower from which a continuous fall of imitation could descend.[3] The German sociologist Georg Simmel, one of the first of his discipline to undertake a serious study of fashion, wrote in 1904:

> *Social forms, apparel, aesthetic judgment, the whole style of human expression, are constantly being transformed by fashion in [a way that] . . . affects only the upper classes. Just as soon as the lower classes begin to copy their styles, thereby crossing the line of demarcation the upper classes have drawn and destroying their coherence, the upper classes turn away from this style and adopt a new one. . . . The same process is at work as between the different sets within the upper classes, although it is not always visible here.*[4]

The downward flow theory has had among its twentieth-century proponents such authorities as Robinson, Laver, Sapir, and Flügel. Flügel, in fact, suggests that sumptuary laws originated with the reluctance of upper classes to abandon the sartorial distinctiveness that to them represented superiority.[5]

To some extent, this theory has validity. Some fashions may appear first among the socially elite. Eager manufacturers then quickly mass-produce lower-priced copies of them which many consumers can afford, and the elite seek newer styles.

Because of radical change in our social

structure, however, today this theory has few adherents. The downward-flow theory of fashion dissemination can apply only when a society resembles a pyramid, with people of wealth and position at the apex and followers at successively lower levels. The social structure today, however, is more like a group of rolling hills than it is a pyramid. There are many social groups and many directions in which fashion can and does travel.

This altered pattern of fashion acceptance is also a result of the speed with which fashion news now travels. All social groups know about fashion innovation at practically the same time. Moreover, accelerated mass production and mass distribution of fashion goods have broadened acceptance of styles. They are available at lower prices and more quickly than ever before.

For these reasons, those who mass-produce fashion goods today are less likely to wait cautiously for upper-class approval of newly introduced styles. As soon as significant signs of an interesting new style appear, they are ready to offer adaptations or even copies to the public.

Horizontal-Flow Theory

A newer theory is the **horizontal-flow theory** (or mass-market theory) of fashion adoption. It claims that fashions move horizontally between groups on similar social levels rather than vertically from one level to another.

One of the chief exponents of this theory has been Dr. Charles W. King. He believes that the modern social environment, including rapid, mass communications and the promotional efforts of manufacturers and retailers, exposes new styles to the fashion leaders of all social groups at approximately the same time. King notes that there is almost no lag between the adoption of a fashion by one social group and another. Paris fashions, for example, are now bought and copied for mass distribution sometimes even before the originals are available to the more elite markets. Trade buyers at couturier openings purchase models, ship them home by air, and get copies into retail stores often before the custom client—whose

garments are made to order by the same couturiers—has had a chance to wear the new clothes.

This horizontal flow also has been observed by some modern supporters of the older downward-flow theory. Robinson, for example, says that any given group or cluster of groups takes its cues from contiguous groups within the same social stratum. He claims fashions therefore radiate from a center of each stratum or class.[6]

IMPLICATIONS
FOR MERCHANDISING. The theory of horizontal fashion movement has great significance for merchandising. It points out the fallacy of assuming that there is a single, homogeneous fashion public in this country. In reality, a number of distinctly different groups make up the fashion public. Each group has its own characteristics and its own fashion ideas and needs. The horizontal-flow theory recognizes that what wealthy society people are wearing today is not necessarily what suburbanites, college students, or office workers will either wear tomorrow or wait until tomorrow to accept. It admits that there are separate markets in fashion goods as in any other type of merchandise.

Retailers who apply the horizontal-flow theory will watch their own customers closely rather than be guided solely by what more exclusive stores are selling. They will seek to identify the groups into which customers can be divided in terms of income, age, education, and lifestyle. Among their customers, they will look for the innovators and their style choices as well as the influentials and their selections. King defines a **fashion innovator** as a person who is quicker than his or her associates to try out a new style. A **fashion influential** is a person whose advice is sought by associates. A fashion influential's adoption of a new style gives it prestige among a group. The two roles may or may not be played by the same individual within a specific group.

The news that socially prominent women are wearing plunging necklines in exclusive New York restaurants will have less significance for the retailers in a small Midwestern

Acceptance of the pillbox hat exemplified the downward-flow theory. The down jacket moved horizontally among groups on similar social levels. And the popularity of traditional work clothes has shown an upward flow to fashionable dressers of all ages.

city than the observation that the leader of the country-club set in their community is abandoning bright colors for black on formal occasions. If the latter is a fashion influential in the community, she is a more important bellwether for them than is the socialite in New York.

INDUSTRY PRACTICE. King draws a distinction between the spread of a fashion within the industry itself and its adoption by consumers. A vertical flow definitely operates within the industry, he concedes: "Exclusive and famous designers are watched closely and emulated by lesser designers. Major manufacturers are studied and copied by smaller and less expert competitors."[7] And, as any reader of *Women's Wear Daily* knows, the hottest news in the industry concerns what the top designers and the top producers are showing.

King points out, moreover, that the innovation process in the industry represents a "great filtering system." From an almost infinite number of possibilities, manufacturers select a finite number of styles. From these, trade buyers select a smaller sampling. Finally, consumers choose from among retailers' selections, thereby endorsing certain ones as accepted fashions.

This process, King maintains, is quite different from the consumer reaction outlined by Simmel and other proponents of the downward-flow theory. The difference lies in the fact that today the mass market does not await the approval of the class market before it adopts a fashion.

Upward-Flow Theory

The third theory that attempts to explain the process of fashion adoption is relatively new. It reflects the enormous social changes that have occurred in the past decade or two and that continue to occur. Because the process of fashion dissemination that evolved in the 1960s and 1970s was exactly opposite to that which prevailed throughout much of recorded history, this theory has important implications for producers and retailers alike.

This theory of fashion adoption is called the upward-flow theory. It holds that the young—particularly those of low-income families and those in higher-income groups who adopt low-income lifestyles—are quicker than any other social group to create or adopt new and different fashions. As its name implies, this theory is exactly the opposite of the downward-flow theory. It holds that fashion adoption begins among the young members of lower-income groups and then moves upward into higher-income groups.

Perhaps the most obvious example of the upward-flow theory in action is the worldwide popularity of blue jeans, denim, and even denimlike material. Acceptance of this fashion began in the 1960s and grew steadily stronger in the 1970s. Blue jeans and denim jackets were traditionally the working clothes of manual laborers. They were first worn as street clothes by teenagers who were members of lower-income groups or who chose to be associated with those groups. The jeans fashion spread rapidly among all young people, regardless of income, and then moved almost as rapidly up the age scale. By the early 1970s, fashionable pantsuits and even evening dresses were made of denim or of costly materials dyed to resemble denim.

Fashions such as long hair, leather and peasant apparel, and styles and designs associated with various minority groups have followed the same pattern. They begin as part of a young and lower-income lifestyle and are then quickly adopted among other people with different lifestyles. In the late 1970s, the "western look" followed a similar pattern, particularly in men's and boys' apparel.

For producers and retailers, this new direction of fashion flow implies radical changes in traditional methods of charting and forecasting fashion trends. No longer can producers and retailers look solely to name designers and socially prominent fashion leaders for ideas that will become tomorrow's best-selling fashions. They also must pay considerable attention to what young people favor, for the young have now become a large, independent group that can exert considerable influence on fashion styling.

As a result, today fewer retailers and manufacturers attend European couture showings, once considered fashion's most important source of design inspiration. Now producers and retailers alike are more interested in ready-to-wear showings. Here they look for styles and design details that reflect trends with more fashion relevance for the youth of the United States.

It would appear that fashion will never again flow in only one direction. Of course, there will always be customers for high-fashion and for conservative fashion. But producers and retailers must now accept that they will be doing a considerable proportion of their business in fashions created or adopted first by the lower-income young and by those who choose to be allied with them.

FASHION LEADERS AND FASHION FOLLOWERS

As different as they may be, the three theories of fashion flow share one common perspective. They recognize that there are fashion leaders and fashion followers in the movement of fashion acceptance. People of social, political, and economic importance here and abroad are seen as leaders in the downward-flow theory. The horizontal-flow theory recognizes individuals whose personal prestige makes them leaders within their own circles, whether or not they are known elsewhere. Finally, the important fashion role played by young, lower-income groups in the last half of the twentieth century is recognized in the upward-flow theory.

Fashion Leaders

The theories of fashion adoption stress that the fashion leader is not the creator of the fashion; nor does merely wearing the fashion make a person a fashion leader. As Quentin Bell explains: "The leader of fashion does not come into existence until the fashion is itself created . . . a king or person of great eminence may indeed lead the fashion, but he leads only in the general direction which it has already adopted."[8] If a fashion parade is forming, fashion leaders may head it and even quicken its pace. They cannot, however, bring about a procession; nor can they reverse a procession.

INNOVATORS AND INFLUENTIALS.

Famous people are not necessarily fashion leaders, even if they do influence an individual style. Their influence usually affects only one striking style, one physical attribute, or one set of circumstances. The true fashion leader is a person constantly seeking distinction and therefore likely to launch a succession of fashions rather than just one. People like Beau Brummel, who made a career of dressing fashionably, or the Duchess of Windsor, whose wardrobe was front-page fashion news for decades, influence fashion on a much broader scale.

What makes a person a fashion leader? Flügel explains: "Inasmuch as we are aristocratically minded and dare to assert our own individuality by being different, we are leaders of fashion."[9] King, however, makes it clear that more than just daring to be different is required. In his analysis, a person eager for the new is merely an innovator or early buyer. To be a leader, one must be influential and sought after for advice within a proscribed coterie. An influential person, says King, sets the appropriate dress for a specific occasion in a particular circle. Within that circle, an innovator presents current offerings and is the earliest visual communicator of a new style.[10]

SOCIAL LEADERS.

In today's world, "society" has replaced royalty in the role of fashion leader. Whether the members of this "society" derive their position from vast fortunes and old family names or from new fame and recent wealth, they bring to the scene a glamour and excitement that focuses attention on everything they do. Their pictures appear in newspapers and magazines; they appear on television, radiating success. The average person seeks to imitate these people in the only way available—by imitating their fashions.

In the past, fashion leadership was the province of royalty. New fashions were introduced in royal courts by such leaders as Empress Eugénie and Marie Antoinette. Today's lists of best-dressed men and women, however, rarely include members of royalty. There are fewer royal houses today, and, except on state occasions, royalty must dress for the many activities of their day-to-day lives.

As monarchies were replaced by democracies, members of the wealthy and international sets came into the fashion spotlight. Later, it was the families of political figures and industrialists who made the best-dressed lists. Today, through the constant eye of television and the newspapers, the average person is able to find fashion leadership in a whole new stratum of society—the Jet Set. This unstructured group cuts across old, established social lines. It is not unusual, for example, to find a princess skiing with a rock star, an oil executive, or a news commentator.

What these socialites are doing and what they are wearing is instantly served up to the general public by the media. For as far as fashion is concerned, these people are not just in the news, they *are* the news. Any move they make is important enough to be immediately publicized. What they wear is of vital interest to the general public. The media tell us what the social leaders wear to dine in a chic restaurant, to attend a charity ball, or to go shopping. As trend setters, their choices are of prime interest to designers and to the world at large.

This inundation of news about what social leaders wear of course influences the public. The average person is affected because so many manufacturers and retailers of fashion take their cue from these social leaders. Right or wrong, fashion merchants count on the fashion sense of these leaders. They know that the overwhelming exposure of these leaders in the media encourages people of ordinary means to imitate them—consciously or unconsciously.

PEOPLE IN THE NEWS. Fashion today takes its impetus and influence from people in every possible walk of life. These people have one thing in common, however: they are newsworthy. Because of some special talent, charisma, notoriety, or popularity, they are constantly mentioned and shown in fashion magazines and on the front pages of newspapers. They may or may not appear in the society pages.

In this group can be found presidents and princesses, movie stars and religious leaders, sports figures and recording stars, politicians and television personalities. Because they are seen so frequently, the public has a good sense of their fashions and lifestyles and can imitate them to the extent of their means and desire.

Prominent individuals have been responsible for certain fashions that continue to be associated with them. Many times, however, these individuals are not what would be considered fashion leaders. In the nineteenth century, the semifitted, velveteen-collared coat style adopted by the Earl of Chesterfield became known simply as a Chesterfield. It continues as such today. The short jacket adopted by General Dwight D. Eisenhower during World War II is still identified as the Eisenhower jacket. Moreover when Dorothy Hamill soared to fame as an Olympic ice skating champion, her short, distinctive hairstyle became known as the Hamill haircut.

Even if particular fashions or hairstyles associated with people in the news do not bear their names, the influence of famous people may be just as strong. In the 1930s, a tremendous impact was felt by an entire menswear industry when Clark Gable appeared without an undershirt in *It Happened One Night*. Practically overnight, men from all walks of life shed their undershirts in imitation of Gable. In the late 1930s, women dared to wear slacks after seeing Greta Garbo and Marlene Dietrich wearing them in the movies. In the early 1960s, when the former Mrs. John F. Kennedy appeared in little pillbox hats, both the style and the hat market blossomed under the publicity.

Today there is strong emphasis on sports. And what prominent sports figures wear is of great importance to the people who seek to imitate them. Television has created the public acceptance of several sports. For example, people have enjoyed going to baseball, football, or basketball games for years. But sports of a more individual nature, such as tennis and

It's hard to believe today, but in 1949 Gussie Moran's lace panties caused a worldwide furor—they were regarded as a daring touch in the until-then strictly utilitarian tennis garb.

golf, were of minor general interest. Now they are brought into the living rooms of an increasing number of viewers. As a result, fashions for participating in those sports have grown remarkably in importance. Tennis is now the country's most popular participation sport and has given rise to an entire specialized fashion industry. It is difficult today to remember that a mere 30 years ago white was the only color seen on a tennis court and that women wore knee-length tennis skirts. When Gussie Moran, a professional woman tennis player, first appeared on the courts with lace-trimmed panties under her shortened skirt, the furor shook the tennis world and reverberated throughout the sports world. Today, every aspiring tennis player has endless fashion styles, colors, and fabrics to choose from. This wide selection of fashions is also available for golf, jogging, swimming, skating, biking, snorkeling, and other sports.

Some fashions that appear in the media are embraced with unanimity by the public. They are quickly produced at every price and in every possible fabric and design and are seen everywhere. They may even become classics. Others are hailed by only a portion of the public. While their immediate impact may be great, they are soon gone from the fashion scene.

Fashion Followers

Filling out forms for his daughter's college entrance application, a father wrote of his daughter's leadership qualities: "To tell the truth, my daughter is really not a leader, but rather a loyal and devoted follower." The dean of the college admissions responded, "We are welcoming a freshman class of 100 students this year and are delighted to accept your daughter. You can't imagine how happy we are to have one follower among the 99 leaders!"

Most people want to be thought of as leaders, not followers. But there are many people who are followers, and good ones. In fact, followers are in the majority within any group. Without followers the fashion industry would certainly collapse. Mass production and mass distribution can be possible and profitable only when large numbers of consumers accept the merchandise. Luckily, more people prefer to follow than to lead. The styles fashion leaders adopt may help manufacturers and retailers in determining what will be demanded by the majority of consumers in the near future. Only accurate predictions can ensure the continued success of the giant ready-to-wear business in this country which depends for its success on mass-production and distribution. While fashion leaders may stimulate and excite the fashion industry, the fashion followers are the industry's lifeblood.

REASONS FOR FOLLOWING FASHION.

Theories about why people follow rather than lead in fashion are plentiful. Among the explanations are feelings of inferiority, admiration of others, lack of interest, and ambivalence about the new.

Feelings of Insecurity.   Flügel writes, "Inasmuch as we feel our own inferiority and the need for conformity to the standards set by others, we are followers of fashion."[11] For example, high school boys and girls are at a notably insecure stage of life. They are therefore more susceptible than any other age group to the appeal of fads. A person about to face a difficult interview or attend the first meeting with a new group carefully selects new clothes. Often a feeling of inadequacy can be hidden by wearing a style that others have already approved as appropriate and acceptable.

Admiration.   Flügel also maintains that it is a fundamental human impulse to imitate those who are admired or envied. A natural and symbolic means of doing this is to copy their clothes. An outstanding illustration of his theory was provided in the 1960s by the former Mrs. John F. Kennedy. First as the wife, then as the widow of the president, her clothes and hairstyles were copied instantly among many different groups throughout this country. On a different level, the young girl who copies the hairstyle of her best friend, older sister, or favorite aunt demonstrates the same principle; as do college students who model their appearance after that of campus leaders.

Lack of Interest.   Sapir suggests that many people are insensitive to fashion and follow it only because "they realize that not to fall in with it would be to declare themselves members of a past generation, or dull people who cannot keep up with their neighbors."[12] Their response to fashion, he says, is a sullen surrender, by no means an eager following of the Pied Piper.

Ambivalence.   Another theory holds that many people are ambivalent in their attitudes toward the new; they both want it and fear it. For most, it is easier to choose what is already familiar. Such individuals need time and exposure to new styles before they accept them.

VARYING RATES OF RESPONSE.

Individuals vary in the speed with which they respond to a new idea, especially when fashion change is radical and dramatic. Some fashion followers apparently need time to adjust to new ideas. Merchants exploit this point when they buy a few "window pieces" of styles too advanced for their own clientele and expose them in windows and fashion shows to allow customers time to get used to them. Only after a period of exposure to the new styles do the fashion followers accept them.

FASHION AS AN EXPRESSION OF INDIVIDUALITY

As the twentieth century entered its eighth decade, a strange but understandable trend became apparent across the nation. People were striving, through their mode of dress, to declare individuality in the face of computer-age conformity.

People had watched strings of impersonal numbers become more and more a part of their lives—zip codes, bank and credit card account numbers, employee identification numbers, department store accounts, automobile registration, and so on. An aversion to joining the masses—to becoming "just another number"—began to be felt. So while most people continued to go along with general fashion trends, some asserted their individuality. This was accomplished by distinctive touches each wearer added to an outfit. A new freedom in dress, color and texture combinations, use of accessories, and hairstyles allowed people to assert individuality without being out of step with the times. Most social scientists see in this a paradox—an endless conflict between the desire to conform and the desire to remain apart.

We have all known people who at some point in their lives found a fashion which particularly pleased them. It might be a certain style of dress, a certain shoe, or a hairstyle. Even in the face of continuing changes in fashion, the person continued to wear that style in which she or he felt right and attractive. This is an assertion of individuality in the face of conformity. Although superbly fashion-conscious, the late and famous actress Joan Crawford never stopped wearing the open-toed, sling-back, wedge shoe of the 1940s. While the pointed toe and stiletto heel of the fifties gave way to the low, chunky heel of the sixties, she continued to wear the same style. She was perfectly in step with fashion when the wedge shoe finally returned to popularity in the early 1970s. Woody Allen has recently achieved special recognition for wearing—anywhere and everywhere—sneakers! At formal occasions he conforms by wearing appropriate formal attire. But his feet remain sneakered, and Woody retains an individuality that he feels strongly about.

Most people prefer to assert their individuality in a less obvious way, and today's ready-to-wear fashions lend themselves to subtle changes that mark each person's uniqueness. No two people put the same costume together in exactly the same way.

Fashion editor Jessica Daves summed up the miracle of modern ready-to-wear fashion. It offers, she says, "the possibility for some women to create a design for themselves . . . to choose the color and shape in clothes that will present them as they would like to see themselves."[13]

The Paradox of Conformity and Individuality

For decades, experts have tried to explain why people seek both conformity and individuality in fashion. Simmel suggests that two opposing social tendencies are at war: the need for union and the need for isolation. The individual, he reasons, derives satisfaction from knowing that the way in which he or she expresses a fashion represents something special. At the same time, people gain support from seeing others favor the same style.[14]

Flügel interprets the paradox in terms of a person's feelings of superiority and inferiority. The individual wants to be like others "insofar as he regards them as superior, but unlike them, in the sense of being more 'fashionable' insofar as he thinks they are below him."[15]

Sapir ties the conflict to a revolt against custom and a desire to break away from slavish acceptance of fashion. Slight changes from the established form of dress and behavior "seem for the moment to give victory to the individual, while the fact that one's fellows revolt in the same direction gives one a feeling of adventurous safety."[16] He also ties the assertion of individuality to the need to affirm one's self in a powerful society in which the individual has ceased to be a measure of the society.

One example of this conflict may be found in the off-duty dress of people required to wear uniforms of one kind or another during working hours, such as nurses, police officers, and mail carriers. A second example is the apparel worn by many present-day bankers. While retaining the customary shirt and tie, many have abandoned the traditional "banker's gray" suit for more individual and often colorful sport jackets and slacks.

Retailers know that although some people like to lead and some like to follow in fashion, most people buy fashion to express personality or to identify with a particular group. To belong, they follow fashion; to express their personality, they find ways to individualize it.

Fashion and Self-Expression

Increasing importance is being placed on fashion individuality—on expressing your personality, or refusing to be cast in a mold. Instead of slavishly adopting any one look, today's young person seeks to create an individual effect through the way he or she combines various fashion components. For instance, if a young woman thinks a denim skirt, an ankle-length woolen coat, and a heavy, turtlenecked sweater represent her personality, they will be considered acceptable by others in her group.

Forward-looking designers recognize this desire for self-expression. Designers say that basic wardrobe components should be made available, but that consumers should be encouraged to combine them as they see fit. For instance, they advise women to wear pants or skirts, long or short, according to how they feel, not according to what past tradition has considered proper for an occasion. They suggest that men make the same choice among tailored suits, leisurewear, and slacks, to find the styles that express their personalities.

Having experienced such fashion freedom, young people may never conform again. Yet despite individual differences in their dress, young experimenters have this in common: a deep-rooted desire to dress differently from the older generations with whom they live and associate.

Most people—particularly those who lack the time, funds, and vital flair for combining different components into a strictly personal look—still tend to accept a fashion or effect as a whole. A touch of novelty in accessories, color, line, or texture within the framework of prevailing fashion is enough to satisfy the feeling of individuality that the average consumer craves.

The fashion merchandising rules expounded by Nystrom years ago thus continue to prove themselves valid in both theory and practice.

MERCHANDISING VOCABULARY

Define or briefly explain the following terms:

Downward-flow theory   **Horizontal-flow theory**

Fashion influential   **Line**

Fashion innovator   **Upward-flow theory**

MERCHANDISING REVIEW

1. Name the three types of designers most commonly serving the American fashion industry today. What are the responsibilities of each?
2. What are the major sources of inspiration for many fashion designers? Give an example of how the designs of a modern apparel designer have been influenced by one such source of inspiration.

3. Into what three groups may fashion manufacturers be classified? Indicate the identifying characteristics of each.
4. What are the three groups or classifications into which most fashion retail firms fall? What are the basic identifying characteristics of each?
5. Briefly explain the downward-flow theory of fashion adoption. How valid is this theory today? Why?
6. Briefly explain the horizontal flow theory of fashion adoption. Discuss its implications for today's merchants.
7. Briefly explain the upward-flow theory of fashion adoption. What are its implications for modern merchants?
8. Why are the following prime candidates for positions of fashion leadership: (a) social leaders, (b) people in the news, (c) sports professionals?
9. For what four reasons do most people follow, rather than lead, in matters relating to fashion? Elaborate on each.
10. How can an individual use fashion as a means of self-expression?

MERCHANDISING DIGEST

1. Discuss the implications of the following quotation from the text: "Another widely held misconception is that designers live and work in 'ivory towers,' dreamily creating their artistic designs. Nothing could be farther from the truth." Cite examples to support your answer.
2. The text states that "famous people are not necessarily fashion leaders, even if they do influence an individual style." Discuss this statement and its implications for the fashion industry. Name at least one recently famous person who has *not* been a fashion leader or influential and at least one who *has* been a fashion leader or influential. Name a specific style for which the latter is famous.
3. Discuss why people today seek both conformity and individuality in fashion. Discuss the implications this has for the fashion retailer.

REFERENCES

1 Bell, *On Human Finery,* pp. 48–49.
2 Robinson, "Fashion Theory and Product Design," p. 129.
3 Tarde, *The Laws of Imitation,* p. 221.
4 Simmel, "Fashion," p. 545.
5 Flügel, *The Psychology of Clothes,* p. 139.
6 Robinson, "Economics of Fashion Demand," p. 383.
7 King, "Fashion Adoption," pp. 114–115.
8 Bell, op. cit., p. 46.
9 Flügel, op. cit., p. 140.
10 King, op. cit., p. 124.
11 Flügel, op. cit., p. 140.
12 Sapir, "Fashion," p. 140.
13 Daves, *Ready-Made Miracle,* pp. 231–232.
14 Simmel, op. cit., pp. 543–544.
15 Flügel, loc. cit.
16 Sapir, loc. cit.

EXPLORING
THE DYNAMICS OF FASHION

A. Wear or bring to class an example of *either a current or outdated fashion* that proves or disproves one of the nine statements below on the dynamics of fashion. Be prepared to present your example and briefly explain (one or two minutes) how it proves or disproves each of the statements. In a short paper (two pages), trace the development and then identify the recurring cycles of your merchandise example. Research your merchandise in a book on the history of costume.

1. Fashions are evolutionary in nature; they are rarely revolutionary.
2. Since fashion changes are outgrowths of changes in consumers' needs, it is seldom possible to force or hold back fashion change.
3. Prevailing psychological attitudes have an important bearing on the extent of fashion interest at any time.
4. All fashions move in cycles.
5. Styles reoccur in fashion acceptance. Occasionally an entire "look" is reborn.
6. Wardrobes vary from lifestyle to lifestyle.
7. An individual derives satisfaction from knowing that the way he or she expresses a fashion represents something special. At the same time, people gain support from seeing others favor the same style.
8. "There can be no disputing taste."
9. A new style is often considered daring and in dubious taste; it is then gradually accepted, then widely accepted, and finally gradually discarded.

B. There seem to be definite correlations between fashions and the times. As times change, so do fashions, and when a fashion changes, the *total look* changes. Accessories, makeup, and hair styles are all part of this total fashion look. When styles are revived, they are revived in new forms, adapted for new lifestyles and occasions.
Study the following chart; then answer the questions about it.

1. Find examples (draw, sketch, photograph, cut and paste) of one or more of the fashion items listed in the right-hand column of the chart.
2. What similarities in fashions and their causes can you find in the decades listed?
3. What environmental changes within the last two decades do you feel will have lasting effects over the next 10 to 20 years?

4. What examples from the decades listed can you find to support the theory that fashion is evolutionary?
5. During what time period was fashion closest to being revolutionary?
6. What additions can you make to the information in any of the decades listed?
7. From your interpretation of the information on past decades, what conclusions can you draw about the evolution of fashions and their relationship to current events?

SOCIAL AND ECONOMIC INFLUENCES ON FASHION IN THE UNITED STATES (1920–1980)

DECADE	EVENTS TAKING PLACE	PUBLIC REACTIONS	INTERPRETATION IN APPAREL & ACCESSORIES
1920's	Post WW I, Paris influence First women's lib Increasing prosperity Modern art, music, literature Birth of sportswear	Daring looks and behavior Freedom for the body Short hair styles Women begin to smoke Dancing (Charleston)	Chemise dresses Short skirts T-strap shoes Cloche hats Luxurious fabrics: silks, satins, crepes Costume looks Long strands of beads
1930's	Depression era Unemployment, little money Hollywood influence: Stars & Designers Rayon and acetate fabrics Big bands, swing music	Frugality, conservatism The little woman Make do	Soft looks: loose, light fabrics Long hemlines, bias cuts Big hats, big brims The housedress Fox, fur-collared coats, wraps
1940's	WW II: government restrictions Exit France as fashion source Shortage of materials Emergence of American designers Radio, records Crooners: Crosby, Sinatra Dior—1947 "New Look"	Women take men's jobs Glamour, pinup girls Strong nationalism Common cause philosophy	Tailored, mannish suits Padded shoulders Knee-length straight skirts Peplum jackets Soft, shoulder-length hair (pageboy) Rolled hair Small hats, perched in front Pants for women
1950's	Population increasing; "baby boom" Firms expanding, going public, diversifying Move to suburbs Incomes rising More imports Improved transportation Improved communication Developments of more synthetics, finishes, textures	Buy new homes, appliances, furnishings Conformity Improve quality of family life Use of increased leisure time for sports and recreation The station wagon	Classics: shirtwaist dress At-home clothes Mink coats Sack dress (too quickly copied) Sportswear Ivy League look, grey flannel suit, skinny ties, button-down shirts Car coats Wash 'n wear fabrics
1960's	Rise of shopping centers New technology: stretch fabrics, new knitting methods Big business expansion Prosperity Designer names Vietnam War: youth rebellion Boutiques London influence: Twiggy, Mod, Mary Quant, Carnaby Peacock Revolution, rock music, youth cult	New sexual freedom Experimentation in fashion Anti-establishment Generation gap Identity seeking, new values Divorce, singles	Street fashions: jeans Vinyls, synthetics, wet-look Mini-skirts Wild use of color and patterns Knits, polyester Ethnic clothing and crafts Unisex clothes Fun furs Long hair, wigs Men: turtlenecks, wide ties, Nehru jackets, golf co-ordinates, nylon printed shirts
1970's	Equal rights, women's lib Women working outside the home Watergate, disenchantment with politics Recessions Ecology, conservation Energy crisis Stabilizing economy End of Vietnam War Disco dancing, clubs Consumerism	Individualism Return to sanity, reaction to 1960's chaos Back to nature, health foods, natural fibers New conservatism Urban renewal, interest in cities & their problems ERA Minority organizations	Pants suits (women) leisure suits (men) Maxi and longuette (1970's disaster) Jeans: bell bottoms, straight leg, tapered leg, peg leg. Jeans acceptable for dress and casual wear T-shirts, tank tops Eclecticism Boots Hair: frizzy or soft Classic Look: blazers, shirts, investment clothing Separates, not coordinates Romantic look: soft, feminine

2

MARKETERS
OF FASHION

Marketing refers to all the business activities that direct the flow of goods from suppliers and producers to consumers. The many processes involved in converting raw materials into finished goods and distributing these goods to consumers are collectively known as the **marketing process.**

The chapters in Unit 2 explain how this marketing process works. This unit explores the various industries involved in marketing fashion goods and discusses their history and development. Also discussed are the organization and operation of these industries, their major market centers, the merchandising activities they engage in, and the trends that indicate what their future may be.

The industries discussed in this unit include those that produce the raw materials of fashion, those that produce semifinished or finished

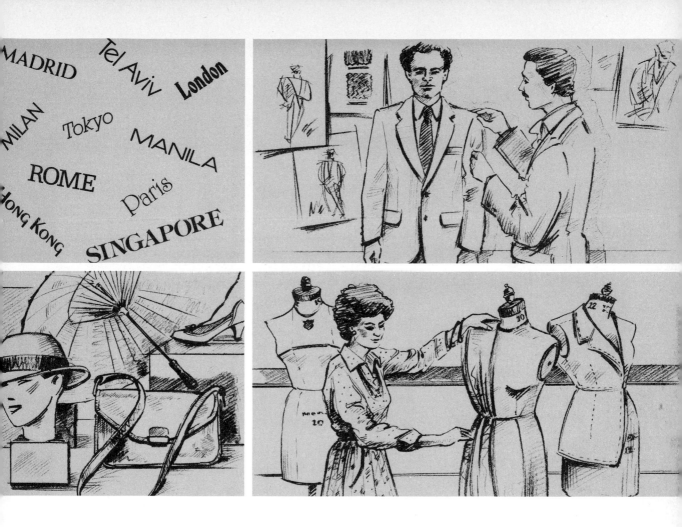

fashion goods, and those that distribute the fashion goods to consumers. Separate chapters are devoted to:

- the primary suppliers: industries supplying fibers, fabrics, leathers, and furs
- the secondary suppliers: industries producing women's and children's apparel, menswear, and women's fashion accessories
- foreign fashion market centers
- retail distributors of fashion goods

All segments involved in the marketing process are affected by the basic principles relating to fashion, as discussed in Unit 1. A working knowledge of the capabilities of each of these segments and their interrelated roles in anticipating and meeting consumer demand is also valuable background information for anyone considering a career in either wholesale or retail fashion merchandising.

5

THE MATERIALS OF FASHION: TEXTILE FIBERS AND FABRICS

A good musical group—be it a rock group or a symphony orchestra—will demand the most flawless, up-to-the-minute recording facilities in order to preserve its performance in as perfect a manner as possible.

So, too, the ongoing success of the fashion industry demands that exactly the right materials be chosen for its endlessly diverse finished product—apparel.

And, just as a musical group must concern itself with the selections it will perform, with the placement of its musicians, and with the balance of instruments for ideal sound, the fashion industry evaluates and chooses materials in terms of their ultimate uses, the cost factors involved, and the acceptance of these materials by the customer.

The designer creating a style at the drawing board must consider the material best suited for the particular silhouette and details of design. The manufacturer then must consider the various weights and patterns currently desired as well as the cost factors. Finally, the retailer must select fashions made of those materials considered appropriate and desirable by specific customers.

Textiles, or fabrics, are used more than any other material, such as leather or fur, in the manufacture of fashion apparel. Fashion textiles are the end product of the close collaboration of an entire field of industries. This network of industries, called **primary suppliers,** produces the many fibers and fabrics that make up the fashion textile world.

The fiber industry processes both natural and man-made fibers. **Natural fibers** are either vegetable—cotton and flax, for example—or animal, such as wool, cashmere, and silk. **Man-made fibers**—rayon, polyester, and others—are produced in chemical plants. The fabric industry knits or weaves these fibers into various fabrics and textiles.

The process by which raw cotton from the field or chemicals from a test tube ultimately become a fashionable shirt or skirt is a remarkable one. To understand these processes, one must know something about the many producers involved as the product moves along toward its ultimate destination—the fashion customer. As Christian Dior, the world-famous haute couture designer, commented, ''Fabric not only expresses a designer's dreams but also stimulates his own ideas. It can be the beginning of an inspiration. Many a dress of mine is born of the fabric alone.''[1]

In the last few years there have been more and more newsworthy developments in the fashion textile industry, affecting every step of the fashion process. These advances range from new methods of producing and blending fibers to the latest solutions to the industry's energy-related problems.

THE TEXTILE FIBER INDUSTRIES

Garments are made from fabrics. Fabrics are made from yarns, and yarns are made from fibers. A single **fiber,** then, is the smallest part of the fabric. It is extremely fine and hairlike in appearance. Although tiny, fibers have a great influence on fashion. When spun into yarn and knit or woven into fabric, it is the fibers that will have a great deal to do with the color, weight, texture, and care qualities of the finished product.

Fibers are divided into two broad categories: natural and man-made. Natural fibers are derived from plant or animal sources. Man-made fibers are produced in chemical factories.

With today's wide array of textile fibers, it is hard to realize that much of what we are now used to has come into existence only within recent decades. Polyester, the most widely used man-made fiber in the world, was first produced by E. I. du Pont de Nemours in 1953. Nylon, the man-made fiber with the second highest use, is also a Du Pont product and was introduced in 1939. Rayon, the first man-made fiber, was produced by the American Viscose Company in 1910, and today is the third most used of the man-made fibers.

Originally the natural fibers were not given the special finishes and properties that we find in them today. Until the introduction of the Sanforized process in 1930, cotton garments shrank significantly. Now an even more revolutionary process, called Sanfor-Set, has been developed. It makes cool, comfortable cotton as carefree as the man-made fibers that were invented to give this ease of care to fabrics. Before the late 1950s or early 1960s, one would never have dreamed of washing a wool skirt or dress. But with advanced technology and innovative chemical processing, this has been changed. All these revolutions and evolutions in textile fibers are of great importance today. The fashion world seeks to offer an increasing variety of goods to satisfy customers' demands for the new natural qualities. At the same time the industry attempts to maintain the easy-care qualities that have come to be expected.

History and Development

The fiber industries are of vastly different ages and backgrounds. The natural-fiber industries are so old that they predate written history. Even primitive human beings are believed to have gathered flax to make yarn for fabrics. The man-made fiber industries, on the other hand, are so young that the oldest among them, rayon, is not yet a century old. Thus natural fibers have had a very long history of extremely slow development, which has speeded up only in recent years. Man-made fibers have had a very short history of amazingly rapid development.

THE NATURAL-FIBER INDUSTRIES. The principal natural fibers used in the production of textile fabrics include **cotton,** a vegetable fiber from the cotton boll of the cotton plant; **wool,** an animal fiber from the coat of sheep; **silk,** an animal fiber from the cocoons spun by silkworms; and **linen,** a vegetable fiber from the woody stalk of the flax plant.

Cotton. Cotton, the most widely used of all the natural fibers, is the vegetable fiber attached to the seed of the cotton plant. Cotton thrives in the United States and is grown in other countries around the world, including Egypt, Russia, China, Brazil, Mexico, and the Sudan.

An archaeological site in Mexico has provided so far the oldest example of cotton's use as a textile—a bit of woven cloth estimated to be 7,000 years old. A 3,500-year-old Hindu hymn refers to cotton. Twenty-five hundred years ago, a Greek historian described how Indian women picked cotton bolls and carded and spun the fiber into yarn.

Cotton was grown in America in Colonial days, but it was Eli Whitney's invention of the

A cotton field in bloom. Cotton is the most widely used of all natural fibers.

cotton gin in 1793 that caused the explosion of the cotton industry. This led to the importation of slaves to handpick the cotton. By the mid-1800s cotton grown in the southern part of our country dominated the world markets. The industrial revolution in England, which had produced the machinery to make cloth, demanded more and more of the South's cotton. Ultimately, the Civil War raged over these cotton fields. When the war ended, the position of cotton as a major national economic factor was adversely affected. Cotton continued to be grown, however, on a more limited scale. In the United States, mechanical pickers and strippers have replaced manual labor, although today the rest of the cotton-growing world still depends on human labor.

Because cotton fibers are composed primarily of cellulose, they have good durability and a pleasing feel in the hand. Because the cotton fiber is hydrophilic, it absorbs moisture quickly. It also dries quickly, giving a cooling effect which makes cotton a good fiber for warm or hot weather. This is why most T-shirts are made of cotton. Cotton fabrics can be washed or dry-cleaned and never produce the undesirable static electricity generated by other fibers.

The cotton boll provides a multitude of products. The longest and finest fibers (up to $2\frac{1}{2}$ inches) are used for sheer cotton fabrics; the shorter fibers are used for coarser goods. The very short fibers, called lintels, are used in the manufacture of rayon and such non-fashion items as paper and absorbent cotton. The cottonseed itself is processed into cottonseed oil, used in cooking, and cottonseed meal, which becomes feed and fertilizer. The fertilizer goes into the ground to start the cotton crop all over again.

Wool. Wool is the fiber that forms the coat of sheep. Being an animal fiber, it is mainly composed of protein. By far the greatest amount of wool comes from Australia, New Zealand, and Russia. However, a considerable number of sheep are also raised for wool in the Western United States, England, Scotland, South Africa, and Uruguay. Good grazing lands in moderate climates are suitable for the growth of higher-quality wool coats. In colder climates, sheep develop coarser wool coats more suitable for carpets than apparel.

Cave dwellers of the late Stone Age probably kept warm by draping themselves in the skins of wild sheep and goats. Later the animals were domesticated specifically for their wool coats. As far back as 4200 B.C., according to available records, there were wool weavers, dyers, and merchants. The wool industry continued as the most powerful in the textile world until the eighteenth century when cotton became its rival.

In the late 1600s, the first woolen mill in the western hemisphere was set up in Massachusetts. Most American woolen mills built since that time have been located in the Northeast and Southeast. The American sheep ranches which provide the wool are mostly located in the good grazing areas of Utah, Colorado, and Montana. Part of the history of the Old West records the range wars between cattle ranchers and sheep ranchers. Most of the West had originally been settled by the cattle ranchers. They fought bloody range wars attempting to

PURE WOOL

The sewn-in Woolmark label is your assurance of quality-tested fabrics made of the world's best...Pure Wool.

WOOL BLEND

The sewn-in Woolblend Mark label is your assurance of quality-tested fabrics made predominantly of wool.

When you buy wool, look for these labels. The one on the left is on pure wool; the other one on fabrics made of wool blends.

keep sheep herders and ranchers from allowing their sheep to graze on cattle land.

Wool shorn from live sheep is called "fleece wool" or "clipped wool" and is considered superior in quality. Wool removed from sheep already dead from disease or slaughter is called "pulled wool" and is not considered as good a grade.

There are over 200 grades of sheep. Wool produced by Merino sheep is considered to be the best grade because it has the softest hand, the most crimp and resiliency, and the best elasticity. The least-desirable wool comes from mongrel sheep. It has the least elasticity and strength and is used mainly for low-grade clothing and carpets.

Wool produces warm fabrics because, just the opposite of cotton, it absorbs moisture slowly and dries slowly. Wool fibers also have a natural crimp which traps air to form insulating barriers against the cold.

Wool fabrics are more expensive than cotton. It costs more to convert wool fibers into fabrics, and raising sheep is more expensive than raising cotton.

Silk. Silk, too, goes far back in history as a fiber with which people adorned themselves. It is said that silk was discovered in 2640 B.C. by a Chinese princess who was studying the formation of the silkworm cocoon.

The silkworm forms silk by forcing two fine streams of a thick liquid out of tiny openings in its head. These fine streams harden into filaments upon contact with the air. The worm then winds the silk around itself. It thus forms a complete covering, or cocoon, as protection during its change from worm into moth. Amazingly, up to 1,600 yards of this continuous fiber are wound into a cocoon by the silkworm. To keep this silk in one continuous length, most of the worms are intentionally killed by heat before they are ready to leave the cocoons. A few moths are allowed to break out of the cocoon, however, to produce eggs for the next crop of silk.

Because of the exclusive, mulberry-leaf diet and the climate preferences of the cultivated silkworm, China, Japan, and Italy are the world's principal producers of silk fiber. And ever since silk was discovered in China, over 4,000 years ago, it has been considered a most important fiber for fashion fabrics. In fact, the ancient Chinese guarded the production of silk and decreed death to anyone who revealed the secret.

During the Middle Ages, the cultivation of silkworms, called sericulture, was brought to Europe from the Far East. Italy, France, and Spain became important silk centers. In the sixteenth century, the explorer Cortez attempted to bring the silkworm to this country but failed. Because later attempts to introduce sericulture to the United States have also proved unsuccessful, all silk used by American mills is imported.

Cultivated silkworms produce the finest real silk. Another type of silk, called "tussah," is produced by wild, uncultivated silkworms. These worms spin an uneven filament that is stronger and thicker than the cultivated type and is used in heavier, rougher fabrics. Still another type of fiber is produced when two silkworms rest together and form one cocoon with a double strand. These unseparated fibers are of uneven thickness and are called "duoppioni" silk.

Silk fabrics all but disappeared from the United States during and after World War II but have recently made a dramatic comeback. Customers once again yearn for the luxurious look and feel of silk. They are willing to forego the easy-care advantages of other fabrics for the glamorous and luxurious qualities that are to be found only in real silk.

Linen. This fabric is made from the stem of the flax plant. Only after the flax fiber is pressed into a fabric is it actually called linen.

Flax is generally considered to be the oldest known textile fiber, having been used in the Stone Age. It may have been first cultivated for its food value but was soon used for its fiber as well. Materials made of flax were used by the ancient Egyptians to wrap mummies.

The cultivation of flax spread throughout Europe into Asia and to the Americas. During Colonial times, flax was a popular crop in this country. It dwindled rapidly in importance, however, after the invention of the cotton gin made cotton cheaper to produce. Today, flax for linen fiber is grown mainly in Ireland and Belgium. It is grown in the United States primarily for the oil yielded by its seeds.

Flax, which is mainly composed of cellulose, has a fiber length which averages from 6 to 20 inches. This means that linen fabrics are lintfree because there are no short fibers. It is the strongest of the vegetable fibers (twice as strong as cotton) and, like cotton, absorbs moisture and dries quickly. This makes linen, too, a good fabric for hot weather, but one which requires a good deal of care.

Linen weaving is an old British craft. Its products were reinstated as successful fashion exports by the Irish designer Sybil Connolly. She also introduced Irish lawn (a fine, sheer linen), embroidered linen, and crochet into the high-fashion catalogue. In 1952 she showed her collection to the Philadelphia Fashion Group. Its instant success led to an increase in the supply of natural Irish weaves, especially "banween," a chalk-white woolen material previously associated with tough country wear.

Today's customer knows fine linens as superb fabrics for women's and men's fashions and for the most elegant table settings.

THE MAN-MADE FIBER INDUSTRIES.

Unlike natural fibers, which can be traced back thousands of years, the oldest of the man-made fibers will not reach its one hundredth birthday for some years to come.

Scientists had attempted to develop synthetic fibers for centuries, however. Just as medieval alchemists persisted in the attempt to make gold from base metals, so did the chemists of the 1700s and 1800s persist in their efforts to create "artificial silk." Unlike the alchemists' dream, however, this dream came true.

No one person gets the full credit. Many chemists and scientists contributed their findings. Finally, in 1886, a French scientist, Count Hilaire de Chardonnet, came up with a fiber made of natural cellulosic substances (doubtless wood pulp and cotton linters). Five years later, in 1891, the count started commercial production in the world's first "artificial silk" plant. Nineteen years later, in 1910, the United States boasted its first such plant in Marcus Hook, Pennsylvania.

For some time the new fiber continued to be called "artificial silk" or "art silk." But in 1924 it was finally given an identity of its own. The National Retail Dry Goods Association (now the National Retail Merchants Association) coined the word "rayon" and registered it internationally. Man-made fibers had finally come of age. They were given names of their own and could be accepted on their own merits. In 1901, the Dreyfus brothers in England developed cellulose acetate.

Nylon, discovered by Du Pont laboratories in 1938, was the first of the noncellulose, man-made fibers. Thus, nylon was truly the first totally man-made fiber in the world. At the same time, a process for making polyester was discovered in England. Terylene had been invented by John Whinfield at the research works of the British Calico Printer's Association in 1941. But for much-needed dollars, the secret was sold to the United States, where the product was produced by the Du Pont laboratories and became known as Dacron. Later, acrylics, such as Orlon, and other synthetic fibers, such as the elasticlike spandex ones, were to join in the man-made fiber parade.

All man-made fibers, cellulosic and noncellulosic, start out as thick liquids. Rayon and

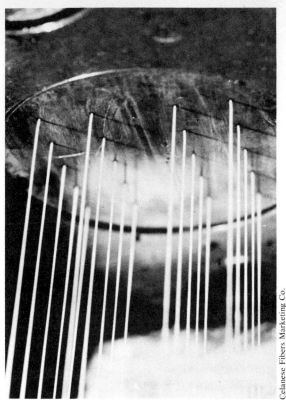

Man-made fibers of varying lengths are produced by the forcing of liquid through the tiny holes of a mechanical device known as a spinnerette.

Celanese Fibers Marketing Co.

Organization and Operation

Because of the vast differences in the origin and characteristics of various fibers, the fiber industries do not have uniform patterns of organization or operation. Although there may be similarity within groups, the practices of the natural-fiber industry differ markedly from those of the man-made fiber industry.

In spite of the differences, however, the goal of both groups is the same: to produce as efficiently as possible the fibers favored by consumers and thus needed by the textile fabric field.

THE NATURAL-FIBER INDUSTRIES. There are four major areas of cotton production in the United States: the Southeast, the Mississippi Delta, the Texas-Oklahoma Panhandle, and the far Southwestern states of New Mexico, Arizona, and California.

Nearly all cotton growers sell their product in local markets, either to mill representatives or, more likely, to wholesalers. The cotton wholesalers then bargain at central markets in Memphis, New Orleans, Dallas, and Houston. Many of these transactions may also take place in New York and Chicago, although the actual cotton goods are not on hand.

The wool produced in this country comes from relatively small sheep ranches in the Western states. But Boston remains the major central marketplace for wool, both domestic and imported.

Both cotton growers and sheep ranchers have been greatly affected by the advent of man-made fibers. The public has become accustomed to fabrics made of fibers specifically created to provide whatever qualities it demands. The cotton and wool producers now must pay close attention to the needs and wants of this public. They attempt to develop and promote in their products those characteristics which will command the best prices in the marketplace. The cotton farmer tries to grow more cotton and cotton of a better quality on each acre. The sheep farmer tries to develop hardier breeds that will produce larger quantities of high-quality wool per clipping.

acetate, the earliest of the man-made fibers, were "cellulose fibers," having as their bases such natural cellulose products as wood pulp and cotton linters. Fibers of varying lengths are produced by forcing the liquid through the tiny holes of a mechanical device known as a **spinnerette.** This is much the same way that spaghetti is made out of dough, or that the silkworm produces its fibers.

In 1979, a scant 70 years after the first artificial silk plant opened in Pennsylvania, man-made fibers in the United States were consumed by the fabric mills at an annual rate of approximately 9 billion pounds. These test-tube fibers have changed the face of fashion. They have also helped to change the living habits of the entire American public.

As the man-made fibers continue to grow in usage, the cotton- and wool-fiber industries continue to compete.

THE MAN-MADE
FIBER INDUSTRIES.

Obviously, climate and terrain have nothing to do with the production of a man-made fiber. Indeed, chemical plants are extremely adaptable, requiring only supplies of raw chemicals, power, and labor. Chemical companies have thus erected their plants in every part of the United States—up and down the East Coast, in the South, the Midwest, and increasingly on the West Coast. Operations are located wherever companies have found good raw materials or railroads and waterways for convenient shipment of those materials. Most of these plants are huge in size.

With man-made fibers, it is also possible for the producing plant to serve as its own market. Not only does the plant create the fiber, it also spins it into yarn and then knits or weaves it into fabric. Burlington Industries, J. P. Stevens, Dan River, and Milliken & Co. are just a few of the giants who incorporate all operations, from raw product to finished fabric.

Fiber Development. Limited quantities of a new or modified man-made fiber are usually first produced in a pilot plant on an experimental basis. If research indicates that both industry and consumers will accept the new product, additional plant capacity is allocated. New applications of the fiber are then explored and new industries are consulted and encouraged to use it.

While this procedure is going on in one chemical company, there is always the possibility that another company may be working along similar lines to develop a competitive fiber. The company that is first to develop a new fiber has no assurance that it will have the field to itself for long. For example, there are many brands of such man-made fibers as nylon, rayon, and acetate on the market and a roster of companies producing various acrylics and polyesters. For example, polyester fibers are produced by Celanese as Fortrel, by Du Pont as Dacron, by Eastman as Kodel, and by Hoechst as Trevira.

One reason why each important man-made fiber is produced by several chemical companies at the same time is that these fibers are engineered to provide whatever characteristics are currently in demand by industry and the consumer. Popular demand for a particular attribute—such as locked-in color, warmth without weight, or imperviousness to wrinkles —sets the same problem before the research laboratories of all fiber producers at the same time. Many of them come up with similar answers.

Consumer products in which textile fibers are incorporated are required by federal law (the Textile Fibers Products Identification Act of 1960) to bear labels specifying their fiber content by generic name and percentage of each that is used. The brand name or trademark of any of the fibers contained may also be stated, although this is not required by law.

Fiber Distribution. There are three ways in which producers of man-made fibers usually sell their fibers to fabric manufacturers:

- As unbranded products, with no restrictions placed on their end use and no implied or required standards of performance claimed
- As branded or trademarked fibers, with assurance to consumers that the quality of the fiber has been controlled by its producer, but not necessarily with assurance as to either implied or required standards of performance in the end product
- Under a licensing agreement, whereby the use of the fiber trademark concerned is permitted only to those manufacturers whose fabrics or other end products pass tests set up by the fiber producer for their specific end uses or applications

Licensing programs set up by different fiber producers and by processors of yarn vary considerably in scope. The more comprehensive programs entail extensive end-use testing to back up the licensing agreement. They exercise considerable control over fabric products that have been licensed and offer technical

FIBER TRADEMARKS

Acetate	**Modacrylic**	Multisheer	Kodel
Ariloft	Acrilan	Qiana	Spectran
Celanese	SEF	Shareen	Strialine
Chromspun	Verel	Ulstron	Trevira
Estron		Ultron	Twisloc
Lanese	**Nylon**	Vecana	Vycron
Loftura	Anso	Zeflon	Zefran
	Antron	Zefran	
Acrylic	Beaunit Nylon		**Rayon**
Acrilan	Blue "C"	**Olefin**	Avril
Bi-Loft	Cadon	Herculon	Beau-Grip
Creslan	Captiva	Marvess	Coloray
Fina	Cantrece	Polyloom	Enkrome
Orlon	Caprolan	Vectra	Fibro
Zefran	Celanese		Xena
	Cordura	**Polyester**	Zantrel
Aramid	Courtaulds Nylon	Avlin	
Kevlar	Crepeset	Blue "C"	**Spandex**
Nomex	Cumuloft	Caprolan	Lycra
	Enkaloft	Dacron	
Metallic	Enkalure	Encron	**Triacetate**
Lurex	Enkasheer	Fortrel	Arnel
	Monvelle	Hollofil	

Source: Man-Made Fiber Producer's Assoc. Inc. 1978.

services to help correct a fabric which fails to pass a qualifying test. Trademarks used under such licensing agreements are referred to as **licensed trademarks.** Celanese's Fortrel is an example of a licensed trademark.

Licensing programs may involve wear tests as well as laboratory tests. They also may specify blend levels, requiring, for example, that a minimum percentage of the designated fiber be contained in the yarn to qualify the product for licensing. Checking products periodically through retail shopping is not unusual.

Merchandising Activities

No matter how familiar fashion fabric and apparel producers and consumers may be with the qualities of each fiber, there is always the need to disseminate information about the newest modifications and their application to fashion merchandise. To do this, producers of both natural and man-made fibers make extensive use of advertising, publicity, and market research. They also extend various customer services to manufacturers, retailers, and consumers.

Usually the producer of man-made fibers, such as Celanese or Monsanto, undertakes these activities on behalf of its own individual brands and companies. The Man-Made Fiber Producers Association also carries on a very active program of consumer education about man-made fibers in general. Producers of natural fibers, on the other hand, carry on related activities through trade associations, each presenting a particular natural fiber. Examples are the National Cotton Council (the central organization of the cotton industry), Cotton Incorporated (the group specializing in promoting the use of cotton by designers and manufacturers), the American Wool Council,

Producers of natural fibers have formed trade associations for many particular fibers. The Mohair Council ran this ad in *Knitting Times,* a magazine directed to the trade.

the Wool Bureau, and the Mohair Council of America. There are also organizations promoting the use of fibers from other countries, such as the Irish Linen Guild and the Belgian Linen Association.

ADVERTISING
AND PUBLICITY.

Both man-made and natural fibers are advertised and publicized, but man-made fiber producers put considerably more dollars into this merchandising effort than do natural-fiber trade associations. They maintain a continuous flow of competitive advertising and publicity directed at both the trade and consumers. Sometimes an advertising and publicity effort will concern the entire range of textile fibers made by a single producer. Sometimes it will concentrate on a single fiber and its characteristics. A good example is the method employed by Milliken & Company to promote its polyester fabrics over a period of 28 years.

In 1953 the company began offering buyers a complimentary breakfast during New York's big June market month. This was served in a showroom setting in the garment district. Tickets were free. Company staff acted as hosts and buyers were encouraged to examine the Millikan fabrics on display around the rooms.

In the 1960's, because of steadily growing interest, Milliken moved the breakfast location from the garment district to New York's Waldorf Astoria Hotel and added a spectacular musical revue as entertainment. The musical's cast of professionally-trained young men, women, and children wore clothes made of company fabrics. They sang and danced to popular songs whose lyrics had been turned into commercials for Milliken fabrics. Well-known persons from the entertainment world appeared as guest stars. Production costs were estimated at more than $2 million.

The world-famous Milliken Breakfast Show was produced exclusively for one group of persons—the garment trade. Apparel buyers, garment and fiber manufacturers, and retailers were the only people invited. Some 32,000 of them attended the 13 performances of the 1979 Show. Tickets still were free, seats un-

reserved. Audiences began lining up at 6 a.m. for good seats and stood cheering at the Show's finale.

In January 1981 Milliken & Company announced to the trade and its employees that it was giving up its Breakfast Show and as a result of test marketing, planned a whole new advertising program, including consumer TV and strong trade advertising.

Among the trade publications used by the man-made fiber producers are *Women's Wear Daily, Men's Wear,* and *Daily News Record.* Serving as consumer media are mass-circulation magazines and newspapers as well as radio and television. Today some giant man-made fiber producers use national television spectaculars to publicize their brand names and get their fashion message across to consumers. However, spectaculars are no longer used to the extent that they were in the 1960s.

Since the names of major fibers are relatively well known today, an increasing number of man-made fiber producers now emphasize the qualities of their products rather than the names of fibers. An outstanding example is Monsanto. The company has used almost every medium including television to publicize its "Wear-Dated" licensed trademark program. The basis of this program is a guarantee that not only the fabric, but also the buttons, belts, buckles, zippers, lining, padding, thread, and all other appurtenances used in the construction of a garment labeled "Wear-Dated" will give satisfactory normal wear for one full year, or Monsanto will provide the customer with either a refund or a replacement. (See illustration on page 84.)

Although natural fibers are not advertised and promoted as aggressively as man-made fibers, some natural-fiber groups are putting more effort and money into campaigns to meet the growing domination of man-made fibers. Because these campaigns are mainly handled by trade groups, they promote the fiber itself, not the products of an individual natural-fiber producer. One of the most eye-catching campaigns is that of Cotton Incorporated. The ads and posters not only underline cotton's advantageous characteristics as a fiber but also point to the cotton industry's importance in the

Monsanto Textiles Company

Monsanto publicizes its licensed trademark policy, thus putting the advertising stress on product quality.

economy, to its interest in ecology, and even to its aid in the fuel crisis ("Cotton: less energy to produce; fed by earth; powered by sun"). All of these subjects are front-page news and billboard topics.

Fiber sources also provide garment producers and retailers with various aids that facilitate mention of their fibers in consumer advertising. This adds impact to the recognition already achieved by the fiber producer's name, trademark, slogan, or logotype. For example, the Wool Bureau encourages the use of its ball-of-yarn logotype in producer and retailer advertising of all-wool merchandise, as well as in displays. See the illustration on page 77.

To help spread the textile-fiber fashion story, producers and trade associations con-

tinually provide the press with newsworthy information, background material, and photographs for editorial features, to facilitate mention of fashion and fiber in the media. Some of this publicity effort is accomplished by direct contact with the press; some of it is done by supplying garment producers and retailers with glossy photographs and other materials to enhance the efforts. A familiar example of fashion publicity on behalf of a natural fiber is the National Cotton Council's annual Maid of Cotton program. A beauty queen is selected to make appearances throughout the country in a fashionable cotton wardrobe designed by famous designers. An example of fashion publicity on behalf of a man-made fiber was Du Pont's introduction of Qiana, a new form of nylon, in 1968. First, members of the Paris couture were encouraged to present dresses in fabrics made entirely of this fiber; then, intensive trade advertising publicized the use of fabric made from Qiana by outstanding United States and European designers. Later, Qiana was advertised and publicized as being used in the production of a wide variety of moderately priced men's and women's apparel and accessories.

Another form of fiber advertising and publicity is the development of seasonal fashion presentations for use by retail stores. Publicity kits and programs specially prepared for local markets are developed. The objective is to support promotions during peak retail selling periods. Producers may also supply fashion experts to do the commentary at fashion shows, to participate in television talk programs, or to address local consumer groups and retail sales personnel. Films about fibers and fabrics also may be used to further dramatize the fiber story.

Another promotional effort is the advertising undertaken by fiber producers in cooperation with fabric and garment manufacturers and retailers. Such **cooperative advertising** or advertising, for which the costs are shared by a store and one or more producers on terms mutually agreed to, benefits the fiber in two ways. First, consumers begin to associate the fiber name with other names already familiar, such as the name of the fiber source or the name of the retail store selling the garment. This is particularly important when a fiber is man-made and still new. Second, fabric and garment producers as well as retailers are encouraged to use and promote the fiber because of the fringe benefit they receive in the form of subsidized local or national advertising.

RESEARCH
AND DEVELOPMENT.
Both natural-fiber producers and man-made fiber producers are constantly seeking ways to improve their products. The large man-made fiber producers handle research and development mainly on an individual company basis. The natural-fiber producers, because of the small size of the average company, often work through group efforts.

The research facilities of the giant chemical companies engineer both existing and new fibers to meet the fashion and performance demands of their expanding and varied markets. The producers of man-made fibers are particularly active in instructing the fabric industry in the manipulation of new yarns, in developing optimum blends and constructions, in improving dyeing and finishing techniques, and in evaluating consumer reaction to the fabrics made from their fibers. Technical bulletins on the proper methods of processing their fibers are issued to the trade. These are supplemented by available expert advice on specific problems relating to yarn, fabric, or garment production.

Research into fabric styling and development is also undertaken by most major producers of man-made fibers. Working with fabric producers, these companies develop experimental constructions and sample weavings and knittings well in advance of each new season. They also make available to their fabric customers the services of fabric construction specialists, stylists, print consultants, color experts, and fashion and market experts.

Producers of natural fibers have increased their research activities in recent years in attempts to impart to their fibers, yarns, and textiles such qualities as dimensional stability, crease retention, wrinkle resistance, luster or matte finish, washability, and any other char-

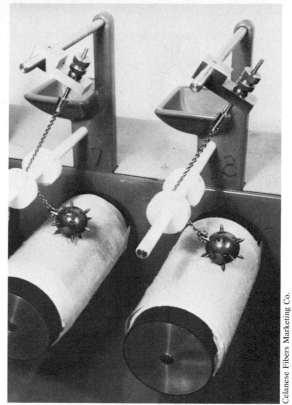

Celanese Fibers Marketing Co.

The mace test is widely used for pulling and snagging of fabrics.

acteristics that improve their acceptance. Some man-made fibers offer dimensional stability, for instance. Wool and cotton can offer the same characteristic when woven into cloth if the fabric is preshrunk. Similarly, wash-and-wear and crease-resistant properties, formerly found only in fabrics made from certain man-made fibers, can now be offered in fabrics made of cotton, wool, and linen.

CUSTOMER SERVICES. All major producers of man-made fibers and many smaller firms offer a number of services to direct and secondary users of their products. Producers of natural fibers, working through their associations, also offer many such services. These include:

- Technical advice to yarn and textile mills as well as to garment producers.
- Assistance to textile and garment pro-

ducers and retailers in locating sources of supply.

- "Libraries" of fabrics that can be examined by manufacturers, retailers, and the fashion press, with information supplied about where to buy these fabrics, what to pay for them, and what delivery to expect.
- Fashion advice and information to the textile industry, retailers, and the public.
- Fashion exhibits, sometimes open to the public, for manufacturers and retailers.
- Extensive literature for manufacturers, retailers, educators, and consumers about fiber properties, use, and care.
- Fashion experts and clothing and textile home economists to address groups of manufacturers, retailers, or consumers, staging appropriate fashion shows and demonstrations.
- Educational films and audiovisual aids for use by the trade, schools, and consumer groups.
- Assistance to retail stores in staging promotions of garments in which one or more of the promoted fibers are used. Such assistance may include finding sources of supply; staging fashion shows; developing customized retail-oriented promotional programs for department and specialty stores, resident buying offices, and chain and mail-order outlets; supplying speakers and retail merchandising representatives to interested groups; providing publicity releases and suggested advertising copy; cooperating with retail stores in the cost of local advertising; advising on store displays; and conducting consumer demonstrations and training meetings for sales personnel in stores.
- Textile processing experts to help solve problems involving fabric production; similarly qualified experts to help solve problems in the production of apparel and accessories.

THE TEXTILE FABRIC INDUSTRY

Between the fiber and the apparel fashion lies the fabric, the basic material out of which the garment or accessory is made. **Textile fabric** is cloth or material made from fibers by one of the following methods: weaving, knitting, braiding, felting, crocheting, knotting, laminating, or bonding. Sometimes one particular method may be in fashion. At other times there may be a trend in favor of a combination of methods. In general, however, most textile fabrics are either woven or knitted.

The textile fabric industry comprises a network of associated industries, each accomplishing one of the steps required to turn fibers into finished fabrics. The production of most fabrics begins with the production of yarn from fibers. **Yarn** is a continuous thread formed by spinning or twisting fibers together. Yarns are made into **greige goods** or unfinished fabrics. Greige goods (pronounced "gray goods") are converted into finished fabrics for industrial or consumer use.

History and Development

The earliest step toward mechanization in the textile fabric industry was in the production of yarn, when the spinning wheel was introduced into Europe from India around the sixth century. Even with this, spinning remained a slow, tedious process and a home occupation for centuries thereafter. Then in the eighteenth century, the British worked out mechanical methods of spinning cotton fibers into yarn. By 1779 Hargreaves, Arkwright, and Crompton each had made a contribution toward the modern factory production of yarn.

Next came mechanization of the loom, which weaves the yarn into cloth. When the British worked out machine methods of spinning fibers into yarns, they were confronted with quantities of yarn much larger than hand-operated looms could use. The first power loom was invented by an English clergyman, Dr. Edward Cartwright, and patented in 1785. It used water as a source of energy.

The same sequence of mechanization was true on this side of the Atlantic. In 1790, Samuel Slater established a yarn mill in Pawtucket, Rhode Island. A present-day giant in the textile field, J. P. Stevens and Company is descended from Slater's famous mill. For some time, however, fabric production remained both a hand operation and a home industry, totally inadequate to meet the demand for apparel fabrics. Then, Francis Cabot Lowell, a New Englander, visited a textile factory in England and memorized the detailed specifications of its power-operated machinery. In 1814 Lowell built the first successful power loom and the first textile fabric mill in the United States.

The demands of a rapidly growing country provided an eager market for the output of United States textile mills, and the young industry flourished. Automation and mechanization techniques developed both here and abroad have greatly advanced production procedures. Today it is possible for a single operator to oversee as many as 100 weaving machines if the fabric is plain.

Organization and Operation

The textile fabric industry in the United States today is composed of between 6,500 and 7,000 mills employing about 900,000 workers. Some of these mills produce yarn; some weave or knit cloth for apparel and other purposes; some do finishing. All are part of an industry that in 1979 delivered over $40 billion worth of goods annually. Even this rate of production, however, has proved insufficient to satisfy this country's appetite for textile products; in 1978 the U.S. imported $7,857 million in textiles, while only $2,903 million were exported.[2]

Textile mills are widely dispersed throughout the country. The industry has tended to seek areas where labor and land costs are low. There has also been little advantage in concentrating production in any one area through the construction of giant mills or complexes. A small mill can operate about as efficiently as a large one, since textile machinery has a long, useful life and its output can be increased by working two or three shifts. There used to be some concentration of textile mills in the Northeastern states, but in recent years the Southeastern part of the country has offered cheaper labor and land.

Because it is necessary for the textile fabric industry to commit itself far in advance to specific weaves, colors, and finishes, it is extremely well informed about fashion and alert to incoming trends. But because they are geared to mass-production methods, most mills are reluctant to produce short, experimental runs for individual designers.

The market centers for textile fabrics are not at the mills but in the fashion capital of the country, New York City. There, on the doorstep of the garment industry, every mill of importance has a salesroom. A fabric buyer or designer for a garment maker, or a retail store apparel buyer or fashion coordinator, only has to walk a block or two to obtain firsthand information on what the fabric market offers.

TYPES OF MILLS. Some mills sort and select the fibers to be used, spin them into yarn, then weave or knit them and finish the fabric. Finishing may include dyeing, napping, and pressing. It may also include treating the fabric to ensure such attributes as nonshrinkage and permanent press. Fashion influences decisions every step of the way.

Some mills produce only the yarn. Others weave or knit fabric from purchased yarn but do not carry the process beyond the greige, or unfinished, state. There are also plants that bleach, dye, preshrink, print, or in other ways impart desired characteristics to fabrics produced by other mills. The plants that handle the various stages may or may not be under common ownership, and they may or may not be geographically close.

For certain effects, yarns may be dyed before being woven or knitted (yarn-dyed); for others, fabrics are knitted or woven first and then dyed (vat-dyed). In some instances, either the warp or the weft (filling) yarns are dyed before weaving. The complete fabric is then dyed to get a cross-dyed effect.

Many mills no longer limit themselves to working with yarns made of a single fiber. Fibers may be used alone or with other fibers, as demand dictates. Any of the types of mills described above may combine a natural fiber with another natural fiber, or, more commonly, a natural fiber with a man-made fiber, to achieve a desired effect. Examination of the fiber content labels on garments will show

how widespread the man-made fibers are. It will also show how rayon, in particular, is combined with almost any other fiber to achieve a specific effect.

THE CONVERTER. It is probably correct to say that the textile converter is the real middle-man of the textile industry. **Textile converters** buy greige goods from the mills, have the goods processed to order by the finishing plants, and then sell the finished goods to garment makers. Therefore, they must be on top of trends in colors, patterns, and finishes. They must fully understand fashion and must be able to anticipate demand. Converters work very quickly since they come on the production scene toward the end of the operation, and are primarily interested in the finish and texture applied to the greige goods.

In recent years, the converter's know-how has helped American textile producers meet the competition of foreign textile producers who offer more fashion-oriented goods in small yardages. Converters can supply apparel producers with fewer yards of selected fabrics than can larger fabric mills. The latter must produce tremendous yardages of a designated pattern or design in order to maintain a profitable operation.

While many converters are truly small operators, others, such as Everfast, Cohn-Hall-Marx, and M. Lowenstein, are large.

Merchandising Activities

It is said that fabric precedes fashion. This means that dress designers, for example, cannot create a garment unless they find just the right cloth. It must drape the way they want it to and have the colors and textures needed to give the desired form to the design.

Since the textile fabric industry must work several seasons ahead of consumer demand, it must be early in recognizing the direction that fashion is taking. Textile firms employ staffs of fashion experts who attend market openings around the world. They work with designers to create fabrics in those weights, textures, colors, and patterns that it is antici-pated consumers will want. And they do this 2 or 3 seasons, or some 12 to 18 months, before the garments made of those fabrics will appear in stores. Two textile fairs of worldwide importance are held semiannually. These are Interstoff, held in West Germany, and Ideacomo, held in Italy. Should the textile producers fail to identify and act upon a trend seen at a major textile fair, retailers and apparel producers can be frustrated in their efforts to serve the fashion consumer.

ADVERTISING
AND PUBLICITY. Large fabric manufacturers advertise lavishly. Their advertising features the brand names of their products and frequently the names of specific apparel manufacturers who use their goods. Either with the cooperation of fiber sources or on their own, these fabric houses sponsor radio and television programs, run full-color advertisements in a wide variety of mass-circulation magazines and newspapers, and share the cost of brand advertising run by retail stores. Their advertising generally makes consumers aware of new apparel styles, the fabrics of which they are made, and often the names of retail stores where they may be purchased.

Fabric producers compete among themselves for the business of apparel producers. They also compete for recognition among retail store buyers and for consumer acceptance of products made of their goods. They publicize brand names and stage seasonal fashion shows in market areas for retailers and the fashion press. They provide hang tags for the use of garment manufacturers. These tags may bear not only the fabric's brand name but also instructions relating to its care. In accordance with federal regulation, fabric producers also supply manufacturers with the required care labels that must be permanently sewn into all garments. Many fabric firms also make educational materials available to schools, consumer groups, and retail sales personnel. They also supply information to consumers and the trade press. All of these are means of publicizing fashion news, fabric developments, and products.

SOME OF THE MOST EXCITING FASHIONS START WITH ENKA'S SPECIALTY FIBERS.

In developing an innovative fiber for the apparel industry, Enka's textile scientists and technicians are as interested in its performance as in its esthetic properties—its ability to fulfill tomorrow's fashion requirements. Fibers that give fashionable apparel star quality:

GOLDEN TOUCH.® The special polyester. It has almost twice as many filaments as ordinary polyester, so it feels like the real thing. Butter-soft suede, silk-like luxury, cottony-soft fleece, velour, corduroy, terry, cashmere richness.

MULTILOBAL ENKALURE® NYLON. Drapable, silky with a lustrous look and a soft, sensuous hand. It's everywhere—from the beaches to the discos.

ENCRON® GOLDEN GLOW.® A bright, trilobal polyester that's

wonderfully radiant, soft and drapable. Available blended with Enkaire® rayon for a mohair-like fabric.

CREPESOFT™ POLYESTER. America's first producer-textured polyester crepe yarn. For knitted or woven fabrics with the crepe permanently built in.

VIVE LA CREPE™ NYLON. Soft, sensuous and static free. It won't bunch, crunch or ride up.

CREPESET® SILVER LABEL™ Possibly the most elegant crepe in the world.

And there's more. Yarns that, when turned into fabric, give fashion a high-styled look. For more information on our star-studded line of fashionable fibers, contact us. American Enka, 530 Fifth Avenue, New York, NY 10036 (212) 730-5362.

ENKA

ENCRON® GOLDEN TOUCH® GOLDEN TOUCH-SUEDE, GOLDEN TOUCH-CORDUROY ENKALURE® GOLDEN GLOW® ENKAIRE® CREPESOFT, CREPESET® SILVER LABEL, VIVE LA CREPE ARE TMs OF AMERICAN ENKA CO., ENKA, N.C. A PART OF Akzona INC

Large fiber manufacturers advertise lavishly both to consumers and to the trade. Their trade advertising features their brand name fibers for use in apparel fabrics.

RESEARCH
AND DEVELOPMENT Fabric producers, like fiber producers, now devote attention to exploring the market potential of their products and anticipating the needs of their customers. Success in the fashion industry depends on supplying customers with what they want. Fashion causes swift changes. Anticipation of such changes requires close attention to the market and a scientific study of trends.

Many of the large fabric producers maintain product and market research divisions. Their experts work closely with both the trade and consumer markets in studying fabric performance characteristics. Many fabric producers provide garment manufacturers with sample runs of new fabrics for experimental purposes. The market researchers conduct consumer studies relating to the demand for or acceptance of finishes, blends, and other desired characteristics. Such studies also help fabric and garment producers to determine what consumers will want in the future, where and when they will want it, and in what quantities.

A recent example of the close cooperation between the fiber houses and the textile manufacturers in the exploration and testing of new processes is Cluett Peabody's Sanfor-Set and Burlington Mills' cotton denims.

Denim producers had not been able to solve the problem of cotton denim's extreme shrinkage when tumble-dried—at least not without giving up the very qualities of cotton their customers demanded. Burlington Mills was one of the producers of cotton denim.

At that point, Cluett Peabody had just developed the Sanfor-Set process and was interested in putting it into practical testing.

The two companies joined forces to initiate the Sanfor-Set process on Burlington's cotton denim fabrics. It was a remarkable success, and other fabric houses joined in. Everyone benefited. Cluett Peabody's Sanfor-Set process actually overcame cotton's stubborn tendency to wrinkle and shrink in the tumble-dryer—a vital step toward a truly care-free garment. Burlington Mills now had a cotton denim fabric that "breathed" as cotton should, remained wrinkle-free through count-less washings and tumble-dryings, and kept its original shape through years of wear.

Thus in 1979 Sanfor-Set became the revolutionary new treatment for cotton fabrics. Its impact upon the marketplace is just beginning to be felt.

CUSTOMER SERVICES. Today's well-integrated and diversified textile companies speak with great fashion authority. They also employ merchandising and marketing staffs whose expertise in fashion trends is available to apparel manufacturers, retailers, the fashion press, and frequently to consumers. Fashion staffs attend foreign and domestic market openings and issue seasonal fashion forecasts. They conduct in-store sales training programs, address consumer groups, and stage fashion shows for the trade and press. They help retail stores arrange fashion shows and storewide promotions featuring their products, and they assist buyers in locating merchandise made from their fabrics. These fashion merchandising experts not only carry the company's fashion message to trade customers but reach retailers and consumers as well.

TRENDS IN THE TEXTILE INDUSTRIES

As the 1980s began, the American textile industry looked back on a decade of staggering events on the domestic and international scene, and, more specifically, on the textile scene.

Uncertain world conditions, particularly in relation to the oil-rich countries, focused all Americans' attention on the energy crisis. The economic indicators of the nation were still predicting a recession. And within the textile industry, there was concern about proliferating imports of foreign goods, burgeoning federal regulations for employee safety and environmental protection, and the ever-present uncertainty about the country's economic stability. The American textile industry turned its eyes to the 1980s with full knowledge that this would probably be the most dramatically changing decade the industry had known since World War II.

Spiraling petrochemical costs would affect the man-made fiber industry. Technology would have to produce increased production while guarding price levels. Mechanization and automation would have to be expanded to turn the industry from a labor-intensive to a capital-intensive one. The trend toward giantism would accelerate. Increased foreign expansion would have to be generated and greater diversification of products planned. And finally, in terms of employee safety and environmental protection, the 1980s would be the decade in which the word became the deed.

Far from fearing the 1980s, the textile industry positioned itself to make the most of this decade. Until then, it had been planning and preparing. Now the stage was set for dramatic action.

Expanded Mechanization and Automation

The trend toward the use of more machinery and less labor is apparent at all levels in the production of textile fibers and fabrics.

In the cotton fields, the goal is a savings in labor costs and a reduction in harvesting time. A mechanical stripper can harvest 50 times as many bolls of cotton as a worker who snaps off the bolls by hand. A mechanical picker can harvest 500 times as much cotton lint as a worker who picks the lint from the plants by hand.

In the mills, machines for mixing fibers for conversion into yarn enable one worker to mix the same amount of fiber in the same amount of time it formerly took four workers. In addition, machines make possible greater standardization of product. New high-speed mechanized yarn twisters are twice as productive as conventional twisters. Automated weaving and knitting machines operate at increasingly higher speeds and require fewer operators. And most of these operators have been trained to repair the machines should problems develop. Automated knitting machines, capable

of producing fabrics with cutting patterns outlined on them in knitted thread, are being developed. Machines for recycling products and converting former waste into usable materials are also being developed.

During the first half of the 1970s, sophisticated electronic equipment for high-speed preparation of designs on fabric became commonplace. More than 75 percent of the total gross knitted fabric output used this technique —which performed in seconds an operation that formerly took hours. The dawn of the 1980s saw the computer revolutionize the dyeing and printing of fabrics. This incredibly fast system transfers the computerized designs from a television screen directly onto the fabrics.

New electronic systems for printing designs on fabric "read" a design and produce a copy in the form of a special negative. These negatives are electronically scanned; in a single hour, rollers—which used to take the printing industry 100 hours to make—are produced. Other electronic systems make it possible for a firm's management to determine the cost price of fabrics before they are knitted or woven. Still other systems provide a fabric firm's management with daily and cumulative figures for year to date or season to date as compared with previous year. These figures are detailed as to orders, stock on hand, and quantities on order. The systems also provide figures on shipments broken down by individual accounts and other pertinent data the firm may require to keep stock in a desired ratio to sales.

All of this means a reduction in labor costs, a reduction in human errors, and a reduction in production time. It means improved productivity per work hour, greater standardization of product, and better quality control.

Improved Technology

Understanding that healthy sales depend upon having what ultimate consumers want, the textile industry is putting increased effort into developing processes that will give products the characteristics consumers find both practical and inviting. New processes have been developed at every level of fiber and fabric production, but some of the most interesting are in the dyeing and finishing areas.

As energy costs continue to spiral upward, dyers and finishers have felt mounting pressure to reduce their consumption of fuels and other raw materials. The increased cost of oil and oil-related chemicals poses a great threat. Fortunately, new dyeing and finishing equipment has helped to reduce energy usage. New methods of reclaiming chemicals from waste streams have also led to further conservation methods. In addition, there are improved dyes and improved methods of dyeing. Some produce better dyeing of fibers and fiber blends that formerly were difficult to dye. Some produce sharper colors; some more subtle colors. Some produce colors that are more resistant to fading or changing under sunlight or after repeated washings. In the 1970s, heat-transfer printing became big news as the way to print designs on that decade's best-selling fiber, polyester.

A number of improved or new finishes have given fabrics more consumer appeal. Some increase soil-resistance. Some reduce the static electricity problem that knits can have, or their snagging problems. Some produce fabric that feels like suede.

Continued Trend Toward Giantism

Mergers, acquisitions, and the trend toward giantism continue. Firms have been expanding horizontally. **Horizontal integration** means absorbing or merging with other companies that function at the same level of production, for example, the merger of two fabric producers. Firms have also been expanding vertically. **Vertical integration** means absorbing or merging with companies at other levels of production, for example, the acquisition of a fiber mill by a fabric firm. As a result, the textile industry shows a decline in the total number of firms but an increase in the number and size of large firms. See Table 5-1.

TABLE 5-1
The 10 Largest Publicly Held U.S. Textile Companies

NAME	ANNUAL SALES (MILLIONS OF DOLLARS)
Burlington Industries	$2,456
J. P. Stevens	1,736
West Point Pepperell	909
Springs Mills	685
United Merchants & Manufacturers	642
Cone Mills	618
M. Lowenstein & Sons	605
Collins & Aikman	557
Cannon Mills	547
Dan River	530

Source: Business Week, April 9, 1979, page 66.

Increased Foreign Expansion

Another trend, limited to fabric producers, is toward the acquisition or establishment of mills abroad. Such foreign-based mills may be wholly owned by a United States firm or may be jointly owned by a United States firm and a host-country firm. Most are located close to fiber sources. To this convenience are added the facilities, fashion knowledge, and technical skill of their United States owners or part owners. The engineers may be American or American-trained, but the rest of the plant is usually staffed by local workers who are paid according to local wage scales. By producing some goods abroad, domestic manufacturers defend themselves against the competition of foreign-made fabrics. They also put themselves in a more favorable position to sell in countries where tariff walls limit or keep out goods made in the United States.

Another trend involves foreign business firms, mainly Japanese, that are buying into fabric or finishing plants here. Some of these firms are becoming partners in or sole owners of new facilities being built here. At least one Japanese firm was said to be thinking of moving into cotton cultivation in the southern United States to secure a long-term, stable supply. One of the world's largest chemical companies—larger even than Du Pont—is the West German-owned Hoechst Group. This company employs 9,000 Americans in 19 states and registers over $900 million in sales here. It makes a diversified group of products, from the polyester fiber Trevira to Foster Grant Sunglasses.

Greater Diversification of Products

Today, the textile industry produces a more diversified range of fibers and fabrics than ever before. The specialization that once divided the industry into separate segments, each producing fabrics from a single type of fiber, has all but faded. To meet the needs of consumers, it is often necessary to blend two or more fibers into a yarn or to combine a warp yarn of one fiber with a weft yarn of another. Mills are learning to adjust their operations to any new fiber or combination of fibers. Illustrating the importance of blends is the trademark developed by Cotton Incorporated that is used on fabrics that contain 60 percent or more cotton fiber but are not 100 percent cotton. The Wool Bureau introduced a trademark for fabrics made of a fiber blend of at least 50 percent wool. (See page 77.)

Two of the largest firms in the field illustrate how the industry is moving toward greater diversification of product. Burlington, originally a rayon mill specializing in bedspreads, now produces and sells spun and textured yarns of both natural and man-made fibers. Their products include a wide variety of finished woven and knitted fabrics, some unfinished fabrics, and hosiery for men, women, and children. They also produce a wide variety of domestic and home furnishings, from bed linens to rugs and furniture. Under the J. P. Stevens banner are both cotton and woolen mills. Some produce spun and textured yarns, others produce finished fabrics for both over-the-counter sales and apparel manufacture, and still others produce women's hosiery. Both companies use the major natural fibers and a large number of the man-made fibers available in this country.

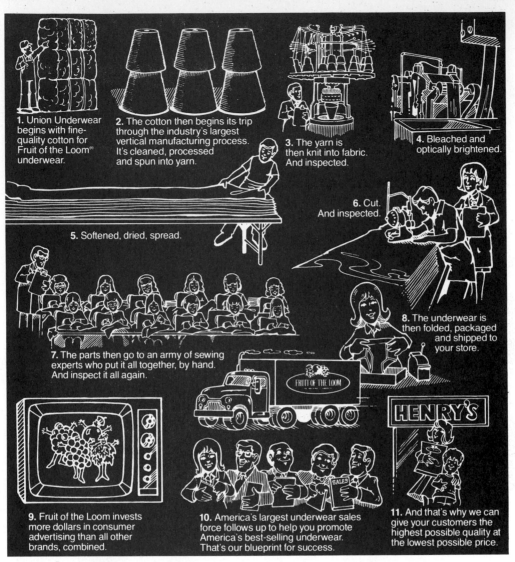

1. Union Underwear begins with fine-quality cotton for Fruit of the Loom® underwear.

2. The cotton then begins its trip through the industry's largest vertical manufacturing process. It's cleaned, processed and spun into yarn.

3. The yarn is then knit into fabric. And inspected.

4. Bleached and optically brightened.

5. Softened, dried, spread.

6. Cut. And inspected.

7. The parts then go to an army of sewing experts who put it all together, by hand. And inspect it all again.

8. The underwear is then folded, packaged and shipped to your store.

9. Fruit of the Loom invests more dollars in consumer advertising than all other brands, combined.

10. America's largest underwear sales force follows up to help you promote America's best-selling underwear. That's our blueprint for success.

11. And that's why we can give your customers the highest possible quality at the lowest possible price.

Quality and value. The fruits of our labor.

FRUIT OF THE LOOM. UNCONDITIONALLY GUARANTEED **#1 in supply, #1 in demand**

Union Underwear Company, Inc., 1290 Avenue of the Americas, New York, N.Y. 10019. (212) 581-9700. An operating company of Northwest Industries.

This ad explains the steps between the raw material and the appearance of the finished product (here cotton underwear) in retail stores.

Increased Government Regulation

Until recently, federal regulation of the textile industry was mainly concerned with the fiber-content labeling of fabrics and products made of those fabrics. In 1954, a Flammable Fabrics Act was passed, but it served to ban from the market only a few very ignitable fabrics and apparel made from those fabrics. The increasing strength and direction of the consumerism movement, however, has resulted in more government regulation of the textile industry, both on the federal and state levels.

July 1972 was the month when two important changes in federal textile regulations became effective: the FTC's rule on "Care Labeling of Textile Wearing Apparel," and the revision of the Flammable Fabrics Act.

The FTC's care-labeling rule requires that all fabrics—piece goods as well as apparel and accessories made of fabric—be labeled to show the type of care the fabric requires. The label must indicate whether the fabric can be washed or should be dry-cleaned. If the fabric can be washed, the label must indicate the temperature at which it should be washed. The label must also indicate whether ironing is required, and if so, at what temperature. The manufacturer must sew a permanent label into each garment.

During the next few years the industry will spend upwards of $2 billion in trying to meet a demand by OSHA (Occupational Safety and Health Administration) that cotton dust in mills be reduced sharply. Cotton dust is believed to cause byssinosis, a pulmonary disorder also called "brown lung" disease.

The following trends in the textile industry are a result of government environmental and consumer regulations:

- Fibers and textile products will be made by larger producers with a resulting decrease in the number of small concerns and marginal operations. This will result primarily from the higher production costs related to complying with the new government regulations and the greater capital investment required to stay competitive in a period of continually rising costs.
- Manufacturing operations will function at higher efficiencies, recycling as much as possible and converting waste to energy.
- Fibers with built-in environmental disadvantages will slowly give way to more suitable replacements, or new processing techniques will be devised to allow their continued use.
- Transfer printing may be an important way to reduce some of the dye-house stream-pollution problems.
- Consumers will be increasingly protected, with particular emphasis on children's apparel and home furnishings.
- Consumers will be better advised on the characteristics of their purchases.

MERCHANDISING VOCABULARY

Define or explain each of the following terms:

Cooperative advertising	**Primary suppliers**
Cotton	**Silk**
Fiber	**Spinnerette**
Greige goods	**Textile converter**
Horizontal integration	**Textile fabric**
Licensed trademark	**Vertical integration**
Linen	**Wool**
Man-made fibers	**Yarn**
Natural fibers	

MERCHANDISING REVIEW

1. Why is it necessary for a student of fashion merchandising to have a basic knowledge of textile fibers and fabrics and of their respective industries?
2. Name the four natural fibers. From what source is each obtained? Indicate at least two countries that are principal sources for each.
3. Compare or contrast natural and man-made fibers on the basis of the following: (a) relative size of their producers; (b) location of production facilities; (c) predictability of supply; and (d) consistent uniformity of product.
4. Trace the steps or stages through which a completely new or newly modified man-made fiber goes from its conception to its general availability. Why are fibers with similar characteristics usually available from more than one producer at the same time?
5. Name and explain the three ways in which producers of man-made fibers usually sell their products to fabric manufacturers.
6. What are the various methods used for converting fibers into fabrics? Which methods are in most common use today?
7. Trace the historical development of the textile industry in the United States. What specific technological advances have been of major importance in its development?
8. Through what processes do fibers usually go in being transformed into fabrics?
9. What is the function of a textile converter? What are the advantages for (a) a fabric mill and (b) the apparel trade of dealing with a converter?
10. Name and describe the provisions of three government regulations that had an important effect on the American textile industry in the past 20 years.

MERCHANDISING DIGEST

1. Compare or contrast the methods employed by natural and man-made fiber producers in carrying out their advertising and publicity activities.
2. Discuss current trends in the textile industry as they relate to (a) expanding use of mechanization and automation; (b) increased foreign expansion; and (c) greater diversification of products.

REFERENCES

[1] Dorner, *Fashion in the Forties and Fifties*, p. 38.

[2] Hodden, "The Textile Economy: Another Drumbeat?" p. 68.

6
THE MATERIALS OF FASHION: LEATHER AND FUR

Cave dwellers who wrapped themselves in animal skins for protection against the elements discovered the warmth of fur and the protective and supple qualities of leather. In fact, animal skins were probably all that cave dwellers did have to wear, since the discovery and art of spinning and weaving material came much later. Leather and fur still play an important role in the fashion business. Leather is particularly important in some of the fashion accessory fields, such as shoes, handbags, and gloves. It has also recently increased in popularity as an apparel material. Fur is used primarily for outerwear apparel either for the basic garment or for its trim.

In contrast to the production of textiles, the processing of leather and fur appears rather primitive and slow. Thus fashion trends have to be spotted and acted upon particularly early. Yet many changes are taking place in these industries, largely in improved production methods and techniques. These changes are giving designers and manufacturers a wider range of products to work with. These changes may also indicate the course that fashions made from leather and fur will take in the future.

THE LEATHER INDUSTRY

Leather making is a time-consuming and very highly specialized process. Because of this time factor, the leather industry has always had to anticipate and predict trends in advance of other fashion material suppliers. Leather producers must make commitments to colors, finishes, and production from 8 to 16 months in advance of the leather's use by apparel and accessory manufacturers. The coordination of colors, textures, finishes, and other fashion variables is vital to the leather industry. Other fashion producers often look to the leather industry for leadership in color direction. They also look to this industry in many instances for long-range forecasts.

The process of transforming animal skins into leather is known as **tanning.** The term "tanning" comes from the Latin word for oak bark, the material used in the earliest known treatment of animal skins. Tanning is the oldest craft known. Primitive people not only killed animals for food, they also devised ways to treat the skins for use as body covering. The modern tanning industry receives many of its hides as by-products of the meat-packing industry. Many other skins come from animals that are raised and bred primarily for milk or wool. After these animals can no longer fulfill their primary function, tanners convert the hides and skins to leather.

Maybe the real reason the cattlemen hated the sheepherders was that they dressed better.

What chance did a scruffy cattleman have to win the favor of the new schoolmarm or the young widder?

Even if the cowboy played the guitar, all a sheepherder had to do was sashay into town wearing a new shearling coat.

Not that the sheepherder had it all that easy coming by a new shearling.

Naturally, he couldn't get them store-bought the way you can today at Barney's.

And each sheepherder had to be his own fashion designer. Unlike today, when fastidious French craftsmen match, cut, and sew specially selected skins according to the patterns of some of the world's leading designers.

For the sheepherder, too, selection was haphazard. Today, the makers represented at Barney's choose only the finest skins from the world's best herds. In fact, of the thousands of skins they inspect, only 3% meet their standards.

Today, also, a sheepherder can choose from hip-length, ¾-length, and full-length shearlings.

And, in reality, Barney's has not left out the cattleman. Because Barney's offers a full range of trench coats, vests, reversible and quilted coats in leathers, along with the finest collections of shearlings.

This town, it would appear, is big enough for both of them.

Barney's, New York

7th Avenue and 17th Street. Open 9 AM to 9:30 PM. Free alterations. Free parking. We honor the American Express Card, Master Charge, Visa. And, of course, your Barney's Card.

Barney's

Inside in or inside out? When it comes to wearing shearling coats, people don't follow like sheep.

History and Development

The use of leather for apparel and other purposes was commonplace in North America long before the first European settlers arrived. The earliest known tanners in what is now the United States were Indians. They made clothing, moccasins, and tents from deerskins. Although they lacked the knowledge to produce leathers of today's variety and quality, they developed tanning techniques that met their own needs.

The first commercial tannery in the American Colonies was established in 1623 in Plymouth by Experience Miller, an Englishman. Peter Minuit, Governor of New Amsterdam, invented the first machinery used for tanning in the Colonies. This was a horse-driven stone mill that ground the oak bark then used in converting animal skins into leather.

Mechanization of the industry took a long step forward in 1809. Samuel Parker invented a machine that split heavy steer hides 25 times faster than was possible by hand. Split hides produce a lighter, more supple leather, desirable in shoes, boots, and other apparel.

Yet mechanization, which developed at about the same rate on both sides of the Atlantic, has not appreciably reduced the time required for the actual tanning process. Hides and skins require prolonged exposure to a series of treatments before they become leather. To produce kid leather, for example, requires several weeks for the actual tanning and finishing process itself. This is in addition to the time required to purchase the skins, ship them to the tannery, receive and inspect them, and start them on their way through the tanning process. However, mechanization has reduced much of the heavy manual labor previously required to stir hides and skins as they soak and for dehairing and defleshing them. There are also machines now that can split hides, emboss patterns, and perform other processes formerly done by hand.

Chemistry has made a great contribution to tanning methods. It has provided new tanning agents that reduce the time required to transform hides and skins into leather and that achieve greater variety of qualities in leather. Modern instruments control solutions for temperature and other factors to assure uniformity of product.

Organization and Operation

Tanning was once a household industry, and still is so in some of the less-developed areas of the world. But today it has become relatively big business in the United States. Nearly 21,000 workers are employed in this country's tanneries, turning out $2 billion worth of leathers a year for widely divergent uses.

The tanning processes at the heart of this industry are basically the same as they have been for thousands of years. Although the grease and brains of an animal are no longer used to treat its pelt, tanners still soak pelts to soften them, remove any flesh or hair that may adhere to them, and treat them to retard putrefaction. As recently as a century or two ago, tanners still relied principally on such natural materials as oak or hemlock bark to process skins. But today there is a vast range of chemical and natural agents at their disposal: chrome salts, synthethic tanning agents, and oils, for example. As a result, the variety of colors, textures, and finishes available to the fashion industries today is infinitely greater than it was even 50 years ago. This is true even though the variety of animals whose skins are used has decreased. Some animals have been placed on state, national, and international endangered-species lists and their commercial uses restricted or banned.

ORGANIZATION. The leather industry in this country is divided into three major types of companies: regular tanneries, converters, and contract tanneries. **Regular tanneries** are those companies that purchase and process hides and skins to the specifications of converters and are not involved in the sale of the finished product. **Converters** buy hides and skins, farm out the processing to contract tanneries, and sell the finished product. **Contract tanneries** process hides and skins to the specifications of converters and are not involved in the sale of the finished product. About half the firms in the industry are regular tanneries; the other half are contractors and converters.

The leather industry is highly specialized because the methods and materials used vary according to the nature of the hides or skins being treated and the end product for which each is intended. Tanners of calfskin do not normally tan kidskins; tanners of glove leathers do not normally produce sole leather.

The mergers, consolidations, and affiliations prevalent in the textile industry during and immediately following World II have also taken place in the leather industry. In 1870 there were 4,500 tanneries in operation in the United States; today there are fewer than 500. The trends toward mergers and toward fewer and larger plants continue.

Leather is largely a by-product of the milk-, meat-, or wool-producing industries in the United States. It therefore has been lower in cost than it would have been had the animals been raised for their skins alone. Some recent developments in world economics, however, have begun to change this. Because of an expanding market for hides in other countries, the trend toward smaller herds of cattle in the United States, and the growing use of leather in other fashion and home furnishings markets, United States leather hides are becoming very expensive. This is leading to imports of less expensive foreign leather.

Most United States tanneries are located in the northeast and north central states. In these regions are also clustered the industry's major customers, such as shoe, apparel, and accessory manufacturers. Like textile producers, however, most leather firms maintain sales offices or representatives in New York City for the convenience of their customers.

SOURCES OF
LEATHER SUPPLY.
Most leather comes from cattle. But fashion also uses the hides and skins of many other animals from all parts of the world. Kid and goatskins come from Europe, Asia, Africa, and South America; capeskin comes from a special breed of sheep raised in South Africa and South America; pigskin comes from the peccary, a wild hog native to Mexico and South America; buffalo comes from Asia.

The variety of glove leathers alone illustrates how worldwide are the sources of leather:

- *Cabretta* from South American sheep
- *Calfskin* from young calves of the United States and elsewhere
- *Goatskin* from South America, South Africa, India, Spain
- *Kidskin* from Europe
- *Pigskin* from Yugoslavia, Mexico, and Central and South America
- *Buckskin* from deer and elk in Mexico, South and Central America, and the People's Republic of China
- *Mocha* from Asian and African sheep

In the United States in 1978, imports of hides and skins exceeded $100 million, but exports were nearly $300 million. The great bulk of raw materials for leather in the United States comes from domestic meat-packing industries.

LEATHER PROCESSING.
The leather trade divides animal skins into three classes according to weight. Animal skins that weigh 15 pounds or less when shipped to the tannery are referred to as **skins.** Calves, goats, pigs, sheep, and deer are among the animals producing skins. Animal skins weighing from 15 to 25 pounds, such as those from young horses and cattle, are referred to as **kips.** Animal skins weighing over 25 pounds, such as those from cows, oxen, buffalo, and horses, are referred to as **hides.**

The process by which skins, kips, and hides become leather is a lengthy one. This is one of the many reasons why the leather industry has to work well in advance of demand. Three to six months are usually required for the tanning of hides for sole leather and saddlery. The time is shorter for kips and skins, but the processes are more numerous, requiring more expensive equipment and more highly skilled labor. Leather for shoe uppers, garments, and accessories is tanned and finished in three to six weeks.

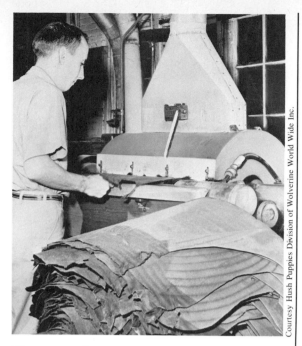

Courtesy Hush Puppies Division of Wolverine World Wide Inc.

The processing of leather requires extensive equipment and highly skilled labor.

Tanning may involve the use of oils, vegetable materials, minerals, or chemicals as the tanning agent. The choice of the agent mainly depends upon the end use for which the leather is being prepared.

Oil. Processing with oil is one of the oldest methods of turning raw animal skins into leather. A fish oil—usually codfish—is used. Today, oil tanning is used to produce chamois, doeskin, and buckskin—relatively soft and pliable leathers for use in making gloves and jackets.

Vegetable Materials. Vegetable tanning, which is also an old method, uses such agents as tannic acids from the bark, wood, or nuts of various trees and shrubs and from tea leaves. Vegetable tanning is used on cow, steer, horse, and buffalo hides. The product is a heavy, often relatively stiff leather used for the soles of shoes, some shoe uppers, some handbags and belts, and saddlery. Vegetable-tanned leather can be identified by a dark cen-

ter streak in the cut edge. It is resistant to moisture and can be cleaned by sponging.

Minerals. There are two important tanning methods that use minerals. One uses alum; the other uses chrome salts. Alum, used by the ancient Egyptians to make writing paper, is rarely used today. Chrome tanning, introduced in 1893, is now used to process nearly two-thirds of all leather produced in this country. This is a fast method that produces leather for shoe uppers, gloves, handbags, and other products. Chrome-tanned leather can be identified by the pale, blue-gray color in the center of the cut edge. It is slippery when wet. It is usually washable and can be cleaned by sponging.

Chemical. Another relatively new process uses formaldehyde for tanning. This is the quickest method of tanning. The leather is white when tanned and thus can be dyed easily. Leather tanned by formaldehyde is washable and often used for gloves and children's shoe uppers.

Combinations. It is possible to combine tanning agents. A vegetable and mineral combination, or retanning, is used for products such as work shoes and boots. Combinations of alum and formaldehyde, and oil and chrome, give leather different qualities.

Merchandising Activities

Because of fashion coordination problems, leather producers do not merely stay abreast of fashion, they must keep ahead of it. As a result, they are among the best and most experienced forecasters in the fashion business. They have to be—especially those who work with the skins or hides of foreign animals. Months before other fashion industries have to commit themselves on matters of color and texture, leather producers have already made their decisions. They have started the search for precisely the right dyes and treatments to produce what they expect will be in demand in a given future period. The time it takes to transform skins, kips, and hides into leather requires that tanneries project fashion demand several seasons into the future.

FASHION
INFORMATION SERVICES.

Having made their assessments of fashion trends very early, leather tanners, like fiber and fabric producers, share their conclusions with their customers. Individually or through industry associations, tanners retain fashion experts to disseminate this information. These experts advise manufacturers, editors, and retailers on future fashion trends in leather.

A typical activity of leather producers is the preparation of fashion booklets for distribution to manufacturers, retailers, the press, and other interested persons. Such booklets are sometimes available a year or more before the consumer is likely to wear or use the leather products described. The booklets include comments on general fashion trends. They describe the leather colors and textures suitable for classics, boutique merchandise, and promotional use. Finally, they include swatches of important textures and looks in leather.

Another typical activity of individual producers and of industry associations is the assignment of a fashion expert to work with retailers, manufacturers, and the press to help them crystallize their fashion thinking. This service might take the form of individual conferences, of participation on a committee of producers or retailers, or of fashion presentations to industry, retail, or consumer groups.

Yet with all this activity, individual tanners are not known by name to the public. A fashion editor describing a leather garment, glove, or shoe is not likely to mention the leather producer. Nor is the leather producer likely to be named in retail store advertising or in the advertising placed by the manufacturers of the finished products. As a result, the consumer who may recall names of several fabric and fiber producers would probably have a hard time naming even one tanner.

The Tanners Council prepares an annual fashion booklet for distribution to manufacturers, retailers, and the press. It contains swatches of important leather textures and colors.

TRADE ASSOCIATIONS. Tanners work together to promote their products. Their industry supports associations whose function is to disseminate technical and fashion information to producers, consumers, and the press. Some associations, like the Sole Leather Council and the Auto Leather Guild, strive to promote a particular kind of leather. Others, such as the Tanners' Council, function on an industry-wide basis, working to promote all kinds of leather.

Formerly such associations were primarily concerned with serving segments of the market that were already customers. Today the major effort is to broaden the market for all types of leathers. Markets that once used only leather, such as the shoe industry, are now using other products as well, making it necessary for the industry to defend its frontiers. Markets that traditionally used little leather, such as dresses, skirts, and coats, now are being actively cultivated by the leather industry.

At the retail level, the leather industry's associations are a valuable source of information in fashion planning and selection. They are also an important source of fashion and technical information for salespeople. For the consumer, the industry associations provide fashion and technical material which is made available to schools, distributed with merchandise purchased in retail stores, and publicized through the fashion press.

RESEARCH
AND DEVELOPMENT. Leather retains and expands its markets by adapting its products to fashion's changing requirements. Before World War II, relatively few colors and types of leather were available in any one season, and each usually had a fashion life of several years. Today, a major tannery may turn out hundreds of leather colors and types each season, meanwhile preparing to produce more new colors and textures for the next season.

To protect and expand their markets, leather producers constantly broaden their range of colors, weights, and textures. They also introduce improvements that will make their output more acceptable where it now has either limited use or no use at all.

Leather has the weight of tradition behind it; people for centuries have regarded fine leather as a symbol of luxury. But today leather shares its hold on the fashion field with other and newer materials. Producers are attempting to meet the competition not only of other leathers but also of other materials through product research and development. The Tanners' Council Research Laboratory at the University of Cincinnati and the Eastern Regional Research Laboratory of the U.S. Department of Agriculture in Philadelphia have expanded research efforts on behalf of the industry. The Tanners' Council has contracted with the U.S. Bureau of Mines for research on chromium in the tanning industry. The objective is to develop improved technology to recycle or recover chromium from tanning wastes.

The Tanners' Council of America also has initiated a fund drive among members and suppliers. Their goal is to raise over $1 million for a stepped-up research and development effort at the Tanners' Council Research Laboratory.

These research programs mark the first use of large amounts of United States funds to resolve ecological and process-modernization problems of the tanning industry.

Industry Trends

Until just a few decades ago, the leather industry concerned itself primarily with meeting the needs of relatively few segments of the fashion industries, such as shoes, gloves, belts, handbags, and small leather goods. The use of leather for apparel was restricted largely to a few items of outerwear, such as jackets and coats. These were stiff, bulky, and primarily functional in appeal.

Today, the leather industry is changing. These changes are the result of several trends: enlarging market opportunities, increased competition from synthetics, and increased foreign trade.

ENLARGING MARKETS. Improved methods of tanning are turning out better, more versatile leathers with improved fashion characteristics. In general, these improvements fall into two categories: (1) the new leathers are softer and more pliable: (2) they can be dyed more successfully in a greater number of fashion colors.

Because of these new characteristics, the personal leather goods and leather furniture markets continue to have the most growth potential. In cowhide leathers, the demand is high for the lighter-weight, mellow, natural-looking, full-grain leathers. Especially desirable are the glazed, rich-colored, aniline-dyed types that accentuate the natural beauty of the grain. These are used predominantly in luggage, portfolios, and men's apparel. The sheep and lamb tanners are very encouraged by the sustained growth and demand for glazed and suede leathers in the leather apparel market.

COMPETITION
FROM SYNTHETICS. Some of the potential market for leather is being taken away by synthetic materials. For instance, synthetics are replacing leather in some shoe parts. The traditional leather heel lift is now almost always made of plastic. Synthetics are also replacing leather in other accessories. Synthetics are used in making handbags that look and feel like leather but are less susceptible to scratches and can be cleaned more easily. Synthetics are even taking over some of the potential leather apparel market. Today fabrics made of natural and man-made fibers look and feel like various types of leather but are easier to clean and care for.

INCREASED
FOREIGN TRADE. The demand for leather throughout the world continues to increase. United States packers or hide dealers, able to get higher prices for their hides from tanneries in countries where demand outstrips supply, have sharply increased their export of hides.

Domestic leather products manufacturers have been severely affected in the last decade by imported products. This in turn has prompted domestic tanners to concentrate on exploiting foreign markets more fully. American tanners' exports increased from $150 million in 1977 to an estimated $250 million in 1979. Canada remains the largest export market for United States leathers, followed by Korea, Hong Kong, and China. These four countries took 62 percent in value of all United States leathers exported during 1978. As a result, prices have gone up sharply. Many American tanneries, caught between a shortage of hides and increased prices, have had to curtail production or even close. In turn, because of higher domestic prices, United States retailers have been turning to synthetics. They are also turning to other countries for leather and leather products, buying principally from Italy, Argentina, India, Brazil, and Uruguay.

Of concern to the leather industries are the Multilateral Trade Negotiations in Geneva. The consensus among representatives of the United States leather industry is that any reduction in the tariffs on leather products will only speed the demise of these domestic industries. They also claim that tariff reduction by other countries will not benefit domestic producers as long as foreign competitors maintain nontariff barriers and continue to subsidize industries. However, developing foreign markets for United States leather products represents growth potential for this industry. Impetus may come from the decline of the dollar against foreign currencies. It may also come from government programs designed to stimulate export expansion for small businesses.

INDUSTRY
GROWTH FACTORS. Factors that can contribute to the growth of the leather industry over the next five years are:

- Consumer demand for products manufactured from genuine, natural-looking leather, which, in contrast to synthetic materials, symbolizes quality and value to the consumer
- A supply of raw cowhide large enough to allow for real growth in production

- Strong industry efforts to develop foreign markets and increase exports
- Success of industry and governmental efforts in securing relaxation or elimination of foreign trade barriers on United States leather
- Expanded research and development functioning to raise the levels of technology.

THE FUR INDUSTRY

People in ancient civilizations not only wore fur, they spread it on the floor as rugs and used it to decorate walls. It was also used as a valuable item of trade with other countries. In the Middle Ages, Russian sable, marten, ermine, and fox were favorite trimmings on the clothes of the rich and noble in England. By this time, furs were well established as visible signs of prestige and were more precious than any cave dweller could have imagined. Italian cardinals wore ermine as a symbol of purity; English nobles wore it as a symbol of power. Northern Europeans were said to value furs more than gold and silver, which were cold comfort in the harsh climate of their countries.

Centuries later, beaver skins were highly valued and became the common currency in North America. In Canada in 1733, one beaver pelt could buy one pound of sugar or two combs or six thimbles or eight knives. Four beaver pelts were enough to purchase a gallon of brandy or a pistol. Fur was still as good as gold as late as 1900 when Chile banked chinchilla skins as security for a loan.

Europe's demand for luxury furs soon far outgrew the continent's supply. Pressure to find new sources played an important part in encouraging exploration and trade in the early development of North America.

The fur industry is mostly a craft industry, involving small firms and highly skilled and trained workers. Advances in technology have produced new colors, new mutations, and less expensive furs.

History and Development

Fur trappers and traders were among the earliest explorers of North America. Originally their goods were the basis of the Colonies' foreign trade. Some of the continent's larger cities were originally founded by trappers such as Champlain, Joliet, and Duluth.

With Jacques Cartier, a French explorer and navigator, came the first realization of North America's fortune in furs. Cartier's quest for the fabled Northwest Passage led him to the mouth of the St. Lawrence River in 1534 where he traded for furs. The next year he returned and, sailing further up the St. Lawrence, found a vast wealth of furs.

The Dutch and the English were not far behind the French. In 1604 Champlain made his first voyage up the St. Lawrence and down the New England coast. Two years later, Charles I of England gave the first patent rights to the Virginia Company. In 1609, the Dutch, who had already been trading along the coast, sent Englishman Henry Hudson to seek out a water passage to the Orient. His report of the Hudson River and the furs he found encouraged the Dutch to establish a trading post on lower Manhattan Island and up the river at Albany.

The English and Dutch organized companies to trade with the Indians for furs, which were often exchanged for colored beads and cheap alcohol. Trading posts that were set up to handle the Indians' catches were the first centers of colonization in some parts of what is now the United States. Major cities like Chicago, Detroit, St. Paul, Spokane, and St. Louis grew from such beginnings.

The colonists and later their descendants used fur for apparel and other purposes. Daniel Boone's coonskin cap and the bear-skin rug are examples of the early use of fur by settlers. For the most part, however, the young country used furs for export purposes, buying from more developed countries those articles it could not yet produce itself.

The historical importance of beaver and the beaver trade still lingers. The trade is commemorated in scores of place names in as many states. There are Beaver Creeks, Beaver Falls, Beaver Kills, Beaver Lakes, Beavertons and Beaver Towns, Beavervilles, and just plain Beavers. England cannot forget its beaver trade either. It has Beverley and Beverstone (distorted beaver names), and Bea-

TABLE 6-1
Popular Varieties of Fur

FUR	VARIETY	FUR	VARIETY
American marten		Lynx	Bay Lynx (bobcat)
Antelope			Canadian
Badger	Feathered		Montana
Baum marten			Russian
Beaver	Natural	Marmot	
	Sheared	Marten	American
Burunduki			Baum
Calf			Stone
Chinchilla		Mink	Mutation
Coyote			Natural ranch
Ermine			Wild
Fisher			Pieced
Fitch		Mole	
Fox	Blue	Muskrat	
	Cross	Nutria	Natural
	Grey		Sheared
	Kitt	Opossum	American
	Platina		Australian
	Red	Otter	
	Silver	Pahmi (Asian	
	White	ferret badger)	
Guanaco		Pony	
Kid		Rabbit	
Lamb	Broadtail	Raccoon	Japanese (Tanuki)
	Broadtail (American	Sable	
	processed)	Seal	Alaskan fur seal
	Karakul (caracul)		Hair
	Mongolian	Skunk	North American
	Mouton		South American zorina
	Shearling	Squirrel	
	Tibet	Stone marten	
	Persian	Weasel	
		Wolverine	

verbrook and Beavercoate, as well as other names that hark back to a time of empire and economic revolution. As for beavers themselves, they never became extinct. They bred in various regions of North America, waiting for their return to the fashion spotlight. Today 25 percent of the furs sold are beavers!

The history of the fur business throughout the world is characterized more by growth than by change. Russia had fur fairs or auc-

tions as early as the thirteenth century. While much has changed in the world, there are still fur fairs. Furs are still sold at auctions attended by furriers from all around the world. Here the world's finest furriers compete for the world's finest furs.

Until recently, fur meant mink, muskrat, or Persian lamb. It meant sable for those who could afford it. Lynx, beaver, raccoon, and skunk were in vogue now and then. Today a wide range of furs are popular. Knowing about furs, then, begins with knowing the variety of furs available, and even the variety in one type of fur (see Table 6-1).

While mink in the classic style still accounts for about 55 percent of the furs sold, a new category of "sport" or "contemporary" furs is growing in popularity. The leading contemporary furs include fox, raccoon, beaver, coyote, muskrat, Persian lamb, Tanuki (Asian raccoon), and nutria. Raccoon is the fastest growing in popularity because the letting-out technique (described on page 108), formerly used only on expensive furs such as mink, is now widely used to eliminate the bulky look of raccoon.

Organization and Operation

The fur industry in the United States can be divided into three groups: (1) the trappers, farmers, and ranchers who produce the pelts; (2) the fur-processing firms; and (3) the firms manufacturing fur products for consumers.

OBTAINING THE PELTS. The first step in the production of fur merchandise is to obtain the necessary pelts. A **pelt** is the skin of a fur-bearing animal. Trappers are the major source of wild animal pelts, which must be taken only at the coldest season of the year to be of prime quality. The trapper sells pelts to nearby country stores or directly to itinerant buyers. In some areas, collectors or receiving houses accept furs for resale on consignment from trappers or local merchants. When enough pelts have been gathered, a fur merchant may export them or send them to an auction house. Private sale or sales through a broker may also take place.

A fairly recent development in the fur industry, and an increasingly important source of pelts, is **fur farming,** or the raising and breeding of fur-bearing animals under controlled conditions. This began in 1880 with silver-fox fur farming on Prince Edward Island, off the eastern coast of Canada. Chinchilla, Persian lamb, fox, and nutria farms as well as mink ranches have grown rapidly throughout the United States during the past 50 years. By careful breeding, strains most likely to win fashion and financial success have been evolved. Some of the most beautiful and exotic colors in fur pelts today are the result of breeding to develop colors and markings that meet the changing demands of fashion. Fur farmers and ranchers usually sell their pelts directly to auction houses.

At auctions, fur buyers and manufacturers bid for the pelts, which are sold in bundles. Those who plan to make garments seek bundles of matched skins similar in color and quality which will make up a garment of uniform beauty.

The auction trail is an international one. It attracts United States fur buyers to England, Scandinavia, and Russia, as well as to various fur market centers in the United States itself and Canada. European fur buyers visit New York, Greensville, St. Louis, Seattle, Minneapolis, and cities in Canada to obtain pelts of animals native to North America. Except for London, each auction center handles primarily the pelts of its own country.

Many people in the United States do some trapping of wild animals every year. For most, however, such trapping represents a very seasonal and minor source of income. The several thousand fur farms and ranches in this country produce by far the greatest number of pelts.

FUR PROCESSING. After manufacturers of fur goods buy the pelts at auctions or from wholesale merchants, they contract with fur-dressing and fur-dyeing firms to process the pelts.

The job of fur dressers is to make pelts suitable for use in consumer products. First the pelts are softened, both by soaking and by mechanical means. Then the "flesher" removes with a blade any unwanted substances from the inner surface of the skin. For less expensive furs, this process may be performed by roller-type machines. At this point, the pelts are treated with solutions that tan the skin side of the pelt into a pliable leather. Also at this stage, the fur side of the pelt may be processed. This involves either plucking unwanted guard hairs or shearing the underfur to make the fur lighter in weight and the pelt still

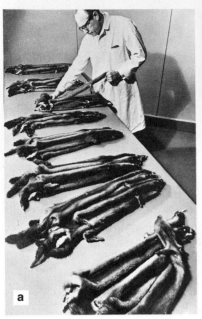

more pliable. Finally, the pelt is cleaned again. Although fur dressing has traditionally been a handcraft industry, modern technology has turned it into a more mechanized process.

After dressing, the pelts may go to a dyer. Fur dyes once were derived from vegetable matter, but today they consist largely of complicated chemical compounds. New dyes are constantly being developed, making it possible to dye fur more successfully and in more shades than ever before.

MANUFACTURING
OF FUR GOODS.
Manufacturing of fur goods is basically a handcraft industry, made up mainly of small, independently owned and operated shops. This is because of the nature of the basic material with which the industry works. No two animals are quite alike, and neither are any two pelts. A pelt, moreover, varies in hair color and quality from one section of the body to another.

Because of the skills and judgments required in working with pelts, the production of fur garments lends itself neither to mass-production methods nor to large-scale operation. After the processing that all fur pelts undergo,

the following steps are required to transform pelts into finished garments:

- Sketching a design of the garment
- Making a canvas pattern of the garment
- Cutting the skins to conform to the designer's sketch, to exhibit the fur to its best advantage, and to minimize waste
- Sewing the cut skins together
- Wetting the skins and nailing them to a board so that they dry permanently set
- Sewing the garment sections together
- Lining and finishing
- Inspection

Nearly all the above steps are done by hand, with consideration for each pelt's peculiarities and the differences in color and hair quality in the various parts of each skin. This is in sharp contrast to the mass-production methods of those apparel makers who cut and sew fabrics.

For some more luxurious furs, the cutting operation may be extremely complex in order to **let out** short skins to a length adequate for garment purposes. Letting-out mink, for example, involves cutting each skin down the center of the dark vertical stripe (the "grotzen stripe"). Each half-skin is then cut at an angle

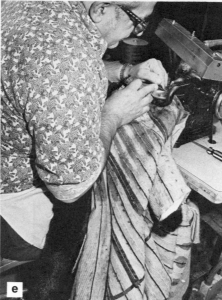

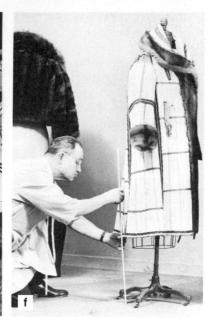

In fur apparel production, pelts are (a) graded by color, size, and hair length to obtain maximum uniformity, (b) "let out" by skilled cutters, (c) sewn into long strips which are (d) wetted and tacked to a board in the exact shape required by the pattern, (e) sewn together, and then (f) made into a garment that is (g) proudly shown to buyers.

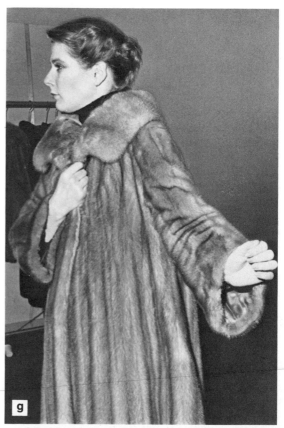

into diagonal strips one-eighth to three-sixteenths of an inch wide. Then each tiny strip is resewn at an angle to the strip above and below it in order to make the skin longer and narrower. The other half-skin is resewn in like manner. The two halves are then joined, resulting in a longer, slimmer pelt, which is more beautiful than the original. Ten miles of thread may be needed to join the strips let-out for a single coat. The nailing process may require as many as 1,200 nails.

RETAIL DISTRIBUTION
OF FUR GARMENTS.
The line between manufacturing and retailing is less clear in furs than in other industries. Retail fur merchants may maintain an assortment of finished garments to show or sell to customers who buy off the rack. But they will also have a supply

(a-d, f) Fur Information and Fashion Council; (e,g) Marilyn L. Schrut of skins and a fur workroom so that they can make up custom garments as well.

Most fur garments are retailed in one of two ways: through leased departments or through consignment selling. Both types of operation permit a retail store to offer its customers a large selection of fur accessory and garment types without tying up vast quantities of capital in inventory.

A **leased department** is one ostensibly operated by the store in which it is located, but which is actually run by an outsider who pays a percentage of sales to the store as rent. In a leased department, the operator or lessee owns the stock. The lessee may also run departments in other stores and can, if necessary, move garments and skins from one location to another. The lessee, a retailer of a special kind, is usually well capitalized and has expert knowledge of both furs and retailing. In **consignment selling,** a manufacturer places merchandise in a retail store for resale but permits any unsold portion to be returned to the wholesale source by a specified date. In consignment selling, the garment producer, in effect, lends stock to a store. If not sold, the furs are returned to the producer for possible sale elsewhere.

In 1980, there were approximately 600 manufacturers, employing about 250,000 workers. United States retail fur sales were over $875 million, an enormous increase over 1970, when sales were $279 million. The center of the fur industry is in New York City, which did over $494 million in retail sales.

Large fur specialty stores include Flemington Fur of Flemington, New Jersey, which carries an inventory of over 6,000 fur garments in sizes 4 to 54, and Schumacher Fur Company of Portland, Oregon. Schumacher sells ready-made furs and also designs and produces its own lines for sale to retail stores.

Merchandising Activities

The fur industry is made up almost entirely of small firms. Thus, it relies to a considerable extent upon group efforts rather than those of individual entrepreneurs for its merchandising and promotional activities. In some instances,

the labor unions, fur traders, dressers, and garment producers all work together to encourage the public's acceptance of furs.

TRADE ASSOCIATIONS. The fur industry relies mainly on the efforts of its trade associations to impress upon consumers the fashion and luxury values of its product. Trade associations also assist retailers in promoting fur to the public. The Fur Information and Industry Council does this for the industry as a whole. Individual types of furs are promoted by such specialized associations as EMBA (organized as the Eastern Mink Breeders Association and now nationwide); GLMA (the Great Lakes Mink Association, a much smaller group than EMBA, specializing in ranch mink); and ECBC (the Empress Chinchilla Breeders Cooperative). EMBA is by far the biggest and most important of these trade groups. It disseminates publicity and produces educational booklets for retailers, schools, and the general public. Both mink associations have heavily advertised slogans for prospective customers. "Wrap yourself in something special," say EMBA ads. GLMA ads ask "What becomes a legend most?"

LABELING. To capitalize on the consumer's interest in whatever furs are currently fashionable, the industry finds ways to treat one type of fur so that it resembles another more desirable or more expensive one. For the consumer's protection, the Federal Trade Commission has issued the Fur Products Labeling Act of 1952 and various rules since then. These have established definite requirements for the labeling of articles made of fur.

By law, the following must be stated, both on a label attached to the merchandise and in all advertising of fur products: (1) the English name of the animal; (2) the country of origin; (3) the type of processing, including dyeing, to which the pelts may have been subjected; and (4) if paws or tails have been used or if parts from used garments have been reused. Thus, a customer who buys a Persian lamb coat made from the most desirable sections of the pelts and a customer who buys a coat made of paws alone both know exactly what they are paying

Swakara is a trademark for karakul and broadtail lamb. Note the number of designers and manufacturers mentioned in this ad. Also, note the invitation to visit the Swakara booth at the International Fur Fair.

for. What was labeled "Hudson seal" generations ago would be labeled "dyed muskrat" today.

Industry Trends

Demand for furs is generally related to a country's economic conditions. During the Depression of the 1930s, fur sales dropped off drastically. In the period immediately following World War II, when the public had money and very little consumer merchandise was available, fur sales boomed.

In the early 1970s, conservationists were in full swing, newly aware of the diminishing wildlife resources of an increasingly civilized planet. As a result, fake fur and petrochemical coats were replacing the genuine articles in the closets of the fashion-buying public.

Since then, the fur industry has made an incredible comeback. Volume has jumped nearly 300 percent from $279 million in the early seventies to $875 million by 1979. Although the number of furriers is half today what it was 10 years ago (more than 600 firms were forced out of the business by the industry's bad times), the fur industry has been revived for a variety of reasons. New fashion interest, increased foreign trade, new legislation, and worldwide shortages are the major trends influencing the growth of the fur industry in the 1980s.

FASHION INTEREST. Once associated only with the rich and formal, furs are now bought and worn by everyone. This fashion demand in recent years has led to an increase in the variety of fur garments, from casual and sporty, elegant and classic, to faddish and fashionable.

Increased interest in fur apparel is found not only among older customers—once the traditional market for furs—but also among young customers. Nor is it limited to women's apparel; the use of fur coats and accessories by men has greatly increased and now accounts for 20 to 25 percent of retail fur volume in some large retail stores. Furs for men have

BADGER BY BIRGER CHRISTENSEN...
B FROM OUR EXCLUSIVE COLLECTION

Natural badger, feathered to give a softness that's breathtakingly luxurious. Just as you'd expect from Denmark's legendary furrier.

The badger coat, 7990.00.

Birger Christensen's Birgitta Ravn-Holm, with us tomorrow, noon to two. Come meet her in our fur lair. New York.

Imported furs labeled as to country of origin.

THE FUR SALON ON 3 bloomingdale's

1000 THIRD AVE., NEW YORK. 355-5900. OPEN LATE MONDAY AND THURSDAY EVENINGS.

Bloomingdale's

Fur that has been feathered was featured in this retail store's ads. The fur designer/manufacturer names are highlighted. Also note the mention of imported fur labeling.

gained in popularity since their acceptance by many male sports figures and celebrities.

There are fur vests, fur jackets, fur suits, fur-trimmed sweaters and dresses, and all types of fur accessories. Fur has been feathered, ribbed, and crocheted.

The famous French and American designers such as Christian Dior, Yves St. Laurent, Givenchy, Bill Blass, Halston, Oscar de la Renta, Pauline Trigere, and Calvin Klein are now designing especially for the fur industry. Italian fur designers such as Soldano and Fendi use innovative techniques. As a result, everyone is thinking of buying a fur fashion garment. And the demand for fur outweighs the supply. Fashion interest has helped to create that demand.

INCREASED
FOREIGN TRADE.

In 1978, export sales (wholesale) of raw, dressed pelts and manufactured goods were $341 million compared to only $233 million in imports—a very favorable balance of trade. European, South American, and Far East furriers buy in America, not only because of the high quality of American pelt dressing, but also for the variety. Europeans come here primarily for mink, muskrat, beaver, and raccoon.

Because of this trend, the first American International Fur Fair was held in New York in March 1979. Attendance was estimated at well over 5,000 people. Exhibiting at the fair were 70 American manufacturers and 55 foreign companies from eleven different countries, including France, England, Italy, Sweden, and Finland. Buyers attending from Germany, Japan, South America, Switzerland, and Canada reflected the importance of the fair to the international market.

NEW LEGISLATION.

The Federal Trade Commission and the fur industry are perpetually engaged in discussions about changes in the fur labeling rules. The most important fur legislation of recent years, however, concerned "endangered species," or those species of animals in danger of becoming extinct. In 1973, the federal Endangered Species Act was passed, forbidding the importation or transportation across state lines of a variety of animals or products made from those animals. Among the species classified as endangered are a number formerly used in making fur products. These include most varieties of leopard, tiger, ocelot, cheetah, jaguar, vicuna, and a few types of wolf.

WORLDWIDE CONDITIONS.

There is more and more talk at fur fairs about an increase in demand for furs at the beginning of the twenty-first century. This prediction is partly based on the increasing world population and a continuing high rate of demand for mink, fox, and sable. Too, many scientists believe that some time in the next century there will be a period, lasting for several decades, during which the average yearly temperature will drop significantly. Naturally, this will bring a greater need for warmer clothing. The last few unusually cold winters in a row in the United States and a number of European countries, for instance, have sent the popularity of furs soaring.

Since the onset of oil shortages, fake fur has become number one on the endangered list. Petroleum products from which the imposter garments are made have become more of an issue for ecologists than skins, which are, after all, a renewable resource.

MERCHANDISING VOCABULARY

Define or briefly explain the following terms:

Consignment selling	Leased department
Contract tanneries	Let-out
Converters	Pelt
Fur farming	Regular tanneries
Hides	Skins
Kips	Tanning

MERCHANDISING REVIEW

1. In what ways have technological advances in machinery and chemistry benefited the leather industry?
2. Name and describe the three major types of firms into which this country's leather industry is divided.
3. Why does specialization prevail throughout the leather industry in this country? Give examples of such specialization.
4. Name the five major agents or methods used for tanning leather. Briefly describe the characteristics of leather tanned by each of these agents or methods. For what consumer products is each of these best suited?
5. Describe the fashion information services provided by leather producers and/or their trade associations.
6. Why is product research and development so important today in the leather industry? What specific benefits to the consumer have resulted from such product research and development?
7. Describe the history and development of the fur industry in this country.
8. Into what three groups is the fur industry divided? Briefly describe the function of each.
9. What is meant by the term "fur farming"? Discuss its importance in the fur industry today.
10. Differentiate between "leased departments" and "consignment selling" as these terms apply to retail distribution of fur garments. What major advantages does each have for retail merchants?

MERCHANDISING DIGEST

1. Discuss the following statement from the text and its implications for leather merchandising: "Leather producers do not merely stay abreast of fashion, they must keep ahead of it."
2. Discuss current trends in the leather industry as they relate to: (a) enlarging markets, (b) competition from synthetics, and (c) increased foreign trade.
3. Discuss: (a) the provisions of the Fur Labeling Act of 1952 and how it protects the consumer, and (b) recent legislation relating to furs.

MANUFACTURERS OF WOMEN'S AND CHILDREN'S FASHION APPAREL

7

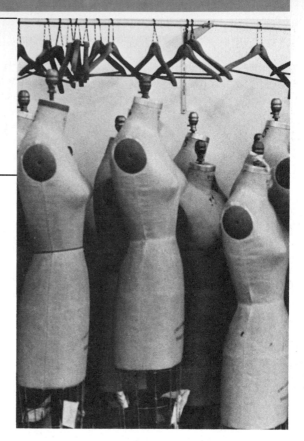

The manufacture of women's and children's apparel is a major industry in the United States. This industry is the sixth largest employer of production workers in the country, accounting for approximately 7.7 percent of all workers engaged in manufacturing. The health of the apparel industry is thus vital to the nation's goal of minimal unemployment and of providing opportunities for women, ethnic groups, and unskilled workers.

The production of ready-to-wear for fashion-conscious consumers is the function of this multi-billion-dollar industry. The apparel industry, described as exciting, challenging, exhausting, and cutthroat, has come to be known by various names—the garment trade, the cutting-up trade, the needle trade, or simply the "rag" business.

The apparel industry includes production of men's and boys' wear (discussed in Chapter 8) as well as women's and children's wear. All categories of apparel in women's, misses', juniors', and petites' size ranges are referred to in the trade as the women's apparel industry or market, although this is technically a misnomer. Children's wear is the trade term for infants', toddlers', girls' (sizes 7 to 14), and pre-teens' apparel.

The women's ready-to-wear industry is relatively young; it was little more than an infant at the turn of the century. Since then it has gained flexibility, grown rapidly in size, and undergone many changes. Trends indicate that the 1980s will bring more dramatic changes in the manufacturing industry than have occurred since the turn of the century. The fast-paced world of the computer, the

emergence of production-intensive industry giants over small, labor-intensive operations, the unsettled economy, and the world market's shifting picture all denote change. The apparel industry is in the midst of its own industrial revolution.

HISTORY OF THE WOMEN'S APPAREL INDUSTRY

Historically, the making of apparel for the entire family was a household job, usually the responsibility of the women. This has been true in most cultures ever since the family home was a cave and garments were animal skins, sewed together with leather thongs.

Although women traditionally did the sewing, men were the first industrial producers of apparel. For many centuries, professional tailors have made a business of producing custom-made clothes for men. It was only a few centuries ago that professional dressmakers began producing custom-made women's apparel. Today, the demand for custom tailoring and dressmaking has been overshadowed by that for less expensive, factory-produced ready-to-wear in great variety.

Growth of Ready-to-Wear

The term **ready-to-wear** refers to apparel made in factories to standard size measurements. This is in contrast to custom-made apparel produced by professional dressmakers or by home sewers to the exact measurements of the individual who will wear the garment.

During the first half of the 1800s, apparel manufacturing was limited to men's clothes. Only after the Civil War did women's apparel begin to be made on a commercial basis. The first garments turned out on a ready-to-wear basis were cloaks and mantles, neither of which required the careful fit that most women's garments require.

By the turn of the century, however, limited quantities of women's suits, skirts, and blouses were made in factories. Within a decade, some manufacturer had the idea of sewing a blouse and skirt together, and the first ready-to-wear dresses were produced.

By the end of World War I, the women's apparel industry—today the heart of the fashion business—had passed the $1 billion mark in product value. By 1980 the factory value of all shipments made by the women's apparel industry in one year totaled over $46.7 billion.

Unionization

An important factor in the growth of the women's ready-to-wear industry in this country was that the right kind of labor was available at the right time and in the right place. In the nineteenth and early twentieth centuries, millions of Europeans sought refuge in the United States, particularly in big cities along the eastern seaboard. They needed to earn a living. Many, trained as dressmakers or tailors in their homelands, turned naturally to the growing apparel industry for jobs.

However, working conditions in the apparel trades at the turn of the century were appalling. Hours were long, pay was little, and factories were overcrowded, dark, unsanitary, and unsafe.

In 1900, workers formed the International Ladies' Garment Workers' Union (ILGWU), the major union in the women's apparel trade today. Strikes in 1909 and 1910 helped pave the way for collective bargaining in the women's garment trade. The tragic Triangle Shirtwaist Factory fire of 1911, which killed 146 workers, rallied support around the workers and eventually led to stricter building codes and revised labor laws.

Characteristic of today's union activities is the ILGWU's participation in joint employer-union committees to set prices for piecework on individual garments. These prices depend on the elements of work involved in each style.

However, the ILGWU has developed into more than a collective bargaining agency. This union has contributed funds for promoting New York as an industry fashion center. It has helped develop schools to train technical workers, designers, and other skilled employees needed in the industry. In addition, the ILGWU has subsidized housing and vacation resorts and has provided other benefits, making it easier and more pleasant for employees to remain in the city and to stay in the garment industry.

ORGANIZATION AND OPERATION OF THE WOMEN'S APPAREL INDUSTRY

Historically, the women's apparel industry has been made up of relatively small firms. Until very recently, there were no giants in this industry comparable to a General Motors or Ford in the automotive industry.

This all began to change at the end of the 1960s. Many marginal firms went out of business, and many mergers took place. The ownership of apparel manufacturing businesses by such conglomerates as Gulf & Western became economically desirable.

International Ladies Garment Workers Union

At the turn of the century, working conditions in the apparel sweatshops were crowded, uncomfortable, often unsafe—and the hours were long.

These changes necessarily brought some restrictive measures to an industry noted for its flamboyant methods of operation. While it is still possible to respond quickly to changing demands in fashion, more planning is now involved. As the apparel industry moves into the pattern of big business, it cannot contract or expand its facilities at a moment's notice. Starting an apparel business with minimum capital in hopes that a particular item will catch on and skyrocket into the fashion success story of the year is today the exception, not the rule.

Certain patterns of organization and operation prevail within the women's apparel industry. First, not all producers of apparel actually perform all the processes necessary to turn out finished garments. Second, firms within the industry have traditionally been highly specialized in terms of their production. Third, new lines, or assortments of styles, are developed for each selling season of the year.

Types of Producers

The fashion apparel industry consists of three types of producers: manufacturers, jobbers, and contractors. A **manufacturer** is one who performs all the operations required to produce apparel, from buying the fabric to selling and shipping the finished garments. A **jobber** handles the designing, the planning, the purchasing, usually the cutting, the selling, and the shipping, but not the actual sewing operation. A **contractor** is one whose sole function is to supply sewing services to the industry, where it is sometimes called an **outside shop.**

MANUFACTURERS. The greater New York area in general and New York City in particular are home to many of the women's apparel manufacturers. More than 60 percent of the women's apparel produced in this country is made in the greater New York area.

In recent years, some manufacturers have set up sewing plants of their own or work with contractors far from New York City. In upstate New York, in Alabama, or in any area where people with sewing skills are available for employment, small plants have been built. The training, supervision, and planning requirements of such plants are minimal compared with those of a main plant. Producers already experiencing labor shortages at their headquarters location find an abundant labor supply both a practical and economical way to expand sewing operations. However, even when a manufacturer moves production facilities out of New York, designers and the major showroom usually remain in the city.

Manufacturers, by definition, are producers who handle all phases of a garment's production. Their staff produces the original design or buys an acceptable design from a free-lance designer. Each line is planned by the company executives. The company purchases the fabric and trimmings needed. The cutting and sewing are usually done in the company's factories. On certain occasions, however, a manufacturer may use the services of a contractor if sales of an item exceed the capacity of the firm's sewing facilities and if shipping deadlines cannot otherwise be met. The company's sales force and traffic department handle the selling and shipping of the finished goods. One great advantage of this type of operation is that close quality control can be maintained. When producers contract out some part of their work, they cannot as effectively monitor its quality.

APPAREL JOBBERS. Apparel jobbers handle all phases of the production of a garment except for the actual sewing and sometimes the cutting. A jobber firm may employ a design staff to create various seasonal lines or may buy acceptable sketches from free-lance designers. The jobber's staff buys the fabric and trimmings necessary to produce the styles in each line, makes up samples, and grades the patterns. In most cases, the staff also cuts the fabric for the various parts of each garment to be produced. Jobbers, however, do not actually sew and finish garments. Instead, they arrange with outside factories run by contractors to perform these manufacturing operations. The sales staff takes orders for garments in each line, and the shipping department fills store orders from the finished garments returned by the contractor. (Note that apparel jobbers are involved in manufacturing, whereas most "jobbers" are middlemen who buy from manufacturers and sell to retailers.)

CONTRACTORS. Contractors usually specialize in just one phase of the production of a garment: sewing. In some cases, contractors also perform the cutting operation from patterns submitted by a jobber or manufacturer. Contractors developed early in the history of the fashion industry, with the beginning of mass-production techniques. Contractors serve those producers who have little or no sewing capability of their own as well as those whose current business exceeds their own capacity.

If a contractor is used, cut pieces of the garment are provided by the jobber or, in some cases, by the manufacturer. For an agreed price per garment, the article is sewn, finished, inspected, and returned to the jobber or manufacturer for shipment to retail store purchasers. The price charged by the contractor is largely determined by the union, which, in collaboration with industry management, sets the piece rates for labor.

In the mass production of ready-to-wear, a single sewing machine operator rarely makes a complete garment. Each operator sews only a certain section of the garment, such as a sleeve or a hem. This division of labor, called **section work,** makes it unnecessary for an operator to switch from one highly specialized machine to another or to make adjustments on the machine. Any change or adjustment in equipment takes time and increases labor costs. In the fashion trade, time lost in making such changes also causes delays in getting a style to consumers. Delays in production could mean the loss of timeliness and sales appeal before an article reaches its market.

Contractors may arrange to work exclusively with one or more jobbers or manufacturers, reserving the right to work for others whenever the contractors' facilities are not fully employed. Such agreements are necessarily reciprocal. If a contractor agrees to give preference to a particular jobber's or manufacturer's work, the jobber or manufacturer gives preference to that contractor when placing sewing orders.

The major advantages of the contractor system are:

- Large amounts of capital are not required for investment in equipment which may soon become obsolete.
- Difficulties in the hiring and training of suitable workers are minimized.
- The amount of capital necessary to meet regular payrolls is greatly reduced.
- By providing additional manufacturing facilities in periods of peak demand, contractors help speed up delivery of orders.

The contractor system has the disadvantages common to most assembly-line productions. No individual has full responsibility for the finished product, and so the quality of workmanship and inspection may tend to be uneven.

Once, most contractors were located in the metropolitan New York City area. Today, they may be located anywhere in the world where labor is abundant, where wages, taxes, and land costs or rents are lower, and where modern facilities and good transportation are available. Today, it has sometimes proved more profitable, for example, to ship fashion goods from New York to contractors in Hong Kong for sewing and finishing, then return them to New York for shipment to customers, than to sew and finish those same goods in metropolitan New York.

Size of Producers

Throughout the history of the industry, many of the firms producing women's apparel have been relatively small in size. For instance, in the early 1970s, there were some 5,000 firms making dresses. Their total output amounted to $3 billion. In contrast, the industry producing radios and television sets had an equal output achieved by only 300 firms.

However, publicly owned giants do exist today in the fashion industries. One of the largest is Jonathan Logan, which has grown from sales of $100 million in the early 1960s to over $426 million by 1979. Cluett Peabody and Warnaco are two other examples of corporate apparel giants.

Currently the trend is toward giantism, simply because the economics of the times demand it. And it is expected that more and more small- or medium-sized firms will disappear or be bought up by larger firms.

There are four basic ways in which giant firms are created and in which large firms become even larger. First, a firm can expand by **going public,** which means a privately owned company becomes a public corporation and issues stock for sale. This enables a company to substantially increase the amount of capital it has available for modernization and expansion purposes.

Second, a firm can expand through horizontal integration—by merging with or acquiring other firms which are doing business at the same marketing level. This enables a company to increase its size without having to learn the intricacies of doing business at other levels of marketing. When a producer of misses' dresses acquires a firm making junior apparel, or a producer of daywear dresses acquires a firm making casual knitwear, this is horizontal integration.

Third, a firm can expand through vertical integration—by merging with or acquiring firms at different marketing levels. For instance, a dress manufacturer might seek a merger with a producer of the kinds of fabrics the manufacturer uses. Or it may merge with a chain of specialty stores that sell the manufacturer's type of dresses. Vertical integration enables a company to gain control of all or part of the development, production, and marketing of a product.

Fourth, a firm can expand through the formation of **conglomerates,** which are groups of companies that may or may not be related in terms of product and marketing level. In fact, the parent company usually seeks to acquire companies that are different in terms of product, seasonal demand, and market level. Thus it protects itself against such hazards as great fluctuations or changes in demand or possible setbacks in any one of its activities.

But despite the presence of giants, it is still possible for a small firm to set up shop and remain in the apparel business. Such companies can survive even with a modest investment and without the full range of talents and facilities required to process garments from original conception to ultimate distribution. A designer can function as a one-person custom business until attracting a manufacturer with the capital and productive capacity to capture the attention of a larger clientele. Producers with limited capital but with a wanted product, a good distribution setup, and a desirable price level can use free-lance designers and farm out sewing to contractors, thus stretching their capital.

Specialization by Product

Traditionally, women's apparel firms were divided into distinct groups according to: (1) types of apparel; (2) size ranges; and (3) price zones. A blouse manufacturer seldom made dresses as well. A dress manufacturer seldom turned out both women's and juniors' sizes. A coat and suit manufacturer rarely produced both expensive and popular-priced lines.

Today, however, the industry is much less specialized. An increasing number of firms are developing diversified lines and crossing previously established price and product lines. Again, Jonathan Logan, originally a dress house for juniors' sizes, is a typical example. It has diversified its product mix to include R & K Dresses, a misses' dress company; Amy Adams, a dress company for half-size women's dresses; Rose Marie Reid, a bathing suit company; and Etienne Aigner, a leather handbag, belt, and shoe company.

Nevertheless, both producers and retail buyers still have to think and work in terms of product specialization. For instance, a producer will choose an inexpensive fabric for a popular-priced line and a more expensive fabric for a better-priced line. A retail buyer will shop one group of resources for sportswear, another group for coats, and still another for bridal wear.

CATEGORIES. The following are the traditional basic categories in women's apparel and the types of garments generally included in each category:

- Outerwear (coats, suits, rainwear, jackets)
- Dresses (one or two pieces; ensembles, meaning a dress with a jacket or coat)
- Sportswear and separates (active, contemporary; town-and-country and spectator sportswear, including slacks, shorts, tops; swimwear and cover-ups; bathing caps; beach bags; sweaters; skirts; shirts; jackets; tennis dresses; casual dresses; pantsuits)
- After-five and evening clothes (dressy apparel)
- Bride and bridesmaid attire
- Blouses (including both dressy and tailored)
- Uniforms and aprons (including housedresses and sometimes career apparel)
- Maternity (dresses, sportswear)

SIZE RANGES. Women's apparel is divided into several size ranges. Unfortunately, the industry has not yet developed standard industrywide size measurements for each of these ranges, although exploratory work has been undertaken in this direction. This is why one

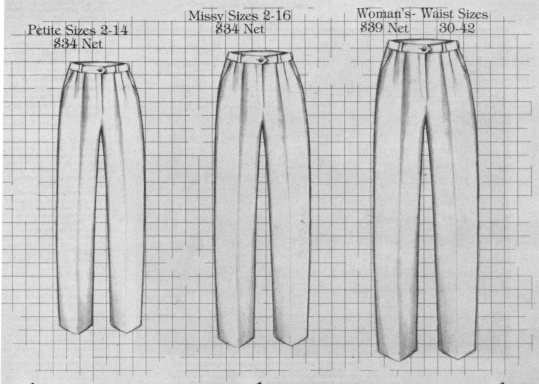

When a fashion is popular, every size wants it. Some manufacturers are responding to this demand by providing garments in three size ranges.

manufacturer's misses' size 12 is likely to fit quite differently than another manufacturer's misses' size 12 in a similar style. The traditional size ranges are:

- Women's (including even half-sizes 12½ to 26½ and straight sizes 36 to 52)
- Misses' (including regular even sizes 6 to 20; tall sizes 12 to 20; and some producers making sizes as small as 2)
- Juniors' (including regular sizes 5 to 17 and petite sizes 3 to 15)
- Petites' (including regular even sizes 2 to 16 and junior sizes 3 to 15)

There is a growing number of customers in this country who wear clothes that are of petite or large sizes. But most department stores, specialty stores, mass merchants, and apparel chains prominently display and sell a great proportion of their total sales in the misses' and juniors' size ranges. Less space and display are devoted to petite sizes, large sizes, and maternity wear.

WHOLESALE PRICE ZONES. Women's apparel is produced and marketed at a wide range of wholesale prices. Major factors contributing to the wholesale price of garments are: (1) the quality of materials used; (2) the quality of workmanship employed; and (3) the amount and type of labor required in the production process.

Within this wide range of prices, however, there are certain **price zones,** or series of somewhat contiguous price lines that appeal to specific target groups of customers. The women's apparel market has traditionally been divided into the following three price zones:

- Better (usually the higher prices; sometimes referred to as the "prestige" market). Includes lines of name designers.
- Moderate (usually the medium prices). Today, this category also usually includes the boutique lines produced by the designers traditionally considered "better" designers. These lines include Geoffrey Beene's Beene Bag line, Bill Blass's Blassport line, and Oscar de la Renta's Miss O line.

- Popular (usually the lower prices; sometimes referred to as the "promotional," "mass," or "budget" market).

Developing and Creating a Line

Two to four months before the apparel for a specific selling season reaches the retail store, the store's buyers are in the wholesale markets. Here they view the lines of manufacturers and make their selections. From six to twelve months before that time, manufacturers begin creating their future seasonal lines. This means that the development of a line may begin as much as a year and a half before consumers have their first look at new seasonal merchandise on a store's selling floor (see Table 7-1).

First, the designer charged with creating the line reviews all available information on trends, materials, and previous fashion successes and failures. From these the designer forms some idea of what the coming season's line should include. Each design is first sketched or developed in muslin. The design is then considered both on its own merits and for its suitability in the line as a whole. Many designs may be discarded at this point.

Designs that seem most likely to succeed are then made up into finished garments. This is done by a **sample hand,** a designer's assistant who is an all-around seamstress. Various executives of the firm (sales, purchasing, and production heads, cost experts, and others) then examine the samples. At this point, several more designs may be discarded while others may go back to the design room for modification.

Producing a Line

When a design has survived these preliminary challenges, a patternmaker makes a production pattern in whatever garment size the firm uses for its samples. From this pattern, one or more samples are cut and sewn. If the sample is acceptable, its production costs are carefully figured and a wholesale price is determined. The design is given a style number and becomes part of the manufacturer's line.

TABLE 7-1
Manufacturer's Line Planning Calendar for the Fall Season

June (*start*)	1. Establish piece goods reserves with domestic mills		4. Final commitment for domestic and imported fabrics
July			5. Approve ads and mailer
August	1. Define and submit product category concept as to: a. Customer b. Body fit/silhouette c. Fashion direction d. Unit volume goals e. Marketing objectives	January	1. Submit plans for new or special labels, hangers, buttons, packages, supplies, etc. 2. Increase commitments for advertised fabrics 3. Costing of new models made in own plants 4. Swatching procedures outlined
September	Show and sell 4th quarter holiday line (Nov.–Dec. delivery) 1. Establish gross margin goals 2. Approve merchandiser's SKU of volume 3. Final approval of volume by brand 4. Commitment from retailer on quantities required		5. Sample orders for in-house production 6. Review construction and packaging of new models 7. Finalize new trimmings 8. Review acceptance of costing/ new models/own plants 9. Sample orders issued with complete specification sheets 10. Model lines cut (for sales staff) 11. Acceptance of cost structure for contracted items, if any 12. Line review for breadth sampling
October	Show promotional goods, holiday, early spring (first quarter) 1. Initial forecast of basic program (style and color) 2. Preliminary marketing plan 3. Prepare master schedule for basics 4. Compare master schedule with production availability (fashion production must fit balance) 5. Initial commitment for 50% of basic fabrics 6. Make initial domestic fabric purchase of fashion piece goods	February	1. Marketing plan by model/pattern (total quantity required plus regional plans according to quotas 2. Final review, cost contracting 3. Gross profit test 4. Updated master schedule for finished goods 5. Synchronize sales plans, marketing plans, master schedule, and manufacturing plans 6. Final line and pricing review at merchandise meeting of executives 7. Final marketing plan 8. Gross profit test (final)
November	1. Approve basics 2. Implement fabric commitment on balance of basics 3. Make initial imported fabric purchases on confined goods		9. Merchandise bulletin and swatch cards 10. Ship sample cards and shirts 11. Sales meeting
December	Sell spring, ship holiday goods, build-up basic stocks 1. Complete imported fabric purchases 2. Merchandising meeting 3. Submit advertised features to Marketing division		12. Follow-up on shipment of late samples
		March	ON SALE

After buyers have viewed a line and placed their orders, the manufacturer usually finds that some style offerings have received considerable buyer interest while others have not. Those in the first group are scheduled for production; those in the second group are usually dropped from the line.

For every style that is to be produced, the original pattern is **graded** or sloped to adjust it to each of the various sizes in which the style will be made. Next, the pieces of the pattern in all its sizes are carefully laid out on a long piece of paper, or **marker,** which is placed on top of the fabric to be cut.

One of the most important processes in the mass production of apparel is that of cutting through many thicknesses of material in one operation. Its success depends on the accuracy with which each layer of material is placed on top of the one directly underneath. A "laying-up machine" carries the material back and forth along a guide on either side of the cutting table, spreading the material evenly from end to end. On top of this pile of laid-out material, which may be anywhere from 50 to 100 layers in depth, the marker is laid to serve as a cutting pattern. A **marker** is a long piece of paper that corresponds in width to the width of the fabric being used. On this paper is traced the outline of each piece of a pattern for each size in which the style will be made. Then the material and marker are secured by clamps at either end and at intervals along the material's selvaged edges.

Among the more revolutionary new pieces of machinery to come along in the 1970s was the computerized pattern marker Camisco. This new computerized system for designing and producing patterns eliminates manual labor. It also reduces fabric needs up to 9 percent by allowing fabric to be cut to much closer tolerances.

Cutting the material around the edges of individual pieces of the pattern's marker is done either by electric knife or, more recently, by laser beam. Individual pieces of each pattern, still with the paper marker on top, are then tied up in bundles according to size. They are then passed along to the sewing operators either in the same plant or in a contractor's shop. After sewing, finishing, pressing, and inspection, the finished garments are ready for shipment.

As the season progresses, retailers reorder popular numbers, and manufacturers may recut them. However, producers recut only the "hottest," or best-selling, numbers in their lines. They drop any others for which there have been only scattered reorders.

WOMEN'S DOMESTIC FASHION MARKET CENTERS

U.S. firms produce over $46 billion worth of fashion apparel and accessories a year, figured in terms of factory shipments. Only a small fraction of this output is exported. Even though an increasing amount of apparel and accessories is imported, well over 75 percent of the vast array of fashion goods spread out before American consumers is made by American producers.

For this reason, domestic market centers are of greatest importance to most American retail store buyers. In these market centers, fashion buyers select most of the merchandise that will be offered for sale in retail stores.

In spite of the influential role that foreign designers have played in the history of fashion, no longer does all fashion inspiration originate outside this country. Today, American producers, as well as some foreign producers, look to American designers for fashion leadership.

Even before World War II, which violently disrupted the traditional pattern and flow of fashion inspiration, designers in this country had begun to fill fashion apparel needs that foreign designers neither understood nor could design for. Prominent among those American retailers who believed wholeheartedly in American designers was the late Dorothy Shaver. She was president of New York's famous Lord & Taylor in the 1940s and 1950s and the first woman to achieve such a position in a major retail store. Dorothy Shaver believed in American designers and supported them fully, inaugurating the first

(a) The pieces of the pattern are carefully laid out on the marker, which serves as a cutting pattern. (b) Many thicknesses of material are cut through in one operation.

American Designer Week. She advertised designers, publicized them, and presented their creations in Lord & Taylor's Fifth Avenue windows, where once only foreign designer creations appeared.

One of the best known American fashion designers of the past was the late Claire McCardell. She designed and produced clothes of special appeal to American women, introducing the easy lines that made the most of their figures while still permitting freedom of movement. Some of the casual clothes created by this world-famous designer before World War II have continued in popularity throughout the years. Shirtwaist dresses and skirts with unpressed pleats are examples.

American designers have no protection against design piracy, and many of them would welcome protective laws. Regulations that shelter the French couture world, however, would violate antitrust laws in our country. But even without such protection, and without the glamorous, centuries-old reputation Paris designers enjoy, American designers continue to flourish. Their interpretations of fashion appear to be in close harmony with what the American people want.

The New York Market

The American apparel industry is as geographically concentrated as it is highly competitive. It originated in New York at the turn of the century and grew with the help of successive arrivals of Jewish, Italian, and Hispanic immigrants. New York City is the fashion apparel production center of the United States, from which goods are shipped to stores throughout this country. It is also the sales headquarters for manufacturers whose design and production facilities may be located elsewhere.

New York's "garment district," as the women's apparel market is called, is that section of the city bounded by Ninth Avenue on the west, the Avenue of the Americas (Sixth Avenue) on the east, 34th Street on the south, and 41st Street on the north. Plans are being developed for an enormous fashion mart on Eighth Avenue between 40th and 42nd streets. It will house the various showrooms now scattered throughout the garment district.

The hub of the garment district is Seventh Avenue. In the year 1972, the industry and the New York City government renamed Seventh Avenue "Fashion Avenue." New York City also launched a campaign to become known as the "Fashion Capital of the World." Enormous quantities of goods are displayed on Seventh Avenue. From here some $12 billion worth of wholesale goods was shipped in 1978 alone. Seventh Avenue also ranks as New York City's largest employer, having provided 145,000 jobs in 1978.

Within the garment district are literally thousands of showrooms displaying various types and price lines of women's and children's apparel. Apparel industry experts say a buyer on Seventh Avenue can find 100,000 to 150,000 different styles of women's and children's clothing from which to choose. Many showrooms are maintained by New York producers. Other showrooms display the lines of manufacturers from around the world.

Because retail merchants and buyers have limited time to spend away from their stores, they find it advantageous to be able to do all their purchasing in one city. New York can provide this one-stop shopping advantage, saving the merchants both time and travel expense. Most major fiber and fabric producers, the publishers of consumer and fashion periodicals, and trade associations also maintain offices and/or showrooms in New York City. These are additional sources of fashion trend information, valuable to a merchant on a buying trip.

In many respects, New York is more expensive and more difficult to work in than any other area in which fashion producers have developed businesses. But despite disadvantages such as crowding and the high costs of space, labor, and living, many segments of the fashion industry continue to operate there. Most of those whose headquarters are located elsewhere consider it essential to show their seasonal lines in New York City, because so many retailers travel there to buy their merchandise.

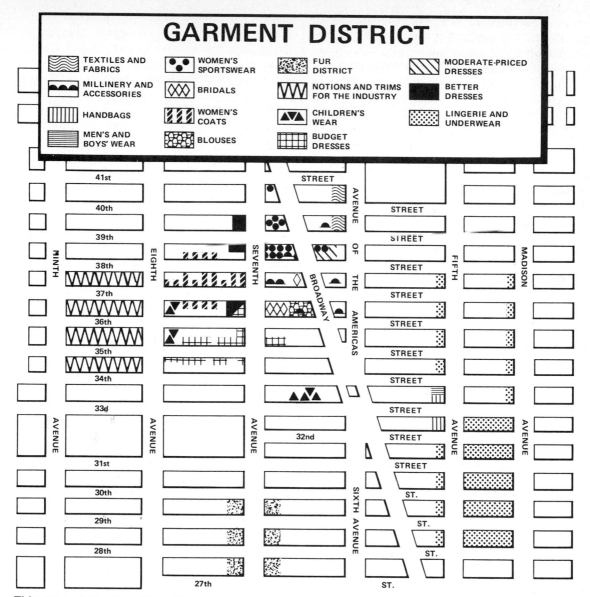

GARMENT DISTRICT

TEXTILES AND FABRICS	WOMEN'S SPORTSWEAR	FUR DISTRICT	MODERATE-PRICED DRESSES
MILLINERY AND ACCESSORIES	BRIDALS	NOTIONS AND TRIMS FOR THE INDUSTRY	BETTER DRESSES
HANDBAGS	WOMEN'S COATS	CHILDREN'S WEAR	LINGERIE AND UNDERWEAR
MEN'S AND BOYS' WEAR	BLOUSES	BUDGET DRESSES	

This map of the New York City garment district shows the number and variety of showrooms available to buyers of men's, women's, and children's wear.

Regional Fashion Apparel Markets

New York is still the major fashion apparel market. The proliferation of regional apparel marts throughout the country, however, is changing the pattern of wholesale fashion merchandising for the first time since the industry was established in New York almost a hundred years ago.

As regional apparel marts expand and multiply, more and more designers and manufacturers are finding it economically advantageous to show their wares at one or more of them. Apparel marts offer hundreds of lines— from high fashion to volume price and from domestic to foreign—all under one roof.

In addition to the economic advantages, these marts provide other advantages for both producers and buyers. The marts usually consolidate the goods of all manufacturers and support services under one roof, allowing a buyer to see a wide diversity of fashions in a short time with a minimum of effort. Concentrated fashion shows highlight the latest fashion message. And useful educational seminars on all aspects of the fashion business are usually sponsored by the members of each regional apparel mart.

Because television informs viewers of the latest trends, consumers today are sophisticated. They are demanding that the latest fashion merchandise be available to them more quickly. The buyers who once bought most of their fashion goods from traveling sales representatives came to New York only twice a year for the newest fashions. Because those buyers now want these goods as soon as possible, producers now show their collections in the regional fashion apparel markets. This places fashion at the fingertips of hundreds of small and medium-size retailers, who can now shop and evaluate many more lines than ever before. The marts are thus helping them to stay competitive with their larger counterparts.

With related travel costs soaring, the self-contained apparel marts will be playing increasingly more important roles in the coming years. However, the marts do not yet dominate apparel manufacturing or selling. New York is still firmly entrenched as the key marketplace and dominant fashion center.

The regional fashion apparel markets are located in several major cities (see Table 7-2).

THE DALLAS MARKET. The Southwest United States today is one of the fastest-growing areas in terms of population, industry, and wealth. It is also the home of several minority ethnic groups—American Indians and Mexican Americans. The cultural contributions to apparel made by these groups are evident in some of the regional dress items and accessories that are widely accepted today. The prevailing climate in the Southwest is conducive to more casual lifestyles, and the preferred apparel for such lifestyles is sportswear.

With the rapid growth in the Southwest, Dallas, the largest city in the region, has become both an apparel production center and a very important domestic fashion market center. It is the third largest market center in this country and advertises itself as the place "where New York and California meet."

In layout, construction, and unique fashion approach, the Dallas Market Center complex is one of the most forward-looking merchandising market centers in the United States. Its vital statistics are staggering. The center is situated on 135 acres, has 7,200,000 square feet of space, and is the largest merchandising complex in the world.[1] The six buildings that comprise the Dallas Market Center complex include the World Trade Center, the Trade Mart, Market Hall, the Decorative Center, the Home Furnishings Mart, and the Dallas Apparel Mart. These buildings house representatives from more than 20,000 firms that handle everything from home furnishings to appliances, gifts, apparel, and accessories. Virtually every conceivable item for the individual or home is available here.

The Dallas Apparel Mart is the Dallas Market Center's building for wholesale apparel manufacturers and exhibitors. It has a total capacity of nearly 1,500 showrooms where over 10,000 lines may be shopped.

Lines shown at the Dallas Apparel Mart during the year include active sportswear, junior and missy sportswear, menswear, children's wear, leather goods and shoes, lingerie, dresses, outerwear, and cosmetics. Each merchandise category is placed in an area of its own to conserve the buyers' time, energy, and legwork.

Many retailers, particularly those located in the middle South, Southwest, and Midwest, find buying trips to the Dallas market less expensive, less time consuming, and also far less overwhelming than trips to the New York market.

TABLE 7-2
Regional Fashion Apparel Markets

	NAME OF FACILITY	NUMBER OF APPAREL SHOWROOMS, LINES	NUMBER OF YEARLY APPAREL MARKETS	PRIMARY TRADE AREA SERVED
Atlanta	Atlanta Apparel Mart	600 showrooms	8	11-state Southeast region
Charlotte	Charlotte Merchandise Mart	225 showrooms	11	N.C., S.C., Virginia, West Va., Tenn.
Chicago	Chicago Apparel Center	800 showrooms 4000 lines	12	Midwest plus Mideast regions
Dallas	Dallas Apparel Mart	1,500 showrooms, 10,000-plus lines	13	10-state South Central region
Denver	Denver Merchandise Mart	300 showrooms	8	14-state Western region
Kansas City	Kansas City Apparel Mart	200 showrooms	5	7-state Central region
Los Angeles	California Mart	2,000 showrooms, 10,000 lines	70+	International
Minneapolis	Hyatt Regency Hotel and Merchandise Mart	350 showrooms, 1,000 lines	11	Upper Midwest region
Miami	Miami International Merchandise Mart	300 showrooms	16	Florida, Caribbean, Latin America
Pittsburgh	Greater Pittsburgh Merchandise Mart and Expo Center	300 showrooms	N/A	Pennsylvania, W. New York, Ohio, Maryland, West Virginia
San Francisco	San Francisco Apparel Mart	800 showrooms 2000 lines (by Spring '81)	9	N. Calif., N. Nevada, Oregon Washington, Idaho
Seattle	Seattle Trade Center	270 showrooms	12	Pacific Northwest including Alaska and Canada

Source: California Apparel News. Friday, February 22, 1980.

THE CALIFORNIA
APPAREL MART.

Much of California's fashion success stems from its ability to promote a certain lifestyle approach to fashion. Today, sales of the sportswear-oriented "California look" are booming as Americans grow more leisure-conscious and drift toward the Southern and Western states known as the Sun Belt. Because of this success, California has become the second largest apparel manufacturing state. Its apparel producers have had a phenomenal growth rate, in part through their relationship with the California Mart, a major regional apparel mart located in Los Angeles.

In late 1979, 15 years after the opening of the California Mart, the facility completed phase four of its development as a regional mart. This phase marked a 50 percent increase in total square footage over the original. The California Mart now boasts over 2,000 showrooms with approximately 10,000 lines represented.

The California Mart is well known for its support of the California garment and apparel industry. Five fashion shows a year are held at the mart to spotlight the lines, draw buyers, and expose thousands to the latest fashion from all over the world. These shows highlight "market weeks," which run as long as two or three months through the entire buying season. A newsletter, with a circulation of over 22,000, and a mart directory keep buyers informed of mart events and schedules.

THE SAN FRANCISCO
APPAREL MART.

The San Francisco Apparel Mart is now building a 16-story tower addition called Pacific II. This is slated to be completed by 1981. The San Francisco Mart will never rival the California Mart because of the large number of manufacturers and producers of apparel in the Los Angeles area. But it may be comparable to the regional marts of Denver, Chicago, and Atlanta.

THE DENVER MARKET.

Denver is the major market center for the 14 Rocky Mountain and Plains states (roughly one-third of the continental United States). It serves as a clearinghouse for goods and services for the entire region. The Denver Merchandise Mart is one of the major marts in this country.

In January, the mart's International Western Apparel and Equipment Market draws buyers from around the world. This event has been named part of the U. S. Department of Commerce Foreign Buyer Program, the first apparel market to be so honored.

The Denver Mart houses 300 permanent showrooms. These are used by local, national, and a few foreign producers of men's, women's, and children's apparel and accessories, as well as textiles.

Regular seasonal market weeks for women's and children's apparel and accessories, as well as for textiles, are held in November for spring, in January for summer, in August for the winter holiday season, and in May for fall. Menswear, boys' wear, and Western wear weeks are held in September for the winter holiday season and spring and in April for fall. The famous Market Week for men's dress and Western dress is held each January. Two shoe shows are also held in the Denver Mart, in September for spring and in April for fall. In addition, an apparel extravaganza and a ski show are held in April, gift and jewelry shows in March and August, and a home furnishings show in February.

THE CAROLINA, VIRGINIA,
AND TENNESSEE MARKET.

Over the last decades there has been an unmistakable movement of apparel and accessories production facilities from the Northeast region of this country to the mid-Atlantic and mid-South regions. With a population movement to these areas as well, it is inevitable that an important apparel and accessories market should develop.

The Charlotte Merchandise Mart in Charlotte, North Carolina, houses over 225 permanent showrooms for producers of women's and children's apparel and accessories. An additional 100 producers take temporary booth space for the regular market weeks held in January, late March, May, late August, and October.

THE ATLANTA MARKET. The newest addition to the Atlanta skyline is the $41 million Atlanta Apparel Mart, completed in late 1979. This new apparel mart houses more than 600 showrooms for fashion apparel for men, women, and children. It serves the 11-state Southeast region.

Located in the heart of downtown Atlanta, the Atlanta Apparel Mart is connected by an enclosed aerial walkway to the 18-year-old Atlanta Merchandise Mart. The entire apparel mart is designed for the information and comfort of buyers, with glass cab elevators, aerial walkways, and a 3,000-seat fashion theater. The mart is divided into sections by merchandise category, such as dresses, sportswear, children's wear, menswear, and accessories. A unique feature of the Atlanta Apparel Mart is the Atrium, specially designed for fashion shows.

THE MIAMI MARKET. Miami, long known as the fun and sun capital of North America, has changed its image. No longer is it merely a playground for people escaping chill winds and snowdrifts. The new Miami has taken on a decidedly business-oriented and international flavor.

In the last several years, Miami has established itself as the marketplace for buyers and manufacturers from Central and South America and many of the Caribbean islands. It has also established a fashion image of its own in the minds of American buyers.

The Miami International Merchandise Mart has begun a campaign to attract more and more buyers to the showrooms of its 300 tenants. The mart offers gifts, apparel, and textiles under one roof. The apparel manufacturers are widely varied, representing top names from across the United States and some foreign designers as well.

A new vehicle for promoting an exchange between manufacturers of domestic and Latin American merchandise is the annual Trade Fair of the Americas. This fair has been extremely successful for domestic manufacturers, most of whom had never sold to Latin American countries in the past. This fair is held at the Coconut Grove Exhibition Center in Miami.

THE CHICAGO MART. The new center, near Chicago's famous Merchandise Mart Plaza, opened in 1976. Before this center opened, women's and children's apparel showrooms had occupied one floor of the Merchandise Mart Plaza.

The Chicago Apparel Center is a double-towered structure with 13 floors of showrooms (over 800) and exhibit halls. It is topped by an 11-story Holiday Inn. There are now 3,000 lines available to buyers 52 weeks a year, and about 4,000 available during market weeks, all under one roof.

In addition to five major women's and children's markets and two men's and boy's markets annually, the Chicago Apparel Center hosts special markets such as the National Bridal Show and a women's large-size market. The latter is the first national market of its kind in this country.

A major goal of the Chicago Apparel Center is to provide a vast pool of information about retailing and merchandising techniques. Seminars, guest speakers, free consultations, and a group called the Retail Advisory Board are all methods the Chicago Apparel Center is using to provide this service.

Other Domestic Fashion Market Centers

In recent years, smaller regional merchandise marts have been built in a number of larger cities and have become important regional trade centers. Like the larger marts already described, these house the permanent showrooms of local, national, and some foreign fashion producers. Regularly scheduled market weeks are also held in these marts. These weeks are usually sponsored by various sales representatives' associations, such as Style Exhibitors, Inc., the American Fashion Association, the Shoe Travelers' Association, and the Men's and Boys' Apparel Association.

The following are some examples of these

The exciting Atlanta Mart is (a) a modern multilevel building (b) with a giant exhibition hall that is used for fashion shows and (c) hundreds of manufacturer's showrooms (d) where buyers examine new merchandise lines and place orders.

domestic merchandise marts that serve as regional fashion markets. The Kansas City Apparel Mart, a new $6.5 million mart, was opened in 1979. Formerly, the Kansas City Trade Mart handled many of the apparel exhibitors. The Seattle Mart, featuring the Pacific Northwest Apparel Association, houses 270 permanent and 300 transient sales representatives representing more than 1,600 lines of apparel, accessories, and shoes. Other regional fashion market centers are the Northeast Trade Center in Woburn, Massachusetts, the Hyatt Regency Hotel and Merchandise Mart in Minneapolis, Minnesota, and the Greater Pittsburgh Merchandise Mart and Expo Center in Pittsburgh, Pennsylvania.

MERCHANDISING ACTIVITIES

Most fashion producers sell directly to retail stores rather than through intermediaries. The pace of fashion in all but a few staple items is much too fast to allow the selling, reselling, or warehousing activities of wholesale distributors or jobbers.

Women's apparel producers aim their sales promotion efforts at both retailers and consumers. Such efforts take the form of advertising, publicity, and promotional aids available to retailers who buy their products.

Advertising

Today, much retail advertising of women's fashion apparel carries the name of its producer. As late as the 1930s, however, nearly all retailers refused to allow any tags or labels other than their own on the fashion goods they offered. A series of governmental regulations, in addition to merchandise shortages during World War II, helped reverse this situation. Today, most merchants capitalize on the producers' labels that are attached to the goods, feature producer names in their own advertising and displays, and set up special sections within their stores for individual producers' lines.

The apparel manufacturing industry spends less than 1 percent of its annual sales total on advertising, but the exposure given to its products is impressive. Some exposure is obtained through ads placed by apparel firms in consumer publications—both fashion and general magazines as well as newspapers. Some is obtained through ads in trade publications. Another important source of exposure is cooperative advertising with retail stores.

Publicity

Whether they spend money on advertising or not, apparel producers have many opportunities at their disposal to familiarize the public with their brand names through publicity. To obtain maximum publicity, producers sometimes hire a public relations person or firm. Photographs of some of their best-selling styles may be distributed to newspapers and magazines. They may supply television and sports personalities with items of apparel in an attempt to attract public attention.

In addition to the individual efforts of firms to secure publicity, the major women's couture firms located in New York City show their collections at semiannual press weeks. There are two press weeks each January and two each June. One is organized by the New York Couture Group, the public relations arm of the New York Couture Business Council. The other is called the American Designers Showings, and is an activity of a public relations firm, Eleanor Lambert, Inc. Both give the country's fashion editors (newspaper, magazine, radio, and television) an opportunity to examine the latest designer collections. Both also provide them with photographs, prepared stories, and interview opportunities that they need to tell the fashion story to their audiences.

Press weeks once exhibited merchandise lines that ran the entire gamut of price levels. Gradually, however, lower-priced merchandise was eliminated. In recent years, New York press weeks have featured almost exclusively the lines of higher-priced producers.

Semiannual press-week showings are now also held in Los Angeles under the sponsorship of the California Fashion Creators.

Promotional Aids

To assist retailers and to speed the sale of their merchandise, many apparel manufacturers provide a variety of promotional aids. The range is vast, and a single firm's offerings may include any or all of the following:

- Display ideas
- Display and stock fixtures
- Advertising aids
- Suggestions for departmental layout and fixturing
- Reorder forms and assistance in checking stock for reorder purposes
- Educational booklets for salespeople and customers
- Talks to salespeople by producers' representatives
- Assistance from producers' fashion experts in training salespeople, staging fashion shows, addressing customers
- Statement enclosures or other mailing pieces for stores to send to customers
- Special retail promotions to tie in with producers' national advertising campaigns

The following is typical of what can be achieved by close cooperation between producers and retailers. A sportswear producer offered assistance to any store that would stage a travel promotion using the firm's merchandise. A major airline joined in the effort; its flight attendants were available in the store to show customers how to pack and to advise them on clothing needs in vacation spots served by that airline. The producer's fashion experts planned minimal wardrobes to meet maximum travel demands. The producer, the store, and the airline all contributed to the promotion, and each profited by the interest generated.

More recently, one apparel producer's retail store customers were shown a 20-minute color videotape featuring the producer's current line. The taped fashion show used four live models, and the producer provided the commentary. It was intended to help educate fashion sales personnel about fabrics, colors,

Dayton's, Minneapolis

Trunk shows make effective promotion.

silhouettes, and skirt lengths in the producer's line, as well as the accessories necessary to complete this fashion message. Videotapes of this kind are sometimes also shown on the selling floor for retail customers.

Another effective promotion an apparel producer can provide for the retailer is a trunk show of the manufacturer's line. A **trunk show** is a showing of samples of most of the producer's line to a retail store's customers. Accompanying the samples are the producer, designer, or special representative of the firm. To dramatize this special event a fashion show is usually part of the trunk show, with the producer or his/her representative on hand to deliver the commentary, meet customers, and discuss actual garments.

Customers then order any of the items shown, and everyone has benefited. The customer has seen fashions that the customer might never have otherwise seen and has experienced the glamour of the fashion world. The retailer has enjoyed a dramatic influx of customers who have come to see the show and place their orders. And finally, the manufacturer has had an opportunity to see just which of the styles shown are hot. If the customer response has been enthusiastic, the manufacturer has also seen these products attain a new status in the eyes of the retailer.

INDUSTRY TRENDS

As the 1980s begin, America's apparel industry faces dramatic change. American designers have finally succeeded in rivaling Paris designers as definers of high fashion. At the same time, however, manufacturers are being challenged by competitors from other parts of the world.

After years of dominating the apparel manufacturing world, the American wholesale apparel market has watched massive imports from countries where labor wages are low continually eat into the market. These imports, increasingly higher in quality, leapt from 6 percent in 1967 to over 22 percent in 1979.

The apparel industry has begun to take action in the face of this threat to its very survival. It is taking giant steps toward internationalization of marketing expertise, structured management of licensing, diversification and decentralization, and automation. These factors represent a major change in the operation of the apparel industry.

In looking ahead to see what is in store for the fashion apparel industry, it is necessary to realize that this fast-moving, complex industry has constantly adjusted to the changing tastes and preferences of consumers. It may be this very ability to respond to change that will result in the emergence of a more successful apparel industry than ever before.

Internationalization of Apparel Marketing

American apparel manufacturers are beginning to think in international terms, because the industry has become increasingly international in scope. The appeal of American garment styling knows no boundaries, as evidenced by the worldwide popularity of the Western look and other classical American looks.

The United States Department of Commerce has developed a Textile and Apparel Export Expansion Program. Its purpose is to help strengthen the international competitive position of the textile and apparel industries. New evaluations of market potentials, manufacturing competition, distribution practices, and markets for major apparel product categories are being compiled and reviewed to provide new and greater opportunities for apparel manufacturers.

In 1981 the New York Apparel Industry will sponsor a prêt-à-porter show of fashion apparel designed by Americans. The purpose of the exhibition (patterned on the French prêt-à-porter shows) is to increase apparel exports to Europe, the Orient, and South America. This is a step designed to help meet the increasing competition of foreign designers and producers who are showing their goods in the United States.

Proliferation of Licensing Arrangements

Licensing is an arrangement whereby firms are given permission to produce and market merchandise in the name of the licensor. The licensor is then paid a percentage of the sales for permitting his or her name to be used. This practice has grown tremendously in the late 1970s and early 1980s. Many well-known women's apparel designers are licensing either the use of their designs or their names for a wide variety of goods. Licensing arrangements by such American designers as Halston, Gloria Vanderbilt, Calvin Klein, and Bill Blass provide current examples of this growing trend.

Licensing is also crossing international borders. An increasing number of American designers are making licensing arrangements with foreign producers. At the end of 1979, Oscar de la Renta signed licenses transferring the production of his entire Miss O line, with an annual volume of about $2.5 million, from New York to Hong Kong.

Decentralization of Production Facilities

In 1978, an industry survey reported that the present 15,000 manufacturing apparel plants in the United States will be reduced to 10,000 by the end of this century. While some of the decrease will probably be caused by mergers and bankruptcies of small firms, the most significant factor will be the number of firms that move their production facilities out of the country.

Offshore production has become one of the biggest threats to the health of the American apparel industry. At the beginning of the 1970s, American manufacturers refused to put their brand names on what they considered to be low-quality products made abroad with cheap labor. But as the decade ended and the industry entered the 1980s, more and more apparel manufacturers were importing goods. These came either from their own apparel plants operating in cheap, labor-rich, foreign areas or from their long-term supply arrangements with foreign producers. United States manufacturers can also take advantage of a special tariff advantage under Section 807 of the Tariff Classification Act of 1962.

Section 807 works like this: An American apparel manufacturer designs the patterns and cuts the fabric in its U.S. plant. This material is then shipped to the offshore country for sewing and is sent back to the United States for finishing and packaging. The company thus takes advantage of cheap labor for the most labor-intensive aspect of the apparel manufacturing process and pays duty only on the value added to the garment by the work done abroad.

Diversification of Product

Traditionally, as mentioned earlier, women's apparel producers were specialized in terms of the types, size ranges, and price zones of apparel they produced. Today, producers are broadening their offerings. For instance, Blue Bell, maker of Wrangler jeans, has broadened its base through acquisition and new product development. It has expanded its lines to include shirts, sport coats, and slacks. Interco, Inc., formerly the International Shoe Company, began diversifying in the late 1960s when footwear was the first apparel industry to feel the sting of imports. Since then, Interco has purchased 11 apparel producers, including London Fog raincoats and College Town sportswear.

PETITES. According to the Health, Education and Welfare department, there are 14 million women in the United States who are in the petite size category. These women are 4'10" to 5'4" tall and weigh between 85 and 115 pounds. Both junior and missy customers can also be petite size customers.

The first show that displayed only petite sizes was held in January 1979 by the California Mart. Here approximately 500 buyers viewed some 20 manufacturers' lines.

LARGE SIZES. Research figures show that approximately 25 percent of all women in the United States wear large sizes—sizes 16 to

20, 12½ to 26½, and 36 to 52. Although we as a nation have been diet- and figure-conscious for many years, there has always been a substantial number of large-size women in this country. However, apparel in these sizes has only made up a small proportion of apparel production. In recent years, more attention is being paid to the larger size, and fuller-figure fashions are gaining in importance at the manufacturing level. Many top-name manufacturers have established special divisions devoted to designing and producing large-size apparel. In the past few years, many of the regional apparel markets have been sponsoring special market weeks for the large-size market.

Decreasing Emphasis on Seasonal Lines

Traditionally, women's apparel producers created two lines a year—one for the spring-summer season and one for the fall-winter season. Rarely were new styles available until the next semiannual line was introduced. Buyers simply reordered those styles that sold well.

However, because of consumer demand, producers gradually began introducing minor seasonal lines (such as holiday, resort and cruise, and transitional wear) between regular semiannual lines. These helped stores bring new styles and new interest to their selling floors throughout the year.

The trend away from strictly seasonal lines is continuing. Although producers of better apparel still tend to develop strictly seasonal lines, producers of moderate-priced apparel keep adding new styles to their lines throughout each season. Producers of popular-priced apparel have just about dropped seasonal lines. They concentrate instead on producing a continuous series of lower-priced items that are copies or adaptations of higher-priced popular styles.

Automation in Apparel Production

The most radical change taking place in the apparel industry today is its belated transfor-

mation, through automation, from a labor-intensive industry to a product-intensive one.

Long after every other major industry's response to the technological explosion of the 1960s and 1970s, the apparel industry is instituting radical changes. These involve refinements in traditional cutting and sewing machinery. The application of new technologies —lasers, computers, and improved management methods, for example—are all aimed at increasing productivity, reducing labor costs, and achieving better standardization of product and better quality control.

CUTTING AND
SEWING PROCEDURES. Laser beam systems for cutting fabric were first introduced in the menswear manufacturing industry. They have now been adapted for use in the production of women's apparel, where the cutting work is more complicated. A laser beam can cut fabric more quickly and more accurately than an electric knife. Since in this method cuts are made by burning, raw edges that might unravel are eliminated.

Equipment is being developed that will automatically lay out a pattern so that the least amount of fabric is used. This will allow maximum usage of each bolt of fabric. Also in use is equipment that records apparel patterns on electronic tape. The patterns can thus be stored easily and safely and can be located quickly. Some equipment in experimental use makes sample duplicates at the same time the original pattern is made.

More automation is also being used in sewing plants. Electronic scanners optically guide sewing machine heads to stitch the pieces of a cut pattern according to programs. Conveyor belts carry the pieces of a garment from one machine to another in the order in which they are to be sewed together. Machines have been introduced that fuse seams by heat instead of by stitching, thus saving time and eliminating raw edges. Other machines, that fit a section of tubular fabric over a three-dimensional metal form, heat-set the fabric, and then cool it, have reduced the labor once involved in sewing by 30 to 40 percent.

TABLE 7-3
Leading Seventh Avenue Designer Firms

COMPANY	DESIGNERS	PRODUCTS
Kasper for Joan Leslie (Division of Leslie Fay)	Kasper	Dresses, jackets, and skirts, $150–$400
Mary McFadden	Mary McFadden	Dresses, $800–$1,200; coats, $800–$2,000; blouses, $200–$400; Suits, $1,200; jewelry, $35–$1,000. Licensed products: including perfume, upholstery, wallpaper, stationery, blouses
Hanae Mori, Inc., U.S.A.	Hanae Mori	Hanae Mori couture, including evening wear, $800–$3,900; Hanae Mori rtw; dresses, $192–$700; separates, $400–$700. Licensed products: including bedcovers and sheets with WestPoint-Pepperel
The Ruffin Companies	Clovis Ruffin	Ruffinwear updated contemporary dresses, $40–$80; Ruffinknit contemporary knit dresses, $40–$80; Clovis young designer dresses, $90–$200
Giorgio Sant'Angelo, Inc.	Giorgio Sant'Angelo	Made-to-order apparel under Di Sant'Angelo label, $1,000–$15,000; Licensed products: Giorgio Sant'Angelo for SDB Creations; rtw dresses, $120–$900; furs by Michael Forrest; various other products, including home furnishings, accessories
Albert Capraro	Albert Capraro	Coats, suits, dresses, $100–$500; sportswear, $100–$200. Licensed products; eye wear with Silor Optical
Bonnie Cashin Weatherwear	Bonnie Cashin	Bonnie Cashin Weatherwear for Russell Taylor: rainwear, $80–$300; Cashin Country coats, suits, dresses, jackets, $100–$400
Halston Enterprises, Inc.	Halston	Halston Originals, rtw, $200–$1,100; Halston sportswear, $75–$300. Halston made-to-order, average price, $1,250. Licensed products: Halston V (dresses) and Halston VI (sportswear) to Manhattan Industries, $30–$110. Other licensed products, including accessories, luggage, toiletries, lingerie, men's apparel
Cathy Hardwick	Cathy Hardwick	Dresses, $75–$150; separates, $60–$150; coats, $120–$400. Licensed products, including blouses, jeans, sheets, towels
Anne Klein & Co., Inc.	Donna Karan and Louis Dell'Olio	Anne Klein & Co. designer sportswear, $50–$600, mainly $100–$300; Anne Klein Design Studio (licenses various products); Anne Klein International (rtw and licensing operation outside U.S.)
Adolfo, Inc. (Adolfo owns the women's rtw operation and Leon of Paris own the men's rtw divisions)	Adolfo	Adolfo women's suits, dresses, evening gowns, $350–$1,300; Adolfo Sport men's sportswear, $60–$150; Adolfo for Leon of Paris men's suits and sport coats, $290–$400. Other licensed products: shirts, ties, leather goods, furs, shoes, fragrances, wigs, hats, tennis wear

Source: Women's Wear Daily, Feb. 5, 1979 to Feb. 8, 1979.

TABLE 7-3 *(Continued)*

COMPANY	DESIGNERS	PRODUCTS
Fashions by John Anthony	John Anthony	John Anthony couture, coats, suits, and dresses, $1,300, evening wear, to $3,000; John Anthony rtw: coats, suits, dresses, and evening wear, $120–$290; John Anthony Petites coats, suits, dresses, evening wear, $120–$290; rainwear, $180–$240; separates, including jackets, pants, blouses, skirts, $240–$850. Licensed products: furs, scarves, Vogue patterns
Barrie Sport, Ltd.	Scott Barrie	Scott Barrie evening wear, $250–$400; Scottie day dresses (cottons and crepes), $110–$130; Scott Barrie Blouserie (silks), $50–$100; Barrie Jean Co. (cotton and denim), $38; Scottie Playwear (sportswear terry cloth and cotton knits), $20–$70
Geoffrey Beene, Inc.	Geoffrey Beene, president	Geoffrey Beene, $600–$2,000; Beene Bag sportswear, $70–$140; Epoca fragrances: Red Flannel perfume, $100/oz; and Grey Flannel men's cologne, $16.50/4 oz
Albert Nipon, Inc.	Pearl Nipon	Albert Nipon dresses, $160–$300; Nipon Boutique day and evening dresses, $110–$160. Licensed products: rtw in Canada, Albert Nipon for Swirl (loungewear); Vogue patterns
Oscar de la Renta, Ltd.	Oscar de la Renta	Oscar de la Renta suits and dresses, $300–$800; Miss O, dresses, $138–$196
Bill Blass, Ltd.	Bill Blass	Designer clothes, $700–$5,000. Furs by Mohl; robes by Royal; tennis clothes by Tennis, Inc.; intimate apparel by Flex-knit; patterns for Vogue; fragrance by Revlon; scarves, jewelry, menswear; sheets and towels; automobiles by Lincoln Mercury
Diane Von Furstenberg Importing, Inc.	Olivier Gelbsmann	Cosmetics and fragrances, $3.75–$55. Licensed products: dresses and sportswear for Puritan Fashions; tops and shirts for Camicetta; rainwear for Main Street; jewelry for DMA; eye wear, furs, sleepwear, luggage, home furnishings
Calvin Klein, Ltd.	Calvin Klein	Women's rtw, $84–$280; outerwear, $180–$500; T-shirts, $20–$40; menswear; cosmetics. Licensed products: various accessories; furs; sheets; blouses, $98–$200; skirts and pants, $84–$180; rainwear, blazers, outerwear, $150–$500; dresses, $94–$280. Jeans by Puritan Fashions Corp.; furs by Alixandre; scarves, belts, handbags, menswear, sheets
John Kloss Design Studio	John Kloss	Licensees include: Lily of France, Cira, Harbor Casuals, Butterick Patterns, Columbia Minerva, John Kloss Sportswear
Ralph Lauren	Ralph Lauren	Women's rtw: blouses, skirts, dresses, jackets, $58–$500. Men's rtw: (Polo Fashions, Inc.)

SALES AND INVENTORY REPORTS. Computer printouts have become extremely important to the entire fashion industry, from the fiber houses to the manufacturers to the retailers. More and more producers of women's apparel are using daily or weekly computer printouts to keep their inventories of piece goods in better balance with unit sales for each style number.

Printouts also provide them with up-to-date information on the number of units—by style, size, and color—that are on hand, in the process of being produced, and on order from each of their retail store customers. Computerized reports can also tell producers the dollar volume of business they are doing this year compared to that in previous years with each of their retail accounts.

Some larger retailers and producers are experimenting with daily or semiweekly transmittal of sales information. Store sales are fed into store computers, sorted by style and producer. Producers are then sent a rundown on the activity of their styles. This enables both stores and producers to keep close track of changes in consumer demand.

For instance, with such current information at their fingertips, producers can update production plans and fabric commitments to correspond with demand trends. Their design departments can keep close track of the acceptance or rejection of individual styles and use this information in their planning of new styles. Their sales staffs can be given more useful and detailed information so that they can tell store buyers about the firm's best-selling styles, fabrics, and colors.

THE CHILDREN'S WEAR INDUSTRY

The production of children's wear is basically a segment of the women's apparel industry. Boys' wear is not considered part of children's wear but rather of menswear.

Children's clothes were once merely scaled-down versions of adult apparel and were made in the home or by professional dressmakers. Portraits and other pictures from the past, such as Godey's famous fashion prints, show children clothed in miniature replicas of adult fashions of the period. Although this is no longer the case, children's wear still takes its cues for styling, colors, fabrics, and other details from the trends promoted by producers of adult apparel.

History of the Industry

As a commercial activity, the children's wear industry is largely a phenomenon of the twentieth century. Prior to this time, the production of infants' and children's clothing was almost entirely a "cottage industry." This clothing showed little concern for the special needs associated with children's activities, or the changing proportions of their growing bodies. While boys' and girls' clothing was different, there was little distinction within either boys' or girls' wear. All little girls, for example, dressed in the same few styles. Clothes were made large enough so that a child could grow into them and sturdy enough to be handed down to younger or smaller children.

Although a few designers specialized in higher-priced children's wear, it was not until after World War I that the commercial production and distribution of children's wear became a recognized industry. This followed in the wake of a developing women's apparel industry, discussed earlier in this chapter.

The same technological, sociological, and economic changes that were responsible for the development of the women's clothing industry were responsible for the development of the children's industry. As more women were working outside the home, they had less time to sew. And a rapidly increasing juvenile population created new markets. These factors encouraged existing companies to expand their operations, brought new companies into the field, and encouraged specialization of products. The development of snaps, zippers, and more durable sewing made more functional apparel possible.

For the first time, attention was directed toward developing standard size measurements in clothing for immature and growing physiques. Since then, commercial standards

Children's wear in 1874 featured miniature versions of adult apparel, usually made at home or by professional dressmakers.

of sizing have been developed for infants' and children's knit underwear, for toddlers' apparel, and also for girls' and pre-teens' apparel.

Changes in the American way of life since the end of World War II have brought about changes in American children. Gone is the child who accepted homemade clothing or clothes bought by parents to suit *their* tastes.

Today's children are customers in their own right. They are in the store at the time of purchase, know what they want, and do not hesitate to express their wishes. They live, more than their predecessors, in the adult world. They are exposed to advertising on television, radio, and in printed media; they are targets of programs and publications. Children are encouraged to express their individuality. And they do.

Organization and Operation

There are over 800 firms in the children's wear industry, employing over 90,000 workers. The majority of these firms are small and in many cases family-owned. Exceptions are such giant companies as Carter's and Health-Tex, as well as the children's wear divisions of large-scale women's apparel producers, such as Danskin, Russ-Togs, Levi Strauss, and White Stag.

Similar in structure to the women's apparel industry, the children's wear industry is categorized by price, size, and type of merchandise. In terms of price, again as in women's wear, the industry is made up of producers of budget-, moderate-, and better-priced goods. By far the greater share of the children's wear business is done by producers of budget-priced and moderate-priced goods. Continuing inflation has greatly decreased the share of the market formerly enjoyed by high-priced goods. Also because of inflation and rising costs of operation, many former producers of budget-priced lines are "trading up" into the moderate-price range. Most of the real budget-priced goods are being produced out of this country.

The children's wear industry specializes in the following size groups:

- *Infants:* Two size categories are used for infants' clothing. One category uses 3 to 36 months. The other uses newborn, small, medium, large, and extra large.
- *Toddlers:* Toddler sizes range from T1 to T4 (the T stands for toddler). A toddler is a young child who is learning to walk.
- *Children:* Children's sizes are usually worn by girls and boys between the ages of 3 and 6. Many manufacturers produce sizes 3 to 6X for girls and 3 to 7 for boys.
- *Girls:* In girls' wear the sizes are 7 to 14, corresponding to the growth and development of girls as they enter their teens. Preteen and teen junior sizes have been developed in recent years to provide the more sophisticated styling requested by some girls.

Boys' wear, sizes 8 to 20, is considered part of the menswear industry and is discussed in Chapter 8.

Another area of specialization within the industry is by type of product. For example, one producer will make only girls' knits, another dresses, another sportswear, and still another coats. Frequently, however, a producer will make a single type of product in more than one size range—sportswear or dresses in toddlers' through girls' sizes, for example, or in sizes 2 to 14.[2]

The same design and production methods that apply to women's apparel are used in the children's wear industry, except that in the latter they are less elaborate.

Most manufacturers produce only two collections a year: fall and spring. However, some of the high-fashion, higher-priced firms are beginning to cater to the needs of a changing market by adding winter and summer lines.

Market Centers

Most of the children's wear firms are located in the North Atlantic states, particularly in New York City. As is the trend in the women's apparel industry, some factories have moved farther south in order to obtain lower production costs. In many cases goods are produced in foreign countries. The design, sales, and distribution centers of such firms remain, however, in New York City. While New York continues to be the most important market center for children's wear, many producers maintain permanent showrooms in the large regional apparel marts and schedule showings there of seasonal lines. Goods made in Europe, except for some infants' and children's quality knitwear items, are considered too expensive by the majority of customers. The Far East is a large marketplace for less expensive children's wear items.

Merchandising Activities

Many of the features and activities of the children's wear industry are similar, if not identical, to those of the women's apparel industry. Sales promotion and advertising activities for children's wear, however, are considerably more limited. A sports personality is used only occasionally, for example, to publicize T-shirts and other items of children's wear.

The few giants in the industry—Carter's, Health-tex, and Danskin—advertise aggressively to the consumer. Smaller firms—the majority in the budget and moderately priced children's wear field—leave most consumer advertising to the retailer. Firms producing higher-priced, name-designer merchandise do a limited amount of consumer advertising. The high cost of this advertising is often shared with textile firms.

In general, the industry limits its advertising to the trade press. Specialized publications that are concerned solely with children's wear include *Earnshaw's, Infants, Girls and Boys Wear Review, McCall's Children's Wear Mer-*

An outstanding example of children's wear advertising by Health-tex, one of the giants in the industry.

chandiser, and *Kids Fashions.* Trade publications that report on adult fashions, such as *Women's Wear Daily* and *Daily News Record,* also carry children's wear industry advertising and news reports of interest to retailers on a regular, weekly basis.

In October 1979, sponsors of The National Fashion and Boutique Show inaugurated a national showcase for the children's wear industry and called it The National Kids' Fashion Show. Now a semiannual event, featuring over 350 children's wear lines, it is held at One Pennsylvania Plaza in New York City. The range of categories shown includes infant, toddler, boys' sizes 4 to 7 and 8 to 20, girls' sizes 3 to 6X, 7 to 14, and pre-teen garments.

Industry Trends

Like the women's apparel industry, children's wear producers are constantly on the lookout for ways to increase productivity and reduce, or at least minimize, current costs, while still maintaining quality. Many producers have found that the way to keep their share of the market is through complete and total modernization, with computerized systems operating throughout the entire production process.

The clear distinction that once existed between budget-, moderate-, and better-priced children's wear has been eroded by continuing inflation. Some of the once major producers of moderate-priced sportswear and dresses, such as Pandora and Girlstown, have recently gone out of business because of inflation and rising operating costs. To have stayed in business under such conditions, they would have been forced to raise their prices beyond the upper limits of the moderate price range. This would have placed them in competition with already well-established producers of higher-priced apparel, a much smaller segment of the children's wear market.

In order to fill the vacuum thus created in the moderate price range, many budget producers are trading up. The vacuum thus created in the budget market is now being filled to a large extent by imports from countries with lower labor costs.

Producers' associations and labor unions, such as the International Ladies' Garment Workers Union, both continue to apply pressure on United States government agencies, demanding greater curbs on imports. According to these groups, burgeoning imports—particularly those involving textiles and apparel—are a potential threat to the survival of the American fashion industries. Trends indicate that industry and labor will continue to demand curtailment of such imports. The government, on the other hand, will view the import-export situation in terms of what is best for the country as a whole.

Children's wear producers are increasingly aware of the importance of the right fashion and styling in their products. This is particularly noticeable today with the licensing of such famous American designer names as Sasson, Calvin Klein, and Gloria Vanderbilt to jeans and other sportswear items for children, boys, and girls. Similarly, licensing arrangements with such top French designers as Yves St. Laurent, Pierre Cardin, Givenchy, and Christian Dior all permit producers to offer exclusivity of product to their retail store customers and help sell designer clothes for children.

Another important trend is that as children grow into their teens, they are looking to their peers and the young adult group—not to their parents—for their fashion direction. This means that successful children's wear producers must be alert not only to the trends and fads of their own target customers, but also to hot items and product styling in the young adult market. These producers must style their products accordingly.

There is a gradual trend away from producing only two lines a year and a growing trend toward introducing additional styles on a continuing basis. Many children's wear manufacturers are now producing ''items'' rather than complete lines. For example, manufacturers may produce T-shirts rather than polo shirts, sweatshirts, etc. Within that T-shirt item, one style may be a best seller or ''hot item,'' a T-shirt with a current saying, for example. While often involving a fad rather than a full-blown fashion, early identification and production of a single hot item can spell the difference between a red or a black bottom-line figure for its producer.

More and more children's wear producers of name-brand lines are increasing their volume of business by developing unbranded goods or additional brands for their discount store customers. Many have already had success in making up goods to the exact specifications of chain organizations. The chains merchandise these goods under their own brand names, thus developing exclusivity of product.

MERCHANDISING VOCABULARY

Define or briefly explain the following terms:

Conglomerates	Marker	Trunk show
Contractor	Offshore production	
Going public	Outside shop	
Graded	Price zones	
Jobber	Ready-to-wear	
Licensing	Sample hand	
Manufacturer	Section work	

MERCHANDISING REVIEW

1. Discuss the effect of extensive immigration on the development of the apparel industry in the United States.
2. What is the name of the major union in the women's apparel industry? List the benefits this union has achieved for its members.
3. In what three ways does the apparel industry in this country differ from other industries also producing consumer goods?
4. Name and describe the function of each of the three types of apparel producers found in the United States today.
5. What is meant by the term *section work*? What are its advantages in the production of fashion apparel?
6. What are the major advantages and disadvantages of the contractor system?
7. Describe the steps involved in developing a line of women's apparel.
8. Why is New York City considered the major fashion market center in the United States?
9. Describe the advertising and publicity activities of fashion apparel producers, indicating specific methods they may use in each activity.

10. Name at least five types of promotional aids that many women's apparel producers provide to their retail store customers.

MERCHANDISING DIGEST

1. Describe the three basic areas into which women's apparel-producing firms have traditionally been subdivided. What changes are currently taking place with respect to such specialization by product?
2. Where are fashion market centers located in this country besides New York City? Discuss at least two market centers, indicating the distinctive characteristics and services each offers retail store buyers.
3. "The women's apparel manufacturing industry is going through a period of dramatic change." Indicate seven significant industry trends and discuss three in detail.

REFERENCES
[1] "Expanding Apparel Marts," p. 11.
[2] Cuccio, "Children's Budget Leaves the Basement," pp. 1 and 24.

MANUFACTURERS OF MENSWEAR

Today, the menswear industry is in a growth pattern, the momentum of which will most likely continue through the 1980s. But this has not always been the case. For many years this industry was very conservative and non-growth-oriented. Twenty years ago, a man was considered well-dressed if he owned a dark suit, white shirts, and a selection of deep-toned ties. Because the menswear industry in the United States was organized and operated to respond to this conservative pattern, changes in both styling and production methods were slow and deliberate. Today, the many needs and wants of the male population are being recognized by designers and manufacturers. The focus on fashion in menswear is transforming this segment of apparel manufacturing into a dynamic and exciting industry.

Throughout history and until the industrial revolution, fashion interest centered around men's apparel rather than around women's. Not only was male dress more distinctive and "stylish" than female dress, but much of it—particularly that worn for ceremonial occasions—was more colorful. Males were regarded as the dominant sex, and their apparel was intended to bear witness to that fact.

In earlier times, as discussed in Chapter 3, both custom and royal decree often dictated that apparel clearly indicate the social class of its wearer. In certain periods, men's clothes also expressed qualities of bravery, strength, and manliness. The apparel of medieval knights shows this. The apparel worn by men in the French royal courts of the seventeenth and eighteenth centuries emphasized high social status, from the curled wigs to the cascades of lace and ribbons on the breeches.

Then came the industrial revolution. Power, both in terms of money and influence, gradually moved from the upper classes into the hands of those who were clever and hard-working. As a result, a new class of industrial rich was created. However, many of the newly powerful chose to identify with the Puritan work ethic; instead of publicizing their newly acquired wealth and power through elegant apparel, they dressed soberly and discreetly.

Gradually, even those not connected with the growth of industry wore subdued clothing styles. They found it wiser, more practical, and more in tune with the times to dress as an accountant rather than as a gallant.

Almost all menswear thus became conservative and remained so for over 150 years. During this period, men saw their wives and daughters become the fashion plates. Women's clothes were styled not only to show off the attributes of the wearer but also to signal the social class, financial achievement, and social success of husbands and fathers.

Menswear through the ages—always a stronghold of fashion interest. Until the late 1800s, the males' fashions often outshone the females' fashions.

It was during this long period of conservatism in men's fashions that the menswear industry was born and took shape. Menswear is the oldest and most traditional of the domestic apparel industries. And although it is the industry in which custom tailoring retained its importance longest, it is also the industry in which ready-to-wear got its start.

At the production level, boys' wear, sizes 8–20, is traditionally considered a separate segment of the menswear industry, just as children's wear is considered a separate segment of the women's wear industry. (See Chapter 7.) Statistical data relating to the production of children's wear and women's wear are rarely combined. In the production of boys' wear and men's wear, however, data are usually combined. The reason for this is undoubtedly the operational structure of the industry as a whole. Some firms produce only men's apparel, some only boys' apparel, and some produce both. Such being the case, this chapter will deal primarily with the men's apparel industry, with references to boys' wear as appropriate.

HISTORY AND DEVELOPMENT

Until the late 1700s, all men's apparel made in this country was custom-tailored. The rich patronized tailors' shops. Those who could not afford tailor-made clothing wore clothing made at home.

The first ready-to-wear clothing produced here probably was made by tailors in ports in the Northeast. Seamen off ships stopping in these ports needed city clothes while on shore, but they lacked the time or money to spend on tailor-made clothes. To meet the seamen's needs, a few tailors in waterfront cities such as New Bedford, Boston, New York, Philadelphia, and Baltimore began anticipating sales. They made suits in advance so that sailors could put them on as soon as they stepped on shore.

These first ready-to-wear shops were called "slop shops," and in comparison with today's apparel, the name was appropriate for the product they sold. These ready-to-wear suits offered none of the careful fit and detail work found in custom-tailored suits. However, sailors had seldom worn anything except homemade clothes, and so the ready-to-wear suits were acceptable, and the prices were right.

Some of today's leading menswear retail organizations got their start in those early days. For instance, Brooks Brothers' first store was a shop opened by Henry Brooks in 1818 in downtown New York. Jacob Reed's Sons' first store was opened by Jacob Reed in 1824 near the waterfront in Philadelphia.

During this period, industrialization resulted in a population movement to urban areas, where people settled around or near factories. Often the adults and older children of a family worked in a nearby factory. Factory work left neither time nor anyone at home to make the family's clothing. However, it often provided enough income so that the head of the house could buy a ready-made suit.

Industrialization also created a rapidly growing new middle class of white-collar factory supervisors, managers, and junior executives. These newcomers to the middle class did not have the income to pay for custom-tailored clothes, but they did want wardrobes that would show off their new class status. To meet this new demand, tailors improved the quality, fit, and variety of ready-to-wear apparel.

Soon the slop shops became respectable men's clothing stores. By the mid-1800s, the upper classes still would not consider buying clothes off a rack, but the middle class—always most important in terms of fashion acceptance—patronized these stores.

The sewing machine, invented by Elias Howe in 1846, helped speed up production of men's ready-to-wear. The Gold Rush of 1848 increased the demand for male ready-to-wear. One name connected with menswear during the Gold Rush is Levi Strauss. He went to the gold fields of California with heavy fabric to sell to miners for tents. Instead, he turned it into pants and overalls, which the miners needed more than tents. The Civil War increased the demand for ready-to-wear even more, this time in the form of uniforms. In addition, the specifications given factories for the production of Civil War uniforms gradually led to the development of standard measurements and a better fit in men's ready-to-wear.

"Store-bought clothes" succeeded in breaking the final class barrier near the end of the 1800s. Several financial crises during that period caused men who had formerly worn only custom-made clothes to patronize ready-to-wear clothing stores. Their patronage helped ready-to-wear to gain widespread acceptance throughout the class structure. Even though custom tailoring remained a vital part of the industry until recently, it gradually declined to its present status as a minor segment of the menswear industry.

Dual Distribution

One operating policy connected with the men's ready-to-wear industry since its early history has been **dual distribution,** which refers to manufacturers' policy of selling goods at both wholesale and retail. This practice has been far more prevalent in the menswear industry than in women's apparel.

Dual distribution of menswear got its start in the early and middle 1800s, when the ready-to-wear business was expanding along with the country's population. New ready-to-wear factories were concentrated in the North, but since population was growing rapidly in the South, particularly in port cities, good business was to be found there.

At first, ready-to-wear clothing manufacturers were content to sell goods to independent clothing stores in the South. However, producers soon decided that it would be doubly profitable to own some of those Southern retail outlets. By the 1830s, a number of New York manufacturers had outlets in New Orleans, then the second largest port in the United States, and in other Southern population centers. At the same time, other manufacturers continued to sell goods on a wholesale basis to independent clothing stores where they did not have outlets of their own.

Interest in dual distribution waned in the last half of the nineteenth century. It again became a popular trend in the boom years following World Wars I and II. Each time, interest lasted for a few years, then sagged.

The most recent interest in dual distribution was seen in the latter half of the 1960s, when producers again began building chains of retail outlets. By the mid-1970s, however, the trend had passed. One reason for this was the economic situation. The pattern was holding true: In good times, dual distribution has been attractive, and in bad times it has been dangerously costly. Another reason (which probably will keep manufacturers from ever again becoming involved with dual distribution) is the increasing possibility of violating federal antitrust laws, which rule against one-company domination of any specific segment of an industry.

The number of stores owned and operated by menswear producers has never been large, nor is it now, in comparison with the total number of menswear retail outlets. However, the best of the quality outlets in many major metropolitan areas are owned by manufacturers and are likely to remain so. This limited dual distribution does not violate federal laws and in most cases is a source of additional profits.

Today one of the most successful dual distribution manufacturers of men's tailored suits is Hart, Schaffner & Marx. This company manufacturers men's suits and coats and retails them in their 275 retail outlets, producing $600 million in annual sales. In addition to its own brand, the firm produces many different lines of men's suits, such as Hickey-Freeman and Austin Reed, as well as the American-made suits and coats that are styled and licensed by Christian Dior and Nino Cerutti. Although the firm functions under the dual distribution system on many of its lines, certain lines are sold only to independent retail stores.

Contractors

As the men's ready-to-wear business grew, so did its attractiveness as a profitable investment. But going into business as a menswear manufacturer required considerable capital in terms of factory construction, equipment, and labor costs. This situation led to the birth of the contractor business described in Chapter 7. By hiring a contractor to do the sewing and sometimes the cutting as well, manufacturers did not need factories or sewing machines or a labor force.

Contractors of menswear handled their work in one of two ways. Usually, they set up their own factories where the sewing was done. But sometimes they distributed work to operators who sewed at home, either on their own machines or on machines rented from contractors. These workers were paid on a piecework basis.

Thus, right after the Civil War and for the next two decades or so, menswear was manufactured in three different ways: (1) in **inside shops,** or garment factories, owned and operated by manufacturers; (2) in contract shops, or contractors' factories, where garments were produced for manufacturers, and (3) in homes, where garments were made on a piecework basis, usually for contractors but sometimes for manufacturers.

A contractor's most important value in apparel manufacturing is the ability to turn out short runs of a style quickly and inexpensively. A **short run** is the production of a limited number of units of a particular item, fewer than would normally be considered an average number to produce. Because short runs are a contractor's specialty, contracting has remained an important factor in women's apparel manufacturing. However it was gradually abandoned by menswear manufacturers until recently, when it again became important in the production of sportswear.

Traditional menswear manufacturers turned away from contractors and stayed away until recently for several reasons. First, the menswear industry had a pattern of very slow style change, and contracting was not as economical as inside-shop production. Second, improved equipment and cheaper electric power helped make production in inside shops more practical and efficient. Third, as quality became increasingly important, menswear manufacturers found it easier to control work within their own factories than in the contractors' factories.

Unions

As the menswear market and industry grew, so did competition among manufacturers. Factory employees became the victims. To produce ready-to-wear clothing at competitive prices, manufacturers and contractors demanded long hours from workers and yet paid low wages. In addition, factory working conditions, which had never been good, deteriorated further. Contractors were particularly guilty, and their factories deserved the names **sweat shops** or "sweaters" that were given to them. According to an official New York State inspection report of 1887:

> The workshops occupied by these contracting manufacturers of clothing, or "sweaters" as they are commonly called, are foul in the extreme. Noxious gases emanate from all corners. The buildings are ill smelling from cellar to garret. The water-closets are used by males and females, and usually stand in the room where the work is done. The people are huddled together too closely for comfort, even if all other conditions were excellent.[1]

The outcome was inevitable. Workers finally rebelled against working conditions, hours, and pay.

Local employee unions had existed in the industry since the early 1800s, but none had lasted long or wielded much power. The Journeymen Tailors' National Union, formed in 1883, functioned (and still functions today) mainly as a craft union. A union representing all apparel industry workers, the United Garment Workers of America, was organized in 1891, but it had little power and soon collapsed. Finally, in 1914, the Amalgamated Clothing Workers of America was formed. It remained the major union of the menswear industry until the 1970s, when it merged with the Textile Workers of America and the United Shoe Workers of America to form the Amalgamated Clothing and Textile Workers Union.

Workers in tailored-clothing plants make up the backbone of the Amalgamated, and the union is a strong force in menswear manufacturing in the North. However, its influence in factories producing men's work clothes, furnishings, and sportswear in the South and other parts of the country was almost nonexistent until the mid-1970s. It was then that a drive to organize support in the South gave the union its first toehold in these areas.

The famous strike during the early 1970s at the El Paso, Texas factory of the Farah Company, the largest manufacturer of men's pants and work clothes, was part of a long and bitter fight. The company had resisted the attempt of the union to organize the Farah workers for many years, and only after a long court battle were the plant and its workers unionized.

ORGANIZATION AND OPERATION OF THE INDUSTRY

The menswear industry traditionally has been divided into firms making five kinds of clothing:

- Tailored clothing (suits, overcoats, topcoats, sport coats, and separate trousers)
- Furnishings (shirts, neckwear, sweaters, knit tops, underwear, socks, robes, and pajamas)
- Heavy outerwear (windbreakers, snowsuits, ski jackets, parkas, and related items)
- Work clothes (work shirts, work pants, overalls, and related items)
- Other (uniforms, hats, and miscellaneous items)

For many years, the Federal Bureau of Labor Statistics did not recognize these divisions within the industry. Instead, all production was grouped under the general heading of "men's apparel" or "men's garments." Since 1947, however, because of strong urging from tailored-clothing firms, the federal government has used these five classifications. In the trade, **tailored-clothing firms** are those producing structured or semistructured suits, overcoats, topcoats, sport coats, and separate slacks in which a specific number of hand-tailoring operations are required. Tailored-clothing firms once dominated the menswear market, both in unit production and in sales. However, in recent years there has been a steady decline in demand for tailored clothing. On the other hand, there has been a steady growth in demand for sportswear, or more casual apparel that is less structured and involves fewer (if any) hand-tailoring operations.

Sportswear and casual wear were the fastest growing segment of the menswear industry during the 1970s. Changes in lifestyles, resulting in a demand for leisure looks, as well as men's increasing interest in more variety and fashion in their apparel all contributed to this growth.

As we move into the eighties, however, the fastest-growing demand is for separates. This appears to represent a shift toward the expression of more individualized taste, as well as a response to economic limitations and apprehensions. Moreover, the separates phenomenon is not limited to popular-priced goods but applies to better-priced goods as well. One authority believes that people who buy separates are more fashion-aware than customers who need the reassurance of a preassembled look, such as that of coordinates or suits.

Size and Location of Manufacturers

The manufacture of menswear and boys' wear, unlike that of women's apparel, is dominated by large firms. In 1979, manufacturers of menswear and boys' wear shipped an estimated $15.1 billion at wholesale costs.

For the past five years Levi Strauss; Blue Bell; Cluett, Peabody; and Interco have been the four largest manufacturers of menswear and boys' wear. Their combined sales of $2.9 billion is more than one-third of the total combined volume of the top 30 companies in the field. In turn, sales of the top 30 firms represent 55 percent of total industry shipments.

Diversification, mergers, and acquisitions by top menswear producers in the past few

Note the evolution of the three-piece men's suit as worn on the college campus from 1920 to 1940 to 1980.

years have also made it more difficult to ascertain the size and production figures of each firm.

Although there are menswear manufacturers in almost every section of the country, the largest number of plants are in the mid-Atlantic states. New York, New Jersey, and Pennsylvania form the center of the tailored-clothing industry, and traditionally over 40 percent of all menswear manufacturers have been located in this area.

However, the industry's center is gradually moving South. A number of Northeastern manufacturers have set up plant facilities in the South, where both land and labor are less expensive. These include not only apparel manufacturers from the mid-Atlantic states but also some men's shoe manufacturers, who once were found almost exclusively in New England.

Some menswear manufacturers have always been located in the South. For instance, firms manufacturing separate trousers—a segment of the tailored-clothing industry—have always been centered in the South, as have many manufacturers of men's shirts, underwear, and work clothes.

The number of firms located in the West and the Southwest is also steadily growing. Most of these plants produce sportswear or casual attire.

The sportswear and casual-wear output within the industry is not clearly defined, because many manufacturers who produce sportswear, including active sportswear, are also involved either primarily or secondarily with other merchandise categories. Also, because official government sources (mainly the U.S. Bureau of the Census) do not specifically report on many important items of sportswear and casual wear, the size and production figures relating to these types of apparel are difficult to estimate.

Designing a Line

For generations, tailored-clothing manufacturers in the United States were known as slow but painstakingly careful followers, rather than leaders, in menswear styling. The typical tailored-clothing manufacturer had a staff of designers or bought free-lance designs. Designers' names were known only within the trade and were seldom considered important by consumers.

Traditionally, the leading fashion influence was English styling. Designers in this country would study the styles currently popular in England, decide which might be acceptable here, and gradually develop a line based on those styles. Production was a slow process because of the amount of handwork involved in producing tailored clothing. Usually, a full year passed from the time a style was developed until a finished product was delivered to a retail store.

The first signs of male rebellion against traditional styling came during the late 1940s and early 1950s. As described earlier, year after year manufacturers had been turning out versions of a style that had long been popular in England—a draped suit with padded shoulders, based originally on the broad-chested uniform of the Brigade of Guards. A number of young men attending well-known Northeastern colleges became tired of the traditional look. They took their objections to New Haven clothing manufacturers, and the result was the natural-shoulder, Ivy League suit.

Importance of Name Designers

However, it was the radical shift in attitudes in the 1960s that brought about men's willingness to wear suits as fashion. The Vietnam protest, student riots, and racial unrest all encouraged American men to express themselves in a nontraditional manner. They led to the era of the "Peacock Revolution," when men, as in days long ago, once again took a great pride in their appearance. Some favored long hair, bold plaid suits, brightly colored shirts, wide multicolored ties, and shiny boots. Others dressed, even for work, in Nehru and Mao jackets, leisure suits, white loafers, polyester double knits, and the "California look"—shirts unbuttoned to the waist and necklaces.

It was during this period that name designers, most of whom were already famous as designers of women's apparel, began to join the

pierre cardin
PARIS • NEW YORK

In the world of designer clothing, we bring you the best of all worlds.

See us at BAMA
Booths H-344, I-341
N.Y. Coliseum
March 23-26

Nationally Advertised...
Co-op Ad Program
Calvin Clothing Corp.
34 West 33rd Street, New York, N.Y. 10001
Phone (212) 279-6244

**Designer clothing seems to be a trend in both men's and boys' wear.
Note that this ad mentions a co-op advertising program for retailers as
well as participation in the BAMA (NAMSB) exhibit.**

ranks of menswear designers. Bill Blass, who has been designing menswear since 1965, won the first Coty Award ever given for menswear design. As expressed in the *New York Times,* "The idea that men would wear clothes designed by a women's apparel designer was never considered seriously, and one thing that men have arrived at today is that being interested in clothes does not carry a stigma."[2]

Other famous foreign and domestic name designers of women's apparel are now actively engaged in entering into **"licensing agreements"** for the production of menswear bearing the famous designer's label. The manufacturer pays for the work (or name) of the designer in royalties based on gross sales. Royalties average from 5 to 7 percent on men's suits and 5 percent on mens' sportswear, according to industry sources.

The French firm of Biderman, S.A. is reputed to be the top manufacturer of menswear produced under licensing agreements. For example, this company holds the worldwide license to produce Yves St. Laurent menswear. YSL suits are produced in France, while sportswear and shirts are made in both the United States and Hong Kong. All carry appropriate labels of origin as well as the famous designer's name. Biderman also holds the license to manufacture Calvin Klein's menswear, producing suits in France and sportswear in Hong Kong. For the past six years, this company has been licensed to produce Daniel Hector's menswear for the European, United States, and Canadian markets.

Status names are changing the shape of the boys' wear industry. It is difficult to tell which came first—boys' demand for designer clothes or the designers' efforts to enter the boys' wear business. Whatever the case, well-known fashion designers are now competing for space alongside traditional branded merchandise in boys' wear departments.

Designer fashions for boys first appeared and gained widespread popularity in the 1970s, which turned out to be a productive and profitable decade for boys' wear. Billy the Kid, for example, the largest branded boys' wear company in the market, grew in sales from $12 million in the early seventies to more than $80 million in 1972.[3] It appears as though this fashion trend will continue into the 1980s.

In the boys' wear industry, fashion is viewed as the key element for success in the eighties. Vibrant color and different fabrics are being used, replacing drab brown and navy apparel with a livelier look. There has also been a conceptual change in boys' wear. More and more established boys' wear manufacturers are moving away from a children's approach to styling to a young men's approach.

Because of the increasing interest in fashion, boys' wear has become a prime area for both European and American name designers. Jeans and other items of apparel bearing the labels of Cardin, St. Laurent, John Weitz, Ralph Lauren, Calvin Klein, and Sasson illustrate this point.

Today the "name game" is big business in all segments of the menswear industry. While there are no hard figures on the amount of designer business done at wholesale, the best market estimates for retail sales are close to $1 billion for all categories combined. (In 1978, menswear and boys' wear, both designer and nondesigner combined, generated a total of $26.5 billion at retail.)[4] Certainly, status labels are extremely profitable for retailers and manufacturers.

With their spectacular rise to popularity in the seventies, designer clothes offered much more than a unique look. Men developed confidence in certain labels, no matter where they might be sold. Labels also gave items an aura of quality, and even if the quality was questionable, designer goods had the look of "old money." Thus, status became the major merchandising tool in the mid-seventies.[5]

Today, designer labels are more easily promoted than the familiar brands of former decades. This is so for a number of reasons, other than the fashion and prestige associated with the label:

- Designers are visible. Their names are household words; their faces appear in newspapers and magazines. They lend themselves to fantasy, a key factor in fashion merchandising.
- Designers have more exposure because

their names often appear in different categories of merchandise in different shops or departments.

- Designer labels usually allow retailers to put a higher markup on merchandise because of the fashion mystique associated with the name.

A large number of European and American designers have thus begun to fulfill the desires of the newly fashion-conscious American man. *The New York Times* classifies leading menswear designers as follows:[6]

- The Old Guard—Bill Blass, Ralph Lauren, Nino Cerutti, Pierre Cardin, Christian Dior
- The New Guard—Giorgio Armani, Basile, Gianni Versace, Yves St. Laurent, Geoffery Beene
- The New Wave—Calvin Klein, Lee Wright, Chaps by Ralph Lauren, Bill Kaiserman's Raphael line

Tables 8-1 and 8-2 list today's leading designers of menswear and boys' wear and the classification of products appearing under their labels.

Producing a Line

A generation ago, it might have been possible to identify tailored clothing as office or formal wear, and sportswear as weekend or vacation wear. Today, the only real difference between the two types of apparel lies in their construction, rather than styling, colors, or fabrics.

A tailored sport coat is "three-dimensional," or "structured." Its construction involves many different hand-tailoring operations. These give it a shape of its own even when not being worn. A sport jacket is "unstructured." Its construction involves few if any hand-tailoring operations. It often lacks padding, binding, and lining. It takes its shape, in part, from the person who wears it.

For this reason, two distinctly different production methods are currently used to produce menswear. One is the older, tailored-clothing method. This segment of the menswear industry has traditionally been slow to react to consumer demand. The other is the newer sportswear method, developed specifically because it can respond quickly to demands for style change.

TAILORED-CLOTHING PRODUCTION. The production of tailored clothing in general and of suits in particular has long been considered the backbone of the menswear manufacturing industry. Suits made by tailored-clothing firms are graded according to the number of hand-tailoring operations required for their production. The grades, from lowest to highest, are 1, 2, 4, 4+, 6, and 6+. The grade-1 suit represents the lowest quality of tailored suit carried by a store that features popular prices. A **grade-6+** suit, which requires between 120 and 150 separate hand-tailoring operations, is the top line of tailored suits carried in a prestige store. Oxxford and Hickey-Freeman produce top-of-the-line, 6+ suits.

However, a revolution has been under way in the production workrooms of the menswear apparel industry. The introduction of the polyester double knit in the 1960s led to new automation processes, including that known as **fusing.** In this process, various parts of the suit can be melded together under heat and pressure rather than stitched. Other new machinery made it possible to produce suits with "cookie-cutter" speed and precision. Today, as a result, a lower-quality, high-volume suit known as a **grade-X suit** can be produced in 90 minutes with only 90 stitching and pressing operations.

The average retail price of the grade-X suit is about $110, while the grade-6+ suit is about $400.

There is a distinct difference between the fit of a traditional suit and that of a designer suit. Designer suits are sized on what is called the "7-inch drop." The term **drop** refers to the difference between the waist and chest measurements of the jacket. For example, a designer suit jacket that measures 42 inches around the chest would measure 35 inches at the waist. Traditional suits are styled with a 6-inch drop which gives the suit jacket a completely different look and fit. However, in some jackets for young men and other customers who work at

TABLE 8-1
Leading Menswear Designers

DESIGNER	COMPANY	CLASSIFICATION	PRICE
Geoffrey Beene	Joseph & Feiss	Clothing	From $200
	Chesa International	Sportswear	From $25
	Mannor Corp.	Slacks	From $40
	Gino Pompeii	Neckwear	From $13.50
	Coberknit	Active wear	From $30
	Jacqueline Cochrane	Toiletries	From $11
Bill Blass	PBM	Clothing	From $210
	After Six	Formal wear	From $235
	Malcolm Kenneth	Coats, rainwear	From $250
	Gates Shirts	Dress, sport	From $30
	J. S. Blank	Neckwear	From $13.50
	Buxton	Small leathers	From $10
	Revlon	Toiletries	From $15
	Royal Robes	Robes	From $60
Pierre Cardin	Intercontinental Apparel	Clothing	From $195
	Harry Irwin, Inc.	Coats	From $235
		Dress shirts	From $24
	Eagle Shirtmakers	Sportswear	From $27
	Smerling	Footwear	From $80
	Swank	Belts, leathers	From $8
	Jacqueline Cochrane	Toiletries	From $9.50
	Sheridane	Neckwear	From $10
	Roytex	Robes	From $50
	Breezy Point	Activewear	From $60
	Gilbert Hosiery	Hosiery	From $2.50
Oleg Cassini	Phoenix Clothes	Clothing	From $195
	Burma Bibas	Dress shirts	From $18.50
		Sportswear	From $20
		Outerwear	From $150
		Neckwear	From $8.50
	Auerback Robes	Robes	From $35
	CBS Apparel	Active wear	From $18
	Jarman	Footwear	From $60
	Lyntone Belts	Belts	From $19
	Jovan	Toiletries	From $4
Christian Dior	Hart, Schaffner & Marx	Clothing	From $280
	Gleneagles	Rainwear	From $130
	Hathaway	Dress shirts	From $25
	Cisco	Sportswear	From $25
	Thane	Sweaters	From $30
	Stern-Merritt	Neckwear	From $12.50

Source: *Men's Wear,* January 28, 1980, pp. 51–52.

TABLE 8-1 *(Continued)*

DESIGNER	COMPANY	CLASSIFICATION	PRICE
Christian Dior (cont.)	State O'Maine	Robes	From $40
	Host Pajamas	Sleepwear	From $25
	Camp	Hosiery	From $2.50
	Destino	Leathers, jewelry	From $10
	Liberty	Umbrellas	From $15
Halston	J. Schoeneman	Clothing	From $195
	Garey Shirtmakers	Dress, sport shirts	From $22.50
	Pacesetter	Neckwear	From $13.50
	Halston Fragrances	Toiletries	From $8.50
	Weldon	Loungewear	From $48
Ralph Lauren	Polo Fashions	Clothing	From $320
		Sportswear	From $35
		Neckwear	From $15
	Trylon	Robes	From $110
	Acme Boot	Boots	From $150
	Chaps—Greif	Clothing	From $225
	Chaps—Hathaway	Shirts, sportswear	From $19
	Chaps—Warner/Western	Fragrances	From $10
	Polo Western Wear	Western apparel	From $10
Oscar de la Renta	K-R Men's Apparel	Clothing	From $210
	Champion	Slacks	From $25
	Excello	Shirts	From $22
	Wembley	Neckwear	From $11.50
Yves St. Laurent	YSL Men's Clothing	Clothing	From $185
		Shirts	From $25
		Sportswear	From $27.50
	Manhattan Accessories	Neckwear	From $13.50
		Belts, leathers	From $10
	Harwyn	Footwear	From $65
	Charles of the Ritz	Toiletries	From $8
John Weitz	Palm Beach	Clothing	From $120
	Casualcraft	Outerwear	From $90
	Excello	Shirts	From $19.50
	Glen Oaks	Slacks	From $20
	State O'Maine	Swimwear	From $14
	Host Pajamas	Pajamas	From $16.50
	Imperial Handkerchief	Handkerchiefs	From $2
	Storm Hero Umbrella	Umbrellas	From $12
	John Weitz Toiletries	Toiletries	From $10
	Camp Hosiery	Hosiery	From $2.50
	Gemini	Footwear	From $60

TABLE 8-2
Leading Boys' Wear Designers

DESIGNER	LICENSEE	CLASSIFICATION
Geoffrey Beene	Lobel/Geoffrey	Clothing, slacks
Pierre Cardin	Adler Pants	Slacks
	Calvin Clothing	Clothing
	Eagle Shirtmakers	Shirts, sweaters
Polo (Lauren)	Calvin Clothing	Clothing, slacks
	Holbrook	Shirts
John Weitz	Adler Pants	Slacks
	Calvin Clothing	Clothing
	Camp Industries	Socks
	Kaynee Corp.	Shirts
	Schachter Salles	Rainwear
	Whitmore Inc.	Ties
Yves St. Laurent (YSL)	Chips & Twigs	Clothing, outerwear

Source: Men's Wear, January 28, 1980, p. 57.

keeping in shape, the drop may be even greater than 7 inches. European styling usually features more fitted jackets that hug the body and have very square shoulders.

Until recently, each menswear manufacturer tended to produce only one type of apparel, such as coats, suits, or shirts. If a large firm produced more than one kind of apparel, each type was likely to be made in a separate factory. For example, the firm would produce coats in one factory and sport coats in another. Today, many large firms are producing various types of menswear, although each type is still usually produced in a separate factory.

Production of tailored clothing is usually a long and complicated process. After selecting the styles to be featured in the next line, a manufacturer orders the fabric in which the various styles are made up. Once the line is set up, the manufacturer shows it to store buyers. Delivery of the fabric may take up to nine months. Even after the fabric is delivered, however, the manufacturer does not start to cut a style until enough store orders are accumulated for that style to make its production profitable. This is because making up a single style in a man's suit, for example, involves cutting a great many sizes—considerably more than are involved in producing a woman's dress style. Men's tailored clothing is produced in the following proportioned sizes:

- Shorts: 36–44
- Regulars: 35–46
- Longs: 37–48
- Extra longs: 38–50
- Portlies: 39–50
- Portly shorts: 39–48
- Big sizes: 46, 48, 50

While it is unlikely that a manufacturer will receive orders that require a single style to be cut in this entire range of proportioned sizes, it is likely that the most popular styles will have to be cut in at least half or more of them.

Even after the cutting is done, the work goes slowly. For instance, a grade-6+ suit may require as many as 15 hours of an experienced tailor's time, and it may take between 1 and 1½ hours just to hand-press this grade of suit before it leaves the factory. This is why the cost of labor makes up approximately two-thirds of the entire cost of producing a tailored-clothing item. Most tailored-clothing firms own their own production facilities. The quality control that such construction requires can only be maintained in an inside shop.

If you're having trouble finding a good tailor these days, perhaps it's because so many are working for us.

The story of most of Barney's tailors started many years ago in Europe.

There a boy didn't learn a trade in school.

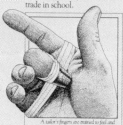

A tailor's fingers are trained to feel and mold the fabric. During his apprenticeship, fingers are actually tied down until pushing the thimble becomes a reflex.

If he chose tailoring as his vocation, he lived with a master tailor and his family and began an apprenticeship.

This education abided no shortcuts.

Before he could call himself a master tailor, a boy learned each phase of suit making. From hand sewing to hand pressing, from cutting the cloth to making the pattern itself.

It took at least 15 years to become a master tailor.

More years, in fact, than are required to become a doctor.

Fitting Tributes.

From all the tailors we interview, only the select are chosen to work at Barney's.

Of our 200 master tailors, only those who are custom tailors as well qualify as fitters.

At Barney's, each floor has its own fully equipped tailor shop and staff of fitters, all under the supervision of a head fitter.

All fitters are carefully chosen for their knowledge of fashion and their ability to interpret it for their customers.

So successful are some of these relationships that many customers ask for their particular fitter by name.

Taking The Long Cut.

If the collar of your jacket doesn't fit snugly against your neck, our tailors don't hesitate to reset it by raising, lowering or shortening the collar.

It sounds simple. But this alteration requires expert handling. The tailor, using nothing more advanced than a needle, thread, and skilled hands, fells the new collar with hundreds of small stitches.

This is just one of the many precise alterations that are offered to you at no additional charge.

Most alterations are hand-basted before the final sewing.

The Basted Try-On.

Such great clothiers as Oxxford, Chester Barrie, Hickey Freeman, and Kilgour, French & Stanbury set an extremely high standard of tailoring.

Our tailors not only uphold this standard but take special pride in extending it.

If it's indicated at your initial fitting, you're invited to make an appointment for a basted try-on.

This time, you'll find all alterations have been sewn with temporary, hand-basted stitches.

If any further adjustments are necessary, they are made.

Only then, after conferring with your fitter and giving your approval, are the alterations completed.

Pressing Issues.

The finest makers of men's clothing apply over 30 hand pressings to a jacket to mold it into its final shape.

In custom alterations, fine hand pressing is equally essential. As such, Barney's tailors never overlook it.

Sewing machines are used where hand sewing is impractical. This operation is done by our tailors on the most advanced equipment.

You see, at Barney's itself, we offer you 7 floors of the finest American and International fashions.

And across the street, on the 5 floors of Barney's tailoring shop, we offer you the services

Hand pressing is an essential part of custom alterations at Barney's.

of the finest American and International tailors as well.

Barney's, New York

7th Avenue and 17th Street. Open 9 AM to 9:30 PM. Free alterations. Free parking. We honor the American Express Card, Master Charge, Visa. And, of course, your Barney's Card.

Barney's

This retailer's ad stresses the importance of expert alterations to complement the expert tailoring of men's high-grade suits.

SPORTSWEAR PRODUCTION. In contrast, many sportswear firms use contractors in exactly the same way and for the same reasons that women's apparel producers do. Sportswear manufacturers, unlike tailored-clothing manufacturers, are interested in short runs and quick response to customer demand. The quality of workmanship is much less important in this area than having the styles, colors, and fabrics that customers want when they want them. It is the style, color, and fabric of a sport jacket that sells it, not the way its lapel, for example, is constructed.

In addition, unstructured sportswear, regardless of what kind of firm produces it, is likely to be made up in a much narrower size range than tailored clothing. For instance, a sport shirt is not produced in the wide variety of neck sizes, sleeve lengths, and collar and cuff styles in which a dress shirt is made. Instead, a sport shirt is usually produced in four basic sizes (small, medium, large, and extra large) and sometimes with a choice between short and long sleeves.

This is the kind of production work that contractors handle most successfully. When contractors are used, the sportswear manufacturer may be the designer, or a designer may be hired, or a design may be bought from a freelancer. The manufacturer buys the needed fabric. Then sometimes the cutting and all of the sewing are done by the contractor, as in the women's apparel field. Finally, the finished goods are returned to the manufacturer, who handles the distribution.

Contractors' plants are located wherever production costs can be kept low. There are many in different locations in this country, and an increasing number of American sportswear manufacturers are using contractors in other countries. The use of the contractor system allows the sportswear manufacturers to provide a steady flow of new styles at moderate prices.

Contemporary Apparel

Contemporary menswear, like sportswear, has not yet been recognized by the Bureau of the Census as a separate category of men's clothing. A product of the 1970s, this category has only recently appeared on the apparel scene. The term **contemporary menswear** relates to a special type of styling which is often also referred to as "updated," "better," or "young men's." It applies not only to coats and suits but to all categories of apparel, from outerwear to furnishings. Although there is no precise definition of the term, it can best be described as new fashion, better fashion, or fashions at the mid- to late-rise stage of their cyclical life span. Although contemporary apparel is not ultrafashionable or "way out" in terms of styling, it is often distinguished by the use of bright colors.

The typical contemporary menswear customer is usually a young man in his late 20s or early 30s. He is a college graduate and is working at a good job with a promising future. He is a sports enthusiast, if not an active participant, and is at least somewhat active in social, business, and community affairs.

Contemporary merchandise is produced by both tailored-clothing and sportswear firms. It is usually produced under a name designer's licensing agreement, rather than being styled by a manufacturer's in-house or free-lance designer. When this type of merchandise is produced by a firm already making other types of apparel and furnishings, new operating divisions are usually created to handle the product, to give it identity, and to enhance its marketability.

Contemporary suits are usually produced in the following sizes:

- Shorts: 36–40
- Regulars: 36–42
- Longs: 38–44

MARKET CENTERS

New York is the traditional and still by far the largest market center for all kinds of menswear, including tailored clothing, sportswear, contemporary lines, and furnishings. Regional markets in other parts of the country—Chicago, Los Angeles, and Dallas, for example—are growing in importance. But the biggest shows and the largest number of permanent showrooms are still located in New York.

The Clothing Manufacturers Association, the trade association of the tailored-clothing industry, holds two market weeks a year in New York. Fall lines are shown in February, and spring lines in late August or early September.

The National Association of Men's Sportswear Buyers, a membership organization founded by sportswear buyers but now including independent store owners, retail buyers, and merchandise managers, holds two week-long showings a year in New York. Fall lines are shown in late March or early April, and spring lines in October. These showings include lines from manufacturers of all types of menswear, including tailored-clothing as well as sportswear and contemporary lines. It is claimed that these showings bring together the offerings of more menswear producers than any other show in the world.

In addition, numerous small regional shows are held around the country. Nearly every area has a Men's Apparel Guild which stages regular seasonal showings in regional market centers as well as in various cities throughout the region.

The delivery terms offered by tailored-clothing firms when taking orders during these market weeks are different from those of sportswear firms, although the former are slowly changing. Tailored-clothing firms traditionally deliver all merchandise ordered from a seasonal line in one shipment. Sportswear firms are moving toward successive deliveries of a seasonal line, sometimes with slight style changes from month to month.

MERCHANDISING ACTIVITIES

Menswear producers, like women's apparel producers, back their offerings with both advertising and publicity. Various fiber firms and associations often cooperate in these endeavors, as discussed in Chapter 7. Advertising is usually done by individual producers or by producers working in cooperation with fiber firms or associations. Publicity is handled mainly by various trade associations.

Advertising

Men's apparel producers turned to advertising in the latter 1800s, using trade advertising to establish direct contacts with retailers. As a result, the business relationships between manufacturers and stores soon became very strong and stable. In most large towns and small cities, each major menswear retailer had an exclusive arrangement with a separate manufacturer. That tie often continued for generations. As a result of this long relationship, most menswear manufacturers in general and tailored-clothing firms in particular have not felt it necessary to do much national consumer advertising. Instead, they have tended to put advertising money into cooperative programs with established retail accounts. This remains the trend among many long-established firms. Cooperative advertising is still an important merchandising activity of the tai-

Graham & Gunn sport coats suggested retail prices from $185 to $265 at these and other fine stores:

F.R. TRIPLER, New York • RICHARD THOMAS, Hamden • PEER GORDON, LTD., Cleveland • FORD'S, Rocky River • NASH'S, Cincinnati • BILL FOGARTY'S, Knoxville • CODY'S, Montgomery • CAPPER & CAPPER, Chicago & Detroit • KNIGHT'S ARMOR, Rockford • JIM HERRON, LTD., Springfield • THE SQUIRE'S SHOP, St. Louis • JACK HENRY, Kansas City • THE MEN'S SHOP OF MERIDIAN, Meridian • LITTLER, Seattle

Graham & Gunn, Ltd., 36 S. Franklin St., Chicago, IL 60606   © 1980 Hart Services, Inc.

This co-op ad was placed in a nationally circulated magazine by the manufacturer, but it mentions the names of retailers across the country who carry the item featured.

lored-clothing segment of the industry. Today, tailored-clothing firms prepare newspaper and magazine ads for use by retail store customers. Some provide the necessary material for radio and television commercials as well.

The sportswear houses, however, are relatively new and have not yet built strong retail ties. Sportswear manufacturers have to compete for retail accounts much as women's apparel manufacturers do. Thus they use little cooperative advertising. Instead, they concentrate on building brand recognition and acceptance by advertising nationally. Some of the ads are aimed at consumers. Others, placed in the trade press, are aimed at retail stores.

Publicity

While most large menswear manufacturers have publicity departments, the major publicity efforts in the menswear industry are organized and carried out by two trade groups, the National Association of Men's Sportswear Buyers (NAMSB) and the Men's Fashion Association of America (MFA). The former handles trade publicity, that is between manufacturers and retailers. The latter handles external publicity, between the trade and consumers.

NAMSB. The main purpose of the National Association of Men's Sportswear Buyers is to help retailers learn what producers are offering. In addition to its show weeks, NAMSB also provides members with a steady stream of pertinent information about developments within the menswear industry. For instance, it distributes a detailed monthly newsletter about fashion trends in menswear to Association members. Twice a year, it prepares fashion-trend slide kits that members can rent for a nominal fee. NAMSB also has a college scholarship program for children of retail members and retail members' employees, intended to encourage young people "to consider menswear retailing as a career."

MFA. The Men's Fashion Association of America represents all segments of the menswear manufacturing industry. The Association aims its publicity and public relations efforts at consumers by providing consumer media with information about the menswear industry in general and about menswear trends in particular.

The MFA holds three major Press Previews a year. In February, it holds a Press Preview in a major Southwestern or West Coast city, such as Houston, Dallas, or Los Angeles, to cover spring-summer trends. In June, it holds a Press Preview in the New York area to cover fall-winter trends. The third Press Preview, added to the schedule in the mid-1970s, is held in the Southwest or on the West Coast in September or October.

Each Press Preview lasts between three and four days. It consists of fashion shows, slide presentations, seminars, and other events intended to tell media representatives about major trends in menswear fashions. These previews became so popular that, in the mid-1970s, the MFA began limiting attendance at the meetings to the country's major media representatives.

In addition, the MFA sends regular publicity to the media in the form of press kits, feature articles, photographs, and even slide shows that can be used on television talk shows and women's programs.

INDUSTRY TRENDS

After more than 150 years, men are once again fashion-conscious. As a result, the menswear industry is finally doing what the women's apparel industry has been doing for years. A wide range of choices in color, fabrics, and styles is now available to men of all ages.

The dynamics of population growth as well as developments in the economy today tend to favor certain segments of the menswear market over others. The fastest-growing age group at the present time includes men 25 to 44 years of age. A large percentage of men in this group have upward mobility in their careers and are interested in projecting the correct image through their fashion selections. Because of this, contemporary styling and tailored separates may benefit in the 1980s. The growing numbers of higher-income, quality-conscious, mature males should create markets for an increasing number of diversified products. Other trends include a greater emphasis on the automation of production processes, an increase in both foreign production and sales, and a growing awareness of factors currently influencing the marketplace.

Diversification of Product

Many menswear manufacturers are increasing the types of apparel they offer. Traditionally, a firm in this industry produced only a single type of garment and sometimes only a single grade of that garment. Now menswear producers are beginning to ignore the tradition of product specialization that both manufacturers and retail stores have followed for so long.

For example, some of the biggest changes have taken place in an area that once was the most rigid: work clothes. For generations, firms like H. D. Lee and Levi Strauss turned out overalls, work pants, and work shirts in approximately the same patterns and the same fabrics, season after season. Now casual clothes have become popular, and the big-name producers of work clothes have found themselves producing fashion goods. In addition to jeans, which had almost completely saturated the market by the mid-1970s, these manufacturers are also producing a wide range of slacks, casual pants, and jackets. They are available in different styles, colors, and fabrics, all carefully selected to sell to today's sportswear-conscious male—and female. By the late 1970s, H. D. Lee and Levi Strauss were as much interested in style sales reports as they were in unit sales reports.

Suits are another example. In the past, manufacturers of traditional suits turned out a selection of styles in one or two grades. Today, the trade calls the traditional tailored suit a ''suit-suit,'' because so many other types of suits have made gains in fashion importance.

Styling

The blazers, vests, and slacks produced by such giant firms as Levi Strauss, Haggar, and Farah introduced separates to the casual menswear market. Popular-priced sportswear was at the forefront of the separates movement in the late 1970s. Today, however, separates in the category of better-priced tailored clothing are beginning to have an increasingly pronounced influence on the marketplace.

Some manufacturers and retailers see separates as a bridge between sportswear and traditional menswear. One retailer sees separates as the trend of the future, satisfying the American consumer's need for instant gratification by allowing a suit to be bought and taken home immediately.[7] Most likely, however, separates will continue to have major impact in the popular-priced merchandise categories (approximately $175 to $195 at retail) and a less significant effect on the $350- to $400-suit market.

How separates will affect the sales of coordinates in the decade of the eighties is an open question. This will be an important trend to watch.

Traditionally, men's long-sleeved dress shirts have been made in neck sizes $14\frac{1}{2}''$ to $17''$, graduated in half-inches. Each size has also been available in a choice of sleeve-length sizes $32''$ to $35''$, graduated in inches. In an effort to reduce inventory levels and increase stock turnover at both the manufacturing and retailing levels, manufacturers have resorted recently to making dress shirts in only two sleeve lengths—regular ($32''$-$33''$) and long ($34''$-$35''$). Half-inch neck sizes have been retained, however. Today more than 50 percent of all men's dress shirts are being produced in regular and long sleeve lengths. This percentage is expected to increase considerably in the future.

Automation of Production

Advances in technology have affected every industry. In menswear, new equipment and systems are helping manufacturers combat

Save $0-$00

Separate connections you mix/match for perfect fit.

00⁰⁰ Coats, reg. $00 **00⁰⁰** Vests or slacks, reg. $00 each.

Buy each in the size that suits you best. All in a superb woven texturized polyester fabric that looks like you paid dollars more. Pattern coat with center vent; solid coat has side vents. Vest reverses from solid to pattern. Pattern or solid slacks. Gray tones. Coat, vest: regs. 36-46, longs 40-46. Slacks in sizes 30-40.

MONTGOMERY WARD **June Sales Parade**

Separates, sometimes called "instant suits," are seen by many retailers as the trend of the future.

one of the most serious problems faced by all apparel producers today: the slow but steady dwindling of an available labor force. Every year it becomes increasingly difficult to find a sufficient supply of workers. Turnover in the industry is tremendous, averaging between 60 and 70 percent in recent years. The time required to train workers has become a crucial factor in estimating productivity.

For these reasons, the industry is gradually turning to automation. Through the introduction of new equipment and systems, increased productivity and quality control can be introduced into the manufacturing process. However, this trend is found only among larger firms. Much of the equipment is still too expensive for smaller manufacturers and is also capable of working at faster production speeds than smaller manufacturers need.

One way that major companies are handling the labor problem is by establishing "clusters" of plants in the South and other areas where land costs are low and labor is relatively cheap. A large central plant turns out the main segments of a garment, such as various parts of a shirt. Bundles of those parts are then trucked to small satellite plants in nearby communities for machine stitching. Since the more intricate work has already been done in the central plant, the work handled at the satellite plants is simple, and the labor cost is relatively low. The satellite plants attract workers because they provide a home-town source of income, with minimum training required. Workers do not have to travel long distances each day as they would be required to do in order to earn slightly more at more distant plants.

It is in the central plant of such a cluster, and in other large apparel manufacturing plants, that automation is beginning to be developed. This is being achieved through the installation of equipment that (1) does jobs by machine that formerly had to be done by hand, (2) cuts down on the number of workers needed to do a specific job, and (3) cuts down on the amount of training and skill that workers need.

For instance, "pocket-setters" sew a pocket on a shirt automatically. "Sequential buttonhole sewers" stitch all buttonholes on a shirt in a single automated operation. "Collarmakers" reduce the number of workers needed to make a collar on a production-line basis from eight to two. Since the equipment is programmed to follow a set pattern of operations and only a few simple tasks are left to the operators, these workers can be trained to run such collar-making equipment in 2 weeks instead of the 10 to 12 weeks once required to teach workers to handle manual collar-making operations.

As mentioned earlier the introduction of polyester double knit in men's apparel in the 1960s led to new automation processes, including fusing.

Automation has also invaded the labor-intensive, better tailored-clothing industry. In the past, 1 to $1^{1}/_{2}$ hours were required to hand-press a man's grade-6 or 6+ suit. Today that time is reduced to a matter of minutes by means of a computer-controlled, automated system which steam-presses each part of the suit.

In general, the industry is gradually becoming more machine-oriented than operator-oriented. This is a vast change for an industry that, throughout most of its history, prided itself on the individual workmanship that went into many of its products.

Foreign Production

Price competition is very strong in the menswear market. A very important factor in setting prices at wholesale is the cost of labor. Because of this, an increasing number of menswear producers, particularly sportswear firms, are building plants or contracting to have work done in areas outside the country where land and labor costs are lower.

The amount and type of work done outside the country vary greatly. Some firms handle everything except the sewing in their domestic plants and contract to have the sewing done in plants outside the United States. Some have both the cutting and sewing done outside the country. Some ship greige goods to one country for dyeing and finishing and then ship these goods to another country for cutting and sewing. Some buy fabric outside the country and have the garments cut and sewn outside the country. In such cases, producers never actually see the products in any form until the finished goods are delivered to this country for distribution.

The disadvantages of foreign production include uncertain quality control and a longer wait for delivery of finished garments. Advantages, as discussed in earlier chapters, include lower production costs because of lower building or renting costs and lower costs of labor. This enables manufacturers to charge lower wholesale prices and enables retailers to pass savings on in lower retail prices. However, since goods produced in foreign countries are subject to import duties, savings are possible only when import duties are relatively low. In the late 1970s and early 1980s, worried by the amount of foreign production in the menswear industry, menswear production workers in this country began demonstrating to get duties raised on imports of menswear from several key areas of foreign production, such as Taiwan and South Korea.

Current Influencing Factors

That designer talents and labels add significant value to women's apparel has now been well established. To what degree this may hold true for the menswear industry will be determined in the 1980s. National brands, together with a good store name, is another factor that will assure the menswear customer of good value.

Imports continue to make inroads in the menswear market. Spiraling prices for domestic production, quality considerations, and the desire for exclusivity are causing more and more retail menswear organizations to build up their direct import programs, as well as to buy indirect imports (clothing made abroad for United States manufacturers).

Merchandise shortages following World War II put most menswear manufacturers in an advantageous position in their dealings with retailers. This situation did not change until the repeal of the Fair Trade Laws and the recession of the late 1970s. Today there are

Sell profit-boosting Major League Baseball sportswear from Champion, your expert in licensed apparel. Champion Products Inc., 350 Fifth Avenue, New York 10001.
See us at the BAMA Show. Booth H333-335

© Champion Products, Inc. 1980 and © Major League Baseball Promotion Corp. 1980

A growing trend in boys' sportswear is a type of licensing agreement in which the product bears the name of a sports team.

many examples of manufacturers' cooperation with retailers that may become established, ongoing activities of the industry. These include Puritan's concurrent showing of goods for Holiday, Spring, Father's Day, and Fall, which allows retailers to see an entire year's styles at one show. Another example is the increase in retail-advertising funding by manufacturers.[8]

The number of menswear shops rapidly increased in the 1960s and decreased in the early 1970s. Recently, however, shops featuring clothing and accessories for men are again proliferating in all areas of the country. Shops featuring active sportswear for jogging and tennis are especially popular.

However, current inflation is forcing the fashion-conscious man to seek shops where his fashion demands and limited finances are compatible. He thus shops in "pipe-rack" discounters, where "fashion at a price" is the motto. Examples of discounters in the East are Syms, BFO (Buyers' Factory Outlet), and NBO (National Brands Outlet); in Houston and Dallas, Kuppenheimer Outlet Store and Menswear House; in Los Angeles, C. & R.

Clothiers, Inc.; in Detroit, National Dry Goods; and in Chicago, The Suitery. All are retailers catering to this new need in the menswear industry.

MERCHANDISING VOCABULARY

Define or briefly explain the following terms:

Contemporary menswear	Inside shops
Drop	Licensing agreements
Dual distribution	Short run
Fusing	Sweat shops
Grade-6+ suit	Tailored-clothing firms
Grade-X suit	

MERCHANDISING REVIEW

1. What effect did the industrial revolution have on male apparel? What socioeconomic factors were responsible for the drastic changes that occurred?
2. What four developments in the nineteenth century were largely responsible for the development of the men's ready-to-wear industry in this country? How did each help to accelerate those developments?
3. Name and describe the three ways in which menswear was manufactured in this country in the latter part of the nineteenth century.
4. For what three reasons did early manufacturers of men's tailored clothing give up the use of contractors?
5. What is the name of the major union in the menswear industry today? Briefly review the conditions that led to unionization within the industry.
6. Name the different segments into which the menswear industry is subdivided, on the basis of the type of product lines each produces. What specific products are produced by each segment?
7. Describe the differences between a tailored sport coat and a sport jacket, from a manufacturing standpoint.
8. Contrast the advertising policies of men's tailored-clothing firms with those of firms producing sportswear.
9. What are the names of the two major menswear trade associations? Describe the function and activities of each.
10. What is the single greatest problem facing producers of menswear today? How are producers attempting to alleviate this problem?

1. Discuss the following statement from the text and cite examples to illustrate it: "Throughout history, and until relatively recently, fashion interest centered around men's apparel rather than around women's."
2. What is meant by "dual distribution" in the menswear industry? Discuss dual distribution on the basis of its (a) history, (b) development, and (c) extent of implementation today.
3. Discuss and give examples of how diversification of product lines, as an increasingly important industry trend, has affected (a) menswear production and (b) the retailing of menswear.
4. Discuss the increased use of foreign production facilities as a trend in the menswear industry. What are its advantages? Disadvantages?

REFERENCES

[1] Quoted in Cobrin, *The Men's Clothing Industry,* p. 67.

[2] Ettorre, "Businessmen and Buttonholes," p. F1.

[3] McGriff, "Fashion Seen Key Element for Success in the 80s," p. 10.

[4] "The Designer Syndrome," 1980, p. 48.

[5] Ibid.

[6] Ettorre, "Businessmen and Buttonholes," p. F13.

[7] Rothman, "Separates—New Tailored Separates Sales Spell Success," p. 56.

[8] Spaulding, "In a Hot Streak? Men's Wear," p. 52.

MANUFACTURERS OF FASHION ACCESSORIES

⑨

The world of fashion is one of constant innovation and change. Fashion accessories manufacturers must forecast these changes so that their goods will mix and match, contrast and coordinate with fashion apparel. The nature of the fashion accessories business, in which items are "in" one year and "out" the next, makes the designers and manufacturers in these industries especially sensitive to trends and customer acceptance. The ability to adapt or change a style or an entire line in midseason is the hallmark of a successful fashion accessories manufacturer.

ACCESSORIES AND CLOTHING COORDINATION

There has always been a strong relationship between fashion accessories and the clothes with which they are worn. Accessories must be designed to be worn with new fashions and also to update fashion apparel already owned. Thus fashion accessories manufacturers must be prepared to produce styles that blend, follow or lead, and innovate. Manufacturers must be aware of the fashion trends in color, silhouette, texture, and design so that retailers and consumers can be offered accessories to complete a total fashion look.

The fashion accessories industries must be highly responsive to fashion and quick to interpret incoming trends. Very often consumer reactions to fashion accessories come first and can signal changes and trends in apparel fashions. Many times an accessory item becomes very successful with the customer early in a season. Other industries take advantage of

this early selling success by manufacturing similar or identical items. When this occurs, the "hot" item will be stocked and sold in many different departments of a store. Past examples of this are shawls, sunglasses, headwear, tops, and bodywear. All have been sold in both accessories departments and in many apparel departments at the same time.

The practice of showing accessories lines during fashion apparel market weeks enables merchants to coordinate the apparel and accessories they purchase. Thus the assortments they display and advertise will reflect the total fashion look they wish to present to their target customers.

Retailers have traditionally viewed accessories as **impulse items**—items that customers buy on an impulse rather than as a result of planning. They are bought because of color, excitement, or newness, or because customers simply want something new to give their spirits and wardrobes a lift. Most large

RECHARGE YOUR WARDROBE WITH HIGH VOLTAGE FASHION ACCESSORIES

Get ready for the jolt of bicolor. Add a finishing touch to any outfit with black and white geometric jewelry in sophisticated new plastics.
$4-$12.50

Then strap on a belt from our collection and your clothes take on an exciting new look in a flash. Blazing belts by Pearl and Jane Klein will ignite your fashions.
$6-$9

You can put pizzazz in your pace with Round-The-Clock® pantyhose by Givenchy. Sparkling Le Fleur textured pantyhose will charge up your fashions with a distinctly unique look.
$5

Energize your fashions with sparkling new purses from Sol Mutterperl and Lumured. Hold on tight to a clutch bag or let it swing from your shoulder. Both styles radiate vitality.
$18-$26

Bolt down to Crowley's where a wide selection of accessories are waiting for you. Choose from a vast assortment of colors, styles and sizes in Costume Jewelry [19], Handbags [21], Fashion Accessories [26], and Hosiery [14] at all stores.

Crowley's

Shop tonight until 9 p.m. at: Westborn, Macomb Mall, Livonia Mall, Lakeside Mall, Farmington and Birmingham. Grand River open until 7 p.m. New Center open until 6 p.m.
Use your Visa, Master Charge and American Express at Crowley's.

Crowley-Milner Co.

Retailers know that customers often buy accessories on impulse to give their wardrobe a new look.

department stores position the fashion accessories departments on the main floor near the front of the store because of this impulse buying pattern. A trend now is to have accessory department "outposts" throughout the store, adjacent to fashion apparel departments. This merchandising technique has proven very successful in helping customers achieve a coordinated look.

The most recent innovation, however, is departments that feature total coordination in accessories and apparel. Often these departments feature name designers' apparel and accessories, allowing one-stop shopping. The concept of one-stop shopping is growing rapidly, because more and more women are entering the work force and have less free time for shopping. Retailers and manufacturers are working hard to coordinate fashions so that customers can buy more in less time.

Many successful boutiques and specialty stores feature fashion accessories. Shoe stores, handbag and hosiery stores, millinery stores, and cosmetic stores are becoming more popular because of the new interest of the customer and retailer in the fashion accessories business. The association of famous designers with fashion accessories is another reason for this growing popularity.

Among European fashion leaders, fine accessories have long been a status symbol and have been considered indispensable to a fashion wardrobe. Americans, however, have just recently become aware of the versatility and uniqueness of fashion accessories. Fashion accessories have now become a major part of fashion in this country and an essential segment of the fashion industry.

The impact of foreign-made merchandise has been very evident in the fashion accessories industries. Whether the foreign merchandise is made to specification for U.S. manufacturers or retailers or is sold directly by importers to retailers, its percentage of total merchandise sold has grown tremendously. In some of the industries, notably shoes, handbags, and neckwear, sales of foreign-made accessories have risen to well over 50 percent of all merchandise sold.

The rise of accessories as a dynamic force in fashion only came about in the past few decades. And their impact grows stronger each year. Fashion accessories manufacturers are continually striving to innovate creative fashion designs that customers can use to give a new fashion look to their wardrobes.

COSMETICS

Throughout recorded history people have painted their faces. A study of face painting among primitive tribes suggests that the first makeup may have been protective. Thousands of years later, protection is still a basic factor in the cosmetics industry, with sales of protective face creams in the billions of dollars. Since the earliest civilizations, cosmetics have also been developed and applied for the enhancement of nature and the perfection of appearance. King Tutankhamen's burial site revealed several types of cosmetics in the form of unguents, creams, and pomades. There is also evidence of cosmetic use in ancient China, Greece, India, and Rome.

As defined by the Federal Trade Commission, **cosmetics** include articles other than soap that are intended to be "rubbed, poured, sprinkled, or sprayed on, introduced into, or otherwise applied to the human body for cleansing, beautifying, promoting attractiveness or altering the appearance without affecting the body's structure or functions." This is an unglamorous definition for an industry that can be traced to Cleopatra's appropriation of her priest's perfumes, powders, and paints to bedazzle Mark Antony.

The relationship between cosmetics and fashion apparel grows stronger each year. Top fashion designers are moving into the creative segment of the cosmetics industry. They work with manufacturers to develop and forecast the color, design, line, and textures of coming fashions. The cosmetics industry then manufactures and promotes exciting new colors to coordinate with the new season's fashion apparel. As changing lifestyles influence the design of apparel, so do they prompt the development of new products by the cosmetics industry.

History and Development

Historically, the pursuit of beauty has been the prerogative of the rich and privileged. Special beauty aids were concocted in the temple, the monastery, the alchemist's cell, or the kitchen.

Only in the past 60 years or so has the age-old pursuit of beauty found its way into modern laboratories. The enhancement of appearance has ceased to be the privilege of the select few. It has now become the necessity of the many. Innovative products created through research and development, together with outstanding advertising and package design, have made cosmetics widely available to consumers of different ages, lifestyles, and economic levels.

The cosmetics industry has undergone a significant change in recent decades. It was once made up of many small firms, none of which owned a significant share of the market. It is now an industry in which a relatively small number of firms command major market shares. Although there are close to 600 companies in the cosmetics industry, the top eight firms account for 50 percent of total shipments. The largest 50 firms account for 88 percent of the total. Although a number of firms have remained autonomous, a large number of national brand cosmetics companies are now part of large drug conglomerates. This relationship between the drug and cosmetics industries continues to grow.

Another change has been the passing of the individual "giants" of the industry. A few flamboyant personalities helped to shape the scope and direction of the entire cosmetics industry. Elizabeth Arden, Helena Rubenstein, Charles Revson, and Max Factor were all legends in their own time and individual rulers of their own special beauty empires. The drive, intuition, foresight, and promotional abilities these entrepreneurs brought to the field known as the "beauty business" is still felt in the industry today. The success of these pioneers in selling hope and beauty to the American public has rarely been duplicated in any other fashion accessories industry. Today, only Estee Lauder still operates her "beauty empire" with the personal drive and decision-making skill of the original innovators. The companies of the other cosmetic giants have become public corporations or divisions of multinational conglomerates. Recently, a new group of farsighted entrepreneurs have begun to take their place in the industry. Adrien Arpel, Madeleine Mono, Diane von Furstenberg, and Irma Shorell are just a few among this new breed.

Organization and Operation

Although dominated by giant producers of nationally advertised brand lines, the industry has many **"private label"** manufacturers, who produce merchandise to specification under the brands of chain stores, mass merchants, or small independent stores. Examples of private label fragrances are Volage, sold by Neiman-Marcus, and Bloomies, sold by Bloomingdale's.

All large, nationally advertised cosmetic firms produce hundreds of items. For sales and inventory purposes, products must thus be divided into broad categories. The typical order form of one large firm, for example, lists all the company's products, in the various sizes or colors available, under such end-use categories as facial makeup, nail care, bath preparations, hair care, fragrances, eye products, body care, and so on. If a firm produces men's as well as women's cosmetics, each of the two lines is given its own distinctive brand name, and separate sales and inventory records are kept for each brand line. Because of fashion and product obsolescence, manufacturers are constantly updating and shipping new items to keep the cosmetics customer buying new products and/or new colors. A system of product returns, unique to the cosmetic industry, aids the retailer in keeping the inventory current. The industry refers to this system as **rubber-banding.** Other industries allow returns to vendors for damages, overshipments, or wrong shipments only. Rubber-banding means that products not sold within a specified period of time are returned to the manufacturer and are replaced with others

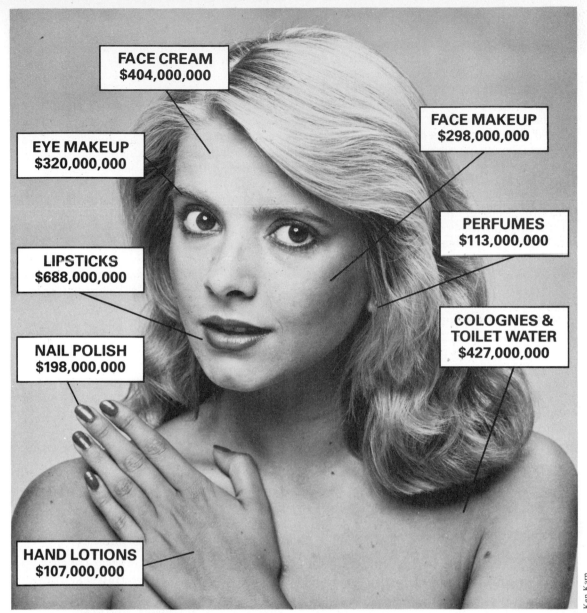

FACE CREAM
$404,000,000

FACE MAKEUP
$298,000,000

EYE MAKEUP
$320,000,000

PERFUMES
$113,000,000

LIPSTICKS
$688,000,000

COLOGNES &
TOILET WATER
$427,000,000

NAIL POLISH
$198,000,000

HAND LOTIONS
$107,000,000

Ken Karp

Cosmetics—a multimillion dollar industry. Here's where the money went.

that will sell. It guarantees that the cosmetics retailer will never have to take a markdown on this merchandise.

FEDERAL COSMETIC LAWS. The major ingredients of cosmetics in any price range are fats, oils, waxes, talc, alcohol, glycerin, borax, coloring matter, and perfumes. Because chemicals are the basis for most cosmetic products, the Federal Drug Administration is the federal agency that polices and regulates the manufacturer. FDA regulations prevent manufacturers from using potentially harmful ingredients and from making exaggerated claims regarding the efficacy of their products.

The Federal Food, Drug, and Cosmetic Act, effective in 1938, was the first federal law controlling cosmetics in the United States. It prohibits adulteration and misbranding of cosmetics. When the act was updated in 1952, new amendments made it more stringent. Additional amendments were then enacted by Congress in 1960, requiring government review and approval of the safety of color additives used in cosmetics.

The Fair Packaging and Labeling Act was passed by Congress in 1966 to prevent unfair or deceptive methods of packaging and labeling. This act covers many consumer industries besides the cosmetic industry. All cosmetics labeled since April 15, 1977, must bear a list of their ingredients, listed in the order of their weight.

Constant surveillance by consumer and industry groups and advisory boards keeps the industry sensitive to product liability. A formal regulatory program for cosmetics is expected to be passed and implemented in the early 1980s. This legislation will require manufacturers to register their products and formulations and to establish their safety before selling to the customer.

TRADE ASSOCIATION. The Cosmetic, Toiletry, and Fragrance Association (CTFA) is the major cosmetic trade association. Its membership markets 90 percent of all cosmetics, toiletries, and fragrances sold in the United States. The CTFA coordinates the industry's commitment to scientific and quality standards. It is the industry vehicle for information exchange about scientific developments among association members, consumers, and those who regulate the industry at federal, state, and local government levels. The CTFA also keeps members informed on government regulations and offers advice on interpretation and compliance.

THE FRAGRANCE MARKET. The fragrance industry is growing and will continue to grow because for many customers fragrance has become a necessity. The designer names associated with many fragrances—Lauren's Chaps for men and Halston for women, for example—lend these products status and an aura of uniqueness. Designer fragrances will acquire a growing percentage of total sales. There has been a rapid pace in the introduction of new fragrances since 1977, and the fragrance market is the fastest growing segment of the cosmetics industry. Its $1 billion in yearly sales is predicted to become $3 billion by 1990.

Continual innovation in fragrances is necessary to maintain growth in a fashion-conscious market. A fragrance is usually offered as both a perfume and a lower-priced cologne. The latter is intended to entice the customer who may be hesitant about experimenting with an expensive product. The success of a perfume or cologne depends in part on attractive packaging and aggressive promotion. The image created by advertising the kind of person who wears a particular fragrance can also be an important factor in the success of the fragrance. This was the case with Revlon's Charlie.

Perfumes are worn predominantly by women between 25 and 44 years of age, because this group is both fashion-conscious and affluent enough to purchase these expensive items. Toilet waters and colognes are worn more informally than perfumes. They are lower in price because the perfume oils are diluted with alcohol. These are popular with younger women. It appears that market growth of fragrances will remain very strong through 1990. An important factor in this growth will be the increasing number of working women, particularly in white-collar jobs, where lighter fragrances are preferable to the heavy perfumes they may wear in the evening. The concept of a "wardrobe" of fragrances to suit the various roles a woman assumes is being promoted and will likely boost demand.

THE MALE
COSMETICS MARKET. Today the market for male cosmetics is expanding and is expected to experience above average growth in the future. The changing male image is opening up new and larger markets in hair

care, cosmetic items, and fragrances. A recent survey showed that the average male today owns from four to six fragrances.[1] Men are also buying more diversified products, such as moisturizers, cleansers, and skin toners. These products are being designed to give a healthy look throughout the year and to keep the skin naturally healthy. Men, like women, are concerned with aging. Unlike women, they have done little about it until now. It is gradually becoming socially acceptable for men to treat their skin to retard the aging process.

Because men have been captivated by the national preoccupation with youthful appearance and bodily fitness, installation of complete men's cosmetics sections in department and specialty stores is a growing trend. Bloomingdale's and Saks, among others, have expanded their men's cosmetics areas. Menswear specialty stores are adding cosmetics areas, and mail-order catalogs are devoting more space to men's grooming aids.

THE ETHNIC MARKET.   Approximately 25 million consumers make up the total ethnic market. Blacks, an important segment of that market, account for an estimated 20 percent of the total cosmetics, toiletries, and fragrances purchased annually in the ethnic market. For years the black cosmetics market was small, dominated by black-owned companies and hair-care products. In 1965, Flori Roberts, a white woman, designed and manufactured the first full line of nationally distributed cosmetics for black women. The largest black-owned cosmetics company is Johnson Products Company, Inc., manufacturers of Afro Sheen hair preparations and Ultra Sheen cosmetics. Naomi Sims, a well-known black fashion model, has promoted, with a fashion-oriented approach, a line of cosmetics for black women that bears her name. More major firms are promoting products designed for the skin tones of the black woman. Revlon has the Polished Ambers line, for example, and Avon has the Shades of Beauty line.

Black women require the same makeup products (except for color) as white women. There are 35 distinctive undertones in the nonwhite skin and only 3 undertones in the white skin. Otherwise there is no basic difference between the two. But there are two special problems in creating makeup for black women, and the major cosmetics houses long neglected them. All skin exfoliates; minute pieces loosen and peel off, resulting in a new coat of skin every 28 days or so. On white women the effect is often unnoticeable. But exfoliation can cause ashen spots to appear on dark skin, unless it is covered with special emollients. Also, the upper and lower lips of black women sometimes differ in color. Even a slight difference is enough to require application of a special base to the lighter lower lip so that a lipstick does not appear to be two different shades.

THE INTERNATIONAL MARKET.   The foreign market for most cosmetics is growing faster than the U.S. market. The best markets for U.S. exports of cosmetics are Canada, South America, the Middle East, the Far East, and Africa. Although cultural differences exist, basically the same types of cosmetics and toiletries are in demand worldwide. As the major companies have discovered, overseas sales are good business. Little or no adjustment need be made in formulas or packaging of items popular in the U.S. to make them best sellers worldwide.

Merchandising Activities

The cosmetics, toiletries, and fragrance business is a highly visible one. The products are used nearly every day by millions of people. In the prestige cosmetics market, competition for restricted distribution to quality department and specialty stores is keen. All of the prestige brand manufacturers want to sell their lines in the most prestigious store in each town. They offer these stores exclusives, specials, and cooperative advertising to guarantee that their products will receive prime locations in these stores. Limiting the stores, or "doors," where their products are available adds to the aura of exclusivity and uniqueness

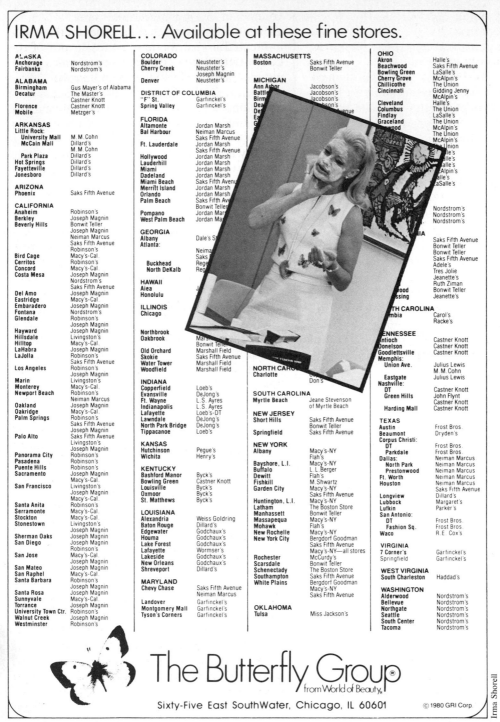
Irma Shorell cosmetics has "doors" in fine stores across the country. Ms. Shorell frequently visits these stores to train their salespeople in the use of her products.

the manufacturer of each line wishes to convey to its target customers. This merchandising technique is used primarily by such prestige cosmetics brands as Estee Lauder, Elizabeth Arden, Clinique, and Irma Shorell.

Since there is a need to inform and educate cosmetics customers, these prestige cosmetics companies place their own **brand-line representatives** behind the counter as "line" salespeople. These line salespeople, also called beauty counselors, are well equipped to perform this important function. They are trained in the end use of the hundreds of items carried in each specific line. In many instances, the salaries of these representatives are paid by the cosmetics company directly. Sometimes the store shares in the payment of their salaries. These representatives are also responsible for stock inventory. They keep detailed records that show what items are and are not selling. The cosmetics companies constantly keep their brand representatives informed about new items, new colors, and new promotions.

National advertising by cosmetics companies is immense. Between television and print media, their advertising will be close to $1 billion in the early 1980s. But advertising in national media is not the only type of sales promotion in which cosmetics firms are engaged. A new product or visiting company specialist or authority is often promoted through editorials in newspapers and magazines. Department stores use charge account mailing inserts and print leaflets to get the customer into the store. Once this is achieved, an "in-store promotion" will entice and intrigue the customer to buy. The in-store promotion may feature makeup artists and beauty authorities from a cosmetic company. Or it may feature purchase inducements such as "gift with purchase" or "purchase with purchase." All of these merchandising activities are widely used to promote the image and sales of prestige cosmetics companies in department and specialty stores.

The mass-distribution cosmetics market involves drugstores, discount stores, variety stores, and large national chains such as Sears, Penney's, and Montgomery Ward. The volume of business done in these stores is growing. As they have become increasingly interested in distribution to these types of retail outlets, large cosmetics companies have planned and implemented new merchandising activities. Until a few years ago, the mass-distribution outlets were limited to selling lines such as Cover Girl, Maybelline, or a store's own label line. At the present time, large, nationally advertised brands such as Max Factor and Revlon are introducing their medium-priced lines into these outlets. This enables customers to select products more easily and thus increases sales. Mass-market retailers are turning to open-access display systems and mass-marketing displays. Max Factor is now selling its Pure Magic line from pegboards. Hanes is test-marketing L'Erin in self-contained units, as it so successfully did with the L'Eggs pantyhose rack display. Revlon's Natural Wonder line has been repackaged for distribution to the mass-market outlets.

The cosmetics industry is attempting to personalize the sale of its products through point-of-purchase information and greater use of samples. More companies are using computerized displays to assist customers on correct choice of makeup and treatment products. Both prestige and mass-distribution lines are using these merchandising activities.

Department and specialty stores are now offering services for hair, skin, and body care. This is a trend that is growing each year. Sales floor salons in department stores, featuring such cosmetic lines as Lancome, Orlane, Payot, and Adrien Arpel, offer the customer advice on complete beauty care and treatment. Beauty regimens, which in past decades have been favored mainly by European women, have today been simplified and modernized to fit American lifestyles. Both products and regimens are becoming more personalized as more and more lines offer analyses of individual needs and tailor their products to these needs.

Industry Trends

The sales volume for cosmetics will reach $10.9 billion in 1981 and is projected to be more than $22 billion by 1990.[2] Some key factors influencing this continuing sales growth in the cosmetics industry are:

- An increased percentage of women in the heavy-spending age group of 25 to 44
- A growing number of women in the work force
- Introduction of new and upgraded products
- An expanded market for male cosmetics
- The growth of the ethnic markets

Competition is very keen in the cosmetics industry, and product obsolescence is rapid. Large research and development departments employed by cosmetics manufacturers are constantly working to improve the quality and performance of their products. The cosmetics business depends upon repeat business, and so a well-made product that performs as claimed means repeat sales and loyal customers. In the prestige cosmetics market, the influence of high-fashion and prêt-à-porter designers continues to grow. This results in a closer tie between beauty and fashion in seasonal color statements. Department and specialty store retailers who are anxious to maintain product exclusivity will be the beneficiaries of this trend toward cosmetics marketed under high-fashion designers' labels.

Fashion has prompted a growing use of cosmetics by both men and women of all ages. Preoccupation with self-image and health will continue to stimulate sales growth. Pollution, especially where populations are highly concentrated, has prompted consumers to become more aware of the protective aspect of face creams and cosmetic preparations. Facial skin-care products are the fastest-growing classification in the cosmetics business, reflecting the emphasis placed on care of the skin by all segments of the buying public. Products carrying a ''treatment,'' or therapeutic, image will continue to grow. Economic affluence also affects the cosmetics industry. More consumers are willing to spend more money in the pursuit of health and beauty and are able to afford complete skin and body care. It is interesting to note that in periods of economic downturn or recession, sales of cosmetics have traditionally been far less affected than have sales of clothing or most other apparel accessories. The reason may be that for only a small investment consumers can still keep in step with new fashion looks and thus they can gain a greater feeling of self-assurance and confidence in their appearance (see Chapter 2).

SHOES

Some primitive peoples wrapped their feet in fur; later, people strapped their feet in sandals. Making shoes was once a painstaking handcraft. But the manufacturing of shoes has developed into an industry with over 300 variations in shoe sizes and widths and over 10,000 different shapes and styles. A fashion which originated in America's early history and which still retains its popularity is the moccasin. It is a shoe that can be worn by both men and women and is one of the first examples of unisex fashion.

Organization and Operation

Shoemaking in America was once exclusively a Yankee industry. The major center for footwear production in the United States is still in New England where the industry had its origin. But another large center of production today is the St. Louis, Missouri, region. The westward movement of the industry came when the Midwest was recognized as an important source of hide supplies and cheaper labor. Brown Shoe Company, the largest American producer of name-brand footwear, is based in St. Louis.

For each type and size of shoe in a producer's line, there must be a **last,** or wooden form in the shape of a foot, over which the shoes are built. The variety of lasts, the quality of materials, and the number and type of manufacturing operations required determine the quality and price of the finished shoe. As many as 200 to 300 operations may be performed by highly skilled workers in the making of an expensive, high-quality shoe.

The range of sizes that shoe manufacturers must produce is enormous. The normal range

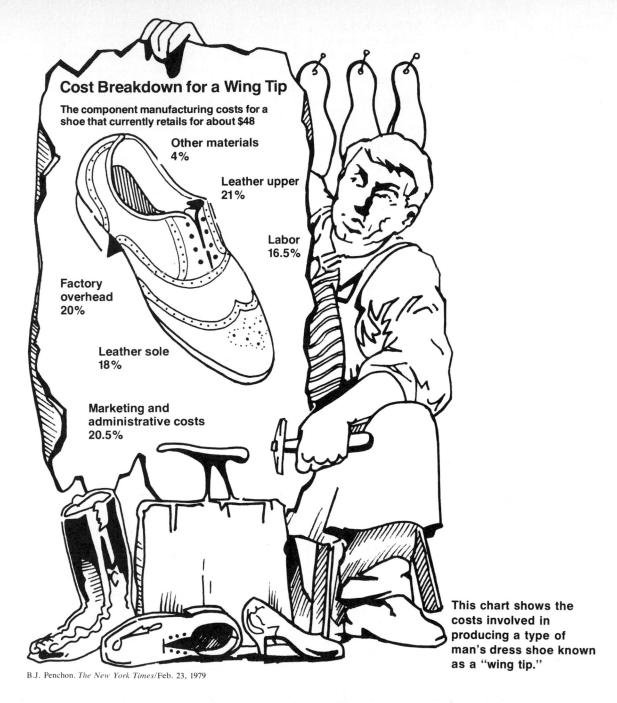

Cost Breakdown for a Wing Tip

The component manufacturing costs for a shoe that currently retails for about $48

Other materials
4%

Leather upper
21%

Labor
16.5%

Factory overhead
20%

Leather sole
18%

Marketing and administrative costs
20.5%

B.J. Penchon. *The New York Times*/Feb. 23, 1979

This chart shows the costs involved in producing a type of man's dress shoe known as a "wing tip."

of women's shoe sizes involves 103 width and length combinations. And this does not include sizes shorter than 4, longer than 11, or wider than D. Inventories, production problems, and capital investments are tremendous compared with those of other fashion-related industries. Thus it is not surprising that giant companies dominate the industry. Among the fashion industries, only cosmetics has a higher percentage of production by giant companies.

However, opportunities for smaller producers do exist in the shoe industry. Unlike manufacturers in most other industries, for example, shoe producers do not have to invest in machinery if they do not want to. Instead they can lease equipment, thus keeping the major portion of their capital available for materials and merchandising activities. Nor do they have to produce lasts, since specialized firms now perform this function. Neither do they have to make every part of the shoe in their own plants; other specialists produce many of the standard components, particularly heels.

Market Centers

As with most fashion industries, New York City is the major U.S. market center for shoes. Most producers maintain permanent showrooms there, regardless of where their manufacturing plants may be located. Foreign footwear producers employ selling agents in the United States who also have showrooms located in this market center. This is also true for United States-based importers. Twice a year, seasonal lines are shown to store buyers and the fashion press. The semiannual shoe show at the New York Coliseum presents lines from many manufacturers, both American and foreign, under one roof. This makes it easy for buyers, store owners, and other fashion-related people to view the whole market. Capsule shoe showings are also held in regional markets such as Dallas, Miami, Chicago, and Los Angeles for the benefit of area buyers and merchants.

Merchandising Activities

The shoe industry has an active national trade association known as the National Shoe Manufacturers Association. Together with the National Shoe Retailers Association, it disseminates technical, statistical, and fashion trend information on footwear. In addition, the leather industry and its associations operate as sources of fashion information for shoe buyers and other retail store executives.

Brand names are a major part of the footwear industry, and manufacturers advertise extensively in national fashion magazines and on national television.

In contrast with most other fashion industries, many of the larger shoe manufacturers operate retail chain organizations of their own. This is a practice known as "dual distribution." The other industry that practices dual distribution is the menswear industry (see Chapter 8). An outstanding example of dual distribution in the shoe industry is the Brown Group, which manufactures Buster Brown shoes for children, Naturalizer and Air Step shoes for women, and Roblee and Regal shoes for men. The Melville Corporation, which manufactures Thom McAn shoes, is another example. All of these shoe brands are sold in retail stores owned by the shoe manufacturers. Frequently these shoe chains also stock related accessories, such as handbags and hosiery.

Some shoe manufacturers also operate in the retail field through leased departments in retail stores. Because of the tremendous amount of capital required to stock a shoe department and the expertise needed to fit and sell shoes, many department and specialty stores lease their shoe departments to shoe manufacturers. Surveys made by the National Retail Merchants Association have repeatedly shown that women's shoe departments are among those most commonly leased by its member stores. Morse Shoe Company, Spencer Shoe Company, and Edison Shoe Company are some of the manufacturers that operate leased shoe departments in stores.

WOMEN'S SHOES. For centuries, little attention was paid to the styling of women's shoes. Their purpose was regarded as purely functional, and it was considered immodest to expose the feminine ankle. Since the 1920s, however, women's feet have been plainly visible, and shoes have developed both in fashion importance and variety. When fashion invaded the shoe industry after World War II, the black or brown all-purpose shoes that were to be worn with any wardrobe disappeared. New and varied leather finishes, textures, plastic and fabric materials, and ranges of colors provided shoe styles that not only kept pace with changes in fashion but in many cases originated fashion trends. Styles have run the fashion gamut from pointed to squared toes, from high to flat heels, and from naked sandals to thigh-high boots.

MEN'S SHOES. A shift in thinking on the part of American men has had a dramatic effect on the merchandising of men's shoes. Dress shoes were once the most important sales category in men's shoe departments in retail stores. They are now being replaced by dress/casual and casual shoes. Casual shoes were once considered appropriate only for the 18 to 25 age group but now are preferred by men of all ages. The return in the 1980s of the classic look, the three-piece suit, and narrower ties is reviving interest in loafers, moccasins, and dressier, classic slip-ons. Although the sales volume for men's shoes is increasing, it is moving at a slower rate than it is in women's shoes.

CHILDREN'S SHOES. Until they are approximately 10 years old, boys and girls take more interest in their shoes than anything else they wear. Maybe this is due in part to the influence of children's stories—the Wizard of Oz, Seven League Boots, and Cinderella, for example—in which shoes have magical powers.

Also, boys and girls must be taken along when shoes are bought and are involved in the purchase decision. From an early age they learn that the correct fit and look of their shoes are important. This early training leads to their view of shoes as the mainstay of a fashion wardrobe.

Industry Trends

The United States is still the world's most lucrative footwear market. Approximately 1 billion pairs retailed at $14 billion in 1979. Sales are projected to be $24 billion by 1985. In 1965 only 12 percent of all shoes sold in the United States were imported. But the number of manufacturing plants in the domestic shoe industry has dropped from 950 in 1969 to about 400 in 1979. The industry now has as many importers as domestic producers. Specification buying by retail buyers and manufacturers in foreign markets, such as Korea, Taiwan, Italy, Spain, and Brazil has been gaining momentum each year. One of the primary reasons for this rise in footwear imports is the continually rising cost of production in the United States.

Domestic manufacturers are experimenting with new and upgraded computer technology to aid in the design and manufacturing of shoes. Producers are thus attempting to meet the problems of foreign competition and to enlarge their market potential. The United States Department of Commerce's Footwear Industry Revitalization program, in operation since July, 1977, is also providing impetus. With a federal grant of $800,000, this program is establishing an industrywide footwear center in Washington, D.C., scheduled to be operational by 1983. The Research Triangle Institute has been commissioned to do an evaluation of shoe-related technologies with the objective of creating a new generation of technology for domestically produced footwear. Another trend, and one supported by the federal government, is the increase in exports of American-made shoes to the rest of the world.

Americans are participating in a greater variety of sports than ever before. This has brought about a proliferation of styles in athletic footwear. Athletic shoes have also become fashion items for people who want to look like athletes, even though they may not participate in any sport. An estimated 90 percent of athletic shoes sold are not strictly used for the purposes for which they were designed. This phenomenal boom in athletic footwear is to a large extent the result of foreign fashion leadership. The success of the Adidas and Puma lines from West Germany and the Tiger line from Japan led American manufacturers to update and restyle their existing athletic footwear lines.

Americans buy about 1 billion pairs of shoes, slippers, and boots a year. About 50 percent are manufactured domestically, and 50 percent are imported.

There is a strong relationship between shoes and the clothes with which they are worn. Greater emphasis on fashion continues to be the major trend in the footwear industry. Shoe designers and manufacturers regularly attend European apparel openings, as do shoe buyers from retail stores, gathering information on international trends in styling. More and more, apparel fashions influence both the styling and color of footwear. Skirt lengths, silhouettes, pants, and sporty or dressy clothes are the fashion keys to shoe designs. It is therefore essential for retailers to coordinate shoes and apparel wherever and whenever they can.

HOSIERY

Until World War I, women's legs were concealed under floor-length skirts and dresses. They were rarely, if ever, seen. When skirt lengths moved up and the female leg became visible, interest in its adornment increased, and the hosiery industry began to grow. However, hosiery's importance as a fashion accessory has been a rather recent development. To a great extent, this has been the result of product improvement, new products, and innovative styling to complement and coordinate with fashion apparel.

History and Development

It was not until the introduction of nylon that hosiery as we know it today became a fashion accessory. Before the introduction of nylon in 1938, women wore seamed silk, cotton, or rayon stockings. Because of its easier care and durability, the new nylon hosiery was eagerly accepted despite its high price.

With the entry of the United States into World War II, nylon production was restricted to war purposes and silk was unavailable. Because the hosiery that was available was heavy and unattractive, women began to go barelegged and used leg makeup to give the effect of sheer stockings. The barelegged look became very popular, and when nylon became available again, the industry developed sheerer weights (deniers) and seamless hosiery which would give this look.

Fashion first entered the hosiery picture in the 1950s with the introduction of colors other than black or flesh tones. But it was not until the 1960s that hosiery became a major fashion accessory. With the shorter skirt—eventually evolving into the miniskirt and micromini—colors, textures, and weights of stockings were created in great variety. It was at this time in fashion history that pantyhose were introduced and became a fantastic success.

The great popularity of pantyhose brought about the introduction of seamless pantyhose and figure-control pantyhose. In the 1970s when the popularity of pants for women was at its peak, knee-high and ankle-high hosiery became popular. Together with pantyhose they captured the major share of the hosiery business.

Organization and Operation

The hosiery industry consists primarily of large firms, many of which are divisions of huge textile or apparel conglomerates. The largest concentration of these hosiery plants is found in the Southern states, with more than half of them in North Carolina.

Most hosiery mills perform all of the steps necessary for the production of finished hosiery. Some smaller mills may perform the knitting operation only, contracting out the finishing processes.

Full-fashioned seamed hosiery is flat-knit to size and length specifications on high-speed machines. These machines shape the hosiery as it is knitted. The outer edges are then stitched together on special sewing machines, after which the hosiery is dyed. Each stocking acquires permanent shape through a heat-setting process called **boarding.** Then the stockings are carefully matched into pairs. Their welts are stamped with a brand name or other appropriate information, and the pairs are packaged.

Seamless hosiery and pantyhose are circular-knit to size and length specifications on high-speed machines. Again, these machines shape the item during the knitting process. Subsequent steps are dyeing, boarding, pairing, stamping, and packaging, as for full-fashioned hosiery.

Since hosiery is knitted in the greige (unfinished) state, most manufacturers can produce branded and unbranded hosiery in the same mill. The greige goods are then dyed, finished, stamped, and packaged to specification for national brand, private brand, or for unbranded customers.

Market Centers

Although most hosiery is produced in the South, New York City is the market center where manufacturers maintain permanent showrooms. Retail buyers visit these showrooms semiannually. Here they select seasonal lines and find out about the national advertising programs of the big producers. Smaller mills frequently employ the services of selling agents. These agents maintain offices in New York City for closer contact with retail and fashion markets.

Merchandising Activities

Traditionally, the women's hosiery industry concentrated its merchandising activities almost exclusively on the promotion and sale of nationally advertised brands. Recently, however, the industry has been merchandising its products for private labeling or for sale in vending machines and from self-service displays in supermarkets and drugstores.

NATIONAL BRANDS. Major hosiery producers sell their brand lines to a wide variety of retail stores across the country. The producers aggressively advertise these lines on a national basis in magazines, newspapers, and television. They also usually supply cooperative advertising, display aids, and fashion assistance to help promote these national brands at the store level. Major national brands include Hanes, Burlington, Round-the-Clock, and Kayser-Roth. Givenchy, Christian Dior, and Schiaparelli are major designers' names now used for prestige lines manufactured by these national companies.

PRIVATE BRANDS. Chain organizations, groups of retail stores, and some individual stores have developed their own private brands in competition with or in addition to nationally advertised brands of hosiery. There are many advantages to a private label brand for the retailer. The cost of the hosiery is usually less because there is no built-in charge for advertising as there is for national brands. The private brand can be made up in colors and constructions that will match customer profile specifications. Because the private brand is not available elsewhere, price promotions are easier. Customer shopping loyalty can also be built upon the exclusivity of the private brand. Some private label brands are Sears' Best, Macy's Supremacy and Marchioness brands, and Lerner's own brand.

MASS-MERCHANDISED BRANDS. More and more self-service stores such as supermarkets, discount stores, and drug chains are beginning to carry hosiery. With this change in the channels of retail distribution, hosiery manufacturers are developing low-priced, packaged hosiery that can be profitably sold in these stores. Each of these brands offers a good choice of styles and colors. Each manufacturer supplies attractive, self-service stock fixtures and promotes its brand through national advertising. Examples of mass-merchandised brands are L'Eggs, made by Hanes Hosiery, and No Nonsense, made by Kayser-Roth.

Industry Trends

Fashion trends have a tremendous influence on sales in the hosiery industry. For example, when skirts are shorter or have leg-revealing silhouettes, texture and color in hosiery become more important. "All-in-ones"—pantyhose with built-in panties—were the answer for the tighter fitting pants and skirts of a recent fashion look. Apparel manufacturers have recently worked with hosiery manufacturers to design pantyhose that are both texture- and color-coordinated to their sportswear. The hosiery is to be displayed with the apparel to convey a total fashion look.

Hosiery manufacturers are devoting more time and money to new developments in product manufacturing and research. The industry is becoming more fashion-oriented and is working very closely with apparel manufacturers to offer the customer a coordinated fashion look.

The inventory of most hosiery departments includes conventional stockings, pantyhose, casual legwear, bodywear, and casual footwear. Bodywear and casual legwear are relatively high-priced retail items, while packaged hosiery is low-priced. As a result, some stores have made separate departments out of these two different categories.

The interest of the buying public in health and body-building activities has produced a new fashion item—bodywear, which consists of coordinated leotards, tights, and wrap skirts. Because bodywear has price and brand-name advantages over competing merchandise in swimwear, active sportswear, and junior sportswear departments, its sales have boomed in many hosiery departments.

The varying needs and wants of hosiery customers have prompted hosiery manufacturers to design entirely new items. Control-top pantyhose, support hose, outsizes (for the stout), and pantyhose/panty combinations are examples.

With the increasing importance of new distribution channels, such as mass merchants and supermarkets, hosiery manufacturers have developed new packaging and marketing strategies for these markets. The success of the L'Eggs and No Nonsense brands has prompted the industry to look to more innovative and technologically advanced methods for introducing and marketing hosiery fashions.

If the girl's wear department has an accessories outpost, these terrycloth bodysuits by Danskin may be carried there as well as with girl's sportswear.

HANDBAGS

The ways in which people carry their belongings reflect the times in which they live. Through the centuries, small sacks vied with pockets as places to keep belongings. In the eighteenth century the **reticule,** forerunner of the modern handbag, was carried by fashion leaders of the day. The modern handbag has become more than a receptacle for needed coins or personal possessions. It is now a fashion item that is used to reflect a person's unique personality and style.

Handbags are used for different needs, moods, fashion statements, and occasions. They are part of the total fashion look. Handbag styles vary from the most casual to the most formal. Well-dressed women use their handbags to dramatize, harmonize, or contrast with their fashion apparel. For example, a woman may have a tailored handbag to wear to the office, a small "disco bag" for evening wear, and a roomy sports sack to wear to the health club.

In recent years, handbags and carryalls for men have entered the fashion picture on a limited basis. It will be interesting to watch the extent to which this fashion develops. At the present time, this fashion has had much more success with European men than with American men.

Organization and Operation

Compared with other fashion industries, the handbag industry is quite small. The number of domestic firms producing handbags is diminishing each year with the increase in imported handbags made in Europe, South America, and the Far East. Domestic firms producing handbags are concentrated in New York and New England. More and more frequently, the smaller firms, employing from 20 to 30 people, are closing. The remaining firms are becoming larger and more diversified in order to obtain a larger share of the consumer market.

The quality of a handbag depends first of all on the quality of the materials used, whether they be leather, fabric, plastic, or novelties. Handbags are constructed in layers of different materials, starting with the outer layer of leather or other goods and finishing with the inside lining. In addition to the physical elements that go into a handbag, the skill of the maker is critical to the quality of the final product.

Fashion and personal taste determine whether a handbag should blend or contrast with apparel color. Shapes may be small or large, pouch or swagger, draped or boxlike. In general they are designed to suit the size of the wearer and the currently popular apparel silhouette.

Market Centers

The handbag market center is in New York City, close to the major garment industries. Permanent showrooms are maintained there, and seasonal lines may be viewed at least twice a year with the seasonal showings of fashion apparel.

Merchandising Activities

Although manufacturers' brand names are relatively unimportant in the handbag industry, there has been tremendous growth in designer-name handbags. Famous fashion designers such as Pierre Cardin, Bill Blass, Calvin Klein, and Diane Von Furstenberg have entered into licensing agreements with handbag manufacturers. It is not always true that a handbag carrying a designer name has actually been created by that designer. But under a licensing agreement, the designer reserves the right to demand that certain quality standards be observed in the production of all handbags carrying his or her name.

Few handbag manufacturers are large enough to advertise on a national basis in newspapers or on television. The customer's impression of what is new and fashionable in handbags is gained primarily through stores where they are coordinated and displayed with fashion apparel. "Total look" advertising in newspapers and magazines also keeps the customer up to date on handbag fashion.

Industry Trends

Unfortunately, the handbag industry is not making a concerted effort to improve manufacturing and marketing techniques. Faced with severe competition from foreign imports, many domestic handbag manufacturers have themselves become importers of foreign-made handbags. These importers employ domestic creativity and expertise to design styles and then have the handbags manufactured in countries where the wage scale is much lower. By the mid-1980s, almost 50 percent of all handbags sold in the United States will be imported. The industry's trade association—the National Handbag Association—is lobbying for tighter import restrictions and for financial adjustment assistance to domestic firms hurt by foreign competition.

Some of the larger manufacturers have recently diversified their lines to include styles for men. Still others are adding luggage, small leather goods, such as wallets and key cases, and coordinated belts to their product lines.

The handbag industry is attempting to provide a complete wardrobe of fashion handbags to fashion-conscious men and women through continued improvements in styling, the use of new and exciting textures and colors, and total coordination with fashion apparel.

JEWELRY

Since the earliest civilizations, jewelry has played a significant and varied role in people's lives. Jewels have been viewed as agents of supernatural powers, as symbols of love, as mediums of exchange, and as effective offerings to the gods. Men as well as women have been intrigued by and have worn necklaces, bracelets, and other jewelry ornaments. The chains and medallions worn by some fashion-conscious men in the last decade are no great departure from the protective amulets worn by men in ancient Rome as necklaces. Tibetan Buddhists wore court necklaces derived from Lamaist rosaries, and Renaissance portraits frequently show men wearing heavy gold necklaces.

Organization and Operation

Modern methods of making jewelry may be less arduous than those of earlier times, but essentially they involve the same steps. Modern jewelry makers melt and shape metal, cut and carve stones, and string beads and shells. Jewelry designers still use enamel, glass, ceramic materials, and natural mineral formations to express their creative ideas.

The jewelry industry in the United States is divided into two groups, primarily on the basis of intrinsic value or quality of product. One group is referred to as **fine jewelry;** and the other is termed **costume** or **fashion jewelry.**

FINE JEWELRY. The counterpart of haute couture apparel is fine jewelry. Only precious metals such as gold and all of the platinum family (palladium, rhodium, and iridium) are used to make fine jewelry. Silver is also considered a precious metal but is not used as widely as gold and platinum. Precious metals are too soft to be used alone. They are therefore combined with one or several other metals to produce an alloy hard enough to retain a desired shape and to hold stones securely.

Stones used in fine jewelry are known as **gemstones** to distinguish them from those stones suitable only for industrial use. Gemstones are natural stones and are classified as either precious or semiprecious. **Precious stones** include the diamond, emerald, ruby, sapphire, and the real, or oriental, pearl. **Semiprecious stones** include the amethyst, garnet, opal, jade, and other natural stones that are less rare and costly but still beautiful. In recent years, chemists have succeeded in creating synthetic rubies, sapphires, and diamonds, but none are yet suitable for use in fine jewelry.

The fine jewelry industry is essentially a handcraft industry. The lapidary, or stonecutter, is an artisan who transforms dull-looking stones into gems of beauty by cutting, carving, or polishing them.

In the creative fine jewelry houses, as in haute couture apparel houses, design, production, and retail sales all usually take place under one roof and one management. Many fine jewelry firms sell only the merchandise they manufacture, much of which is custom designed.

COSTUME JEWELRY. Costume or fashion jewelry may be compared to mass-produced apparel. Materials used in the manufacture of costume jewelry are plastics, wood, glass, brass, or other base metals (such as aluminum, copper, tin, and lead). Some of these materials may be coated with more costly metals like gold, rhodium, or silver. Stones and simulated pearls used in costume jewelry are made from clay, glass, or plastic. While they are attractive and interesting in surface appearance, they are less costly and have none of the more desirable properties of natural stones.

Before the 1920s, most jewelry worn by both men and women was made from gold. It was often set with precious or semiprecious stones. Silver was seldom used as a jewelry metal because it was too soft to hold stones securely. It also quickly tarnished. Rarely was jewelry in those days designed to accessorize or complement apparel styles of a period. Coco Chanel has been credited with changing this. In the 1920s she introduced long strands of frankly-fake pearls to be worn with the widely popular short, sleeveless, collarless, elongated-torso dresses of that period. It is interesting to note that Chanel not only introduced this jewelry style but wore it herself throughout the rest of her life. Long strands of pearls became her trademark. The new type of jewelry was aptly called "costume," since its design was originally intended, and still continues, to be influenced by the neckline, bodice, and sleeve details of apparel design. In the 1960s, Kenneth Jay Lane designed costume jewelry that looked so real that social and other fashion leaders preferred to wear it rather than their own authentic jewels.

Most of the large, popular-priced costume jewelry houses employ stylists who design seasonal lines or adapt styles from higher-priced lines. Most of this jewelry is produced in New England and the Middle Atlantic states, with Providence, Rhode Island, as the major production center of the costume jewelry industry. Facilities concentrated there produce jewelry to the specifications of individual firms, much the same as apparel contractors work with apparel manufacturers and jobbers. Mass-production methods prevail. In contrast to the handshaping of metal used in fine jewelry, the metal used in costume jewelry is usually cast by melting it and then pouring the molten metal into molds to harden. Finally, designs may be applied to the hardened metal by painting its surface with colored enamel or etching the metal by machine.

A great portion of costume jewelry is mass-produced by large companies such as Monet, Marvella, Swank, Accessocraft, and Bergere. But there is also a trend toward smaller manufacturers in this market. Individuals with creative talent open small retail and/or wholesale operations catering to customers interested in individualized styling and trend-setting fashions. This is an outgrowth of the handcraft movement of the 1960s and 1970s, when single entrepreneurs designed, created, and sold their own designs and merchandise.

BRIDGE
JEWELRY DEPARTMENT.

With the dramatic increases in the price of gold and silver in the 1980s, jewelry designers and retailers sought ways to meet the public's demand for reasonably priced authentic jewelry. A solution was the creation of "bridge" lines and "bridge" departments. The general definition of a **bridge jewelry department** is a department that forms a bridge—in price, materials, and newness—between costume and fine jewelry.

The recognition of sterling silver as a precious metal and the boom of the American Indian turquoise jewelry from 1970 to 1975 also prompted some of the larger department and specialty stores to create bridge departments for these new categories. More recently,

The natural splendor of coral. Here, our stunning, two-strand fantasy necklace of lustrous branch coral. It's just one from our uniquely elegant collection. And because it's semi-precious, it's of paramount import to glamour now! In angelskin red, by Carol for Eva Graham. 18", $75. Semi-Precious Boutique, Fashion Jewelry Collections, Street Floor—where we are all the things you are.

Saks Fifth Avenue

Bridge jewelry departments often feature semiprecious jewelry.

bridge jewelry departments are those in which merchandise is classified on the basis of one of the following: (1) price points, (2) precious metal, (3) fashion newness, (4) karat of gold.

Stores such as Marshall Field, Neiman-Marcus, Broadway Department Stores, and the May Company have bridge departments that carry gold-filled, vermeil, sterling silver, and some 14-karat fashion jewelry. Ivory, turquoise, coral, and other semiprecious stones set in high-fashion designs are also part of bridge departments' inventories.

Marketing Centers

New York City is the principal market center for both fine and costume jewelry. Major firms maintain permanent showrooms there as a convenience to store buyers and also to keep in close contact with developments in other segments of the fashion industry. Los Angeles also has a fast-growing jewelry center that has become an important source of Asian jewelry, particularly jade and pearls.

Seasonal showings, held semiannually, are sponsored by the industry's trade association, the Jewelry Industry Council. Retailers of both fine and costume jewelry attend these showings to preview fashion trends for the coming season, to keep abreast of developments in the industry, and to buy for their seasonal needs.

Merchandising Activities

Fine jewelry manufacturers traditionally have concentrated on providing a wide range of fairly basic items, such as diamond rings and watches. They provide their store customers with a wide range of services and, in many cases, some form of advertising assistance. With the exception of watches, brand names are relatively unknown in this branch of the jewelry industry.

Leased jewelry departments are fairly common in the merchandising of fine jewelry. A large amount of capital is required to provide adequate assortments, and specialized knowledge is needed to sell this merchandise. Therefore, large-scale operators, who in many cases

are also manufacturers, provide retail stores with stock, trained personnel, and advertising. They return a percentage of sales as rent to the host store. An example is the Zale Company, which operates leased departments in many stores.

The larger costume jewelry firms offer seasonal lines so broad that they can easily adapt to whatever trend fashion may be taking. Because they contract the production of most of their merchandise, emphasis can swiftly be switched from less popular items to those in greater demand. The larger firms also market much of their merchandise under brand names and advertise widely in national consumer publications.

Some of the larger costume jewelry firms offer advertising assistance in the form of advertising mats or cooperative advertising allowances. Some firms help to plan and maintain retail store assortments. Others supply display fixtures. Still others offer fashion guidance and traveling representatives to help train retail salespeople and to serve customers on the retail selling floor.

Industry Trends

Today, all branches of the jewelry industry are placing greater emphasis on producing designs that complement current apparel fashions. As an example, when turtlenecks became popular, jewelry producers began designing and offering long chains and pendants that looked graceful on high necklines. When sleeveless apparel is in fashion, bracelets are prominent in producers' lines. When prints are popular in apparel, more tailored jewelry styles are usually featured.

Some fine jewelry firms are broadening their lines. Traditionally known for prompt service, fine workmanship, and high prices, several such firms today also offer costume jewelry of original design and excellent quality at modest prices.

Some of the larger costume jewelry manufacturers, especially in the men's field, have begun to adopt a "big business" attitude toward diversification of product, although this is not yet a general industry practice. For example, Speidel, traditionally a watchband producer, has had excellent response to their line of men's colognes. Swank, traditionally a producer of men's cuff links, tie tacks, tie clasps, and related jewelry items, has diversified into colognes, sunglasses, travel accessories, and a variety of men's gifts.

The jewelry industry, like most other fashion accessories industries, is attracting the attention of an increasing number of apparel designers. Pierre Cardin and Christian Dior are examples of designers who are entering into licensing agreements with better costume jewelry producers.

GLOVES

Historically, gloves have served many purposes besides the obvious ones of protection and warmth. At one time, an English knight going into battle carried his lady's glove on his sleeve as a good luck charm. In the exchange of property, giving a glove once symbolized good faith in the transaction. Gloves have also been used to denote rank or status. Prior to the sixteenth century, for instance, only men of the clergy or of noble rank wore gloves.

Today, gloves are worn both as a costume accessory and for protection and warmth. To be in fashion, gloves must closely relate in styling, detail, and color to current apparel fashion. For example, fashions in women's glove lengths are largely determined by the fashionable length of sleeves, particularly coat and suit sleeves. Fashionable apparel trimmings also often find their counterparts in glove ornamentation. Just as there are classic styles in apparel, so, too, are there classic styles in gloves. Examples are the untrimmed, white, wrist-length glove for wear on dress occasions, and the "suit" glove, which extends a few inches beyond the wrist, for more general wear.

Organization and Operation

In the early days of the twentieth century, fashion interest focused on the well-gloved hand, and the glove business flourished in the United States. The glove material most favored by fashion at that time was leather. Today, however, knit and woven fabric gloves dominate the field.

In the production of leather gloves, most of the manufacturing operations are hand-guided. In some cases, they are done completely by hand. As a result, glove factories have remained small, few machines are required, and comparatively few workers are employed in any one factory. Moreover, producers tend to specialize, performing just one manufacturing operation, such as cutting or stitching. The other operations are farmed out to nearby plants, each of which performs its own specialty.

In contrast to the methods employed in the production of leather gloves, much of the production of fabric gloves is mechanized. The most favored and durable glove fabric used today is a double-woven fabric. It is possible to use almost any fiber in producing this particular type of fabric. Knit gloves are usually made of woolen, acrylic, or cotton string yarns.

Today fabric gloves are produced in various parts of the country. Gloversville, New York, however, remains the major production center for both fabric and leather gloves, with several plants producing both types.

Market Centers

The major market center for both leather and fabric gloves is in New York City. Here many glove firms maintain permanent showrooms where they show seasonal lines to buyers. The typical glove firm offers a very wide and versatile assortment of both domestic and imported gloves in a wide range of prices.

Some better-known glove resources are Hansen, Kayser-Roth, and Aris Glove. Kayser-Roth produces gloves at many price points, including expensive designer lines under the Halston label. Aris Glove manufactures fine leather gloves and also the Isotoner glove. A special construction and fabric cause the hand to be "massaged" during the wearing of this glove.

Merchandising Activities

In general, the merchandising activities of the women's glove industry have tended to lag behind those of other fashion accessories industries. Compared with the dollars spent on consumer advertising by other segments of the fashion industry, outlays for glove advertising are quite modest. Only a few large producers with nationally distributed brand lines have actively promoted their products or offered even limited merchandising services to their retail store customers. In recent years, however, because of stagnating sales and competition from imports (particularly of leather gloves), many glove producers have begun to reevaluate their merchandising techniques. For example, some producers are now packaging many styles of stretch gloves that can be sold from self-service fixtures. Another technique is the packaging of matching gloves, hats or caps, and scarfs in sets for self-service sales. This is a means of increasing the market for glove manufacturers as well as building volume. To help reduce the amount of inventory many store departments carry knit gloves in small, medium, and large sizes only and have many styles in stretch fabrics where one size fits all.

To add interest and variety to the glove selection, many manufacturers now produce gloves lined with fur, silk, and cashmere. They are also designing and manufacturing styles for specific sports—ski gloves and mittens, golf gloves, tennis gloves, and driving gloves, for example.

Although most of the larger producers of women's gloves employ fashion stylists, few make their services available to retail store accounts except on rare occasions. Sales-training aids have been limited mainly to color charts.

For years the glove industry has maintained a trade association known as the National Association of Glove Manufacturers, with headquarters in Gloversville, New York. This association's activities, however, have focused mainly on tariff questions and federal agency regulations and rulings rather than on industry and product publicity.

Industry Trends

Sales of domestically-produced leather gloves have suffered considerably in recent years from the competition of less-expensive imports. To meet this challenge, the industry is trying to improve manufacturing procedures in order to reduce costs. In addition, improved materials are resulting from product research and development in the leather industry. These are expected to increase the market potential of domestically-produced leather gloves. For example, many leather gloves today are hand washable and come in a wide range of fashion colors.

MILLINERY

At one time, a woman did not consider herself dressed unless she was wearing a hat. After decades of prosperity, the millinery industry began to decline in the years following World War II. Because of the more casual approach to women's dress and the popularity of beehive and bouffant hairstyles, millinery sales hit bottom in 1960. During the freewheeling 1960s and 1970s a hat was worn only on the coldest of winter days, and strictly for warmth, not for fashion.

During this time, the millinery industry and its active trade association, the National Millinery Institute, researched, publicized, and campaigned in an extensive effort to reverse the trend, but with little success. This situation served as an example of the fashion principle that no amount of sales promotion can change the direction in which fashion is moving.

However, accelerated interest in a variety of fur head coverings for both men and women during recent years has improved and extended the market potential of millinery. With the return of glamour and the classic looks predicted for the eighties, a new breed of young, versatile, millinery designers is working toward the return of millinery as a fashion necessity. It is also predicted that, after a generation of hatlessness, men's headwear will be the hottest item in haberdashery.

INTIMATE APPAREL

Intimate apparel, sometimes referred to as "inner fashions" or "body fashions," is the trade term for women's foundations, lingerie, and loungewear. As a rule, intimate apparel is not usually considered a fashion accessory by producers, retailers, or even customers. It is considered so in this chapter, however, because these garments are as important in achieving a desired look or effect as the more visible accessories such as handbags or shoes. Also, in the past two decades, both sleepwear and loungewear designers have created styles of significant fashion interest.

Historically, women's intimate apparel was produced by three separate industries: the foundations industry, the lingerie industry, and the robe industry. Today, however, the close fashion relationship between foundation garments, lingerie, and robes (now called loungewear) has brought the industries closer together. It has encouraged mergers among firms that formerly specialized in only one type of intimate apparel. And, as with other segments of the fashion business, the designer name has had major impact.

The Foundations Industry

Classified as **foundations** are such undergarments as brassieres, girdles, panty-girdles, garter belts, corsets, and corselettes (one-piece garments with a brassiere top and a girdle bottom).

HISTORY
AND DEVELOPMENT. The foundations industry began with the factory production of corsets just after the Civil War, when Warner Brothers opened its first plant in Bridgeport, Connecticut. At that time, the bell-shaped silhouette was at the height of its popularity. To achieve the tiny waist required by the fashionable bell silhouette (and its successors, the bustle-back silhouette and the Gibson Girl look), women wore foundations of sturdy, unyielding cotton. These were reinforced with vertical stays of whalebone or steel. Front or back lacing permitted varying degrees of waist constriction to achieve the desired effect.

The foundations industry experienced a drastic change in customer demand in the 1920s when the fashion shifted to straight, loose styles in apparel. These required little corseting but did demand flattening of the bosom. Bandagelike bras were worn to minimize the bust, while girdles controlled any conspicuous bulges below the waistline.

In the 1930s, the silhouette again became more feminine and softly curved. Women coaxed their figures into the appropriate lines with two new types of foundations, more comfortable than anything available before: the two-way stretch girdle and the cup-type brassiere. These innovations heralded a trend toward foundations that molded the figure gently while permitting freedom of movement. They also reflected the fashion for easy fit in outerwear, with definite but not exaggerated curves. In the past three decades, further technological advances have enabled the foundations industry to produce softer, more comfortable, and lighter-weight undergarments. These garments come with better shape-retention properties and in a wider assortment of styles for various figure types.

Brassieres are a good example of the radical style changes that have occurred in foundation garments in the last 50 years. During this period, brassiere styling has evolved from the original bandage type, to cup form, to fiber-filled, to wire-supported, to the "no-bra" bra, to the molded (rather than seamed) bra.

Today, foundation garments coax or mold a body; they do not harness it. Moreover, they can be comfortable, light, soft, and pretty, all at the same time.

MARKET CENTERS. The foundations industry, like nearly all other fashion-influenced industries, has its principal market center in New York City. Here the major firms in the industry maintain permanent showrooms. The industry's trade associations, the Associated Corset and Brassiere Manufacturers and the Intimate Apparel Council of the AAMA schedule and publicize market weeks here in January and in June.

MERCHANDISING
ACTIVITIES. Brand names have always been important in the foundations industry, and much of the industry's merchandising activity has been directed toward their promotion. The major foundations producers widely advertise their brand names—such as Lily of France, Formfit, and Warner—in both trade and consumer publications. Ads in consumer publications often mention the names of retail stores that stock the featured merchandise. In addition, many firms offer cooperative advertising arrangements to their retail store customers. Merchants use such cooperative allowances to stretch their own advertising budgets and to tie in at the local level with national advertising of the brands they carry.

Historically, the foundations industry has supplied many services to its retail store customers. Producers have helped train retail salespeople and have offered retail store buyers assistance in planning assortments and controlling stocks.

INDUSTRY TRENDS. Trends in the foundations industry are similar to those of other fashion-related industries. The trend toward mergers in other industries during and immediately following World War II, however, did not develop in the intimate apparel industries until the late 1950s. At that time, customers began demanding color-coordinated foundation garments. Many small firms that made either brassieres or girdles saw an advantage in joining with one another to produce matched colors. In time, many such collaborating firms merged their ownership and operations in order to meet the competition of larger firms. Some merged with lingerie producers. Others explored the advantages of merging with ready-to-wear producers. Since the introduction of figure-control features in bathing suits, some foundations firms have merged with swimsuit makers or set up their own swimsuit divisions. In addition, some are making "body suits,"—control garments that are completely made of stretch material, with a panty-type bottom and a T-shirt or camisole-type top. Although intended as undergarments, if done in attractive materials they closely resemble ready-to-wear "body shirts" and often can be used as such.

The Lingerie and Loungewear Industries

Lingerie is the undergarment category that includes slips, petticoats, panties of all types, nightgowns, and pajamas. Slips, petticoats, and panties are considered "daywear," while nightgowns and pajamas are classified as "sleepwear." **Loungewear** is the trade term for the category that includes robes, bed jackets, and housecoats. However, some lingerie firms have expanded and diversified their product lines to include loungewear items, and some lingerie and loungewear firms have merged. It is therefore sometimes difficult to draw a clear-cut line between the two industries.

Until the 1930s, most mass-produced lingerie and loungewear were purely functional, with little variety in style or seasonal change. Cotton was the principal fabric, but wool was also used in extremely cold climates. Silk appeared only in luxury styles. In the 1930s, rayon began to be used extensively and remained a basic fabric material throughout the 1940s. During all of this time, lingerie and loungewear were considered staple items, relatively untouched by fashion and produced in limited styles and colors.

The introduction of easy-care, man-made textile fibers in the 1950s revolutionized these industries, and lingerie and loungewear stepped into the fashion spotlight. Previously, only the largest companies had sent fashion experts to the Paris openings to report on the lines and colors featured in new apparel styles. As fashion interest began to center around a total look or fashion theme, women began to develop a feeling for color and design harmony in everything they wore. Consequently, the lingerie and loungewear industries became increasingly aware of the need to keep in touch with the total fashion picture.

Creative lingerie firms today employ top designing talent, often recruiting them from the apparel field. Styling in all three categories —daywear, sleepwear, and loungewear—

Art as Lingerie...on with the Show!

A new kind of gallery opens today, devoted to the concept that art you can wear may well be your most valuable asset (and your most beautiful!)

With this thought in mind, we challenged a group of young artists to play out their fantasies in lingerie. And, what a collection they've created. Daywear, loungewear, dreamwear, all-out entertainment wear in silks, satins, laces, handknits. Embellished with personal touches like hand-painting, appliqué, embroidery. Glorious pieces of art... preciously one-of-a-kind. 100.00 to 2000.00.

Our gallery includes the works of:
Alison Abbott/Lynn Weinberg
Charles Batte
Patt Baumgarten
Carole and Sarelle
Susan DeNoble
Jennifer R. Dule
Lisa Fidler
Beth Goodman
Lorraine Jackson
Claudia Jemmott
Christine Lightfoot
Mary Manly
Jane Nelson
Ria Romano
Robcynth
Ruth Suyenga
Vinette Varvaro
Jean Ward
Marcos Merehi
Lynn Greene

Tomorrow from noon to two, many of the stars of our show will be with us to chat about how they've interpreted Art as Lingerie. Do stop by.

Lingerie Level, New York (355-5900). Open late Mondays and Thursdays.

Art as Lingerie at **bloomingdale's**

It is sometimes difficult to draw a clear-cut distinction between lingerie and loungewear. This elegant robe is really a work of art.

closely follows that of apparel. For example, when silver touches are important in evening and after-five apparel, silvery gowns and negligees are shown in the more expensive lingerie lines. When color-mad prints predominate in apparel, wildly-patterned slips, sleepwear, robes, and panties are featured.

MARKET CENTERS. The principal market center of the lingerie and loungewear industries is New York City. Major firms in these industries publicize market weeks in January and June, held on the same dates as the foundations industry's market weeks. Since many store buyers purchase all three types of merchandise, concurrent market weeks enable them to plan and coordinate purchases and promotions simultaneously. If stores employ separate buyers for each category, those buyers usually work closely with one another in the market, coordinating their purchases and promotional plans for the coming season.

MERCHANDISING ACTIVITIES. Brands are as important in the lingerie and loungewear industries as they are in the foundations industry. In fact, store purchases of lingerie and loungewear are often figured in terms of brand resources rather than categories of merchandise. Like the foundations industry, lingerie and loungewear firms widely advertise their branded lines in both trade and consumer publications. Most firms also offer cooperative advertising arrangements to their retail store customers. While some lingerie and loungewear brands such as Vanity Fair, Barbizon, Lady Lynne, Miss Elaine, and Olga (formerly a foundations designer) continue in popularity, merchandising activities focus more on styling, color, fabric, and well-known designer names than on brands.

Both the American loungewear and lingerie industries cover the major U. S. and European fashion markets today. They provide stores with seasonal color and style charts and with suggestions for relating intimate apparel styles and colors to those of ready-to-wear. Some firms offer assistance in planning and controlling retail assortments. Some of them also help in staging retail sales promotion events, often in cooperation with a textile fiber or fabric producer.

INDUSTRY TRENDS. Trends in the lingerie and loungewear industries parallel those in the foundations industry. There have been an increasing number of mergers, both between lingerie and loungewear firms and between these firms and foundation producers. There also has been an increasing emphasis on fashion-oriented styling and use of fabrics such as chiffon, satin, and panne velvet.

Another trend has been the strong diversification and expansion of product lines. Daywear has now been expanded to include body shirts, chemises, camisole tops, and packaged "little nothings." The latter are bras, bikinis, and halters that are "nonconstructed," in contrast to the more conventional "constructed" brassieres and foundations. Sleepwear has added matching robes and hostess gowns, some of which can be worn for social occasions outside the home as well as for at-home parties. Loungewear has added matching robes and lounging pajamas, both of which can be worn outside the home as well as for at-home occasions.

Increasing quantities of bras, panties, and bikini sets of the nonconstructed type are being produced and packaged for sale on self-selection racks in both conventional and mass-merchandising stores. These enable the stores to increase unit sales without increasing selling expenses.

Fashion continues to be the major competitive tool in the marketing of intimate apparel. Nevertheless, vast quantities of intimate apparel are still sold on the basis of function and in slowly changing styles. These involve minimum risk for producer and retailer and minimum price to the consumer. But in the medium to upper price brackets, fashion rather than intrinsic value is the motivating element. It is in these categories that the work of name designers is beginning to appear. Halston, Diane Von Furstenberg, Christian Dior, Geoffrey Beene, Clovis Ruffin, and Givenchy have all designed or sponsored the design of women's lingerie and loungewear in recent years.

Keeping in step with fashion has multiplied the industries' problems. But it has also enlarged their opportunities to sell more goods at higher prices while giving greater satisfaction to consumers.

OTHER FASHION ACCESSORIES

Other fashion accessories include neckwear, belts, umbrellas, small leather goods, handkerchiefs, sunglasses, and wigs. While once some of the industries producing these accessories were quite large, today they are relatively small. The output of industries producing these accessories tends to fluctuate in direct relationship to the fashion importance of each to the current popular look. The main showrooms of the producers are in New York City, although much of the merchandise in these categories is manufactured in foreign countries.

One innovative and successful approach to merchandising these fashion accessories has been to group them all together into one store department. This department is usually called the dress accessories department and features the merchandise in current fashion in each of these classifications. Depending upon the accepted fashion of the season, one or more of these dress accessories may be prominently featured. When the emphasis is on neck and shoulders, scarfs become important. When emphasis on the waistline is important, belts are featured.

TRADE ASSOCIATIONS—ACCESSORIES

- American Footwear Industry Association
  1611 North Kent Street
  Arlington, Virginia 22209
- Associated Corset and Brassiere Manufacturers
  535 Fifth Avenue
  New York, New York 10017
- Association of Umbrella Manufacturers and Suppliers
  11 West 32 Street
  New York, New York 10001

- Belt Association
  300 West 40 Street
  New York, New York 10018
- Jewelry Industry Council
  608 Fifth Avenue
  New York, New York 10020
- Lingerie Manufacturers Association
  41 East 42 Street
  New York, New York 10017
- Millinery Institute of America
  200 Madison Avenue
  New York, New York 10016
- National Association of Glove Manufacturers
  52 South Main Street
  Gloversville, New York 12078
- National Association of Hosiery Manufacturers
  516 Charlottetown Mall
  Charlotte, North Carolina 28204
- National Handbag Association
  350 Fifth Avenue
  New York, New York 10001
- National Shoe Retailers Association
  200 Madison Avenue
  New York, New York 10016
- Cosmetic, Toiletry and Fragrance Association
  1133 15 Street N.W.
  Washington, D.C. 20005

TRADE PUBLICATIONS—ACCESSORIES

- *Beauty/Fashion*
  48 East 43 Street
  New York, New York 10017
- *Body Fashions/Intimate Apparel*
  757 Third Avenue
  New York, New York 10017
- *Cosmetics & Toiletries*
  Allured Publishing Corporation
  P.O. Box 318
  Wheaton, Illinois 60187
- *Cosmetic, Toiletry and Fragrance Association Journal*
  1133 15 Street N. W.
  Washington, D.C. 20005

- *Drug & Cosmetic Industry*
  757 Third Avenue
  New York, New York 10003
- *Fashion Accessories*
  Business Journals, Inc.
  22 South Smith Street
  Norwalk, Connecticut 06855
- *Footwear Focus*
  National Shoe Retailers Asso.
  200 Madison Avenue
  New York, New York 10016
- *Footwear News*
  7 East 12 Street
  New York, New York 10003
- *Hoisery-Underwear*
  757 Third Avenue
  New York, New York 10017

- *Intimate Fashion News*
  McKay Publishing
  95 Madison Avenue
  New York, New York 10016
- *Jewelers Circular-Keystone*
  Bala Cynwyd, Pennsylvania 19004
- *Leather and Shoes*
  30 Church Street
  New York, New York 1013
- *Wigs, Hats and Accessories*
  22 East 42 Street
  New York, New York 10017
- *Women's Wear Daily*
  7 East 12 Street
  New York, New York 10003

MERCHANDISING VOCABULARY

Define or briefly explain each of the following terms:

Brand-line representatives	**Intimate apparel**
Boarding	**Last**
Bridge jewelry department	**Lingerie**
Cosmetics	**Loungewear**
Costume or fashion jewelry	**Precious stones**
Fine jewelry	**Private label or brand**
Foundations	**Reticule**
Gemstones	**Rubber-banding**
Impulse items	**Semiprecious stones**

MERCHANDISING REVIEW

1. Name the three major industries that make up the intimate apparel, or inner fashions, industry. What types of garments are produced by each? Why are they often regarded, and their products often merchandised, as a single industry?
2. Describe the various merchandising activities currently engaged in by the intimate apparel industries.
3. Name and briefly describe three methods of merchandising women's hosiery.

4. Discuss the merchandising activities of the domestic shoe industry in terms of (a) advertising, (b) maintenance of retail outlets, and (c) leased departments.
5. What is considered the most significant trend in the cosmetics industry today? Briefly discuss other trends of special importance to the cosmetics industry.
6. Name the two major categories of merchandise, produced by the jewelry industry and describe the distinguishing product characteristics of each.
7. What are the major materials used in the production of gloves? Give several examples of how women's apparel fashions influence glove fashions.
8. Discuss the fashion importance of handbags. Of what materials are handbags made?
9. What categories of merchandise are usually to be found in fashion accessories departments today? Discuss the current fashion importance of each category.
10. What factors have contributed to the popularity of "non-constructed" bras, bikinis, and halters in recent years?

MERCHANDISING DIGEST

1. Discuss the following statement and its implications for retail merchants of fashion accessories: "Fashion today emphasizes the total look, and accessories are an essential part of that look."
2. Discuss current trends in the intimate apparel industries as they relate to (a) mergers, (b) diversification of product lines, and (c) styling.
3. Discuss how changing fashions and technological advances have influenced the styling of women's hosiery.

REFERENCES
  [1] From a report by Arthur D. Little Co., *Product Marketing,* January 1978.
  [2] Ibid.

10
FOREIGN FASHION MARKET CENTERS

Relationships among nations today are characterized by technological, economic, and social exchange. As a result, people of the world are more knowledgeable of how others live, what they are concerned about, and what they are wearing. Fashion has become a worldwide force in this exchange of ideas and ideals.

Since World War II, fashion centers and fashion innovation have developed worldwide. Although Paris had traditionally been the center of the Western fashion world, France and the Paris designers were isolated by the war from the rest of the world. Therefore, designers in other countries were forced to develop their own creative abilities to satisfy the fashion needs of their people. Wartime shortages also created the need for innovation in materials, designs, and styles. These in turn led to the acceptance of new fashions.

As World War II came to an end, countries began to rebuild their economies. One of the most important exports that can be developed is a fashion image. Through a fashion image, a country is able to interest consumers in many or all of the factors that contribute to this fashion image—natural resources, local customs, native design, and fashion materials characteristic of that particular country.

Many new or emerging countries use exports as a means to help them develop their technological and economic status. Because textile production and garment production are labor-intensive and require relatively inexpensive machinery, they are usually the first technology-related efforts of an emerging nation. In order to make their exports more attractive and competitive, many foreign governments subsidize their producers of fashion exports. Also, the United States offers lower custom duties on merchandise from emerging or underdeveloped nations to help them become economically more independent. Among these nations today are Malaysia, Sri Lanka, Thailand, and Guatemala.

SHOPPING FOREIGN MARKETS

American fashion merchants are constantly seeking creative and innovative styles to offer their customers. They find that a concept of merchandising fashions from all over the world gives their customers a wider and more economically satisfying choice.

Now that exciting fashion merchandise and fashion designs can be found anywhere in the world, the manner in which American retailers shop these foreign markets is very important. To guarantee that they have the best possible coverage in worldwide fashion markets, buyers use many different shopping methods. The five methods most used for buying foreign fashion merchandise are: (1) buyers' visits to foreign fashion markets; (2) foreign commissionaires or agents; (3) store-owned, foreign buying offices; (4) foreign exporters or selling houses at import fairs or with U.S. showrooms; and (5) American importers.

Each method has many factors in its favor. But because foreign fashion goods are so important to the image of a store, all five methods are generally used to guarantee the most complete coverage of the foreign fashion scene.

The buyer's visit to each foreign fashion capital ensures that a store's foreign fashions will suit the special needs of its target customers. Many times, foreign production and styling have to be adjusted to suit American requirements. Thus the approach to foreign merchandise must be creative. Preparations at home and development work abroad by the buyer help each store maintain this individual approach. Most stores encourage their buyers to spend time investigating the cultural, economic (including retail), and social climate of each foreign country visited. This flavor can then be translated to their customers in the form of imports.

Foreign commissionaires or agents are used by retailers to represent and assist their buyers in a foreign country. A **commissionaire** organization is usually located in a major city of a foreign market area. It is staffed by market representatives, each of whom specializes in a particular category of merchandise. These market representatives keep in constant touch with market developments. They work with visiting retail buyers who want to locate specific types of goods or who simply want to see what the market has to offer. The commissionaire does not make purchases for its store clients, however, unless authorized to do so by an appropriate store executive. The store pays the commissionaire a fee that is usually a percentage of the **first cost** (which is the wholesale price in the country of origin) of any purchase made. The commissionaire then follows up to make sure that the merchandise deliveries are made, and made on time, since this is critical in fashion merchandising.

Store-owned foreign buying offices are maintained by:

- Large department store organizations such as Macy's, Gimbels/Saks, and the May Company department stores.
- The big general merchandise chains such as Sears and Montgomery Ward
- Large resident buying offices such as the Associated Merchandising Corporation

These are used by all the buyers of each company. The store-owned office works year round, advising buyers about new trends and items. It also functions as a follow-up service to ensure prompt delivery and quality control of the foreign merchandise bought in each country. Most large stores and chains maintain a foreign buying office in each of the large fashion capitals of the world, such as Paris, Rome, London, Hong Kong, and Tokyo.

Another way that buyers can shop foreign markets is to attend the foreign import shows produced in the United States. The European Fashion Fair—a semiannual event in New York City—is one of the largest and most prestigious of these. Many foreign countries now participate in or stage their own fashion fairs in the United States. Here buyers and retailers unable to make trips to these countries can view fashions and talk to the designers and manufacturers of each country. France, Italy, Greece, Germany, Israel, Brazil, and Hong Kong are some of the countries that participate in such foreign import fairs.

American importers offer another method of covering foreign fashion markets. Many small retailers do not make overseas trips or use any of the other methods of foreign buying. Shopping the lines of American importers gives them the opportunity to purchase foreign fashion merchandise that would not otherwise be available to them. Although this method limits the opportunity for individualized styling available through the other methods, it allows smaller retailers to offer their customers some of the excitement of foreign styling and merchandise.

Today foreign fashions are selected from one of two categories: "haute couture" and "prêt-à-porter." **Haute couture,** a French term, literally means "fine sewing" but actually has much the same meaning as our own term "high fashion." That is, it includes original styles or designs accepted by a limited group of fashion leaders. These designs are often very expensive, one-of-a-kind creations made for particular customers. The term haute couture is generally used in connection with those design houses that combine luxury fabrics and fine handiwork to create original and trend-setting styles. **Prêt-à-porter,** another French term, means "ready-to-wear," and is similar to our domestic ready-to-wear. Both categories of foreign fashions will be discussed in detail throughout the chapter.

For many years, haute couture was the unchallenged leader of fashion innovation and creativity. Although the term is French and the Paris couture was the world leader, other countries, such as Italy, England, and Spain, had similar groups of fashion designers for prestigious private customers. Fashion started with these designers. The couture showings were reported to loyal and eager fashion-conscious customers worldwide, who immediately demanded replicas and adaptations.

The international character of current designers can be seen from the following chart.

The Twenty-Two Top Talents

The Clairvoyant. Yves St. Laurent
The Cult Characters. Calvin Klein, Ralph Lauren, Geoffrey Beene
The Classicists. Halston, Givenchy, Missoni
The Dramatists. Bill Blass, Mary McFadden, Galanos, Oscar de la Renta, Marc Bohan of Dior, Valentino
The Cut-Ups. Karl Lagerfeld, Claude Montana, Thierry Mugler, Sonia Rykiel, Armani, Perry Ellis, Betsey Johnson, Norma Kamali, Kenzo.
Other talented designers with loyal fans: Jean Muir, Zandra Rhodes, Gianni Versace, Krizia, Fernando Sanchez, Stephen Burrows

Source: Designers selected by Carrie Donovan, *The New York Times,* January 6, 1980.

The new fashion designs were copied overnight in New York, Tokyo, and around the world. The original creators, such as Chanel, Cardin, and Dior, then realized the mass appeal of their work and the potential financial rewards of more extensive production. In the 1960s they began to make prêt-à-porter lines in addition to the couture. These lines were less-expensive, mass-produced versions of their signature looks, but which still reflected the designers' artistic and quality control.

FRANCE

The reputation of Paris as a prime source of fashion inspiration began to develop several centuries ago as the result of many interrelating factors. As an artistic center, Paris was considered ideal by creative apparel designers. Skilled garmentmakers were abundant. Luxury fabrics were readily available, and their producers were willing to work closely with designers to create exclusive materials. Suppliers of high-quality trimmings—laces, embroideries, buttons, sequins, ribbons, and feathers—were plentiful. The court, nobility, and wealthy merchants, along with international visitors to Paris, all supported the growth of the fashion industry.

Historically renowned for original and trend-setting high-fashion collections, today Paris is also an important fashion center for innovative ready-to-wear apparel. In fact, the traditional differences between the worlds of couture and ready-to-wear are fading. These reasons will be discussed later in this chapter.[1]

Among all the fashion collection capitals in Europe, Paris is still the cradle of the fashion world. The major fashion changes are usually born there. They are then seen, reported on, adopted, and adapted throughout the rest of the world.

The cultural development of France in the last several centuries has led to this fashion leadership. French culture during the reign of the Bourbons and through the time of Napoleon III set the standard for elegance.

Paris Couture

A **couture house** is an apparel firm for which a designer creates original styles. The proprietor or designer of a couture house is known as a **couturier,** if male, or **couturiere,** if female. Most Paris couture houses are known by the names of the designers who head them—Yves St. Laurent, Givenchy, Ungaro, and Cardin, for example. Sometimes, however, a couture house may keep the name of its original designer even after the designer's death. Marc Bohan, for example, designs under the Dior name.

France has been a fashion leader from the year 1858, when the house of Charles Frederick Worth, generally regarded as the father of the Paris couture, opened its doors. Following Worth and beginning about 1907, Paul Poiret contributed to and continued the great fashion legend that was Paris. Poiret was the first to stage fashion shows. His oriental balls were all part of the opulence that characterized Paris as the center of the fashion scene. Paul Poiret was also the first to branch out into the related fields of perfume, accessories, fabric design, and interior decoration.

In 1868, an elite couture trade association called the Chambre Syndicale de la Couture Parisienne came into being. Membership in the **Chambre Syndicale** was by invitation only and was restricted to couture houses that agreed to abide by strict rules. For membership in the Chambre Syndicale today:

- A formal written request must be presented to and voted on by the body.
- Workrooms must be established in Paris. (It is preferred that the creative production be based in Paris also.)
- Collections must be presented twice a year on the date in January and July established by the Chambre Syndicale.
- A collection should consist of 75 or more designs.
- Three models must be employed by the house throughout the year.
- A minimum of 20 workers must be employed in the couture operation.

The Chambre Syndicale has remained strong in France by providing many needed services for the entire French fashion industry —for ready-to-wear as well as couture. For the ready-to-wear designers there is the Fédération Française de la Couture du Prêt-à-Porter des Couturiers et des Createurs de Mode, part of the official Chambre Syndicale. Many services are provided by the Chambre Syndicale:

- It represents all members and advises on law, taxes, and on many aspects of employment.
- It lobbies by carrying on negotiations with the various branches of government that cover the industry.
- It polices the industry itself to prevent misuses of creative design.
- It registers designs and serves as the protection agency against design piracy. A garment made by a Syndicale member is photographed from the back, front, and sides. The design is registered with the Chambre Syndicale. If a registered design is copied in France, the act is punishable by law.
- It coordinates openings, setting the dates and hours to avoid an overlapping of designers' showings.
- It issues credentials for authorized buyers and the French and foreign press.
- It establishes the delivery dates of merchandise ordered by trade buyers. Merchandise is usually shipped 30 days after its showing.
- It regulates press release dates, which are set approximately six weeks after showings. This gives the buyers of expensive models time to receive the models and have copies manufactured.

COUTURE SHOWINGS. The major Paris couture houses show their semiannual haute couture collections in late January (for spring-summer) and in late July (for fall-winter). Four types of customers attend:

- Private customers, who may select a model (garment) from a designer's collection and have it made up to individual measurements
- Retail store buyers, who may buy models from a collection for resale to their own customers or, in many cases, so they can have the model copied or adapted into ready-to-wear garments for their store's exclusive use

- Ready-to-wear producers, who may buy models for purposes of inspiration or adaptation when designing styles for their own lines
- Pattern manufacturers, who may buy models or paper patterns of models for reproduction as patterns for home sewers

Private customers and the press are admitted free, although the latter have to apply for admission passes. Retailers and manufacturers, who must also apply for admission, are charged a stipulated caution. A **caution** is a fee charged for viewing a couture collection. The caution may be stated as a dollar fee, or as an agreement to purchase a certain number of models, or as an agreement to purchase a certain number of paper patterns, or any combination of these three requirements. The amount of the caution usually varies with the importance of the couture house; less well-known houses usually require considerably lower cautions than do more famous houses.

Other Couture Business Activities

While the traditional haute couture collections continue to make fashion news, actual sales volume has steadily declined in recent years. More and more, private customers whose wardrobes might once have consisted almost entirely of exclusive, couture-made garments are now turning to ready-to-wear. This has occurred partly because (1) many private customers have become impatient with the numerous and lengthy fittings couture garments require; (2) the figures of potential private customers now tend to be so slender and well-cared for that they can easily be fitted with ready-to-wear garments; (3) general economic trends have made many long-time private customers balk at the money required to be dressed by the couture; and (4) an increasing number of talented, ready-to-wear designers are creating more and more fashion news.

COUTURE BOUTIQUES. The first step in meeting this challenge was the creation of couture boutiques, usually located on a lower floor of the same building that houses the couture showrooms. Most well-known Paris couture houses now have these couture boutiques. They feature unusual and exclusive fashion accessories as well as limited lines of apparel. Boutique items are usually designed by members of the couture house staff, are sometimes made in the couture workrooms, and all bear the famous couture house label. Couture boutiques can be as profitable as they are popular. For example, St. Laurent is said to have grossed well over $2 million in 1978 through sales in the boutique owned and operated by his couture house.

COUTURE READY-TO-WEAR. Couture is exclusive and so expensive to produce that all of the couture designers have now begun to design ready-to-wear. Styling of these lines was originally the responsibility of the design staff of a couture house. But today couture designers say they design their most outrageous, creative, and innovative designs for ready-to-wear, with the haute couture collection serving as prestige earners.

Some couture ready-to-wear is sold in special shops operated by the couture house in major cities around the world. Large quantities are sold to department and specialty stores, which often set aside special departments or areas for displaying and selling couture-designed ready-to-wear and accessories. Modern couture designers create lines that fall between what most people are actually wearing and the designer's own private imaginings of how people might be persuaded to clothe themselves. Fashion for them combines fantasy and fact. Rather than widening the gap between the past glories of haute couture and the vitality of ready-to-wear, these designers have worked to join the two by creating and presenting these ready-to-wear collections.

Ready-to-wear operations have become major money-makers for many couture designers. Yves St. Laurent with his partner, Pierre Berge, launched the firm St. Laurent Rive Gauche in 1964. Through a licensing arrangement with Rive Gauche, Didier Grumbach produced and distributed apparel and accessories under the Rive Gauche label. There are now more than 230 Rive Gauche boutiques worldwide, and annual income is estimated at

Paris couture: loss leaders

Dior claims its profits are almost as slim as its models

PARIS—The biggest secret to slip out of the Paris couture closet is the first clear picture of where the money goes. With another lavish round of collections underway for spring, while France faces its highest unemployment rates in years, the designers decided to explain away those out-of-sight prices in their luxury industry.

To prove that couture is merely a flagship prestige operation on which to float a hundred-and-one products from ready-to-wear and cosmetics, baby clothes and bathroom accessories, Dior has thrown open its books.

So we took a close look at the case history of model number 49, an average example of the last collection, free of costly beading or embroidery. It sold "nicely" in the words of a Dior spokesman—which means 27 times.

The balance sheet shows that this simple two-piece in rosewood pink crepe, priced at $2,790, dropped exactly $27.26 profit in the Dior coffers.

To begin with, the French treasury took $312 in sales tax. Then the 85 hours of skilled labor that go into model 49 account for more than $1,000. Overhead and utilities take about $600, with another $500 for fabric and materials, including that much prized pure silk Dior label. So, when the vendeuse has collected her commission of $120, it is time for the couture business to ring up that meager profit!　　　　**—Monique**

Breakdown of a $2,790 Dior dress

French sales tax	$312
Labor (includes social security, meals, medical facilities)	$1,112.62
Dior overhead (offices, administration, utilities, insurance)	$619.50
Workroom expenses	$99.12
Fabric and materials	$495.60
Sales commission	$123.90
Profit	$27.26

Read this news story for an insight into the economics behind the luxury label.

about $50 million. However, all the boutiques, except those owned personally by Berge and Yves St. Laurent, are franchised operations.[2]

COUTURE LICENSING AGREEMENT. A number of couture designers not only sell their own accessories and ready-to-wear lines but also license the use of their names on a wide variety of other producers' goods. These goods range from apparel and accessories to bed, bath, and table linens, to home furnishings, fabrics, and more.

A licensing agreement is a contract whereby the licensor usually agrees to pay the licensee a royalty (which is most often a percentage of the wholesale price of the goods sold) for the use of the licensee's name. The latter may or may not actually provide designs for the product and is not in any way involved in its production.

In 1957, the year Christian Dior died, Dior's annual couture sales amounted to just over $8 million. By 1978, the House of Dior reported a gross annual income of $242 million, with a projection of $625 million by 1983. Most of this income has and will come from over 200 worldwide licensing agreements. In 1980, Pierre Cardin was the undisputed king of couture licensing, with over 375 separate agreements. His name appears on such diverse products as chocolates and bed sheets.

Jean-Claude Givenchy, brother of Hubert and business manager of the couture house, was quoted as saying, "That we continue in couture is often a condition of the licensee contracts that we sign—and through these licenses, the couture can pay for itself."[3]

French Ready-to-Wear

The ready-to-wear operations of Paris couture houses represent only a part of the burgeoning French ready-to-wear industry. The ready-to-wear houses in Paris began attracting world attention around 1960 by emphasizing change. The major change involved throwing out the conventions set by couture houses in favor of a natural way of dressing. This attracted the new, young generation of fashion-oriented consumers who were intent upon making their own fashion image. Through the decades of the sixties and seventies, French ready-to-wear turned out designs that were kicky, funky, anti-Establishment, and just as good-looking as those that the couture showed. Sometimes they were better-looking. As the customers increased, all designers viewed the ready-to-wear business as more creative and free, and the concept of French ready-to-wear grew.

The strength and importance of the French ready-to-wear industry is obvious today. More than 30,000 trade buyers attend the showing of the prêt-à-porter collections. And the press gives more coverage and attention to these showings than to the couture showings.

DESIGNERS. Paris ready-to-wear showings are increasingly more important to American fashion merchants as a source of fashion inspiration. New, young, innovative Paris designers, such as Claude Montana, Thierry Mugler, Sonia Rykiel, Karl Lagerfeld, and Kenzo Takado, are making big fashion news with their trend-setting styles. French ready-to-wear firms, such as Cacharel, MicMac, Dorothee Bis, and Chloe, have become very important fashion resources for American fashion retailers.

TRADE SHOWS. Two large Paris trade shows take place simultaneously in March and October:

(1) the showings of those known as fashion leaders and innovators—the more famous prêt-à-porter designer names, who also produce couture, and
(2) the many mass-producing, ready-to-wear firms and boutiques.

These semiannual trade shows draw thousands of store buyers and apparel manufacturers from all over the world. They also attract approximately twice the number of press representatives as their nearest competitors—the ready-to-wear shows in Milan and London.

The two groups do not exhibit in the same place. Traditionally the couture designers' shows are held throughout the city. In 1979 the couture designers held their fashion shows in huge tents erected in a centrally located area of Paris known as Les Halles (literally "The Hole"). Once the site of the Paris food market, this area is being redeveloped as a shopping and cultural center. Adjacent is a recently completed multi-level building, the Forum des Halles, one level of which is reserved for showrooms of leading Paris designers. Nearby are facilities for boutique showrooms.

The group of mass-producing designers has traditionally exhibited at the Porte de Versailles Exhibition Center. (See the illustration on page 207.) Their trade show, known as the Salon du Prêt-à-Porter Feminin is held in the Palais Sud building in the Porte de Versailles. This trade fair brings together more than 1,000 exhibitors, not only from France but from all over the world.

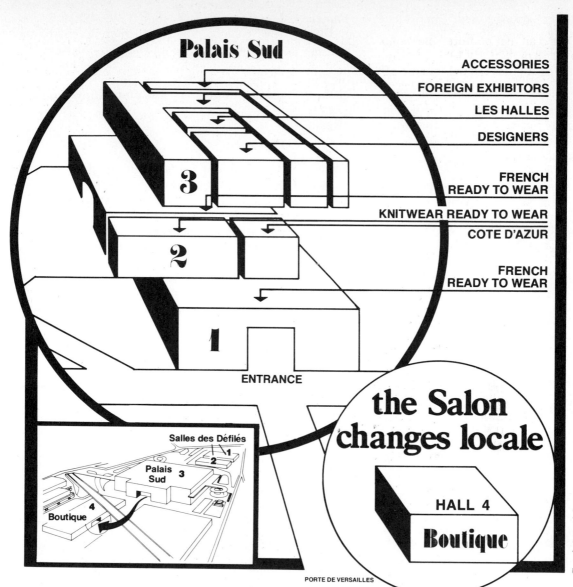

Palais Sud

ACCESSORIES

FOREIGN EXHIBITORS

LES HALLES

DESIGNERS

FRENCH READY TO WEAR

KNITWEAR READY TO WEAR

COTE D'AZUR

FRENCH READY TO WEAR

3

2

1

ENTRANCE

Salles des Défilés

Palais Sud 3

2 1

Boutique 4

PORTE DE VERSAILLES

the Salon changes locale

HALL 4

Boutique

French Apparel Center

The Porte de Versailles Exhibition Center in Paris has four buildings used for fashion trade shows for the many mass-producing ready-to-wear firms and boutiques. The first two buildings, Les Salles des Défilés, are the sites of major fashion shows. The three-level third building, Palais Sud, is shown in detail here. It is the major site of the famous Salon du Prêt-à-Porter Feminin as well as the major men's exhibit, SEHM. The fourth building, the Boutique, features high-styled boutique merchandise.

The strength and importance of French ready-to-wear is growing each season, with more and more trade buyers attending the shows. But the couture is also regaining some of its former importance and prestige with the 1980 revival of romance, elegance, and sophistication. The fit and construction of clothes is once again more important, and elegant clothes design still has its finest practitioners in the haute couture.

The semiannual men's ready-to-wear show, Salon de l'Habillement Masculine (S.E.H.M.), is held in February and September and is as important to the men's industry as prêt-à-porter is to women's wear. It is also held at the Porte de Versailles while the designers hold their special shows in their showrooms or in large salons around the city. The S.E.H.M. itself is international, and all of the leading European menswear designers can be seen there. These include George Rech, Daniel Hechter, MicMac, Browns of London, Alain Paine, Giorgio Armani, and Versace. The show covers every aspect of men's clothing, from the most casual to the most elegant, including suits, dress shirts, ties, and accessories. The French designers who also work in the men's field include Claude Montana, Thierry Mugler, and Kenzo Takado.

EXPORT EFFORTS. In an effort to promote the export of more ready-to-wear for both men and women, French apparel manufacturers formed a trade association in the early 1970s. Called Fédération Francaise des Industries de l'Habillement, this is roughly the equivalent of the American Apparel Manufacturers Association. In order to carry on its work, this association maintains offices in major countries throughout the world. When the French Apparel Center opened in New York in 1972, its main function was to help the federation publicize and promote French ready-to-wear to the American market. These offices play a major role in helping member firms find agents for their products. They also assist in planning retail store promotions featuring French apparel products and carry on a number of other related activities.

Many major French designers and ready-to-wear firms—including Yves St. Laurent's Rive Gauche, Daniel Hechter, Cacharel, and MicMac—now have their own offices in New York. This enables them to handle the volume of business done in the United States and to reach those buyers who do not travel to Paris.

ITALY

Although not as large or as prestigious as France, Italy has come a long way in the past decade in the minds of the fashion world and is now considered a major fashion market. In the past few years, new and extremely innovative designers, such as Tai and Rosita Missoni, Giorgio Armani, and Gianni Versace, have made the Milan showings a "must" on the European fashion tour. The Milan showings have had a major impact on worldwide fashion trends and now generate an excitement and fashion newness that once only emanated from Paris. Not only are the showings considered a major market for women's apparel, Italy has also achieved an outstanding fashion leadership in menswear and accessories.

Italy's reputation for fine knitwear and leather accessories has always kept Italian fashion creators active. Today, when one thinks of fine leather handbags and shoes, beautifully designed and handsomely crafted, Italian designers such as Ferragamo and Gucci come to mind. In the last few years, the growth in exports of Italian-made and designed men's apparel to the United States has rivaled that of Italian-made women's wear. Italian menswear designers responsible for this growth include Basile, Giorgio Armani, and Gianni Versace. Fendi's innovative designs and expert execution of fur fashions have made this name an international synonym for exciting and creative fur designs.

Italian Couture

Like France, Italy has long had couture houses named for the famous designers who head them—Galitzine, Valentino, Heinz Riva, Tiziani, Fabiani, and Andre Laug, for example. These houses are all members of

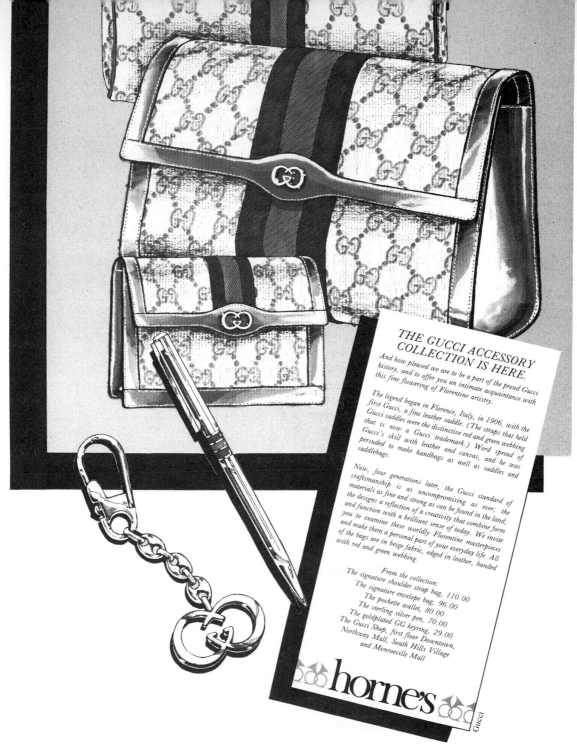

THE GUCCI ACCESSORY
COLLECTION IS HERE.

And how pleased we are to be a part of the proud Gucci history, and to offer you an intimate acquaintance with this fine flowering of Florentine artistry.

The legend began in Florence, Italy, in 1906, with the first Gucci, a fine leather saddle. (The straps that held Gucci saddles were the distinctive red and green webbing that is now a Gucci trademark.) Word spread of Gucci's skill with leather and canvas, and he was persuaded to make handbags as well as saddles and saddlebags.

Now, four generations later, the Gucci standard of craftsmanship is as uncompromising as ever; the materials as fine and strong as can be found in the land; the designs a reflection of a creativity that combine form and function with a brilliant sense of today. We invite you to examine these worldly Florentine masterpieces and make them a personal part of your everyday life. All of the bags are in beige fabric, edged in leather, banded with red and green webbing.

From the collection:
The signature shoulder strap bag, 110.00
The signature envelope bag, 96.00
The pochette wallet, 80.00
The sterling silver pen, 70.00
The goldplated GG keyring, 29.00
The Gucci Shop, first floor Downtown, Northway Mall, South Hills Village and Monroeville Mall

horne's

Gucci

Italy has a reputation for fine leather accessories. American buyers eagerly shop Florentine producers like Gucci and then offer their products in U.S. Stores.

Italy's couture trade association known as the Alta Moda Italiano. Unlike French couture houses, however, Italian houses are not all located in a single city. Many are in Rome, but others are in Milan, and a few are in other Italian cities.

Both Italian and French couture heavily depend on Italian fabric and yarn design. Much of the innovation in print and woven textile design is created and produced in the fabric mills of Italy. Innovation also characterizes both the yarn mills (note the international importance of the Pitti Màglia or Italian Yarn Show) and the knitters who buy the yarns and produce the world famous Italian knits.

COUTURE SHOWINGS. Members of the Alta Moda show their high-fashion collections semiannually in Milan and Rome to private customers, retailers and manufacturers, and the press. The showings are scheduled to take place just before the Paris couture-collection showings, so that foreign visitors can cover both important fashion markets in a single European trip. Italian couture houses not participating in the Milan showings usually arrange to show their collections either in their own salons or in some other location during the same period, also for the convenience of foreign visitors.

As in Paris, buyers and manufacturers are required to pay a caution to attend the Italian couture showings. Private customers and the press are admitted free, although cards of admission are required for the latter.

OTHER COUTURE
BUSINESS ACTIVITIES. Many Italian couture houses, like their Paris counterparts, have set up boutiques for the sale of exclusive accessories and limited lines of apparel. The designs are usually those of the couture house staff, and the apparel and accessories are sometimes made in the couture workrooms. All items offered in the boutique bear the couture house label.

In addition, many Italian couture houses now have high-fashion, ready-to-wear lines. These are sold either in their own shops or to retail distributors throughout Europe, in the United States, and, to an increasing extent, in Japan. For example, Valentino's ready-to-wear is sold in more than 20 stores in the United States and is also distributed in Japan.

More and more Italian couture designers also have licensing agreements with foreign producers. Some design and produce uniforms for employees of business firms, such as airlines. Some accept commissions to create designs for a wide range of fashion products, from menswear to home furnishings.

Italian Ready-to-Wear

Italy began to develop both its women's and men's ready-to-wear industries, separate from that of the couture, earlier than France did. As a result, it started exporting earlier, and today its economy relies heavily on its exporting program. In 1978 the United States imported more than $4 billion worth of Italian merchandise, one-fourth of which was in fashion merchandise. Much of this merchandise is in the medium price range, especially in knitwear and accessories.

DESIGNERS. Innovative Italian ready-to-wear designers make their shows as exciting as the Paris ready-to-wear shows have become. Among the better-known Italian designers who may work for one or more ready-to-wear firms are Walter Albini, Gianni Versace, and Muriel Grateau. Among widely known designers who head their own firms are Emilio Pucci, Giorgio Armani, Giovanna Ferragamo, and Rosita and Tai Missoni. Among well-known Italian ready-to-wear firms are Krizia, Gianfranco Ferre, Basile, Callaghan, Ken Scott, Cadette, Mirsa, Tiktiner, and Fendi.

TRADE SHOWS
AND MARKET CENTERS. Preparing a calendar of Italian showings of women's ready-to-wear was a fairly simple matter until the late 1960s. As interest in ready-to-wear grew and Paris initiated its semiannual prêt-à-porter showings, Italian ready-to-wear producers followed suit. Since many of these producers were located in Florence—a city that already had an established reputation as a fashion cen-

ter—regular, semiannual showings of both ready-to-wear and accessories began to be held in both the Pitti and Strossi palaces in Florence. The showings were scheduled for the week before the prêt-à-porter showings in Paris, for the convenience of foreign visitors.

In the early 1970s, however, a group of Milan-based firms began holding semiannual shows of their own, just before the Florence showings. The Milan shows have now become regular events. They are growing in fashion importance because of the increasing number of important firms who have decided to exhibit in Milan rather than Florence. Some firms exhibit in both.

Along with the exhibits and showings of regular ready-to-wear lines both the Florence and the Milan shows include some ready-to-wear collections of Italian couture houses. These collections are known as the Alta Moda Pronto. In addition to the couture and ready-to-wear shows, the more volume-oriented knitwear show (MAIT) is held in Florence in February. This is well attended by American buyers because of its importance in sweater design.

Men's ready-to-wear shows are held in Florence in February and in September. In 1980 Uomo Modo, the twice a year show of Italian Menswear Manufacturers, gave American and Canadian buyers a preview of their spring 1981 designs before they were shown in Italy. These shows are increasing in importance with the growing number of talented designers producing menswear apparel and furnishings.

Accessories

Italy has always been a fashion leader in the design and manufacture of leather accessories. Shoes, handbags, gloves, and small leather goods are a major part of Italy's fashion industry. Other accessories that are world-famous are silk scarfs and knitted hats, scarfs, and gloves. Because of the Italian finesse in designing these accessories they have become major exports to the rest of the world. The importance of accessories to the well-dressed European public is well known, and this mes-

sage has been carried to the United States by buyers shopping Italian fashion markets. Today, well-designed accessories are a fashion must for the well-dressed, fashion-conscious American public. Because of the importance of Italian fashion accessories, many accessories fairs are held all over Italy. The most famous of them are held in Lake Como, Florence, Milan, Bologna, and Rome.

COUTURE GOODS. When the Alta Moda couture collections are shown in Rome, a special accessories fair is held at the Grand Hotel, also in Rome. This features handbags, gloves, belts, umbrellas, and hats to be worn with the couture apparel. In this way, Italian designers promote the importance of accessories to the total picture of Italian couture. Similar fairs are held in Florence and Milan when the Italian couture collections are shown in these cities.

TRADE GOODS. At every major ready-to-wear trade fair there are always a large number of accessories exhibits to compliment the ready-to-wear being shown. In addition to these exhibits, certain of the accessories industries have special trade fairs of their own.

Mipel is the name of the trade show for Italian-produced handbags and other accessories such as luggage, belts, umbrellas, hats, and scarfs. This important show is held in Milan twice each year, in January and in June. The Mipel show is sometimes too late to allow some American buyers to place orders and be sure of receiving delivery by the start of the coming season. For this reason, an earlier show, called Europel, was instituted in 1974. This show concentrates on handbags and small leather goods and features exhibitors from all over Europe, as well as Italian producers. Although originally sponsored by Italian handbag manufacturers, Europel has held shows in Paris, Dusseldorf, and Berlin, as well as in Rome and Florence.

The famous shoe show held in Bologna in March is considered very important by foreign buyers because of the importance of Italy's shoe industry and the large quantity of shoe exports. The glove industry, centered around Naples, is represented in many fashion fairs, as is women's neckwear, produced mainly in the Lake Como and Milan areas.

Another interesting fashion fair is the famous Ideacomo, held at Lake Como in early May. It is here that the Italian fashion fabric producers show new designs and fabric textures for use in the following year's fashion apparel and accessories.

GREAT BRITAIN

For many years, London was for menswear what Paris has been for women's apparel—the fountainhead of fashion inspiration. In recent years its dominance has diminished, and Italy has become the main source of European-styled menswear. But London still remains the major fashion center for impeccably tailored custom apparel for men.

Britain's most important fashion strength, however, lies in tweeds, woolens, and knitwear for both men and women. The materials for these garments come not only from the mills of the Midlands of England but also from Scotland and Northern Ireland. Britain is also a growing market center for leather apparel for both women and men.

London Couture

The fashion market center of Great Britain has always been London. For a number of years, a small but important British haute couture group, known as the Incorporated Society of Fashion Designers, had their headquarters in London. This group was modeled after the Chambre Syndicale de la Couture Parisienne. It showed semiannual collections by its members to private customers, foreign buyers, and the press just before or after each of the Paris showings. For some years, two members of this group, Hardy Amies and the late Norman Hartnell, had the distinction of being designated "Dressmakers to the Queen." Upon request, they took selections from their haute couture collections to the Queen and the royal family, who selected models to be made up to their individual measurements.

British women's apparel styling had always been considered less trend-setting than that of France or Italy. London showings of haute couture collections thus attracted far fewer foreign visitors than did the Paris and Italian collections. As a result, in the early 1970s the Incorporated Society of Fashion Designers ceased to exist as a formal trade association. Several former members, however, continue to show their collections in their London showrooms at times that are convenient for foreign visitors to the French and Italian collections.

The London fashion houses are today making a major effort to regain the position in the world fashion market they had achieved in the 1960s. It was during these years that London's mods and rockers, with their wide ties and miniskirts, set the fashion tone for the youth revolution.

In the 1979 London Fashion Exhibition, 400 manufacturers and designers gathered at Olimpia, a large exhibition hall. This was the largest number of fashion companies ever to show under one roof in Britain. Only three years before, there had been a mere 80 exhibitors.

Like their continental counterparts, most British haute couture designers are now producing high-fashion, ready-to-wear lines. Some have entered into licensing agreements with foreign producers. Some design and produce uniforms for employees of business firms. One, Hardy Amies, has emerged in recent years as a trend-setting designer of menswear.

British Ready-to-Wear

England was long a nation in which people relied heavily on made-to-measure apparel. Its ready-to-wear industry was of minor fashion importance both at home and abroad until after World War II. The British government is given credit for having played an active role in its growth. In fact, the British government has for many years been engaged in nurturing its apparel industries. According to one of England's best-known fashion authorities, Britain's Board of Trade has been "the fairy godmother to whom is due the survival of their

Brilliance from Britain!

John Bates. Zandra Rhodes. Janice Wainwright. Yuki. Our celebrated guests from Britain. Each distinctive. Each recognized for their unique influence on international fashion. All part of N-M's tribute to style in the British manner. Come to a fashion show featuring the designs of our special guests with commentary by Prudence Glynn, Fashion Editor for the The Times of London, tomorrow at 2:00 p.m. Couture, Second Floor

Neiman-Marcus

ZANDRA RHODES
Ambassadress of fantasy. Fashion that is poetic. Feminine. Instantly recognizable. And always provocative! Her talents are multi-faceted. Her motifs a wonderful interplay of pattern, color and sparkle. All distinctively Zandra!

JOHN BATES
Daring drama for entrancemaking evenings. His designs are recognized and applauded the world over. His colors — striking and rich. Contributing a distinctive brand of excitement to fashion.

YUKI
Preferring to work fashion as sculpture. Japanese-born Yuki manipulates delicate, pliable fabrics. Exhibiting an almost architectural flair. Surprising planes of pleats and fluted columns. Unique dimensions from Yuki.

JANICE WAINWRIGHT
Sophistication and control. Structured, tailored looks for day. Luxury glamour for night. Bright brocades and silks with shimmering black as a common denominator. Cosmopolitan ease — the appeal of Wainwright's disciplined elegance.

A CELEBRATION OF BRITAIN

BRITISH FORTNIGHT HOURS: DOWNTOWN, OPEN MONDAY THROUGH FRIDAY 9:30 TO 8 AND SATURDAY 9:30 TO 5:30.

Neiman-Marcus, Dallas

British designers produce unique fashions that go around the world. Here they are deep in the heart of Texas.

couture and the rapid development of their large and excellent ready-to-wear trade.''[4]

WOMEN'S APPAREL.   Like its American and continental counterparts, British ready-to-wear for women is divided into three categories: high fashion (usually high-priced), moderate-priced, and mass-produced (popular-priced). High-fashion ready-to-wear is usually the product of couture houses in Britain, but it rarely has been considered trend-setting. British moderate- and popular-priced ready-to-wear was considered of little fashion importance until the 1960s.

Early in the 1960s, however, a London designer named Mary Quant recognized an emerging youth trend and began designing clothes for the young. Other London designers quickly followed her lead, and almost overnight London became the world's fashion market center for junior apparel.

The fashion trend in the early 1970s, however, moved toward longer, softer, more romantic styles. When the British ready-to-wear industry failed to follow, London began to lose fashion importance again. But backed by the British government and led by three London designers—Jean Muir, Zandra Rhodes, and Ossie Clark—who had sprung to prominence in the 1960s, a new group of young designers began to exert impact on the London fashion scene. Janice Wainwright, Yuki, and John Bates are popular in the early 1980s. Because the English are more individual in their approach to fashion, they express themselves on a more individualized basis.

London is the center of Britain's women's ready-to-wear industry, and the major manufacturers' trade associations have headquarters there. Most permanent showrooms of ready-to-wear producers are located there, although there also are showrooms in The Midlands and in Scotland. The major ready-to-wear shows take place in London. The International Fashion Fair, sponsored by the Clothing Export Council of Great Britain, is held each April and October.

MENSWEAR. Both London and Harrogate are important market centers for menswear. The major trade associations are located in London. So are many of the permanent showrooms of menswear producers, although others are located elsewhere in England and in Scotland. One important trade show, the International Men's and Boys' Wear Exhibition, has some 200 British and continental firms exhibiting and is held in London in February. However, a bigger menswear show, the Mens-wear Association Convention and Exhibition, is held in Harrogate in September. At this show, about 300 exhibitors (90 percent British and 10 percent from the Continent, Australia, Japan, and Yugoslavia) show their lines. For the American customer, the major British menswear designers and manufacturers can be seen at the previously referred to S.E.H.M. show in Paris. The best-known companies also have showrooms or representatives in the United States to work with their customers.

British Accessories

Most British accessories industries have their headquarters and permanent showrooms in London, and most accessories trade fairs are held there. The Leather Expo is usually timed for June. The London International Footwear Fair is held in September. There is a British Glove Fair in February and a Millinery Guild Show in May and November. These are relatively small shows, however.

Although Britain does have some interesting accessories, particularly in leather products, they do not dominate the country's fashion goods offerings as they do in Italy.

SPAIN

Even though Spain's apparel offerings are at present only of limited interest to American retail buyers, Spain is one of the few countries that still maintains a haute couture group.

The couture group is known as the Alta Costura and maintains headquarters in Madrid. Member firms show their collections either in Madrid's Palacio Nacional or in their own Madrid salons in late July and in January. These showings are timed to precede those of Paris, so that foreign buyers will be encouraged to put Madrid on their travel itineraries. The best known of Spain's fewer than 20 designers are Pertegaz, Elio Bernhanyer, Carmen Mir, Herrera y Ollero, and Pedro Rovira.

The women's and children's ready-to-wear

association in Spain is the Cámara de la Moda Española, with headquarters in Madrid. Its member firms, however, are located in major cities throughout the country. Besides their regular showings to the trade in Madrid in March and October, several members of this association show at fashion fairs throughout Europe.

Spain is an important fashion market for moderate-priced knitwear and leather products, particularly the latter. At times in recent years, the United States has bought almost three-quarters of all shoes exported by Spain. There is increasing production of fur, leather, and suede garments in Spain. Gloves, handbags, travel items, and small leather goods are accessories of special interest to foreign buyers.

An important shoe fair is held in Alicante each year, and there is an annual handbag fair in Barcelona. Iberpiel, the Spanish Festival of Fashion in Leather, is an annual trade fair held in Madrid each January.

SCANDINAVIA

The four countries that make up Scandinavia are closely grouped geographically but quite different in character. Sweden and Finland are the most closely allied, not only historically but also through joint business ventures. Denmark, generally regarded as the link between Scandinavia and the rest of the world, is in many ways more internationally oriented than the other Scandinavian countries.

While each country has its own fashion industries and specialties, the four countries do form a single identifiable market center. This is partly because they tend to have the same basic materials with which to work: leather, fur, some wool, an increasing amount of textiles made of man-made fibers, some gold, and silver. However, the main reason is that the four countries, while they do make individual marketing efforts, hold major trade fairs and maintain permanent showrooms in one central location: Copenhagen. This is the dominant center of the Scandinavian fashion world.

Fashion Products

Conservative, high-style wool apparel, including coats, dresses, and suits, has long been the specialty of the Danish apparel industry. Prices are generally high.

Moderate-priced apparel is particularly strong among the Swedish, Finnish, and Norwegian offerings. Some is cotton knit, but man-made fibers and cotton blends are more common. Styling is often youthful; one Swedish sportswear producer is among those who claim to have introduced the string bikini to the United States in the fall of 1973.

Leather apparel, primarily in menswear, is a popular Swedish product. Both Sweden and Norway are among the important suppliers of mink and other furs to countries around the world.

Scandinavia offers some interesting textile designs. Both American producers and retail buyers, interested in finding unusual fabrics to have made up for special promotions, watch the Scandinavian textile offerings very closely.

Excellent jewelry in all price ranges is available in Scandinavia. The area has long been known for its clean-cut designs in gold and silver. Today, an increasing amount of costume jewelry and "fun jewelry" is being produced there, particularly in Sweden.

Trade Shows and Showrooms

Each Scandinavian country holds its own national fairs in the city that is considered its trade center. For instance, Borås is the center of the Swedish textile and apparel industry. Some permanent showrooms are located there, and regular exhibitions of Swedish textiles and apparel are held there.

In addition, the Scandinavian countries encourage exports by taking their goods to show in other countries. For instance, Sweden and Finland cooperate in an annual Scandinavian fashion show in New York and in Canada.

However, the major market center for the whole of Scandinavia is Copenhagen. In Copenhagen is located the Bella Centret, where the international Scandinavian trade fairs are held. In Copenhagen is the Scandinavian Fashion Center, where the major fashion producers from all Scandinavian countries have their permanent showrooms. Copenhagen is also the city where producers of such accessories as jewelry and handbags have their permanent showrooms and hold their trade fairs.

The apparel fairs are organized by the Scandinavian Clothing Council, headquartered in Copenhagen and made up of representatives from the national clothing associations of each Scandinavian country. The important women's apparel fair, called the Scandinavian Fashion Week, is held semiannually, usually in March and in September. The Scandinavian Menswear Fair is also held twice a year, usually in February and in September. Both draw exhibitors from all the Scandinavian countries and from a number of other countries as well.

OTHER EUROPEAN COUNTRIES

Hardly a country in Europe does not produce some type of fashion goods of interest to foreign buyers. Many goods, however, are produced by firms in widely separated geographic areas that a foreign buyer on a short business trip does not have time to visit. Other goods are produced in countries that are still in the development stage of their fashion importance; therefore, fashion buyers do not spend the time and money to explore their potential. For these reasons, European trade fairs have become important sources of fashion inspiration and merchandise. At these events American fashion retailers seek out goods to offer their customers. American fashion producers search for new resources for materials and new contract production facilities.

Western Europe

There has always been considerable trade between the United States and Western Europe. However, until recently, American buyers looked only to France, Italy, and Spain for fashion inspiration and merchandise. Now other European countries, including Germany, Portugal, and Austria, are increasing in importance as fashion market centers.

WEST GERMANY. The Federal Republic of Germany is better known to American producers than to American retail buyers. The huge Interstoff textiles fair held in Frankfurt each May and November is a very important place to find new fabrics and new fashion ideas. Many major American manufacturers (of both men's and women's apparel) send their designers here to buy; others come to copy. Frankfurt is also one of the four big fur auction centers of the world, and its fur fair is held in April.

Germany is just beginning to increase its apparel exports beyond Europe. The center of its women's ready-to-wear industry is Dusseldorf. Here four fairs a year are held, each with 900 to 1,200 exhibitors and up to 30,000 retail buyers. There is also a newly established fashion fair in Munich each March, and an Overseas Export Fair in Berlin each September. The center of the menswear industry is Cologne, where major menswear fairs are held in February and August. There are numerous accessories fairs; the most important is probably the Leathergoods Fair held in Offenbach in February and August.

AUSTRIA. Austria has some interesting offerings in junior fashions and in accessories. Salzburg is the city where most apparel and accessories producers have permanent showrooms. It is also the city in which the trade fairs are held: the Leathergoods Fair in December, the Junior Fashions Fair in February, and the Jewelry Fair (fine and costume jewelry) in May.

PORTUGAL. American retailers buy some Portuguese products, most of which are lower-priced knitted goods, such as women's knitted ready-to-wear and men's knitted sportswear. Portugal's knitwear industry is located mainly in the Oporto area.

MADEMOISELLE magazine

INTERSTOFF FABRIC REPORT
SPRING/SUMMER '81

Glorious sunny weather prevailed for the 43rd Interstoff held in Frankfurt, Germany, which helped to ease the heavy atmosphere overshadowing the Fair. Some observations:

● Attendance was off; consequently, there was no waiting (nor was it necessary to set appointments) at the trend-setting showrooms. Space and assistance were readily available. Without all the excitement of the celebrity designers in the miles of aisles or the crowded showrooms, the ambience was dull.

● Only Pearl Nipon, Perry Ellis, Don and Caroline Simonelli from the U.S., and Jean-Claude de Luca, Jacqueline and Corine Jacobson from Paris were the few designers we saw.

● Timing, and perhaps too many fabric fairs (Paris' PremierVision, Como's Ideacomo and New York's Texatalia) piggy-backing each other at the end of the Pret, figured prominently in the poor attendance.

● Very much on everyone's mind was the unhealthy economy, despair with the state of the world and a lethargy about fashion per se. Fashion seems to be going through a revolution from which will emerge a new set of fabric standards and fashion values. The fashion trend is for quality fabrics . . . and simplification of fashion. This seemed to be the theme emerging for 1981 at the Fair.

● And there was the American point of view . . . "think internationally." Many American mills are looking to the world for their marketplace, not just Seventh Avenue, U.S.A. These forward-thinking mills have been frequenting the Fair for the past several years. However, new this year were some American mills sponsored by the United States Government, a fabric industry breakthrough. The seasoned reps and the new reps expressed their thoughts on Interstoff in varying degrees of optimism: the seasoned American mills booked sizeable business due to the devalued American dollar—and, in some cases, doubled their European business through Interstoff. And, for the new reps, the fair was greater than ever anticipated.

NEWS FROM INTERSTOFF

. . . COLOR, COLOR, COLOR and more COLOR continues to make news
. . . LINEN, the newest fabrication
. . . CRINKLE, the newest texture

● Printed stripings . . . deck chair, oversized awning (unexpected on voile)
● Candlewick
● Scrim weaves . . . flour sifter, kitchen strainer
● Rustic rag rugs
● Dishrag knits . . . cotton bouclés, raechel meshes

TRANSPARENT, TRANSLUCENT, OPALESCENT Summer 1981's fashion fantasy!
The TRANSPARENTS
● Clear sequins
● Crystal yarns
● Nail enamel sheers
● Shellacked satins
● Saran wrap nylons
The TRANSLUCENTS
● Onion skin voiles
● Tissue paper plain weaves
● Burnout batistes
The OPALESCENTS
● Pearlized taffetas
● Iridescent lamés

As American as the Stars and Stripes, Apple Pie, Blue Jeans and jogging are the American Sportswear KNITS which were visually obvious at the Fair.
"The Active Sports" Jerseys
● Ready-for-action, active-sports jerseys. Functional sweatshirt has come full cycle, from out of the locker room and into the fashion circle.
● No-sweat dressing . . . warm-up jerseys (brushed one side and backed for action)
● Thick and thirsty terries and velours continue
● Think: walk-a-thon, marathon, bike-a-thon jogging, and roller skating
"The Spectator Sports" Knits
● Slim Sweater dressing: sweater sets, sweater jackets
● T-shirt dressing (T-shirt, T-skirt)
● Spare-part jerseys
● Summer knits take on all the right curves

● Crepons are crinkled
● Canvas is wrinkled
● Chintzes are crumpled
● Sheetings are rumpled
COLLECTING, COLLECTIONS, COLLECTIBLES
collecting for now, the next decade, the

LINEN . . . the most sought-out and sought-after fabric at the Fair. Its influence was everywhere.
● The linen fibers . . . hair follicle denier to coarse potato sack
● Linen fabrications . . . flat plain weaves in a variety of weights from delicate christening gowns to rough peasant smocks
● The linen fashions . . . puttied/faded pastels, handkerchief and mill blanket plaids, linen shantung, trousseau treasures, the linen melanges
WRINKLE/CRINKLE SURFACES
No wrinkles have been taken out of next season's flat fabrics. Instead a few new ones have been added to last season's puckery seersuckers.

return in depth as the jean influence reaches epidemic proportions.
For wilting summer temperatures, the AJOURÉS with all their airy-white innocence have instant appeal.
● Drop-stitch knits (pointelles)
● Suggestive sheers (a bit naughty, a bit demure)
● Naive Swiss cottons (drawnwork, clips, ruffles and flounces)
Coming into fashion focus, **DECORATIVE FABRICATIONS** and **INTERIOR INFLUENCES**
● Floral chintzes
● Casement curtain fancies
● Woven stripings . . . mattress tickings, tea towel tattersalls

were there and their influence was obvious. Pure classic.

In conclusion, why the Interstoff? Why, because where can you see all this concentration, saturation, centralization and focalization of fabrics? Only at Interstoff. It is the only international fabric fair that has been consistently able to handle with efficiency 850-plus exhibitors for a period of 26 years, totalling 43 shows. And with this terrific track record, hopefully we can all look forward to a more optimistic atmosphere when the dates will have been moved forward three weeks next fall.

DJ White
Fabric Editor

Irene Silvagni
Paris Editor

A *Mademoiselle* report stresses the importance to fashion buyers of Interstoff, the huge textiles fair held in Frankfurt each May and November.

Eastern Europe

Although Eastern European countries are not considered important fashion market centers, some American producers and retail organizations have begun on a limited scale to explore their potential. The best way to start such exploration is by visiting the trade fairs held by each country in its major industrial city. For example, Poland holds an annual International Fair in Poznań, providing an excellent showcase for that country's products. Yugoslavia held its first annual International Fair in Tragir in 1974, featuring mainly the lines of Eastern European producers.

Since the mid-1970s, Eastern European countries in general, and Poland in particular, have begun to actively promote their ready-to-wear export trade. In 1974 Poland sent to New York the first government-sponsored export show ever to be held by an Eastern European country. Today most of this area's ready-to-wear exports go to Western European countries. The small amount that finds its way to this country consists mainly of utilitarian–type outerwear in medium- to lower-price ranges. Perhaps of greater significance to American fashion producers and retail organizations is the fact that these Eastern European countries are now developing as an area where a good grade of contract work can be done.

ISRAEL

In actual dollar value, Israeli fashion products are not of major importance when considering total U.S. fashion imports. However, the United States is very important to the total Israeli export effort. Therefore, Israeli producers are eager to work with our buyers and to produce apparel that will appeal to the American public. Two of the most successful fashion exports from Israel are swimwear and leather outerwear. Recently, Israeli jewelry also became very popular. Stores all over the United States featured jewelry made of precious and semiprecious metals and stones fashioned in the original and unique manner of Israeli handicrafters.

Gotex in swimwear and Beged-Or in leather outerwear are two of the Israeli manufacturers best known in the United States. Israel is also becoming a good source of lower- to moderate-priced knitwear and swimwear both in cotton and man-made fiber blends.

Because of its interest in becoming a world-renowned fashion center, Israel, with the help of the American fashion industry, has instituted an Israeli college of fashion and textiles. It is known in Israel as Shankar College of Fashion and Textile Technology. Here, young Israeli men and women study the art of fashion design and textile science. They are working to make Israel a center of innovative design and construction in textiles and clothing. This school is patterned after the famous Fashion Institute of Technology in New York City.

Through the government-sponsored Israel Company for Fair and Exhibitions, Israeli producers have been promoting their lines aggressively in other countries as well as in the United States. Israeli producers are now represented at the Paris Prêt-à-Porter, at the Frankfurt Interstoff, at the Milan Camis, at the Munich Fashion Week, and at Israeli Fashion Week shows held in London and New York.

Presently, Israeli manufacturers and designers are engaged in the production of higher-styled, higher-priced fashion apparel and accessories and expect to produce a greater impact upon foreign fashion centers all over the world.

LATIN AMERICA

French and Italian have been the traditional foreign languages of fashion. By the mid-1970s, however, Spanish and Portuguese, spoken in Latin American accents, had been added to the list. Fashion merchants began visiting such market centers as Rio de Janeiro, Buenos Aires, São Paulo, and Bogotá.

Two factors encouraged fashion merchants in the United States to pay attention to Latin America, which includes Central America, South America, and the Caribbean area. One factor was inflation. The other was the level of achievement reached by the developing nations of Latin America.

Inflation in the 1970s cut sharply into the American fashion merchant's traditional sources of textiles, apparel, and accessories. Because of inflation, Japan was temporarily priced out of its textile and textile products export business. American producers and retailers had to look elsewhere for goods at more reasonable prices.

Many countries of Latin America have reached a level of development where they can offer foreign buyers the goods they want at attractive prices. These countries have important raw materials, such as cotton, wool, leather, and the materials for man-made textiles. They have built networks of industries that are eager for export opportunities so that they can expand. These industries are being encouraged by their governments, because additional exports mean both an increase in gross national product and an increase in international trade status. These industries also have a good labor supply. Because the standard of living in these countries is not as high as elsewhere, the cost of this labor is not as high.

As a result, Latin America has emerged in recent years as a market center for three different kinds of fashion goods. First, its most advanced countries already have industries producing a variety of internationally styled fashion goods. Second, many countries in this geographic area offer increasingly greater quantities of unusual fashion goods that reflect each country's national heritage in arts and crafts. Third, the countries' production facilities and labor can turn out a variety of fashion goods to the specifications of American producers and retailers at attractive prices.

Fashion Products

Important industries producing both women's and men's apparel already exist in Argentina, Brazil, Colombia, and Uruguay. Argentina and Uruguay are probably the largest South American producers of apparel in both the moderate and upper price ranges, wool being a very important fabric. Brazil is particularly strong in sportswear. Colombia is an important market center for menswear. Together with the Dominican Republic and most of the Central American countries, Colombia produces popular-priced lines of men's sport shirts, particularly of the shirt-jac variety. Bolivia has a somewhat smaller apparel industry than the other three major countries of South America, but it offers some unusual styles of excellent quality.

Handbag buyers are likely to go to Argentina for better-quality goods, to Brazil for moderate-quality goods, and to Colombia for inexpensive goods. Uruguay is another source of handbags, producing moderate- to high-quality goods.

Perhaps the single most important market center for shoes in Latin America is Brazil. Brazilian shoe manufacturers concentrate on producing well-styled merchandise in lasts that fit North American feet. For belts and small leather goods, some of the major market centers are in Brazil, Argentina, and the Dominican Republic.

Jewelry buyers find tortoiseshell jewelry in Jamaica and both tortoiseshell and amber jewelry in the Dominican Republic. For costume jewelry, the major market center is Brazil. A number of Latin American countries produce silver and gold jewelry of native design, with Ecuador and Peru having some of the most interesting offerings.

Fashion Production

For those producers or retailers who are interested in having contract work done in Latin America, there are many possibilities. Considerable contract work is already being done in Mexico, San Salvador, Costa Rica, and Honduras. The Dominican Republic has five free zones, and contract work for U. S. fashion merchants is being done in each one of them. There is also a free zone in Colombia, where one Japanese firm has a plant employing 600 workers.

Most of the countries mentioned above have facilities that specialize in high-volume, moderate-quality, and low-price goods. However, there are also opportunities for those who want to have top-quality work done. Ecuador, for instance, can only handle a small amount of contract work, but it specializes in producing top-quality goods.

Trade Shows

Probably the single most important market center in South America is São Paulo, Brazil. An international textile and textile products fair is held there every January and June, with exhibitors not only from Latin America but from other areas of the world as well. This trade show draws some 60,000 buyers from around the world.

Other important international fairs featuring textiles and textile products as well as fashion accessories are held in Bogotá, in Lima, and in San Salvador. All three are annual fairs.

THE FAR EAST

When fashion buyers refer to the Far East, they are talking about a large group of countries, each well known for its styling and workmanship in different price points and qualities. The major countries of the fashion buyer's Far East are Japan, Hong Kong, Korea, Taiwan, Sri Lanka, India, Singapore, Malaysia, China, and the Philippines.

The United States imports more apparel from the Far East than from any other area in the world. However, a great deal of these imports have been contracted for by American producers or retailers and made to individual buyers' specifications. In general, the Far East has been a source of low-price, moderate-quality, high-volume production. However, the more developed Asian countries, such as Japan and Hong Kong, are becoming part of the mainstream of fashion and sophistication. As they take on Western standards of living, technology, and customs, their direction turns more and more to designing and creating rather than to copying. Drawing on their long history of beautiful design, the Japanese have produced some outstanding international designers, such as Hanae Mori, Kenzo Ta-

kado, and Kansai Yamamoto, Hong Kong has produced new, young, talented designers whose work can be seen at the annual Hong Kong Festival. Many of their lines are now being bought by United States retailers.

In the past, American buyers came to depend upon the Far East as a source of low-cost production. Because of rising domestic costs, lower production costs became imperative for fashion buyers if profit margins were to be maintained. Buyers also used the Far East as a market in which to have fashions they saw in the European fashion centers copied and adapted. When buyers found an interesting fashion item, they would ship a sample to a manufacturer in the Far East. Here a "development sample" would be made up so that it could be copied or adapted for sale at a popular price in the United States. This is called **contract or specification buying** and is prevalent in the Far East. Although contract prices have increased in some parts of the Far East, much of this type of work is still done there for American producers and retailers.

A fashion retail buyer needs to know which areas in the Far East are best equipped to handle specific types of contract work. Japan and Hong Kong were once the two major contract countries. But these countries have upgraded their fashion images, so that today they are outstanding fashion producers of high-styled, high-priced fashion apparel. They still do some contract work, but it is high in quality and therefore more expensive.

Japan

Because most major American manufacturers of moderate-priced apparel produce some items in the Far East, the fashion impact of Tokyo has become extremely important. Many Japanese boutiques in Tokyo have their own design staffs, who create exciting new looks. The Tokyo boutiques are very individualistic, and because of their ability to turn their fashion goods very quickly, the Tokyo fashion scene is often six months to a year ahead of other fashion centers. For this reason, many American designers, retailers, and manufacturers work in Tokyo before going on to their contractors in other parts of the Far East. They are inspired by Japanese designs and they create similar ideas for the American market. For example, the "fifties" fashion was evident in Tokyo in the year 1977–1978, well before the American fashion scene adopted it.

Since 1970 Japan has sponsored a Tokyo Fashion week. This semiannual fashion fair is held in January and July as a combined effort of over 120 Tokyo fashion apparel producers. In 1980, the 11th Tokyo Fashion Week included 30,000 items representing 2,000 brands and 120 producers.[5]

The Japanese textile industry has become as innovative and sophisticated as the American textile market. A classic example is the impact of Ultra Suede—a Japanese creation—on the American designer market. Japanese print designers also have a major impact on American fashion through the textiles produced in Japan. The fabric may be bought in Japan and then used in producing apparel in the United States or in other parts of Asia.

Japanese yarn mills are also highly developed and sophisticated, although less so than the textile industry. All of the major Asian knitters and American designers who work in the Far East travel to Tokyo to work with the major yarn mills. Much of the original inspiration and design come from Italy through the Pitti Maglia, much as the fabric inspiration may come from Interstoff in Germany. But the translation and much of the innovation are Japanese.

In many cases a design concept may originate in Paris, Milan, or New York. But a unique, innovative process must take place between the original designer and the Asian technician in order to produce fashions for the volume market. Some of these innovations in yarns or knitting techniques have had a major impact on the moderate American sportswear market.

Hong Kong

Hong Kong has made a dramatic shift from carrying out copying and contracting work to creating and producing its own fashion de-signs. Hong Kong sponsors a fashion week each year, inviting buyers from all over the world to come to Hong Kong and view the exotic fabrics and fashions of its designers and manufacturers. Hong Kong has also presented a fashion show here in the United States, taking it from coast to coast to show American buyers innovative and exciting styling and designs.

Korea

With much of the same design history as the Japanese, Korea has some exciting young designers creating for the local fashion-conscious market. One of them, Maria Kim, has established a successful volume-priced knitwear business in the United States.

Much of the production of ready-to-wear in Korea is still contract work. But because of the fashion design movement among young Koreans, this is slowly beginning to change.

Taiwan

In Taiwan there is a definite upgrading in the quality of work being produced. Taiwan closely follows Hong Kong in the variety and innovation of knitwear technology. To stimulate and build a more fashion-oriented and higher-priced market, the Taiwan Textile Federation has been established. Under its aegis, young Taiwanese designers and technicians are being trained in fashion design and execution. In addition, GarmenTaipei, an interesting showcase of what is being produced in Taiwan, is held in Taipei in the Republic of China each October.

India

The traditional fabric designs and garments of India have had a profound impact on world fashion. Gauze, madras, and the native kurta (tunics over casy pants) had a tremendous influence on American fashion in the mid-seventies and are reemerging in importance in the eighties.

Both Pink Glo mink sets were designed and made by one of Hong Kong's leading manufacturers of ready-to-wear fur garments. Today Hong Kong is an outstanding producer of highly styled high-priced fashion apparel.

People's Republic of China

In the future, the People's Republic of China may become one of the most interesting market centers of the Far East. As yet, only a small amount of buying is taking place in China by American retailers. However, many retailers expect Chinese–United States trade to increase tremendously, especially since the United States reestablished diplomatic and trade relations in 1978. For example, in 1980, Bloomingdale's launched a $10 million promotion featuring imports from the People's Republic of China.

The People's Republic of China holds a very important semiannual trade fair in Guangzhou (formerly Canton). But admission is by invitation only, and just a few hundred foreign firms are invited. Today, more American buyers and producers are being invited to visit China with the long-range purpose of establishing a flourishing trade.

MERCHANDISING VOCABULARY

Define or briefly explain the following terms:

Caution	**Contract or specification buying**
Couture house	**First cost**
Couturier, couturiere	**Haute couture**
Chambre Syndicale	**Prêt-à-porter**
Commissionaire	

MERCHANDISING REVIEW

1. What are the three different methods that American retail stores may employ when shopping foreign markets?
2. Distinguish between a store's own foreign buying division and a commissionaire organization.
3. Name and describe the four different types of customers who attend the showing of couture designers.
4. Give four reasons why the sales volume of European couture houses has declined in recent years.
5. How have most Paris couture houses attempted to meet the growing challenge and competition of a rapidly developing ready-to-wear industry? To what extent has each of these business efforts been successful?
6. For what fashion products is Italy best known?
7. Discuss the developments of the British ready-to-wear industry. What designer was credited with making London the world's fashion market center for junior apparel?
8. For what fashion products is Spain best known?
9. What countries make up what is commonly referred to as Scandinavia? What city is the major market center of that geographic area? For what fashion products is it best known?
10. What countries are included in the geographic area referred to as Latin America? Name and discuss several reasons why Latin America has become an important fashion market center in recent years.

MERCHANDISING DIGEST

1. It is stated in the text that the "reputation of Paris as a prime source of fashion inspiration began to develop several centuries ago as the result of many interrelating factors." Identify those factors and discuss their importance in the development of any major fashion design center.

2. What major countries make up the Far East? Discuss the importance of that geographic area to producers and retailers of fashion goods.

REFERENCES

[1] McCarthy, "YSL to Pay $7 Million for Rive Gauche," p. 27.

[2] "Eye" Column, p. 8.

[3] Morris, "Fashion Report," p. 8.

[4] Garland, *Fashion*, p. 73.

[5] Tokyo Women's and Children's Wear Manufacturer's Association, "Tokyo and Fashion," p. 22.

11
RETAIL DISTRIBUTORS OF FASHION

In 1980, changes in world affairs made it clear that the new decade would bring dramatic changes in every phase of American life. The complacency of the fifties, the spirit of revolt of the sixties, and the "me" attitude of the seventies had vanished. In the eighties, people were faced with the possibility of a drastic alteration in lifestyle caused by economic conditions more stringent than any the nation had known since World War II.

The threat of war, an ongoing energy crisis, continuing inflation, and the necessity of conserving the nation's resources were brought home to a people who had grown accustomed to the idea that more and bigger is better. The adjustment to a "small is beautiful" philosophy was a difficult one.

Detroit car makers watched in dismay as skyrocketing prices and conservation concerns caused the American people to turn more and more to smaller, fuel-conserving foreign cars. The nation's fashion retailers also had cause to consider how the buying habits of their customers might be affected by economic conditions. Fortunately, retailers had faced the challenge of ever-accelerating changes over the past two decades. Flexibility in their merchandising positions had long been the key to their success and growth. Retailers that had not been able to adjust to change in recent decades no longer existed. Those that had been able to change were stronger than ever. Now, department stores, specialty stores, great chain stores, and discount stores all faced yet another challenge. This time, however, the challenge was brought about by forces from beyond the nation's borders as continuing unrest in the Middle East threatened world oil supplies.

HISTORY AND DEVELOPMENT OF FASHION RETAILING

The term **retailing** refers to the business of buying goods from a variety of resources and assembling those goods in convenient locations for resale to consumers. It logically follows that **fashion retailing** refers to the business of retailing fashion-oriented merchandise.

The term **merchandising** refers to the planning necessary on the part of a retailers in order to have the right merchandise, at the right time, in the right place, in the right quantities, and at the right prices (that is, prices which the firm's customers are both willing and able to pay). It logically follows, therefore, that fashion merchandising refers to this planning where fashion-oriented merchandise is concerned. The merchandising function is the most important function in all retail organizations because, in almost all cases, sales are the sole source of a store's revenue.

In this chapter we will explore how various forms of retailing have developed and the means by which modern retail organizations seek customer patronage.

Early Retailing

To better understand the position of retailing in the 1980s, it is necessary to understand how this remarkable business started and how it evolved.

Retailing began in the outdoor bazaars of the Orient and the marketplaces of the Mediterranean. Here people came together to buy, sell, and barter goods of all kinds. The modern version of such bazaars and marketplaces is the shopping center.

Some early tradespeople, such as weavers, potters, and goldsmiths, were masters at their crafts who produced the goods they offered for sale to customers. Each of them was usually responsible for the training of a number of apprentices. They lived, worked, and maintained shops in their homes, which were often located on a street or in an area crowded with other people who produced similar goods. Customers seeking a particular type of product would shop for it on that street or in that area. The modern counterpart of those craft shops is the specialty store. The staff of today's version is expected to be as knowledgeable about specific types of merchandise as those early masters and their apprentices.

Other early retailers bought rather than made goods for resale purposes. They obtained their stock from traders who brought the merchandise by ship or caravan from distant countries. Each retailer offered, in one location, many different types of merchandise. The modern counterparts of those early shops are department and variety stores.

Other early retailers deliberately sought out their clientele. These were peddlers, who purchased limited assortments of goods from a variety of tradespeople. Peddlers carried the goods on their backs or on pack animals or in wagons. They called on customers who lived in sparsely settled areas far removed from the urban shops in an effort to resell those goods.

The modern version of the early peddler is the house-to-house salesperson.

Development of Retailing in the United States

From the time of the first explorations, it was obvious to the European nations that the New World was a rich source of many goods. Not the least of these were luxury furs and skins that were in great demand in the Old World. As a result, trading posts were set up in the New World to collect pelts from trappers and Indians in exchange for food, liquor, and ammunition. This North American phenomenon led in 1670 to the formation, under the royal decree of Queen Anne of England, of the Hudson Bay Company of Canada. Located south of what we now know as the Canadian border, these trading posts later developed into such cities as Chicago, Detroit, and St. Louis.

Towns that soon developed along the eastern coast of North America had shops and stores much like those of European towns. But along the frontier and in sparsely settled farming areas, different forms of retailing developed. The general store, which carried a wide variety of consumer goods, became an important retail distribution center in those early days. Peddlers also played an important role, going from town to town and from farm to farm with their assortments of merchandise. Later, when mail service became more reliable, a third method of rural retail distribution developed: mail-order selling.

GENERAL STORES. The rugged frontier and the widely scattered farming areas of North America created the need for a special kind of retail establishment. Thus was born the **general store,** carrying stocks of utilitarian items that the frontiersmen and women needed, from salt pork to saddles, from lamp oil to ladies' bonnets. Soon the general store became the community social and economic center, as well as the gathering place for political debate. Since money was a scarce commodity on the frontier, bartering became an important way of doing business; the general store took goods as well as cash in payment.

As the frontier pushed westward and attracted more farmers and ranchers and their families, general stores began adding new kinds of goods to their assortments, such as basic dress fabrics and sewing notions.

Then, as settlers grew more prosperous, many sent away to stores on the East Coast for their fashion purchases—new dresses or shawls for the ladies, for example, and even "dress up" suits for the men. They also patronized the local specialty shops that appeared as the frontier towns grew. In the rural areas, however the general store continued to thrive. To this day, it exists on a reduced scale as a focal point of many communities in remote areas of the South, West, and Northeast.

Gradually, these general stores turned from a barter system to a cash-only system. They thus became strictly dispensers of merchandise. Such were the beginnings of many of the nation's great general merchandise and department stores. An outstanding example is Meier & Frank Co., Portland, Oregon.

PEDDLERS. Even with trading posts scattered along the frontier and general stores in towns there was need for another kind of retailer. Rural homesteads, far from towns or well-traveled roads, welcomed the peddler with his pack full of necessities and "luxuries."

In the peddler's pack were pots and pans, shoes and boots, pins, thread, combs, ribbons, and laces. He also brought news, including information on the latest fashions in the cities back East. And he took orders along the way for items to be delivered on his next trip, although his route was often so long that a year might pass before his return. The peddler also reported back to producers in the East about the items which pleased or displeased his customers. Thus he became the first "market analyst."

The peddler disappeared as the nation

The peddler's creed was "You can't do business from an empty wagon."

grew. He was replaced by the traveling salesman who took samples of merchandise to stores and shops along his route. Actual door-to-door sales are used to this day, but only for certain types of fashion merchandise. Cosmetics are probably the number one fashion product that is sold in this manner today.

Yet it was one of those early peddlers who founded one of the country's largest retail organizations. Adam Gimbel, tired of a life of travel, set down his peddler's pack and opened a retail store in Vincennes, Indiana, in 1842. From this beginning grew the giant retail dynasty that later encompassed all Gimbel Brothers, Inc., stores as well as the prestigious and ultrafashionable chain of stores known as Saks Fifth Avenue.

MAIL-ORDER SELLERS.   Certainly no aspect of the retail business has had a more remarkable, ongoing role in the buying activities of the American people than mail-order selling.

The mail-order business was begun in the late 1800s specifically for the millions of rural Americans who could not go to a store. It was made possible by the introduction of Rural Free Delivery of mail to far-flung points across the nation and of Parcel Post, which allowed packages of goods to be delivered by mail.

The first **mail-order company**—that is, a company which does the bulk of its sales and deliveries by mail—was Montgomery Ward, founded in 1872. It was followed in 1886 by Sears, Roebuck and Company, and the mail-order business was soon in full swing.

The mail-order catalog brought a new world to the lives of rural Americans. Hundreds of fashion items, furnishings for the home, and tools for the farm were illustrated, described, and priced. The fashions were not necessarily exciting. But the variety and prices delighted rural women, who had been limited to the scant provisions of the general store or the peddler's pack. A whole new world of fashion was opened to these women, and they eagerly responded. By 1895, only nine years after its first issue, the Sears, Roebuck catalog boasted 507 pages. The fledgling company posted sales at three-quarters of a million dollars that year.

By the 1920s, the automobile had made its presence felt even in rural areas. Mail-order companies began to open retail stores in these areas to meet the competition of city stores now accessible by automobile. By the 1930s, mail-order companies began to open catalog centers. Here customers could come and write up their own orders. Salespeople were available to help them in selecting merchandise from the catalog. Today customers can shop at any of the major mail-order companies in person, by mail, or by phone.

The convenience of shopping at home by mail order is still widely used today. Where it once was the province of the rural areas, mail-ordering has gained new customers in the nation's cities. Department stores and specialty shops direct a considerable amount of money and effort to generating business through mail-order sales. Their catalogs and mailing pieces have become increasingly more elaborate and more frequent. Mail-order offerings are now also made by oil companies, American Express, and Visa and MasterCard credit cards.

Today, the catalog contents of the major mail-order houses bear no resemblance to those early offerings to rural America. Famous designers now create exclusive fashions for these catalogs. Mail-order companies possess the most up-to-date testing laboratories to assure that the fit, fabric, color, workmanship, and wearing qualities of the merchandise they offer are of the quality customers want. Because these mail-order houses print and distribute millions of each catalog, they have tremendous purchasing power and prestige in the fashion market.

Mail-order business is big business, and it is here to stay. Even greater success can be expected as the energy crisis limits automobile travel to shopping centers or downtown stores.

The Retail Scene Today

The function of retailers is to meet the needs and wants of their target customers. Just as the success of a style depends upon customer acceptance, so does the success of retailers depend upon customer acceptance of the goods and services they offer. The success or failure of even the greatest and most prestigious of retailers depends upon the level of customer satisfaction. In the words of the late Marshall Field, ''Give the lady what she wants!'' In today's retailing, however, it is not only the lady, but the man and child as well.

Various types of retailers have evolved from the early days of retailing. Each type has a certain organization and method of operation which enable them to give their customers what they want. There are retailers who stock many different types of merchandise and retailers who specialize in limited types of merchandise. There are retailers who serve those who casually spend large sums of money for their fashions and retailers who concentrate on customers who carefully watch every dollar. There are retailers who own no retail outlets of their own but operate departments in the stores of others.

Today there are hundreds of thousands of retail organizations of various kinds in the United States that specialize in apparel and accessories for men, women, and children. There are almost as many general merchandise organizations that include apparel and accessories among their offerings. Many specialized retail firms also handle limited varieties of fashion merchandise. Examples are the food stores and drugstores that also sell hosiery, toiletries, cosmetics, and such prepackaged, basic fashion items as T-shirts and underwear.

The forces of change are reshaping the retail trade. At one time, each type of retailer had a different organizational structure and hence a distinctive appeal to customers. However, retailers have had to change their retailing strategies in response to the changing environment. Clear-cut differences and distinctions that existed between retailers 20 or 30 years ago are now blurred. Most of today's successful retailers are characterized by their alertness to changes in the environment and in customer buying habits and by their effective response to these changes.

ORGANIZATIONAL STRUCTURE OF RETAIL FIRMS

The organizational structure of retail firms does not follow the clean-cut lines of authority and responsibility that one often finds in other types of business firms. Therein lies one of the strengths of retail firms. Management recognizes that retailing is a ''people business''—a service to a firm's customers. A tightly structured and rigid organizational system could inhibit the kind of creative awareness retail executives need to understand the changing needs of a store's customers and to respond effectively to them.

Organization Chart

An **organization chart** is a visual presentation of the manner in which a firm delegates responsibility and authority within the organization. A retail organization may adopt an organizational structure with anywhere from two to six major functions or areas of responsibility. Each of these functions is headed by a top-management executive. This person is responsible to the chief executive of the firm, usually called the general manager, the executive vice president, or the president.

The organizational structure of most medium-size department stores today is based on a four-function plan, as follows:

- Finance and control division, with responsibility for the credit department, accounts payable, and inventory control
- Merchandising division, with responsibility for buying, selling, merchandise planning and control, and usually fashion coordination
- Sales promotion division, with responsibility for all advertising, display, special events, publicity, and public relations
- Operations division, with responsibility for maintenance of all facilities, store and merchandise protection, customer services, receiving and marking, and personnel

The number of major functions established by a retail firm as a basis for its effective operation depends upon its sales volume, number of employees, and how many store units it operates. The smaller the sales volume and the fewer the employees, the more varied are the responsibilities of each of its employees, including executives. The larger the sales volume and number of employees, the more specialized become the responsibilities of each employee.

In the smallest retail firms, an owner, a part-time bookkeeper, and a salesperson or two may handle all the work necessary to keep the firm operating successfully. In somewhat larger firms, an owner or manager is often responsible for both the sales promotion and merchandising activities, but turns over responsibility for financial and operational activities to one or two others in the firm who have experience in these fields.

Retail firms with larger than medium sales volume, a larger number of employees, and perhaps several branches usually find it necessary to increase their major functions from four to five. They remove responsibility for personnel from the operations division and elevate it to major functional status under the direction of a personnel executive. When this is done, personnel, as a separate function or division within a retail firm's organizational structure, is responsible for employment, training, employee records, executive recruitment and development, and related activities.

Retail firms with the largest sales volume and number of employees, and usually operating more than six branches, often add a sixth major function to their operating structure: branch store coordination. The executive responsible for this function serves as the link between parent and branch store executives and sees that the firm's merchandising, personnel, and public relations policies are carried out in the branches. The organization of such a retail operation is shown in the figure on page 231.

A chain's organizational structure is much more extensive than that of even the largest branch-operating retail firm because of the more complex nature of its activities. For example, in a branch-operating retail firm, transportation and warehousing activities are usually part of the operations function. But in a chain, these two activities are usually considered a major top-management function under the direct supervision of a top-management executive.

Overlapping authority and responsibility occur frequently in the retailing field. For example, salespeople are trained by personnel executives in ringing up sales, writing up sales checks, and handling delivery requests. But they are given merchandise and fashion training by their buyer and often by the fashion coordinator.

Where there are several branches, overlapping can become even more complex. In an effort to adapt the merchandise assortments and presentations of each individual branch to the preferences of the community each serves, branch-operating stores can develop relationships within their organizational structure that defy charting. For example, in branch stores, department managers are assigned to supervise the merchandise assortments and selling activities in one or more merchandise areas. They also are responsible for reporting to the appropriate parent-store buyers the customer reaction to departmental assortments in their assigned areas. A department manager's immediate superior in the branch store may be a group manager or the branch store manager, but he or she also works with and receives directions from the parent-store buyer of each department managed.

TYPES OF RETAILERS OF FASHION MERCHANDISE

Many different types of retail stores sell fashion merchandise. There are small, independently owned and operated stores. Others are part of large corporations that have many stores. The stores which dominate the fashion retail world today are those known as general merchandise stores and specialty stores.

General merchandise stores are retail stores which sell a number of lines of merchandise — apparel and accessories, furniture and home furnishings, household linens and drygoods, hardware and appliances, and smallwares, for example — under one roof. Stores included in

Legal Counsel
Research Department

Other Advisory Services

STOCKHOLDERS

BOARD OF DIRECTORS

PRESIDENT

VICE PRESIDENT & GENERAL MANAGER

FINANCE & CONTROL DIVISION — Treasurer & Controller

ACCOUNTING OFFICE
- Accounts Payable
- Cash Office
- General Accounting
- Inventory Taking
- Insurance & Taxes
- Payroll Office
- Sales Audit
- Statistical

CREDIT OFFICE
- Billing Customers
- Cashiers in Office
- Charge Accounts
- Charge Authorization
- Credit Interviewers
- Deferred Payments

CREDIT UNION
EXPENSE CONTROL
LAYAWAY OFFICE
MERCHANDISE STATISTICS

OPERATING DIVISION — Store Superintendent

ADJUSTMENTS
ARCHITECT'S OFFICE
CUSTOMER SERVICE
- Salespeople
- Service Desks
- Telephone & Mail Orders
- Bridal Registry

DELIVERY
ELEVATORS
HOUSEKEEPING
MAIL DIVISION
MAINTENANCE
PACKING & PICK-UP
PRINTING
PURCHASING DEPARTMENT
RECEIVING AND MARKING
RESTAURANTS
STORE PROTECTION
TRAFFIC DEPARTMENT
WAREHOUSE
WORKROOMS

PERSONNEL DIVISION — Personnel Director

EMPLOYMENT OFFICE
- Interviewing
- Placement
- Termination

HOUSE ORGAN
PERSONNEL BUDGETS
PERSONNEL TESTING
RECORDS AND REVIEWS
- Budgets & Records
- Job Analyses
- Rating & Reviews

TRAINING
- Induction & System
- On the Job

WELFARE & HEALTH

MERCHANDISING DIVISION — General Merchandise Manager

BUYING OFFICES
COMPARISON BUREAU
DIVISIONAL MANAGERS
- Department Managers
- Assistant Buyers
- Salespeople

FASHION COORDINATION
HOME PLANNING BUREAU
MERCHANDISE PLANNING & CONTROL BUREAU
MERCHANDISE RESEARCH

SALES PROMOTION DIVISION — Sales Promotion Manager

ADVERTISING DEPARTMENT
- Artists
- Copywriters
- Direct Mail
- Layout
- Radio & TV

DISPLAY DEPARTMENT
- Interior Displays
- Sign Room
- Window Displays
- Exterior Displays

PUBLIC RELATIONS
- News Releases
- Public Fashion Shows
- Special Events
- Use of Auditorium

BRANCH STORES — Executive in Charge of Branches

Audit
Credit
Store Planning
Maintenance
Receiving
Transfer of Merchandise
Employment
Training
Merchandising
Sales Planning
Advertising
Displays
Special Events
Liaison With Main Store

Adapted from NRMA

This organization chart for a large department store is typical of stores with six divisions or areas of responsibility.

TABLE 11-1
Retail Performance by Type of Store

COMPANY	$ SALES (in 1000s)	COMPANY	$ SALES (in 1000s)
Mass Merchandisers		Tiffany & Co.	73,252
Sears, Roebuck and Co.	17,946,336	Sterchi Bros. Stores, Inc.	45,230
K-Mart	11,695,539	Kenwin Shops Inc.	18,897
J. C. Penney Co. Inc.	10,845,000	Totals	2,675,789
F. W. Woolworth Co.	6,102,800		
Montgomery Ward & Co.	5,014,000	**Discount Stores**	
Totals	51,603,675	Zayre Corp.	1,394,109
		Wal-Mart	900,298
Department Stores		G. C. Murphy Co.	711,996
Federated Dept. Stores	5,404,621	Vornado, Inc.	702,377
Dayton-Hudson Corp.	2,961,884	Kings Dept. Stores	540,608
May Dept. Stores Co.	2,582,540	Roses Stores, Inc.	500,005
Carter, Hawley, Hale	2,116,586	Caldor, Inc.	475,733
Allied Stores Corp.	2,082,686	Alexander's Inc.	451,743
R. H. Macy and Co.	1,958,333	Kuhn's Big K Stores Corp.	328,127
Assoc. Dry Goods Corp.	1,605,607	Pamida, Inc.	318,833
Mercantile Stores Co.	922,141	Hartfield-Zody's	315,726
Marshall Field & Co.	762,590	Heck's Inc.	285,536
Carson Pirie Scott & Co.	412,080	Ames Dept. Stores	232,536
Strawbridge & Clothier	335,643	Jamesway Corp.	202,293
Dillard Dept. Stores	331,212	Gaylord's National Corp.	112,451
Goldblatt Bros. Inc.	304,617	Masters Inc.	82,788
Woodward & Lothrop	271,010	Friendly Frost	46,700
The Higbee Co.	188,298	M. H. Lamston, Inc.	31,341
Wieboldt Stores	166,119	Totals	7,633,473
Glosser Bros. Inc.	146,025		
Hess's Inc.	142,481	**Miscellaneous**	
J. B. Ivey & Co.	122,734	City Prod. Corp.	3,313,000
Zion's (ZCMI)	108,624	Gamble-Skogmo, Inc.	1,954,644
L. S. Good and Co.	72,272	McCrory-Rapid American	1,543,000
Crowley-Milner & Co.	55,183	Beneficial Corp.	1,115,863
Walker-Scott Co.	43,279	SCOA Industries Inc.	780,333
Totals	23,096,565	Outlet Co.	307,096
		New Process Co.	213,103
Specialty Stores		Elder-Beerman Stores	178,651
Levitz Furniture Corp.	498,194	Dollar General	161,694
Petrie Stores Corp.	435,872	Totals	9,567,384
Garfinkel, Brooks Brothers,			
Miller & Rhoades Inc.	390,916	**Summary**	
Lane Bryant	365,552	Mass Merchandisers	51,603,675
The Gap Stores, Inc.	259,888	Dept. Stores	23,096,565
Miller-Wohl Co.	167,742	Discount Stores	7,633,473
Rockower Bros, Inc.	125,769	Specialty Stores	2,675,789
Brooks Fashion Stores, Inc.	113,737	Miscellaneous	9,567,384
Haverty Furniture Stores, Inc.	96,983	Grand Total	94,576,886
Winkelman Stores Inc.	83,757		

Source: Women's Wear Daily, Aug. 23, 1979. Figures reflect 1978 sales.

this group are commonly known as mass merchandisers, department stores, discount stores, variety stores, general merchandise stores, or general stores.

Specialty stores carry only limited lines of related merchandise. They define their customers more specifically—in terms of age range, size range, or common interest. These specialty stores differ from general merchandise stores in that their customer groups are more homogeneous, at least in respect to the particular merchandise that the store offers. Table 11-1 shows sales volume for a sample listing of retail stores by type.

The general merchandise and specialty store groups account for the greater share of fashion retailers. But modern retailing has also seen the rise of leased and franchise departments and stores, catalog showroom stores, and the broad realm of nonstore retailing. The latter includes mail-order operations of all kinds, door-to-door or in-home selling, fashion merchandise offerings to credit card customers, automatic vending machine merchandising, and the use of telecommunications in the sale and delivery of merchandise.

DEPARTMENT STORES

Department stores are the type of retailer most familiar to the buying public. Department stores in large cities all over the world are often among the most famous landmarks. Few people visit New York without seeing Macy's or Bloomingdale's, for example. Such stores as Marshall Field in Chicago, J. L. Hudson in Detroit, John Wanamaker in Philadelphia, Lazarus in Columbus, Rich's in Atlanta, The Broadway in Los Angeles, Eaton's in Montreal, Harrod's in London, and Galeries Lafayette in Paris are other well-known names. See Table 11-2 for the top department stores in the United States.

Department stores are so named because they present each of their many different kinds of merchandise in a separate area or department. A department store usually leads other types of stores in terms of overall status and importance in a community. It usually serves a larger segment of the local population than

do other types of stores because its merchandise covers a wide range of categories and prices.

In addition, department stores are always very interested in finding ways to serve their local communities. If a department store can stage a fashion show for a local charity or lend space for an art show or club meeting, for instance, it usually does so willingly. Such community service generates goodwill. It also creates an awareness of the store and its merchandise that represents an addition to the efforts that the store makes specifically to publicize and sell its merchandise.

Definition

A **department store** is defined by the U.S. Bureau of the Census as an establishment that normally employs 25 or more people and is engaged in selling general lines of merchandise in each of three categories:

- Furniture, home furnishings, appliances, and radio and TV sets
- General lines of apparel and accessories for the entire family
- Household linens and drygoods (an old trade term meaning piece goods and sewing notions)

Organization for Buying and Merchandising

In department stores, various categories or related merchandise are grouped together into departments—sportswear, dresses, men's clothing, or furniture, for example. In most cases, a separate buyer is assigned to purchase all stock for each department. In the very largest of the department stores, each category may be more specifically defined and departmentalized. In some sportswear departments, for example, the categories become blouses, skirts, pants, etc., with a separate buyer and department number for each category.

In most nonchain retail organizations that have fewer than 12 branches, a department buyer is headquartered in the parent, or

TABLE 11-2
Top Department Stores in the United States

COMPANY/DIVISION	AFFILIATION	NUMBER OF STORES	VOLUME (MILLIONS)
1. Macy's, New York	(RHM)	15	$715
2. Bamberger's, New Jersey	(RHM)	21	660
3. Hudson's, Detroit	(D-H)	16	652
4. May Co., California	(May)	29	610
5. Broadway-Southern California (new Broadway-Southwest listed separately)	(CHH)	40	595
6. Marshall Field & Co., Chicago	(MF)	17	520
7. Bloomingdale's, New York	(Fed)	15	518.2
8. Abraham & Straus, Brooklyn	(Fed)	11	512
9. Macy's California	(RHM)	17	490
10. Foley's, Houston	(Fed)	9	412.2
11. Burdine's, Florida	(Fed)	19	407
12. Bullock's, Los Angeles	(Fed)	20	405.3
13. Lord & Taylor, New York	(ADG)	34	405
14. Dillard's, Little Rock	(Ind)	44	391.3
15. Emporium-Capwell, No. California	(CHH)	18	390
16. Joske's, Texas	(All)	27	360
17. Dayton's, Minneapolis	(D-H)	15	357
18. Hecht's, Baltimore-Washington	(May)	20	355
19. Jordan Marsh, New England	(All)	14	340
20. Rich's, Atlanta	(Fed)	15	328.8
21. Lazarus, Columbus, OH	(Fed)	14	325.4
22. Wanamaker, Philadelphia	(CHH)	16	325
23. Famous-Barr, St. Louis	(May)	12	315
24. Goldblatt's, Chicago	(Ind)	46	306.6
25. Bon Marche-Northwest, Seattle	(All)	27	300
26. Woodward & Lothrop, Washington	(Ind)	14	295.2
27. Filene's, Boston	(Fed)	19	267.7
28. Carson, Pirie Scott, Chicago	(Ind)	26	255
29. J. W. Robinson, Los Angeles	(ADG)	18	245
30. Sanger-Harris, Dallas	(Fed)	11	240.7
31. Gimbels-New York	(BAT)	11	240
32. May Co.-Cleveland	(May)	10	220
Strawbridge & Clothier, Philadelphia	(Ind)	11	220
34. Shillito's, Cincinnati	(Fed	9	211.6
35. Kaufmann's, Pittsburgh	(May)	10	210
36. Maas Bros., Florida	(All)	18	205
37. H. C. Prange Co., Sheboygan, WI	(Ind)	28	200
38. Jordan Marsh, Miami	(All)	12	195

Source: Stores, July 1980, page 22. Figures reflect 1979 sales.

Affiliation Code: RHM, R. H. Macy; D-H, Dayton-Hudson; CHH, Carter Hawley Hale; MF, Marshall Field; Fed, Federated; ADG, Associated Dry Goods; Ind, Independent; All, Allied; BAT, Batus, Inc. Retail Division; CAC, Carter Associates Corp.; EI, Equitable of Iowa.

TABLE 11-2 *(Continued)*
Top Department Stores in the United States

COMPANY/DIVISION	AFFILIATION	NUMBER OF STORES	VOLUME (MILLIONS)
Stix, Baer, Fuller, St. Louis	(ADG)	14	195
40. Joseph Horne, Pittsburgh	(ADG)	15	190
B. Altman & Co., New York	(Ind)	6	190
42. Higbee's, Cleveland	(Ind)	12	185
43. Frederick & Nelson (Inc. Lipman's)	(M-F)	13	180
44. D. H. Holmes, New Orleans	(Ind)	13	176.5
45. Elder-Beerman, Dayton, OH	(Ind)	20	170
G. Fox, Hartford	(May)	7	170
47. Wieboldt's, Chicago	(Ind)	13	169.7
48. Davison's, Atlanta	(RHM)	11	165
49. Thalhimer's, Richmond	(CHH)	23	160
Gimbels-Philadelphia	(BAT)	10	160
P. A. Bergner, Peoria, IL	(Ind)	24	160
52. Hess's, Allentown	(CAC)	17	159.8
53. Younker Bros., Des Moines	(EI)	28	155

"main," store. This buyer is responsible for purchasing stock for the branches as well as for the parent store. In addition, the buyer is responsible for departmental sales in all locations, for the merchandise training of all departmental salespeople, and for the profitable operation of the department in all stores.

BRANCH STORES.   One of the most significant changes in department store retailing involves the growth and development of branch stores. Originally branches were, for the most part, small replicas of the parent (main) store. Most had limited stocks and contributed only a nominal percentage of the firm's total sales volume. Also these branches were located close enough to the parent store so that the departmental buyers could visit each store frequently.

Today many branch stores are as large or, in some cases, even larger than the parent store, contributing in most cases more than 50 percent of the firm's total annual sales volume. In addition, branches are being established farther and farther away from the parent store, making meaningful buyer responsibility for sales and training supervi-

sion and management impossible. In such cases each branch, as well as the parent store, are treated as separate entities, each with its own individual management. Departmental buyers' responsibility is limited to the merchandising and replenishment of stocks as needed by each store.

Merchandising Policies

Merchandising policies are guidelines established by store management for merchandising executives to follow in order to win the patronage of specific target groups of customers. Each type of retail organization has its own characteristic merchandising policies. The following shows how a department store's policies, in each major area of merchandising activity, differ from those of other types of retail organizations.

FASHION-CYCLE EMPHASIS.   Small or moderate-size department stores place major emphasis in their fashion assortments on styles that are in the late-rise and early culmination stages of their fashion cycles. Larger

Some large department stores feature styles in the early-rise stage of their fashion cycles, as in this department shop set up at the beginning of a "new look."

department stores, however, often expand their fashion offerings to include both prestige and budget departments as well. Their prestige departments feature styles in the early-rise stage of their fashion cycles; budget or basement departments feature styles that are well into the culmination stage or may even have begun their decline.

PRICE RANGES.   Small or moderate-size department stores tend to concentrate on merchandise assortments within moderate price ranges. However, larger department stores will feature higher price ranges in their prestige departments and lower price ranges in their budget or basement departments.

DEPTH AND
BREADTH OF ASSORTMENTS.   A department store's policy in relation to the type of fashion assortments it carries must follow the merchandising policies of the store as established by top management. There are two types of fashion assortments used by retailers. One is known as "narrow and deep" and the other is known as "broad and shallow." A **narrow and deep assortment** is one in which there are relatively few styles, but these few styles are carried in all available sizes and colors. A **broad and shallow assortment** is one in which there are many styles but only limited sizes and colors are carried in each style.

Outstanding examples of narrow and deep fashion assortments are those carried in department store chains, such as Sears, Roebuck and Co. and Montgomery Ward. Bloomingdale's and Marshall Field & Co. are good examples of department stores whose fashion assortments may be characterized as broad and shallow. Most department store buyers, especially when placing orders for goods prior to the start of a selling season, begin with broad and shallow assortments. As the selling season advances the assortments are later changed to narrow and deep assortments of those styles or similar styles and colors to which customers show good response. Conversely, the assortments of department store prestige apparel salons, which consist of styles in the introductory or early-rise stages of their fashion development, are always maintained at a fairly wide and very shallow level. In some cases only two or three pieces of a style may be carried, with each piece in a different size and color.

BRAND POLICIES.   Nationally advertised brands usually play an important role in a department store's fashion stocks and are prominently featured in its displays and advertising. In order to minimize competition from local stores that feature the same brands, department stores may seek items from branded lines that will be **confined,** or exclusive with them in their own communities.

CUSTOMER SERVICES.   Department stores were pioneers in offering customer charge and return privileges. This willingness to accept merchandise returns was one of the foundations on which the late John Wanamaker built his business. His first store, opened in Philadelphia in 1876 in an old freight station, was a men's clothing store. A year later he had added such departments as ladies' goods, household linens, upholstery, and shoes, for a total of 16 departments. Wanamaker advertised that any article that did not fit well, did not please "the folks at home," or for any other reason was unsatisfactory could be returned for cash refund within 10 days.

Today, department stores offer an increasing number of services because of increased competition for customers. The more familiar customer services include a variety of credit plans, free local delivery, free parking at suburban branches, and alterations. New customer services may include travel bureaus, ticket agencies, post office facilities, art and needlework instruction, child-care centers, expanded telephone-order facilities, and extended shopping hours.

SELLING SERVICES. Modern department stores may offer a variety of selling services within a single store. This depends upon the nature and sometimes the price level of the merchandise involved. In prestige apparel departments, a salon type of selling service often prevails. In this type of service, merchandise other than that used for display purposes is kept out of sight. A salesperson chooses styles from the stockroom to bring out for individual customer's inspection. Self-selection is the type of selling service most commonly employed by department stores today, however. Merchandise is arranged on open racks, counters, or shelves for the customer's inspection. Salespeople are available to assist customers by providing information about the merchandise and by completing the sales transaction once a customer has reached a buying decision. A few department stores offer self-service with check-out counters for certain types of merchandise, but this is the exception rather than the rule.

PROMOTIONAL ACTIVITIES. Department stores engage in a moderate amount of promotional activity. For this reason, they generally are referred to as semipromotional stores. This means they regularly feature individual items in their advertising and displays. They also do a moderate amount of "special sale"

and "special purchase" promotion, such as anniversary sales, end-of-month clearances, and traditional seasonal events such as White Sales and Back-to-School promotions.

FASHION COORDINATION. Department stores usually place only a moderate emphasis on coordination of fashion accessories with apparel, other than in fashion shows and in window and interior displays. However, as competition increases, particularly from specialty stores and discount stores, department stores place greater emphasis on the coordination of their fashion assortments as a means of creating a distinctive fashion image.

SPECIALTY STORES

Specialty stores vary widely in both size and type. They range from the tiny **Mom-and-Pop store,** run by the proprietor with few or no hired assistants, to huge departmentalized institutions that resemble large department stores. Some are single-unit stores; some are units of chains; some are suburban branches of central-city stores or branches of a parent store located in a distant city.

Most specialty stores are individually owned. They have no branches and are not units of chains. The composite sales of these single-unit stores, however, represent less than half the total sales volume of all specialty stores. The larger share of business is done by multiunit specialty stores or local, regional, or national chains. J. W. Robinson is an example of a Los Angeles based multibranch specialty store. For other examples of multiunit chain operations with units throughout the country, see page 239.

Definition

According to the Bureau of the Census, a **specialty store** is one that carries limited lines of apparel or accessories or home furnishings. A shoe store, a jewelry store, or one handling only women's apparel and accessories is classified as a specialty store. In the trade, however, retailers use the term "specialty store"

Specialty stores come in many sizes and varieties; what they have in common is fashion awareness.

to describe any apparel and/or accessories store that exhibits a degree of fashion awareness and that carries goods for men, women, and/or children.

Organization for Buying and Merchandising

In large specialty stores, as in department stores, merchandise is usually grouped into separate departments. In these stores, a buyer is assigned to purchase stock for each department and has the same responsibilities as does the buyer for a single or multi-branch department store.

Smaller specialty stores, however, may not be departmentalized. In this case, all merchandise is usually bought by the owner or store manager, sometimes with the help of one or two assistants.

Like department stores with few branches, specialty stores generally merchandise their branches from the parent store. Specialty stores with great numbers of branches use the chain-store type of organization. Specialty-store branches enjoy the same advantages over local competition that department store branches do: a skilled fashion merchandiser who directs the operation from the parent store and a large stock from which to draw styles, colors, and sizes.

Merchandising Policies

Specialty stores generally concentrate on pleasing a specific, carefully profiled customer rather than trying to serve a broad range of customers as department stores do. Most non-chain specialty stores employ this merchandising policy in their efforts to win maximum customer patronage.

FASHION-CYCLE EMPHASIS. The customer selected by the specialty store as its target may be high-fashion or budget-minded, a fashion innovator or a follower, a teenager or a senior citizen, to give just a few examples. Each specialty store builds its fashion assortments around merchandise that is in the particular stage of its fashion cycle most likely to appeal to the majority of the store's target customers.

PRICE RANGES. Some specialty stores feature lower price ranges, but many specialty stores carry only current and high fashions and feature moderate to high price lines. Stores of the latter type are so widely known and function so effectively that consumers tend to associate the term "specialty store" with slightly higher prices and newer fashions than those found in department stores.

DEPTH AND
BREADTH OF ASSORTMENTS. The usual merchandising approach of specialty stores is to have broad and shallow assortments within

the categories that their target customers may be expected to accept.

BRAND POLICY. Most specialty stores place major emphasis on their own store label or, in some cases, on designer labels. If specialty stores select merchandise from nationally advertised brand lines, they usually avoid the **fords** (styles that are widely copied at a variety of price lines). Because they often buy only a few units of a given style, many specialty stores can and do make greater use of smaller fashion resources with limited production than do department stores.

CUSTOMER SERVICES. Customer services offered by specialty stores tend to be fairly similar in both type and number to those offered by department stores with equivalent sales volume.

SELLING SERVICES. Self-selection selling is used in specialty stores where it is appropriate, but there is likely to be more emphasis on personal selling than in department stores. In the medium- to higher-priced specialty stores, emphasis is placed on remembering what individual customers and their friends have purchased. The accent in such stores is on personal service.

PROMOTIONAL ACTIVITIES. Advertising and display activities of specialty stores tend to be less promotional than those used by department stores. Rather than featuring individual items, moderate- to higher-priced specialty store ads and displays usually feature designer collections, ''looks,'' and trends in coordinated apparel and accessories. Lower-priced specialty stores, and particularly those that are units of a chain, tend to feature in both their ads and displays the fashion-rightness of the styles carried in their assortments.

FASHION COORDINATION. In most specialty stores, accessories are carefully related to apparel, and fashion coordination is stressed in ads, displays, and selling services.

CHAIN ORGANIZATIONS

Chains that deal in fashion merchandise may be national, regional, or local. They may be department store chains, with only a portion of assortments devoted to fashion goods. They may be mass-merchandise chains that emphasize the quality and durability of their fashion goods and distribute impressive quantities of merchandise. Or they may be general merchandise chains known for selling nationally advertised fashion goods below suggested retail prices. There are specialty store chains that deal exclusively with fashion merchandise at high prices. There are also apparel specialty chains that focus on a special size, age, or income group. Outstanding examples of mass-merchandising chains are the J. C. Penney Co., Sears, Roebuck and Co., and Montgomery Ward. Outstanding examples of general merchandise chains are K-Mart and Zayre. Saks Fifth Avenue, Neiman-Marcus, and Lord and Taylor are examples of prestige specialty chains. The Limited, The Gap, Lerner Stores, and Casual Corner are examples of apparel specialty chains appealing mainly to the junior customer.

Definition

According to the Bureau of the Census, a **chain organization** is a group of 12 or more stores, centrally owned, each handling somewhat similar goods and merchandised and controlled from a central headquarters office. The difference between a chain organization and a department or specialty store organization with multiple branches is that the former is merchandised and controlled from a central office, while the latter is merchandised and controlled from a parent store.

Organization for Buying and Merchandising

Centralized buying, merchandising, and distribution of fashion assortments prevail among retail chain organizations. The majority of chain stores are departmentalized. But a chain buyer located in a central buying office is usually assigned to purchase only a specific category or classification of merchandise, instead of buying all categories carried in a single department as a nonchain buyer does. For example, a sportswear buyer for a department or specialty store might be responsible for buying all the various categories of merchandise usually carried in a typical sportswear department, such as swimwear, tops, jeans, sweaters, and slacks. In contrast, one chain organization buyer might be assigned to purchase swimwear, another to purchase sweaters, and so on. Category buying, rather than departmental buying, is necessary because of the huge quantities of goods in each category that are needed to stock all the individual units of a chain. These units sometimes number in the thousands.

Centrally purchased merchandise is usually distributed to the units of a chain from central or regional distribution centers. Most larger chains have set up elaborate systems of supervision and reporting so that their central-office buyers are kept informed at all times of what is selling and what remains in stock at each of their many units.

Unlike single-unit or multibranch department or specialty store buyers, central buyers are not directly responsible for sales. These are the responsibility of the store manager of each unit in the chain and the appropriate department manager. Neither are central buyers responsible for the merchandise training of salespeople in each unit. However, they do supply trend and other information to chain units about the merchandise distributed to them. And, since central buyers are usually responsible for providing stock in only one or limited merchandise categories, they are not responsible for the profitable merchandising of a department as a whole.

Merchandising Policies

A chain organization's merchandising policies depend upon the type of target customer the chain has chosen to serve. Most department store chains, with a few important exceptions, establish merchandising policies that appeal to customers with limited or moderate income. Most specialty store chains, on the other hand, mold their merchandising policies to attract customers with average to above-average incomes and usually above-average interest in fashion apparel and accessories.

FASHION-CYCLE EMPHASIS. Most department store chains do not try to be fashion leaders. Instead, they place emphasis on fashion styles that have reached the culmination stage of their cycles. Some large specialty store chains such as Lord and Taylor, however, assert fashion leadership by offering styles in earlier stages of their fashion cycles at moderate- to moderately-high prices.

PRICE RANGES. Most department store chains tend to emphasize consistent values and promotional prices in their fashion offerings, as do lower-priced speciality store chains. Therefore, they feature prices in the low to moderate ranges. Speciality store chains with more fashion leadership, however, stress moderate to higher price ranges.

DEPTH AND
BREADTH OF ASSORTMENTS. Both department and lower-priced specialty store chains usually concentrate their assortments on a narrow range of proven styles with depth (in color and size) in each style. The fashion assortments of specialty store chains that stress greater fashion leadership tend to be broader and more shallow.

Rapid and accurate stock and sales reporting is essential to profitable chain operation. The "system," or method of reporting used, is viewed by a chain, large or small, as the vital artery that carries its lifeblood. For this reason, electronic systems now handle the tremendous flow of merchandising data in most chain organizations.

BRAND POLICY. Private labeling is used to a large extent by both department and specialty store chains. In offering its own brands, each chain can maintain certain quality standards and provide the merchandise characteristics most in demand by its customers. At the same

SAVE 25%

Active kids sport a winning look in terry shorts and tops

Summer basics: cool, comfy terry shorts and tops of polyester, cotton and polyester acrylic and polyester or polyester and cotton. Lots of styles.

for little kids
$3.49 girl's sunsuit, S-M-L . .2.59
$2.99 boy's sport short, 3-6x, 2.19
$5.99 boy's short-sleeve top, S-M-L 4.49

for bigger boys and teens
$3.99 boy's shorts, S-M-L . .2.99
$4.99 boy's short-sleeve shirt, 8-16 . . . . .3.69
$4.99 boy's shorts, S-M-L . .3.69
$4.99 boy's top, S-M-L . .3.69
$5.99 teen boy's shorts, S-M-L, 4.49
$6.99 teen boy's shirt, XS-S-M-L 5.19

for bigger girls
$4.99 shorts, S-M-L 3.69
$5.99 top, S-M-L 4.49

Ask about Sears credit plans
Sale ends (date)

Sears

© Sears Roebuck and Co., 1980

Most department store chains emphasize promotional prices in their fashion offerings.

time, private labeling can ensure that the merchandise assortments are not readily comparable with the offerings of competing stores.

CUSTOMER SERVICES.   Customer services are usually more limited in chain organizations than in most nonchain stores. Free delivery of fashion merchandise is rarely provided. The usual credit plans prevail, with greater emphasis on installment plans. Chain organizations may take the lead or follow the lead of other prominent stores in the community in establishing business hours.

SELLING SERVICES.   With rare exceptions, selling services in department store and low-to moderate-priced speciality store chain organizations are usually of a self-selection type.

Clerks simply answer questions and ring up sales. Higher-priced specialty store chains, however, tend to place more emphasis on personal selling techniques.

The three major mass-merchandise chains supplement floor sales in their retail outlets with catalog sales. A special catalog desk or counter is usually maintained in each retail store unit. Customers may phone, mail, or come in person to order merchandise not regularly carried in that store's stock.

Each chain prepares seasonal catalogs—as many as five or six a year. Selection of fashion merchandise for catalog selling has to be done much further in advance than selection for store floor sales, because of the time required to develop and print catalogs. Central buyers for each chain's retail stores may assist in the planning and buying of catalog merchandise.

Today's catalogs differ vastly from those 20 to 50 years ago, especially in the case of fashion merchandise. More pages are now devoted to apparel and accessories for men, women, and children. Merchandise is more closely related to current fashion trends, and illustrations are usually in full color.

PROMOTIONAL ACTIVITIES. Promotional activities of most chain organizations are coordinated with their central buying activities. The advertising staff at a chain's central or regional headquarters prepares advertising layouts and provides display suggestions for all chain units. These are designed to promote the fashion merchandise purchased by the central buyers for the various units.

Department store chains concentrate mainly on item advertising of fashion goods with frequent off-price promotions. Specialty store chains that carry higher-priced fashion merchandise usually follow the promotional pattern of nonchain specialty stores operating at the same price level; they feature looks and trends in ads and displays.

FASHION COORDINATION. Larger department and specialty store chains may employ the services of a fashion coordinator. This person searches both domestic and foreign markets for new fashion trends and for unusual styling that can be adapted or incorporated into their private label merchandise offerings. In the largest chains, a fashion coordinator has a staff of assistants. Each assistant is assigned responsibility for a specific type of fashion apparel, such as dresses, sportswear, menswear, or children's wear.

The fashion coordinator of a chain, working closely with the central buying and merchandising staffs, is also responsible for periodic fashion reports to the managers and staff of each unit. These highlight current fashion trends and coordination possibilities in apparel and accessories for the coming season. (For further details about fashion coordination in chain operations, see Chapter 20.)

DISCOUNT STORES

Discount stores are a twentieth-century development. Originally the term "discounter" applied only to dealers in durable or hard goods who sold merchandise below manufacturers' list prices. The procedure was considered illegal in those days, although the fair trade laws in most states have since been changed.

Every facet of the early discounters' operations were designed to keep costs low. They dealt only in low-risk merchandise. Their stores were situated in out-of-the-way locations where rent and real estate taxes were low. Minimum facilities and basic "pipe rack" fixturing were the rule. Sales were handled on a central-cashier basis that eliminated the need for a sales staff. They did little paid advertising, depending mainly on word-of-mouth promotion. As a result, they could price merchandise much lower than conventional retailers and still operate profitably. Factory outlet discount stores originated as places for manufacturers to sell their "irregulars" and slow-moving merchandise directly to the public.

During the latter 1950s, many of the early hard-goods discounters began adding limited lines of soft goods and fashion goods to their offerings. At first these efforts met with only mediocre success, because most discounters lacked the necessary merchandising experience with these types of goods. As a result, a number of them turned over the merchandising of soft goods and fashion departments to leased operators who had more expertise along those lines. By using lessees, the discount store owners also did not have to invest the firms' capital in high-risk inventory nor in the expenses involved in merchandising such inventories. Instead, they simply collected a share of each leased department's sales volume as rent. Today, more and more discount stores are buying up the companies that were the lessees of their fashion departments or are simply hiring their own buyers for these departments. The markup and profit these fashion departments generate allow discount stores to be more competitive in the pricing of their durable goods.

In the last two decades, many of the old-line discount organizations have substantially expanded their fashion assortments, improved their housekeeping and services, modernized facilities and fixturing, and upgraded advertising and display in an effort to establish a definite fashion image.

In addition, in recent years many conventional retailers and large ownership groups have entered the discount field with wholly-owned discount operations as separate divisions of parent firms. For example, Target Stores is the discount operation of the prestigious Dayton-Hudson department store group. K-Mart is the highly successful discount chain operation of the S.S. Kresge variety chain.

Although most discounters started as durable goods merchants, a few started out as women's apparel fashion discounters and still retain prominence in that field.

Today, a new type of fashion discount operation is making its appearance on the retail scene. These are stores that offer odd lots of higher-priced fashion apparel—frequently designer-label apparel—at prices considerably less than those charged in conventional stores. One of the oldest, best-known, and largest of these is Loehmann's; it has a parent store in the Bronx and a number of branches along the Eastern Seaboard.

Whether they be creative merchandisers or dealers in producer overstocks, discount stores serve an important fashion function in selling enormous quantities of fashion goods.

Definition

Discount Merchandiser, the magazine of the discount industry, defines a **discount store** as a departmentalized retail establishment using many self-service techniques to sell hard goods, health and beauty aids, apparel and other soft goods, and other general merchandise. It operates at unusually low profit margins. It has a minimum annual volume of $500,000 and is at least 10,000 square feet in size. It may be an independent store or a unit of a department, specialty, or variety-store chain.

Organization for Buying and Merchandising

In departments owned and operated by a chain discount organization, buying and merchandising activities are basically the same as those previously described for chain organizations. Centralized buying prevails. Discount store buyers, however, are usually responsible for buying for several departments rather than for only a single category of merchandise. The nonchain discount stores, which are far less numerous than chains, follow the same basic buying and merchandising pattern as that of similar volume nonchain department or specialty stores.

Early discounters searched the market for closeouts and special-price promotions. In many cases, their inventories consisted almost entirely of this type of merchandise. Today, however, the fashion stocks of many discounters consist of regular goods bought in either the low-end open market or special lines made up exclusively for discount operations by producers who sell their regular lines to conventional stores. Most conventional retail firms will not allow their buyers to purchase fashion goods from producers who sell the same goods to mass-merchandised operations. Many producers, however, have found it profitable to create a second line for such customers because of the huge quantities of fashion goods they can use.

Merchandising Policies

Nearly every discount store has the same target customer: a person who wants value at prices lower than those charged by conventional retail stores. Discount store merchandising policies are designed to serve this kind of customer.

FASHION-CYCLE EMPHASIS. Most discount stores today concentrate on styles that are well into the culmination stage of their cycles. However, a few offer some styles that are still in their early fashion stages.

PRICE RANGE. In most cases, discount operations feature lower prices than those offered by conventional retailers.

DEPTH AND
BREADTH OF ASSORTMENTS. The fashion assortments of stores that buy mainly manufacturers' closeouts and discontinued styles tend to be broad and shallow. The fashion assortments of discounters that have goods made up especially for them and regularly buy low-end merchandise tend to be narrow in ranges of styles but great in depth.

BRAND POLICY. Until recently, nationally advertised brands were usually not available to discounters. As a result, some producers made up secondary lines under different brand labels for distribution through discount firms. Recently, however, some nationally advertised fashion apparel and accessories may be found in discount store assortments, at the same prices as marked in competing, conventional stores.

CUSTOMER SERVICES. Transactions in discount operations are usually made for cash, although a number of such stores today accept checks or bank credit cards or offer credit plans of their own. Refund policies are generally liberal: money back if the goods are returned unused in a specified number of days. Delivery service, if available, is usually restricted to bulky items and often involves an extra charge. Limited fitting-room service for trying on apparel may sometimes be found. Paperwork is kept to a minimum. The cash-register receipt often serves as a sales slip, and refunds are usually made in cash, eliminating credit slips and extensive bookkeeping.

SELLING SERVICES. In discount store selling, frills are eliminated. Merchandise is stocked on racks or tables and customers help themselves. Self-service prevails. Employees are present only to direct customers and straighten the stock. Customers make their selections and then take them to a cashier's desk where sales are rung up.

PROMOTIONAL ACTIVITIES. Today, discount stores are highly promotional. They place their emphasis on all types of advertising, including newspaper, radio, and direct mail. Advertising always emphasizes low price and, in many cases, comparative prices.

Interior displays are used mainly to identify the location of merchandise; they play a relatively minor role in the store's promotional efforts. Window displays in some leading discount chains, however, are well planned and attractive.

FASHION COORDINATION. In spite of the gradual upgrading of some merchandising techniques, there is little evidence that discount stores try to coordinate their fashion apparel and accessory offerings.

VARIETY STORES

Variety stores once referred to themselves as "limited price variety stores," to underscore the fact that they carried a wide range of merchandise in a limited number of low price lines. Some literally were 5-and-10-cent stores, with all merchandise priced at either a nickel or a dime. Others sold goods priced up to a dollar. Fashion merchandise was represented in their assortments only by such utilitarian articles as socks and underwear, ribbons and buttons, and simple hair and dress ornaments. Chain operations dominated the field.

In the 1930s, the larger variety chains began to broaden their assortments and extend their price ranges. They grew into what are now known as general merchandise stores.

Definition

A **variety store** carries a wide range of merchandise in a limited number of low or relatively low price lines. Some variety stores are independent organizations, but most are units of chain organizations.

Organization for Buying and Merchandising

Since most variety stores are units of a chain, their buying and merchandising techniques are identical with those described for chain organizations (see above). These include centralized buying and distribution handled by headquarters office personnel.

Merchandising Policies

Variety stores serve a wide range of customers. They provide one-stop shopping for many different basic personal and household necessities, all relatively inexpensive. Following are the merchandising policies which make variety stores the convenience they are for many different groups of customers.

FASHION-CYCLE EMPHASIS. The fashion apparel and accessories that variety stores carry are usually limited to styles that are well into the culmination stage of their fashion cycles.

PRICE RANGES. The fashion assortments carried by variety stores are low or relatively low in price.

DEPTH AND BREADTH OF ASSORTMENTS. Fashion assortments in variety stores tend to be narrow in range of styles and generally shallow in depth of size and color in each style.

BRAND POLICY. Many variety stores use their own private labels on merchandise made to specification or bought from unbranded manufacturers.

CUSTOMER SERVICES. The earlier variety stores had bare wooden floors, no fitting rooms, and few, if any, customer services. Today, however, modern units of such variety chains as F. W. Woolworth Company or S. S. Kresge are well-lighted, air-conditioned, and carpeted or surfaced with resilient floor coverings. Only the larger chains, however, offer such customer services as charge privileges, delivery, and a basic kind of ready-to-wear fitting room.

SELLING SERVICES. Self-service generally prevails in variety stores as a selling technique, although some limited personal selling may be provided. Well-labeled merchandise is packaged, binned, or hung for customers' inspection and selection.

PROMOTIONAL ACTIVITIES. Variety stores seldom, if ever, advertise fashion goods. Their promotion of fashion goods is largely limited to displays. Though mainly functional, these attempt to emphasize the important fashion points of the merchandise.

FASHION COORDINATION. Variety stores make no attempt to coordinate fashion assortments since the styles they feature are already widely accepted. In units of the larger chains, however, a concerted effort has been made to feature coordinated apparel and accessories both in window and in interior displays.

Because the fashions that are featured have already proved successful before making an appearance in these stores, and also because of their low pricing policies, variety stores

Here is an ad that appeared in a trade journal directed to retailers. It would interest store owners wanting to lease their accessories department.

make their major appeal to lower-income customers who are fashion followers.

LEASED DEPARTMENTS

Department stores tend to lease both merchandise and service departments, as do chain and discount organizations. Specialty stores usually restrict leased operations to services.

Services commonly leased include the beauty salon, shoe repair, and jewelry repair. Merchandise departments most frequently leased include millinery, shoes, fine jewelry, and furs. There are also some leased departments that handle women's apparel. But these are likely to be found in discount stores, and they usually concentrate on lower-priced goods.

Glemby Company and Seligman and Latz lease many of the beauty salons in department, specialty, and chain stores throughout the country.

In Alexander's, in New York City, "Fred the Furrier" leases the fur department. He has used many innovative advertising and selling techniques to build up the fur business in all the Alexander's stores.

Definition

As indicated in Chapter 6, a leased department is merchandised by an outside organization rather than by the store itself. That organization owns the department's stock, merchandises and staffs the department, pays for its advertising, is required to abide by the host store's policies, and pays the store a percentage of sales as rent. In general, the operator of a leased department is an expert in some merchandise or service that a retail store finds unprofitable to handle directly.

Organization for Buying and Merchandising

The operator of a leased department may be a local person functioning in a single store or a giant organization doing business in hundreds of stores across the country. Central buying and merchandising prevail. In larger operations, traveling supervisors regularly visit their various locations to confer with both the host-store management and the department manager, to help them cope with problems that may arise, and to plan for future growth.

Leased-department operators are in a unique position with respect to the fashion industries. They are usually in daily contact with their markets and are sometimes established in a wide variety of stores. They can give impetus to incoming styles or clear producers' stocks of declining styles, according to the merchandising policies of their host stores. The successful, long-established operators sometimes know their industries better than the producers themselves. Such operators are equipped to give fashion guidance to their sources of supply as well as to the stores they serve.

Merchandising Policies

The fashion merchandising policies of a leased department are dictated by the terms of its lease and must conform to the policies of the store in which it operates. Assortments and services must be on a level with those of all other departments in the host store, so that customers have no indication that the department is not owned and operated by the host store.

Some larger leased-department organizations are immensely flexible in their approach to individual store policies and can function on almost any level of fashion and service that may be required. Others limit themselves to narrow fields, such as popular-priced shoes. These seek connections only with stores whose merchandise and service policies are compatible with their own.

Table 11-3 outlines the merchandising policies of the types of retail firms discussed in this chapter.

TRENDS IN RETAIL FASHION DISTRIBUTION

The successful retailers of the future will be those who anticipate and adapt to environ-mental change. This will require the development of flexible organizational structures and internal communications programs which monitor demographic shifts and corresponding changes in consumer preferences. The closing of stores such as W. T. Grant, Robert Hall, Franklin Simon, Bond stores, E. J. Korvettes, and the J. M. Fields stores has resulted from misguided expansion or misjudgments of social and economic trends.

Consumerism is a controlling element in retail stores' operating policies and procedures. Traditionally the retailer was concerned with product quality, variety, and pricing. Now retailer responsibilities include product information and safety, compensation for unsatisfactory purchases, and electronic systems for transfer of funds. Retailers are recognizing that every facet of a store's organization must concern itself with consumer needs and wants. As a result, retailers are developing coordinated strategies for satisfying consumers' interests.

A major trend in fashion distribution is the movement toward bigness—in size and scope of organization, in number of units, and in breadth of assortments. This trend affects department stores, specialty stores, chain stores, discount stores, and all other forms of retailing. The 1980s will also bring computerization beyond the store and into the customer's home. Selecting merchandise at home by computer will be one of the shopping alternatives in the eighties.

Organizational Structures

Retail fashion distributors face a great challenge in the next two decades—the challenge of monitoring the demographic shifts of consumers and their constantly changing merchandise preferences. Retailers need to rethink and reevaluate merchandising decisions made in the sixties and seventies and update their marketing strategies for new target markets. Retailers will need to use better planning methods and tighter inventory and expense controls in the coming years if they are to survive and grow. More professional management structures, better communication with

TABLE 11-3
Merchandising Policies of Various Types of Retail Firms That Sell Fashion Merchandise

MERCHANDISING POLICIES	NONCHAIN DEPARTMENT STORES	NONCHAIN SPECIALTY STORES	CHAIN ORGANIZATIONS	DISCOUNT ORGANIZATIONS	VARIETY STORES	LEASED DEPARTMENTS
Fashion Cycle Emphasis	Mainly late rise and early culmination; early rise in prestige departments; full to late culmination in budget departments	Particular stage of cycle favored by, majority of its customers	Mainly culmination stage; some specialty chains feature styles in earlier stages of cycle	Styles well into the culmination of their fashion cycles	Styles well into the culmination of fashion cycles	Same as in host store
Price Ranges	Mainly moderate; high in prestige departments; low in budget departments	Mainly moderate but depends on stage of fashion cycle its customers prefer	Department store chains: lower and promotional pricing; some specialty chains: moderate to high price ranges	Lower than conventional retailers	Low to relatively low	Same as in host store
Depth and Breadth of Assortments	Broad and shallow at start of new selling seasons; narrower and deeper as customer preferences become known	Typically broad and shallow	Department store chains: narrow range of proven styles in considerable depth; moderate- to high-priced specialty chains: broader and shallower	Mainly broad and shallow	Narrow and shallow	Same as in host store
Brand Policies	National brands emphasized	Major emphasis on own store labels or designer labels	Own private labels emphasized	Unbranded; own brand or with brand label removed	Private label or un-branded	Same as in host store

Customer Services	Pioneer in offering customer charge and return privileges; increasing in number and types offered	Similar to those offered by department stores of equivalent sales volume	More limited than in independent stores	Limited	Minimal	Same as in host store
Selling Services	Mainly self-selection; some personal selling; salon type in prestige depts.	More emphasis on personal selling than in department stores	Mainly self-selection in department store and low-priced specialty chains; more personal selling in higher-priced specialty chains	Self-service	Self-service	Same as in host store
Promotional Activities	Semipromotional; feature items and annual sales events	Less promotional than department stores; more emphasis on "looks" and trends	More promotional than independent stores; feature items, values, lower prices in department stores and low- to moderate-priced specialty chains	Highly promotional; low prices featured	Very limited	Same as in host store
Fashion Coordination	Moderate amount; trend to more as competition increases	Stress coordination of fashion assortments	Mainly minimal at local store level; efforts largely confined to central buying and merchandising level	Little, if any	Little, if any	Same as in host store

TABLE 11-4
How Consumers are Shifting Where They Buy

| APPAREL CATEGORY | RETAIL OUTLETS | | REASON |
	FROM	TO	
Women's	Traditional women's dress shops	Department stores Junior/misses specialty chains	Consumer shift to sportswear
	Department stores	Discounters	Pricing
	Department stores	Junior/misses specialty chains	More focused marketing and merchandising
Men's	Traditional men's tailored clothing stores	Department stores	Consumer shift to sportswear
	Traditional specialty stores Department stores	National chains Discounters	Pricing
Children's	Department stores	National chains Discounters	Pricing

Source: Booz, Allen & Hamilton.

Reprinted in *Chain Store Age,* General Merchandise Edition, January, 1980, p. 67.

the consumer, and specialization of channels of distribution and merchandise will also be some of the methods used. For many years, retailers and small entrepreneurs thought of themselves as "merchants," not as managers. With increased competition and more complex distribution problems, large and small retailers have found that the need for professional, well-trained, and educated managers is growing.

Competition

Growing chains, specialized retailers, and the increased sophistication of shoppers have made competition more keen. The era of the "loyal" customer has passed. No longer do customers shop in only one store or expect that only one store will satisfy their needs. No longer do customers shop without checking to see what other stores are selling. Today's customers are alert observers of what is offered in the marketplace and choose to shop where

they believe they will get the most for their money. (See Table 11-4, which indicates that changing tastes and prices are key factors in the shift in shopping habits.) Therefore it is imperative for management to continually re-evaluate the wishes of the customer and keep themselves competitive in all areas. Only with professional and well-structured organizations will retailers be able to keep themselves abreast of consumer wants and needs.

Growth of Large-Scale Retailing

Both department and specialty stores in their early history were primarily single unit, independent, and family owned. In the 1930s, a trend toward bigness and mergers began. Federated Department Stores, Allied Stores, and other corporate ownership groups were formed and began acquiring stores that were formerly independent. At that time the Macy interests owned several stores, each in a different city, as did the Gimbel family and May

Department Stores. This trend has not only continued but accelerated. By the mid-1970s, only a few of this country's largest stores were still independently owned.

During the late 1920s and early 1930s, companies that had formerly been exclusively mail-order houses began opening store units. These retail units represented the entry of chain organizations into the retail distribution network.

MERGERS AND ACQUISITIONS.

Mergers and acquisitions in the retail field normally are carried out in the financial arena, through exchange of stock or purchase of controlling interests. The operations and image of the acquired store or chain remain apparently unchanged in the public eye.

For example, there is nothing about the operations of the New York-based Bergdorf Goodman or Dallas-based Neiman-Marcus specialty stores to indicate that they both are under the same corporate ownership (Carter Hawley Hale) as The Broadway department store chain based in Los Angeles and the Walden bookstore national chain. Most customers are unaware that Joske's, Texas, stores are owned by Allied Stores Corporation, who also owns Jordan Marsh, Boston, Bon Marche, Seattle, and Maas Brothers, Florida. The Bullock stores in California and the Burdine stores in Florida are among those owned by Federated Department Stores. New York-based Lord & Taylor, Los Angeles-based J. W. Robinson, and Phoenix-based Goldwater's are among the stores owned by Associated Dry Goods Corporation. Although operating under their original owner's names, Kaufmann's in Pittsburgh and G. Fox in Hartford are both owned and operated by May Department Stores.

VOLUNTARY ASSOCIATIONS.

On another level, there is a growing trend among smaller stores to affiliate loosely with one another on a voluntary basis. The purpose of this is to exchange information as well as to secure certain group-buying advantages such as early delivery and sometimes lower prices.

In voluntary associations, each store retains its own identity, and owners retain complete control of their stores. No financial joining is involved. However, the heads of stores that are affiliated in this manner get together regularly to compare methods and results. They feel such meetings result in better and more profitable storekeeping for all concerned. Affiliations of this type are often organized and guided by an accounting firm or by a management consultant firm that specializes in the retail field.

CHAIN EXPANSION.

Chain organizations are continually replacing older, smaller units with larger, newer units that contain considerably expanded fashion assortments. They are also expanding into such foreign markets as Spain, Belgium, Italy, South America, Canada, and Japan.

BRANCH EXPANSION.

Until recent years, branches were located principally in suburbs of the cities in which the parent stores were located. The trend today, however, is toward opening branches far from the trading area of the parent store. Lord & Taylor, for instance, now has branches in Pennsylvania, Massachusetts, Maryland, Connecticut, Illinois, Texas, Georgia, Virginia, and New Jersey. Additional branches in other states are in the planning stage. Bloomingdale's, New York, has established branches in Connecticut, New Jersey, and suburban New York City areas. It also opened a branch in Washington, D.C., and has plans for more branches in other cities far removed from the main store.

Both branching and merging have not only increased stores' volume but also stores' fashion impact. The trend in branch store operation today is toward an increasing merchandising and operational autonomy.

However, the energy crisis and the possibility of gasoline shortages for some years to come have introduced new problems to be considered. Retailers are facing a situation in which customers are making fewer trips to the regional shopping centers but shop in their branch stores. To go with or against the trend toward branch store expansion has been a difficult, major management decision for almost all large retail distributors.

Many retailers are projecting that their growth and expansion will have to come from existing stores, rather than new branch stores. A revitalization of downtown shopping areas, stimulated in many parts of the country by the infusion of county, state, and government financial aid, is regarded by many retailers as the trend of the eighties. The resurgence of smaller-sized, more economically operated stores is another alternative for many retailers.

Consumerism

The term **consumerism** refers to the efforts of consumers to promote their own interests. To be successful, retailers must develop a heightened awareness of consumer needs and attitudes and a responsiveness to consumer values. New consumer protection regulations are added each year—not only federal regulations, but state consumer protection laws as well.

The trend in retailers' support of consumer protection laws and in retailer education of both buyers and sellers is growing. The consumer now wants information on expected product performance, on guarantees and warranties, on energy consumption, on product care, and on probable product life. Because retailing is a labor-intensive industry, supplying such information to the work force in retail establishments throughout the country becomes an all-important goal for retailers in the 1980s.

Consumerism can have a very positive effect on retailing in the future. Knowing what the customer wants and being able to satisfy this want—with none of the customer disappointment in quality, service, and operation of the past—constitutes one of the most positive and important objectives in retailing.

Expanded Fashion Assortments and Service

Top management decisions on retail stock assortments and services are determined by the all-important target customer. The number of retailers using marketing research to determine who their target customer is continues to increase. Once the needs of this customer are clearly defined, inventories can be trimmed and the assortment clearly tailored to that customer's needs and wants.

The forecast for the coming decades is that fashion assortments will be more finely tuned to precise customer needs and wants. Value-conscious customers will help retailers to define these assortments, and in some cases there will be a return to the basics.

With consumer protection laws, energy crises, decreased spending, and growing unrest among countries around the world, every retailer faces a tremendous challenge in keeping fashion assortments and services appealing to the customer. New, exciting, and forcefully presented fashions can be the springboard for large sales increases for retailers, since fashion is usually a key motivation behind consumer spending.

Retailers will also expand the types of services offered the customer. It will be the service-oriented retailer, constantly upgrading and innovating store services, who will experience increasing sales volume and profit in the future.

Expanded shopping hours and days, fashion shows, in-store fashion events, and community-related services are all important ways to build a firm and positive image in the minds of targeted customers.

Increasing Use of Automated Data Processing Systems

In many areas of their operations, an increasing number of retailers are using automated data processing. However, in terms of fashion merchandising, perhaps the most important trends are in the expanding use of electronic cash registers and other automated methods for capturing sales information at point of sale. These enable retail executives to obtain faster, more accurate reports on sales and inventory. Further developments in these data processing systems are making greater use of manufacturer preticketing of merchandise.

YOU'LL LIKE OUR STYLE
as well as our clothes.

Browsing? Buying? Need one of our free services? We do everything we can to make shopping—or just looking—an unhurried, hassle-free pleasure at Wallachs. That's our style. Lost a button? Sat on your hat? Need a collar stay? Jammed a zipper? Pop in. We'll sew on the missing button, steam out your hat, or get your zipper on the right track again. The charge? A smile.

Walked out of a restaurant with the wrong raincoat? Or no raincoat at all? Make it the last time with one of our handy name and address tags. Pop in and we'll button one into yours, no matter where you bought it.

Wallachs, you'll like our style, as well as our clothes, all from names as famous as these; Hart Schaffner & Marx, Hickey Freeman, Austin Reed of Regent Street, Christian Dior, Pierre Cardin, Nino Cerruti, Countess Mara, Bill Blass.

wallachs

You'll like our style as well as our clothes.

Courtesy of Wallachs

Service-oriented retailers are constantly seeking new and upgraded services to offer their target customers.

This should considerably reduce store marking and receiving expenses and make possible faster delivery of purchases to the selling floor.

Changing Retail Patterns

A theory expounded by Dr. Malcolm P. McNair, retailing authority and professor emeritus of Harvard University Business School, suggests that many retail organizations originate as low-priced distributors of consumer goods, with strictly functional facilities, limited assortments, and minimum customer services. As time goes on, each successful firm begins to trade up in an effort to broaden its consumer profile. Facilities are modernized; store decor becomes more attractive. Assortments become more varied and higher in quality, greater emphasis is placed on promotional efforts, and more customer services are introduced.

In this process of trading up, considerably greater capital investment in physical plant, equipment, and inventory is required. Operating expenses spiral. As a result, retailers are forced to charge higher prices to cover the increased costs of doing business.

As retail organizations move out of the low-priced field and into the moderate- or higher-priced fields, a vacuum is created at the bottom of the retailing structure. This vacuum does not exist for long, however. Enterprising new firms move quickly into the vacated and temporarily uncompetitive low-priced area to meet the demands of customers who either need or prefer to patronize low-priced retail distributors. The pattern keeps repeating itself, with successful retail firms trading up and new firms moving into the bottom level of the retail price structure.

This pattern of movement is very obvious in today's retail scene. Department and specialty stores are expanding their facilities, services, assortments, and price-line offerings. Discount stores are trading up. As a result, a vacuum has appeared at the bottom of the retail price structure. It is being filled by such low-priced operations as the outlet store, the warehouse store, and the catalog showroom.

The outlet store is the oldest of these low-priced operations, having originated as an odd-lot, low-priced, factory-owned outlet in the early days of industrialization. Today these outlets are growing in number, and many handle products of more than one manufacturer. The warehouse store, a newer development, handles mainly odd lots of major appliances and furniture. The catalog showroom, the newest entry in the low-priced field, is set up like a trading-stamp redemption center, with merchandise catalogs for customers to study and samples of the merchandise on display in the showroom. Orders are filled from a stockroom on the premises, and customers take their purchases with them. Although only a minimal amount of fashion goods is offered in such catalog showrooms, it is likely that in the future more soft goods will be available.

There is now a great resurgence in mail-order retailing. The automobile once helped to free the customer from shopping by mail-order catalog. It has now slowed or stopped the customer from shopping in the stores because of the energy situation.

New mail-order catalog houses are emerging every day. Established retailers such as department stores, specialty stores, boutiques, apparel chains, and mass merchandisers are also adding mail-order type booklets and catalogs to their advertising and sales promotion budgets.

MERCHANDISING VOCABULARY

Define or briefly explain the following terms:

Broad and shallow assortment   **Confined styles**

Chain organization   **Consumerism**

Department store

Discount store

Fashion retailing

Fords

General merchandise store

General store

Mail-order companies

Merchandising

Merchandising policies

Mom-and-Pop store

Narrow and deep assortment

Organization chart

Retailing

Specialty store

Variety store

MERCHANDISING REVIEW

1. What are considered the modern retail versions of the following types of early retail distributors: (a) outdoor bazaars of the Orient and marketplaces of the Mediterranean, (b) medieval craft or guild shops, (c) tradespeople who purchased goods from traders for purposes of resale rather than producing such goods themselves, and (d) peddlers?

2. Name and briefly explain the characteristics and importance of three early forms of rural retail distribution in this country.

3. Describe the organizational structure of most medium-size department stores and the responsibilities of executives in charge of each major function.

4. How did department stores originally get their name? What are the four major responsibilities of a departmental buyer for an independent retail firm with fewer than 12 branches?

5. What is meant by the term "merchandising policies"? Who is responsible for establishing them? What important purposes do they serve?

6. Compare and/or contrast the merchandising policies of department and specialty stores in regard to the depth and breadth of assortments during a selling season.

7. Compare and/or contrast the responsibilities of nonchain departmental buyers with those of central buyers for chain organizations.

8. What is a leased department and how does it operate? Name the departments in a retail store that are frequently leased.

9. What stage or stages of the fashion cycle would most likely be emphasized in the fashion assortments of: (a) a small or medium-size department store; (b) a higher-priced specialty store; (c) a department store chain; (d) a discount store?

10. In which major type of retail store would you be most likely to find the following emphasized in its merchandise assortments: (a) nationally advertised brands; (b) private brands; (c) low-price branded or unbranded goods?

MERCHANDISING DIGEST

1. Discuss the following statement from the text and its implications for retail merchants: "Many retailers are projecting that their growth and expansion will have to come from existing stores, rather than new branch stores."
2. "The number of major organizational functions established by a retail firm . . . depends upon its sales volume, number of employees, and how many store units it operates." Discuss this statement from the text, citing specific examples of how these three factors not only affect the organizational structure of a firm but also the responsibilities of its various employees.
3. Discuss any two major trends in fashion distribution and how each reflects specific changes in consumer demand.

EXPLORING
THE MARKETS OF FASHION

The following can be used as an assignment or as a project, depending on the amount of research and detail requested by your instructor.

You are the buyer for the medium-priced sportswear department of a large, nationally advertised chain of stores. Your target customer chooses goods at the peak of their fashion cycle. Because of your enormous buying power and many retail outlets, you have determined that featuring new, exciting, and different merchandise in your stores is essential.

A. Explain why you have made the decision to use new, exciting, and different merchandise. What factors relating to the dynamics of fashion were used in your decision?

B. Draw a flowchart showing the markets you would have to research for your merchandise. Be sure that you carefully represent the movement and interrelationship, as you see them, between each market. See the sample chart below.

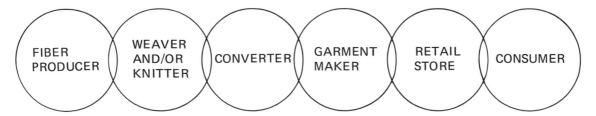

3
RETAIL MERCHANDISING OF FASHION

Merchandising in its most general sense means buying and selling goods for profit. More specifically, modern merchandising means having the right merchandise, at the right price, at the right time, in the right quantities, and in the right place for your target customer.

All retail merchandising begins with a specific estimate of what the target customer will want. The merchandising of fashion goods involves all of the same problems that the merchandising of many other types of goods involves. In addition, however, fashion merchandising attempts to satisfy customer demands that are constantly changing. The essential activities involved in retail merchandising of fashion goods are discussed in Unit 3. These discussions include:

• Consumer motivation: analyzing what prospective consumers will want in a future selling period
• Merchandise planning: determining what and how much merchan-

dise will be needed and when to act upon the estimates of consumer demand

· Selection and buying factors: using all appropriate factors in developing the estimates and goals in merchandise planning

· Sales promotion: promoting, through various methods, the sale of goods which have been ordered in anticipation of demand

· Competition: meeting the difficult problems relating to merchandising competition by establishing a distinctive fashion image

Merchandising in its oldest sense implies trading. Good merchandising calls for effective trading, both with sources of supply and with customers. Successful retail merchandising requires careful planning, intelligent selecting and buying of goods for resale, and effective selling of those goods in order to win and keep customers, provide the funds necessary to pay all of the store's operating expenses, and, in addition, achieve a reasonable profit on the capital invested.

12
INTERPRETING CUSTOMER DEMAND

When you walk into your favorite retail store today to buy a pair of jeans, a blouse or a jacket, the chances are very good that you will have an amazing array of styles, fabrics, and colors to choose from. Certainly, you would expect to find such a large selection, for we have become accustomed to choosing from a cornucopia of goods on our shopping rounds. Manufacturers and retailers vie with one another for our business through new styles, fabrics, and colors. Through television, radio, magazines, newspapers, and store displays, they present an endless array to satisfy our every fashion preference. This has not always been the situation, however. Until quite recently, the preferences of the customer had little or no influence in the manufacture and sale of consumer goods.

Prior to the turn of the century, manufacturers concentrated, of necessity, on the production of industrial goods. The country was growing rapidly. Factories were springing up, and farm machinery was in demand. The production of consumer goods was not equal to the demand for them, and manufacturers who did produce looked to their own needs first. Consumer goods that were produced were of the kind and quality that could be made most easily, at the least expense, and for maximum profit. As a result, retailers had little variety in the products available to them in the wholesale markets. Therefore, they, in turn, could offer the consumer very scant assortments from which to choose.

America was a fast-growing country, and in the first three decades of this century, rapid technological advances took place. Many of these involved the development of mass-production techniques. These soon made increasing quantities and varieties of consumer goods available in the wholesale markets. In addition, the ongoing entry of new companies into the manufacturing field, made more and more products available in the retail marketplace. Thus, by the mid-1920s, the supply of consumer goods began to approach the level of consumer demand for those goods. This brought about an increase in competition among producers and retailers for the consumer's dollar.

The Depression of the 1930s brought about a radical change in the philosophy relating to the marketing of consumer goods. Marketing, once producer-oriented, now became oriented to the consumer. With the economy in chaos and millions of people unemployed, the consumer had little money to spend, while producers and retailers had ample goods to sell. There were too few dollars "chasing" too much merchandise. For the first time in America's history, the competition for these scarce consumers' dollars became intense.

Advertising and other sales promotion efforts were sharply increased. Marketing efforts became more consumer-oriented at every level. Department stores vied with one another to sell their wares through off-price sales. The movie houses lured people in with promises of giveaways such as dishes and glassware. The struggle to meet the public's demands was tremendous. Those businesses that produced or sold what the public wanted were the ones that survived the difficult years of the thirties; those that ignored the trends in consumer demand did not.

It is not surprising, therefore, that this period produced increased protection for the consumer. While consumerism—the efforts of consumers to promote their own interests—has existed as long as there have been buyers and sellers, the rights of consumers to be protected from unfair marketing practices was just beginning to be acknowledged. The stark realities of the Depression helped to strengthen the consumerism movement. Because people had so few dollars to spend, they were increasingly determined to get good value for their money. This demand on the part of consumers led Congress to pass three major pieces of legislation in the 1930s. The Robinson-Patman Act of 1936 concerned unfair practices that tended to limit competition in the marketplace. The Wheeler-Lea Act of 1938 outlawed fraudulent advertising of any products involved in interstate commerce. And, most important, the Food, Drug, and Cosmetics Act of 1938 required detailed and accurate labeling of food, drugs, and cosmetics. The turbulent 1930s saw the end of many fortunes and the beginning of what would become a global war. This decade also saw the beginnings of a new era in the history of marketing. The age-old warning *caveat emptor,* or "let the buyer beware," had begun to give way to the marketing philosophy expressed in the words *caveat venditor,* or "let the seller beware."

Unfortunately, World War II brought with it an artificial, wartime economy which persisted into the boom years immediately following the war. Lessons that had been hard-learned by manufacturers and retailers during the years of the Depression were forgotten or pushed into the background. Producers and retailers grew accustomed to having consumers lined up to buy the scarce goods offered during the long war and for months thereafter. They began to believe that anything they determined to be the fashion would be purchased by consumers, who had no choice but to accept it. This did not happen, however. Many promotions failed because the products were not in line with demand. Other promotions succeeded because they involved products wanted by consumers. These products would probably have been purchased even if they had not been promoted. Two classic examples come to mind. In 1947, Christian Dior gambled that the women of America and Europe, weary from years of war, scarcity, and of clothing that was skimped on to save fabric, would welcome a dramatic change. He brought out his "New Look." The look was full and lush, and women embraced it wholeheartedly. They were tired of the lean years and of doing without. They wanted something totally new and exciting, and Dior sensed that want and filled it. Overnight, skirts plunged to midcalf. In contrast, soon after the war ended several new American automobiles, such as Tucker, Kaiser, and Frazier, were introduced and heavily promoted to the American public. But these cars did not meet the needs and wants of the American public. They therefore failed to achieve lasting acceptance and their producers went out of business.

In more recent years, several fashion promotions have proved futile because they tried to force the consumer into unwanted fashions. No case is more dramatic than that of the midi-length skirt of the early 1970s. This was a style designed to compete with the mini and the maxi-length skirts. But even the unceasing efforts of the most powerful generator of fashion news, *Women's Wear Daily,* could not successfully launch the midi. American women stayed away from it. Those manufacturers and retailers who felt that their combined energies could force-feed the style were left with heavy stocks and heavy markdowns.

In the 1980s, however, producers and retailers of fashion know they must first find out what consumers want and need if they are to be successful in making and selling their merchandise. In the light of fashion principles and the factors that are known to influence fashion movement and dissemination, merchants study customer demand within the particular segment of the population that they seek to serve. Retailers must be alert both to obvious consumer demands and to the subtle changes in those demands if they want their assortments to win continued customer approval.

Thus, it is the consumer, not the merchant or manufacturer, who now determines which styles become fashions. Consumers let merchants know not only what goods should be included in their stock, but in what quantities, at what time, and at what price these goods are wanted. Consumers, by accepting or rejecting what is offered to them, indicate to the retailer not only their present wants but also the direction in which their preferences are headed.

TIMING AND OBJECTIVITY IN MEASURING CUSTOMER DEMAND

The needs and wants of consumers, as discussed in Chapter 2, are influenced by various economic, sociological, and psychological factors. These environmental factors constantly change, and as they change, so do the needs and wants of consumers. For instance, American consumers today are vastly different from consumers a few decades ago. They have a higher standard of living, are better educated, enjoy a wider range of interests, travel more, and have greater social mobility. And they are continuing to change.

Because of the constantly changing needs and wants of customers, a merchant's job of identifying those needs and wants and interpreting them in terms of specific items of merchandise is a constant, continuing process. It cannot be a one-time or once-in-a-while research project; instead, it must be as much a part of day-to-day business operations as keeping sales or inventory records.

As merchants chart the trends in customer demand, they must be ready to change their goods and services in accordance with important changes noted. Changes may require, for instance, the addition of new categories of apparel, such as ski wear or tennis outfits. Or they may require the addition of lower price lines or the introduction of luggage in patterns and colors related to apparel fashions. As changes occur in customers' interests or lifestyles, merchants must make corresponding changes in their assortments.

Among the changes most difficult for merchants to recognize are those that occur as a result of changes in taste. Since taste is a very personal thing, good merchants cannot let their own tastes dominate their assortments. They must make every effort to recognize and cater to the tastes of their customers.

Adapting to the tastes of others is not always easy, especially when that taste differs radically from one's own. Yet objectivity in choosing merchandise in accordance with the tastes of a store's customers is one of the most important qualifications a retail merchant in general, and a retail buyer in particular, must develop. Buyers cannot buy according to their own tastes. They must constantly keep the customer's preferences in mind when making merchandise selections.

This does not mean that every fashion retailer should rearrange assortments to reflect every new fashion trend. How far a retailer should go in changing assortments to meet a new trend depends upon customers. At the end of the 1970s and beginning of the 1980s, many retailers serving customers with avant-garde tastes quickly filled their stocks with extreme, wide-shouldered fashions. These were designed to invoke the philosophies of the 1940s and thus cash in on the nostalgia trend. Other stores recognized that this fashion was not one their customers would accept and so resisted it. Another trend of the period was extremely tight jeans, which were accepted by some customers and rejected by others.

Some merchants always "edit" their assortments, eliminating those styles which they consider to be in poor taste, because this is what their customers expect them to do. Other retailers, regardless of personal preferences, accept even the most extreme of fashions, because they know that their customers' tastes run in that direction. Successful fashion merchants accept change only to the degree that they expect customers to accept it. Thus the key to successful merchandising lies in an ongoing study of customer demand and an objective interpretation of the precise nature and extent of the demand.

ELEMENTS OF CUSTOMER DEMAND

In determining the potential demand for fashion merchandise among a store's customers, the retailer must consider a number of factors. The merchandise itself must be analyzed in terms of the various elements and characteristics that may either contribute to or work against its acceptance by customers. The merchandise must be studied in the light of customer buying motives, particularly those influencing a store's target customers. The store's own image, its regional location, and the season of the year must also be taken into consideration.

It is not enough for merchants to merely keep abreast of general fashion trends and general customer demand. They must carefully study and evaluate each item of merchandise offered in the market, in competing stores, and in their own inventory in terms of its particular appeal to customers. Fashion merchandise offered in any store must meet the fashion demands of its target customers in styling, in quality, and in pricing.

Selection Factors

Selection factors refer to the various characteristics or components of an item of merchandise that influence a customer's decision to purchase or not to purchase it. Customers make these decisions based upon the composite value they attach to the various elements or characteristics of individual items. Listed below are the major selection factors that significantly influence a customer's choice when contemplating the purchase of most fashion goods:[1]

- *Silhouette* refers to the degree to which an item is considered moderate or extreme in form in relation to the currently popular silhouette.
- *Decoration or trim* refers to the presence or absence of buttons, bows, piping, ruffles, or other types of decorative trimmings. Some customers prefer strictly tailored apparel, while others prefer various degrees of decoration.
- *Material or fabric* refers to the "hand" of the material or fabric, its bulky or slenderizing effect, its weight when worn, its sheerness or opacity, its fiber content, and its durability in use (Will it stand up under hard wear? Is it easily snagged? How likely is it to "pill?")
- *Surface interest* refers to the roughness or smoothness of the material, the degree to which the material is dull or shiny, whether the surface is patterned (as in jacquard), plain, or deep (as in velvet or corduroy).
- *Color* refers to the actual color or color combinations used and the hue or value of each, the intensity of color, whether the item is solid or multicolored, whether the color or colors are complimentary to the wearer, and whether the color or colors blend with, mix, or match accessories or wardrobe items already owned.
- *Workmanship* refers to the degree of quality in construction, stitching, shaping, finishing. Subjective judgment is often involved here. Not all customers have the same quality or value standards relating to workmanship.
- *Size* refers to preciseness of fit, degree to which the graded measurements of ready-to-wear apparel correspond to the actual body measurements of customers, the relative size of accessories in relationship to the size and shape of the apparel with which the item will be worn.
- *Sensory factors* refer to odors (such as the pleasant scent of leather or perfume, or the unpleasant scent of some leather substitutes), sounds (such as the pleasant crackle of taffeta, the unpleasant squeak of a poorly-made pair of shoes).
- *Ease and cost of care* refers to such easy-

We didn't make this sweater, but we did insist that it be available in blue lovat.

This classic cable-stitched crew neck sweater was made in Scotland of the highest quality, hand blocked cashmere. Perhaps, the warmest, softest, most sensuous material in the world.

The second most important thing about these sweaters is the fact that we thought about, and selected, the unusual range of colors that is exclusively available at Dunhill Tailors.

Along with red, yellow and light blue, we offer old rose, mint green, pink, lavender and the above-mentioned blue lovat—originally created for use in tweeds to match the Scottish landscape—and said to have been Bonnard's favorite color. For the diffident, we also have beige or camel.

These sweaters cost one hundred and fifty dollars. And we have a beautiful shetland wool sweater from the same maker in a different range of Spring colors at only sixty.

For your approval now at Dunhill Tailors, just west of Park Avenue on East 57th Street.

We welcome the American Express card and the pleasure of your company.

DUNHILL TAILORS
65 East 57th Street · New York · New York · 10022 · (212) 355-0050

This retailer recognizes that color can have a significant influence on a customer's decision to buy.

Dunhill Tailors

care and economical features as wash-and-wear and permanent-press finishes, as well as to the future expenses involved in fabrics that have to be dry-cleaned or furs that have to be both cleaned and stored.

Brand refers to customer confidence or lack of confidence in a brand name because of previous experience with the brand, familiarity or lack of familiarity with the brand, status or lack of status of the brand.

- *Utility* refers to the extent of usefulness of an item (such as the degree of warmth and protection provided by a coat, the support provided by a well-fitting shoe, the capacity and carrying devices of a handbag), the number of different uses for such an item.
- *Appropriateness* refers to the degree of suitability and acceptability of an item for specific occasion use.
- *Price* refers to the value placed by an individual customer upon the above factors, plus any other factors that a customer may consider important, in relation to the retail price of the item. For example, in a child's swimsuit, a high quality of workmanship may not be as important as price. The suit may be worn only a few times one summer, outgrown in the following season or two, and discarded. On the other hand, a high quality of workmanship is usually important when purchasing work shoes, as they are likely to have to withstand long, hard wear.

Thus merchants have to determine whether or not to stock a fashion item by first examining a number of factors relating to the item itself. They have to look at the styling and detail, at how the item is constructed and finished, and at its practicality. They then must gauge whether or not it would have appeal to their customers at the price that must be charged for it.

Buying Motivation

The great philosopher George Santayana addressed himself to the elements which shape us and motivate us in our lives. He showed that each of us takes with us through life a history of causes and effects which makes us react differently from, or the same as, our friends, neighbors, and members of our own family. These causes and effects also motivate us in our fashion selections. If merchants are hopeful of gauging why one item appeals to customers while another does not, they must comprehend **buying motivation,** or why people buy what they buy.

One of the early marketing authorities to study buying motivation was Dr. Melvin T. Copeland. He divided consumer buying motives into two classes: rational motives, or those based on appeal to reason, and emotional motives, or those originating in instinct and emotion, representing impulse or unreasoned promptings to buy.[2] Rational motives, according to Dr. Copeland, included such factors as durability, dependability, comfort, economy of operation, and price. Emotional motives were thought to include such factors as imitation, emulation, quest for status, prestige, appeal to the opposite sex, pride of appearance, the desire for distinctiveness, ambition, and fear of offending.

As a result of more recent market research and the findings of experimental psychology, it has become obvious that buying motives are neither as simple nor as easily categorized as was believed when the variety of consumer goods was considerably less than today.

A more recent marketing authority, Jon G. Udell, has developed a much more valid theory. He claims buying motives arise out of both conscious and unconscious reasoning and can best be measured along a bar scale of motives.[3] Udell's bar scale runs from **operational satisfactions,** which are those derived from the physical performance of the product, to **psychological satisfactions,** which are those derived from the consumer's social and psychological interpretation of the product and its performance.

MIDPOINT

OPERATIONAL SATISFACTIONS — PSYCHOLOGICAL SATISFACTIONS

Every purchase is made for a variety of reasons that can best be measured along a bar scale of motives

When selecting fashion goods, utility is seldom of as much concern to consumers as the psychological satisfactions to be derived from ownership and use of the product. Yet fashion buying decisions are not always clear-cut. Operational motives may also be present.

A recent, typical example of this is the remarkable acceptance of down-filled, quilted outerwear. As late as the early 1970s, the vast majority of those who purchased this form of clothing were involved in sports—hunting, fishing, and camping, for example. Quilted, down-filled vests, jackets, and coats provided the necessary warmth without weight that was desired by active outdoors people. For the most part, these garments were in natural colors or colors that served a practical purpose such as hunter's red or nautical yellow or orange. For years those not involved in outdoor activities paid little attention to this type of clothing. In the late 1970s, however, other people began to try these garments and discovered the convenience of warmth in the coldest weather with very little weight. Demand accelerated rapidly, resulting in a proliferation of styles and colors designed to meet the demands of people from all social and economic levels. Myriad new colors were introduced into the now-fashionable outerwear. Totally reversible styles were designed with interchangeable snap-on patch pockets and hoods. The down-filled quilted garments were also available in every possible length, from bomber jacket to floor-length coats. The fashion was worn by men, women, and children. It was seen in every walk of life, worn as freely to the concert as to the office or the sports arena. This type of apparel is now being worn by most people as much for its fashion appeal as its practicality. It is this multiplicity of uses that has ensured the continued importance of down-filled quilted apparel in the fashion picture.

Patronage Motives

Patronage motives is the name given to the reasons that induce customers to shop in one store rather than another—it refers to "why we buy where we buy."

For such "pickup" items as cosmetics or inexpensive hosiery, people often depend on the neighborhood drugstore or supermarket, or any other nearby store, even if its selection is limited. For fairly routine fashion merchandise, such as moderately priced blouses, slacks, and sweaters, the suburban shopper is likely to go to a nearby shopping center for a good selection of such items. For the more important fashion purchases, such as furs, fine jewelry, or designer clothes, it may be necessary for people who live in the suburbs or in small towns to go to stores in the nearest large city or in a not-too-distant high-fashion shopping center.

There are countless reasons why a customer chooses one store over another when the locations and merchandise offerings are comparable. A store's fashion reputation, its assortments, and its price ranges all come into play. So do the services offered (such as credit, delivery, adjustments, and parking) and the attitudes of the salespeople. Each of these factors can help to sway a customer toward one store and away from another. Even the size of a store and the way it is laid out have a bearing on whether or not a customer chooses to shop in it. A customer will award fashion patronage to the store that best fills a need and supplies the motivation needed to buy.

Variations in Demand

The geographical area where people live, their life styles, the prevailing climate, and numerous other factors influence both the type and the extent of customer demand. These factors explain, for instance, why two specialty stores—one in a metropolitan area of the Northeast and one in a Midwestern city, both serving customers of approximately the same income group—cannot offer similar assortments. They also explain why a nearby branch may need an assortment somewhat different from that of the parent store or other branches.

REGIONAL VARIATIONS. Variations in the composition of the population and in the prevailing climate vary the demand for fashion goods in different parts of the United States. For instance, people in the Western states are often quicker than most to adopt new

THE FANTASIES AND THE FACTS

Neiman-Marcus

FANTASY: You need your own oil well to shop Neiman-Marcus. FACT: Lots of our customers are millionaires. But we also take pains to please school teachers and secretaries and students and budget-conscious moms and junior executives, etc. Everybody's looking for good value these days.

We're opening in White Plains on September 8th.

NEIMAN-MARCUS WESTCHESTER

Bozell & Jacobs—agency; Neiman-Marcus—client

As this ad recognized, a store's fashion reputation and its price ranges are important reasons why a customer chooses one store over another.

styles, especially if they are casual and informal. Sometimes regional preferences in apparel reflect the racial stocks from which the population is mainly drawn. In the Great Lakes region, for example, many residents are of German and Scandinavian ancestry. Blue-eyed and fair-skinned, they are partial to the color blue, whether it is in or out of fashion.

Sometimes climate is responsible for variations in demand. San Francisco, for example, is famous as a "suit city," whether or not suits are fashionable elsewhere. It is also known as a city whose women never store their furs. The city's climate makes a removable jacket comfortable for daytime wear. Chilly evenings make the warmth of a fur welcome even in summer.

URBAN AND SUBURBAN DEMAND.

Fashion demand in suburbs is usually different from that in central cities. Too, there may be notable differences in demand among the various suburbs of a single city. Although branch customers may be in similar income brackets and have essentially the same taste levels as city customers, most retail stores find that apparel preferences of the two groups differ. Living is more casual in suburbs than in cities.

When department stores first branched out vigorously into the suburbs in the 1950s, stores were small in size compared with today's giant branch stores. Because the first branches were small, merchandise selections were necessarily limited and often featured the store's higher-priced lines. As the population movement from cities to suburbs continued, stores found small branches inadequate. They replaced them with larger units that were either free-standing or else served as anchor stores for new regional shopping centers. Because of the larger size of these new branches, the parent stores were able to increase the depth and breadth of the branches' assortments and offer a greater range of price lines.

To stimulate business in their branches and lend additional emphasis to the fashion image they wish to project, stores occasionally feature special fashion promotions at branch stores. This gives suburban customers the opportunity to attend fashion events that traditionally had been held only in center-city stores.

Perhaps the most important fact about consumer demand that branch store expansion has taught retailers is that people prefer to make fashion purchases from plentiful assortments. When a branch offers only a limited assortment, customers are more likely to visit several stores before making their purchasing decision. Thus, the branch store with the limited assortment runs a greater risk of not getting their patronage.

SEASONAL VARIATIONS.

In areas where the change of seasons is strongly marked, the demand for warmer or cooler apparel follows the calendar. In regions like southern Florida or Hawaii, however, there is practically no seasonal climatic change. Thus there is little reason for seasonal variations in the weight or type of garments offered for sale. Some northern parts of the country have short springs and summers, and most of their fashion demand is for cold-weather clothes. In the South and Southwest the reverse is true; there is only a short winter season and little demand for warm clothes. As a result, fashion interest concentrates mainly on styles, materials, and colors that provide summer comfort.

Seasonality has once again become an important factor in consumer demand for fashion goods. The demand for clothes designed specifically for hot or cold weather had diminished in the 1960s and early 1970s because of improved heating and air-conditioning systems in offices and homes. But this changed with the energy crisis of the late 1970s and early 1980s. Outdoor climate became a factor in the type of clothing the consumer chose. Styles and fabrics that help the consumer face differences in seasonal variations are important now to meet consumer demand.

A factor that upsets the traditional impact of the calendar upon fashion demand is the ease and speed of travel. Consumers can take a brief vacation—even a weekend trip—and quickly reach a climate radically different from the one at home. Today, customers who live in a mild climate turn to the stores they regularly patronize in search of warm clothing for a ski weekend. Customers who live in a cold climate and are planning a quick trip south descend upon their favorite store in midwinter looking for cool, lightweight apparel and accessories to wear with that apparel.

Successful merchants must provide at all times what their customers want. The timing and nature of customer demand today is subject to constant change. It requires that fashion assortments include the various types of merchandise that customers want, no matter when they want them.

OTHER VARIATIONS.

In every part of the country, regardless of climate, certain periods of the year have gradually become traditional for the selling of certain fashions. Also, customers have come to expect special sales at certain times of the year.

Special Occasions and Holidays. In the torrid days of late August, parents across much of the nation are busy outfitting their school-age children in warm pants, sweaters, skirts, and coats. The calendar shows that school days are fast approaching, and parents become aware that new clothes are needed for the fall term. This is a natural peak in fashion demand that is completely determined by the calendar, and stores are quick to satisfy it. The back-to-school period represents the single largest selling period of the year for clothing for all students from first grade through college. Therefore, stores traditionally offer greatly enlarged assortments and usually run special-price promotions on selected merchandise.

With year-in and year-out regularity, May, June, September, and December are the traditional wedding months. Stores peak their assortments of gowns and accessories for the bride and her attendants at specific periods in advance of those months to accommodate this demand. Such preplanning also takes place in order to provide suitable clothing for the social events that are part of such holidays as Christmas, New Year's, and Easter.

Although travel today is practically an everyday affair, vacation needs are still a seasonal spur to fashion selling. Summer travel clothes and accessories are still the basis of vacation fashion planning. There is an ever-growing demand for winter vacation fashion needs as well.

Special Sales Events. Because stores have established an annual pattern of promotions, customers have come to expect and patronize special preseason or postseason sales. These have little relation to the natural pattern of demand but have become traditional off-price sale periods. Merchants need to stimulate sales during normally slow periods and to clear out odds and ends of old stock before bringing in styles for the new season. This has led to a traditional pattern of special sales events in many merchandise categories, ranging from bed linens to furniture and including such fashion items as apparel, lingerie, and shoes. Even elegant shops whose policies are firmly against off-price promotions find it necessary to stage semiannual or annual clearances.

Another example of artificially stimulated demand is the summer preseason sale of winter coats and furs. The history of such sales goes back to the 1920s and perhaps even earlier. Coat factories had long layoffs between peak selling seasons and periods of intense activity and expensive overtime work. To reduce the need for overtime work and provide their workers with more regular employment, manufacturers made concessions in price to retailers who ordered and accepted delivery of goods in advance of the normal selling period. This enabled the retailers, in turn, to offer winter garments to their customers at lower than regular prices if they bought such garments in the summer. In the days before air conditioning, a considerable price inducement was necessary to entice women into stores to try on winter coats in mid-summer heat. Nonetheless, customers came and made their selections, and summer coat and fur sales became a tradition.

AIDS IN DETERMINING CUSTOMER PREFERENCES

The fashion sense of successful merchants is the fruit of hard work. These merchants check their own stores' past merchandising records. They determine general trends in consumer demand through every available source. And on occasion they solicit information on local demand from representative groups of their own customers. In fashion merchandising, instinct and intuition are no match for facts and conscientious research.

Although most stores base their fashion merchandise selections on systematic research, such research is particularly important in larger stores. In a small specialty store, the owner is usually also the merchandise manager. He or she can collect customer preference information by studying stock and sales records, talking to customers, and listening to vendors. In larger stores, determining customer preferences is a more complex research job. The customers served may number in the hundreds of thousands instead of just the hundreds. The number of fashion items offered and vendors involved may be multiplied proportionately. Smaller stores may need only pencil and paper to do a good customer research job from their sales and stock records. Larger stores use electronic data processing systems to collect and analyze such customer demand information on a continuing basis.

Information From Store Sources

Any store that has been in business for more than a season has in its records a treasury of information about its customers' responses to previous merchandise offerings. This information, properly interpreted, shows what customers have bought and what has not interested them. It also indicates what fashion trends may be developing and what trends may be passing their peak.

It is assumed, of course, that the store or department being studied has a clearly defined target group of customers. These are not necessarily the same individuals month after month or year after year, but they are people of similar incomes and taste levels who prefer styles at approximately the same point in their fashion cycles. If a store's customers are too heterogeneous a group, or if a store has been shifting its sights, aiming first at one and then at another type of target customer, its past history will not be a reliable basis on which to build future plans.

PAST SALES RECORDS. It can be assumed that those items which sold at the fastest rates in the past had the strongest natural appeal to customers. If fast sellers have some features in common, such as color, price, detail, or texture, these features can be an important indication of the nature of customer demand. For example, if the "jewel" neckline is a feature of nearly all best-selling blouses, at several prices, and in several colors, it can be assumed that the jewel neckline is gaining in demand over other types. On the other hand, if beige blouses are the best sellers, regardless of

neckline or sleeve treatment, then it is color that is influencing the customers, beige being the most important color in the tide of demand.

PRETESTING. New styles are first bought in wide variety but in small quantities. Customer reaction and sales are then observed. Styles that sell promptly are reordered. Other similar styles are ordered, and the slow sellers are dropped.

There are many other ways to pretest new styles. One way is to stage fashion shows early in the season, observe customer reactions, and note their purchases. Another way is to show vendors' lines to salespeople and invite their comments. Still another is to hold preseason sales, such as summer coat sales, in order to determine which styles are most popular.

The trunk show, as discussed in Chapter 7, is a dramatic form of pretesting new season styles. Samples of the producer's lines are exhibited at scheduled, announced showings. People who attend see every style the producer has available, not just those styles the merchant has already chosen to stock. If customers see a style they want that is not carried by the store, they can order it. Merchants, meantime, have a chance to see how their selections from the producer's line compare with those that interest their customers. Retailers thus can tailor their assortments to more adequately reflect their customers' wants.

MARKDOWNS. Downward revisions in the selling prices of merchandise are **markdowns.** Good retail practice requires that all markdowns be entered on a store record and a reason given for each markdown. Since markdowns are often used to clear out slow-moving stock, an analysis of the styles that had to be reduced often shows what merchandise features failed to attract sufficient customers. This indicates how the merchant should readjust the assortments in the future. For example, a line of vividly colored vinyl jackets may do well in a high-priced version in a boutique setting and in a low-priced version in the budget department. A moderate-priced version offered in the regular sportswear department, however, may be such a slow seller that most of the stock ends up on the markdown rack. A logical assumption, then, is that the extreme in sport jackets, properly priced, is acceptable to the top and bottom strata of the store's customers. But the group in the middle, who are traditionally conservative, are not interested in this type of merchandise.

WANT SLIPS. When a customer requests something that is not in stock, salespeople report the situation on forms that are known as **want slips.** (See below.) These can be particularly interesting as a means of studying current customer demand, for they are one of the few indications a store has of what customers would buy if available. Study of these unfilled customer wants helps a merchant correct possible errors in filling demand for particular sizes, prices, colors, or types of items. A dress department, for instance, might stock only conservative styles in larger sizes. But want slips might show that customers wearing these sizes would like to find more lively colors and youthful styles from which to choose.

ADVERTISING RESULTS. Stores try to determine the amount of business that has been transacted as a direct result of advertising. This is often hard to determine, unless a customer arrives at the store with ad in hand or mentions the ad to a salesperson. However, if an ad promotes a particular line or item, increases in sales immediately after the ad appears are usually attributed to the promotion. The response to the advertising of a specific style is usually an indication of the degree of customer interest in the style. This is particularly true if several styles receive equal advertising emphasis but show considerable differences in arousing customer interest.

In a departmentalized store, a buyer for one department sometimes can obtain valuable guidance from the results of advertising done by related departments, in addition to the results of his or her own ads.

RETURNS, COMPLAINTS, ADJUSTMENTS. When a store accepts a return from a customer or makes an adjustment on goods that failed to give satisfaction, all the details about the

---

MERCHANDISE WANT SLIP

Department No. _42_   Name _Sara Davies_

Date _8/17_

The following Requested Merchandise is not in Stock:

Description (Item, Color, Size, Price)	No. of Calls	Buyer's Remarks
After five, chiffon, beige, sweetheart neckline	2	Order placed for #417 with Silhouette Dress Co. on 8/20

The following Stock is getting low:

Mfr., Style, Color, Price	Pieces On Hand	
Aiken, #6192, red, $26.00	3	Discontinued
R & K, #1001, 2/10, 1/14 $55.00	4	Reordered 24 pieces

SUGGEST A SUBSTITUTE

Salespeople fill out want slips when customers request merchandise that is not in stock. Buyers respond to each request and return the slip.

transaction are recorded. These records are warnings for store buyers, telling them which goods have not been found acceptable by customers and why. For example, if customers return laminated fabrics because they separated in cleaning, then the buyer should consider finding a more reliable source for laminated fabrics. In addition, the buyer would have to accept the fact that a certain degree of prejudice might have developed against laminates, thereby influencing customer demand. Additional promotion, stressing the reliability of the new fabrics, might be needed.

CUSTOMER SURVEYS.   Many customers are quite willing to tell a retailer what they like and what they do not like about the store. They will point out what does and does not interest them in the merchandise assortment. Such customer surveys can be quite informal and yet provide a clear indication of trends. The buyer or store owner who talks with customers on the selling floor, observes expressions, and listens to remarks made by customers learns a good deal about the nature of customer demand and how the store's assortment is viewed by the customer. Formal surveys can be made by mail or personal interview to determine, for example, what price lines are favored, what types of merchandise are wanted by regular or potential customers, and what services are expected.

SALESPEOPLE.   Because of their constant, direct contact with customers, salespeople usually can provide valuable information about what customers want. In larger stores, salespeople are really the stores' only links with their customers, for store buyers seldom can spend much time on the selling floor. Salespeople can report whether customers bought certain styles eagerly or reluctantly and whether they asked for any particular items that were not immediately available. Sometimes the information gathered from salespeople is the first indication a store may have of a change in a trend. At other times, what the salespeople report will reinforce and amplify what a merchant may already have

suspected from observations and from store records.

Information from Sources Outside the Store

Merchants also look beyond their own doors for indications of consumer demand. What they learn from outside sources may confirm what they deduce from their own experience —or it may indicate points they have missed or perhaps misinterpreted. A typical case would be one in which certain styles or items are not yet stocked in a store but which are enjoying good acceptance in other stores.

There are many specific sources to which merchants turn for information, including their competitors and suppliers. To alert retailers, however, almost everything has fashion significance. What people wear to the theater and restaurants, what important local people are wearing, and what national celebrities are wearing are among the many guides that help a fashion merchant identify current trends in customer demand.

COMPETITORS.   Merchants and their buyers regularly study the advertising of other stores. They visit the selling floors of competing stores to see what is stocked, what is featured in displays, and what appears to be selling.

Some stores rely on their buyers and merchandise managers to do this job. Others prefer to set up a separate comparison bureau or office, believing that its staff can perform the work involved more extensively and more objectively than can the store's merchandising executives. These comparison shoppers visit the stores of local competitors, check prices, assortments, services, and customer response. They then report their findings to executives in their own store for appropriate action.

RESIDENT BUYING OFFICE.   A **resident buying office** is a business organization, located in a major market area, that provides its noncompeting client stores with many market-related services. It provides those stores with a steady flow of current information on general trends in consumer demand. Such information takes the form of market bulletins, reports on new items, fashion forecasts, and lists of styles and items that are best-sellers in other client stores. During periods when store buyers are in the market to view producers' lines, the resident buying offices hold clinics, or meetings, at which buyers from the buying office's various client stores can discuss fashion, merchandise, and merchandising. Separate clinics are held for buyers specializing in each category of merchandise, so that the discussions can be detailed. There are also group meetings for heads of stores and for merchandise managers.

In addition, individual store managers and their buyers may consult the market representatives of the buying office about vendors and best-selling items. At the resident buying office, store buyers meet informally and frequently compare notes on consumer demand. Buying offices are still further discussed in Chapter 17.

MANUFACTURERS AND
THEIR SALES REPRESENTATIVES. The producers with whom a store deals can contribute information in discussing why they sponsor certain styles and trends. Their lines have been planned to meet anticipated consumer demand and tested against the reactions and sales experience of many retail buyers. Well-prepared sales representatives usually are eager to provide retail buyers with detailed information about their line and also about response to it.

Some of the most accurate information about consumer demand comes from producers. Today, major producers in each branch of the fashion business are large enough to use modern electronic equipment in collecting and analyzing information about sales trends quickly. Such producers thus are in a position to tell merchants what styles are selling at what rate in each part of the country. They can give advice about the styles that might prove to be best for each store and when they should be offered. They can also give the buyer helpful details about ways other stores have presented similar merchandise and what the results have been.

RESEARCH
STUDIES AND SURVEYS. Individual manufacturers, industry associations, publications, and government agencies occasionally conduct research studies in which consumers are polled about what they want to buy, where and when they prefer to buy, and their reasons for buying or not buying. The purposes of these surveys are varied, but each contributes some useful information about customer buying patterns.

One typical survey was made by a foundation and lingerie producer to ascertain ages, heights, weights, and dress sizes of customers. This survey also gathered information about the kinds of foundations, lingerie, and sleepwear customers preferred.

CONSUMER AND
TRADE PUBLICATIONS. Fashion merchants obtain insights into consumer demand from publications—both those that are intended for the general public and those intended for readers within some specific sector of the fashion business.

Fashion news is reported in almost all consumer newspapers and magazines. Merchants keep track of this news. They also follow the fashion advertising in such publications, so that they will know what influences may be creating or discouraging demand for certain fashion products among their customers. Magazines that give special emphasis to fashion, such as *Vogue* and *Harper's Bazaar,* or to fashions for specific groups of customers, such as *Glamour* or *Mademoiselle,* make considerable efforts to keep fashion merchants informed about the merchandise to be featured in future editions. These publications also can provide merchants with assessments of fashion trends among particular segments of the public and with information about how merchants can best influence them. Many consumer magazines spend enormous amounts of money on research in order to know their readers better. They are usually more than

MADEMOISELLE

HARPER'S BAZAAR

VOGUE

ESSENCE

TOWN & COUNTRY

Esquire

GLAMOUR

L'OFFICIEL USA

seventeen

These magazines give special emphasis to fashion.

willing to share these studies with merchants.

One type of survey used regularly by some consumer magazines and sporadically by others determines how many of certain items their readers buy per year and what they pay for each.

Trade publications are expert in assessing fashion and market developments. Some of these publications are directed primarily at retailers, telling them what merchandise is new and good, and how stores are promoting it successfully. Examples are *Intimate Apparel, Handbags and Accessories, Jewelers' Circular-Keystone,* and *Boot and Shoe Recorder.* Others, like *Women's Wear Daily,* address themselves to all branches of an industry, from the retailers to the primary sources of materials used in manufacturing the products concerned. From both types of trade publications, a fashion merchant can get a highly professional assessment of consumer demand and the influences that are being exerted upon it.

REPORTING SERVICES. There are services to which merchants can subscribe to keep up to date on store happenings, ideas, trends, and market news. For example, Retail News Bu-

reau supplies regular reports on the ads run by New York stores. Its other services include market forecasts, hot-item bulletins, general market news, a merchants' newsletter, and a variety of other bulletins and news releases about women's apparel and accessories. Another example is the *Fashion Calendar,* published weekly and available on a subscription basis. It lists and gives details about all important fashion events. The same source also publishes a monthly fashion newsletter for retail executives called *Fashion International.* Similar market information is also available on a fee basis from Tobé Associates, Inc., one of the older services in the field, founded by the late Tobé Coller Davis.

FASHION CONSULTANTS. Independent fashion consultants sell their expertise to merchants to supplement that of a firm's own executives. Fashion consultants may be hired by merchants on a regular retainer basis or to assist with a single project. Some consultants specialize in certain areas of fashion, while others offer a wide range of fashion services. Most of these experts have years of experience in the fashion business.

RETAIL NEWS BUREAU

'A *Confidential* Reporting Service'

ITEM (S)—

YOUNG CONTEMPORARY SPORTSWEAR
SIZES S,M,L
$36.00

RESPONSE*			
FAIR	GOOD	STRONG	SELLOUT
	x		

SPYC	**RESOURCE**

WAYNE ROGERS
1441 BROADWAY
NYC

REPORT NO. JF-MS523-6

STORE BERGDORFS

PAPER TIMES 5-21

AD. SIZE 3 x 5"

WEATHER RAINY

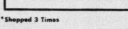

*Shopped 3 Times

Our shetland wool cardigan,
fair isle style. Faring beautifully
in a season of clean-cut collegiate
looks in graduated pales of
powder blue, dusty rose or
natural. From Wayne Rogers,
S,M or L. $36.
Sixth Sense, Sixth Floor.

BERGDORF GOODMAN

On the Plaza in New York

DETAILS: NEVER PUT ON HOLD

STYLE #6654R: SHETLAND WOOL SWEATER IN GRADUATED PALES
OF DUSTY ROSE,POWDER BLUE, OR NATURAL.
FOR SIZES S,M,L, $36.00.

ADVERTISED MERCHANDISE AVAILABLE AT BERGDORFS IN SIXTH SENSE
ON THE SIXTH FLOOR.THIS IS AN INITIAL ORDER FOR THEM. OTHER
STORES CARRYING THE SWEATER ARE ROBINSONS,MACYS,A & S,
AND BLOOMINGDALES. DELIVERY IS A/R 8-30.

Errors subject to correction

● MERCHANDISE REPORT OF **RETAIL NEWS BUREAU**, 232 MADISON AVE., NEW YORK N. Y. 10016 ●

Copyright   *An Independent Agency Reporting the News of Retailing—Promptly, Accurately, Completely.*   MU 6-2134

Published by Retail News Bureau, 232 Madison Ave., New York, N.Y. 10016

Independent reporting services provide buyer subscribers with up-to-the-minute information on the fashion market.

Customer Advisory Groups

A third source of useful information for retailers is supplied by various customer groups organized by some stores. These groups give retailers a consumer's view of store policies, services, assortments, and fashions. In addition, they assure the store of a flow of favorable publicity among the circles in which group members move. If group members or their activities are considered newsworthy, they also provide the store with publicity in the news media.

COLLEGE BOARDS. Perhaps the oldest and most firmly entrenched consumer advisory group is the college advisory board. A college board is made up of at least one upper-class student chosen from each college that is important to residents of an area. In the August and September selling rush, these young women and men serve both as salespeople and as advisers to college-bound customers. They may also informally model apparel.

TEEN BOARDS. Stores often set up teen or high school boards. Activities of these boards differ from those of college boards in several respects. Actual sales work usually is not involved. Activities are also year-round, since the high schools are located in the store's trad-

THE RAM® REPORT LISTINGS
LISTING IS LIMITED EXCLUSIVELY TO THE BEST SELLING 20%

MISSES SPORTSWEAR & SEPARATES CLASSIFICATION ANALYSIS

Fashion Merchandising Area: South & So. Calif.   Season: HOLIDAY

KNIT & WOVEN TOPS

					SO.	S.C.
SHIRT NECKLINE	LADY ARROW	4345	12.75	String tie lace collar L/S poly sheen in solid pastels. Sold out.	X	
	LADY ARROW	4170	10.75	Solid Ultressa® long sleeve shirt w/detachable bow. Av. for Holiday.	X	
	LADY ARROW	4346	12.75	Poly sheen lace trim L/S solid colors. Sold out.	X	
	COPPERFIELD	2118	25.00	Solid georgette smock shoulder notch collar L/S shirt. Sold up.	X	X
	A KALLINS	4308	6.75	Arnel®/nylon brushed velour placket collar L/S rib trim. Av. 6 clrs.	X	
	COPPERFIELD	2902	20.00	Solid L/S square collar shirt pleat front & back yoke. Av. for Spr. 3/15.	X	X
	C.P. INC	9705	13.75	Solid poly crepe de Chine shirt 2 patch pkts roll tab slv. Sold up.	X	
	CARRY BACK LTD	9013	14.50	100% silk shantung darted cap slv sm notch coll; new clrs for Spr.		X
	LADY ARROW	6482	12.75	Striped Ultressa® L/S shirt w/detachable bow. Sold up.	X	
	BODIN APPAREL	12110	11.50	100% poly multicolored classic print shirt in navy, red & white.	X	
JEWEL, U & V NECKLINE	JINNY JIN	9390	10.00	Shimmer terry V neck band bottom P/O. Av. new hot candy colors.	X	X
	A KALLINS	5032	5.50	L/S terry chenille V neck, rib bottom & cuffs. Av. new brights.	X	
	I Q ORIGINALS	4012	15.00	Cotton/rayon L/S jewel neck honeycomb front knit top.	X	X
	KENAR	1582	24.00	L/S V neck silk crepe de Chine sweatshirt. Jewel tones. Av. S/S #1583.		X
	COPPERFIELD	2104	17.50	Double darted shaped V nk L/S blouse in solid palace crepe. Sold up.	X	X
	KENAR	3910	16.00	Silk & cotton sweater top V neck L/S. Available 7 bright colors.		X
HIGH & BOW NECKLINES	JINNY JIN	7190	10.75	Shimmer terry band collar roll slv w/tab. Av. in new hot candy colors.		X
	HERALD HOUSE	8150	6.50	50% Dacron®/50% cotton L/S turtle neck top in 10 colors.	X	X
	LADY HOLIDAY BLOUSE	999	7.75	L/S poly dot bow blouse; for Spr. S/S #720. Av. prints & solids.		X
	SAINT PIERRE LTD	4953	32.00	Silk crepe de Chine jacquard L/S bow blouse. Matching skirt avail.		X
TUNICS	ECCOBAY	8251	7.85	Eccobay's fashion velour L/S raglan V nk band bottom rib trim top.	X	X
	ECCOBAY	8252	8.35	Eccobay's fashion L/S crew nk placket frt rib trim. P/O top.	X	
	BODIN APPAREL	12132	10.50	100% poly knit stripe S/S tunic. Avail. multicolor red/wht/navy.	X	
JACKETS	ECCOBAY	8540	20.00	Eccobay's fashion poly stretch gab 2 button patch pkt lined blazer.	X	X
	CENTURY	9901	31.50	Chanel-type L/S jacket in solid velveteen w/trapunto details. Sold up.	X	X
	BODIN APPAREL	12140	29.00	100% poly SuperSuede® fully lined L/S blazer. Av. navy, red & white.	X	
SKIRTS	CENTURY	9497	19.00	Side pleat tartan plaid kilt w/fringe & pin. Av. 2 week delivery.	X	X
	CENTURY	9432	14.50	Wool blend flannel slim skirt side slits. Av. poplin #7123 for Spring.	X	X
	ECCOBAY	8120	8.35	Eccobay's fashion poly/wool basic 4 gore belted skirt.	X	X
	CENTURY	9824	17.00	Sold up. Long wool blend plaid slim skirt w/side slits.	X	
	SIDNEY GOULD	9780	15.00	Solid chenille A line pull... Holiday 2 week delivery.	X	

From information taken from over 44 million consumer purchases and about $1.2 billion in annual sales, the RAM data system generates the top 20 percent of best selling items by classification on a weekly basis in the pages of *Women's Wear Daily*. The listings are paid for by the manufacturers who qualify to participate in these listings.

ing area. Teen boards, unlike those for college students, often engage in activities beyond fashion merchandising alone. For example, working through their teen boards, stores may sponsor such projects as charm schools and the preparation of fashion columns for school newspapers. Some stores have similar activities for pre-teens on a more restricted scale.

Accustoming younger age groups to regular store visits increases the likelihood that they will become fashion customers in their college, career, and married years. And the store, having "watched them grow up," is better able to anticipate their wants. It can also encourage them to comment freely to management if assortments or services are lacking.

CAREER WOMEN. Never in the history of retailing has so much attention been paid to the working woman as in the last few years. The reason is obvious. Working women make up a very large part of a retailer's business. Because they are working, these women are out of the house and in close proximity to retail stores. They also have dollars to spend.

In the 1960s, programs existed in a few major department stores. These usually consisted of a career club with a board of directors chosen from the city's leading women in business. Programs, fashion shows, and "how-to" clinics were held on a regular basis for the club members. In return, the members helped the store by offering reactions to merchandise and by suggesting how the store could become more popular with working women.

By the end of the 1970s, career women programs had been started in almost every major store in the U.S.—from Dayton's, with its Brown Bag, week-long series of meetings, to Saks Fifth Avenue, Foley's, Abraham and Straus, Macy's, Weinstock's, Jordan Marsh, Gimbels, and many others. Programs varied from store to store, but among the special services usually offered were famous guest speakers, how-to clinics, fashion shows, seminars, and career guidance round-tables.

One store runs a club for career women which holds meetings devoted to informative programs emphasizing fashion. One club member is chosen by lot every second week to select and accessorize several stock garments she considers ideal for working women. Her selections are then featured in the store's boutique for career women.

Retailers now realize that the ranks of working women are going to swell in the next decade. This extremely valuable market has placed its demands for recognition squarely in front of the country's retailers—who have responded with programs like those mentioned above.

MERCHANDISING VOCABULARY

Define or briefly explain the following terms:

Buying motivation	**Patronage motives**
Caveat emptor	**Psychological satisfactions**
Caveat venditor	**Resident buying office**
Markdowns	**Selection factors**
Operational satisfactions	**Want slip**

MERCHANDISING REVIEW

1. Trace the rise of the consumer movement and the practices, at both production and retail distribution levels, that gave the movement impetus.

2. How is today's typical American consumer different from one of a few decades ago?
3. Name and describe any five elements or selection factors that significantly influence a customer's choice when contemplating the purchase of most fashion goods.
4. How does Udell's theory of buying motives differ from an earlier, widely held theory? Do you agree? Why?
5. Name five reasons why customers patronize a store.
6. What factors are primarily responsible for (a) regional variations and (b) seasonal variations in demand?
7. What factors, other than regional and seasonal differences, contribute to variations in customer demand?
8. What sources in a merchant's store yield information about customer demand? Briefly note the specific type(s) of information provided by each source.
9. What sources outside a merchant's store yield information about customer demand? Briefly note the specific type(s) of information provided by each source.
10. How are customer advisory groups valuable to a fashion merchant in obtaining relevant information on customer demand? Give at least one example of how each group can provide a merchant with helpful information.

MERCHANDISING DIGEST

1. Discuss the following statement from the text: "It is not enough for merchants to merely keep abreast of general fashion trends and general customer demand." What else should a merchant carefully consider?
2. Discuss the importance of price as a selection factor.
3. Discuss the following statement and its implications: "Seasonality has once again become an important factor in consumer demand for fashion goods that are designed specifically for hot or cold weather . . . ."
4. Trace the development of the rise of the career woman and discuss the implications for fashion designers, manufacturers, and retailers.

REFERENCES

[1] Based on Wingate and Friedlander, *The Management of Retail Buying*, p. 92.
[2] Copeland, *Principles of Merchandising*, pp. 155–167.
[3] Udell, "A New Approach to Consumer Motivation," pp. 8–9.

13

THE DOLLAR MERCHANDISE PLAN

Each year, fashion buyers are responsible for investing many thousands of their stores' dollars in acquiring stock for resale. This responsibility is a big one and one that stores do not take lightly. Fashion implies change, and fashion buyers must stay one step ahead of customer demand in order to make a profit for their stores. If a buyer misjudges customer demand and invests money in the wrong type of merchandise, this almost certainly means lost sales, large markdowns, and decreased profits for his or her store.

WHAT IS DOLLAR MERCHANDISE PLANNING?

To aid both the buyer and the store in planning carefully for stock purchases, the buyer prepares a dollar merchandise plan. The **dollar merchandise plan** is a specific budget that projects both sales goals and the amount of stock that is required to achieve those goals. It is the most important plan the buyer works with, and in some ways it is similar to a buyer's contract with the store.

Employment contracts spell out in detail the responsibilities of the employee and the reward that the employee will receive for fulfilling those responsibilities. The dollar merchandise plan is a projection of the sales a buyer expects to achieve over a specific period of time, usually six months. It shows the amount of stock the buyer expects to have on hand, the expected necessary markdowns, and the stock purchases planned throughout the period. In return for fulfilling the responsibilities outlined in the dollar merchandise plan, the buyer receives a predetermined salary and/or commission.

Although the dollar merchandise plan is a formal projection, it can be changed if necessary. If actual sales are below those planned, the buyer makes every effort to improve merchandising techniques so that the projected figures will be achieved. But if conditions differ from those that existed or were anticipated when the plan was drawn up, the plan should be revised.

Goals of Dollar Merchandise Planning

The major goals of careful, scientific planning in retail merchandising are:

- To maintain an inventory that is neither too large nor too small for anticipated customer demand
- To time the delivery of purchases so that merchandise is available for sale neither too early nor too late for customer demand
- To keep purchases in line with the store's ability to pay for them
- To have funds available for the purchase of new goods when they may be needed

Tools of Dollar Merchandise Planning

The dollar merchandise plan is one of two financial tools that retail merchants use to achieve these goals. The other is the dollar open-to-buy. The dollar merchandise plan looks to the future; it is drawn up to serve as a guide for a selling period that has not yet begun. The open-to-buy is concerned with the present; it is a control device to keep stocks in line with actual sales. The term **dollar open-to-buy** refers to the dollar value of planned purchases for a given period minus the dollar value of all orders scheduled for delivery during that same period but not yet received. Planned purchases are defined and discussed later in this chapter. A detailed discussion of open-to-buy will be found in Chapter 16.

Use of Retail Figures

The majority of department stores and departmentalized specialty stores operate under an accounting system known as the **retail method of inventory** evaluation. In this system, all transactions affecting the value of a store's, department's, or merchandise classification's inventory—such as sales, purchases, markdowns, transfers, and returns-to-vendor—are recorded at their retail values. Stores on the older "cost" method of inventory evaluation (usually only small stores) keep their records on the basis of the cost of the merchandise, rather than the retail price.

Stores operating under the retail method plan their merchandise budgets and assortments entirely on the basis of retail values. Since the majority of departmentalized stores use the retail method of accounting, all figures used in subsequent discussions of dollar merchandise planning are at retail values, unless otherwise indicated.

HOW IS THE DOLLAR MERCHANDISE PLAN PREPARED?

As already defined, the merchandise plan or budget is a careful integration of a sales program and projections for the stock needed to achieve those planned sales during a specific period of time.

In a small store, where the owner is in constant touch with all operations, a formal merchandise plan may be unnecessary. However, even in a small store with limited capital resources, some preplanning of purchases and other elements of the merchandising operation is necessary.

In large retail organizations, a carefully detailed plan or budget is essential. The very size of the establishment requires the distribution of merchandising responsibilities among many individuals. The merchandising plan thus provides a guide for each of these individuals in their efforts to secure desired sales and profit results. A carefully prepared merchandise plan serves as a contractual agreement between the buyer and the store. It also furnishes a standard against which store management can measure the performance of the executives responsible for the merchandising operation.

Procedures for Preparing the Plan

In a small organization, dollar merchandising plans for the store as a whole are usually drawn up. In larger stores, separate budgets are first developed for each department. Later these separate budgets are incorporated into a master plan at the divisional level, or the storewide level, or both.

The merchandise plan, whether for a single department or for a store as a whole, should be prepared in a form that is clear to all who must work with it. While the format of the plan may vary considerably from store to store, both in scope and degree of detail, the ideal is a plan presented in the simplest form possible and in terminology familiar to everyone who will be using it.

The period covered by a merchandise budget may vary from one month to a year, but the usual planning period is six months. The spring season—February through July—is usually planned in one budget. The fall season—August through January—is planned in another budget. In most cases the seasonal plan is later broken down into monthly or, in some cases, weekly subdivisions.

Merchandise plans are drawn up several months in advance of the period to which they refer. The length of time varies from store to store, but plans must always be completed and approved before actual buying for the season begins.

Departmental buyers usually play an active role in the initial preparation of merchandise plans. First, a store's accounting department supplies each buyer with a planning form. On it are the figures from that department's merchandising operation during the corresponding season of the previous year. Many stores, particularly larger ones, also include in their plans last year's actual and this year's projected figures for seasonal merchandising goals. These figures include gross margin desired, the number of stock turns desired, and certain departmental operating expenses. These seasonal merchandising goals are established by store management, not by departmental buyers. They will be discussed later in this chapter. Figure 13-1 is typical of a six-month merchandising planning form as it might be presented to a buyer of junior sportswear.

Using the planning form, the buyer then prepares figures on anticipated sales, stock, markdowns, and purchases for the department in the upcoming six-month season. The buyer employs his or her specialized knowledge of market conditions, trends, and demand cycles in completing the plan. It is important that the completed plan fit within the framework of management's goal figures for the season.

When a buyer has completed work on the merchandise plan it is reviewed by the divisional merchandise manager, who may make revisions before approving it. Next, the merchandise manager consolidates into a divisional plan the approved plans of all the departments under his or her supervision. The divisional plan is then submitted to the general merchandise manager for review and approval. Finally, all plans are subject to review by the store's controller (or other chief fiscal officer) and usually the chief executive (the general manager or president). When they are approved, departmental plans are combined into a master plan for the store as a whole.

Departmentalized stores with several large branches usually make separate merchandise plans for each department in each branch. These plans are usually drawn up by departmental buyers in cooperation with respective branch store managers. Separate branch plans may then be incorporated into the parent store's departmental plan. Or individual branch store plans may be incorporated, together with the total parent store plan, into a companywide plan. Stores with only a few branches generally combine branch store merchandising plans with the plans of each parent store department.

A good merchandise plan is both specific and flexible. Since the plan is an attempt to forecast customer demand and develop strategies far in advance of the period covered, the plan cannot be completely rigid. As the season actually gets under way, figures in the plan are frequently reviewed, both in relation to actual results and in relation to more current information about the balance of the season. For example, if the supply of certain types of goods appears to be threatened by a lengthy strike, store management might decide to increase their stocks of such goods immediately, rather than waiting for the previously planned purchase time. Or, if important business firms lay off large numbers of employees, retail stores in that area can probably expect a decrease in customer demand. These stores would probably decide to reduce their sales projections and stock requirements. Such reductions in the seasonal plan would result in decreased purchases for the affected departments.

Elements of the Plan

Merchandise plans vary considerably from store to store in format, scope, and detail. The basic elements included in most seasonal merchandise budgets, however, are sales, stocks, markdowns, and purchases. In addition, as previously mentioned, the merchandising plan

		PLAN (This Year)	ACTUAL (Last Year)
Dept. Name Junior Sportswear	Dept. No. 145		

<table>
<tr><td colspan="3" rowspan="3">SIX MONTH
MERCHANDISING
PLAN</td><td></td><td>PLAN
(This Year)</td><td>ACTUAL
(Last Year)</td></tr>
</table>

Dept. Name Junior Sportswear   **Dept. No.** 145

SIX MONTH MERCHANDISING PLAN		PLAN (This Year)	ACTUAL (Last Year)
	Initial markup (%)	48.5	47.5
	Gross margin (%)	42.3	41.8
	Cash discount (% cost purch.)	8.0	7.8
	Season stock turnover (rate)	2.8	2.6
	Shortage reserve (%)	1.5	1.8
	Advertising expense (%)	2.8	3.0
	Selling salaries (%)	8.0	8.5

SPRING 198—		FEB.	MAR.	APR.	MAY	JUNE	JULY	SEASON TOTAL
~~FALL 198—~~		~~AUG.~~	~~SEP.~~	~~OCT.~~	~~NOV.~~	~~DEC.~~	~~JAN.~~	
SALES	Last Year	12,100	14,200	17,300	15,500	14,100	10,800	84,000
	Plan							
	Percent of Increase							6.0%
	Revised							
	Actual							
RETAIL STOCK (BOM)	Last Year	34,500	35,500	39,000	35,000	34,000	29,000	21,000*
	Plan							*
	Revised							
	Actual							
MARKDOWNS	Last Year	2,000	2,500	2,800	2,200	2,200	2,100	13,800
	Plan (dollars)							
	Plan (percent)							14.0%
	Revised							
	Actual							
RETAIL PURCHASES	Last Year	15,100	20,200	16,100	16,700	11,300	4,900	84,300
	Plan							
	Revised							
	Actual							

Comments

   *Represents stock end of period.

Merchandise Manager _____   Buyer _____

Controller_____

Figure 13-1

may include other seasonal goal figures affecting operating profit such as initial markup, gross margin, stock shortage reserves, cash discounts, and stock turnover. Also often considered essential in planning are such operating expenses as selling salaries and advertising expense.

PLANNING SALES. The first step in the preparation of a merchandise plan is to make a realistic estimate of prospective sales during an upcoming season. This estimate is based upon external factors, internal factors, and general fashion trends that are likely to influence a department's sales volume. Finally, seasonal sales goals are broken down into sales goals for each month in the season being planned.

External Factors. External factors are those outside of the store or its control. They include employment prospects, general economic conditions, population changes, and the competitive situation. The opening of a new plant in an area, for example, is likely to increase spending power in the community. Conversely, the possibility of strikes or shutdowns among local employers means a potential loss of spending power in the trading area.

Optimism regarding the future encourages consumer spending. Threats of new taxes, higher interest rates, or declines in economic activity tend to discourage spending.

Sales prospects are affected by the growth or lack of growth in an area's population. They are affected by changes in the proportion of high-income to low-income families and by changes in the age composition of a population. A new housing development for young families, for example, provides a potential increase in sales in children's, juniors', young women's, and young men's departments. A new, center-city highrise apartment building appealing to older couples may favor departments selling higher-priced, more conservative apparel and accessories, as well as home furnishings.

The competitive effect of new or expanded stores and shopping centers in the trading area is evaluated. Consideration is also given to the possibility that stores in other communities within easy traveling distance may be gaining or losing power to draw off some of the local retail business. On the other hand, if any local competitors have closed up shop, or if new highways or parking facilities have made it easier for customers to get to the store, there is reason to anticipate sales growth.

Internal Factors. Internal factors are those within the store or its control. They include physical changes within the store that either enhance or diminish the sales prospects of individual departments. They also include the opening of new branches, the general trend in store sales, and the number and extent of promotions the store's management expects to undertake during the season being planned.

Physical changes within a store can affect the sales prospects of various departments within the store. For example, if new escalators are being installed with landings at the entrance to department X, sales of that department will probably benefit. On the other hand, if department Y had to be moved to a less prominent location or perhaps had its floor space reduced because of the alteration, department Y's sales may suffer. Relocation, expansion, or contraction of a department's selling space aren't the only physical changes that affect sales. The acquisition or elimination of display fixtures, a change of decor, and any change in its proximity to departments carrying related merchandise can also affect sales.

If a new branch is to be opened within the planning period, the additional anticipated sales in that branch should be taken into account. The fact that there may be a shift in the location of sales—a possible decrease in the main store sales as a result of the transfer of some patronage from there to the new branch—should not be overlooked in the planning procedures.

If the store as a whole is enjoying expanded sales, each department within the store usually profits from the increased customer traffic. The reverse is true if the store as a whole is attracting less traffic.

A department's sales are also affected by the amount of promotion the store plans in its behalf. Its sales opportunities are enhanced if the store as a whole plans increased promotional effort, since this usually will bring increased customer traffic. Such efforts may be general, intended simply to bring more people into the store. Or they may be aimed at specific groups, such as career women, young mothers, or teenagers. In the latter case, only those departments in which the merchandise has particular appeal to the group being courted can expect significant sales benefit.

Fashion Trends. Fashion trends are frequently the most important factor influencing sales. These usually affect the sales of several departments at one time, pushing up the sales potential of some and depressing the sales prospects of others. For example, if the trend is toward dressier apparel, dress departments can budget optimistically. But departments selling sportswear and other casual attire will plan more cautiously. Similarly, fashion trends in ready-to-wear affect the sales planning of other fashion departments. For example, a trend toward fitted waistlines undoubtedly will increase the sales potential of the belt department as well as that of the foundations department. A trend toward longer skirts places less emphasis on legs, thereby decreasing the sales potential of hosiery departments. At the same time this trend increases the sales potential of shoe departments, particularly in such merchandise as higher heels to wear with longer skirts.

Monthly Sales Goals. Retailers usually express sales goals in dollars. These sales goals are translated into percentages of increase or decrease in actual sales compared with the corresponding period of the previous year. The percentage of change, however, is not necessarily the same for each month of the season. Each month's sales goals are separately set within the framework of the seasonal plan. In setting goals, careful consideration must be given to the previous years' sales for the same month, to the percentage each month has usually contributed to total annual sales, and to any other factors influencing a department's sales potential.

Since the pattern of consumer demand varies both seasonally and monthly, this fact must also be taken into account when planning monthly sales goals. If there were no such variations, each month would contribute an equal number of dollars to the year's total sales volume. A glance at Table 13-1 will show this to be far from the case. In planning sales, merchants allow for the fact that not only does the number of business days vary from month to month but that there are some months in which customers buy more freely than in others.

Monthly sales volume, as a percentage of the total year's sales, also varies from depart-

TABLE 13-1

Estimated Percentage of Annual Sales Made in Each Month of Years 1978 and 1979 in Apparel and Accessory Stores

	1978	1979
January	6.1	6.5
February	5.7	5.9
March	7.8	7.7
April	7.4	7.9
May	7.7	7.8
June	7.6	7.7
July	7.3	7.3
August	8.4	8.8
September	8.5	8.2
October	8.7	8.6
November	9.7	9.5
December	15.1	14.1

Source: Estimated and projected figures based on data collected by the Monthly Retail Trade Branch, Business Division, of the United States Census Bureau.

ment to department. This is explained by the seasonality of the merchandise that each handles and the curve of consumer demand for that merchandise. For example, toy departments and often fur departments do the bulk of their annual business in a relatively few months of the year.

Holidays and other special days such as Valentine's Day, Mother's Day, and Father's Day also give rise to variations in demand. The extent to which each influences monthly sales planning depends upon the nature of the merchandise and the extent of the department's promotional plans.

In estimating the sales potential for each month, a buyer or store manager also considers any special circumstances that may have affected sales the previous year but that can be ignored in this year's planning. For example, some sales may have been lost in the previous year because of delivery delays. If no delivery problems are anticipated this year, sales may be appreciably better because of this one factor alone. Other factors affecting sales in previous years such as unseasonable weather, special promotions held in competing stores, and special attractions that drew customers to one's own store should also be taken into account.

Most buyers keep some kind of personal notebook in which they list special conditions that have affected sales. Weather, their own advertising and that of their competitors, and changing market conditions are some of the factors noted.

Another familiar device is a departmental "Beat Last Year" book, in which comparative daily sales are recorded for as many as five successive years. Notes like "rain," "parade," and "half-page ad" (noting the item advertised) remind the buyer of the story behind sales figures for each day.

In the case of a new store, a new branch, or a new department within an established store, past sales records are not available as a guide. Research—formal or informal—combined with careful judgment must take the place of experience. Market studies, consultations with other merchants or other buyers, and discussions with bankers and vendors are all helpful in arriving at sales goals for the new enterprise.

Figure 13-2 indicates how the seasonal merchandise plan looks when seasonal and monthly sales goals have been set.

PLANNING STOCK. The next step in dollar merchandising planning is to estimate the amount of stock that will be needed to support the planned monthly sales. In terms of dollar investment, this planning and control of stocks is an essential part of the merchandise plan or budget.

The objective in planning a beginning-of-the-month inventory is to keep stocks in a desired ratio to sales planned for that month. This makes it possible to achieve the seasonal stock turnover goals, which will be explained later in this chapter. At the same time, placing realistic limits on the beginning-of-the-month investment makes possible a steady flow of new merchandise into stock throughout the month as inventory is depleted by sales.

Considerations in Planning. Since sales during any month can only be realized if there is stock to sell, it is good practice to plan stocks

				PLAN (This Year)	ACTUAL (Last Year)
Dept. Name Junior Sportswear Dept. No. 145					
SIX MONTH MERCHANDISING PLAN		Initial markup (%)		48.5	47.5
		Gross margin (%)		42.3	41.8
		Cash discount (% cost purch.)		8.0	7.8
		Season stock turnover (rate)		2.8	2.6
		Shortage reserve (%)		1.5	1.8
		Advertising expense (%)		2.8	3.0
		Selling salaries (%)		8.0	8.5

SPRING 198—		FEB.	MAR.	APR.	MAY	JUNE	JULY	SEASON TOTAL
FALL 198—		AUG.	SEP.	OCT.	NOV.	DEC.	JAN.	
SALES	Last Year	12,100	14,200	17,300	15,500	14,100	10,800	84,000
	Plan	12,700	17,700	16,500	17,000	15,500	11,600	91,000
	Percent of Increase	5.0	24.6	−4.6	9.7	9.9	7.4	8.3%
	Revised							
	Actual							
	Last Year	34,500	35,500	39,000	35,000	34,000	29,000	21,000*

Figure 13-2

for the beginning of each month rather than for the end of the month. In any event, the planned beginning-of-the-month (BOM) stock is identical with the end-of-month (EOM) stock for the preceding month.

Two major considerations influence fashion merchants in planning BOM stocks. First, there must be an adequate opening assortment on hand, in sufficient quantity, to meet anticipated customer demand until stock replacements for goods sold can be secured. The best dollar stock plans for fashion departments are those in which minimum quantities of each item needed are detailed by classifications, price lines, types, colors, and sizes. (Assortment planning is discussed in detail in Chapter 14.)

A merchant's second consideration in planning BOM stocks is anticipated sales. The planning must be such that the desired seasonal stock turnover may be realized, markdowns minimized, and a steady flow of new, interesting merchandise assured throughout the month.

The same external, internal, and fashion factors that influence the planning of monthly sales also influence the planning of monthly stocks and must be evaluated accordingly.

Variations in Monthly Stock Goals.   In planning monthly stock goals, stocks should be brought to a peak just prior to the time when sales are expected to reach their peak. By peaking stocks before consumer demand reaches its crest, merchants are able to present maximum assortments in needed styles, sizes, and colors when the public is in the mood to buy.

Similarly, beginning-of-the-month stock plans are reduced as a selling season approaches its close and demand decreases. Two other factors help the merchant to reduce inventory as the season ends. Unsold seasonal goods are marked down. Any new goods that may be brought into stock are usually manufacturers' closeouts. These are usually purchased and resold at prices lower than earlier in the season.

Stock-Sales Relationships.   Departmentalized stores are guided in their stock planning by

two stock-sales relationships: monthly stock-sales ratios and a desired rate of seasonal stock turnover.

The first of these relationships, known as a **monthly stock-sales ratio,** is defined as the number of months that would be required to dispose of a beginning-of-the-month inventory at the rate at which sales are made in (or planned for) that month. The formula used for calculating this relationship is:

$$\text{stock-sales ratio} = \frac{\$ \text{ BOM stock}}{\$ \text{ sales for month}}$$

Applying this formula to the February planned sales and stock figures appearing on Figure 13-3:

$$\text{stock-sales ratio} = \frac{\$32,500}{\$12,700}$$
$$= 2.56$$

The stock-sales ratio is an important tool in stock planning in that it directly relates stock requirements to planned sales. Appropriate stock-sales ratios may be derived from a store's own experience. Or they may be based on the experiences of other stores as compiled by such trade associations as the National Retail Merchants Association, or from combinations of the two. Ratios will vary, of necessity, from month to month, from department to department, from one type of retail operation to another, and from one type of merchandise to another. They depend primarily upon the cycle of demand for various types of merchandise and the merchandising policies of an individual store. Once a sales goal has been set and a desirable stock-sales ratio is established, the stock needed at the beginning of any month can be determined as follows:

$$\$ \text{ BOM stock} = \$ \text{ planned sales} \times \text{stock- sales ratio}$$

Using the figures from Table 13-2 as an illustration of the application of this formula, assume that a merchant plans February sales at $2,000 in each of three departments: Women's Dressy Coats, Lingerie, and Men's Furnishings. Applying the February stock-sales ratios listed in this table, the amount

		PLAN (This Year)	ACTUAL (Last Year)
Dept. Name Junior Sportswear	Dept. No. 145		
SIX MONTH MERCHANDISING PLAN	Initial markup (%)	48.5	47.5
	Gross margin (%)	42.3	41.8
	Cash discount (% cost purch.)	8.0	7.8
	Season stock turnover (rate)	2.8	2.6
	Shortage reserve (%)	1.5	1.8
	Advertising expense (%)	2.8	3.0
	Selling salaries (%)	8.0	8.5

SPRING 198—		FEB.	MAR.	APR.	MAY	JUNE	JULY	SEASON TOTAL
FALL 198—		AUG.	SEP.	OCT.	NOV.	DEC.	JAN.	
SALES	Last Year	12,100	14,200	17,300	15,500	14,100	10,800	84,000
	Plan	12,700	17,700	16,500	17,000	15,500	11,600	91,000
	Percent of Increase	5.0	24.6	−4.6	9.7	9.9	7.4	8.3%
	Revised							
	Actual							
RETAIL STOCK (BOM)	Last Year	34,500	35,500	39,000	35,000	34,000	29,000	21,000*
	Plan	32,500	39,500	37,000	36,000	34,000	26,000	21,000*
	Revised							
	Actual							
	Last Year	2,000	2,500	2,800	2,200	2,200	2,100	13,800

Figure 13-3

of stock at retail value that should be on hand February 1 in each of these departments would be:

Women's Dressy Coats $2,000 × 2.6 = $ 5,200
Lingerie $2,000 × 4.6 = $ 9,200
Men's Furnishings $2,000 × 6.7 = $13,400

Unlike the stock-sales ratio, which is used in planning beginning-of-the-month stocks, **stock turnover** refers to the number of times that an average stock of merchandise (inventory) has been turned into sales during a given period. The formula for determining the rate of stock turnover during any given period is:

$$\text{stock turnover} = \frac{\$ \text{ net sales}}{\$ \text{ average inventory}}$$

For example, using Figure 13-3, we can find that the average stock for the spring season being planned is $32,286. This figure is ob-

tained by adding all six beginning-of-the-month stocks (February–July) to the end-of-season stock ($21,000) and dividing that sum by 7 (the number of inventory figures used):

$$\frac{\begin{aligned}32,500 + 39,500 + \\ 37,000 + 36,000 + \\ 34,000 + 26,000 \\ + 21,000\end{aligned}}{7}$$

average inventory = $32,286

Then, by dividing the season's total planned sales of $91,000 by the average stock of $32,286, a stock turnover rate of 2.82 is found for the six-month period:

$$\frac{\$91,000}{\$32,286} = 2.82 \text{ stock turnover}$$

TABLE 13-2
Typical Monthly Stock-Sales Ratios

MONTH	WOMEN'S DRESSY COATS	LINGERIE	MENS-WEAR
Jan.	2.1	4.7	6.3
Feb.	2.6	4.6	6.7
March	2.3	5.5	5.7
April	2.4	5.2	6.3
May	3.8	3.8	6.2
June	4.7	4.3	3.8
July	3.9	4.3	6.0
Aug.	4.5	3.9	5.6
Sept.	5.0	5.0	5.1
Oct.	3.3	4.7	5.6
Nov.	2.7	4.0	3.6
Dec.	1.9	1.8	1.5

On a storewide basis, the typical stock turnover figure for all department stores is somewhat better than three turns a year. Rate of stock turnover, however, varies widely from one department to another within a given store. The rate depends upon the type of merchandise handled, its price ranges, and the depth and breadth of assortments carried.

In general, the rate of stock turnover is higher in women's apparel than in men's clothing or home furnishings. It is also higher in departments featuring lower-price ranges than in those featuring higher-price ranges. Typical average turnover figures for various types of goods are widely used by retail merchants in evaluating the proficiency of their merchandising operations (see Chapter 16). The following average turnover figures illustrate how the annual turnover varies on the basis of type of merchandise handled:

Misses' dresses	4.5 turns
Men's clothing	2.5 turns
Sleepwear and robes	7.8 turns
Millinery	6.5 turns

As an example of how the rate varies according to the price ranges of merchandise, the average turnover rate for budget dresses in a recent year was 4.6, compared with 4.1 for higher-priced dresses. When the nature of the merchandise requires that considerable depth and breadth of assortments be carried in relation to sales, turnover is low. As an example, the average stock turnover in women's shoes remains fairly constant at 2.0. This is because it is often necessary to stock as many as 100 pairs of women's shoes in a single style and color in order to have an adequate stock of the most popular combinations.

The rate at which stock is turned into sales directly affects retail profit objectives, since no income is realized until merchandise is sold. A direct attempt to achieve a desired rate of stock turnover is made by limiting beginning-of-the-month stock to a predetermined stock-sales ratio, as further discussed in Chapter 16.

PLANNING MARKDOWNS. Having planned monthly sales and beginning-of-the-month inventories, the fashion merchant is now almost ready to calculate the amount of stock that should be purchased throughout each month in order to achieve planned sales and stock goals. Before this is done, however, the merchant may decide to estimate the dollar value of markdowns it will be necessary to take each month. Markdowns reduce the retail value of the inventory just as sales do.

Purpose of Markdowns. Wise fashion merchants use merchandise markdowns to speed the sale of slow-moving, damaged, and out-of-season goods in order to make room for new merchandise. Markdowns are also used as a means of meeting price competition and for adjusting retail prices to declining market values. *Markdowns are most useful if regarded as a tool rather than as a curse.* They help to release capital that would otherwise be tied up in stock and make funds available for reinvestment in more salable stock.

Because of rapidly changing consumer demand, markdowns are generally larger and of greater importance in fashion goods departments in which the merchandise is more staple, such as blankets or housewares. By using markdowns judiciously to clear out seasonal goods promptly, fashion merchants avoid the heavy risks involved in carrying the goods beyond their normal selling period.

Dept. Name: Junior Sportswear				Dept. No. 145			

		PLAN (This Year)	ACTUAL (Last Year)
SIX MONTH MERCHANDISING PLAN	Initial markup (%)	48.5	47.5
	Gross margin (%)	42.3	41.8
	Cash discount (% cost purch.)	8.0	7.8
	Season stock turnover (rate)	2.8	2.6
	Shortage reserve (%)	1.5	1.8
	Advertising expense (%)	2.8	3.0
	Selling salaries (%)	8.0	8.5

SPRING 198— ~~FALL 198—~~		FEB. ~~AUG.~~	MAR. ~~SEP.~~	APR. ~~OCT.~~	MAY ~~NOV.~~	JUNE ~~DEC.~~	JULY ~~JAN.~~	SEASON TOTAL
SALES	Last Year	12,100	14,200	17,300	15,500	14,100	10,800	84,000
	Plan	12,700	17,700	16,500	17,000	15,500	11,600	91,000
	Percent of Increase	5.0	24.6	-4.6	9.7	9.9	7.4	8.3%
	Revised							
	Actual							
RETAIL STOCK (BOM)	Last Year	34,500	35,500	39,000	35,000	34,000	29,000	21,000*
	Plan	32,500	39,500	37,000	36,000	34,000	26,000	21,000*
	Revised							
	Actual							
MARKDOWNS	Last Year	2,000	2,500	2,800	2,200	2,200	2,100	13,800
	Plan (dollars)	1,900	2,000	2,500	2,000	2,000	2,100	12,700
	Plan (percent)	15.0	11.3	15.0	11.8	12.9	18.1	14.0%
	Revised							
	Actual							
	Last Year	15,100	20,200	16,100	16,700	11,300	4,900	84,300

Figure 13-4

Markdown Terminology. As discussed in Chapter 12, the term markdown refers to the dollar difference between the previous price and the reduced price at which merchandise is marked. To express the relationship between the value of accumulated markdowns and net sales for a given period, a markdown percentage figure is used. **Markdown percentage** may be defined as the dollar value of the net retail markdowns taken during a given period, expressed as a percentage of net sales for the same period. For example, Figure 13-4 shows that February markdowns are planned at $1,900 and February sales at $12,700. Ex-

pressed as a formula, markdown percentage is calculated as follows:

$$\text{markdown \%} = \frac{\$ \text{ markdown}}{\$ \text{ net sales}}$$

$$= \frac{\$1,900}{\$12,700}$$

$$= 14.96\% \text{ or } 15\%$$

Retailers use the term **retail reductions** for all reductions that occur in the retail value of the inventory. These include merchandise markdowns, discounts allowed to employees and other special customers, and stock shortages. Merchandise markdowns, however, constitute the major part of retail reductions. They vary considerably from month to month, particularly in the case of fashion goods. Anticipated markdowns are usually included when seasonal budgets are drawn up. Estimates of special discounts may be included with merchandise markdowns or shown separately. Estimates for reductions caused by stock shortages are made by setting up special monthly reserves for such contingencies as explained later in the chapter.

Factors in Planning Markdowns. A certain percentage of any retail store's stock will always have to be marked down before it can be sold. Some stock may have to be marked down more than once. Since markdowns result in lowered gross profit (the difference between the cost of the merchandise and the price at which it is finally sold), they must be planned for and controlled.

Markdowns are usually planned as a percentage of each season's planned sales. They may then be allotted to individual months, according to the merchant's estimates of when and to what extent monthly markdowns are going to be needed to sell the goods. In establishing the markdown estimates, the experience of previous seasons and of other stores is considered, together with the general business outlook for the period ahead.

The chief factors to be considered in establishing seasonal markdown goals are:

- The past experience of the store or department.
- Trends in wholesale prices. (Markdowns tend to increase during periods of falling wholesale prices and decrease when wholesale prices are rising.)
- Comparative figures of similar stores.
- Amount of old stock on hand at the beginning of a new season.
- Changes in merchandising policies and methods that may have occurred since the previous year or that are about to occur.

In allocating a season's markdown estimate to individual months, a merchant considers not only dates throughout the season when changes in customer demand are expected to occur, but also store policy in taking markdowns. Large stores tend to take markdowns while there is still sufficient customer demand to move the goods quickly at minimum price reductions. Small stores tend to postpone taking markdowns, preferring to clear their stocks only at the end of a selling season.

PLANNING PURCHASES. Having entered monthly sales, beginning-of-the-month stocks, and monthly markdown figures on the planning form, the merchant is now ready to calculate the value of the purchases that can be made each month if stocks and sales are to be kept in balance. **Planned purchases** is the term used to indicate the amount of merchandise that can be brought into stock during a given period without exceeding the value of the inventory planned to be on hand at the end of that period.

In most large stores, purchases are planned on a monthly basis. However, some smaller fashion merchants, particularly those who make infrequent market trips, budget purchases on a seasonal or market-trip basis. In either case, the procedure for planning purchases is the same. Planned purchases are derived from planned sales, stocks, and, when applicable, markdowns, by simple math.

The calculation of monthly purchases begins with planned sales for that month. To this figure is added planned markdowns for the month. These two figures represent the amount by which the retail value of the BOM stock is expected to be decreased during the month. To these figures are added the planned end-of-the-month stock (the same as the BOM stock for the following month), because these three factors—planned sales, markdowns, and EOM stock—represent the value of all merchandise needed during the month. From the total of these three figures is subtracted the BOM stock for that month, which is the amount already available for sale. The remainder represents the purchases that can be made for delivery during that one month if there is to be on hand at the end of the month the amount of stock that has been previously planned.

The formula for calculating planned purchases, then, is as follows:

$$\text{planned purchases} = \begin{array}{l} \text{planned sales for month} \\ + \text{ planned markdowns} \\ + \text{ planned EOM stock} \\ - \text{ BOM stock} \end{array}$$

Applying this formula to the February figures given in Figure 13-5:

$$\text{planned purchases} = \$12,700 + \$1,900 \\ + \$39,500 - \$32,500 \\ = \$21,600$$

Dept. Name __Junior Sportswear__   Dept. No. __145__

SIX MONTH MERCHANDISING PLAN

	PLAN (This Year)	ACTUAL (Last Year)
Initial markup (%)	48.5	47.5
Gross margin (%)	42.3	41.8
Cash discount (% cost purch.)	8.0	7.8
Season stock turnover (rate)	2.8	2.6
Shortage reserve (%)	1.5	1.8
Advertising expense (%)	2.8	3.0
Selling salaries (%)	8.0	8.5

SPRING 198—		FEB.	MAR.	APR.	MAY	JUNE	JULY	SEASON TOTAL
~~FALL 198—~~		AUG.	SEP.	OCT.	NOV.	DEC.	JAN.	
SALES	Last Year	12,100	14,200	17,300	15,500	14,100	10,800	84,000
	Plan	12,700	17,700	16,500	17,000	15,500	11,600	91,000
	Percent of Increase	5.0	24.6	−4.6	9.7	9.9	7.4	8.3%
	Revised							
	Actual							
RETAIL STOCK (BOM)	Last Year	34,500	35,500	39,000	35,000	34,000	29,000	21,000*
	Plan	32,500	39,500	37,000	36,000	34,000	26,000	21,000*
	Revised							
	Actual							
MARKDOWNS	Last Year	2,000	2,500	2,800	2,200	2,200	2,100	13,800
	Plan (dollars)	1,900	2,000	2,500	2,000	2,000	2,100	12,700
	Plan (percent)	15.0	11.3	15.0	11.8	12.9	18.1	14.0%
	Revised							
	Actual							
RETAIL PURCHASES	Last Year	15,100	20,200	16,100	16,700	11,300	4,900	84,300
	Plan	21,600	17,200	18,000	17,000	9,500	8,700	92,000
	Revised							
	Actual							

Comments

*Represents stock end of period.

Merchandise Manager __T. J. Evans__   Buyer __Jane Dean__

Controller _____

Figure 13-5

Although most stores plan their purchases at retail value, as was done here, some smaller stores still use cost value. If desired, the equivalent cost value of retail purchases can be calculated easily by multiplying the retail value of the planned purchases by the cost complement of the planned markup percentage for the period. (The cost complement is 100 percent minus the retail markup percent.) For example, if the February initial markup is planned at 48.5 percent and February retail purchases are planned at $21,600, the cost value of the $21,600 retail figure may be determined as follows:

$$\begin{aligned} \$ \text{ cost} &= \$ \text{ retail} \times (100\% - \text{retail markup } \%) \\ &= \$21,600 \times 51.5\% \\ &= \$11,124 \end{aligned}$$

WHAT SUPPLEMENTAL ELEMENTS RELATE TO DOLLAR MERCHANDISE PLANNING?

As previously stated, many retail stores, particularly large departmentalized stores, expand budgeting procedures beyond the four basic elements discussed above. They frequently include in the dollar merchandise plan goal figures for any of the several additional elements that directly relate to the profit of the operation. Important among these elements are cash discounts earned as percentage of purchases or sales, the rate of stock turnover desired, initial markup, the gross margin, shortage reserves, and operating expenses as a percentage of net sales.

In most cases, only seasonal goal figures for these supplemental elements are planned. In fewer cases, additional seasonal dollar and percentage-to-sales goal figures are worked out. Goal figures of each of these supplementary elements of the dollar merchandise plan, together with the figures representing the previous year's actual performance, are supplied by the store's controller or fiscal division. (See the top, right section of the Six Month Merchandising Plan shown in Figure 13-5.) Since such goal figures reflect the financial objectives of the store as determined by top management, they are rarely left to the discretion of departmental planners.

Guidelines in budgeting these additional elements of the dollar merchandise plan are obtained from the store's own experience, from the *Merchandising and Operating Reports* of the National Retail Merchants Association, and frequently from figures supplied by the store's resident buying office.

Markup

Markup is the difference between the cost and the retail price of merchandise. ("Markon" is a term used by some large retail stores as a designation of the difference between cost and selling prices.) Most stores express markup as a percentage of retail value, thus:

$$\text{retail markup } \% = \frac{\$ \text{ retail} - \$ \text{ cost}}{\$ \text{ retail}}$$

Some smaller stores and most manufacturers, however, calculate markup percentages on the basis of cost, or:

$$\text{cost markup } \% = \frac{\$ \text{ retail} - \$ \text{ cost}}{\$ \text{ cost}}$$

As previously stated, most fashion merchants use the retail system of accounting and employ the first formula given here in their calculations. But they need to be familiar with the second formula as well, since it may be used in discussions with suppliers and other retailers.

The dollar difference between the delivered cost of merchandise and the retail price placed on it when it is first brought into stock is called the **initial markup.** Retail stores plan initial markup percentages to ensure that the income derived from sales (the difference between the cost of goods and the retail prices at which they are first marked) will be adequate to cover: 1. all expenses incurred in the operation of the business; 2. anticipated reductions in the retail value of the inventory, such as markdowns, stock shortages, and employee discounts; and 3. a reasonable margin of profit to the store.

Some purchases may yield a higher or lower percentage of markup than was planned. But a buyer's aim throughout the season is to *maintain an average markup* on purchases no less than the goal figure indicated on the dollar merchandise plan. This predetermined average figure is intended as a guide for the buyer, not a figure which a buyer must apply to all purchases.

Gross Margin

Instead of initial markup percentage, or sometimes in addition to it, some stores plan gross margin of profit. **Gross margin** represents the dollar difference between net sales for a period and the net cost of merchandise sold during that period:

$$\begin{array}{r} \text{\$ net sales} \\ - \text{\$ net cost of mdse. sold} \\ \hline = \text{\$ gross margin} \end{array}$$

Gross margin percentage is calculated by dividing the dollars of gross margin by the net sales for the period:

$$\frac{\text{\$ gross margin}}{\text{\$ net sales}} = \% \text{ gross margin}$$

Gross margin is a very important figure in dollar merchandise planning. It represents the amount of money left from sales income after deducting the total cost of merchandise sold during a given period. The gross margin represents the amount of money available to pay all operating expenses and taxes with a reasonable profit left over.

Cash Discounts

Cash discounts are the percentages or premiums allowed by manufacturers off their invoices if payment of the invoice is made within a certain specified period of time. Such discounts are allowed to encourage the prompt payment of invoices.

Cash discounts earned are an important source of additional income for a store or department. For that reason they are included in most dollar merchandise plans, representing either a percentage of net sales or a percentage of the cost of purchases. Cash discounts increase gross margin, because they reduce the actual cost of merchandise purchases.

TERMS OF SALE. The combination of allowable discounts on purchases and the time allowed for taking such discounts is referred to as **terms of sale.** The percentage of cash discount allowed and the length of time allowed for the taking of that discount are fairly standardized within each industry. However, they vary widely from industry to industry.

For example, in the women's apparel industry, the usual terms of sale are 8/10 EOM (8 percent cash discount allowed if the invoice is paid within 10 days following the last day of the month in which the invoice is dated). In the handbag industry, terms of sale are usually 3/10 EOM; in the millinery industry, 7/10 EOM; in the glove industry, 6/10 EOM.

ANTICIPATION. An additional discount granted by some vendors for the payment of their invoices before the end of the cash discount period is called **anticipation.** Because anticipation further reduces the cost of purchases, retail stores can make profitable use of their capital by taking anticipation whenever the anticipation date is higher than current bank interest rates.

Stock Shortages and Overages

Stock shortages or overages represent the dollar difference between the **book inventory** (the value of inventory on hand as indicated by the store's accounting records) and the physical inventory (the value determined by taking a physical count). When the book inventory is greater than the physical inventory there is said to be a **stock shortage.** When the physical inventory is greater than the book inventory there is said to be a **stock overage.** Stock shortages are experienced with consistent regularity by retail stores. Stock overages occur very seldom. Both are discussed in detail in Chapter 16.

Stock shortages or overages can be determined only when a complete physical inventory is taken, which is usually only once or twice a year. But most stores set up interim monthly reserves for tolerable, or anticipated, shortages. This means that a certain percentage of monthly net sales is set aside in a special reserve account. The accummulated reserve fund is then applied as an offset to any actual difference between the book inventory and the actual physical inventory when the latter is taken.

Shortage reserve percentages are usually based upon past experience. The maximum allowable percentage is determined by store management at the beginning of a season or year, and does not change from month to month. Actual differences between the value of the book inventory and the value of the physical inventory, as determined from an actual count, are compared with the accumulated shortage reserve when the physical inventory is taken. If the actual shortage is less than the reserve, gross margin is increased by the amount of the difference. If the actual shortage is greater than the reserve, gross margin is thereby reduced by an equivalent amount.

Stock shortages decrease a department's gross margin and ultimate profit and are essentially the responsibility of the buyer. For these reasons, many stores include seasonal shortage reserve figures in their dollar merchandise plans.

Operating Expenses

Two kinds of expenses are incurred in the operation of a selling department: direct and indirect.

Direct expenses are those that occur as a direct result of the operation of a specific department. These are the types of expenses that would cease if the department itself ceased to exist. Examples of such direct expenses are salespeople's salaries, buyer's and assistant's compensation, expenses incurred in connection with buying trips, advertising expenses, and delivery charges.

Indirect expenses are those that do not directly result from the operation of an individual department, but are shared by all departments of the store. Examples are compensation of top management executives, utilities, maintenance, insurance, and receiving and marking expenses.

Many stores that include operating expenses as an element of the dollar merchandise budget make it a practice to plan advertising expenses and selling salaries separately. They are planned as seasonal or monthly percentages of planned sales, since these expenses are most intimately related to the actual production of sales. The six-month plan in most stores does not include a budget for indirect expenses, but they are included in the planning of initial markup.

MERCHANDISING VOCABULARY

Define or briefly explain the following terms:

Anticipation	**Markup**
Book inventory	**Monthly stock-sales ratio**
Cash discount	**Planned purchases**
Direct expenses	**Retail method of inventory**
Dollar merchandise plan	**Retail reductions**
Dollar open-to-buy	**Stock overage**
Gross margin	**Stock shortage**
Indirect expenses	**Stock turnover**
Initial markup	**Terms of sale**
Markdown percentage	

MERCHANDISING REVIEW

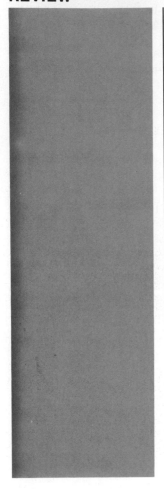

1. How is the dollar merchandise plan similar to a buyer's contract with the store?
2. What are the four goals of dollar merchandise planning?
3. The dollar merchandise plan is one of two financial tools that retail merchants use to achieve these goals. What is the other? What is the difference between these two financial tools?
4. Briefly describe the usual procedures for preparing and approving the merchandise plan.
5. What specific factors or conditions should be carefully considered in estimating the sales potential of a department or a store in a given future period? How may each of these factors or conditions actually influence sales potential?
6. Why do fashion trends frequently have a more important bearing on a fashion department's sales potential than do economic conditions? Give examples to illustrate your answer.
7. What two major considerations influence fashion merchants in planning BOM stocks? Why are BOM stock levels planned instead of EOM stock levels?
8. Differentiate between the two types of stock-sales relationships that are of major importance in dollar stock planning. Why is each considered important? What is the formula used in calculating each of these two relationships?
9. What is meant by the term "stock shortage?" What provisions are usually made on a six-month merchandise plan for anticipated stock shortages?
10. How might a knowledge of terms of sale save a retailer some money? Give examples.

MERCHANDISING DIGEST

1. This chapter states that the dollar merchandise plan is the most important plan the buyer works with. Discuss this statement in terms of the purpose of the dollar merchandise plan and its practical use.
2. Discuss the way in which both external and internal factors affect the planning of sales. Give examples of these factors from your own experience as a customer in retail stores.
3. Discuss markdowns on the basis of the following: (a) their purpose; (b) factors to be considered in budgeting; and (c) their effect on profit.

Based upon the information discussed in this chapter, prepare a 6-month merchandising dollar plan using the following figures and information. Rule a plan like the one shown below.

Assume you are the moderate-price dress buyer for the store. Your merchandise manager informs you that the store is planning on a small sales increase this year over last year and expects you to plan accordingly. Dresses this season have become a more wanted fashion item and therefore you feel that an increase in sales will not be too difficult to obtain.

Calculate sales figures for each month to total your 6-month total sales plan. Also calculate beginning-of-the-month stock necessary to obtain planned sales, monthly markdowns within the prescribed limit, and the retail value of purchases that can be made in each of the 6 months being planned. From your planned stock turnover for the period, determine what will be your average stock for this season. Also, compute the stock-sales ratio for each of the months being planned and enter them under Comments.

Dept. Name __Dresses__ Dept. No. __172__

	PLAN (This Year)	ACTUAL (Last Year)
SIX MONTH MERCHANDISING PLAN Workroom cost		
Cash discount %		
Season stock turnover	3.5	3.8
Shortage %		
Average stock		380,000
Markdown %	15	15

SPRING 198–	FEB.	MAR.	APR.	MAY	JUNE	JULY	SEASON TOTAL
FALL 198–	AUG.	SEP.	OCT.	NOV.	DEC.	JAN.	
SALES $ Last Year	135,000	125,000	100,000	125,000	210,000	100,000	825,000
Plan							985,000
Percent of Increase							
Revised							
Actual							
RETAIL STOCK (BOM) $ Last Year	400,000	380,000	300,000	450,000	400,000	350,000	
Plan							
Revised							
Actual							
MARKDOWNS $ Last Year							123,750
Plan (dollars)							147,750
Plan (percent)							15%
Revised							
Actual							
RETAIL PURCHASES Last Year	115,000	45,000	250,000	105,000	160,000	130,000	
Plan							
Revised							
Actual							
PERCENT OF INITIAL MARKON Last Year							
Plan							
Revised							
Actual							
ENDING STOCK July 31 Jan. 31 Last Year	380,000						
Plan							
Revised							
Actual							

Comments

Merchandise Manager _____ Buyer _____
Controller _____

14

PLANNING THE FASHION MERCHANDISE ASSORTMENT

The successful fashion buyer provides customers with the right merchandise, at the right time, in the right place, in the right quantities, and at prices customers are willing and able to pay. Needless to say, this important job of merchandise selection cannot be left to chance. Successful buyers work with carefully prepared plans that spell out the merchandise assortments they strive to maintain.

A **merchandise assortment** is a collection of varied types of related merchandise intended for the same general end use, such as coats or sportswear. A merchandise assortment is usually grouped together in one selling area of a retail store. An **assortment plan** is a comprehensive and detailed listing of all items to be carried in stock during a given period by size, type, and price line. For example, 24 raincoats, sizes 8-16, at $100.

The major objectives of assortment planning are similar to those of dollar planning, namely:

- To buy and maintain an inventory of those styles, sizes, colors, and price lines that accurately reflect the customer demand throughout a given period
- To time the delivery of purchases so that each individual component of the inventory is available for sale neither too early nor too late for customer demand
- To keep purchases in line with the store's ability to stock, display, promote, and pay for those purchases
- To keep funds available at all times for the purchase of new or additional goods as they may be needed
- To relate demand for each type of fashion goods to the demand for all other types of goods in an inventory, so that similar fashion influences and price levels will be reflected throughout the entire assortment

CONSIDERATIONS IN ASSORTMENT PLANNING

The major responsibility of a buyer is to plan and maintain through purchases an assortment of merchandise so well balanced to the preferences of customers that sales goals will be achieved and a reasonable profit will result from the merchandising operation.

A **balanced assortment** is one in which types, quantities, and price lines of merchandise in an inventory during a given period of time closely match the demand of target customers. A balanced assortment is the goal of all merchandising efforts.

To achieve balanced assortments, fashion merchants must always be guided by the merchandising policies of their stores. They consider the same factors that they weigh in drawing up the dollar merchandise plan. They decide how each factor will affect the size and composition of their assortments. They carefully consider the variations in demand arising out of the divergent preferences of different customer groups. They also consider those variations in demand occasioned by seasonal change. They study and evaluate planning information from a wide variety of sources, and particularly information gathered from the market. Once they have given careful consideration to each of these factors, fashion merchants are ready to plan assortments for the coming season, in dollars or units or both.

Store Merchandising Policies

Senior executives of a store are responsible for establishing and clearly defining a store's merchandising policies. These policies are detailed statements about how the store chooses to implement its specific business objectives. No retail enterprise can be all things to all people or supply all the needs of all people in a given trading area. Each store must select one or more specific segments of the area's total population that it wants to serve. Then it must establish merchandising policies that best serve the interests and preferences of those target customers.

Merchandising policies are management directives to employees about how the store elects to carry on its business. These are drawn up primarily to serve as guidelines for buyers to follow in developing and maintaining merchandise assortments.

As discussed in Chapter 11, merchandising policies relate to:

- The degree of fashion leadership for which the store or department wishes to be known—fashion leader, fashion follower, emphasis on specific items such as fads
- The price ranges offered—high, moderate, popular, low
- Its quality standards—finest available, acceptable, unimportant consideration
- The depth and breadth of its assortments—shallow, deep, broad, narrow, or a combination

- Its brand policies—national, private, unbranded
- Exclusivity of merchandise—emphasized or nonemphasized
- Maintenance of basic assortments—always in stock, usually in stock, unimportant consideration

Factors Influencing Assortment Planning

In planning assortments, as in preparing the dollar merchandise plan, merchants review the probable impact of external, internal, and fashion factors. These factors affect not only how much customers may be expected to spend in an upcoming season, but also the types of goods they will purchase.

EXTERNAL FACTORS. The economic condition of both the country in general and the local community have a marked effect on the planning of fashion assortments. These conditions might indicate to the retailer that there will be greater affluence in the trading area or a larger proportion of affluent customers than previously served. As a result, the retailer would include more high-priced goods in the assortment than before. He or she would also include a larger proportion of new and relatively untried fashions and probably a more generous representation of strictly "fun" apparel.

On the other hand, the community may have suffered financial setbacks. There may be a generally pessimistic attitude toward the future of the economy. Perhaps the unemployment rate is increasing, or taxes, interest rates, and prices are escalating. As a result of this pessimistic attitude on the part of customers, the retailer would feature styles in the assortment that are versatile enough to make a limited wardrobe adequate for many, varied occasions. In this case, the most expensive goods included should involve minimum fashion risk.

The local competitive situation is also taken into account. Changes in that area may have a direct bearing on the makeup of a fashion assortment. For example, supermarkets and drugstores in a local trading area may be prominently featuring limited styles of low-priced hosiery on self-service racks. In response, the hosiery buyer for a local quality department or specialty store may decide to play down utility items and increase the offerings of finer quality and newer styles.

INTERNAL FACTORS. Internal factors also affect the assortment plans for any or all parts of a store's inventory. An enlarged and remodeled selling floor may accommodate deeper and broader assortments than were previously possible. Relocating related departments so that they are next to each other may encourage each to plan larger assortments of matching colors and patterns.

The opening of new branch stores also directly affects the planning of fashion assortments. The merchandise preferences of potential customer groups in the new trading areas must be recognized and provided for.

The extent and type of promotional activities the store intends to engage in during the period for which fashion assortments are being planned is another factor that has a direct bearing on the makeup of those assortments. For example, if the store intends to increase its use of television presentations during that period, departmental fashion assortments should carry generous quantities of the merchandise that is to be featured. If a store's management has decided to initiate an advertising campaign stressing the values to be found in its merchandise offerings, then value must be of prime consideration when planning each department's assortment.

FASHION FACTORS. Fashion trends, of course, exert a powerful influence on assortment planning for fashion departments. Fashion makes the difference between what was the right assortment yesterday and what can be expected to be the right assortment tomorrow. This is true of both apparel and accessory assortments for men, women, and children. Whatever the trend, fashion rarely affects one department in the apparel or accessories groups without influencing the assortments in all the others.

The degree to which a store's customers show a marked preference for fashions in the introductory, rise, culmination, or decline phases of their cycles becomes a prime factor in assortment planning for fashion departments. While many customers choose apparel and accessories at more than one phase of a fashion cycle, each tends to favor merchandise at one phase more than any other. Fashion assortments should always be planned with such customer preferences in mind.

Variations in Assortment Planning

Assortments carried in similar departments will vary from store to store. They depend upon the merchandising policies of each store, the preferences of each store's target group of customers, and often the geographic location of the store.

For a highly simplified example, consider two merchants who are planning assortments for college shops catering to similar groups of customers in similar geographical areas. Each merchant had identical sales of $10,220 in skirts, sweaters, slacks, and pantcoats the previous year. Table 14-1 shows two of the many ways in which that $10,220 could have been distributed among the four categories. This is assuming, again in the interest of simplicity, that there were only two price lines carried in each category.

Shop A's customers showed considerable interest in blazers last year. Shop B's customers had little interest in these garments, but showed considerably more interest in sweaters than did shop A's customers. Shop A's customers showed considerable interest in lower-priced goods. Shop B's customers had a pronounced interest in higher-priced goods.

In developing assortment plans for a six-month period, the fashion buyer must always carefully consider the important selling seasons that will occur during that six-month period. The buyer must gauge the effect of each on the demand for a specific department's merchandise. Seasonal variation in demand is a primary consideration of fashion buyers as they undertake planning departmental assortments.

TABLE 14-1
Foundation for Assortment Planning
Review of College Shop Sales for Previous Year

	SHOP A		SHOP B	
	UNITS	DOLLARS	UNITS	DOLLARS
Skirts at $20 each	30	$ 600	35	$ 700
Skirts at $30 each	50	1,500	40	1,200
Total skirts	80	2,100	75	1,900
Sweaters at $25 each	28	700	26	650
Sweaters at $35 each	40	1,400	70	2,450
Total sweaters	68	2,100	96	3,100
Slacks at $20 each	50	1,000	32	640
Slacks at $30 each	60	1,800	80	2,400
Total slacks	110	2,800	112	3.040
Blazers at $50 each	50	2,500	18	900
Blazers at $80 each	9	720	16	1,280
Total blazers	59	3,220	34	2,180
Grand total	317	$10,220	317	$10,220

Sources of Planning Information

In collecting facts to guide assortment planning, fashion merchants study records of what they have bought, sold, and marked down in corresponding past seasons. They also seek information from buyers in similar but noncompetitive stores, from vendors, and from their store's resident buying office. These sources supply information about what other customers, similar to their own, may be expected to purchase in the coming season.

At best, however, all indications of consumer preferences in the past can only serve as a rough guide to fashion merchants as they go about identifying future fashion trends, both in general and on the local scene. Merchants compare notes with buyers of related departments. They analyze what they read about fashion trends in trade and fashion publications. They note what is to be featured in future editions of consumer publications. They find out what fashion themes are being planned for future editorial coverage in those publications. And if their stores serve customers who want to be first with the newest styles, the merchants will seek even more information. In addition to covering the better domestic markets, they may visit couture houses and ready-to-wear producers in foreign market centers for indications of incoming fashion trends.

METHODS OF SEASONAL PLANNING

There are two methods of planning sales and the amount of stock necessary to produce those sales during a given six-month period. The first method, known as dollar planning, has been discussed in Chapter 13 and is merely reviewed here. The second method, known as unit planning, is discussed in detail as follows.

Dollar Planning

For purposes of review, the six-month merchandise plan is based on the dollar value of anticipated sales, optimum stock levels, necessary markdowns, and allowable purchases. The dollar plan is an essential part of merchandise assortment planning for the following reasons:

- It indicates the minimum sales objectives of the store or department.
- It serves to guide management in planning for and controlling the capital needed for inventory investment throughout the period.
- It serves as a guide in making purchases.
- It provides a base against which sales-related operating expenses can be measured.
- It serves as a guide in planning promotional expenditures.
- It provides management with a means of measuring the results of merchandising efforts by establishing seasonal goal figures such as planned sales, rate of stock turnover, and gross margin.[1]

Under the dollar method of planning, it becomes the responsibility of departmental buyers to provide, within dollar limitations, a merchandise assortment that is at all times balanced to customer demand in terms of classification and price line.

Unit Planning

However, dollar planning does not ensure assortments that are well-balanced to demand. This is because it does not pinpoint the nature and extent of customer demand at specific times within the planning period. As a result, an increasing number of retailers are now combining dollar merchandise planning with unit planning, especially in fashion departments. Under unit planning, sales and beginning-of-the-month inventories are first planned in terms of units of merchandise by classifications and price lines. When these units are multiplied by their respective price lines, they yield dollar classification figures for planned sales and stock. Unit purchases are then planned in the same way that dollar planned purchases are determined.

The advantages of planning by units rather than dollars are:

- It is more consistent with the way sales are actually made, since customer purchases are made in units of merchandise.
- It serves as a guide to the types and quantities of stock needed to achieve unit sales goals for each price line in each class.
- It helps reduce inventory investment in slow-moving merchandise.
- It provides a base for developing monthly open-to-buy figures so that active classifications and price lines are not penalized because of the more sluggish ones.
- It helps to minimize departmental overbuying.

Table 14-2 illustrates how a casual dress department with two major classifications might construct its sales plan for February using unit planning. Price lines and classifications are fully explained in the next sections.

First, the number of unit sales anticipated at each price line within each classification is determined. Next, the dollar value of the unit sales planned at each price line within each classification is computed by multiplying the price line by the number of units. Finally, both the units of planned sales and their dollar equivalents are totaled to produce the overall, departmental planned sales for February.

The unit sales plan will also help in planning the stock needed at the beginning of each month or season. Stock-sales ratios may be applied to the unit sales planned at each price line. Totals are derived in both units and dollars, as in sales planning. Finally, planned purchases in both units and dollars may be calculated for each price line in each classification, and for the department as a whole. The procedure described in the explanation of dollar purchase planning in Chapter 13 is used for these calculations.

PRICING ASSORTMENTS

The first factor to be considered in planning assortments is the price structure around which the assortment is to be built. The second factor is the depth and breadth of merchandise assortments to be offered at each of the various price points within that structure.

TABLE 14-2
Dept.: 40
Name: Casual Dresses

Season: Spring 198___
Month: February

CLASS	PRICE LINE	DESCRIPTION	PLANNED SALES UNITS	PLANNED SALES DOLLARS
12301	$29	Dresses, misses'	30	$ 870
12302	36	Dresses, misses'	36	1,296
12303	42	Dresses, misses'	40	1,680
12304	48	Dresses, misses'	38	1,824
12305	56	Dresses, misses'	15	840
12306	65	Dresses, misses'	12	780
12300		Total, dresses, misses'	171	7,290
12801	$29	Dresses, juniors	25	725
12802	36	Dresses, juniors	32	1,152
12803	42	Dresses, juniors	36	1,512
12804	48	Dresses, juniors	30	1,440
12805	56	Dresses, juniors	18	1,008
12806	65	Dresses, juniors	10	650
12800		Total, dresses, juniors	151	6,487
		Total, Casual Dresses	322	$13,777

The price structure of a store or department is determined by management. It is designed to attract the customer groups which the store has chosen to serve. Therefore, the price structure of a store or department is a very important aspect of its overall image. It provides the foundation upon which all assortments should be based.

Price-Related Terminology

For a clearer understanding of retail pricing and its importance in assortment planning, it is necessary to understand the meaning of several price-related terms and their relevance in assortment planning.

PRICE-LINING. The term **price-lining** refers to the practice of determining the various but limited number of retail prices at which a department's assortments will be offered.

PRICE LINE. The term **price line** refers to a specific price point at which an assortment of merchandise is *regularly* offered for sale. For

example, if a department selling Misses' Dresses regularly offers a selection of dresses in a variety of styles, colors, and sizes at $29, $36, $42, $48, $56, and $65, each specific price is known as a price line.

PRICE RANGE. The term **price range** refers to the spread between the lowest and the highest price line carried. The price range in the Misses' Dresses department mentioned above is $29 to $65.

PRICE ZONE. The term price zone refers to a series of price lines that are relatively close to each other and that are likely to appeal to one particular segment of a store's or a department's customers.

The three most widely accepted retail price zones are:

- Promotional (lowest price lines carried)
- Volume (middle price lines, where the largest volume of sales occur)
- Prestige (highest price lines carried, usually to lend importance to the assortment as a whole)

All three price zones are normally found within any departmental price range, regardless of what or how many price lines may be included. They apply to the price structures of basement or budget departments, to prestige or high-fashion departments, as well as to moderate-priced departments.

For example, within the price range of the Misses' Dresses department mentioned above, the price lines included in the three typical price zones might be:

- Promotional (or lowest): $29, $36
- Volume (or medium): $42, $48
- Prestige (or highest): $56, $65

The number of units sold in each price zone, as a percentage of total department sales, will vary, however, from one department to another, from one store to another, and from one selling season to another. For instance, a department store tends to do 50 to 60 percent of its business in the volume price zone, 35 percent in the promotional price zone, and 5 to 15 percent in the prestige price zone. But in a high-fashion specialty store, the largest volume of business would be done in the prestige price zone, a moderate amount in the medium price zone, and almost none in the lower price zone.

Considerations in Pricing

A departmental buyer is responsible for establishing specific price lines within the range assigned to a particular department. The buyer is also responsible for the pricing and repricing of individual items included in the assortment.

ESTABLISHING
PRICE LINES. In establishing retail price lines, a buyer should be careful to establish significant dollar differences between price lines. Customers should be able to readily distinguish differences in quality that exist, or should exist, in the merchandise at various price lines.

While it is advantageous from the standpoint of customer goodwill to maintain the same price lines on a continuing basis, this is not always possible. Higher wholesale prices inevitably result in higher retail prices. Higher costs of doing business at the retail level inevitably result in a wider spread between an item's wholesale and retail price.

PRICING ITEMS. Once price lines have been established, a buyer usually "buys into" those price lines. This means that the buyer prices merchandise at the established price line that comes closest to covering the wholesale price of an item plus the initial markup which may be required. For example, if the wholesale price of an item is $20.50 and the initial markup required is 48 percent, the buyer calculates the item's retail price to be $39.42.

$$\text{Retail} = \frac{\$ \text{ Cost}}{100\% - \text{Markup } \%}$$
$$= \frac{\$20.50}{100\% - 48\%}$$
$$= \$39.42$$

Quite obviously, $39.42 is not a customary retail price line. Assuming there are established price lines in the department of $39 and $43, the buyer would consider the item's sales potential at one of these prices. It might first appear that the item should retail at $39. However, if the buyer thought the quality of the item was comparable to other items in stock priced at $43, the item might be retailed at $43, thus achieving a higher initial markup.

In addition to wholesale cost and quality, other factors influence retail pricing practices. These factors include:

- Competitors' prices for the same or similar merchandise
- Manufacturers' "suggested" retail price (for example, those of nationally advertised brands)
- The home store's pricing policies (low, medium, or high) and the required correlation of prices between its departments
- Nature of the goods (exclusive, high markdown risk, fragile)
- Demand and supply

BEST-SELLING
PRICE LINES. Among each department's price lines, there are always a limited number that account for the greater share of the de-

partment's dollar and unit sales volume. These are referred to as **best-selling price lines.** These lines are usually concentrated in the middle of the department's price range. Customer preference usually is targeted into these best-selling price lines.

In planning assortments, successful buyers clearly recognize best-selling price lines. They plan the assortments so that the greatest number of units in the greatest variety of types, colors, materials, and sizes are included at these price lines. Other price lines are then planned on the basis of the relative sales importance of each price line to the department's total volume.

CLASSIFYING ASSORTMENTS

As stated in the NRMA *Standard Classification of Merchandise,* a **classification** is "an assortment of units or items of merchandise which are all reasonably substitutable for each other, regardless of who made the item, the material of which it is made, or the part of the store in which it is offered for sale."[2]

Purposes of Classification

There are two major reasons for subdividing merchandise into classifications. First, it is a way to more precisely define the nature and extent of customer demand so that merchandise is readily available to satisfy that demand. Second, it provides for better planning and control of the merchandising operation.

To achieve these aims, it must be clearly understood by the buyer, as well as by superiors and subordinates, that the department is composed of many different types of merchandise. Each different type, although generally related, is intended for a somewhat different use. For example, a Men's Furnishings department is usually made up of such diversified types of merchandise as dress shirts, sport shirts, underwear, hosiery, robes, hats, accessories, and so on. In terms of end use, none of these types of merchandise can be substituted for any other. Each type, therefore, should be designated as a separate classification for assortment planning and control purposes.

Establishing Classifications and Subclassifications

Authorities agree that, as a first step in establishing classifications for assortment planning purposes, every item at every price line that is currently in stock should be listed. In addition, the list should include items not currently in stock but which have been included in the department's assortment during the preceding 12-month period. The next step is to sort out the listed items by classification, or end use. Figure 14-1 show seven classifications of rainwear/all-weather coats carried in a four-store group.

When broad classifications have been established on the basis of end use and nonsubstitutability, it then usually becomes necessary to set up subclassifications. These identify the merchandise within each classification according to various product characteristics. In this way, specific areas of customer demand within the broad classification can be identified. It also may be necessary to indicate the seasons or months each classification and subclassification is carried, since many items, especially fashion goods, are seasonal in nature.

For merchandise planning and control purposes, each classification and subclassification is assigned a permanent identification code, usually a number. In most cases, the code for a classification consists of a fixed range of consecutive numbers. Each subclassification is assigned a specific range of numbers within the wider range assigned to the broad classification.

Careful study of the price lines at which each classification and subclassification will be offered is considered essential in assortment planning. This ensures that (1) all price lines within a department's price range are represented in the assortment plan; (2) the best-selling price lines are appropriately represented with the widest variety of types, colors, materials, and sizes; and (3) duplication of merchandise has been minimized, if not prevented.

According to a well-known authority on merchandise planning and control, the goal of

--STORE--		ALL CLS	CLASS 1	CLASS 2	CLASS 3	CLASS 4	CLASS 5	CLASS 6	CLASS 7	CLASS 8	CLASS 9	CLASS 0
BRIDGEPO	WEEK	311	201		110		150					42-
	*PTD	800	271		379		400					
	*SEASON	1682	355		969							
	*TR% CURR	526.31										
	*TR%-1 MO	109.97										
	*TR%-2 MO	112.64										
	*STOCK	7277										
	*% SALES	3.65	33.87		47.37		18.75					100.00
	*% STOCK	3.51										
BAY SHORE	*WEEK	190	154		150		40	50				134
	*PTD	938	238		560		240	50				116
	*SEASON	1612			968							
	*TR% CURR	107.07										
	*TR%-1 MO	223.17										
	*TR%-2 MO	154.47										
	*STOCK	6494										
	*% SALES	4.28	16.41		59.70		4.26	5.33				14.28
	*% STOCK	3.13										100.00
STAMFORD	*WEEK	412	75		337		50		126			22-
	*PTD	1043	145		744		209		378			4
	*SEASON	2519	153		1775							
	*TR% CURR	195.68										
	*TR%-1 MO	103.72										
	*TR%-2 MO	114.41										
	*STOCK	9294										
	*% SALES	4.76	13.90		71.33		4.79		12.08			
	*% STOCK	4.48										100.00
COMMACK	*WEEK	120	154		100		80	42	42			38
	*PTD	511	154		235		130		42			
	*SEASON	1609			1245							
	*TR% CURR	56.33										
	*TR%-1 MO	113.90										
	*TR%-2 MO	65.65										
	*STOCK	6232										
	*% SALES	2.33	30.13		45.98		15.65		8.21			
	*% STOCK	3.00										100.00
COMBINED	*WEEK	8034	2871	126-	4072		947	50	144			112
	*PTD	21897	4570	126-	14034		2229	50	1028			116
	*SEASON	63644	5866		47321		8000		2417			
	*TR% CURR	74.19										
	*TR%-1 MO	116.32										
	*TR%-2 MO	113.06										
	*STOCK	207060										
	*% SALES	3.00	20.87		64.09		10.17	.22	4.69			.51
	*% STOCK											100.00

267 RAINWEAR ALL WEATHER COATS   SEPARATE SALES AND STOCK ANALYSIS-AUDITED THRU-NOAUD   PER-02.WK-4.W/E-02/29   PG   4

**** CLASS LEGEND ****

1-BASIC LONG
2-BASIC SHORT
3-STORM LONG
4-STORM SHORT
5-ZIPOUT LONG
6-ZIPOUT SHORT
7-NOVELTIES
8-UNASSIGNED
9-UNASSIGNED

Figure 14-1 This printout shows rainwear classified into seven different groups, with space for adding three more groups in the future.

all classification and assortment planning is to carry "stocks that provide the customer with the combination of [selection] factors that to [that customer] are most significant."[3]

ASSORTMENT PLANNING IN FASHION DEPARTMENTS

The assortment plan for a fashion department, like that for a staple or semistaple goods department, should be based on a well-conceived classification and price-line plan. However, planning ready-to-wear or accessories assortments involves considerably more study, time, and effort on the part of the buyer than does planning assortments for carpets and rugs or housewares. This is so for several reasons. In a fashion department:

- Both the rate and pattern of sales vary considerably within a given season and from one season to the next.
- Customer preferences vary dramatically from one season to the next and from year to year.
- Merchandise frequently cannot be reordered during a selling season.

For these reasons, fashion buyers have three major responsibilities with regard to planning and maintaining a well-balanced merchandise assortment. First, they must be able to estimate, with reasonable accuracy, the peaks and valleys in customer demand that will occur during the season being planned. Second, they must be constantly on the alert for even the slightest sign of change in customer preferences. And third, they must continually evaluate the assortment in terms of newly developing trends in the wholesale market and in customer demand.

Classifying a Fashion Department

The principles of classifying and subclassifying items to develop balanced merchandise assortments can be applied both to fashion goods and to merchandise that varies less dramatically in type, styling, or color from one season to the next. The techniques used in applying the principles differ, however, in several respects.

First, customer preferences for product characteristics such as styling, color, and fabric usually vary from one season to the next and always vary from one year to the next. A fashion buyer can therefore use past sales experience only as a rough guide in planning assortments for a coming season. Planning must be based more on the recognition of major fashion trends and on an evaluation of those trends in respect to the store's target groups of customers. This sharply contrasts with the development of seasonal assortments for departments handling more staple goods. Products carried in these assortments have longer demand cycles, and style changes are far less frequent. In departments handling more staple goods, the rate of sale of most items can be plotted with reasonable accuracy. Thus the availability of merchandise remains fairly constant throughout a season and often from one season to the next.

Second, the demand for certain fashion classifications and subclassifications is highly seasonal; so, too, is the availability of this type of merchandise. An effective classifications system for fashion goods clearly indicates in which season or seasons of the year each classification or subclassification should be included in the assortment.

Third, fashion assortments are often geared to and effective for a specific period of time. Thus, an age limit, or length of time that each item should be allowed to remain in stock (before being closed out), should be established. This policy can be implemented by coding the day of receipt and age limit of each item on its price ticket for easy reference. For example, the age code for a dress, received on April 25, and for which a six-week time limit has been set, might read "4256W." For most other types of assortments, a regular **season code,** indicating the month and season of receipt of the merchandise, is usually considered sufficient. An example would be X13, with X indicating the 1981 spring season and 13 indicating the thirteenth week of that season.

Finally, price-line planning by classification and subclassification is as important for fashion assortments as it is for other types of merchandise. In many cases it may be more important. The financial risks involved in acquiring merchandise that is so highly seasonal, fragile, and vulnerable to loss in value are great. Fashion merchants can therefore ill-afford duplications in their stock or limited assortments in their most popular price lines. As one authority puts it,

> Developing a classification plan for a fashion department involves the exercise of considerable imaginative effort prior to the start of each season, yet its creation is essential. It becomes, in effect, the foundation stone upon which the entire structure of assortments and a store's "level of service" must perforce rest.[4]

Procedures in Seasonal Planning

Classifications in fashion departments remain relatively unchanged from one season to the next. However, their subclassifications, or variables, and the corresponding composition of the departmental assortment do not remain constant. For this reason, fashion buyers cannot make firm decisions about their seasonal assortments until they have thoroughly appraised what the market has to offer. In addition, they should become familiar with what related markets are offering. Once they have shopped the market, exchanged ideas with other fashion buyers in their own and noncompetitive stores, and learned what fashion themes their store plans to promote during the coming season, they are in a position to start planning their assortments.

As a first step, a buyer might list all the fashion trends he or she has observed or learned about. The buyer lists them in what is judged to be their order of importance for the store's customers in the approaching season. Next, the buyer might rank each fashion variable offered in the market—new styles, fabrics, colors, price lines, and any other significant characteristic—according to what he or she believes to be their prospective sales potential. As we have seen, past selling experience is only a rough guide for the buyer. In planning an assortment for a new season, the buyer must be primarily concerned with recognizing when and to what extent newly developing fashion trends will be of interest to the store's target customers.

Based on their market work and considered judgment of the importance of each fashion trend to customers, fashion buyers can develop a preliminary seasonal classification plan—but only in broad terms. Final decisions regarding details of the departmental assortment plan can come only after a new season is under way. Customer demand alone will determine which styles should be reordered and which should be dropped. It will determine in which subclassifications selections should be increased or reduced and which subclassifications should be eliminated entirely from the assortment.

Evaluating Fashion Trends

All alert fashion buyers are well aware that their customers tend to purchase fashion goods at a certain stage in their fashion cycles. Buyers, therefore, must carefully analyze the fashion trends observed in market offerings and decide when, and to what extent, their customers will be ready to accept new fashions.

For example, if a store's customers want only newly introduced fashions, they will not be satisfied with fashions once they are rapidly rising in popular acceptance. But if customers will not consider purchasing fashion goods until the goods have won widespread acceptance, they will look at, but not buy, fashions in earlier stages of the fashion cycle.

However, it is good merchandising policy for each fashion department to include in its assortment some merchandise that is in earlier stages of fashion development. The newer fashions may be just what the few fashion leaders or influentials among the store's customers are looking for. These leaders can thus give impetus to those fashions on the local scene. Too, a small percentage of merchandise that is more advanced in styling, color, and fabric than that which appeals to most customers lends an aura of fashion leadership to the store's image. Moreover, it helps to adjust customers' eyes to new fashion features and prepares them to accept those features earlier than they might otherwise.

Components of a Fashion Assortment

It is essential to bear in mind that a classification represents merchandise in general demand for a specific end use. Subclassifications represent variable or distinguishing characteristics of merchandise within each broad classification.

CLASSIFICATIONS. As an example of classification, let us consider Misses' Dresses. The primary classifications into which such a department's merchandise might be broken down, on the basis of end use, are:

• Casual
• Streetwear
• Late day
• Formal
• Resort

Other classifications, also based on a specific end use but for which no classification has yet been made, can be added whenever a new type of misses' dress becomes important in the assortment.

SUBCLASSIFICATIONS. Subclassifications, indicating fashion characteristics or variables of each class of dress, can then be made. Sub-subclassifications, if the need for this information is worth the time and cost involved, may also be made.

A few examples of possible subclassifications and sub-subclassifications might be:

• *Style:* basic, coatdress, costume (dress with jacket or coat), two-piece, jumper, princess, sheath, tunic, etc.
• *Neck:* bateau, jewel, portrait, scoop, square, V, cowl, etc.

• *Skirt:* circular, draped, gathered, gored, pleated, slim, tiered, wrap, full, etc.
• *Sleeve:* sleeveless, long sleeve, short sleeve, dolman, rolled, gathered, etc.

SIZING. Size is one aspect of fashion apparel that is unaffected by changing seasonal demand. What is known in the trade as "women's apparel" is manufactured in five basic size ranges:

• *Women's half-sizes:* $12\frac{1}{2}$ to $24\frac{1}{2}$ (and sometimes larger, in even-numbered half-sizes)
• *Women's straight sizes:* 36 to 52 (and sometimes larger, in even-numbered sizes)
• *Misses:* regular sizes 4 to 20 (even-numbered)
• *Juniors:* regular sizes 3 to 17 (odd-numbered sizes)
• *Petites:* misses sizes 2 to 16; junior sizes 1 to 15

In any department where the merchandise is sized, size is often the key selection factor, taking precedence over color, price, styling, or any other fashion variable. A woman who requires a size 14 dress can scarcely be expected to buy a size 10 even if that is the only size available in the style that attracts her. Neither can a man whose foot requires an 11-D shoe be satisfied with the fit of a size 10-C, even if the style pleases him.

Not all sizes enjoy the same rate of sale. Nor is any one color or color combination equally popular in each size in which it is made. Great care must be exercised by a fashion buyer of sized merchandise to see that all sizes are at all times well represented in stock in proportion to the needs of target customers. According to a saying among retailers, "If you're out of a size, you're out of stock."

Alert fashion merchants have found they can bolster their store's fashion image and acquire faithful customers by including in their assortments a well-rounded variety of styles, fabrics, and colors in less popular sizes or in size ranges largely overlooked by competitors in the trading area.

FASHION TRENDS. Fashion buyers are aided in planning their assortments by the knowledge that fashions are largely evolutionary rather than revolutionary in their movements. Fashion change tends to be fairly gradual. While changes may occur in one or more fashion element (silhouette, detail of design, texture, or color) from one season to another, rarely does change occur in all four elements simultaneously. Actually, such change is readily predictable once the elements of fashion are isolated and examined in detail. Fashion buyers who are well-acquainted with fashion principles, as discussed in Chapter 1, and with the way in which fashions move and disseminate, as discussed in Chapters 3 and 4, are prepared to identify trends. They are also prepared to gauge the future relevance of these trends for their target customers and departmental assortments.

NEW-SEASON TESTING. At the start of each season, all fashion stocks should include testing quantities of newly introduced styles, colors, and fabrics. At this time, much of the speculative risk involved in merchandising fashions can be reduced by using only a conservative portion of the open-to-buy until customer preferences can be established more definitely. These preferences are established by customer acceptance or rejection of the choices offered in the opening assortments.

Once the most popular styles, colors, and fabrics become obvious, then these and merchandise with similar characteristics should be bought in depth and aggressively promoted. At the same time, other items in the starting assortments in which customers have shown little interest should either be narrowed down or eliminated from stock.

Expanding and Contracting Fashion Assortments

Assortment planners must always consider the fact that sales in fashion departments vary considerably from month to month throughout a six-month planning season. This is because of the highly seasonal nature of fashion demand and because more than one fashion selling season often occurs within a six-month budget season. The assortments in most fashion departments run a peak-and-valley course throughout a six-month season. Special consideration must be given to this fact when planning fashion assortments.

Early in a season, the variety of styles, colors, and often price lines in an assortment should be broad and in small quantities, in preparation for the selling peak ahead. As this peak approaches, the variety of styles carried in inventory should gradually be reduced so that the assortment includes only those in most popular demand. At the same time, depth of stock in sizes and colors should be increased for each of the best-selling styles. As the peak is reached, buying for that season is discontinued. Stock on hand is sold off in order to have a substantially smaller stock once the peak has passed. When the peak is passed, only minimum assortments of basic styles, colors, and sizes at the most popular price lines should be continued in stock, and then only as long as reasonable customer demand prevails. All other merchandise from the just-ended season's assortment should be marked down and closed out. Then, broad and shallow assortments of new-season styles, colors, materials, and price lines should be introduced into stock. The cycle of expansion and contraction of assortments thus begins all over again.

Reviewing the Plan

Planning, establishing, and maintaining a complete fashion assortment should be an ongoing program rather than one that is only undertaken when sales are down and inventories up. Formal, end-of-season reviews of departmental assortment plans—with buyers and their merchandise managers participating—serve a very beneficial purpose for future planning. Less formal reviews conducted on a regular basis throughout each six-month season are also essential in fashion departments.

Fashion is rarely static, and neither should a fashion assortment plan be static. Fads come and go. Fashion trends follow a fairly normal pattern of development or fade quickly into

Fashion buyers must constantly review plans to be sure they are still up to date in light of unexpected changes in customer preference.

obscurity. ''Hot items'' appear unexpectedly. These and other changes in customer preference often take place after a planned season is under way. To be successful, a fashion buyer must be constantly on the alert for, and receptive to, such changes.

FASHION ASSORTMENT PLANNING IN MULTIUNIT RETAIL ORGANIZATIONS

Multiunit retail organizations are of two types: (1) branch-operating department and specialty stores and (2) chain organizations. Each of these two types of organizations has traditionally used merchandising and operating methods that are almost completely different from those of the other. Each is gradually adopting some of the other's methods, however, and while still very distinct, these organizations are not as different today as they once were.

Branch-Operating Department and Specialty Stores

In branch-operating department and specialty stores, assortment planning and control are essentially as described above. Planning techniques, however, may vary from one retail organization to another, depending upon the number, size, and location of branches.

ASSORTMENT PLANNING. In smaller retail organizations with only a few, relatively small branches in nearby locations, responsibility for merchandising all stores in the group is vested in the parent store executives. Branches are considered ''outposts'' and concentrate solely on selling. Buyers and other executives of the organization are headquartered in the parent store. Communication with branches is maintained mainly by telephone and periodic visits by parent store executives. All merchandising records are kept in the parent store for the convenience of buyers and other store executives. Buyers are ultimately responsible for transmitting merchandising information to all sales personnel, wherever located, and for departmental sales results.

In operations of this size, seasonal departmental merchandise budgets are prepared by the parent store buyers and include figures for branches as well as the parent store. There is little formal planning of assortments for each of the branches, since branch and parent store stocks are usually considered as one.

In developing a preliminary seasonal assortment plan for all stores in the group, fashion buyers proceed as already described. They study records and reports on sales, stock, markdowns, and promotions in the corresponding season of the previous year. They carefully shop the market. They consider the different preferences of customers of each store in the group, through personal observation and discussions with store personnel at the branches. Guided by these considerations, they develop a preliminary assortment plan for their departments, regardless of where the merchandise will be located.

In retail operations of this size, fashion merchandise is usually tested only in the parent store at the start of a new season. Once the season is under way, buyers rarely place merchandise orders for specific branches. Instead, they simply select from newly received shipments those styles, colors, sizes, and price lines most suitable for each branch, and the merchandise is transferred to that branch.

In larger retail organizations with larger, more numerous, and often more distantly located branches, planning is much more formal. Usually, separate merchandise budgets are prepared, separate assortments are planned, and separate unit controls are maintained for each branch. Customer preference may vary widely from branch to branch, especially in the case of fashion goods. Therefore, branch store managers, merchandise managers, and department managers are usually consulted when seasonal assortment plans are being developed.

It is important that a branch-operating organization, no matter how widely dispersed its branches are, maintain a distinctive fashion image. To do this, it must always have in stock certain fashion assortments and price lines in keeping with that fashion image. However, this merchandise need not make up the total fashion assortments of any one branch. Basic fashion assortments can be provided to all stores by the parent store's departmental buyer. But other items in a branch store's assortments should be more directly related to specific local demand at that branch.

TRENDS. Large branch organizations today are allowing their individual branches greater autonomy in developing their own fashion merchandise budgets and in developing and maintaining their own assortment plans. This has come about for one or more of the following reasons:

- Many branches today are as large as, or even larger than, the parent store.
- Sales volume of branches now far exceeds that of most parent stores.
- Many branches are located at considerable distance from the parent store, thus complicating communication.
- Patterns of demand and competitive practices vary from branch to branch according to the trading area in which each branch is located.

In general, therefore, the more numerous a store's branches, or the larger their size, or the greater their distance from the parent store, the greater is the need for fashion assortments that are precisely tailored to the needs of the customers of each branch.

Among branch-operating department and specialty stores, chiefly those with numerous, large branches that are distant from the parent store, there is also a definite trend toward relieving buyers of sales supervision responsibility for all store locations. Another trend is the increasing use of electronic data processing for merchandising purposes, particularly in inventory control. Adoption of an increasing number of the successful operating techniques practiced for many years by chain organizations is also a current trend.

Chain Organizations

A chain organization has previously been defined as a group of retail stores that are centrally owned, each handling similar goods and merchandised from a national or regional headquarters office.

Chain operation is chiefly characterized by central buying and merchandising. Individual units of the chain are engaged only in selling. Central buyers, located in major market areas or a headquarters office, are responsible for providing merchandise for all units of the chain. Centrally purchased fashion merchandise is usually sent to a distribution center, where merchandise is allocated and distributed to the various units of the chain.

Methods of planning fashion assortments for each unit vary from one chain to another. This is particularly true with respect to the amount of autonomy granted individual units in determining the composition of their assortments. For example, in one chain, assortment planning for all units may be the responsibility of the national or regional headquarters office. In another chain, all regular assortments may be planned by the headquarters' merchandising staff, with store units only permitted to make decisions relating to the timing, type, and extent of promotions in which they may wish to engage. In yet another chain, what is considered a basic, seasonal, fashion assortment is detailed by the headquarters staff. Suggestions for additional items, classifications, subclassifications, and price lines that are available through the buying office, to round out and complete the seasonal assortments of each unit, are offered in the form of a listing prepared and distributed by the chain's headquarters or regional merchandise office. In this case, complete descriptions, costs, and retail prices of suggested merchandise are provided to assist the unit management in making selections best suited to that particular store's customers. In such cases, the chain's district manager usually works with the store manager, the fashion (or soft-goods) merchandise manager, and the appropriate department manager in finalizing a seasonal fashion assortment plan.

Individual store merchandise budgets, seasonal assortment plans carefully detailed by classifications and price lines, and weekly or biweekly sales and stock-on-hand reports provide the framework within which fashion merchandise is distributed to each store unit. The success of a chain operation depends on the continuous flow of accurate sales and stock information from its store units to its headquarters office. Only in this way can inventories be properly balanced with demand.

Chain organizations were pioneers in the use of automated data processing systems to control retail inventories. Only data processing can handle the tremendous flow of merchandising data generated in a chain's operation. And only such systems can rapidly convert that data into accurate and timely reports for use by chain executives in decision making.

CATALOG OPERATION. The three largest department store chains in the country—Sears, Roebuck and Company, J. C. Penney Company, and Montgomery Ward—sell impressive quantities of fashion merchandise through seasonal catalogs as well as in their stores. Sears, Roebuck and Company and Montgomery Ward were originally mail-order retailers. They sold merchandise only through catalogs until they opened retail stores in the late 1920s and early 1930s. The J. C. Penney Company, on the other hand, started as a retail store and fairly recently added a catalog operation.

In chain organizations, the planning of fashion assortments to be offered in catalog issues is the responsibility of a separate catalog buying and merchandising staff, located in the headquarters office. The reason for maintaining separate staffs for store sales and catalog sales is the timing of the offerings. However, both staffs work closely with each other. Catalog assortments have to be decided upon many months before those that are offered in the chain's retail stores. This is because of the amount of time involved in the assessment of trends, the selection of individual items, the printing of the catalog, and the delivery of that catalog into the hands of the customers. All of this must take place before the peak of demand for the merchandise offered in the catalog. Fashion merchandise offered in catalogs thus has to be planned and priced far in advance of its actual availability in the wholesale market. For this reason, its planners not only have to excel in accurate prediction of fashion trends, but in most cases have to buy fabrics and have them made up to the chain's specifications. In addition, the catalog buying and merchandising staff has to make sure that stock of each item in the catalog will be available upon demand.

TRENDS. Today the major chain organizations are expanding their use of automated data processing equipment to include electronic cash registers. Point-of-sale information, almost errorproof, can be fed into this type of register, either by punching the register's keys or by use of a "wand" that electronically "reads" a price ticket. This information is transmitted to a computer's memory banks. The computer can then quickly and accurately produce, on demand, selected sales and stock reports. Such reports are essential to good merchandising decisions about the inventories of individual store units, regional divisions, or the chain as a whole.

Conventional retail organizations are adopting many chain store techniques for more profitable merchandising results. At the same time, chain organizations have begun to adopt, to an increasing extent, some of the more successful techniques of traditional retail merchandising. In particular, many chain organizations are now allowing executives of store units more autonomy in merchandising and operating decisions.

Chain organizations are also becoming increasingly fashion-minded. They are devoting considerably more space in their stores and in their catalogs to apparel and home furnishings. They are expanding and upgrading their fashion assortments. They are emphasizing fashion coordination more in their advertisements and displays. Their newer stores are bright, spacious, and colorful, with attractive fixtures, fitting rooms, and carpeting. Many have beauty salons and a variety of other fashion services. All indications point to a continuation of this trend.

MERCHANDISING VOCABULARY

Define or briefly explain the following terms:

Assortment plan   **Price line**

Balanced assortment   **Price-lining**

Best-selling price lines **Price range**

Classification   **Season code**

Merchandise assortment

MERCHANDISING REVIEW

1. What are the major objectives of assortment planning?
2. The chapter says that a balanced assortment is the goal of all merchandising efforts. What is a balanced assortment? How is it achieved?
3. Name and briefly discuss five major areas of merchandising policy that importantly influence the composition of a store's fashion assortments.

4. Name at least five sources of information available to fashion merchants as they go about developing seasonal assortments. What kind of information does each source provide?

5. Name and briefly describe the two major methods of planning merchandise budgets and assortments. Which method is considered best for planning fashion assortments, and why?

6. What is meant by the price structure of a store or department? Why is it important in planning assortments? By whom is it determined? What factors must a buyer carefully consider when pricing goods?

7. What is price-lining? What is a price line? Why do stores use price lines, and what are some considerations in establishing price lines?

8. In addition to the wholesale cost of an item, what other factors must a buyer consider in assigning a retail price? Briefly discuss how each factor might effect a buyer's decision in pricing an item.

9. Briefly discuss the reasons why assortment planning for fashion departments is more difficult than assortment planning for more staple goods.

10. Discuss the procedures for and importance of testing fashion merchandise at the start of a new selling season. Why are expanding and contracting fashion assortments necessary in fashion merchandising?

MERCHANDISING DIGEST

1. Discuss merchandise classification on the basis of the following: (a) purposes, (b) procedures in setting up a system, and (c) establishing subclassifications.

2. Compare and contrast fashion assortment planning in (a) smaller, branch-operating department or specialty stores, (b) large, branch-operating department or specialty stores, and (c) chain organizations.

3. The chapter states that "Once price lines are established, the buyer 'buys into' them." Demonstrate this principle using the information in the following situation: Your store has established price lines of $35, $40, $48, $55, and $62. You have been asked to price a new item that has a wholesale cost of $26.50 and a markup of 48 percent. Be prepared to defend your answers to this problem.

REFERENCES

[1] Taylor, *Merchandise Assortment Planning*, p. 25.

[2] NRMA, *Standard Classification of Merchandise*, p. 15.

[3] Wingate, "What's Wrong with the Planning of Stock Assortments," p. 6.

[4] Taylor, op. cit., p. 15.

15

CONTROLLING FASHION ASSORTMENTS: UNIT CONTROL

Because of the rapid changes in fashion demand, past sales and stock records can only serve as rough guides in planning fashion assortments that meet the demands of target customers. Much more useful as guides are current, detailed reports on unit sales, stock on hand, and stock on order. These reports must reflect merchandise classification, subclassification, and price line. The system for recording the number of units of merchandise bought, sold, in stock, and on order is called **unit control.** Fashion merchants can use the information gathered through unit control to identify developing trends in customer demand. They can also use it to adjust their assortments accordingly as the season progresses and as they plan for upcoming seasons.

Unit control systems isolate and identify "centers of demand" around which properly balanced assortments can be built or reshaped. However, it is important to remember that unit control is a merchandising tool, not an inventory accounting procedure. As used in retailing, it does not and cannot serve as a substitute for regular inventory accounting procedures.

There is no standard unit control system. Systems vary in format from store to store and from one type of merchandise to another. They also vary widely in terms of the methods used for collecting and reporting data and in the amount of detail collected.

In a single small store, unit control is relatively simple and informal. Because the amount of stock is limited, a merchant can often use "visual inspection" to see what is

selling rapidly, slowly, or not at all. As stores grow in physical size and sales volume, however, the need for a formal unit control system becomes increasingly important. And as branches are opened, the need for a good unit control system that provides sales and stock information about all store units—regardless of their number, size, or location—becomes absolutely essential.

TYPE OF INFORMATION RECORDED

Regardless of the type of system used or the type of merchandise involved, a unit control system is set up to show:

- Net sales in number of units
- Stock on hand and on order in number of units
- Additional breakdown of this sales and stock information in whatever detail is considered relevant, such as cost and retail

price, style number, size, color, vendor, and merchandise classification or subclassification

The kind of sales and stock information and the extent of details collected depend upon the type of merchandise involved. They also depend on what the merchant needs to know in order to properly gauge changes in customer demand. Changes in styling or rate of acceptance for staple goods, for instance, are relatively slow. For this reason, unit control systems used for staple goods may be set up to collect only general information which may be quite adequate for their purpose. Because fashion merchandise, however, is subject to rapid change in demand, systems for this type of merchandise are usually set up to collect information in considerable detail. With this detailed information, the merchant will be alerted to the slightest change in demand for specific designs, colors, or other basic fashion factors.

Some types of fashion merchandise require more detailed controls than others. Inexpensive blouses, for example, may require only the recording of unit sales and stock figures by size, price line, and color. For moderate-priced dresses, on the other hand, a system probably would be set up to collect sales and stock information in terms of sizes, colors, classification, vendor, and retail price for each individual style. In men's shirts, it may be necessary to keep sales and stock records by collar size, collar style, sleeve length, color, fabric, and price line or price range.

Each merchant seeks to develop a system that provides the essential facts yet does not collect unnecessary details. The system must provide meaningful assistance in the form of current and accurate information if assortments geared to customer demand are to be maintained.

Forms used for the manual recording of unit control data vary from store to store. Those shown in this chapter are typical. Each store or department within a store needs unit control information that meets its particular needs. Sometimes a merchant examines a number of forms used by other stores and then draws up the type of forms that fit the store's exact requirements. In actual retail practice, there are many variations of forms serving similar unit control purposes.

TYPES OF SYSTEMS

There are two basic types of unit control systems used to record fashion assortment data: perpetual (running or continuous) control and periodic stock-count control. The types of merchandise for which each is best suited and the procedures involved in maintaining each are discussed below.

Perpetual Control

In a **perpetual control** system, purchase orders, receipts of merchandise, and sales are recorded, as they occur, by individual style numbers. From these figures, stock on hand is computed. This system eliminates the need for actual stock counts except for regular physical inventories.

Perpetual controls are best suited for goods that are subject to frequent style change. They are also suited for goods requiring that the degree of fashion acceptance of specific design features and color be carefully watched. Finally, perpetual controls are used for goods that are high or relatively high in unit price. Examples of such merchandise are men's, women's, and children's ready-to-wear and outerwear. Furs and fine jewelry are other examples. The cost of maintaining a perpetual control system is substantially higher than that of a simpler unit control system. It is not high, however, in terms of its value to fashion merchants who need and use its detailed information.

PROCEDURES. A perpetual control record begins when an order is placed for merchandise. A separate record is kept for each style in each classification. On this record, or form, identifying information is noted. This might include classification, style number, brief description of merchandise, vendor, and cost and retail prices. When an order is placed, the number of pieces ordered and the date of the order are noted. As goods are received against this order, the number of pieces originally noted as "on order" is reduced accordingly. An entry is also made to show the total number of units received and their date of receipt. Sales are recorded in units and by date of sale, and the number of units "on hand" is automatically reduced. Returns-to-vendor, which decrease the stock on hand, are also recorded by date and number of units involved. Returns from customers, which increase the stock on hand, are also recorded by date. Thus, at any time, a buyer can tell from looking at the perpetual control records how many units of an individual style have been sold to date, were purchased, are on order, and remain in stock.

On most manually maintained perpetual control forms, a breakdown of each style by size and color can also be kept, if needed. A common practice is to indicate the number of units on order in each size and color with a penciled dot or diagonal line for each individual unit. When shipments are received against a purchase order, the number of units received in each size and color is indicated by inking a diagonal line over the penciled mark. As each unit is sold, the appropriate tally line is crossed off, making it easy to see how many of each size and color have been sold and how many remain in stock. Merchandise returned by customers is re-tallied by adding another diagonal line, usually in red this time, in the appropriate column on the form. Returns-to-vendor are indicated by circling the appropriate tally lines. Thus, it is easy to see at any point how many units, by size and color, have been sold, are in stock, and are on order.

BRANCH OPERATIONS. Stores with only one or a few branches and with a central unit control system usually tally the number of units in each style, by size and by color, that are transferred to each branch. This may be done by using a tally mark of a different color for each branch, such as brown for branch A, yellow for branch B, and so on. The parent store then records branch store sales by style, size, and color, from the sales records received from the individual branches.

Stores with larger and more numerous branches usually adopt a unit control form that permits them to keep sales and stock-on-hand information for each branch as well as for the parent store on separate forms. This enables merchandising executives of the parent store to calculate sales and stock data by style, size, and color for each store and for all stores combined.

FORMS. Figure 15-1 shows how a manually kept perpetual control record of an individual style might look after the buyer has received into stock 86 pieces of that style. On August 15, 86 pieces were ordered, and at that time dots were made in pencil in the applicable color and size block for each unit ordered. When the merchandise was received on September 5, the "on order" entry was circled to indicate that it had been received in full. An entry was also made to this effect in the "received" block. Penciled tallies of the units of sizes and colors ordered were then inked over with a diagonal line to indicate the exact number of pieces received by color and size.

Figure 15-2 shows how the control card for the same style number might look after the style had been on sale for two weeks. Sales have been recorded daily, noting the total number of units sold each day as well as their size and color distribution. Customer returns have also been noted and reentered into stock on hand by size and color. Net sales for each week have then been totaled. Any return-to-vendor has also been noted, indicating date of return and the number of pieces involved. Lines corresponding to each size and color returned have been circled to indicate this action.

In this case, the buyer could see that the demand for larger sizes and for the color black was underestimated. When reordering the style, the buyer will note the date and the number of pieces in the "on order" section of the form. Again, appropriate dots in pencil will serve to indicate the number of units reordered in each color and size.

Unit sales summaries take various forms. They may be either manually or automatically prepared and are based on the information

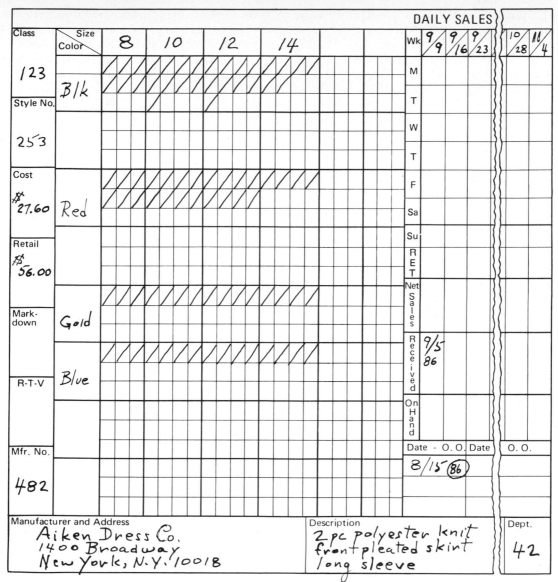

Figure 15-1 The buyer ordered 86 units of a dress, in sizes 8 through 14, in four different colors. When the order was placed, this perpetual inventory card was prepared, with full details about composition of the order, the vendor, classification and style number information, cost price, and the retail price at which the units are to be sold. This is the way the card looked right after the order was received into stock. The receipt date has been entered, the "on order" number circled to show that the order has been received in full, and the original pencilled tally marks have been inked in.

available in the inventory control records. They may be issued to report the total number of units sold and on hand by department, clas-sification, selling price, vendor, style, and store. In addition to these breakdowns, they may be further detailed in terms of color and

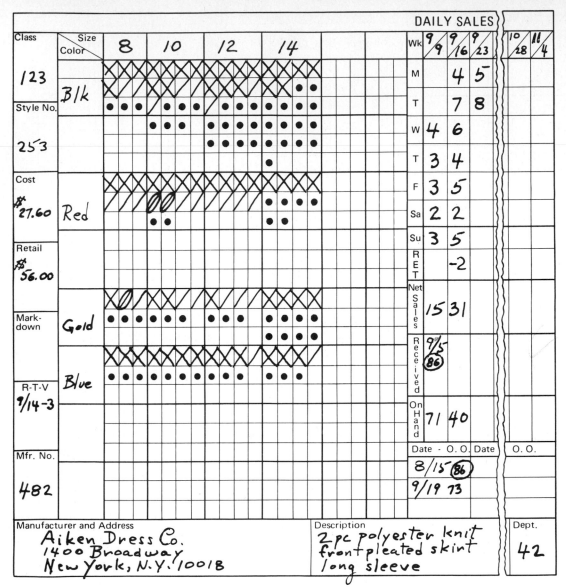

**Figure 15-2 This is the inventory card two weeks later. Sales by
size and color have been entered daily by cross-hatching of the tally
marks, appropriately noting any returns that have been made. Daily
and weekly unit sales have also been entered so that stock on hand can
be readily computed. The result is a detailed day-by-day record of how
this style is selling by size and color. Dots have been entered to indicate
additional merchandise on order but not yet received.**

size. Figure 15-3 is a computer-prepared example of a color and size unit control report.
In fashion departments, sales summaries may
be issued daily, twice a week, or weekly.

Whatever the exact method, a perpetual
control system enables a merchant to compare
the total number of units sold of each style or
group of styles from day to day and week to

Berry's

COLOR AND SIZE UNIT CONTROL REPORT

Dept. 42 Three Days Ending 12/08/8- Page 3 01

SELLING PRICE	CLASS	VENDOR	STYLE	STORE NO.	NET STORE TOTALS	COLOR CODE	06	08	10	12	14	16
48.00	40	012	0555	2	-1	01				-1		
				1 3	2	01					2	
58.00	40	018	0699	4	1	01					1	
64.00	40	018	0753	3	1	01					1	
32.00	40	020	0401	1	3	01				1	1	1
				4 5	1	01					1	
32.00	40	020	0406	1	1	22				1		
				2 3	1	22						1
26.00	90	020	0422	3	1	50						1
26.00	90	020	0424	4	1	50					1	
				2 3	1	50						1
32.00	40	020	0458	1	1	01					1	
32.00	90	020	1120	1	-1	00						-1
				4	3	01			1	1		1
					1	47					1	
					3	01				1	2	
				5 3	-1	40			-1			
44.00	43	020	1206	1	1	15				1		
				0	-1	34				-1		
44.00	43	020	1217	1	1	01					1	
40.00	90	020	1401	4	2	34		2				
40.00	90	020	1403	4	1	01				1		
					4	34				2	2	
				3	1	00				1		
				7	1	01			1	1	-1	

Figure 15-3 Part of a computer-prepared color and size unit control report.

week. It also shows the total number of units sold thus far in the season. The importance of this knowledge becomes apparent if one considers the example of two styles, each of which has had sales of 60 pieces during a 10-week period. If weekly sales reports are available, a situation such as that shown in Table 15-1 becomes obvious: One style is dwindling in acceptance, while the other is increasing in popularity. Without such weekly reports, this very important difference could be missed.

Periodic Stock-Count Control

A unit control system in which stock is counted and recorded at regular intervals and the results used to compute sales for the intervening period is known as **periodic stock-count control.** This type of unit control system is best suited for merchandise that is moderate to moderately low in price and less subject to fashion change than ready-to-wear. It is also suitable for merchandise that does not lend itself to easy tagging by multipart or print-punch tickets. Examples of this kind of merchandise are children's socks, cosmetics, hosiery, and notions. This type of stock control is considerably less expensive to maintain than a perpetual control system.

PROCEDURE. In periodic stock-count control, sales are not recorded as they occur. They are calculated from the inventory changes that take place between counts. The results of this calculation are not as accurate or detailed as the results provided by a perpetual control system. However, they are sufficiently detailed and accurate to indicate trends in demand and the level of demand for less volatile merchandise. They also enable a merchant to maintain stock levels consistent with the sales rate of individual items or groups of items.

In a manual periodic stock-count control system, stock is counted at designated time intervals. The number of units on hand and on order—by classification, price, style number, size, and color (if applicable)—is recorded. Also recorded are the orders placed and merchandise received since the previous count

TABLE 15-1
Sales of Two Separate Styles

	UNITS SOLD	
	STYLE A	STYLE B
Week 1	10	2
Week 2	10	2
Week 3	10	2
Week 4	8	3
Week 5	7	5
Week 6	6	7
Week 7	3	8
Week 8	2	8
Week 9	2	10
Week 10	2	13
Total, 10 Weeks	60	60

was taken. Unit sales can then be computed and recorded as follows:

Units of stock at previous count
+ units received since previous count
− units on hand at present count
= unit sales during intervening period

For purposes of periodic stock-count control, a department's assortment is first divided into sections of related merchandise. Next, the buyer decides how often to count the stock in each section, more active items being counted more frequently. Specific dates are established for each section's count. These must be adhered to faithfully if this system of unit control is to be effective. Responsibility for planning and carrying out counts of specific sections of stock is usually distributed among department personnel. Different dates are usually set for different counts, so that no one person is overburdened and no one day finds the entire stock in the process of being counted.

FORMS. Forms used for a manual system of periodic stock-count control differ from those used for manual perpetual control. Most widely used for the former is a looseleaf notebook with a pair of facing pages assigned to each style or group of items. (See Figures 15-4R and 15-4L.) On the left-hand page (15-4L) are listed style numbers, classification codes, descriptions, vendor's name and address, cost and retail prices, and other information needed for writing up an order. Such information may include the minimum packaging for each item. This is an important factor to consider in reordering, because an item may be retailed individually but purchased by the half-dozen, the dozen, or the gross. Vendors may ship quantities as small as a half-dozen or dozen. The cost of ordering and the shipping charges on such small orders, however, may make it wiser to order in lots of three or six dozen.

Also noted on the left-hand page are maximum quantities of each item that should be in stock and on order at all times during the item's selling season. Careful analysis of sales in previous corresponding seasons, plus specialized knowledge of current production and market conditions, guide a buyer in determining "coverage" of each item needed throughout a selling season. The term **coverage** refers to the maximum quantity to which each item's stock should be built after each regular stock count. It is expressed either in terms of a certain number of weeks' supply or a specific number of units or both.

In determining coverage needed for each item under periodic stock-count control, buyers first estimate the weekly rate of sale of an item during a given selling season. Then they note the number of weeks established between scheduled stock counts. Next they estimate, in terms of weeks, the normal delivery period from the date of reorder to the date of actual receipt of the merchandise. They also estimate, in terms of weeks, the safety or reserve stock needed at all times to allow for an unexpected increase in sales or an unexpected delay in delivery.

In terms of weeks' supply needed, coverage is calculated as the sum of the number of weeks between counts, the number of weeks required for delivery of reorders, and the number of weeks' supply estimated as a necessary safety or reserve factor. Unit coverage is determined by multiplying the estimated weeks'

coverage by the estimated weekly rate of sale of each item.

Assume, for example, that in Figure 15-4 the weekly rate of sale of style 140, white, is estimated at six pairs. If the delivery period is estimated at two weeks, the interval between counts at two weeks, and the safety or reserve period at two weeks' supply, then the coverage needed is a six-weeks supply, or:

$$
\begin{aligned}
\text{maximum units to be} \\
\text{on hand and on order} &= 6 \times (2 + 2 + 2) \\
&= 6 \times 6 \\
&= 36
\end{aligned}
$$

Stock counts should be checked immediately after they are taken and reorders promptly placed to bring the stock of each item up to its designated coverage figure. At all times during a selling period, the quantity of an item on hand and on order should equal the maximum quantity established for that item. In this way stocks can be maintained in direct relation to anticipated demand.

The right-hand page of the control form (see Figure 15-4R) lists the date and quantities of merchandise ordered, the quantities on hand on the dates counts were taken, and receipts of merchandise since the previous counts. On the basis of these figures, sales are calculated for the period between counts. The right-hand page of this form is often punched in both margins so that it can be turned and used on the second side. This page carries only the briefest identification of each item—often only a page number—since all necessary details are on the facing page.

The right-hand page is usually columnar, with blocks of columns available for successive counts. There is a space above each block for the date on which the count was made. The columns are usually headed:

OH Quantities *on hand* when count is made

OO Date and quantity *ordered* since previous count was made

REC Date and quantity of merchandise *received* since previous count was made

Department No.	15								

Vendor   Ricci Glove Company   **Ship via**   Lee Transport
Gloversville, New York 12078

Manufacturer No.   102   **Terms**   6/10/E.O.M.

Class	Style	Cost	Unit Retail	Description	Color	Min. Pack	Coverage	
							Weeks	Units
268	140	41.50dz.	7.00	Driving glove	White	1 dz.	6	36
268	140	41.50dz.	7.00	Driving glove	Black	1 dz.	6	24
268	140	41.50dz.	7.00	Driving glove	Beige	1 dz.	6	24

Figure 15-4 (left-hand page) Periodic stock count control record: identifying and reorder information.

SOLD   *Sales* made between counts, a figure calculated by adding receipts to previous count and then subtracting present count

RESERVE REQUISITION CONTROL.

For fast-selling, low-priced items, particularly those that are packaged, reserve requisition control is often used. **Reserve requisition control** is a form of periodic stock count in which the stock on the selling floor is considered sold and only the reserve stock is counted. A reasonable amount of stock is kept on the selling floor, but the main supply is kept in a stockroom. As the forward (selling-floor) stock runs low, more is requisitioned from the reserve.

Under this system, sales are calculated by adding up the requisitions since the last count and by considering as sold everything that has reached the selling floor. Periodic stock counts are made, but only the reserve stock is counted and considered "on hand."

The reserve requisition control system is especially useful in high-volume, small-unit sales departments, such as hosiery or notions. It is much faster, for example, to count one carton of 144 pairs of hosiery in the reserve stock than to make a count on the selling floor

of 48 boxes, each containing from 1 to 3 pairs. And it is much easier and faster to record requisitions for 36 pairs of one style and 24 pairs of another than to record possibly 30 individual sales transactions involving the same 60 pairs.

VISUAL CONTROL.

What merchants call "eyeball control" or "visual control" is another form of periodic stock count. In **visual control,** a rack, shelf, drawer, or bin is assigned to each style, size, or classification. A periodic check is made to see whether each of these *looks* too empty or too full. The merchant makes an on-the-spot judgment about action to be taken when the bins, shelves, drawers, and racks are checked.

Fashion merchandise does not usually lend itself well to visual control. An exception might be a very small operation in which the proprietor's memory serves as the record. Another might be a boutique or specialty shop that never stocks styles in depth because its customers only want one-of-a-kind items or the newest and most unique styles. Still another exception might involve the stock of special-purpose, lower-volume merchandise, such as cocktail dresses or theater ensembles. In these cases, visual control, rather than more formal and detailed controls, might

		Date 5/3				Date 5/17				Date 5/31			
Class	Style	O.H.	O.O. 5/6	Rec. 5/14	Sold	O.H.	O.O. 5/20	Rec. 5/28	Sold	O.H.	O.O. 6/2	Rec. 6/10	Sold
268	140 White	20	⑫	12	10	22	⑫	12	12	22	⑫	12	
268	140 Black	20			8	12	⑫	12	4	20			
268	140 Beige	30			10	20			8	12	⑫	12	

Department _15_

Manufacturer No. _102_

Figure 15-4 (right-hand page) Periodic stock count control record: on hand, on order, received, and sales information.

prove satisfactory for determining sales and stock-on-hand information.

SOURCES OF UNIT CONTROL INFORMATION

Unit control refers to procedures for collecting data on additions to or subtractions from stock from the time an order is placed with a vendor through the time the item is sold to a customer. Principal sources of such information are purchase orders, sales records, merchandise transfers, returns from customers, returns-to-vendors, order cancellations, and price changes. The use of each in a unit control system is described below.

Purchase Orders

A **purchase order** is a contract between a store and a vendor to purchase certain specified merchandise under certain specified conditions. When signed by an authorized executive of the store and accepted by the vendor, it becomes a legally binding document.

When a purchase order is placed, the original copy is given to the vendor. The store executive who places the order retains one or more carbons for future reference and for making appropriate entries in the unit control records. (See Figure 15-5.) The amount of in-

formation about each order that is entered in the unit control records depends on the type of system used. In general, however, the purchase order is the source of such important control information as:

- Date of order
- Department number
- Classification of merchandise ordered
- Vendor's name and address
- Number and description of each style ordered
- Cost and retail prices of each style ordered
- Quantities ordered of each style
- Details of color and size, if any, in each style

Multiunit stores, such as department and specialty stores with several branches, usually prepare order forms with separate columns for each store unit for which merchandise is purchased. In this way, a single order can cover purchases made on behalf of as many store locations as need to be served. On orders placed for distribution to specific branches, quantities and applicable details of color and size distribution are specified for each location. The more units to be served, the wider the form becomes. With such a form, however, a buyer can see if the order results in a balanced assortment of styles, sizes, and colors for each store unit. Merchandise for specific branches

Berry's

STORE NAME	DEPT. NO.	ORDER NO.
Berry's #1	42	M 184925

BILLING, PACKING, AND SHIPPING REQUIREMENTS
1. INVOICE MUST BE ENCLOSED WITH SHIPMENT, AND CARTON CONTAINING INVOICE MUST BE SO MARKED ON THE OUTSIDE
2. MERCHANDISE FOR TWO OR MORE DEPARTMENTS, SHIPPED AT THE SAME TIME, MUST BE BILLED AND PACKED SEPARATELY, AND INVOICES AND CARTONS PLAINLY MARKED FOR THE SEPARATE DEPARTMENTS. HOWEVER, ALL SUCH SHIPMENTS MUST BE COMBINED UNDER ONE BILL OF LADING.
3. DEPARTMENT, ORDER NUMBER AND WEIGHT MUST BE SHOWN ON THE INDIVIDUAL CONTAINERS
4. ALL GARMENT PACKAGES MUST CONTAIN COLOR AND SIZE LISTS BY STYLE NUMBER

NAME: Aiken Dress Co.
ADDRESS: 1400 Broadway
CITY AND STATE: New York, N.Y. 10018

TERMS: 8/10 EOM
WITH ANTICIPATION FOR PREPAYMENT

DATE OF ORDER	DUE DATE AT STORE	CANCEL BY	HOUSE NUMBER
8/15/8-	9/10/8- Complete	9/10/8- Will be cancelled or shipment returned at vendor's expense	482

SHIP TO: Main Store Cincinnati, Ohio

STYLE NUMBER	CODE OR CLASS	DIS LETTER	DESCRIPTION	SIZES 8	10	12	14		TOTAL QUANTITY	UNIT COST	TOTAL COST	UNIT RETAIL
253	123		2 pc polyester knit front pleated skirt long sleeve									
			Black	6	9	9	6		30			
			Red	6	8	8	4		26			
			Gold	3	4	4	4		15			
			Blue	3	4	4	4		15			
									86	27 60	2373 60	

ROUTING INSTRUCTIONS

FOLLOW OUR ROUTING · WE CHARGE BACK ANY EXCESS TRANSPORTATION COSTS TO YOU.

☑ F.O.B. STORE NAMED OR WAREHOUSE
☐ 1 TO 20 LBS. · PARCEL POST DIRECT TO STORE · DO NOT INSURE
☐ 21 TO 50 LBS. · REA EXPRESS DIRECT TO STORE · MINIMUM VALUE (SPECIFY COMMODITY TARIFF ON WAYBILL)

OVER 50 LBS. (TRUCK ROUTING) I O U Service
SPECIAL ROUTING INSTRUCTIONS Hangers
VALUATION EXCEPTION: NO DECLARATION OF VALUE IS TO BE MADE BY THE VENDOR EXCEPT ON FURS AND JEWELRY, IN WHICH CASE ACTUAL VALUE UP TO $1000 SHOULD BE DECLARED.

FORM 312 REV. 12-63

This order subject to conditions of purchase appearing on the reverse side and is a contract only when confirmed by merchandise office signature.

GRAND TOTAL COST	2373 60
GRAND TOTAL RETAIL	
% MARK UP	

Jane Dean — DEPT. MGR.
T. J. Evans — DIV. MDSE. MGR.

Figure 15-5

may be sent directly to those stores. Or, the order may specify that all merchandise be delivered to the parent store.

Receiving Records

Good retail practice requires that a record be made of each unit of merchandise received by a store. (See Figure 15-6.) A copy of this record is turned over to the unit control clerk, who updates the "on order" entry by indicating the number of units received and the date of receipt. If the total order is received, in some systems the "on order" entry is circled.

The many purposes served by receiving records can be seen in Figure 15-6. This form is in two parts: one above and one below the horizontal, perforated line. In the upper right-hand corner of both parts is a number—one of a consecutive series—that is assigned to an incoming shipment. This number is used for all future identification of that shipment. The right-hand corner also has space for recording the number of cartons or packages in the shipment, the name of the carrier, and the date of delivery.

The upper left-hand section of the form provides space for a variety of information that

RECEIVING RECORD

No. 16181

Received From _Aiken Dress Company_

Address _1400 Broadway_ City _New York, N.Y._ 10018

Date Received: _9/5/8-_

Department	Order No.	Transportation Charges		Buyers Approval or Remarks	Received Via
		Total Paid	Charge Shipper		
42	M 184925	48.00		_Jane Dean 9/16_	I O U Service

Invoice Date	Terms	Invoice Passed	Discount		Amt. of Invoice	Retail Value	Pkg's.	Pieces	Cartons
			Date	Amount					
9/5/8-	8/10 EOM	9/12/8-	10/10	189.89	2373.60	4816.00		86 (hangers)	

ATTACH INVOICE HERE

- -

Received From _____

No. 16181

Vendor No.	Unit Cost	Color	Description	Size 8	10	12	14	Quantity Amt.	Unit	Class	Unit Price
482	27.60	Blk	Style 253, 2 pc.	6	9	9	6	30	ea.	123	56.00
482	27.60	Red	Style 253, 2 pc.	6	8	8	4	26	ea.	123	56.00
482	27.60	Gold	Style 253, 2 pc.	3	4	4	4	15	ea.	123	56.00
482	27.60	Blue	Style 253, 2 pc.	3	4	4	4	15	ea.	123	56.00

Order Checked		Mdse. Checked		Price Tickets		Mdse. Marked		Cost Extension	Retail Extension	Merchandise Received/Date	
	Date		Date		Date		Date			Stock Room	Department
HLC	9/6	FBJ	9/6	MPR	9/6	mng	9/9	2373.60	4816.00	a JL 9/10	

Figure 15-6

will be needed by the accounting department in processing the invoice for payment. When the upper part of the receiving form is detached from the bottom part and attached to an invoice, it is called a "receiving apron." A **receiving apron** is a sequentially numbered form designed for incoming information about each shipment of merchandise. Included on this form are the signatures of persons handling the shipment. These are required by the accounting department before it can enter an invoice for payment.

The bottom part of the receiving form provides space for the receiving clerk to indicate how many pieces of each size and color have been counted in the shipment. (Some forms have two or three printed size scales. The receiving clerk cancels those that do not apply. If necessary, the clerk cancels all three and writes in an appropriate scale.) From this in-

formation, the purchase order can be checked, and the work of making price tickets and affixing them to the merchandise can proceed. This lower section, or a copy of it, is then passed to the unit control clerk, supplying the details needed to keep the unit control style records up to date.

Sales Records

In manual perpetual control systems, the unit control clerk receives for every sale either a sales check or a price-ticket stub identifying the specific article sold. This information is then recorded on the appropriate style record. In periodic stock-count control systems, sales figures are not recorded as they occur. Instead, sales for a specific period are calculated as the difference between one stock count and the next.

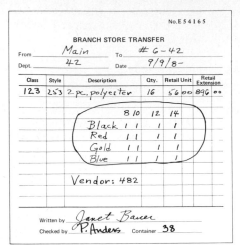

No. E 5 4 1 6 5

BRANCH STORE TRANSFER

From _Main_ To _# 6 - 42_
Dept. _42_ Date _9/9/8-_

Class	Style	Description	Qty.	Retail Unit	Retail Extension
123	253	2 pc. polyester	16	56 00	896 00
			8 10 12 14		
		Black 1 1 1 1			
		Red 1 1 1 1			
		Gold 1 1 1 1			
		Blue 1 1 1 1			
		Vendor: 482			

Written by _Janet Bauer_
Checked by _P. Anders_ Container _38_

Figure 15-7

Merchandise Transfers

Departmentalized stores frequently transfer merchandise from one department to another or from one store or branch to another. Special forms are used to report such transactions. For unit control purposes, transfers are equivalent to sales for the department or store unit releasing the goods; transfers are equivalent to purchases for the department or store unit receiving the goods. The stock on hand of the former is reduced, and the stock on hand of the latter is increased.

Figure 15-7 illustrates a report of the movement of merchandise between various branches. An appropriate entry for all such transfers is made on the style's unit control record.

Berry's

66375

REFER TO ABOVE
NUMBER IN ALL
CORRESPONDENCE

BEFORE SHIPPING GOODS TO A VENDOR ON A CLAIM. DETACH ALL CARBONS. THE FIRST THREE COPIES OF THE CLAIM MUST ACCOMPANY THE GOODS TO THE CLAIM ROOM OR THE WRAPPING DESK.

VENDOR: PLEASE FOLLOW CAREFULLY THE PROCEDURE CHECKED BELOW

CREDIT: THIS MERCHANDISE ☑ IS RETURNED FOR CREDIT. DO NOT SEND A CREDIT MEMORANDUM UNLESS THERE IS A DISCREPANCY IN QUANTITY OR PRICE.

EXCHANGE: THIS MERCHANDISE IS RETURNED FOR EXCHANGE. SEND A NEW INVOICE TO COVER THE REPLACEMENT ON RECEIPT OF OUR PURCHASE ORDER.

REPAIR YOUR MDSE: THIS MERCHANDISE IS RETURNED FOR REPAIR. SEND A NEW INVOICE FOR THE MERCHANDISE WHEN YOU RETURN IT TO US ON RECEIPT OF OUR PURCHASE ORDER.

INVOICE

ALL CLAIMS AGAINST THIS INVOICE MUST BE FILED WITHIN 60 DAYS

SEND TO _Aiken Dress Co._
1400 Broadway
New York, N.Y. 10018

CHARGE (IF OTHER THAN SEND TO)

STORE NO.	Main
DEPT. NO.	42
AS AGREED WITH	L. Salzman
DATE	9/14/8-
PER	M. L. Smith

TERMS	8/10 EOM
AMOUNT OF INVOICE	$ 2373.60
DATE OF INVOICE	9/5/8-
REGISTER DATE	9/14/8-
REGISTER NUMBER	66375

VENDOR: THIS IS AN INVOICE. WE ARE CHARGING YOUR ACCOUNT AS FOLLOWS:

CLASS	VENDOR	STYLE	DESCRIPTION	QUANTITY	COST UNIT	UNIT COST	TOTAL COST	UNIT RETAIL	TOTAL RETAIL
123	482	253	2 pc. polyester front pleated skirt	3	ea	27 60	82 80	56 00	168 00
				TOTAL QUANTITY 3	SUB – TOTAL		82 80	TOTAL RETAIL	168 00

SPECIAL INSTRUCTIONS TO VENDOR _For credit only. Do not replace_

| SHIPPING CHARGES | 2 44 |
| TOTAL | 85 24 |

Figure 15-8

Merchandise Returns

When merchandise is returned by a store to a vendor, a form known as a "return-to-vendor" or "charge-back" is issued. (See Figure 15-8.) A **return-to-vendor** is a store's invoice covering merchandise returned for cause to its vendor. A **charge-back** or **claim** is a store's invoice for claims against and allowances made by a vendor. In most stores, the same form is used for either returns or charge-backs. Copies of return-to-vendor forms go to the unit control clerk so that stock on hand of individual styles may be appropriately decreased on the unit control records.

Should a customer make a merchandise return to the store, a charge credit or cash refund is issued. A copy of these forms goes to the unit control clerk, who adds the returned article to the record of the total number of that style presently in stock.

All returns are carefully recorded on the forms used in perpetual control. If periodic stock count is the control method used, however, small adjustments like these are usually ignored. Only a transaction of major propor-

tions, such as the return of an entire shipment from a vendor, is likely to be entered under the latter systems.

Cancellation of Order

A store may cancel an order for justifiable reasons, such as a vendor not shipping the designated merchandise by the shipping date specified, or a vendor eliminating a style from an order. When an order is cancelled in whole or in part, a covering entry must be made promptly on the appropriate unit control form. This ensures that whoever studies the control records will not mistakenly think that an additional supply of merchandise is still on order.

Price Changes

Unit control records indicate the retail prices at which merchandise is placed in stock. They also show any price changes that occur later. In most stores, a special form is required for reporting all upward or downward revisions in retail prices so that the retail value of the inventory may be adjusted accordingly. (See Figure 15-9.) Copies of these forms are routed

(X) TO SHOW TYPE			PRICE CHANGE							DEPT. NO. 42		B 29001	

Figure 15-9

to the unit control clerk as well as to the inventory control office for appropriate action. Most stores use a single **price-change form** for recording markdowns, markdown cancellations, or additional markups. A few stores provide a separate form for each type of price change.

AUTOMATED UNIT CONTROL

Retailing was slower than some other areas of business to investigate the value of automatic data processing in general and electronic data processing in particular. However, in the 1980s there is increasing evidence that automated unit control has gained widespread acceptance.

Large retail organizations were among the first in the retailing business to use automated systems and equipment. They started by automating the processing of accounts receivable. Once they had developed a system for handling this tremendous bookkeeping chore, they used the same equipment to automate other basic bookkeeping jobs, such as accounts payable and payroll. Then they began working out automated systems in the area of merchandise statistics, which includes unit control systems. An automated unit control system is simply a mechanized version of a manual unit control system. The sales and stock records kept in the system's memory banks may be updated weekly, daily, or as transactions occur. At any point the system can be instructed to print out periodic reports in as much depth as needed on a department's sales and stock by classification, vendor, style, and price line.

Today a number of large retail organizations have electronic data processing systems that handle, among many other jobs, the automatic collection and processing of merchandise information. An increasing number of medium-sized and smaller stores are also benefitting from electronic technology because of the increasing number of independent computer service centers. These centers provide computer knowledge, standardized data processing programs (including unit control

programs), and computer time to companies not large enough to need or afford this expensive equipment, yet large enough to make good use of it on a part-time basis.

Coding

An automated unit control system collects exactly the same kind of sales and stock information that a manual system does, although it is often programmed to collect more detail than is feasible in a manual system. The major difference, then, is that a manual system uses people to record and process data, while an automated system uses machines.

However, before merchandise information can be used in an automated system, the information must be coded. This code usually consists of numbers, since automated equipment works mainly with numbers. Although no two retail organizations use exactly the same coding system, most fashion merchandise is coded for unit control purposes to identify department, classification, vendor, style, color, size, price, and season in which received.

Take another look at the sample receiving record, Figure 15-6. It shows the receipt by department 42 of six black dresses in size 8, classification number 123, style number 253, at $56 retail, from the Aiken Dress Company, which is vendor number 482. Classification, style, size, price, and vendor already are expressed in numbers. Suppose the color black is assigned the number 4, and the season code is 33. Then the code numbers appearing on the price ticket of each of those six black dresses received into stock would be:

Department	42
Classification	123
Vendor	482
Style	253
Color	4
Size	8
Season	33
Price	$56

A growing number of large retailers today identify their merchandise with SKU numbers. A **stockkeeping unit,** or **SKU,** is either a single item of merchandise or a group of items within a classification to which an identifying number is assigned and for which separate sales and stock records are kept. An SKU is the minimum level of merchandise identification and takes the form of a two- to four-digit number. Under this type of control system, an identifying SKU number is assigned within each merchandising classification to each item or group of items of merchandise on order or in stock that has specific characteristics which distinguish it from all other merchandise.

For a retailer working with an automated system, the code or SKU number assigned to a unit of merchandise is as descriptive as a handwritten or verbal description.

Examples of Automated Systems

There are a number of different forms of automated unit control. Some of the more basic forms have been in use for many years, and some of the more complex have come into widespread use only recently. Three examples of automated systems are described below. One of the most basic systems uses the punched price ticket. A more complex system uses the computerized register. And a still more complex system employs a hand-held wand together with the computerized register.

PRINT-PUNCH
PRICE TICKETS. In one of the oldest systems of automated unit control, printed price tickets are coded with a series of punch holes. These holes correspond to the printed information on the price ticket and can be read and interpreted by an electronically controlled machine. (See Figure 15-10.) These tickets are often referred to as "Kimball tickets" after the company that first introduced this type of price ticket or tag. Each price ticket consists of 2 to 4 perforated sections, all of which contain identical printed-punched information. When an item is sold, the end section of the ticket is removed. This removed section is then fed into a machine that "reads" and sorts

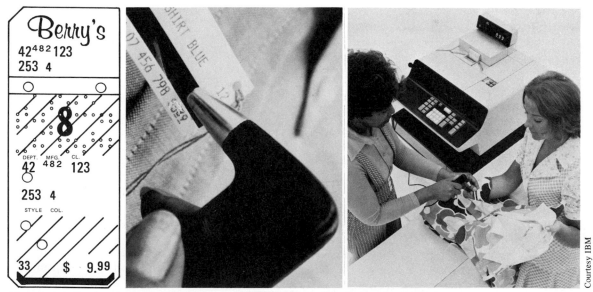

Figure 15-10 (a) Today's price tickets often contain detailed information. This information can be (b) read by a hand-held wand and (c) transferred to an electronic register that figures the transaction and relays information about it to the company's computer system.

out the coded information punched on it. This makes it possible to obtain a detailed unit control report in which all of the precoded information from the punched tickets is listed for all of the items that have been sold that day.

COMPUTERIZED REGISTERS. A more complex system involves the indexing of SKU numbers into the computerized register. The information captured by the SKU coding cannot be as detailed as that coded into individual price tickets, because the number can only extend to four digits. But the unit control information is an up-to-the-minute source of sales trends.

HAND-HELD WANDS. In a still more complex system of automated unit control, each item's price ticket is coded with a magnetic strip or a series of magnetic bars. This coding can be "read" by a hand-held wand that is "hooked into" the computerized register. As the wand is passed over the magnetic coding on the price ticket, the coded information is transferred into the register. (See Figure 15-10.) The register records the transaction and relays the information to the company's computer system.

This type of electronic system has several advantages. First, there is little chance of salespeople making errors as they record sales, because all of the sales information, including the price, is automatically entered into the register by means of the wand. When all items for a particular sale have been recorded, the computerized register automatically computes the total. Second, the detailed information on each price ticket provides the store with a detailed and up-to-the-minute system of perpetual inventory control. Third, the store's computer can be programmed with an economic ordering quantity for each item of merchandise. When the stock for an item reaches a predetermined level, or **economic ordering quantity (EOQ),** a reorder is automatically triggered. Stated another way, when enough units of an item have been transferred from the "on hand" record to the "sold" record, a new order is automatically generated.

Value of Automated Systems

The automation of unit control systems offers retailers the same benefits as the automation of other data-collecting and data-processing chores. First, automated systems in general, and electronic computer systems in particular, are infinitely faster than manual systems. Second, automated systems are almost infallibly accurate, as long as the right information is fed into them. Third, automated systems can collect and process more detailed information than typical manual systems can. This means that more useful reports for evaluating merchandise assortments can be produced.

However, there are also several problems related to automated systems. First, they are expensive, even when the number of clerical personnel the system replaces is considered. Second, if inaccurate information is fed into the system—and this can happen, in spite of the elaborate controls of such systems—errors can be very hard to track down. Third, because of the tremendous capabilities of these systems, store managements sometimes program the systems to turn out reports containing far more detail than merchandisers need or can use. Too much information can be as confusing and misleading as too little. The key to a good automated unit control system is accuracy in recording data and a program that produces reports which are as useful and as succinct as possible.

EVALUATING UNIT CONTROL

In evaluating unit control, it is usually helpful to remember that the word "control" is somewhat misleading. However, traditional trade terms do not readily change. A better term might be "unit records," since the various systems are set up to collect sales and stock information from which reports can be drawn. These systems do not serve as controls in themselves. They only provide information that merchants use to determine how closely their assortments meet customer demand and what they can do to improve those assortments.

Advantages

The major value of unit control is that its records enable a buyer to refer to a detailed analysis of sales and inventory while sitting at a desk or working in the market. The records are usually maintained by style numbers. Reports can be prepared that show departmentalized sales by classification, price line, vendor, size, color, or any other merchandise characteristics helpful to buyers. Thus a buyer can go into the market armed with such facts as: most of vendor A's styles were reordered, while vendor B's had to be marked down before they sold; or fewer size 16s were sold this season than in the previous season; or the department sold as many $40 units this year as last year.

Facts are a much more reliable guide than memory about the nature of consumer demand, even for the immediate past. Facts, not guesses, are essential in keeping track of consumer demand. The correct interpretation of facts enables merchants to meet the needs and wants of consumers.

Properly used, unit control systems contain a built-in reminder that encourages immediate action when conditions require it. The reminder prompts the merchant to check the assortment for completeness and balance in terms of current indications of consumer demand.

An assortment plan, like the dollar merchandise budget, is necessarily subject to change as often as conditions show that the original guidelines need adjusting. Unit control records and reports provide the means for regularly checking previously planned projections against actual results.

Problems Related to Unit Control

Unit control systems, however, are not always properly run or properly used. Moreover, they cannot be expected to do some jobs.

In working with unit controls, carelessness can result in inaccurate and misleading figures. As mentioned above, this is true even with electronic systems, since a computer can digest only the information fed into it.

Manual systems are slow, and sometimes the clerks handling them are so far behind in their work that their reports are of little use by the time buyers receive them. Electronic systems, on the other hand, are sometimes programmed to give so much detail, and so rapidly, that merchants are drowned in data. They are unable to digest it all and are therefore unable to make effective use of it.

Another problem is that it is difficult to estimate the true costs of unit control systems. A number of people are involved in some aspect of the unit control job—clerical workers, technicians, supervisors, buyers, assistant buyers, and sales and stock people—yet no part of their salaries is charged to the unit control expense.

Cost, however, is a relative factor. In general, a merchant weighs the costs of maintaining a unit control system against the benefits derived from the system. If a store provides its buyers with accurate and correct information and the buyers use that information to good advantage, then the cost is likely to be considered worthwhile. However, if the buyers do not use that information, the store has a costly system. On the other hand, if a buyer is deprived of useful information, the store is probably practicing a costly economy.

The last problem relating to unit control systems is that they cannot reveal one very important facet of consumer demand: what items, colors, and sizes customers wanted to buy but could not because they were not present in the assortments. To a point, unit control records may show unfilled demand. They may show, for example, that a certain style enjoyed brisk sales for a period, then was out of stock for a week or two, and then, when restocked, resumed its brisk sales. But unit control systems are not set up to show the requests made by customers for merchandise that was never part of the assortment. The only means by which buyers can find out about unfilled wants of customers is through want slips, customer surveys, and comparison shopping, as discussed in Chapter 12.

MERCHANDISING VOCABULARY

Define or briefly explain each of the following terms:

Charge-back or claim	**Receiving apron**
Coverage	**Reserve requisition control**
Economic ordering quantity (EOQ)	**Return-to-vendor**
Periodic stock-count control	**Stockkeeping unit (SKU)**
Perpetual control	**Unit control**
Price-change form	**Visual control**
Purchase order	

MERCHANDISING REVIEW

1. What are the two basic types of information any unit control system is set up to provide? What additional types of merchandise information can it also provide?
2. Name the two basic types of unit control systems used for the recording of fashion data. How do they differ in method of operation?
3. For which specific types of merchandise is each of the above systems best suited, and why?
4. Name at least 10 kinds of information that can be recorded on most perpetual unit control forms.
5. In what ways do forms used for periodic stock-count control differ from those used for perpetual control? How are sales determined in a periodic stock-count control system?
6. What is meant by the term "coverage?" How is it determined? Discuss its importance in a periodic stock-count control system.
7. What is meant by "coding" as the term applies to automated unit control systems? Discuss its importance and give examples of its use in such systems.
8. What is meant by the term "SKU"? Discuss its use and advantages in automated or electronic data processing systems.
9. Give three examples of automated systems of unit control. Which system is least complex? Which system is most complex? Describe the advantages of each system over the conventional, manually prepared unit control process.
10. What is meant by the term "EOQ"? Discuss its use and advantages in electronic data processing systems.

MERCHANDISING DIGEST

1. Discuss the following statement from the text: "Some fashion merchandise requires more detailed control than others." Do you agree or disagree? Defend your answer.

[handwritten: → HIGH FASHION MORE CONTROL]

2. Identify and discuss the kinds of unit control information that can be obtained from the following store records: (a) receiving records, (b) sales checks, (c) price ticket stubs, (d) merchandise transfers, (e) customer charge-credit and cash-refund forms, (f) price-change forms, (g) return-to-vendor forms, and (h) cancellation of order.

3. Discuss the major advantages and disadvantages of automated unit control systems.

16

CONTROLLING FASHION ASSORTMENTS: INVENTORY CONTROL

As the preceding chapters have demonstrated, the responsibilities of the buyer are not small ones. First, he or she must have the right merchandise in the right place, at the right time, in the right quantities, and at the right price. At the same time, the buyer must carefully control the dollars the store invests in inventory.

To be sure that the buyer's job is done in the most effective way, retail management has established a number of control procedures and devices. These provide means for the supervision of the merchandising function (having the right merchandise in the right place, etc.) and for the ongoing control of the money invested in inventory.

All stores use the same procedures and criteria for evaluating the merchandising function in each selling department. The appeal of fashion merchandise, however, is highly changeable compared with other consumer products, such as furniture and housewares. As a result, the risks and rewards involved in merchandising fashion goods and services are correspondingly greater than those involved in merchandising more staple products.

Close inventory controls and the ongoing evaluation of stock on hand in relation to customer demand are essential to profitable fashion merchandising. Every merchandising executive involved with apparel or accessories has a special need to become thoroughly familiar with the inventory control procedures and various management tools discussed in this chapter.

DOLLAR INVENTORY CONTROL

Retailers plan their dollar investments in fashion assortments well in advance, as discussed in Chapter 13. Each seasonal plan or budget then becomes the base for evaluating actual results. Once the selling season gets under way, purchases of additional inventory are controlled by actual dollar sales as compared with planned dollar sales, and by the dollar value of stock on hand as compared with the planned dollar value of stock on hand.

Retail Method of Inventory Evaluation

The accounting system used by most retail organizations today is known as the retail method of inventory. Under this system, unlike most accounting systems, all records of transactions affecting the value of inventory on hand—such as sales, purchases, markdowns, transfers, and returns-to-vendor—are added to or subtracted from inventory at their retail values. The retail method of accounting developed as a necessity for handling large, departmentalized retail operations. Because of the huge quantities and varieties of merchandise handled by each firm, the wide range of cost prices of that merchandise, and the increasing number of store locations in which that merchandise was being sold, it became impossible to keep track of each item, in terms of its cost price, in a large retail organization's inventory.

Some small stores still use the older cost method of accounting, keeping their inventory records on the basis of the cost price, rather than the retail price, of each item in stock. The cost method is satisfactory only for nondepartmentalized small stores or shops that handle limited varieties of merchandise in fairly shallow depth.

The Book Inventory

Under the retail method, each selling department is a separate accounting unit for which separate records are kept. These records contain details relating to the cost and retail value of each department's inventory, as well as operating expense data.

The term **book inventory** refers to the dollar amount of inventory that should be in stock at any given time, as indicated by each department's accounting records. The figures used to compute the book inventory are derived from various records submitted to the accounting department. These records report additions to and subtractions from the inventory as they occur.

Systems for computing book inventories may be manual or automated. Under either method, figures relating to inventory value are usually shown as separate monthly and cumulative year-to-date totals. Figure 16-1 shows how a manually kept master inventory ledger for a department might appear after the first two months of a fiscal year. Each department's buyer is responsible for initiating all records used by the accounting department to maintain a book inventory. The buyer is also responsible for guaranteeing the accuracy of these records. This responsibility represents a major portion of a buyer's job.

Entries are made in the book inventory as changes are reported to the accounting department. Management can thus have a current evaluation of the retail value of its inventory investment at any time—monthly, weekly, or whenever wanted—either for the store as a whole or for any accounting subdivision. In stores that use electronic data processing systems, inventory values are adjusted instantly when relevant figures are fed into the system. Reports can then be printed out as frequently and in as much detail as desired.

BEGINNING INVENTORY. Under the retail method, a physical count of each department's merchandise is taken annually. Sometimes it is taken more frequently, particularly in fashion departments. From this count of each item in the inventory and the listing of each by the retail price at which it is marked, the total retail value of the inventory is calculated. If the retail value derived from the physical count differs from the book inventory figure as of the same date, the physical count figure is accepted as correct, and the book inventory figure is adjusted to conform. The procedures for taking a physical inventory are discussed later in this chapter.

INVENTORY TRANSACTIONS. Once a beginning inventory has been established, all subsequent transactions affecting the value of that inventory are entered in a department's book inventory as they are reported to the accounting department.

Purchases. Purchases are recorded at both cost and retail. This procedure requires that the unit retail price of goods be entered on each invoice covering shipments received from vendors. For example, items purchased at a cost of $8 a dozen might be assigned a retail price of $1.25 each. The addition of one dozen of this item to a department's book inventory would be entered as a cost value of $8 and a retail value of $15.

DEPARTMENTAL INVENTORY LEDGER

Dept. *159* Year Ending Jan. 31, 198—

Period Ending	Purchases and Transfers			$ Freight Costs (4)	$ Add'l Markup (5)	Accumulated			Deductions at Retail					EOM Inventory		
	$ Cost (1)	$ Retail (2)	% Markup (3)			$ Cost (6)	$ Retail (7)	% Cum. Markup (8)	$ Net Sales (9)	Markdowns $ (10)	% Sales (11)	$ Shortage Reserve (12)	$ Total (13)	$ Cost (14)	$ Retail (15)	% Maint. Markup (16)
Beg. Inv.	32,276	52,227	38.2	—	—	—	—	—	—	—	—	—	—	—	—	—
Feb.	6,000	10,000	40.0	37	120	—	—	—	11,500	590	5.1	173	12,263	—	—	—
YTD	38,276	62,227	38.5	37	120	38,313	62,347	38.5	11,500	590	5.1	173	12,263	30,802	53,084	38.5
Mar.	7,200	12,000	40.0	45	—	7,245	12,000	39.6	13,000	650	5.0	195	13,845	—	—	—
YTD	45,476	74,227	38.7	82	120	45,558	74,347	38.7	24,500	1,240	5.1	368	26,108	29,571	48,239	38.7
Apr.																
YTD																
Oct.																
YTD																
Nov.																
YTD																
Dec.																
YTD																
Jan.																
Year																

KEY:

YTD = Year to Date
Column 1 = Billed Cost of Purchases
Column 2 = Retail Value of Purchases
Column 3 = $\dfrac{\text{Col. 2} - \text{Col. 1}}{\text{Col. 2}}$
Column 6 = Col. 1 + Col. 4

Column 7 = Col. 2 + Col. 5
Column 8 = $\dfrac{\text{Col. 7} - \text{Col. 6}}{\text{Col. 7}}$
Column 9 = Net Audited Sales
Column 10 = From Markdown Book
Column 11 = $\dfrac{\text{Col. 10}}{\text{Col. 9}}$

Column 12 = as % of Col. 9
Column 13 = Col. 9 + Col. 10 + Col. 12
Column 14 = Col. 15 x complement of Col. 8
Column 15 = Col. 7 – Col. 13
Column 16 = $\dfrac{\text{Col. 15} - \text{Col. 14}}{\text{Col. 15}}$

Figure 16-1

To facilitate this bookkeeping procedure, most stores require buyers to **pre-retail** their orders, that is, to indicate the intended retail prices of all items on each purchase order. Thus, when goods are received at a store, the retail value of each vendor's invoice can be calculated and the goods can be marked and placed on sale, even if the buyer is away from the store. This is important because, with the varied demands on buyers' time, particularly in large stores, it is practically impossible for them to be present to "retail" each shipment of goods as it arrives. Another advantage to having buyers pre-retail purchase orders is that invoices can be processed more quickly. The store is thereby less likely to lose the opportunity of taking cash discounts offered by the vendor for prompt payment.

Sales. Sales are recorded either on cash registers or sales checks. From register tapes or duplicate sales checks, a total sales figure for each department or classification is obtained daily. This is entered as a "credit," or decrease, in the value of the book inventory.

Customer Returns. Returns made by customers are recorded on sales credit forms. These figures are totaled daily and entered in the books as a "debit," or increase, in the retail value of the book inventory.

Price Changes. When price changes are made on merchandise after it has originally been placed in stock, a record of each such change is made on price change forms. (See Figure 15-9.) These forms are forwarded to the accounting department, which then increases or de-creates the value of the inventory by an appropriate amount. Price changes may take any of the following forms:

- Additional markups or increases in retail prices above those at which the goods were marked when first received into stock.
- Cancellations of additional markups previously taken and recorded.
- Markdowns or reductions in the retail price of goods currently in stock.
- Markdown cancellations, or increases in price to offset all or any part of previously taken markdowns. (Such cancellations may occur, for instance, after a special sale for which goods from regular stock were briefly reduced.)

Net additional markups (total additional markups minus total cancellations of additional markups) increase the retail value of a book inventory. Net markdowns (total markdowns minus total markdown cancellations) decrease the retail value of an inventory. In either case, only the *retail* value of the inventory is affected. There is no change in the cost value. Accuracy in recording price changes is very important, because mistakes can result in stock shortages or overages.

Transfer of Goods. Any transfer of goods from one department or accounting unit to another is recorded as a decrease in the inventory value of the issuing department and an increase in that of the receiving department. If there are branch stores, transfers of merchandise from one to another are similarly reported and entered on the records. (See Figure 15-7.)

Returns-to-Vendor. Merchandise returned to vendors for credit is reported to the accounting department on a return-to-vendor or charge-back form. (See Figure 15-8.) A description of the merchandise being returned and the quantities are listed on this form at both unit and total cost and retail prices. The total cost value of each return-to-vendor decreases the cost value of the book inventory. The total retail value of the return decreases the retail value of the book inventory. It is important to understand, however, that most vendors will refuse to accept returns unless their permission is first granted.

Some charge-backs are not concerned with actual return of merchandise but with claims or allowances, as when a vendor agrees to a lump-sum allowance toward transportation costs. In this case, the amount of the allowance reduces the transportation cost of purchases by a corresponding amount. There is no change in the retail value of the inventory.

Merchandise on Order

Stores also keep careful records of the cost and retail values of outstanding orders placed for current as well as future delivery. Figure 16-2 is an example of a typical, manually prepared report of a department's outstanding orders. It indicates the date of each order, the order number, the vendor to whom issued, the total cost and total retail values of the order, and the month or months in which delivery of merchandise is intended. Stores with electronic data processing systems usually process departmental merchandise on-order reports on a weekly basis.

Merchandise on order does not affect the book inventory because it represents merchandise that has not yet been received in stock. But outstanding orders are kept on file and carefully watched, since they represent future upward revisions in inventory value as well as future financial obligations. If an order is cancelled by either store or vendor, equivalent cost and retail amounts are deducted from the on-order figure for the month in which delivery originally was expected.

The Physical Inventory

Errors inevitably creep into records, even those maintained by computers. Sales may be rung up at the wrong prices; price changes and transfers may be made for more or fewer pieces than were actually involved; and transactions may be incorrectly identified as to department or classification. Real shortages also occur through pilferage and shoplifting.

WEEKLY REPORT OF OUTSTANDING ORDERS

Department 42   Date 3/17/8— Sheet No. 1

Orders of $50.00 and over must be reported individually. Orders under $50.00 should be reported collectively under "Small Purchases." Report all cancellations in Red.

Order No.	Order Date	Vendor	Total Retail	March Cost	March Retail	April Cost	April Retail	May Cost	May Retail
91428	3/4	Aiken Dress Co.	450	252	450				
91478	3/11	Supreme Dress Co.	1,600			896	1,600		
91464	3/8	Lane Dress Co.	1,080	322	540	322	540		
91514	3/15	Casualaire	3,200					1,856	3,200
		Total Small Purchases	130	70	130				
		Total on Order	22,268	876	1,511	9,361	16,140	2,678	4,617
		Open to Buy			(261)		29,700		43,100

BUYER'S SIGNATURE *Jane Dean*

MDSE. MANAGER'S SIGNATURE *T. J. Evans*

Figure 16-2

With the multiplicity of items and transactions involved, the book inventory is never exactly the same as the true, marked retail value of all goods currently in stock. This is the reason for taking a physical count of all merchandise in a department at the end of each fiscal year. The count is sometimes taken more often if a special situation, such as excessive shortage, warrants it.

INVENTORY PROCEDURE. Taking a physical count of all merchandise on hand in a store or department requires a precise cutoff date on the handling of records affecting inventory. Every merchandise shipment received by that date must be counted, marked, and entered in the book inventory before an actual count takes place. Every sale, every return, and every price change up to that date must also be entered. This assures that the book inventory is updated to the exact time of the physical inventory.

In a physical inventory, every piece of merchandise belonging to a department must be accounted for. This is not limited to merchandise on the selling floor and in the department's stockrooms. Merchandise on loan to the advertising department, the display department, in "will call," and in other selling departments must also be counted. Furthermore, all items of merchandise should have been examined and carefully identified as to classification, season letter, and current retail price before the counting and listing starts. Care should be exercised to see that all items of stock are easily accessible for counting and listing. Guesswork is not compatible with a thorough physical inventory of stock.

The actual count is best made after store closing hours or on a holiday when the store is not open for business. In this way, selling does not confuse the stocktaking. Ideally, the count should be made by crews who do not normally work with the merchandise they are assigned to count and list. After the count has been completed, spot checks should be made to verify the original counts.

INVENTORY FORMS. Sheets or cards on which the counts are recorded are provided by each store's accounting office. These are usually sequentially numbered, and the de-

INVENTORY SHEET

FLOOR ☑
STOCK ROOM ☐
WAREHOUSE ☐

No. 59987

FIXTURE No. | SHELF No.
10 | A

DEPT. No. | CLASS.
201 | B

	Description	Number of Units	Kind of Unit (ea., pr., dz., etc.)	Selling Price per Unit Dollars	Cents	Season Letter	Check in Pencil	Inventory Signatures
1	Velour shirts STYLE 951	20	ea	48	00	M5	✓	Listed By N. Jones
2	Velour shirts STYLE 821	16	ea	36	00	M4	✓	
3	Knit shirts STYLE 785	15	ea	26	00	M3		Counted By J. Costello
4	Knit shirts STYLE 640	10	ea	24	00	M5	✓	
5	Knit shirts STYLE 689	13	ea	26	00	M4	✓	Merchandise Recounted By M. Murphy
6	Sweaters STYLE 942	18	ea	32	00	M4	✓	
7	Sweaters STYLE 865	19	ea	36	00	M3	✓	Listing Checked By L. Pappas
8	Knit shirts STYLE 785	17	ea	26	00	M3	✓	
9								Last Line Used Was Number → 8
10								FOR OFFICE USE ONLY
11								AGE ANALYSIS

		Age in Months	Dollars	Cents
12				
13		Current		
14		7 thru 12		
15		Over 12		
16				
17				
		GRAND TOTAL		

Figure 16-3

partment buyer is responsible for seeing that each issued sheet or card is accounted for at the conclusion of the inventory period. (See Figure 16-3.)

In most cases, only one classification of merchandise is listed on each sheet or card. A typical inventory form may require, at the left, an identifying style number or other identifying information for each item listed. To the right of the description are usually columns in which the counter enters the exact number of pieces of each specific item by the retail price and season code indicated on each item's price ticket. Each inventory sheet is also carefully identified as to department, classification, or other requested subdivision.

When the counts have been completed, the forms are returned to the accounting office.

There, totals are calculated and compared with book inventory figures. If the two do not agree, the book figure is brought into agreement with the physical inventory figure.

Stock Shortages and Overages

In the normal course of business, the physical inventory rarely tallies precisely with the book inventory figure. If the physical inventory figure is less than that of the book inventory figure, the discrepancy is a stock shortage. If it is greater than the book figure, the difference is a stock overage.

Overages are rare: they are found most commonly among stores with several branches. For example, a stock overage is created by transferring merchandise to one branch while charging that merchandise to the inventory of another branch.

Shortages are common and are on the increase. In the past, stock shortages might have averaged 1 to 2 percent of net sales. Today this figure has more than doubled in many cases and is still on the rise.

Some departments, of course, have higher shortage percentages than others, mainly because of the nature of the merchandise handled and the selling techniques employed. Open selling and self-service tend to increase departmental shortages because they permit greater opportunities for undetected theft. Some departments, such as jewelry and cosmetics, have higher-than-average shortages because their merchandise is more susceptible than others to theft, damage, and spoilage. In some fashion departments today, for example, shortages run well above 3 percent of net sales.

Stock shortages are an important factor influencing retail pricing. The initial retail price of merchandise must be set high enough to compensate for loss of income due to stock shortages.

Stores constantly strive to reduce shortage figures by stressing greater accuracy in physical inventory taking. They also stress more care in recording purchase, price-change, and sales data. Greater precautions against theft, such as the use of sensitized price tags and increased security staff, are also being taken. It is an old saying in the department store business that although shortages may not be directly the fault of the buyer in whose department they occur, more buyers have been fired for high shortages than for any other reason. Shortages reduce profits, and a profitable operation is the buyer's responsibility.

Two major causes of stock shortages and overages are clerical errors and merchandise losses. Common clerical errors include:

- Failure to take or record markdowns properly
- Mistakes in calculating retail values of invoices
- Mistakes in charging or crediting department sales

- Mistakes in recording merchandise transfers
- Mistakes in recording returns-to-vendor
- Mistakes in recording physical counts of inventory

Physical merchandise losses occur through:

- Internal theft (pilferage)
- Shoplifting
- Failure to obtain receipts for merchandise loaned
- Breakage and spoilage
- Providing samples of yard goods, perfume, etc. from stock

The Purchase Journal

In departmentalized stores, the accounting office issues to each department a monthly or semimonthly report known as a **purchase or merchandise journal.** On this report are listed all invoices for purchases, transfers of merchandise in and out, and returns to or claims against vendors that have been charged or credited to the department's book inventory during a stated period. (See Figure 16-4.)

Entries made for each invoice for merchandise received include:

- Department name and number
- Vendor name and number
- Shipment receiving number and date
- Invoice number, date, and amount
- Freight costs
- Discounts earned
- Total cost
- Total retail
- Markup percentage

Information on merchandise transfers and returns to or claims against vendors includes the following:

- Issuing department number
- Document number and date
- Name and number of department or vendor to which issued
- Details of transaction
- Total cost and total retail value of each document
- Transportation costs

Dept. 320 Fashion Accessories   **Division 2**   Page No. _1_

Vendor No.	Vendor Name	Type Trans.	Apron/KeyRec No.	Apron/KeyRec Date	Invoice No.	Invoice Date	Invoice Amount	Freight Costs	Discount	Net Cost	Total Retail	M%
1140-1	Baar & Beards	Inv.	55504	01/06	7132	01/04	243.00		19.44	223.56	504.00	
	Vendor Total						243.00		19.44	223.56	504.00	55.6
1192-4	Ben Goodman	Inv.	54707	12/29	9211	12/27	360.00		28.80	331.20	720.00	
		Dum.	55155	12/28		12/28	3.00			3.00	6.00	
		Inv.	22823	01/10	9697	01/08	135.00		10.80	124.20	288.00	
	Vendor Total						498.00		39.60	458.40	1,014.00	54.8
1822-8	Glentex	RTV			3441	01/18	−183.31		−14.40	−168.91	−336.00	
		Inv.	52852	12/14	8761	12/12	360.00		28.80	331.20	672.00	
		Inv.	52852	12/14	8708	12/04	945.00	9.22	75.60	869.40	1,764.00	
	Vendor Total						1,121.69	9.22	90.00	1,031.69	2,100.00	50.4
2795-2	Regina Products	RTV			3439	01/18	−32.70		−.05	−31.05	−55.00	
		RTV			3438	01/18	−422.90		−8.46	−414.44	−706.00	
	Vendor Total						−455.60		−9.11	−446.49	−761.00	41.3
3013-9	Society Mills	RTV			3442	01/18	−72.49		−5.70	−66.79	−133.00	
	Vendor Total						−72.49		−5.70	−66.79	−133.00	49.8

Figure 16-4

Buyers are instructed to carefully check each item on those reports against their own copies of receiving aprons, transfers, and return-to-vendor forms. Any errors are to be reported immediately to the accounting office. Any undetected error on these reports represents a potential stock shortage or overage. For example, an invoice for merchandise received by department X, but incorrectly charged to department Y, represents a stock overage for department X and a stock shortage for department Y.

PERIODIC FINANCIAL REPORTS

Each buyer in a departmentalized store receives a number of periodic reports on the actual results of the department's merchandising operation. The purpose of these periodic reports is to guide the buyer in operating the department more profitably. The same reports go to top management and, in large stores, to appropriate divisional merchandise managers as well. Thus the figures are available to both buying and management levels for study and for decisions on the actions that should be taken to improve results, if necessary.

Four major types of financial reports are usually issued on a regular basis to departmental buyers in medium- and large-volume stores. These reports vary widely from store to store in both format and extent of information presented. They are usually known as sales reports, sales and stock reports, departmental operating statements, and open-to-buy reports. Small stores may use similar reports, but they are usually more informal than those used in larger stores.

Sales Reports

As indicated in Chapter 13, sales constitute the basis of all merchandise planning and control. Therefore, actual sales results are studied closely to evaluate their effect on other elements of the merchandise budget. A number of sales reports are usually available to the buyer for this purpose.

Berry's
BUYERS' SALES REPORT

Dept. 42 **3 Days Ending 12/18/8-**

SELLING PRICE	CLASS	VENDOR	STYLE	STORE NO.	LAST 3 DAYS	THIS WEEK	ONE WEEK AGO	2 WEEKS AGO	TOTAL LAST 4 WEEKS	TOTAL TO DATE	ON HAND	INITIAL DATE OF RECEIPT	TOTAL CUSTOMER RETURNS	ACTIVITY INDICATOR
40.00	51	001	8527	1	1	2	5	4	23	26	31	11/13/8-		
				6			1	3	1	1		11/24/8-		
				5	-	1	-	1			1	11/17/8-		
				7		3		4	7	10	8	11/13/8-		
				2			1	1	3	4		11/13/8-		
				3			1	4	5	6	12	11/17/8-		
				T		5	8	11	39	47	52		7	SLOW 1
44.00	51	001	8533	1	2	2	1	3	9	35	8	10/06/8-		
				5						3		10/16/8-		
				7				4	3	9	9	10/06/8-		
				2						5		10/06/8-		
				3	1	1	1	3	7	13	12	10/06/8-		
				T	3	3	2	10	19	65	29		8	
44.00	51	001	8537	1	3	4	2	3	10	19	20	10/16/8-		
				6			1		1	1	13	11/13/8-		
				5							6	11/17/8-		
				7			1	1	2	3	7	10/16/8-		
				2	-	1	1	1	2	8	15	10/16/8-		
				3		1			1	3	6	10/16/8-		
				T	2	5	5	5	16	34	67		1	
40.00	51	001	8539	1	3	5	4	4	16	16	8	11/24/8-		
				2		1			1	1	5	12/11/8-		
				3			1	1	2	2	8	11/24/8-		
				T	3	6	5	5	19	19	21		2	
44.00	51	001	8540	1		2	5	4	11	14	1	11/13/8-		
				6					2	3	15	11/13/8-		
				5	1	2	1		3	3	3	11/17/8-		
				7	1	2	1		4	5	6	11/13/8-		
				2	2	3	3	1	7	7	4	11/13/8-		
				3	2	2			4	5	7	11/17/8-		
				T	8	14	9	1	31	37	36		1	
40.00	51	001	8541	1		1	2	1	2	13	15	10/06/8-		
				6						5		10/06/8-		

Figure 16-5

FLASH SALES. Daily reports of sales, by department, are routinely developed from the unaudited saleschecks and cash-register tapes for the previous day. They usually include the dollar sales of the corresponding selling day in the previous year. These reports are circulated early the following business day to all merchandise executives and are generally referred to as **flash sales** reports. If a store has branches, sales of each branch are usually shown separately from those of the main store, plus a total sales figure for all locations.

PERIODIC SALES REPORTS. More detailed sales reports are prepared on a one-day, three-day, weekly, or semimonthly basis. In large stores that have several branches, this review shows sales of both the main store and individual branch stores. It also shows customer returns in units or dollars or both, by classification, price line, style number, and vendor. (See Figure 16-5.) In smaller stores, departmental sales may be reported simply in units and dollars by classification.

Weekly reports give buyers a quick, on-the-spot review of sales at all locations. This encourages earlier action than would be possible if sales were reported less frequently. In addition to these figures, some reports, particularly those that are obtained from computers, sometimes show cumulative sales for the month or season to date and sales for the corresponding period of the previous year.

"BEAT LAST YEAR" BOOK. The simplest form of daily sales record kept by a buyer is the "Beat Last Year" book. This may be a single-sheet, monthly record of daily sales or a three-year or five-year diary. Sales figures are entered day by day, and subtotals are inserted to show sales to date during the month. Special conditions affecting sales, such as bad weather, transit strikes, and ads or other promotional efforts, are usually noted as well.

Sales and Stock Reports

Sales alone tell only half the merchandising story. The other half concerns stocks. Therefore, retailers have developed sales and stock reports that are supplied to buyers weekly, semimonthly, or monthly. These show sales for the period, inventory on hand and on order, planned sales and stocks, and the sales and stocks for the corresponding period of the previous year. In addition to the figures for the current period, some reports may show cumulative figures for the year to date. Others may show dollar purchases and markdowns for the current period and year or season to date.

If electronic data processing is available, reports may show not only departmental totals but also classification and subclassification totals. (See Figure 16-6.) Thus a buyer whose total departmental sales and stocks are about at the level of planned figures may see that

WEEKLY SALES AND STOCK REPORT

DIV. 1 | DEPT. NO. 15 | DEPT. NAME Handbags | WEEK ENDED 01/07/8– | PAGE 6

CODE	CODE DESCRIPTION: PRICE GROUP	PRICE		SEASON TO DATE SALES: PLAN	SEASON TO DATE SALES: THIS YEAR	TREND	BEGINNING ON HAND	ADJUSTED PHYSICAL INVENTORY	CURRENT WEEK: SALES	CURRENT WEEK: RECEIPTS	CURRENT WEEK: ADJUSTMENTS PLUS	CURRENT WEEK: ADJUSTMENTS MINUS	CURRENT WEEK: ENDING ON HAND	INTRANSIT	COVERAGE PERIOD	SALES FOR COVERAGE PERIOD PLAN	BALANCE OF SALES FOR SEASON PLAN
241	DRESS PLASTIC																
	1	3.00	5.00	32	16	50-	15		4				11	24	9	29	6
	3	6.00	8.00	85	36	58-	13						13	36	5	11	1
	5	9.00	11.00	20	9	55-	32						32		8	6	
	7	12.00	999.00		1		1-						1-		8		
	9	4.97													7		
241	TOTAL UNITS			137	62		59		4				55	60		46	7
	TOTAL DOLLARS*			897	408	55-			16				440	324		249	31
242	CASUAL PLASTIC																
	1	3.00	5.00	8	11	38	20						20		9	13	1
	3	6.00	8.00	199	72	64-	24		3				21	24	5	11	2
	5	9.00	11.00	56	25	55-	25		1				24		8	6	
	7	12.00	999.00		6		6						6		8	6	
	9	3.97	4.97	49	10	80-	6-						6-		7		
242	TOTAL UNITS			312	124		69		4				65	24		36	3
	TOTAL DOLLARS*			2065	868	58-			29				504	168		255	17
352	FRENCH PURSES																
	2	2.00	3.00	22	3	86-	14						14		6	5	1
	3	3.50	UP	6	3	50-	21		1				20		7	5	
	9	.97			7		19		2				17		6		
352	TOTAL UNITS			28	13		54		3				51			10	1
	TOTAL DOLLARS*			87	27	69-			6				133			34	3
	DIVISION TOTAL																
	TOTAL UNITS			1191	536		92		46	48			94			193	1929
	TOTAL DOLLARS*			4807	2365				198				377			667	7409

* CENTS OMITTED IN DOLLAR FIGURES

Figure 16-6

DEPARTMENTAL OPERATING STATEMENT

Department No. 20

Month March Year 198-

Line		This Month				Year to Date						Line
		Plan		Actual		Plan		Actual		Last Year		
		$	%	$	%	$	%	$	%	$	%	
1	Gross Sales	38,000	108.0	39,476	108.6	69,120	108.0	71,396	108.2	72,669	108.3	1
2	Customer Returns	3,000	8.0	3,142	8.6	5,120	8.0	5,411	8.2	5,569	8.3	2
3	NET SALES	35,000	-9.3	36,534	3.8	64,000	-4.6	65,985	3.1	67,100	2.1	3
4	Beg. Stock @ Retail	66,500	39.6	65,816	39.6	82,800	—	81,950	39.5	86,520	39.2	4
5	Net Retail Purchases	60,200	40.0	68,960	40.0	76,400	40.0	76,102	40.0	78,559	39.5	5
6	End. Stock @ Retail	86,900	39.9	83,541	39.8	86,900	—	83,541	39.7	88,720	39.3	6
7	Markdowns	4,450	12.7	4,565	12.6	7,660	12.0	7,868	11.9	7,590	11.3	7
8	Employee Discounts	350	1.0	336	.9	640	1.0	658	1.0	669	1.0	8
9	Shortage Reserve	525	1.5	545	1.5	960	1.5	990	1.5	1,141	1.7	9
10	Workroom Costs	350	1.0	340	.9	640	1.0	690	1.0	672	1.0	10
11	Cash Discounts	2,890	8.3	2,830	7.8	3,667	5.7	3,653	5.5	3,707	5.5	11
12	GROSS MARGIN	13,056	37.3	13,446	37.0	23,912	35.8	23,092	35.0	23,322	34.8	12
13	Advertising	1,120	3.2	1,417	3.9	2,048	3.2	2,111	3.2	2,416	3.6	13
14	Special Events	210	.6	291	.8	384	.6	396	.6	537	.8	14
15	Buying Salaries	1,155	3.3	1,200	3.3	2,112	3.3	2,178	3.3	2,214	3.3	15
16	Buyer's Travel	175	.5	218	.6	320	.5	397	.6	402	.6	16
17	Selling Salaries	2,660	7.6	2,854	7.8	4,864	7.6	5,015	7.6	5,299	7.9	17
18	Stk & Cler. Salaries	280	.8	284	.8	512	.8	530	.8	604	.9	18
19	Supplies	70	.2	75	.2	128	.2	135	.2	135	.2	19
20	Delivery	140	.4	185	.5	256	.4	270	.4	268	.4	20
21	Other Direct Expense	1,050	3.0	1,091	3.0	1,920	3.0	1,992	3.0	2,015	3.0	21
22	TOTAL DIRECT EXPENSE (13 thru 21)	6,860	19.6	7,595	20.9	12,544	19.6	15,014	19.7	13,390	20.7	22
23	DEPT. CONTRIBUTION (12 minus 22)	6,196	17.7	5,851	16.1	10,368	18.2	10,078	15.3	9,432	14.1	23
24	Indirect Expense	4,095	11.7	4,178	11.5	7,488	11.7	7,536	11.5	7,851	11.7	24
25	TOTAL EXPENSES (22 plus 24)	10,955	31.3	11,773	32.4	20,032	31.3	20,620	31.2	21,741	32.4	25
26	OPERATING PROFIT (12 minus 25)	2,107	6.0	1,673	4.6	2,880	4.5	2,492	3.8	1,581	2.4	26

Figure 16-7

some classifications are far enough above or below plan to require appropriate action. Similarly, where there are branches, a separate set of figures for each location may reveal a need for action at one or more sites, whereas over-all figures for all stores combined would mask such a need.

Departmental Operating Statements

Buyers and their management also receive regular summary reports from the accounting office on the financial aspects of each department's total merchandising operation. (See Figure 16-7.) The format of these reports varies from store to store, but most include actual and planned dollar figures for all phases of the merchandising operation, such as gross sales, customer returns, net sales, mark-downs, purchases, gross margin of profit, operating expenses, cash discounts earned, and so on. Departmental operating statements are usually issued monthly, but in some large stores a midmonth flash report is also provided. Figures are usually stated both in dollars and as percentages of net sales. Some stores also include the retail value of all merchandise on order; others include the number of transactions and the average gross sale for the month.

Open-to-Buy Reports

For buyers and store management, the open-to-buy report is the most important merchandising tool in keeping the inventory investment in line with plans and a desired ratio to actual sales. (See Figure 16-8.) When a promising new item or trend appears, the buyer who wishes to exploit it must move promptly, particularly if it is a fashion item. If the buyer does not have enough open-to-buy, purchase plans may be rearranged to make room for the new item or management may be asked for extra purchasing funds.

Open-to-buy, as previously discussed, refers to the amount of purchases that can be made for delivery in a given period, minus orders already placed for delivery during that same period but not yet received. Open-to-buy may be expressed in dollars or units or both. Dollar open-to-buy reports are usually issued weekly to departmental buyers and may cover future periods as well as the current period.

UNIT OPEN TO BUY REPORT

Dept. 42 Casual Dresses — WEEK ENDING FEB. 21,198—

CODE	PRICE RANGE	E.O.M. INV. 1/31/8–	FEB. ON ORDER	AVAILABLE FOR SALE	PLANNED SALES	ANTICIPATED MARK DOWNS	PLANNED 2/28/8– INV.	OPEN TO RECEIVE FEB.	MAR.	APR.	MAY	JUNE-JULY	OPEN TO BUY MAR-JULY
700	28.00	771	100	871	500	40	750	419	300	800	1000	100	2885
702	32.00	621	85	706	425	30	900	649	500	1000	250	0	2625
704	36.00	1412	210	1622	800	70	1500	748	200	1400	1400	50	3410
706	42.00	3201	610	3811	1600	120	3000	909	800	800	0	0	4310
707	48.00	2120	350	2470	1000	80	2500	1110	1000	750	500	0	4820
708	56.00	1409	300	1709	600	50	1200	141	150	150	100	100	2530
TOTAL MISSY		9534	1655	11189	4925	390	8850	3976	2950	4900	3250	250	20580
710	28.00	494	500	994	700	50	1050	806	1000	1000	500	500	3405
712	36.00	1464	1000	2464	1000	80	1500	116	850	850	550	550	4460
714	48.00	2026	800	2826	1100	100	1700	74	1500	1200	700	0	4795
716	56.00	2251	100	2351	850	70	1500	69	1000	200	100	0	3620
TOTAL JUNIOR		6235	2400	8635	3650	300	5750	1065	4350	3250	1850	1050	17280
TOTAL CASUAL		15769	4055	19824	8575	690	15600	5041	7300	8150	5100	1300	37860

Figure 16-8

The following is an example of how open-to-buy is calculated at any point during a month.

Planned sales for balance of month	$1,000*
Planned end-of-month stock	+ 2,000*
Total stock requirements for balance of month	= $3,000
Stock now on hand	− 1,500
Purchases for balance of month	= $1,500
Orders previously placed for delivery this month	− 1,000
Open-to-buy for balance of month	= $ 500

* From Dollar Merchandise Plan.

From the viewpoint of top management, the open-to-buy report reflects the buyer's competence and efficiency. The overly optimistic buyer tends to buy too heavily and to be chronically overbought, even when the selections are excellent. Another type of buyer who overstocks is the one whose selections tend to fall just short of being right and therefore sell more slowly than planned. Some buyers tend to underbuy, even though they have a gift for anticipating what customers will want and for presenting it to them temptingly. They may have too little confidence in their own judgment or too much confidence in the ability of resources to deliver additional stock in a rush. Accuracy in planning and skill in merchandising to the plan reveal themselves in a department that has adequate stocks yet always has some open-to-buy available for unexpected developments.

MANAGEMENT DEVICES FOR EVALUATING THE MERCHANDISING OPERATION

Management and the individual buyer use many other devices to measure the success of a department's merchandising operation and to guide it toward greater accuracy in meeting consumer fashion demand. Among these are basic stock lists, age-of-stock reports, markdowns, analyses of customer returns, vendor analyses, stock turnover figures, and others. Each is a way of keeping track of or exploring the significance of some facet of the merchandising operation that affects that operation's overall profitability.

Basic Stock Lists

An item of merchandise is described by merchants as **basic stock** if it enjoys such consistent demand that it should be in stock in a complete range of sizes and colors at best-selling price lines throughout a year or season. A basic may be a specific item or a group of substitutable items, such as women's pantyhose in neutral shades, nurses' oxfords, women's white tailored slips, or men's white dress shirts.

When a store runs short of an item that enjoys consistent demand, both customer goodwill and sales are at stake. Stores therefore encourage or require their buyers to list specific items in their departments that are considered basic each season. The buyers are asked to set up periodic stock counts or similar ways of making sure there is always an adequate supply of these goods. Many stores require that a list of such items be retained in the merchandise manager's office. At unannounced intervals, the merchandise manager sends someone into a department to check the basic stock and report any listed items that are not on hand or are in low supply. A buyer whose department repeatedly makes poor showings on such checks is subject to criticism.

To ensure adequate stocks of basic merchandise, some stores draw up two separate budgets for each department or classification: one for basics and one for fashion merchandise. Executives of such stores believe that an overstock elsewhere in a department should not deprive the buyer of needed open-to-buy for basics. Other stores have a policy of permitting basics to be reordered regardless of the state of the departmental open-to-buy. Still others leave the entire matter in the buyer's hands, expecting them to reserve part of their budget and enough of their open-to-buy for basics.

Prior Stock Reports

Retail stores usually place a code for the season on each price ticket. The season code, as previously defined, is a figure indicating the month of the year in which the merchandise was received into stock. In fast-moving fashion categories, the season code may also include a numeral to indicate the week, in addition to the month, in which the article arrived in stock. Some stores put the complete coded date of receipt on the price ticket of each piece of fashion merchandise.

By flipping through the tickets on a rack of garments, a merchant can quickly see which ones have been in stock too long and should be given prompt attention. In some stores, and for some merchandise, a week is considered a long time. In other cases, a month may not be considered long.

Prior stock reports are reports that summarize information about the amount of stock still on hand in each of a number of prior seasons. The report is in units as well as dollars,

and information is gathered from the season letter on each price ticket. Such reports may be prepared by the accounting office from data listed on inventory sheets or from special inventories taken of all or part of a department's stock for age-record purposes. The reports are created by dividing the listing of stock into age groups, totaling each group, and then showing what percentage of the total inventory each age group constitutes. Buyers are required to recheck these reports periodically, indicating what steps have been taken to dispose of prior season stock. (See Figure 16-9.) Some stores, particularly those using electronic data processing equipment, run off actual lists of the specific items of merchandise that are "old." These lists are presented to the appropriate buyers for action.

Women's apparel departments rarely have inventory that is more than six months old. One larger chain organization requires that all women's apparel remaining in stock 10 weeks after its receipt must be marked down.

PRIOR STOCK

Department No. 42
Sheet No. 1

Class.	Style No.	Article (List each classification separately)	Season Letter	Inventory Date 1/31/8– Qty.	Price	First Month Date 2/28/8 Qty.	Price	Second Month Date 3/31/8 – Qty.	Price	Third Month Date 4/30/8 – Qty.	Price
12301	1234	Dress	H4	5	28.00	2	18.88	0	—	—	—
	789	Dress	H5	7	28.00	4	18.88	1	12.88	0	—
	1401	Dress	H5	3	28.00	3	18.88	1	12.88	0	—
12302	239	Dress	H4	6	35.00	4	26.88	2	18.88	1	12.88
	141	Dress	H5	8	35.00	4	26.88	1	18.88	0	—
	984	Dress	H5	1	35.00	0	—	—	—	—	—
12308	957	Dress	H3	1	56.00	1	39.88	1	26.88	0	—
	245	Dress	H4	2	56.00	1	39.88	1	26.88	0	—
	698	Dress	H5	2	56.00	1	39.88	0	—	—	—
Season			H3	27	862.00	14	558.00	3	72.00	0	—
Season			H4	41	1625.00	22	868.00	7	120.00	3	48.00
Season			H5	64	2959.00	31	1440.00	11	228.00	3	84.00
Total				132	5446.00	67	2866.00	21	420.00	6	132.00

NOTE: These sheets must be returned to the Merchandise Office on the 5th of each month with all data shown complete.

Figure 16-9

Once it was common for management to record and pursue slow sellers until each item was finally eliminated from stock. But today fashion moves at a faster pace and the cost of clerical help is higher. As a result, stores now tend to rely instead on spot checks and unit control records to make sure that buyers locate and act upon slow-selling fashion merchandise.

Markdown Analyses

Downward revisions in retail prices are reported to the accounting office whenever they are made. To provide data for further study, stores provide price change forms on which reasons for taking the markdowns may be indicated. Analyses of markdowns and reasons for them yield clues to a buyer's proficiency in gauging customer demand. They also indicate the quality of departmental supervision.

MARKDOWN CAUSES.   Common causes of markdowns are:

- Promotional purchase remainders
- Fabrics or quality
- Style or pattern
- Color
- Sizes
- Quantities (including overstock conditions as well as excessive quantities of specific styles)
- Special sales from stock
- Broken assortments, remnants, shopworn goods
- Price adjustments to meet competition, because of generally falling prices, or to consolidate or eliminate price lines
- Allowances to customers on adjustment claims

BUYER RESPONSIBILITY
FOR MARKDOWNS.   Hardest to recognize but most in need of correction are markdowns due to poor timing. These stem from offering merchandise too soon or too late for its normal selling season or for that stage of the fashion cycle to which the store's customers are attuned. Such markdowns may be reported under almost any of the headings above. But the discerning eye of an experienced merchandise manager will usually recognize them for what they are and search out the roots of the buyer's problem.

Errors in timing the presentation of merchandise to the customer are not always solely the fault of the buyer. There are occasions when tardy deliveries or uncertain weather conditions are to blame. Since late deliveries frequently represent potential markdowns, buyers are expected to weigh the advisability of accepting overdue shipments against the possibility of slackening customer demand.

Delay in taking markdowns or failure to take adequate markdowns, however, is definitely the fault of the buyer. Fashion merchandise deteriorates so rapidly that stores caution their buyers against postponing markdowns or making only timid reductions once they recognize that goods are not readily salable. Yet buyers often engage in wishful thinking; they postpone the inevitable and then have to slash prices drastically in the end. The markdown book records it all, and management finds in that book an index to the buyer's competence.

Customer Returns

The extent to which goods are returned in a fashion department is also an important index of the buyer's competence. If a large proportion of the goods sold is brought back for credit, there is something obviously wrong with the assortment, the merchandise, the selling techniques used, or a combination of all three. Sometimes a persuasive salesperson or a low price may encourage a customer to purchase a dress. If the dress is unflattering, unfashionable, or poorly made, however, the customer is likely to have second thoughts about it after getting it home, and back it goes to the store.

The nature of the merchandise also affects the ratio of returns to sales. In departments devoted to women's and misses' apparel, the rate of returns to gross sales normally exceeds 10 percent. In departments devoted to menswear and boys' wear, the rate of returns is well below 10 percent.

Vendor Analysis

A retailer rates suppliers in terms of how accurately their merchandise meets the needs of customers. Sometimes there is an affinity between one vendor's merchandise and the preferences of a store's customers that persists for seasons and even years. Sometimes the affinity is fleeting.

To help evaluate his or her department's resources, a buyer may, with the help of the store's accounting office, maintain records of dealings with each vendor. Typical forms used for this purpose show vendor name and address, purchases at cost and retail, and the year's or season's total purchases. Vendor returns and claims, as well as markdowns, are also reported by season or year. Thus a buyer can see if a resource has added to the past season's profits or to its problems. (See Figure 16-10.)

Buyers also consolidate and list the yearly totals for their principal vendors so that they can compare one with another. They rank them according to amounts purchased, initial markup, percentage of markdowns, or other criteria. The list of principal resources has another function. The management executives of departmentalized stores usually contact, at least once a year, the few best resources for each of their many departments. Often such contact between the heads of the store and the heads of the manufacturing firm leads to better understanding and to long-range planning that benefits vendor, store, and customer.

Stock Turnover

The more rapidly its retail stock is sold, the more profitably a store operates. Good turnover is the fruit of careful planning and wise management. Retailers are very conscious of the stock turnover in each of their departments.

As explained in Chapter 13, turnover rate, or stock turn, is calculated by dividing net sales for a year by the average retail value of the inventory for that year. A common error, however, is to use only season-end or year-end inventories, omitting the intervening months. At the end of a year or season, fashion inventories are at a low point. To base the average only on these lows would be to calculate a deceptively low average inventory and therefore a deceptively high turnover rate. This would cause the store to congratulate itself on what actually may have been a poor performance.

IMPROVING TURNOVER. The only sensible way to improve turnover is to first examine the details of the assortment and identify the slow-selling classifications or items. The latter must be then disposed of through better display, better selling techniques, or as a last resort, markdowns. The buyer should then use the funds released through the disposal of slow sellers to build up stocks of fast sellers.

Turnover cannot be improved merely by slashing the buying appropriation. And elaborate classification and unit control data can do no more than direct the attention of the merchandising executive to those parts of the stock with the best and the worst turnover. The merchandise itself must be inspected. When the extremely slow-selling numbers are gathered on one rack and the very fast-selling ones on another, the differences between them generally stand out sharply. Buyers can see that their clientele is accepting certain lines, colors, and prices and rejecting others. Better assortment planning then becomes possible, and better turnover results.

Not all causes of slow turnover are correctable, however. Some imports must be bought and paid for long before they reach the selling floor. Domestic merchandise in irregular supply must also often be bought well in advance to ensure timely delivery. Turnover in these cases necessarily suffers. This deliberate sacrifice of turnover in order to secure desirable merchandise is not considered an error of the same magnitude as is the slowing of turnover through inept management of the fashion assortment.

IMPORTANCE
OF GOOD TURNOVER. In explaining the value of good turnover, more than one merchant has compared fashion merchandise to

VENDOR ANALYSIS

VENDOR NUMBER	NAME	MARK UP %	YTD NET PURCHASES RETAIL	COST	FREIGHT	DISCOUNT	YTD MARK DOWNS $	%	YTD RETURNS-TO-VENDOR RETAIL	COST	FREIGHT	DISCOUNT
3529-7	TRALEE	34.2	1400	921					4000	2175		174
3006-6	SMITH DISTRIBUTORS INC	37.9	24600	14654	1173	613						
2499-6	MODERN GLOBE INC	38.3	48600	30000	600					3000	60	
4484-9	BAGS BY MR ROBERTS	41.4	358800	205800	16464	4393	45	9.3		825	66	
4439-3	CASSIE COTILLION	43.1	38800	21760	17408	3596	360	10.0	1500			
2184-9	KID DUDS	43.5	6000	3451	58		10	16.7				
3776-1	METRO NOVELTY CO	43.5	525000	296650	23732		423	10.9				
4264-1	CHERRI LYNN	44.4	51380	29128	5649		420	8.0		640	390	
2142-3	K M T CO	44.4	574000	318575	6346	7039	649	12.6				
3352-9	WILLIAM CARTER CO	44.6	129600	69450	1389	2319	341	5.9	31000	19463	535	
1002-2	A D SUTTON & SONS	44.6	34800	18770	370	512			49700	26710	26	
2140-7	K GIMBEL ACCESSORIES INC	44.7	52200	27360	547	1431	52	15.0	3800	1320		
4274-9	SOFTSKIN TOYS	44.8	119500	65273	657							
3187-9	TOM FIELDS INC	45.1	143600	81157	3558	639	137	11.5	800	445	104	
1045-6	ALEX LEE WALLAU INC	45.5	329200	180209	3603	2260	87	6.1	3300	2761	36	
2244-6	LE ROI HOSIERY CO	45.7	-36000	-18000		-1438	265	8.1	300	146	03	
4062-2	JUST ACCESSORIES	46.0	15000	6600								
4981-7	EARL BERNARD INC	46.1	105000	56860	132	3098	30	25.1				
4272-2	PILLOW PLAYMATES	46.7	99000	52850	349	4838	120	11.4				
1622-5	EASTERN ISLES	47.4	734000	386076	32999	924	975	13.3				
1557-1	DETERMINED PRODUCTIONS	48.6	1390700	715050		868	259	26.2				
1931-3	HER MAJESTY IND INC	48.6	945400	494158	65743	11692	1529	11.0	70400	42403	3194	
1756-6	FREDERICK WHOLESALE CORP	49.9	36000	18000	31738		756	18.0	87500	43958	879	
1618-7	E K WERTHEIMER & SON INC	50.0	72000	36000	540							
4207-2	GIANT UMBRELLA CO INC	50.0	34800	17995	1080	1490	40	6.0				
2741-3	PYRAMID LEATHER GOODS CO	50.1	14400	7355	2044		39	11.2				
3654-4	GAYSTONE PRODUCTS	50.4	100800	50397	216							
1862-7	GUILD LINGERIE OF CALIF	51.2	24800	12134	4296		187	13.6				
2759-6	R G BARRY CORP	51.4	40000	19440	2588	-379	278	11.1				
1755-8	FREDERICK ATKINS INTERNTL	51.7	-40000	-19340								
4233-1	A M A EXPENSE TRANSFER	51.7	-40000	-19340								
3531-9	VELVA SHEEN	53.5	143900	66975	3504		156	10.8				
4920-4	HOLLYWOOD CHILDRENS DRESS	54.0	87600	43800			98	11.2				
	DEPARTMENT TOTAL	47.7	7298300	3955628	226793	43895	7258	10.4	252300	143346	5267	

Figure 16-10

Courtesy Hess's Department Store

Courtesy Liberty House

Retailers use sales per square foot as a measuring device to evaluate a department's effectiveness. Note how these vertical display fixtures make very effective use of space, thus contributing to higher sales per square foot.

fresh fish: both deteriorate rapidly! A good rate of turnover results in:

- Minimum loss of sales appeal of merchandise
- Reduced hazard of soilage and damage from handling
- Increased open-to-buy and the opportunity to freshen assortments with new goods, especially important when the same customers visit a given store or department frequently
- Renewed interest on the part of salespeople, most of whom become bored with lingering stock
- Increased interest of customers in constantly changing stock
- Reduced inventory investment (which, in turn, means a reduction in interest costs, need for borrowed capital, insurance rates, and opportunities for pilferage)

EXCESSIVELY
HIGH TURNOVER. A good turnover rate, however, is not always the highest rate possible. While fashion merchandise turns at a higher rate than more staple merchandise, there are disadvantages in an excessively high rate of stock turnover. Too high a rate implies inadequate stocks, unbalanced assortments, and loss of goodwill when customers cannot find wanted styles, colors, and sizes. In addition, high handling and billing costs may have been incurred by placing many small orders rather than a few large ones. The added expense reduces operating profit.

Other Measuring Devices

Other figures are used by retail management in evaluating a department's merchandising effectiveness. These include the number of its sales transactions, the average gross sale, and dollar sales per square foot. Each of these sheds light in its own way on one or more aspects of a buyer's competence and the efficiency of the merchandising operation.

TRANSACTIONS. The more transactions a department rings up in a year, the more customers it is assumed to have served. If the number falls off from one year to another, this is a possible indication of failure to attract or sell customers. The transaction figure itself is not an index of major importance, but increases or decreases are useful guides when hunting for the strengths or weaknesses of a department.

AVERAGE GROSS SALE.   On an annual or sometimes a seasonal basis, stores divide the net sales of a department by the number of its sales transactions. The result is known as the **average gross sale.** A rising average gross sale may indicate rising prices, successful efforts to sell higher-quality goods, successful efforts to sell more than one item to a customer, or all three. An average gross sale that is higher than the previous year's figure can indicate a better merchandising operation or simply rising prices. When combined with a rising transaction figure, however, it usually means that a department really is pleasing its customers.

SALES
PER SQUARE FOOT.   Stores annually calculate the number of square feet of selling space assigned to a department and divide that number into the department's total net sales for the year. The resulting figure, in dollar sales per square foot, is an index to how well the department has paid its "rent" to management. This figure is becoming increasingly important as store rents continue to escalate. The goal of every department is to have an increasing number of sales per square foot over the preceding year.

In a recent study by the National Retail Management Association, watches and fine jewelry achieved the highest sales per square foot for the year studied. Apparel fabrics achieved the lowest.[1] While not listed among those departments with either the highest or the lowest sales per square foot, misses' apparel departments in department stores usually have figures above those of the store as a whole.

As a means of combating increasing rents, new display fixtures are being used to make use of every inch of selling space. Suggestions from buyers for rearranging their departments or installing new fixtures will meet with little resistance from management if the changes are likely to increase sales per square foot. In departmentalized stores, management may even agree to expand the selling area of a department or classification that shows exceptionally high sales per square foot. On the other hand, management may condense those departments that do poorly in this respect.

MERCHANDISING VOCABULARY

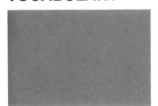

Define or briefly explain the following terms:

Average gross sale	**Pre-retail**
Basic stock	**Prior stock reports**
Book inventory	**Purchase or merchandise journal**
Flash sales	

MERCHANDISING REVIEW

1. The chapter states that it became impossible for large retail organizations to keep track of each item in their inventory by means of the cost-price method of inventory evaluation. Explain how this can be so and give examples. Why is the retail method of inventory evaluation better? Give examples illustrating your answer.

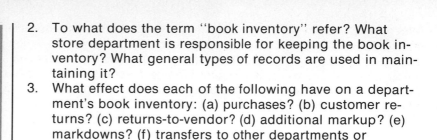

2. To what does the term "book inventory" refer? What store department is responsible for keeping the book inventory? What general types of records are used in maintaining it?

3. What effect does each of the following have on a department's book inventory: (a) purchases? (b) customer returns? (c) returns-to-vendor? (d) additional markup? (e) markdowns? (f) transfers to other departments or branches? (g) transfers in from other departments or branches? (h) merchandise on order? (i) merchandise loaned to other departments?

4. What is a departmental buyer's responsibility with regard to stock shortages and overages? What are the two major causes of shortages and overages? Give at least four examples of each cause.

5. What is a purchase or merchandise journal? Why should it be carefully checked by a buyer or assistant buyer? What is involved in checking it?

6. Name and briefly describe the purpose of each of the four periodic financial reports commonly used today in departmentalized stores.

7. What is the primary purpose served by a departmental operating statement? How often is it usually issued? What specific information does it contain?

8. What factors do retailers take into account when evaluating resources (vendors)? What purpose or purposes do such evaluations serve?

9. Why is age of stock a very important consideration in fashion merchandising? Discuss various ways in which old season or slow-selling fashion merchandise can be kept to a minimum.

10. Why are sales per square foot becoming an increasingly important measure of success for individual departments within a store? What are stores doing to increase sales per square foot?

11. It is stated in this chapter that markdowns and customer returns are vital indexes of a buyer's competence. Explain and give examples for each.

MERCHANDISING DIGEST

1. Discuss markdowns with respect to (a) major causes, (b) "poor timing" of merchandise offerings, (c) delays in taking, (d) size of markdown of individual items, and (e) departmental profits.

2. Discuss stock turnover with respect to (a) how a buyer can achieve a higher rate, (b) benefits resulting from an improved rate and (c) disadvantages of an excessively high rate.

3. The chapter states that the open-to-buy report is the most important merchandising tool in keeping the inventory investment in line with plans and a desired ratio of actual sales. What is meant by this statement? How is open-to-buy calculated?

REFERENCES
[1] Dubbs, Edward S. ''NRMA's New MOR,'' pp. 24–30.

17

SELECTING AND BUYING FASHION MERCHANDISE

The most exciting and rewarding moments in a fashion retail buyer's career are when customers buy the merchandise that the buyer has selected. At these moments, customers reinforce the qualitative decisions and selections made by the buyer in the fashion marketplace.

Up until the actual selection of styles in the market, the buyer's decisions are mostly quantitative. They involve the number of units and the dollars that should be invested in the total stock of fashion apparel and/or accessories the buyer plans to offer the consumer. Others at the store may help the buyer with the planning by supplying or suggesting certain data, expressing opinions, or setting policies and limits on the quantities of merchandise to be purchased. It is in the selection of styles, however, that the buyer begins to make qualitative decisions, and in most cases these decisions are made by the buyer alone.

The selection and buying of fashion merchandise is a constant and never-ending process. The process takes place at the buyer's desk, in manufacturers' showrooms, and in regional and foreign market centers. If successful, the process ends with customer purchases. New items, reorders, and the buyer's own creativity lend excitement to market selection and buying.

In order to be fully aware of current fashion and to operate an exciting fashion shop or department, the buyer must make at least two or three market trips a year. When and how often a buyer goes to market are determined by the size of the shop or department, the fashion-cycle stage and turnover of the merchandise carried, and the store's distance from the market. A store that wants to build or maintain a strong fashion image may send its buyers to

market many times during a year or a season. Buyers will thus be aware of even the slightest changes in the market and will be prepared to act upon these changes when a fashion is in the early stages of its cycle. Retailers who feature price above all else may also send their buyers to the market frequently in search of buys with special price advantages. Promotions, fashion innovations, and newly emerging categories of merchandise may require buyers to make extra market trips in search of these special buys.

THE BUYING PLAN

A merchant or buyer on a trip to the wholesale markets leaves the store prepared to spend a considerable amount of money. To make sure this money is not spent haphazardly, and to show that there is need for the trip, most stores require that a written buying plan be drawn up and approved prior to departure. A **buying plan** is a general description of the types and quantities of merchandise a buyer expects to purchase for delivery within a specific period of time. It also sets a limit on the amount of money to be spent, so that purchases will be kept in line with planned sales and desired inventory levels.

The more enthusiastic a retail buyer is about fashion merchandise, the more the stabilizing influence of a written buying plan is needed. It is a constant reminder to avoid spending too much on the first new and exciting goods encountered while neglecting other sectors of the assortment.

A buying plan makes all the difference, for example, between going to market to see what is offered in coats, and going to market to find coats at specific retail price lines, in specific quantities, with specific delivery dates—all in accordance with budget limitations, assortment plan, present inventory, present commitments, and sales potential of the coat department. Until a buyer or store owner actually inspects producers' lines, the buying plan cannot be completely explicit. To be without one, however, invites unplanned assortments that are poorly related to customer demand.

The buying plan is part of the homework that every retailer undertakes before making any major commitment of funds to buy fashion merchandise. Department stores generally do not release travel funds to their buyers until a plan has been made and has been approved by

BUYING PLAN   Page __1__

Dept. _42, Misses Dresses_ Date _Feb. 20, 198–_

Planned MU% _48.5_

Buying trip to: _New York_

From: _Feb. 24_   To: _Feb. 27_

Reason for trip: _Additional Easter Mdse;_ _Review Mar. – Apr. O.O., New Mdse for early Apr. delivery_

Mo. of Delivery	O.T.B. 2/20/8–	Planned Purchases	O.T.B. Balance	Actual Purchases Cost	Retail
March	$9,300	$7,900	$1,400		
April	13,600	6,700	6,900		

APPROVED: GMM _ABD_ Date _2/22/8–_ DMM _TJE_ Date _2/21/8–_

(1) Class	(2) Unit Retail	(3) Description	(4) Actual Sales L.Y.	(5) Planned Sales T.Y.	(6) Planned Stock 4/15/8–	(7) Total (5+6)	(8) O.H. 2/20/8–	(9) O.O. 2/20/8–	(10) Total (8+9)	(11) O.T.B. (7-10)	(12) Plan to buy	(13) Purchases No.	Cost	Retail
123	22		141	150	250	400	176	90	266	134	Mar 60 / Apr 60			
	26	Street, business and	163	175	300	475	202	100	302	173	Mar 90 / Apr 80			
	30	general occasion wear	155	160	225	385	162	80	242	143	Mar 80 / Apr 60			
	35	dresses	94	100	180	280	112	60	172	108	Mar 60 / Apr 42			
140	30		42	45	80	125	94	36	130	—				
	35	Dressy and after-	30	35	65	100	80	18	98	—				
	40	5 dresses	19	25	50	75	60	18	78	—				

Figure 17-1

the merchandise manager or senior store executive. Figure 17-1 illustrates a simple buying plan that might be used in a moderate- or large-volume store.

Information Required for a Buying Plan

In addition to identifying data such as department number and name, date of trip, destination, and length of stay, a typical buying plan requires detailed information about a number of other points. These include various projections in either dollars or units of merchandise or both, based on both the department's merchandise budget and the merchandise assortment plan.

When a buyer has supplied all the information required in a buying plan, the merchandise manager or senior store executive is in a position to evaluate the need for the trip and also to bring greater experience and judgment to bear upon the tentative decisions that a buying plan represents.

REASON FOR TRIP. The purpose of a buying trip may be to attend regular seasonal openings of vendors' lines, to seek out special values for a forthcoming promotion, or to bolster a section of the assortment that is enjoying an unexpected burst of demand. The reason given for making the trip, as well as some of the other data in the buying plan, also shows management whether the trip is urgent or routine.

OPEN-TO-BUY. Open-to-buy, as discussed in Chapters 13 and 16, is the amount of merchandise that can be purchased for delivery during a given period minus outstanding orders scheduled for delivery during that same period. The formula for calculating open-to-buy is

$$
\text{OTB} =
\begin{array}{l}
\text{planned sales for period} \\
+ \text{ planned markdowns} \\
+ \text{ planned closing stock} \\
- \text{ stock on hand} \\
- \text{ merchandise on order for delivery this period}
\end{array}
$$

Open-to-buy can be calculated and shown on a buying plan either in dollars or in units of merchandise or both. It is usually shown by classification and price lines or price ranges within each classification. The total dollar figure on the buying plan automatically shows management whether or not the proposed purchases are within the dollar limits established in that season's merchandise budget. The unit figures are based on the season's unit assortment plan. In some cases, open-to-buy figures may be shown for one or more months into the future. This is a useful guide if the buyer is authorized to make commitments for delivery of goods beyond the current period for which buying is then being done.

STOCK ON HAND
AND ON ORDER. For each classification of merchandise to be purchased, current merchandise on hand and on order for delivery during the period for which purchases are being planned are indicated on a buying plan. Usually each price line in each classification at which purchases are planned is entered separately, with the stock on hand and on order indicated in units or dollars or both. In moderate- and large-volume stores, unit price and total amounts to be purchased are shown at retail values, while smaller stores tend to use cost figures. By comparing these figures on the buying plan with those in the merchandise budget and the assortment plan, management can determine whether or not the intended purchases are within the budgetary limits set for the department or classification and are in line with its assortment plan.

SALES FOR
THE PERIOD. The buying plan, prepared just before a market trip, includes the most recent sales estimates and reports available. These may be shown in units or dollars or both. If the buying trip is made before the start of a season, the sales figures in the plan will be those projected on the dollar merchandise budget and the merchandise assortment plan. If the selling season has already begun, these figures will have been adjusted to reflect anticipated sales for the balance of the period for

which buying is to be done. If the merchandise budget and the assortment plan have been revised to meet current conditions, the revised figures are used. The important point is that the buying plan includes the most up-to-date sales, stock-on-hand, and stock-on-order figures available at the time it is prepared.

PLANNED STOCK
AT END OF PERIOD. The planned end-of-period inventory figures, in both dollars and units, are very important in planning the buying of fashion goods. Because demand rises rapidly to a peak in fashion goods and falls off even more sharply after the peak has been passed, it is essential to keep the inventory within the established limits. If a fashion merchant brings in too much stock and has more than planned at the close of a selling period, it is likely that heavy markdowns will be needed to get rid of that excess stock.

If the buyer plans to make purchases for more than a month or two, the planned stock for the end of that period is entered in the buying plan. If buying is short term, only the current month's closing stock estimate may be needed.

QUANTITIES
TO BE PURCHASED. Fashion merchants indicate on their buying plans, in terms of both units and retail dollars, how much of each type of merchandise they want to purchase on this trip in order to maintain an assortment that will meet anticipated customer demand. These figures are based on merchants' judgment of sales potential, availability of merchandise, market conditions, and other factors. Quantities to be purchased vary with the timing of a market trip, the store's merchandising policies, the type of merchandise, and delivery conditions. At the start of a selling season, perhaps only trial quantities are ordered, while larger quantities may be purchased with more assurance as the season advances. Most stores establish loosely defined percentages of the seasonal open-to-buy that may be purchased early. The experienced buyer saves a good part of both the unit and dollar open-to-buy for later in the season, for unexpected and opportune purchases, for reorders, and for purchases required by changing customer demands.

ADDITIONAL DATA. Some plans provide space in which the buyer enters the amount of actual purchases after shopping the market. As illustrated in Figure 17-1, these entries are usually placed alongside the approved, planned figures. A number of stores require the buyer to submit, at the conclusion of each trip, a detailed reconciliation of all orders placed, by classification and price line, with quantities approved on the original buying plan. Either of these procedures underscores the importance of adhering to planned figures unless there is good reason to do otherwise.

A few store managements require a list of resources the buyer intends to visit on the market trip. Such a list is usually expected to include the names of one or more resources with which the store has not yet had dealings, but whose potential the buyer will explore. It also includes resources with which the department has already dealt, sometimes for years.

This requirement serves a double purpose. It stimulates the buyer to make realistic plans as to which and how many producers to visit in the time available. In addition, it is a reminder to inspect the lines of resources that have proved successful in customer acceptance and yet avoid the danger of going only to regular resources. Just as any business constantly seeks new customers, so an alert store seeks new and gifted resources to add fresh and interesting items to its assortments.

Some buying plans also include a figure provided by management representing a total dollar limitation for the market trip. This amount may be higher than the total of the planned purchases listed and may actually exceed the open-to-buy, since it may include a provisional allowance for opportune purchases. In a store commited to fashion leadership, this leeway permits buyers more flexibility should they find a new trend developing in the market. For stores serving bargain hunters, this extra money may permit buyers the opportunity to snap up good buys in the market without ignoring the needs of their regular assortments and without having to contact the store for permission to exceed planned figures.

Detailed descriptions of purchases to be made are not necessarily included on buying plans. Buyers, not knowing precisely what they may find, often only note general classifications, such as skirts, tops, pants, jackets, etc.

How a Buyer Plans

Before actually drawing up a buying plan, fashion merchants or buyers review the stock in several respects. They check their basic stock requirements. They study any overstock conditions. They note any items that are winning strong acceptance. They take upcoming sales events into consideration. This overall review is intended to give a good idea of exactly what is needed and what should be sought in the market.

OVERSTOCK. Any section of the assortment on hand that exceeds its planned size requires analysis. The adjustments needed to reduce such overstocked conditions may affect buying plans for categories in which sales are proceeding according to plan. For example, slow sellers in higher-priced lines may have to be marked down into lower-priced lines. In such cases, buying plans for the lower-priced line may have to be adjusted to take such additions to the existing stock into account. There also may be some common factor among a department's slow sellers which can be regarded as a warning against further purchases of a disappointing price line, color, fabric, detail, or other features customers have not favored.

"HOT" ITEMS. Items, new or otherwise, that have demonstrated greater customer acceptance than was anticipated receive thoughtful consideration from the buyer. Even though they may not have been prominent in the original assortment plan for the season, it may be necessary to make an important place for them. To do that, buying plans for other items may have to be cut back.

If the hot item is one the buyer has heard about but has not yet actually had in stock, judgment on its sales potential may be reserved until it has been studied in the market. Then approved buying plans for the more predictable and familiar items may be adjusted, and the buyer may decide to add the hot item to the assortment.

SPECIAL EVENTS. If the buying trip for which the plan is drawn involves preparation for a promotional event, special sale, catalog distribution, or similar activity, the buyer is fortified with details on what was offered to and bought by the store's customers on similar occasions in the past. If a buyer is about to purchase children's gloves, for example, for the store's Christmas catalog, it is important to know how many of those sold from the previous year's catalog were knitted or leather, bright colors or neutrals, matched to caps and scarves or sold separately, and how many were sold at each price. This information then has to be weighed against what appear to be this year's trends in children's gloves.

IMPORTANCE OF
COMPLETE DATA. When drawing up a buying plan, the buyer is in the store. Here all the sources of information on present conditions and past experience, described in Chapters 13 and 14, are available. Once in the market, however, only the condensed data of the buying plan itself can be consulted. The more thoroughly the buyer checks while still at the store, the more valuable the capsulized data on the buying plan will be.

TIMING OF THE MARKET TRIP

Most fashion buyers feel that the more often they are able to view and compare manufacturers' lines, the better they are prepared to implement their assortment and unit plans for their target customers.

Most apparel and accessories firms sponsor two major market periods: Spring/Summer and Fall/Winter. During these market periods, buyers from all over the country, and in many

Advertisement reprinted courtesy of The California Mart, Los Angeles, California

Trade showings are exciting occasions for buyers; they plan months in advance for their visits to markets such as this holiday market held at the California Mart.

cases from all over the world, come into the major market areas to view producers' lines. This creates an exciting and stimulating atmosphere for the visiting buyer. Trade showings are occasions for exhibiting new styles in their greatest variety and with a maximum of showmanship.

Dates of such openings and market weeks vary from one segment of the fashion industry to another. They are scheduled according to the lead time required for production and delivery of goods, the convenience of the buyers involved, and the seasonality of consumer demand for the goods.

In order for the retailer to have the merchandise in stock at the time the customer wants to buy it, it is imperative that both buyer and manufacturer clearly understand the lead time required and the stage of the fashion cycle the retailer's customers prefer. Fashions that are already established and at the peak of the fashion cycle require fast design and production schedules to satisfy consumer demand. Classics and styles in the early stage of their cyclical development require a less demanding schedule.

Recently, earlier market openings with a longer spread between showings and delivery completion dates have been the trend. Manufacturers claim that longer lead time is necessary to get the goods produced and into the stores for early testing purposes. Hot items and fashion goods that are short-lived in appeal—those nearing or at the culmination stage of their development—must of necessity be produced and shipped to the retailer so that they are available to the customer at the peak selling period for these items.

RESIDENT BUYING OFFICES

Most buyers of fashion merchandise, with the possible exception of those from the smallest and perhaps the most exclusive shops, make resident buying offices their first port of call on a market trip. A resident buying office, as noted in Chapter 12, is located in a major market area that provides market information and representation to its noncompeting client

mutual / MAIN FLOOR

BUYING SYNDICATE, INCORPORATED

Bulletin #8129-EA-May 14

DEPT.: Dress Accessories

EXCELLENT INCENTIVE PRICE ...

FROM RIDA

A fantastic incentive price from Rida is being
offered to all Mutual stores for the entire Fall
season. Because this resource has been such a
"winner" with us in the past, we are sure the
advantageous price will allow you to increase
your markup.

The entire Fall line of polyester and poly knits
has met our highest expectations in both quality
and fashionability once again this season.

The featured blazer collar top has been chosen
because the Ready-to-Wear silhouette for Fall
is geared toward tailored, suit-dressing ...
A PERFECT CHOICE.

Style#:   800 ... Sizes: S-M-L
Blazer Collar Soft Shirt.

Original Price: $5.00
Incentive Price: 4.75

Colors: White, Bone, Navy, Red, Black,
          Chocolate, Dorset Blue, Wild Berry,
          Spruce, Amber, Bardolino, Rustic

Also featured (at regular price) is #812, a softly
gathered front skirt at $5.00 ... CAN'T BEAT
IT! This style is a perfect color coordinate with
#800, and many other styles in the line.

Resource: RIDA INDUSTRIES
            1410 Broadway, NYC

Terms: 8/10 eom
FOB: Reading, Pa.
Delivery: June 25th

EILEEN AHERN
Divisional Merchandise Manager

11 West 42nd Street, New York, N.Y. 10036 · Phone 212 564-4200
/zz

Mutual Buying Syndicate, Incorporated.

**Bulletins describing new items are sent by buying offices to their client
stores. Note that resource, price, terms, and delivery information are included as well as sizes and colors available.**

361

stores. These stores are usually fairly similar in size and class of trade but are located in different towns and cities throughout the country.

Nearly all resident buying offices have their headquarters in New York City; some have branches in other important market centers both in the United States and abroad. Most of the major offices cover the whole range of department store merchandise, from fashion accessories to home furnishings. A number, however, serve only specialty stores. A few restrict themselves to a narrow range of merchandise, such as infants' and children's wear.

Types of Resident Buying Offices

There are two major types of resident buying offices—independent offices and store-owned offices. An independent resident buying office actively seeks out noncompeting stores as paying clients, while the store-owned office is entirely owned by the store or stores it represents and works exclusively for them.

INDEPENDENT OFFICES. There are many more independent resident buying offices than there are store-owned resident buying offices. The most common of the former type is the **salaried office,** or **fee office,** which is independently owned and operated and charges the stores it represents for the work it does for them. Such offices usually enter into annual contracts with noncompeting stores to provide market services in exchange for an annual, stipulated fee or "salary" based upon each individual store's sales volume.

This type of office strives to familiarize itself with each client store's individual operation and needs and to meet those needs with a broad range of services. These services include the development of private brand merchandise as well as group purchasing of merchandise, store equipment, and store supplies. Among the oldest and best-known offices of this type are the Mutual Buying Syndicate and Felix Lilienthal Co. Also in this category are a number of specialized offices, such as the

Youth Fashion Guild, which serves only children's shops.

STORE-OWNED OFFICES. Resident buying offices that are owned and operated by the stores they represent divide into three groups: private offices, associated or cooperative offices, and syndicate offices.

An office that is owned and operated by a single, out-of-town store organization and performs market work exclusively for that store is called a **private office.** Such an office is actually a staff bureau of the store, located in the market rather than in the store itself. Because of the investment involved and the high cost of operation, only very high-volume department and specialty store organizations maintain their own private resident buying offices.

A second type of store-owned office is an **associated office,** which is one jointly owned and operated by a group of privately owned stores. Membership is by invitation only and is considerably more expensive than if the store were a client of a salaried office. Stores that belong to an associated office, however, are usually highly homogeneous as to sales volume, store policies, and target groups of customers. As a result, their relationship is generally an intimate one, which includes an exchange of operating figures and the sharing of merchandising experiences. The operating expenses of an associated office are allocated to each member store on the basis of sales volume and amount of services required. Typical of this type of buying office are the Associated Merchandising Corporation, Frederick Atkins, and the Specialty Stores Association. However, there are relatively few associated resident buying offices, and their number is steadily decreasing as more and more privately owned store organizations are being absorbed by syndicates and holding corporations.

A third type of store-owned resident buying office is generally known as a syndicate office. A **syndicate office** is an office maintained by a parent organization that owns a group of stores. The office performs market services exclusively for those stores that are owned by the syndicate or holding corporation. Some offices of this type have more authority than do salaried or associated offices for the placing of merchandise orders to be delivered to member stores. In others, authorization from store buyers is required, despite the close corporate relationship. Examples of syndicate offices are those maintained by Allied Stores Corporation, Associated Dry Goods Corporation, and May Department Stores.

Some stores maintain a private office within the facilities of an independent, associated, or syndicate buying office to which they belong. In this way, a store has access to all the services of the larger office, while the private office provides adequate working space for its visiting buyers. Such an office is usually under the direction of a manager who is on the store's payroll and is directly responsible to the store's management.

Table 17-1 is a selected list of independent and store-owned buying offices.

Organization of the Resident Buying Office

The typical resident buying office is organized along lines similar to those of a department or specialty store. In the merchandising division, there are market representatives, whose positions parallel, to a degree, those of retail store buyers. There are also merchandise managers, who supervise groups of market representatives, just as store merchandise managers supervise a limited number of store buyers. There is a fashion coordinator who is respon-

TABLE 17-1
A Selected List of Resident Buying Offices

INDEPENDENT	ASSOCIATED	SYNDICATE
Anstendig & Weinberg	Associated Merchandise Corp.	Allied Stores Marketing Corp.
Apparel Alliance	Frederick Atkins Co.	Associated Dry Goods Corp.
Atlas Buying Corp.	Mercantile Stores	Independent Retailers Syndicate
Jerry Bernstein	Specialty Stores	Macy Corporate Office
Jack Braunstein		May Merchandising Corp.
Carr Buying Office		
Certified Buying Service		
Clothiers Corp.		
Harold Cohen Associates		
Henry Doneger Associates		
Sophie E. Feltz		
Charles Gillenson		
Gordon & Horowitz		
Felix Lilienthal Co.		
Loweth-National Buying Service		
Magerfield-Chernoff		
Mutual Buying Syndicate		
N.R.C. Fashion Merchandising		
Retailers Representative Inc.		
Steinberg-Kass Inc.		
Van Buren-Newman Inc.		
Young Innovators		
Youth Fashion Guild		

sible for information on the overall fashion picture. All of these specialists are available to store buyers who visit the market, although most of a visiting buyer's needs can be handled by the market representative alone.

Other executives in the typical buying office provide sales promotion ideas and aids to client stores, while still others provide assistance in the purchase of supplies and equipment. Some maintain overseas offices and commissionaires in key cities throughout the world. There is a personnel office responsible not only for selecting staff for the buying office itself but also for recruiting junior and senior executives for client stores. In most offices, there also are facilities for exchange of information on the retail operations of the various client stores. The latter are supplementary services, performed in addition to the resident buying office's primary function of keeping in close and constant contact with markets and merchandise.

The Market Representative

A **market representative** is a specialist who covers a narrow segment of the total market and makes information about it available to buyers of stores served by the resident office. Market representatives "live" in their markets and make themselves authorities on supply, demand, styles, prices, deliveries, and any conditions affecting supply and service to retailers. They visit resources, see lines, check into general conditions of supply and demand, verify trends, seek new, hot items, hunt up specific items requested by client stores, and follow up on delivery or other problems referred to them by client store buyers.

Although the market representative's responsibility is similar in many respects to that of a retail store buyer, it differs in one important aspect: Market representatives cannot place orders for client stores except at the explicit request of the appropriate store buyer.

The market representative spends the early hours of each working day at a desk, reviewing mail from stores and seeing items and lines brought to the office's sample rooms by ven-

dors' sales representatives. The market representative is also available to store buyers who may be in the market.

Afternoons are usually spent in the market, tracking down items, reviewing lines in producers' showrooms, and keeping in touch with what is happening in the industries assigned for coverage. In the late afternoon, the market representative returns to desk work, often to prepare a special bulletin to the stores on something they should know about immediately. It might be an opportunity for a special buy from a manufacturer who is closing out remainders, for instance, or the discovery of a new and exciting item that buyers should have a chance to consider without waiting for a market trip.

Merchandising Services

Among merchandising services they provide to their client stores, resident buying offices report on current market information, conduct buyer clinics, in some cases provide central merchandising facilities, arrange for group purchases, and place and follow up on orders.

CURRENT
MARKET INFORMATION. The market representatives are responsible for keeping appropriate buyers and merchandise managers of client stores continually informed of developments and trends in the market or markets that they are assigned to cover. They usually do this by sending out descriptive bulletins about new items, best sellers, and special price offerings, as well as market surveys.

When buyers arrive in the market, they check in first with their store's resident buying office and review their buying plans with the appropriate market representative. In the light of current supply and demand situations, fashion developments, and other pertinent factors, the buyer and market representative determine what changes, if any, should be made in the buying plan.

A great deal of market time is saved for buyers through such early conferences, since the market representative can direct them to those resources best able to fill their needs. If the buyers come to market hoping to locate some item they have not yet seen but have heard about and hope to find, the market representative will either suggest appropriate resources or advise against hunting for it, depending upon the availability and marketability of the particular item.

BUYER CLINICS. Just prior to the start of major market weeks, the resident offices usually arrange a series of meetings or clinics for client store buyers of certain types of merchandise. These sessions are designed to give the buyers an idea of current fashion and market situations before they visit the showrooms of individual producers.

At such meetings the market representatives and other speakers discuss fashion trends, supply, retail prices, and market conditions. Often samples of the new season's merchandise are put on display. Occasionally a manufacturer comes before such a meeting to present a line, a new sales promotion program, or an idea for more effective product merchandising. In the course of such discussions, buyers may develop a new perspective in relation to their buying plans that enables them to make adjustments to improve the plans. Or they may emerge from the meeting with increased confidence in the advisability of following their plans.

CENTRAL MERCHANDISING. With the information that unit controls provide, even a knowledgeable outsider, remote from a store, can gain sufficient insight into the preferences of a store's customers to be able to plan assortments and select merchandise for them. If a resident buying office is given this information about such fast-moving fashion categories as inexpensive dresses and budget sportswear, the buying office can perform this merchandising service for subscriber stores anywhere in the country. The advantage of a central merchandising operation of this type is that the buying office's representatives are in the wholesale markets daily and can make fresh selections or follow up on deliveries of orders constantly. This service, while not as extensively used today as it once was, is ex-

tremely valuable for smaller stores. They usually cannot afford to send their buyers into the market more than twice a year, which is not often enough to keep a stream of fresh, newsworthy fashions coming into stock.

In such a central merchandising operation, each store provides the buying office with a dollar merchandise budget and an assortment plan, to which it adds general observations about its customers' preferences, such as "no sleeveless dresses" or "our people like wide necklines." Using these guides, the resident buying office orders the garments it considers appropriate for each store. The store regularly reports to the buying office all receipts of merchandise, sales, markdowns, and customer returns, just as if it were reporting to a unit control department under its own roof. The records are kept in the buying office, however, so that the merchandiser in charge of the central merchandising operation has a finger on the pulse of demand in each store.

GROUP PURCHASES. Sometimes the market representative or the store buyer may suggest group action in a buying situation. Through **group purchase,** identical merchandise is bought by several stores at one time from a given resource, so that all participants may share in the advantages of a large-volume purchase. Such a group purchase might involve developing special merchandise for the exclusive use of member stores, pooling purchases in order to obtain financial benefits, or encouraging production of a new fashion item not yet widely available in the market but in which the stores have confidence.

A buying office may organize a group purchase when a manufacturer offers closeout merchandise in a quantity that is too large for one store to handle but might be adequately apportioned among several stores. Group purchasing may also be used when the office prepares a group catalog for such occasions as Christmas or back-to-school promotions. When the catalog is one that can be used by a number of stores, a substantial reduction in printing costs can be realized by all the participating stores. Items selected for such a catalog, however, must be agreed upon by all the buyers, and each must plan to set aside sufficient open-to-buy for the styles chosen by the group. Thus participation in group purchases may, on occasion, involve adjustments in the planned assortments.

ORDER PLACEMENT
AND FOLLOW-UP. Market representatives for resident buying offices, other than those maintained by syndicate or corporate holding companies, are not empowered to place orders for client stores. They may do so, however, at the request of store buyers. Frequently, a market representative will send out an illustrated bulletin on a new or hot item, suggesting that the appropriate buyer authorize a sample order for that store. Sometimes, store buyers may allocate a portion of their available open-to-buy to market representatives to be used at the discretion of the latter.

Store buyers often send special orders to market representatives for placement with vendors. This is done to ensure faster service. Vendors might be inclined to overlook an order for one or two pieces of merchandise placed by a store buyer, but they are less apt to do so when that order is personally placed by the representative of a resident buying office that may have numerous potential store customers.

Some stores send copies of orders to resident buying offices for follow-up regarding delivery. Market representatives maintain tickler files on such orders and check with vendors to ensure that deliveries are made as specified.

OTHER SOURCES OF INFORMATION IN THE MARKET

Successful fashion merchants are constantly looking for information to aid them in satisfying their customers' demands. It is usually the fashion buyer well-prepared with additional data and trend information who can best present an exciting, fashion-right assortment of merchandise to the customer. Although buyers come to market with information on their own store's sales and stock experience and are guided by carefully developed buying plans, good buyers are continually collecting additional facts and opinions throughout their market trips. Their major sources of information include the experience of other buyers from their home store, fashion periodicals, manufacturers, trade associations and trade shows, and other, noncompeting stores and their buyers.

Experience of Other Home-Store Buyers

In addition to their own departments' experiences, department or specialty store buyers also call upon the market experiences of other fashion buyers within their own organization. Some retail merchandising executives make a point of having all fashion buyers confer at the end of each day in the market to exchange information and promotional ideas.

For example, a dress buyer's report that many varieties of the bulky-top look are being offered in the market will influence the coat buyer's selection of styles to carry out the bulky look. Furthermore, the fashion accessories buyer will be encouraged to stock varieties of long, bulky scarfs. Each buyer's evaluation of current market fashion trends helps the others evaluate what they find in their markets and results in a more coordinated store-wide fashion image.

Consumer Magazines

The editorial offices of consumer magazines, both those that devote themselves primarily to fashion and those for whom fashion is but one of many subjects of editorial coverage, are usually located in New York City and therefore are a good source of fashion information for visiting buyers. They are in a position to give advance information on the fashion trends to be featured editorially in upcoming issues and on the specific styles to be used as illustrations of those trends. In addition, fashion magazines share with the retailer their considerable knowledge of fashion itself and of the particular segment of consumers to which their pages are addressed.

The editors of these magazines, like the fashion buyers themselves, do not rely upon intuition to guide their selection of fashions. They study their readers carefully, often with the aid of elaborate consumer research projects, observing how their readers live, dress, work, and relax. Like successful fashion merchants, they are in such close rapport with their readers that they can forecast with a high degree of accuracy the styles that will win acceptance in the months ahead.

EDITORIAL CREDITS. When a magazine editor selects a garment or an accessory item to be featured in a forthcoming issue, the usual policy is to invite one or more stores to have their names appear as retail sources for the merchandise that is being editorially featured. Such a mention is known as **editorial credit.** If a store decides to accept such a credit, or mention of its name, it is expected to stock the featured item in sufficient quantity to satisfy local demand. A well-chosen credit does not affect the buying plan, however, since such merchandise normally would be part of the regular assortment. Ideally, a credit simply highlights an item the store would have selected anyway on its own merits.

TREND INFORMATION. Buyers in the market who call at the offices of magazines usually can see photographs or samples of fashion styles to be featured in future issues. A talk with any fashion or merchandising editor will give the buyer information about the trends the selected merchandise exemplifies, reasons why these trends are important to the magazine's readers, and suggestions about possible promotional tie-ins.

RESOURCE INFORMATION. Consumer magazines, as a matter of course, provide retailers with lists of those manufacturers who produce the garments and accessories to be shown in future issues. Their service to the retailer often goes beyond this point, however. As a result of having spent many hours in the market, the fashion editor of a magazine often can direct a buyer to resources for the particular merchandise sought.

FASHION
NEWS AND INSIGHT. Whether or not retailers accept an editorial credit or seek suggestions as to resources, they still can profit by visiting the offices of those periodicals whose readers most closely resemble their own customers in tastes and interests. They are almost certain to come away with information and insights that aid their market work. If nothing else, in the case of publications whose impact is strong among their customers, they will know what merchandise and fashion news will be given magazine exposure in upcoming months, and they can plan to reflect similar influences in their assortments, if they choose to do so.

All this, of course, is in addition to the fashion buyer's required reading of periodicals devoted exclusively to fashion news in both consumer and trade categories. Magazines such as *Vogue, Harper's Bazaar, Glamour,* and *Gentlemen's Quarterly Magazine* provide the buyer with a background on incoming fashions, as do such trade publications as *Women's Wear Daily* and *Men's Wear.* Regardless of the stage of the fashion cycle at which their customers buy, all merchants need to keep abreast of the newest trends. Only in this way can they evaluate the sales potential of their current stock and decide what purchases to make.

Manufacturers

There is much that producers of fashion merchandise can give buyers by way of useful information. The manufacturer who is a major one in the field and who has fairly wide distribution has experience, activities, and marketing plans that provide invaluable assistance to buyers who are in the market to select merchandise.

FASHION PROJECTIONS. Top-ranking producers usually have carefully thought-out reasons behind their decisions to make up certain styles, to use certain materials and colors, and to ignore others. They can also indicate which numbers in their line are frankly experimental and possibly prophetic, which ones are new but nevertheless definitely expected to develop fashion acceptance, and which are carryovers of styles that are no longer new but remain in demand. Equally important is information explaining why they have perhaps ignored some of the ideas that others in the field have taken up. All this becomes part of the background data buyers process in order to arrive at decisions concerning their own assortments.

STORE EXPERIENCE. Manufacturers often pass along valuable information about what other retailers have bought, promoted, and displayed and how they have trained their salespeople. For example, in a certain category of merchandise, a vendor may tell a buyer how one store achieved exceptional turnover and did many times the volume of equivalent stores elsewhere by keeping rigidly to a rule of frequent stock counts and fill-ins. In another instance, the buyer may be told the details of a spectacular promotion through which a store sold more units of higher-priced merchandise than it had ever previously sold. By picking up ideas about how other stores have achieved good results with a line or styles in that line, buyers may find a way to promote their own merchandise assortments more advantageously.

PROMOTIONAL PLANS. The promotional efforts that a vendor plans to invest in a line, style, or trend can have a bearing upon buying decisions. Buyers should weigh the possible impact of a particular type of promotion upon their own stores' customers. For example, a vendor may have plans for a series of advertisements in various consumer magazines. If one or more of these publications is influential among the store's customers, this fact may cause the buyer to buy that line more freely. On the other hand, if the buyer believes that the vendor's promotional program will have little effect upon the store's customers, it will have equally little effect upon the amount purchased from that firm.

Occasionally, without attempting to relate the vendor's advertising directly to its impact on the store's customers, buyers may find their confidence in a certain style reinforced by the fact that the vendor has enough confidence in it to plan an entire season's promotional outlay around it.

PROMOTIONAL TECHNIQUES. Buyers are more likely to purchase radically new merchandise with greater confidence if they have some well-defined ideas for its display and sale. Manufacturers often can offer such ideas. For example, more and more manufacturers are providing counter-sized videotape machines to instruct the customer in the uses of their products. These aid the buyer in sales of new and innovative merchandise. Intimate apparel buyers have also been greatly aided by the new hanging fixtures supplied by manufacturers that encourage sales of matching panties and bras.

TESTED
CONSUMER PREFERENCES. A resource with national distribution is usually completely familiar with regional variations in timing of consumer demand for merchandise, color preferences, and other marketing matters. Certain apparel, for instance, may be purchased earlier and may enjoy a longer selling season in the South than in the North. Certain colors may be perennial favorites in some areas but may fluctuate in popularity in other areas. A buyer who is new to a store or department can obtain helpful guidance on such points from dependable manufacturers. Records left by the preceding buyer may not clearly show the reasoning that governed timing and assortment choice in the past, but a manufacturer often can clarify the situation in a few words.

Trade Associations and Trade Shows

Associations of manufacturers and of retailers assist fashion buyers in many ways. The nature and frequency of the assistance available, however, are not uniform throughout the fashion industries. Some associations offer more help to buyers than others, and buyers learn to familiarize themselves with the degree of as-

Counter-sized videotape machines instruct customers in the uses of a product.

Ken Karp

sistance they may expect in the industries from which they buy.

RETAIL BUYERS' GROUPS. Associations or clubs for buyers of a single classification of merchandise provide an opportunity for the exchange of opinion with others. At the very least, such an opportunity aids buyers in clarifying their own ideas about fashion and market conditions. In some instances, groups of this kind provide a medium through which buyers can transmit to an entire industry their preferences in matters ranging from the dates when lines should be opened to the sizes of stock boxes to be used. Many such associations are subsidized by the industries concerned, or by trade publications, or both.

TRADE SHOWS. Retail or manufacturer groups, and sometimes independent organizations, establish trade shows at which a great many manufacturers in a given industry exhibit their lines under one roof and at the same time. "Under one roof" usually means a hotel, or two or three hotels, in which several floors are set aside for exhibit space. With a minimum of time and travel, buyers can see almost every line they want to see. They can make comparisons and can exchange opinions in "corridor talk" with other buyers from all over the country. The impact of seeing so many lines in so short a space of time is great, and a clear impression of what the market offers can be readily gained. This is especially helpful in industries in which small firms predominate. The buyer can look in on dozens of them in one day at such a show, instead of trekking from building to building, up and down elevators, and possibly covering only four or five showrooms in as many hours.

Among the industries in which such shows are regularly staged for retail buyers are shoes, notions, piece goods, and men's sportswear.

FASHION BULLETINS. Many trade associations publish fashion bulletins for buyers, to alert them to fashion trends and to explain their significance in terms of retail opportunities. Since whatever helps the retailer to sell an industry's products also helps the industry itself, some of these associations retain experts in retail merchandising and promotion. These experts contribute suggestions to buyers about advertising, selling, and display related to current fashions. Especially noteworthy are the bulletins of some of the associations in the raw materials fields, which discuss colors and textures to be featured in coming seasons.

RETAIL CONVENTIONS. Retailers' associations regularly hold conventions or meetings for their members. Some of the sessions are devoted to subjects of interest to fashion merchants and buyers, especially in areas that present unusual problems or opportunities. The National Retail Merchants Association, at its annual convention (always held in New York City in early January), devotes sessions to various selected categories of merchandise whenever fashion developments (or the lack thereof) in the merchandise concerned make these worthwhile. For many years, also, a regular feature of NRMA conventions has been a discussion of outstanding retail fashion promotions during the previous year and the elements that made each successful.

Other Stores, Other Buyers

Buyers meet with representatives of noncompeting stores through the resident buying office. In the market, they find themselves also in contact with a host of other buyers. Informal conversations can become the medium for exchange of opinions and experience with other retailers.

In addition to such contacts, buyers visiting a market city make a point of looking over the merchandise and displays of local stores. Chatting with a local buyer about some of the new ideas or new merchandise seen in the department may prove stimulating and profitable to the visiting buyer.

Making the rounds of the stores in a large city also provides buyers with an opportunity to gauge the progress of various fashions. They can observe where each stands in its life cycle and how much or how little emphasis is given to them in stores of varying degrees of fashion leadership.

Visiting other stores is also a way to check how far the copying-down process has gone for styles that interest a buyer. Buyers for a medium-priced store, for example, may decide against ordering an otherwise acceptable style because they see that it has been "knocked off" (copied) at low prices and may already be carried in basement departments and discount houses.

WORKING THE MARKET

Shorter but more frequent trips are becoming increasingly important to fashion buyers. During these shorter trips buyers make the decisions that are so vital to the profitability of their departments and to their stores. Maximizing the productivity of these short trips in the market is imperative.

Buyers develop their own techniques and procedures for covering many resources and for doing so with a minimum of physical strain. Because of the time limitation, certain basic procedures should be followed. These involve planning each day's activities in advance, note-taking, and writing up orders.

Order of Seeing Lines

Before setting out each morning, a buyer should have a tentative itinerary set up for calls to be made that day. The schedule cannot be too rigid, since delays are bound to occur. Nevertheless, some sort of itinerary helps a buyer to make sure that each day in the market produces its quota of calls.

GEOGRAPHICAL. Some buyers, keenly aware of time limitations, visit showrooms in what might be called geographical order: one building at a time. With dozens of vendors' showrooms in each skyscraper in Garment Town (as the area in which apparel and accessories showrooms are located is affectionately named), the calls made in one building alone can often make up a good day's work for the buyer. On the other hand, the building-by-building technique may fail to produce an overall impression of trends, because each building tends to draw tenants dealing in the same type and price range of goods. To get a

Many buyers plan to visit the showrooms of their prime resources first. There they examine the vendor's line carefully.

more general view, several buildings must be visited.

BY TYPE
AND PRICE LINES. Other buyers, at some cost to themselves in terms of effort, ignore geography. They instead concentrate their efforts on shopping as much of the market as possible for the specific types and price lines of merchandise in which they are interested. The advantage of this type of shopping is that buyers can compare one vendor's merchandise with that of others while impressions are fresh in their minds.

BY PRIME RESOURCES. A third approach is to first visit **prime resources,** those from which their departments have consistently bought a substantial amount of merchandise in past seasons. Under normal circumstances, buyers can expect to continue to purchase an important share of their goods from these resources as long as the merchandise continues

to meet the customer demand and quality standards of their stores.

Rapport between buyers and such resources is usually excellent, and the exchange of ideas and information fairly rapid. Hopefully the buyers can find much of the merchandise for which they are shopping in the showrooms of their prime resources and can proceed to complete their market tour in a more relaxed frame of mind. Also, when they know what their prime resources are showing, buyers are in a better position to evaluate the styles they see later in other showrooms.

BY PRICE LINES. Still another approach is by price line, or visiting the showrooms of higher-priced resources in each class of merchandise first and then continuing the visits through successively lower-priced markets. Although this approach has obvious disadvantages, buyers usually find more fashion news, more original styling, and more fashion information among the higher-priced vendors than among those in the lower-priced brackets. Buyers who prefer this method point out that it gives them a quick overview of fashion trends as an important base for evaluation of all other lines to be seen during the remainder of the trip.

The choice of method is usually left to the buyer, unless the store has established a preferred method. In a store that strives for fashion leadership, buyers may be required to see the showrooms of the fashion leaders among their resources first. They then meet with the store's other fashion buyers to evaluate what they have seen and to decide which fashions or looks appear right for their store. Only then are buyers free to go on with the rest of their market work.

Showroom Procedures

When important resources first show or "open" a new seasonal line for retail buyers' inspection, most buyers review the line in its entirety, usually taking notes on styles of special interest. Buyers of stores that are regular customers of individual vendors then usually make an appointment for a return showroom visit. At that time, they work with their regular salesperson in reviewing the vendor's line. Styles that originally impressed the buyer are again evaluated, as well as any others that the salesperson believes, because of past experience, would be of special interest to the customers of the buyer's store. Such showroom visits usually are quite time-consuming, and buyers have to plan accordingly.

As each season advances, buyers may make additional market trips for reasons previously discussed. They may visit vendors' showrooms to check on orders placed when the new line was opened, portions of which have not yet been delivered. The purpose of such a visit may be to revise undelivered orders in light of actual store sales experience. Or they may wish to reorder styles that have sold well. Or they may be searching the market for specific merchandise in line with their buying plans. Such showroom visits must be brief. Wise buyers see to it that they do not permit eager salespeople to take up more valuable time on this type of market trip than the buyer can afford. In the interest of maintaining good vendor relations, however, the buyer should never appear curt, impatient, or rude with either vendors or their sales staff.

Managements urge buyers to listen to the sales staff's comments and suggestions and to avoid cutting off what might prove a source of useful information. They instruct them, also, to tell their resources about the success they have had with the line and to express appreciation of business courtesies extended—if only to prepare for some possible future day when they have to request a favor from the resource. Business, and especially the exchange of information about the fashion business, proceeds best in an atmosphere of mutual respect. And respect is what store managements expect their buyers to establish in the market.

Taking Numbers

Normally buyers do not write up orders when they are looking at lines in vendors' showrooms. Instead, they take numbers. **Taking numbers** means writing an adequate description of each style the buyer is considering for possible purchase, including style number, size range, available colors, fabric, wholesale price, and any other details the buyer considers relevant to the style.

It is important to note here that when buyers are viewing a vendor's line, they are mentally converting the quoted wholesale price into an established retail price line at which that merchandise should be marked if they are to maintain the average departmental markup required by their merchandising plans. They must also evaluate whether the item under consideration compares favorably in quality with the merchandise they now own or have on order at the same retail price line. Furthermore, they must consider whether the new item has a limited or excellent sales potential in their stores. Should the new item fail to meet any of the above requirements, the buyer would be well advised to postpone the decision about purchasing the item or perhaps even eliminate the item from further consideration.

In some classifications, such as scarfs, gloves, hosiery, and costume jewelry, the lines buyers view may be very extensive, and they may find it difficult to write a sufficient description of each number for later recall. For such merchandise, a buyer separates the samples into three groups: desirable, less desirable, and least desirable. Later, when the entire line has been examined, the buyer takes the numbers of those styles of greatest interest.

At the end of their trips, buyers compare descriptions of similar merchandise they have seen during their market trip, eliminate duplications and less desirable styles, and make their decisions as to exactly which styles they wish to purchase. If such restraint is not exercised, a buyer may order too lavishly from the first few resources, leaving no funds for possibly more desirable merchandise later. Buyers retain for future references, however, those numbers they have taken but decided not to order at the time. These may serve a valuable purpose should the style the buyer did order be cancelled or should customers request merchandise that was seen but not ordered.

After eliminating the less desirable styles and developing what they believe to be the best possible list of numbers from those they have seen, some buyers work again with the buying office's market representative. They call on the latter's intimate knowledge of a specific market for further guidance before actually writing up their orders.

Writing the Order

Until an order has actually been placed, buyers are free to change their mind about what they want to order. Once they have placed an order, however, it is considered a contract between the store and the vendor, and buyers have committed their stores to take the merchandise. Any change of mind at some later date requires the written permission of the vendor with whom the order has been placed.

Atlanta Apparel Mart

Buyers need the ability to take ample notes quickly, even during the excitement of a fast-paced fashion show.

To ensure that an order covers all required points and to avoid committing the store to unacceptable conditions, buyers should write up orders only on the forms provided by their own stores (or, in some instances, on the forms of their resident buying offices) and not on the vendor's form. The common practice is to write up orders after leaving the market and to have them countersigned by the merchandise manager or other responsible store official.

Buyers should always determine from the vendor exactly when the latter expects to ship each style of merchandise that is being ordered. This is of utmost importance for two reasons. First, the buyer's open-to-buy is reduced by the retail value of all merchandise ordered for delivery each month. Second, the buyer needs this information in planning ads and other promotional activities.

The typical store order form requires the buyer to specify:

- The date of the order.
- The vendor's name and address, together with the shipping point, if different from the showroom address. (A vendor may maintain a sales office in New York City but produce and ship from elsewhere.)
- Shipping instructions, including the date by which all shipments should be completed or the order can be legally cancelled, the route by which shipments should be sent, and all arrangements relating to shipping costs.
- The terms of sale (how soon after shipment the invoice must be paid, and with what discount).
- The department for which the goods are purchased.
- The address of the store unit to which shipment should be made (if store wishes deliveries to be made to other than the main store).
- Any special directions about packing and shipping. (For example, a store with several branches may request each branch's goods to be separately packed and labeled, even though all merchandise is to be received at a central location.)
- Details of styles purchased, including classification, number, description, and cost price. Descriptions, depending on the article, should specify color, fabric, size, or other relevant points. There should be enough information to make it easy for the store's receiving department, as well as for the vendor's shipping room, to know exactly what the order specifies. Failure to include this information on an order leaves the vendor free to ship anything.
- The retail price (shown only on the store's copies of the order, not on the vendor's copy). The buyer indicates the unit retail price intended for each style number. Thus the total retail as well as the total cost value of each order can be calculated, and the initial markup percentage can be worked out. On copies of the order that are intended for the marking room, the column of cost figures is blacked out, and only the retail prices, needed for making up price tickets, are visible.
- Any special arrangements concerning the purchase. (For example, the vendor may agree to contribute a specified amount, under specified conditions, toward the advertising of a purchase; or as is sometimes the case, particularly in orders for such merchandise as furs and high-ticket jewelry items, the buyer may have the privilege of returning unsold goods by a specified date. This is known as **buying on consignment**.)
- Standard trade practices. Established many years ago by the National Retail Merchants Association in cooperation with the associations representing the apparel trades, these practices are usually printed on the back of each store's order blank. The provisions spell out the obligations of buyer and seller to one another and define what constitutes fair or unfair practice in relation to an order.

Merchandising Notes

At the time they write up their orders, buyers also should write up brief notes about the merchandise ordered, the reasons for choosing it, and the overall impression gained from the market trip. From these notes they later prepare training talks for their salespeople about incoming merchandise and fashion trends. These notes also may serve as memos about the selling points of the goods for salespeople as well as for the advertising and display departments. If they do this work while the merchandise is fresh in their minds and while enthusiasm for it is strong, some of the excitement of the market trip will spread to everyone else at the store who will eventually be concerned with the sale of the merchandise.

TESTING NEW FASHIONS

Astute merchants avoid taking too many chances in deciding which fashion will be accepted by their customers. There is risk in letting oneself be carried away by enthusiasm for a new fashion that one has seen in the market. The same risk is present when buyers assume that their own ideas of the right color, line, or texture are identical with those of customers. Merchants risk their fashion reputation in the community, as well as capital, every time they select a new style for stock.

Most merchants greet a new fashion with the sample-test-reorder technique. They buy in small quantities in a wide range of possibly acceptable styles to observe customer reaction. Then they reorder in substantial quantity those styles and colors that appear to have won an initial favorable reception; the rest are quickly marked down and cleared out.

For example, suppose that every indication points to a growing popularity of pale, neutral shades in wool dresses. A buyer may feel very strongly that off-white will be the season's preferred neutral shade and that shirtwaist types will be the preferred styles. Instead of buying off-white shirtwaists alone, however, the buyer will perhaps try white, off-white, and pale beige and will purchase each color sparingly in several styles. When the goods arrive at the store, customer comments as well as actual sales will determine which colors and styles are best received. The buyer may find that pale beige is as well received as off-white; therefore, ample quantities of both colors should be ordered.

At this point, the buyer places additional orders for the most acceptable styles. These may or may not be the same styles originally thought to have the greatest sales potential. Actual experience now gives the buyer more confidence to purchase in larger quantities.

The testing procedure is not entirely risk-proof, however. In offering customers a wide range of styles at the start of the season, a merchant inevitably stocks certain numbers that will have to be marked down because they are hard to sell. In general, however, the losses that occur are far less than they might have been had no testing been done.

An increasingly difficult problem facing all retailers today is that producers of budget and moderate-priced fashion goods are becoming reluctant to accept reorders for any but the most classic of their styles. Instead they prefer to offer newer styles throughout a selling season. Customers, too, are making it plain that they want to see new styles each time they shop a fashion department.

If a market trip is not scheduled for the immediate future, the astute buyer can usually handle such problems in one of two ways. First, the buyer can consult merchandising notes and check with the producers of style numbers taken but not ordered on the last market trip. What the buyer is looking for is merchandise with the same or similar characteristics (details of design and colors) as that which already proved successful on the selling floor and which will apparently continue in appeal if the merchandise is available for immediate delivery. Second, the buyer can consult the appropriate market representative at the store's resident buying office for sources of newer styles with similar characteristics.

MERCHANDISING VOCABULARY

Associated office

Buying on consignment

Buying plan

Editorial credit

Group purchase

Market representative

Prime resources

Private office

Salaried, or fee, office

Syndicate office

Taking numbers

MERCHANDISING REVIEW

1. What factors usually determine how often buyers go to market? For what reasons, other than viewing seasonal lines, do buyers make market trips?
2. What are the major purposes served by a buying plan? What information, other than identifying data, is usually required on a buying plan?
3. In preparation for drawing up a buying plan, what specific aspects of the present stock assortment must the buyer carefully review?
4. What is the major function of a resident buying office? Describe the four major types of resident buying offices.
5. Name and briefly describe the five major merchandising services provided by resident buying offices to clients.
6. What is a "market representative"? Distinguish between the responsibilities of a market representative and those of a store buyer. Name at least five activities engaged in by a market representative.
7. Name five valuable sources of fashion information available to a buyer on a market trip. In what specific ways can each of these sources aid a buyer?
8. Why is it necessary for buyers, while on a market trip, to carefully plan their daily itineraries? What options do buyers have in working the market?
9. What is meant by the term "taking numbers"? What important factors must a buyer consider when viewing a line and taking numbers? Why is it advisable to take numbers rather than writing an order at once?
10. What is the sample-test-reorder technique? What are its advantages to fashion merchants and buyers?

MERCHANDISING DIGEST

1. Discuss the various reasons why buyers visit vendors' showrooms and the typical procedures involved. What are the buyer's responsibilities in vendor relations?
2. Discuss the legal aspects of a purchase order, the types of information required on most order forms, and the possible penalties for not completing forms accurately.

MERCHANDISING ASSIGNMENTS

1. You are a market representative for a resident buying office whose clients are large-volume department stores located mainly in the Southern states. Many of the stores have questioned the benefits of their office affiliation. Their arguments have been that the information they receive from the office is not additional data, but frequently a duplication of facts obtained from various other sources.

Therefore, the office has requested that all market representatives evaluate their function in relation to the services and information offered to their clients.

It is July 15, and the divisional merchandise manager of the fashion accessories' division of the resident buying office has asked each market representative to indicate at their weekly divisional meeting the information on developments that each will be submitting in the August 1st report to the store buyers.

    a. You are the market representative for _____.
List the *possible reports* that would be significant at the beginning of the fall season.

    b. *Prepare a market bulletin* appropriate for the information you want to provide to the stores. Invent any facts you don't have (name of manufacturer, cost, colors, etc.). Be sure to include all pertinent facts the store buyer would need in order to take action on your communication. Bring into class (attached to report) the actual picture of the merchandise featured in the bulletin.

    c. Prepare a *list of services* that are, or should be, offered to store buyers, whether in the market or the store.

2. A blouse buyer is required to make a special purchase of 50 dozen blouses for a storewide sale. The merchandise manager's instructions are that blouses of the quality for which the store regularly paid $96 a dozen should be purchased, but that in this instance not more than $84 a dozen should be paid. The buyer is also directed not to buy discontinued numbers, seconds, poor colors, or odd sizes.

It is the height of the selling season, and the buyer is at a loss in deciding which merchandise resource to approach. Consider the following possibilities:

Resource A: A manufacturer from whom the buyer has made occasional purchases, at regular prices
Resource B: A manufacturer with whom the buyer has not been doing business, but who has been "drumming" the store for the past year, anxious for the account
Resource C: A manufacturer who has obtained, over a period of years, a good share of the buyer's business
Resource D: A jobber who frequently has "specials" and from whom the buyer has bought only on rare occasions

Problem:
a. Determine which resource is most likely to fulfill the buyer's request.
b. List the above resources in the order in which they would be most likely to meet the buyer's wishes, and explain your indicated order.
c. List the resources in the order you think the buyer would *prefer* them to be, regardless of their actual willingness.

18
PROMOTING FASHIONS: ADVERTISING AND DISPLAY

Planning to sell fashion goods to consumers without sales promotion is like planning a party without inviting the guests. Although everything may be ready, nobody comes. Fashion merchants do not assume that customers will come to their doors without encouragement or reminders. "Goods well-bought are half-sold" is a familiar saying among retailers. They know that half the job of selling fashion to the consumer consists of recognizing what the consumer wants and offering assortments geared to those wants. They also know that the other half of the selling effort is sales promotion—the business of arousing the consumer's buying impulses. This half requires just as much careful planning and execution as the other. Because fashion today is fast-moving and very highly competitive, everyone in the fashion business, from the designer with a new sketch to the merchant with new styles in stock, is eager to talk about, show, and promote the sales of new goods. Sales promotion is an essential tool in the ongoing efforts to attract customer patronage.

How sales are promoted varies with each fashion merchant. A small, exclusive shop may rely on word-of-mouth to bring in new customers. The loyalty of established customers can be reinforced by an occasional call from the owner to announce the arrival of new styles. On the other hand, it is likely that a large, low-priced retail store will make extensive use of all media—radio, television, newspaper, and throw-aways—to bring in crowds of customers.

In the 1970s a number of the nation's larg-est, branch-operating retailers began to dramatize and expand their sales promotional efforts in order to meet increasing competition, improve customer patronage, and enhance store image. As part of their stepped-up program, they invested millions of dollars in renovating and upgrading both the layout and decor of their stores. It was at this time that a number of the stores coined a new name for their expanded sales promotional activities— **visual merchandising.** As the term is used it includes everything visual that is done with, to, or for a product and its surroundings to help sell that product. Visual merchandising includes display; print, broadcast, or film advertising; publicity; store layout; and store decor.

Visual merchandising concerns itself with the "store as theater." It uses theatrical techniques to entice customers into impulse buying. Its purpose is to turn stodgy stores into exciting bazaars for shoppers, and to provide expert showcasing for the merchandise. According to Stephen L. Pistner, while president of the huge Dayton-Hudson Corporation, "The store as theater is more important for the 1980s than ever before. The customer wants excitement. And, despite all the demands on a person's time, shopping still is one of the most important leisure-time activities."[1]

Visual merchandising, as it is carried out in the larger stores, is an expensive approach to merchandising that is not financially feasible for a great number of stores. The concept of including store layout and decor with the more traditional sales promotion activities of advertising, display, and publicity, is a valid one, however, even for stores with considerably lower sales volume and limited budgets.

No matter how it is done, however, sales promotion must be ongoing if fashion goods are to be sold while they are still desirable.

SALES PROMOTION DIVISION

Traditionally, in medium-to large-volume stores, there is a sales promotion division which is responsible for promoting sales through advertising, display, and publicity. (See Chapter 10.) In some stores, personal salesmanship is also considered part of this function. The function of **sales promotion,** therefore, may be defined as the coordination of advertising, display, publicity, and personal salesmanship in order to promote profitable sales.

Organization

In small stores where there is a relatively modest amount of promotional activity, there is usually a sales promotion manager who is directly involved in managing all of these activities. Where the volume of promotional activity is too large for such an arrangement, an advertising manager and a display manager usually function under the direction of the sales promotion director. The director may personally handle publicity and its close relative, public relations. Very large stores have a publicity manager as well, who supervises special events, the activities of consumer boards, and so on. In this case, the sales pro-

motion director, often a vice-president, is free for policymaking and for long-range planning.

Operation

The chief executive of the sales promotion division is responsible for preparing storewide sales promotion plans and budgets in conference with the advertising manager, the display manager, the publicity or special-events manager, the merchandise managers, and, if there is one, the fashion coordinator. Such plans and budgets are based on storewide sales goals, which have been developed earlier from six-month dollar merchandise plans (as explained in Chapter 13).

These storewide sales promotion plans indicate, by specific type of activity such as advertising, display, and special events, the extent to which the store intends to employ each in its effort to produce the total storewide sales planned for the upcoming season. Included in the master sales promotion plan are such regularly scheduled events as Anniversary Sales, White Sales, and Back-to-School promotions. Also included are other important and timely storewide, divisional, or departmental promotions for Easter, Father's Day, Mother's Day, and so on. Each department of the sales promotion division—advertising, display, and special events—then prepares its own seasonal plan and budget based on the amount of money allocated to it in the storewide promotional budget. This department plan designates in general terms how that money shall be used to implement the master plan.

The percentage of planned dollar sales allocated to sales promotion varies from store to store. It depends on the type of store and the policy of the store with respect to the nature and extent of promotional activities it chooses to employ. The percentage of departmental planned dollar sales allocated to sales promotion expense also varies from department to department. This depends mainly on the merchandise involved and sometimes on the extent of local competition as well. Sales promotion budgets for fashion departments are usually higher than those for departments selling semistaple or staple goods. For instance, an active sportswear department may have a budget as low as 2 percent of planned sales, while a fur department may have a budget as high as 5 percent of sales.

By far the largest share of the sales promotion division's budget each season is allocated to advertising, and the major share of the advertising budget is usually allocated to newspaper space. In spite of the emphasis given to newspaper advertising, however, it is not the only promotional medium used by stores. Rarely does a fashion merchant rely solely on a single type of sales promotion. Instead, most merchants use every available method and carefully coordinate their efforts.

Thus, when a newspaper advertisement is run, good retail practice requires that the same merchandise and its selling points be featured in departmental displays and possibly in window displays as well. It also requires that salespeople be briefed on what is being featured, as well as when and why the ad is being run. In addition, whenever possible, publicity is sought to back up sales promotion efforts. The effectiveness of a store's promotional efforts depends on the effectiveness of each separate activity in motivating customers.

FASHION ADVERTISING

Advertising is the paid use of space or time in any medium. Advertising may appear in newspapers, magazines, direct-mail pieces, shopping news bulletins, theater programs, catalogs, and bus cards. It may appear on billboards and on radio and television. Retailers make use of some or all of these media to promote the sale of fashion merchandise.

Most large department stores and specialty stores have an "in-house" advertising department. This department is supervised by the sales promotion manager with the aid of a copy chief and art director. The benefits of having an in-house advertising department are many, one of the most important being the ability to act quickly on changes in fashion. By working in a store, copywriters and artists can also develop and maintain a familiarity with the store's target customer.

Because it is very costly for a store to operate an advertising department, however, many smaller stores, including furniture and men's specialty stores, prefer to use an outside advertising agency. The advertising departments referred to in this chapter are those traditionally maintained in-house by large department and specialty stores.

Types of Advertisements

There are two basic types of ads used by stores. One is designed to sell items, the other to "sell" a store's image.

A **merchandise** or **promotional advertisement** is one that endeavors to create sales of specific items. Goodwill, store image, and enhancement of the store's fashion prestige are incidental, although these are nevertheless considered when any such ad is planned and prepared. Figure 18-1 is an example of a merchandise, or promotional, advertisement.

A **prestige** or **institutional advertisement** is one that "sells" the store rather than specific merchandise. It may discuss a new fashion trend. It may point out the store's value as a headquarters for fashion news, for bargains, or for clothes for the family. Perhaps it may publicize a community event. Any merchandise mentioned in the ad is usually considered incidental. The ad's value to the store is measured solely in terms of such intangibles as prestige, goodwill, and enhanced store image.

Advertising Plan

An **advertising plan** is a projection of the advertising that a store intends to use over a period of time, such as a season, quarter, month, or week, in order to attract business. In general, such a plan outlines the dates on which advertisements will be used, the departments and items to be advertised, the estimated sales expected to result from such ads, the media to be employed, the amount of space or time to be used in each medium, and the cost thereof. The cost is usually estimated both in dollars and as a percentage of the sales expected to be realized.

Berry's

Downtown and All Branches.

CANVAS
the City, the Country,
the World—Totes Always Get The Vote!

Canvas is the one. Our spacious, weightless, cotton canvas bags carry not only the vote, but any number of town and travel necessities. Though we don't suggest you vote on the basis of good looks alone, we know you'll flip for the great colors, done with zippy contrasting webbing trims.
Clockwise from bottom left:

Roll: red, navy, black or natural, 17×10, 17.00
   Shoulder Bag: natural, tan, navy or red, 11½×10½, 16.00
     Maxi Tote: red, navy, black, natural or tan, 16½×13, 18.00
      Ring: navy, natural, black, yellow, Kelly green, pink, red or tan, 11½×10, 15.00
       Kangaroo Pocket Tote: natural, black, navy, red, yellow, Kelly green, pink, brown or beige, 17×12½, 17.00

Figure 18-1

The outlay for newspaper space, the most widely used medium among fashion retailers, amounts to more than 3 percent of the typical department store's annual net sales. In individual fashion departments, newspaper space costs vary. On an annual basis, they amount to about 4 percent of sales in coat departments, 3 percent of sales in junior dress departments, and 2.5 percent of sales in handbag departments. The amount of newspaper advertising done, expressed as a percentage of net sales, varies considerably from month to month throughout any given year.

PREPARING THE PLAN. The storewide advertising plan is a general guide to the timing and amount of advertising to be done by each department in the store during a specific season or other period of time. Exact dates, selection of media, decisions on ad sizes, writing of copy, and other details are worked out later, closer to publication time.

Both the budget and the schedule of the general plan are prepared with the understanding that unforeseen developments may require sudden adjustments. These are the same kinds of adjustments that merchandise plans sometimes require. An advertisement that produces spectacular sales results may be repeated promptly, even if the original plan did not call for a second run. Conversely, a planned ad may be scrapped if the merchandise to back it up is not in stock or for some other sound reason.

After the storewide advertising plan has been prepared, it is broken down first into seasonal plans for each selling department and then into monthly plans for those departments. The monthly plans are drawn up about a month in advance. They specify the item or items to be advertised, the dates on which ads will appear, the size of each ad, and the medium in which it will appear.

SOURCES OF
INFORMATION FOR PLANNING. Like the merchandise plan, the advertising plan is based on past experience, present conditions, and future expectations. The advertising department keeps careful records in scrapbook form of what was advertised last year, how it was advertised, at what cost, and with what results. Such a scrapbook contains tear sheets of all advertising previously run. On each ad is noted the dollar cost of the ad and the sales that resulted from it, as reported by the department for which the ad was run. When drawing up an advertising plan for a new season, the planner goes through the scrapbooks for similar periods in previous years and studies both the ads run and their sales results. Each season's plans incorporate as many features as possible of successful advertising used in the past. They avoid the features of that advertising which did not produce desired sales results.

The same factors that buyers and merchandise managers review when preparing their merchandise budget and plan are important in preparing promotional plans. These factors include conditions inside and outside the store; management's goals; indications of promotions planned by resources, publications, and competitors; and any other factors that might affect the store's own plans.

The experience of other retailers is also used in planning. In addition to the store's own advertising scrapbook, the advertising manager studies the advertising of other stores, particularly that of competitors whose advertising results have been observed. Also studied is the advertising of friendly noncompeting stores in other communities which are willing to exchange advertising information.

Through such sources as the store's resident buying office, the National Retail Merchants Association, and various trade publications, each advertising executive keeps in touch with the promotion experience of other stores. Reports of what is being advertised, shown, and sold in the country's top fashion stores are eagerly studied. So, too, are the advertising pages of consumer fashion magazines. Such reports are often a source of inspiration to advertising managers. Managers evaluate them, however, in terms of their own store's target group of customers. They know that the spectacular results from an ad placed by Saks Fifth Avenue, for example, might not be duplicated in their own stores if they placed an identical ad. Yet the approach used by another retail store may trigger an idea that can be used.

Finally, advertising staffs constantly need information from the merchandising division in order to develop effective copy and illustrations. They expect buyers and merchandisers to give the advertising department details about specific fashion trends and to indicate noteworthy features of items that are to be advertised.

Newspaper Advertising

Retailers use local newspapers extensively in promoting fashion merchandise because their customers are mainly from within the areas served by such newspapers. Producers whose fashion goods have national or at least regional distribution tend to favor national magazines for their ads. Some may cooperate with their retail store customers, however, by helping the stores pay for ads of their merchandise in local newspapers.

Newspapers are the retailers' preferred advertising medium because they provide immediate impact and broad local exposure. The time between preparation and insertion of an ad can be quite short, and last-minute changes can be handled readily. Compared with a monthly magazine whose ad pages ''close'' weeks before publication, a daily paper normally can accept changes almost up to the moment that its presses begin to roll. And this is only a matter of a few hours before the edition is on the streets.

Speed is vital in promoting fashion merchandise. A newspaper ad can be prepared for new fashion merchandise even before the goods are in stock, provided the resource has made a firm promise of delivery and can be relied upon. Should there be an unforeseen delay in the availability of the merchandise, the ad can be pulled at the eleventh hour. The importance of this last-minute flexibility is obvious in view of the many kinds of sudden changes that can require a change in advertising plans.

In a community where several newspapers are published, each attracts a particular readership in terms of income, education, and interests. Fashion retailers advertise in the paper that appeals to the readers who are most similar to their own clientele in fashion awareness and income level. In New York, for example, stores that feature fashions in the early stages of their cycles usually buy space in *The New York Times,* which reaches affluent, city-oriented, fashion-aware customers. Stores or departments that offer fashions at the peak and in the declining stages of their cycles have less reason to use the *Times* and therefore rely upon other city or suburban papers. Occasionally an enterprising suburban or small-town store will advertise its newest fashions in a prestigious, big-city paper that has circulation in its community. Much of the paper's circulation is wasted as far as such a store is concerned, but the use of a city newspaper dramatizes the store's fashion authority in the eyes of city-oriented members of its community.

PREPARING THE AD. The preparation of a newspaper ad can begin in one of several places in the advertising department. If the ad depends upon visual impact to get its point across, it will probably first go to the art director for rendering. If it is a routine presentation of fashion, however, or demands that an imaginative tone be set, chances are that the copywriter will be the one to start it on its way. But in either case, it is the buyer who actually initiates an ad. Only the buyer can set in motion the complex process that begins with the arrival of a sample fashion and ends with an advertisement that motivates the public to purchase the fashion.

A buyer may verbally introduce a fashion item at the weekly advertising meeting of the advertising manager, copywriters, and art staff. The divisional merchandise manager and other buyers from that division may also be present. The buyer must then make a formal **advertising request.** A typical example of the form used for such a request is shown in Figure 18-2.

Copywriters are constantly asking buyers to include more information in their advertising requests. Buyers, pressed by other duties, often urge the copywriters to make do with

ADVERTISED MERCHANDISE INFORMATION

Berry's

Advertising information and the merchandise to be illustrated must be in the Advertising Department two weeks prior to the week in which the ad runs in the newspaper.

Department No.	**74**
Date Ad Runs:	**June 1, 198–**
Paper(s):	**Tribune**
Space:	**7-col. full**

Item	Regular Price	Sale Price
Cotton canvas tote bags Matching webbing belts	Bags $15-18 Belts $6	No

List features in order of importance

1. Spacious, weightless, cotton canvas totes for town or travel

2. Five featured styles, wide assortment of colors, darks, neutrals, high shades

3. Webbing trim in contrasting colors, belts in cotton webbing matching bag trim

Sizes: Roll: 17 × 10, #17, Kangaroo pocket, 17 × 12-1/2, #17; Shoulder: 11-1/2 × 10-1/2, #16; Ring: 11-1/4 × 10, #15; Maxi: 16-1/2 × 13, #18

Colors: Roll: red, navy, black, natural; Shoulder: natural, tan, navy, red; Kangaroo and Ring: natural, black, navy, red, kelly green, pink, tan; Maxi: red, navy, black, natural, tan

Art Instructions: Sketch woman's torso showing belt, bags, cascading down length of page

At What Stores: At all stores

Submitted by: Dorothy Smith, buyer

Date Received in Advertising Department: May 15, 198 –

Does manufacturer share cost of ad? Yes Is credit claim attached? Yes

Reason for Advertising:

- ☒ New Line
- ☒ Fashion News
- ☐ Sale
- ☐ Special Purchase
- ☐ Staple Stock
- ☐ Clearance

Quantity on Hand Date Ad Runs	Date Merchandise will be in Stock	Total Retail value of Merchandise	Use Trade Mark or Label	Is Manufacturer Paying for Ad?	Extra Delivery Charge?	Telephone Orders?	Mail Orders?	Mail Order Coupon?
250 pcs	5/26 complete	$3,750	Yes ☐ No ☒	Yes ☒ No ☐ 20 % of Payment	Yes ☐ No ☒ Amount? ___	Yes ☒ No ☐	Yes ☒ No ☐	Yes ☐ No ☒

Figure 18-2

what they have. In fact, a brief description of the item, together with a few words that describe its importance and why the customer will want to buy it, are all that the advertising copywriter needs to write attention-getting copy.

For instance, a buyer may write: "Sleeveless, rayon crepe dress with surplice top. White, polyester linen jacket. Dress in red print. Jacket with 3/4 roll sleeve. Sizes 6 to 14. $100." The copywriter then translates this into: "Our jacket dress doesn't keep 9 to 5 hours . . . here are two pieces that will dance you right out of the office and into the evening ahead." The fashion artist who sketches the garment may choose to show the wearer obviously ready for an evening out, with the costume as fresh and elegant as when she arrived at the office in the morning.

Periodically, fashion advertising in newspapers goes from less copy and more art to more copy and less art. In the 1970s, several department stores elected to rely on heavy copy to get their fashion points across. This followed the approach of the 1960s, when large-scale art and photography were used with a bare minimum of copy to achieve the same purpose. At the start of the 1980s, the approach seems to be a balance of the two.

Whether artwork or photography is used to illustrate fashions is usually a decision arrived at by the sales promotion director with the approval of the merchandise managers and, in some cases, top management. Many times the change from one form of illustration to another is made as much from a desire for "something different" as from any particular analysis. Manufacturers sometimes provide glossy photographs or sketches of their garments, along with suggested copy layouts, or mats, to assist in ad preparation. A **mat**, short for matrix, is a paperboard mold on which picture and/or copy are impressed and from which a plate can be made for reproduction purposes. The decision to use a specific aid provided by the manufacturer is made by the advertising department. These advertising aids are almost never used by major retailers, however. They prefer that only their own particular style and quality of artwork and copy appear in newspapers.

WHEN AN AD BREAKS. At the same time that an ad is to be run, promotion plans may also call for window and department displays. In such cases, the buyer works with the display department to ensure proper presentation of the merchandise in the windows. It is also the buyer's responsibility to order appropriate signs from the store's sign shop and to arrange for departmental displays of the advertised merchandise. Thus, on the day that an ad breaks, customers will find the item or items on display and properly identified. Figure 18-3 shows an example of the forms buyers use to request signs for departmental displays.

Some stores post tear sheets (clippings) of each day's ads on walls in or near elevators, escalators, restrooms, and other areas of heavy customer traffic for additional exposure. Each department usually exhibits its current ads on its own selling floor where customers may see them. Each buyer is responsible for making sure that his or her salespeople know what is advertised, where it is stocked, and what the selling points are, so that they can talk intelligently to customers about the merchandise.

In stores that do a considerable amount of telephone-order business, each day's ads are also posted in the order board area to aid the telephone operators. Today, many larger urban stores have their telephone-order boards manned 24 hours a day, 7 days a week, for customers' convenience.

REPORTING RESULTS. Advertising departments generally request, for future guidance, a report from the buyer on the results achieved from each merchandise ad. Figure 18-4 is an example of a buyer's report to management on the results of a particular ad. These results are measured in terms of net dollar and unit sales. Buyers are expected to report, usually on a printed form, such points as: the number of advertised items in stock before and three days after the ad ran; the number sold; total dollar sales of the department for the three-

SIGN REQUISITION

SIGN SIZES

(1/16 = 5-1/2 x 7)
1/8 = 7 x 11
1/4 = 11 x 14
1/2 = 14 x 22
FULL SHEET = 22 x 28

QUANTITY
14

- PLEASE PRINT PLAINLY
- ORDER SIGNS AT LEAST A WEEK IN ADVANCE
- ORDER ONLY ONE SIZE CARD ON THIS REQUISITION
- GIVE COMPLETE INFORMATION

FOR DEPT.	TEL. EXT.	DATE ORDERED	DATE NEEDED
74	3615	May 14, 198–	May 23, 198–

COPY:

CANVAS HANDBAGS
FOR
TOWN AND TRAVEL
$15 TO $18

REMARKS:

WHAT SPECIAL EVENT *Tribune ad June 1st*

CHECK APPROPRIATE BOX:

PROMOTION	CLEARANCE	SPECIAL PROMOTION	NEW LINE	FASHION NEWS
			X	X

ORDERED BY *Dorothy Smith*

APPROVED BY *H.L. Reiss*

Figure 18-3

day period following the ad; weather conditions; special display efforts; and any other pertinent data that would help evaluate the ad's pulling power.

Buyers and advertising executives learn from such reports which items and approaches produce the most sales among the customers of the store and department concerned. Thus a sound basis for future planning is laid.

PLANNING IN SMALLER STORES.
Planning and reporting are less formal in relatively small stores where there is no advertising specialist to concentrate on promotions. Even in the smallest shop, however, good management demands at least a rough guide indicating what is to be spent, in which media, for what merchandise, and with what expectations. A record of ad results also needs to be kept so that past experience can guide future decisions. Often all that is needed is a scrapbook of ads run, with marginal notes on costs and results.

The store with no staff advertising expert or agency often finds that many aids in constructing ads are available free or at little cost. Part of the work on a market trip involves canvassing the possibilities for obtaining suitable ad-

ADVERTISING RESULTS

Department _74 – Handbags_
Date of Ad _June 1, 198-_
Media _Tribune_
No. of Stores _5_
No. of Units Sold _175_

DOLLAR SALES:
Advertised Item _$ 2,625_
Total Department _$ 7,824_

Note: *This form must be turned in to Merchandise Manager before noon the 4th day after ad has run. Merchandise Manager will initial and send promptly to Sales Promotion Manager.*
Buyer's Signature _Dorothy Smith_
Merchandise Manager's Initials _H.L.R._

Figure 18-4

vertising material, so that when buyers or owners return to the store, they know not only what merchandise to advertise but also how best to present it in an advertisement.

Smaller stores often use media that larger ones may ignore. The cost of a newspaper ad looms large in the budget of a tiny establishment, so its proprietor often uses less costly media such as direct mail. Considerable use is also made of such resource-provided aids as low-cost statement enclosures, display cards, package enclosures, and the "as advertised in" posters supplied by consumer magazines.

Cooperative Advertising

Figure 18-5 is an example of a notice of paid advertising that shows details of a store's cooperative advertising agreement with a manufacturer. Cooperative advertising offers advantages to both parties, but it also presents some problems or opportunities for abuse.

ADVANTAGES OF
COOPERATIVE ADVERTISING. Among the advantages that cooperative advertising offers to the fashion merchant are the following:

- More money is made available for advertising. Cooperative money is usually considered to be in addition to whatever amount the store has budgeted from its own funds for promotion.
- Additional advertising funds may enhance the impact of the store's advertising in two

ways. First, larger or more frequent ads may be placed, thus increasing the impact of the store's name upon the public. Second, the additional space purchased with co-op money may help the store to qualify for a lower cost rate on all its advertising and thus be able to buy more space for the same cost. Newspapers usually give progressively lower rates as the total linage purchased increases.
- Cooperation from producers in other respects is more certain once they have invested funds of their own in the store's advertising. Prompt deliveries, assistance in training the selling staff, and other services are more likely to be available.
- If the advertised brand, or line, or item is new to the area, the producer shares introductory promotion costs with the store and thus shares the initial risk.

From the producer's point of view, the benefits include the following:

- The producer's money buys more advertising space than if the ad was placed directly. The retailer, as a consistent buyer of space, commands lower rates than does a producer with occasional advertising.
- The prestige of the store's name reinforces on a local basis the acceptance an item may enjoy on a regional or national basis. This is especially valuable when lines or brands are being introduced in a new area.
- The retailer, having invested funds in advertising the merchandise, can be more readily counted upon to carry adequate stocks, provide window and departmental displays, and brief the salespeople on the selling points of the goods.
- In large cities, where the manufacturer's line may be sold also through small neighborhood stores, the impact of a major store's advertising helps the sale of the line in the smaller stores as well.

DISADVANTAGES OF
COOPERATIVE ADVERTISING. From the store's point of view, the major drawback in cooperative advertising is that buyers have

Department __42__

NOTICE OF PAID ADVERTISING

Manufacturer's Name __Aiken Dress Company__

Attention of __Jack Shapiro__

Manufacturer's Address __1400 Broadway__
__New York, N.Y. 10018__

Newspaper Date __May 16, 198-__ Name __Tribune__

Date _____ Name _____

Describe Merchandise __Silk shantung dresses, styles 420, 674, 1060__

ADVERTISING AGREEMENT

Manufacturer Agrees to Pay:

☐ 1. Full Charge   4. Your Share as Agreed _____

☐ 2. One-half Charge   5. Up to Amount of _____

☒ 3. __25 %__ Charge   6. Other _____

Person with Whom Agreement Made __Jack Shapiro__ Date __Feb. 16, 198-__

Special Billing Instructions __Send tear sheet with duplicate of invoice.__
__Deduct from Aiken Dress Co. account payable__

Buyer's Signature __Dorothy Smith__

To Be Filled Out By The Advertising Department

Lineage, Total Ad __600__ Rate $ __2.20 line__

Cost, Total Ad $ __1,320__ Amount to be Billed $ __330.—__

Treasurer's Bill No. __A61729__

Figure 18-5

been known to "buy" advertising rather than merchandise. Because of limited advertising funds and their own eagerness to see their departments promoted, some buyers pass up good merchandise for which there is little or no cooperative money available in order to buy what may turn out to be less desirable styles but for which there are cooperative advertising funds. This practice may result in poor assortments.

From the standpoint of the vendor, a major drawback of cooperative advertising is the danger of inadvertently discriminating against some customers in favor of others. Participation in the advertising of a well-known store that uses a big metropolitan daily may be worth much more to a vendor than participation in the advertising of a small shop that uses only a local suburban weekly. Yet, under the provisions of the Robinson-Patman Act (a section of the antitrust laws), a producer in such a situation might seem to be granting discriminatory allowances to the larger store. Rather than leave themselves open to charges of making offers for which only large stores can qualify, a number of apparel firms have simply abandoned cooperative advertising entirely.

Other Fashion Media

While newspaper advertising continues to dominate the average retail department store's use of advertising dollars, the last two decades have seen a dramatic increase in the use of other media to advertise fashion merchandise. Radio, television, magazines, and direct mail have all made their bid for the advertising dollar. The decision as to which of these will be used, as well as when and for what merchandise, usually rests with the sales promotion manager. It is usually found, however, that buyers, merchandise managers, and advertising people all have a sense about what will and will not work. Their combined perspectives on changing times and changing needs have led to the multimedia practices now common to most of the country's major retailers.

RADIO. By the early 1980s, the youth of the country had made its media preference known —radio. As stations playing the top 40 hit songs proliferated, so did teenagers' listening time increase. With transistor radios came round-the-clock involvement with the rock stars of the day. Retailers quickly realized that the newspaper was not the medium to use to attract youth; the radio was. Now, years later, radio advertising is recognized as a must by the retailers interested in reaching the youth group. The car radio is also used to reach the working adult. Morning and evening "drive-time" radio is accepted by retailers as the best

means of reaching this group with their message.

There are no hard-and-fast rules indicating which means of communication retailers should use. Each store, each area, and each customer profile presents a different situation. Simply stated, when radio reaches customers more effectively than other media, stores are quick to use it.

TELEVISION. While a brief relationship between retailers and television existed years ago, most retailers have only recently embraced this medium as a means of conveying their fashion messages to consumers. This may seem surprising, considering the constant, daily impact that television has on our lives and the benefits that such an exciting and colorful medium can offer.

Several factors, however, kept retailers and television apart for almost two decades. In the late 1940s and early 1950s when television stations were new and inexperienced, the costs of commercial and program time were very small. Television stations, needing to fill daytime hours with programming, turned to experienced retailers for help. The famous department store, Rich's in Atlanta, actually provided three hours of programming a day for a new Atlanta television station in 1950 and 1951. The station brought its cameras and lights to Rich's as a television studio. The store programmed the three hours with fashion shows, lectures, how-to demonstrations, autographing teas, cooking lessons, and many other activities which involved showing the store's merchandise on camera.

But such an arrangement could not last. As television caught on and more and more sets were purchased, the cost of programming and advertising time began its upward climb. Within a relatively short time, the cost was beyond the range of practically all advertisers except giant, national manufacturers. Retail stores, as always, had to spend their advertising dollars carefully to ensure the best results. They could not afford the astronomical cost of each 60-second or even 30-second commercial. In addition to their expense, such "one-time shots," unlike newspaper ads, could not be set aside for use again later. Thus retailers, who had at first embraced and supported the new medium, decided that it was too costly and its selling results too uncertain. This disassociation with television lasted, with few exceptions, until the 1970s.

By the 1970s, some of the nation's leading retailers were returning to TV advertising for several reasons. First, the medium had grown up and had achieved a commanding influence in the lives of the American people. Second, newspaper costs had risen alarmingly, to the point that, in some cases, television had become less expensive for the stores to use. Third, increasing numbers of firms now specialized in the production of TV shows and commercials for buyers of television time. Some of these firms were specifically geared to retailer's needs. Fourth, and probably most important, the broadcasting systems, desirous of a larger share of retailers' advertising dollars, were constantly demonstrating the pulling power of television to these retailers.

Stores in areas served only by weekly newspapers found television a means of reaching their customers more frequently. Stores located in large cities found that television enhanced the pulling power of their print advertising and helped them tell their fashion story more effectively.

By the mid-1970s, national chains, such as Sears and the J.C. Penney Company, were buying prime time on national shows to tell customers around the country about their merchandise offerings. In addition, many major department stores around the country were routinely using television spot advertising on a local basis, as well as sponsoring such programs as the local newscast or weather report. Not to be outdone, many small specialty shops found that constant exposure on a specific television station at a specific time of the day was a means of fixing their names firmly in the public's mind.

After a strong start followed by a period of separation, retailer and television had established a permanent relationship.

DIRECT MAIL. As the contents of our mailboxes clearly indicate, direct mail continues to proliferate at a staggering rate, despite increases in mailing and printing costs. As a means of reaching a target customer, direct mail is outstanding. Direct mail also lends itself extremely well to fashion promotion whether in the form of a single-item enclosure that arrives each month with the store's bill or an elaborate catalogue showing a store's fashion assortments. These full-color illustrations of fashion items together with brief but explicit descriptions are geared to motivate immediate customer response.

Manufacturers and their cooperative dollars play a major part in a store's use of direct mail. Statement enclosures, often colorfully printed, are provided by many garment and accessory makers to show items in their current assortments. These are produced by the hundreds of thousands, with blank spaces reserved for the addition of specific store information. These preprinted enclosures provide a valuable means of advertising for smaller stores. However, some stores prefer that any printed material going out with their names attached be produced within their own facilities. These stores reject any preprinted manufacturers' inserts but frequently develop the contents of such inserts in their own style and mail them out to customers. For many years, stores produced one catalog each year, usually for a Christmas season mailing. Today, in many cases, stores send out several catalogs each year in a number of mailings. While the Christmas catalog is usually the largest, there are countless smaller catalogs dedicated to off-price offerings, seasonal needs, specialized areas, and exceptional purchases. Into this category fall Back-to-School catalogs, Home Furnishings and White Sale catalogs, and the yearly Anniversary Sale catalogs. Recently, some stores are mailing out catalogs to their charge customers and a few days later using the additional run of printed catalogs as inserts in the newspaper, thus multiplying the number of potential buyers.

Another form of direct mail used by stores is postcards or letters to inform valued charge customers in advance of upcoming events. Other forms include inserts which are tucked into a customer's package by salesclerks or in the packing room, and personal notes sent by salespeople to special customers, alerting them to new items in which they might be interested.

Direct mail has been a favorite medium for selling bridal fashions for many years. Notices are sent to engaged women, inviting them to attend a bridal show or to visit the store's bridal salon for advice on wedding plans and for selection of clothes for the wedding party.

The effectiveness of the direct-mail medium is difficult for most stores to pinpoint, since customer response may take the form of a telephone order or a personal visit to the store. Occasionally, stores will advertise an item by direct mail only, to measure the medium's pulling power, but this procedure is not common practice.

Catalogs issued by department and specialty stores at Christmas and for back-to-school merchandise are familiar to everyone. The explosion of the specialty catalog has been one of the greatest sales promotion developments of all time.

MAIL-ORDER AND
TELEPHONE SOLICITATION.
Years ago it was common for stores to include easy-to-use mail-order coupons in their advertisements for certain types of apparel and accessories. Since then, however, most department stores have installed telephone-order boards, operating 24 hours a day, 7 days a week. As a result, the coupon, which had to be clipped, placed in an envelope, and mailed to the store, has dwindled in importance. The ads in some Sunday newspapers, especially in magazine supplements, may include coupons for items that do not have to be tried on, such as some intimate apparel, hosiery, handbags, and scarfs. Otherwise, the use of coupons is no longer common.

While the telephone is used by department stores and specialty shops for receiving orders from customers, it is seldom used for soliciting orders. Telephone solicitation has been overused by dance instructors, carpet cleaners, and magazine sales people, among others, and has aroused so much resentment that its value for retailers has been sharply reduced.

Generally, the only fashion promotion done by telephone is the occasional call by a salesperson to a customer when new fashions or specific items arrive. In this case, the customer has specially requested this service.

MAGAZINES. Retailers are generally best served by local advertising media, but there are occasions when they seek to augment their fashion prestige by placing ads in consumer magazines with national circulation. Preferred for this purpose are fashion publications, brides' magazines, and national magazines of general interest. Such advertising is rarely expected to sell the fashion item shown, although sales may well occur. Its purpose is to emphasize that the retailer's fashion message is sufficiently important to be carried in the pages of a publication whose fashion authority is nationally recognized. This prestige advertising is intended to emphasize the store's image—as a place to buy one-of-a-kind jewels, as a salon for the latest in high-fashion apparel, as a headquarters for travel clothes and accessories, or whatever the case may be.

The merchandise selected for such treatment must be carefully chosen because of the length of time that elapses between the magazine's closing date (when all copy and illustrations must be in the hands of a publication) and its date of issue (when the magazine reaches the newsstands or the mailboxes of its subscribers). Apparel or accessories that are advertised in such magazines are either styles typifying incoming trends or timeless classics.

Such advertising implies that the shop or store, regardless of its location, is on a par with the country's best in fashion authority and desirable fashion assortments.

FASHION DISPLAY

The visual presentation of merchandise is called **display.** The purpose of fashion display is to highlight a trend, tell a fashion story, or demonstrate just how apparel fashions should be accessorized and worn.

Retailers use display in two forms: window display and interior display. Window displays

Dress Campbell   Black Watch   Royal Stewart

Scotch Plaid Shirts
(For Men, Women and Children)

Soft, strong and comfortable all-cotton flannel. Woven, yarn dyed plaids are especially clear and attractive. Crease resistant and machine washable.

An excellent shirt for active outdoors use or casual wear. Sportshirt style with breast pocket, double needle stitching, square tails and long sleeves. Weight about 12 oz.

Three tartans, **Dress Campbell** (Green and White with Yellow overplaid.) **Black Watch** (Green, Blue and Black.) **Royal Stewart** (Red with Blue, Green, Yellow and White overplaid.)

Men's Regular Sizes: Sm., Med., Lg. and XLg.

1653E Men's Regular Scotch Plaid Shirt, $14.00 postpaid.

Men's Long Sizes: Med., Lg. and XLg.

1666E Men's Long Scotch Plaid Shirt, $15.00 postpaid.

Women's Scotch Plaid Shirt. Made with same material and make as Men's shirt style but with long tuck-in tails, dress style collar and front placket. No pocket. Three tartans.

Weight about 8 oz. Women's sizes: 8, 10, 12, 14, 16 and 18.

4318E Women's Scotch Plaid Shirt, $14.00 postpaid.

Children's Scotch Plaid Shirt. Children's sizes: 8 to 18. Three tartans.

4332E Children's Scotch Plaid Shirt, $10.25 postpaid.

Trail Model Vest
(For Men and Women)

Provides warmth over a wide range of temperatures when worn alone or under a shell garment. Light in weight (about 9 oz.) and easily packed, it should go along on any camping, fishing, or cold weather outing.

Filled with about 5 ounces of high quality goose down. Goose down breathes for comfort and is the lightest, most efficient insulation available. Shell fabric of wind resistant, water repellent, high thread count nylon taffeta. Snap front closure, down filled collar and kidney warmer back. Length about 27½". Men's vest has self closing pockets, women's has slash handwarmer pockets.

Three colors, Scarlet. Navy. Green.

Women's sizes: Sm.(30-32), Med.(34-36), Lg.(38-40). Wt. 9 oz.

4238E Women's Trail Model Vest, $36.75 postpaid.

Men's sizes: Sm.(34-36), Med.(38-40), Lg.(42-44), XLg.(46-48). Wt. 12 oz.

1419E Men's Trail Model Vest, $36.75 postpaid.

Lee Riders®
(For Men and Women)

Rugged 14 oz. all cotton Lee Cowboy Denim for long, hard wear. Heavy duty stitching with reinforced pockets, 2¼" belt loops and zipper fly. Guaranteed dependability.

Neat and comfortable. Gets better with each washing. Sanforized®. An all around pant for active sports and casual wear. Wt. 28 oz.

Color, Indigo Dyed Blue Denim.

Regular Cut Lee Riders®

Cut on conventional patterns with regular rise and straight legs. Bottom circumference 17⅞". Men's waist sizes: 28, 29, 30, 31, 32, 34, 36, 38 and 40. Inseams: 29", 30", 32" and 34". 29" inseam available in waist sizes 30, 32, 34, 36 and 38 only.

1831E Regular Lee Riders®, $17.00 ppd.

Boot Cut™ Lee Riders®

Cut slim through the thighs and knees with regular waist and rise. Slightly flared from knees to fit over boots. Bottom circumference 19⅞". Men's even waist sizes: 30 to 40. Inseams: 30", 32", 34".

1832E Boot Cut™ Lee Riders®, $17.00 postpaid.

Women please state waist, hip and inseam measurements for Lee Riders® and we will send correct size for proper fit.

The explosion of the specialty catalog has been one of the greatest sales promotion developments of all times. L.L. Bean, one of the nation's oldest catalog sales firms, now offers a wide range of sports apparel and sporting goods for men, women, and children.

are created to catch the eye of people passing on the street and to persuade them to enter the store. Interior display is used to encourage impulse buying, to create customer interest at point-of-sale, to carry out a promotional theme, as well as to enhance the store's decor.

Whereas a newspaper fashion ad is seen at home, on a bus, or in the office, a fashion display is seen by the customer when he or she is inside or just outside the store. By the time people see a display they have already made the preliminary moves of leaving their homes and places of business and of approaching the store. They are already on the retail scene, whether idly strolling by or on a buying errand. Display, if it is effective, can reap dividends from this proximity by sparking a buying impulse that leads to a sale.

Window Display

To a fashion retailer, a store window is useful for selling merchandise, promoting an idea, or publicizing the store as a place to patronize. Its primary function, in one of retailing's puns, is "to make the passer buy." For this purpose it must be arresting and as dramatic as it can afford to be in the context of the store personality and the merchandise involved. Older stores were constructed with many display windows at street level. Newer, free-standing stores may have only a few or no windows at all. Stores in modern regional shopping malls have no separate display windows; instead, customers are presented with a sweeping view of an entire selling floor as they approach a store's entrance.

Fashion windows in stores that have street-level display windows are planned many months in advance, usually when storewide promotional plans are being drawn up. At that time, sales promotion and merchandising executives determine what looks, colors, and other fashion features they wish to promote during the coming season. The display department then draws up a seasonal calendar, based on the storewide promotional plan, indicating the dates on which specific themes and merchandise are to be featured and the num-

ber and location of windows assigned to carry selected messages. Departments compete for window space on the basis of how well their merchandise assortments convey the messages or themes the store has elected to promote during a given season.

Windows are rarely assigned to certain departments on a regular basis, although older stores with many display windows often allot certain banks of windows to certain store divisions on a fairly regular basis. For example, windows featuring ready-to-wear and accessories usually flank the main entrance to a store because of the general interest of customers in these types of merchandise. Household textiles and home furnishings, on the other hand, are often displayed in window areas where there is less traffic. During special sales events, such as White Sales, household textiles may be allotted windows in the areas of higher traffic as part of the store's promotional efforts.

As in the case of newspaper advertising, the store may require from the buyer a form stating what is to go into each window assigned to that department and what signs are to be used with the merchandise. If related items from other departments are used, the buyer or assistant may have the responsibility of selecting and signing for such items and seeing that they are eventually returned to the lending departments. Some stores have display coordinators who are responsible for securing merchandise to be used in displays.

Windows, like ads, are not always used for direct selling. They may be used to set the mood of a season, as are some of the merchandise-free windows that large stores install for Christmas. Some of the most famous of these are the Fifth Avenue windows of Lord & Taylor and B. Altman & Company that usually are devoted to animated Christmas scenes each December. Windows that show Santa Claus bringing gifts or families opening packages on Christmas morning are quite commonly used by large stores during this period of the year. Rather than suggesting specific purchases, these windows remind customers that it is a gift-giving season and that the store is a place to buy gifts.

Ken Karp

The primary purpose of the store window display is "to make the passer buy." Window displays also show the trends of the season in fashion.

TYPES OF WINDOWS. Window displays are designed to convey one of several different kinds of messages to the customer. Window displays featuring fashion merchandise may be designed to show seasonal trends in fashion colors or looks, or to show how to wear specific fashion merchandise to achieve a particular "look," or simply to show what the store has available at what price.

Fashion Messages. Windows are an excellent medium for conveying a fashion message. They may be used to dramatize a new color, for example, by showing garments and accessories in a particular springtime yellow, an autumn brown, or a bold print in which a certain color predominates. They can dramatize a new look, skirt length, or season of the year.

Because the window should arouse interest and stimulate customers to refresh their wardrobes, the actual styles selected for display are usually more extreme and in earlier stages of their fashion cycle than much of the assortment inside the store. If the window merchandise is not too different from what already hangs in customer's closets, it cannot be stimulating. Arresting qualities are essential.

A familiar summary of this philosophy is "Show royal blue; sell navy." The royal blue catches the customers' eye, but once inside the store, they buy their familiar, wearable navy. If navy alone had been in the window, their eyes might have glanced off it without receiving the message that it was time to buy some new spring clothes.

How-to-Wear-It Windows. Among the most rewarding types of window display are those illustrating how to wear new fashion merchandise. While a few people have fashion sense which enables them to innovate and to quickly grasp the right way to put together a look, by far the great majority do not. The effective window display answers their unspoken questions and shows them clearly what to do by presenting several versions of a new look. By showing a mannequin dressed in all the elements of that look, and in the surroundings for which the new fashion is intended, a window can provide customers with an overall picture of the look. It allows customers to judge whether or not they want to wear the new look and if they do, gives them confidence that they can achieve it.

In 1980 the "preppie look," or "prep-dressing," arrived on the fashion scene. This sporty approach to dressing combined both innovation and tradition, but its name alone was enough to turn some customers away. In passing windows that cleverly and correctly displayed this look, however, women saw that many elements of the "preppie" look were old familiar favorites. They were thus able to visualize themselves wearing it.

At no time do windows do a better job of conveying fashion news than when new color combinations or pattern combinations are introduced. Many of the customers' prejudices against certain colors or patterns can be swept away in an instant when these colors and patterns are displayed in ways that they can relate to their own lifestyle and environment.

Over the past decades, a remarkable number of innovations in dress have swept across the fashion scene. To some extent, their acceptance by consumers of all ages and economic and social levels has been the result of effective displays presented in how-to-wear-it windows.

Direct-Sell Windows. Window displays that aggressively attempt to make sales also have an important function in promoting fashion merchandise. Not all customers are concerned with newness and glamour; most are concerned with price as well, particularly in times of economic stress. Thus many customers are drawn by the windows of less expensive stores that feature poster-size signs announcing, for example, that dresses are "all reduced to $19" or that the store is having a "Special! Matching knit hats and gloves . . . $5." Also for the price-conscious customer are the windows that present a veritable cornucopia of items—many kinds and many classifications, arranged with only the thought in mind of showing as much as possible in a small space. Display people who do windows for neighborhood shops of modest size are experts at such techniques; so are the display staffs of shoe, hosiery, and general merchandise chains.

That windows of this type rarely convey fashion excitement does not in any way diminish their importance in the promotion of fashion merchandise. Vast quantities of apparel and accessories are sold as a result of such windows. These windows are the workhorses of fashion window display, and the merchandise they promote, even though it may be at or past the peak of its cycle, constitutes a substantial share of the total volume of fashion goods sold at retail.

PRINCIPLES OF GOOD WINDOW DISPLAY.

A window display is a work of art, created with merchandise and fixtures instead of paint, ink, or clay. This is why window displays are usually the work of professionals who know the basic elements of design and understand how to use those elements to achieve specific artistic effects. However, there are also some principles completely divorced from artistic ones to which window displays, if they are to be effective, must adhere.

First, a window display should feature merchandise that is both timely and in current demand. Fashion merchants pick the newest and most dramatic items and looks in their fashion assortments to feature in their window displays. For the higher-priced merchant, these are the eye-catchers—the styles people have already seen in the fashion news but have not yet had a chance to examine in a store's assortment. For the more moderate-priced merchant, these would be the styles that have gained fairly wide acceptance but are still showing strong popularity.

Next, both the number of items shown and the way they are presented should reflect the fashion image of the store. Stores with higher-priced lines will often put only a single coordinated look or even a single item in a window. That store will use a minimum of props, but both props and background decoration will carry out the "exclusivity" or "prestige" theme. A store with moderate-priced lines, however, will put a number of items in each window to show that they carry a wide assortment of currently popular styles.

Perhaps most important, the items chosen for window displays should be backed by adequate stock on the selling floor. If customers are drawn into a store by an item in a window display, they expect to find in the store's stock a good selection of that item. In higher-priced fashion stores, the assortment on the selling floor does not have to contain a large number of the exact item that is in the window display, but it should contain a reasonable number of items that are similar in their styling and fashion appeal. In more moderate-priced stores, the emphasis should be on having the featured item in a wide variety of styles, sizes, and colors.

Interior Display

Once customers have entered a store, the chances of converting their browsing activities into buying impulses can be increased by interior displays. These may be point-of-sale efforts at the actual spot where the goods are sold, or they may be displays in such places as overhead ledges, corners, platforms, or entrances to departments. Often they repeat a theme expressed in windows and once again drive home the message, whether it be the approach of a new season or the opportunity to buy a bargain. In large stores, such displays are again the work of professionals on the display staff.

Within a department, however, displays of fashion merchandise are usually the responsibility of buyers, their assistants, or the sales-

Ken Karp

This interior ledge displays one item with self-service racks below it. The giant prop adds eye appeal and interest, while the sign clearly points out the sizes carried there.

people. Ingenuity, knowledge of the merchandise, and proximity to the point of sale make up for the absence of the professional's touch.

MAJOR TYPES
OF INTERIOR DISPLAYS. There are several basic types of interior displays. These include displays that present a coordinated look, displays that suggest merchandise for a specific end use, displays that present a single item or an assortment of items, and displays arranged for easy selection.

Vignettes. A product or group of products shown in use is a **vignette.** A typical vignette might display a mannequin in a nightgown and matching peignoir, wearing slippers of appropriate style and color and seated on a boudoir chair to complete the suggestion of a woman preparing for bed. The impact of such a display at the entrance to an intimate apparel department is often enough to draw passing customers to its counters or racks.

Item Displays. A single garment or accessory may be featured in an **item display.** The display may be created by putting one piece on a form. Or, several versions of a style—a shoulder bag in several sizes, for instance, or a style of body shirts in several colors—may be shown on a display fixture.

Assortment Displays. A display that shows, identifies, and prices one of each of the styles currently in a section of stock is an **assortment display.** Such a display is generally used for basic items and permits the customer to make at least a tentative selection while waiting to be served. A classic example is the usual wall display of white shirts behind a men's furnishings counter. The windows of shoe chains follow the same pattern, and their interior displays of slippers, boots, or shoes are also of this type. Scarf departments use assortment display when they fan out their folded stock of each price and type, permitting customers to see the entire color range at a glance.

Self-selection Racks. Although they are not usually thought of as such, self-selection racks are definitely a type of departmental display. In order to emphasize the breadth of the color assortment, several garments, each in a different color, may be displayed on a rack or T-stand. To feature mix-match possibilities, as in sportswear separates, all items of a particular style, pattern, or color may be grouped in one area. The first arrangement says, "Choose from our rainbow assortment." The second says, "See how many components we offer in each color." If the rack is merely a hodge-podge, the implication is that the assortment is broken or unplanned, as on a clearance rack. The buyer, within the framework of store policy, decides which message should be conveyed in departmental displays and instructs stock and sales personnel accordingly.

OTHER TYPES OF DISPLAYS. Interior display makes use of many additional small but effective aids: a counter card, describing the qualities of the goods; a sign atop a rack of clothes, stressing a major selling point; a garment laid open across a lighted, glass-topped counter, emphasizing its sheerness and perfect weave; a sample article attached to a rack of packaged articles, inviting the customer's examination. Attractive displays inside the store as well as large, dramatic windows are all part of the effort to promote the sale of fashion merchandise by means of display.

Vendor Aids

Producers of fashion merchandise, from coats to cosmetics, are keenly aware of the selling power of good retail display. Eager to help stores harness this effective tool in behalf of their merchandise, many vendors in the fashion business develop dealer aids which they supply free or at modest cost to stores. Vendors may also provide speakers and demonstrators to create a live display.

COUNTER AND WINDOW CARDS. Intended to be used in windows, on counters, or with interior displays of the vendor's merchandise, counter and window cards usually name the brand and describe the selling points of the item or brand. Cards of the "as advertised in" variety bear a mounted reprint of the producer's advertisement in the publication concerned. Smaller retailers are generally likely to use these to supplement their limited display facilities. Larger stores are likely to have a policy against the use of such cards, preferring that all announcements be made in their own sign shop and in the store's own style.

FORMS AND FIXTURES. To facilitate the display of specific merchandise, resources sometimes offer stores free or inexpensive forms and fixtures on which to display their merchandise. This equipment often bears the brand name of the fashion producer who supplies it. Familiar examples are the bust and torso forms provided by makers of women's foundation garments and the self-selection racks for packaged bras, gloves, or pantyhose.

The development of self-selection fixtures is a process requiring a large investment in research and design that only a large store is willing or able to make. Smaller stores that do not have capital available for such an investment may willingly use forms and fixtures supplied by vendors who do.

The fixtures developed by vendors generally prove to be very effective in displaying the merchandise, highlighting its sales appeal, and providing ample space for an orderly supply of stock on the selling floor.

Although the fashion industries are now quite active in the use of fixtures, they by no means pioneered in the development of this display technique. That effort was made in earlier years by industries such as those producing greeting cards, notions, and some types of housewares. By the mid-1950s, however, prepackaging and self-selection had been widely adopted in fashion industries, and by the 1980s, such techniques had become common.

DEMONSTRATIONS AND EXHIBITS.

To help consumers understand the virtues of new materials, vendors may sometimes provide exhibits or demonstrations on retail selling floors. Experience has proved this approach an excellent one for getting the message across to consumers.

Speakers and exhibit material supplied by vendors have been particularly useful to retail stores in explaining new fibers, fabrics, and finishes. When the first synthetic fibers were developed for textile use, for example, some producers sent representatives into the stores to explain how their fibers were made and how they should be handled. Wash-and-wear apparel, stretch fabrics, durable press, and other fabric developments have also inspired store demonstrations organized by producers. So, too, have complexion care treatments, false eyelashes, and new types of makeup.

Recurring problems, such as the selection and packing of travel wardrobes, also prompt vendors to develop talks and demonstrations for use in retail stores. The retail selling floor provides an auditorium, and many fashion vendors are eager to perform there.

MERCHANDISING VOCABULARY

Define or briefly explain the following terms:

Advertising	**Mat**
Advertising plan	**Merchandise or promotional advertisement**
Advertising request	**Prestige or institutional advertisement**
Assortment display	**Sales promotion**
Display	**Vignette**
Item display	**Visual merchandising**

MERCHANDISING REVIEW

1. What activities does sales promotion include? Describe the organizational structure of a large store's sales promotion division.
2. Discuss (a) how master storewide sales promotion plans and budgets are developed; (b) how each department of the sales promotion division prepares its plans; and (c)

why it is necessary to coordinate plans and budgets of the departments making up the sales promotion division.

3. What types of advertising media are used by retailers to promote the sale of fashion merchandise? What are the advantages and disadvantages of each type?
4. Name at least three sources from which fashion merchants may obtain information for developing their advertising plans. What type of information does each yield?
5. Discuss a buyer's responsibility for running an ad.
6. What information is usually requested in an advertising results form? What purposes are served by this report?
7. Discuss the advantages and disadvantages of cooperative advertising.
8. Name three forms of direct-mail advertising. Discuss the effectiveness of each in advertising fashion goods.
9. Name three types of window display and explain the purpose and most suitable type of merchandise for each.
10. Identify three types of aids supplied by vendors, either free or at low cost, to stores selling their merchandise. Of what value is each of these to a retail merchant?
11. Discuss the three types of interior display. State the purpose and list the advantages of each. Give at least two examples of merchandise that can be used in each type.
12. What are the advantages of newspaper advertising? How does the fashion retailer select which newspaper(s) to use? Give examples from your community.

MERCHANDISING DIGEST

1. Discuss the following statement from the text and its implication for fashion merchants and buyers: "Goods well-bought are half-sold."
2. Distinguish between a merchandise or promotional ad and a prestige or institutional ad. What purpose or purposes are served by each? Clip examples of each type from newspapers or magazines to bring to class for discussion.
3. You manage a small shop for women's apparel and accessories. What activities might you undertake in promoting the sale of sportswear? Of scarfs? Of handbags? Cite the costs involved for each type of promotion for each item.
4. Explain the resurgence of interest in television advertising by retailers. With your instructor's permission, visit two local fashion retailers that use television to find out their reasons for using this medium.

REFERENCES
[1] Ettorre, "Stores Try Theatrical Selling Techniques," p. D1.

19

PROMOTING FASHIONS: PUBLICITY AND PERSONAL SELLING

Advertising and display are two vital means of promoting the sales of fashion merchandise. The former is used to capture the consumer's attention, while the latter is used to convert that attention into action in the form of making a purchase. Two other important sales promotion tools that are available to fashion merchants are publicity and personal selling.

Although differing in approach, publicity and personal selling are both extremely powerful tools in selling fashion merchandise. Publicity, like advertising, makes its impersonal bid for the consumer's attention through the use of newspapers, radio, television, and even conversation. Like display, personal selling meets the consumers at the most advantageous of all possible points—in the buying situation. Unlike the other types of sales promotion, personal selling is completely consumer-oriented, with each salesperson attempting to recognize and satisfy the individual customer's needs and preferences.

FASHION PUBLICITY

Publicity is the free and voluntary mention of a firm, brand, product, or person in some form of the media. The purpose of publicity is to inform or to enhance interest. The broad purpose of fashion publicity is to make every facet of the fashion business better known to and more readily accepted by the public. The specific purpose of such publicity is to promote the sale of fashion merchandise by informing consumers about the importance of a trend or style, a designer, a manufacturer, or a retailer.

Since publicity, unlike advertising, is given free by the medium concerned, it can bring extremely valuable sales results at little cost. Many retailers, along with entertainers, political aspirants, and authors, now look upon publicity as the most vital key to their success.

Paid advertising is placed in a medium at the request of the advertiser, who decides where and when it will appear. In the case of free publicity, however, the medium concerned decides whether or not the material will be used at all, and if so, the amount of time or space that will be allotted to it and what words and pictures will be used.

In the fashion world, vendors or merchants —the major sources of fashion publicity and information—merely make the facts available to the media and suggest how these facts might be presented. They retain the right to specify a **release date,** which is the earliest date that the announcement can be made. Whether the announcement concerns a new and exclusive fashion design or a personal appearance by a well-known fashion figure in a store, the media usually honors the specified release date as a matter of policy.

The way in which fashion news is originated by designers, vendors, and fashion leaders has been discussed in earlier chapters. This chapter is concerned with the efforts of retailers to publicize fashion in general and their own fashion assortments in particular.

Methods of Obtaining Publicity

Retailers call attention to newsworthy developments within their stores or actually create news by causing something newsworthy to happen, such as fashion shows or personal appearances of celebrities. Stores provide selected media with information about such events in hopes they will be of potential interest to the media's audiences. In turn, these media may then devote space or time to telling their readers or listeners about such happenings.

In their attempts to gain publicity, retailers make news available promptly and, preferably, in advance of the expected event. In addition, they refrain from flooding media with information that is not really newsworthy, for to overdo the publicity effort may cause print and broadcast editors to be less cooperative.

Following are several methods of passing fashion news along to print or broadcast media.

PRESS RELEASES. Retailers may issue press releases before or after such newsworthy events as a visit to the store by a designer, the opening of a new department, or the introduction of a new fashion development. A **press release** is a written statement of news that has occurred or is about to occur, specifying the source of the information and the date after which its use is permissible. Press releases may originate with the store or may be provided to the merchant by vendors whose products are involved.

PHOTOGRAPHS. Vendors frequently send directly to newspaper fashion or women's

Many companies provide editors with glossy photos of their latest fashions. Here a textile company gives a photo and description of a sweater made of their fiber by a sweater manufacturer.

page editors glossy photographs of a model dressed in one of the styles in the vendor's line. Attached to each of these glossies is a short description of the style, the fabric in which it is made, the color and sizes in which it is available, occasionally some information about the designer, and often the local store or stores where that particular style may be found. Reproduction of such a photograph, accompanied by information on the item, its fashion importance, and where it may be purchased locally, often results in favorable publicity for both the vendor and the local store customers of that vendor. Unfavorable publicity, however, may result if an editor does not check with the credited local store or stores as to the actual availability of the style and its selling price before printing or broadcasting the related publicity. No customer enjoys making a trip to a store and finding that the publicized style is not in stock, or finding it in stock but at a higher price than stated in the publicity.

TELEPHONE CALLS.   Sometimes retailers may alert news media to happenings with only a telephone call. If the store is staging a fashion show to raise funds for charity, a call to the editor of the fashion or women's page of the local newspaper may bring a photographer and a reporter to the show.

FASHION CONSULTATIONS.   Fashion merchants often make their expertise available to the media to encourage accurate and stimulating publicity for their stores. Retailers do this by welcoming questions on fashion subjects from the press and answering them as completely as possible, thus encouraging editors to check with them on the accuracy and completeness of fashion news from other sources. Merchants can also achieve some of the same results by being available to speak on fashion subjects before school or consumer groups. In each case, they help stimulate both the public's fashion interest and the assortments of the store the merchant represents.

Media Used

Retail merchants look to both print media and broadcast media when seeking fashion publicity. Most retailers find that the publicity given their activities by local newspapers engenders greater consumer interest than any other media they use. Magazine publicity can be of considerable value but often lacks the news quality and local impact of newspaper coverage. Radio and television publicity also can be very useful, but again, the approach may not be as localized as newspaper publicity. Also, radio or television publicity cannot be preserved for future reference.

NEWSPAPERS.   As a consistent user of advertising space in local newspapers, a retailer often gets preferential treatment in obtaining publicity. For maximum effect from publicity, the retailer selects the paper that seems most likely to reach the readers who will be interested in the particular publicity message. Which paper appeals to which group of readers is something the retailer already will have learned in the course of selecting media for advertising.

Newspapers are also generally more receptive to store requests for publicity than are other media because of the frequency of their publication. Fashion editors and women's page editors have daily pages to fill and Sunday features to prepare. They usually welcome information about store events that have local news value.

The local fashion publicity efforts of retail merchants gain strength from such industry efforts as the semiannual press week showings in New York and Los Angeles, described in Chapter 7. If fashion editors or women's-page editors of newspapers have attended either or both events, they have seen the lines of the sponsoring vendors well in advance of their presentation to the public by retail stores. They have brought back with them the vendors' press releases and photographs of styles the individual vendors consider the most indicative of developing trends. Such editors are not only conversant with fashion trends as a result of their press week experience, but have also become somewhat personally involved in helping these trends develop on their local scenes. With this background and this attitude, they are more receptive than they might otherwise be to the fashion publicity efforts of local merchants.

MAGAZINES.   Fashion and consumer magazines make a practice of showing fashions editorially and of mentioning one or more stores as sources for purchasing that merchandise. These mentions, discussed in Chapter 17, are known as editorial credits. The decision to offer an editorial credit to a store rests with the publication. The decision to accept or decline the credit is made by the store, which takes the following factors into consideration:

- The value to be derived, in terms of publicity among its customers and in the market, from accepting a credit in the periodical concerned. Not every periodical has equal value in these respects.
- The confidence the store places in the style that is being considered for credit. If the sales potential of a style does not warrant purchasing, displaying, and promoting it on its own merits, a store will undoubtedly decline the credit. The store may still carry the style but simply prefer not to give it the merchandising and promotional emphasis that the acceptance of a credit requires.
- The crediting of other stores. Some merchants prefer not to accept a credit if other stores also are mentioned, or if the other stores mentioned are of an appreciably different type from their own.
- The importance of the vendor to the store. A store may accept a credit as a means of strengthening a relationship with a new vendor. Conversely, it may decline a credit rather than share editorial mention with a resource not otherwise important to it.
- The number of concurrent credits the store may have already accepted in other publications. Too many credits appearing at approximately the same time can upset the store's own assortment and promotion plans.

Accepted and acted upon, an editorial mention publicizes the store and its fashion merchandise among readers of the magazine who are within its trading area. Properly managed, such credits enhance the prestige of both periodical and retailer among consumers and producers.

Advertising credits are also available in most magazines. They are mentions of one or more store names, in connection with the advertisement of a vendor, as the retail sources for the merchandise being advertised. Such an ad might also include the names of fiber and fabric sources or other appropriate producers whose products contributed to the featured item of merchandise. The factors a store considers in accepting or rejecting such a credit are much the same as those considered in the case of editorial credits.

RADIO AND TELEVISION. A retailer who is a consistent user of radio and television advertising sometimes enjoys preferential treatment in obtaining broadcast fashion publicity from local stations, as is also the case with newspapers. And just as each newspaper has special appeal to certain groups of readers, so does each radio and television program or station have special appeal to more or less clearly defined groups of listeners.

Retailers become familiar with the nature of such specialization through observing the results their own advertising has achieved. They augment what they have learned from their own experience by studying the research material prepared by each broadcast medium to indicate the number and kind of people who tune in to its programs. Then, to achieve maximum benefit from fashion publicity placed with broadcast media, fashion retailers seek to obtain mentions from those stations and programs whose listeners they believe will be most responsive to their message.

Sources of Fashion Publicity Material

In today's publicity-oriented society, there are countless outlets for a store's fashion message. So, too, are the sources of fashion publicity almost unlimited. Some sources are more important than others, however, in terms of the consistant flow of materials they supply to the media. The most important source is a store's fashion coordinator or ranking fashion authority. Also of great importance are events such as fashion shows and visits to stores by fashion designers and vendors. Further publicity can originate with vendors themselves and with trade associations or their publicity agents.

THE FASHION COORDINATOR.

In any retail organization, much of the fashion publicity obtained is a result of the fashion coordinator's activities. The **fashion coordinator** is the store's ranking fashion authority. The coordinator's duties, which are discussed in detail in the next chapter, include such publicity-generating activities as staging fashion shows, in or out of the store, and arranging clinics or demonstrations at which visiting designers or vendor representatives will speak. The coordinator may also represent the store as a speaker on fashion before consumer or business groups in the community.

FASHION SHOWS.

Whether the retailer's store is a high-fashion, big-city salon or a small shop on Main Street, there is nothing that tells the fashion story to customers quite so clearly and dramatically as does a fashion show. The usual presentation employs models, music, and a commentator, allowing the audience to both see and hear about fashion merchandise. Simpler ways of running shows are possible, of course, and some very effective presentations have been done by commentators who simply hold up each item as it is being discussed. The glamour treatment, however, is more likely to draw larger audiences and win more publicity, and this method is the one stores usually like to use.

Such fashion shows may be held to benefit a local charity or to highlight the store's own assortments. In the former case, admission is charged and the proceeds are turned over to a designated charitable organization. In the latter case, admission is free and may be open either to the general public or only to those who have been invited to come.

Fashion shows may be held on a selling floor or in the store's restaurant or auditorium. Or they may be held outside the store, according to the occasion and the facilities required. Some shows feature the fashions of a single vendor or designer; in others the styles of several vendors are modeled. Shows may be general in nature, appealing to a cross section of the store's customers. Or they may be planned for specialized audiences, such as teenagers,

Courtesy of Hong Kong Trade Development Council

Nothing tells the fashion story more clearly than the fashion show.

college or career men or women, prospective brides, expectant mothers, or people with special interest in travel or sports.

Ways in which retailers assemble audiences for these shows are as varied as the kinds of shows they stage. If the event is on behalf of a charity, the sponsoring organization sells the tickets and usually offers the services of some of its members as models. If the event is geared to a relatively small, special-interest group, such as brides or expectant mothers, personal invitations may be mailed out. For across-the-board audiences, announcements may be placed in the store's advertising, in its windows or elevators, or on radio broadcasts, inviting all interested persons to attend.

Cooperation in the staging of a fashion show may be provided by a consumer publication, a merchandise vendor, a fiber or fabric producer, or any other organization with a reason to help the retailer convey a fashion message.

Publicity is achieved by word-of-mouth and by informing the press and broadcast media, through direct contact or through press releases, about an upcoming event and why it is being undertaken. Occasionally, fashion shows are so original in some aspect that the publicity lingers long after the fashions themselves have gone. Such was the case in recent years when models on moving escalators displayed the fashions of a famous New York specialty store in a newly opened suburban branch of that store.

VISITS FROM
DESIGNERS OR VENDORS.

A visit from a designer, a vendor, or their representatives can often help a store earn considerable publicity for itself, for the vendor, and for the particular fashion area involved. Some representatives are capable speakers and appear on local television shows or give press interviews on fashion trends. These fashion authorities may address groups of customers or school groups, act as commentators for store fashion shows, or hold clinics and act as consultants to individual customers.

In periods of economic uncertainty and increased competition, higher-priced vendors or their designers tend to schedule more trunk shows and increase the number of their visits to customer stores in large urban areas throughout the country. A trunk show, as described in Chapter 7, is a presentation by a designer, vendor, or vendor's representative of samples of a line. The show is held in the store department that is featuring the line. The representative brings samples of the complete line to the store, puts on several scheduled showings, and takes special orders from any customers who choose styles, colors, and sizes not in the store's stock. In this way, designers or vendors' representatives have an opportunity to pinpoint regional variations in fashion demand and to get customer reaction to the vendor's overall fashion philosophy. Trends in demand can be gauged more accurately from face-to-face customer contact than they can from within the narrow limits of a design room or a vendor's showroom.

Advance announcements about trunk shows are made in press releases and store ads. During and after the event, word-of-mouth publicity inevitably grows out of the customers' excitement over the special treatment accorded them. Further opportunities for publicity may be created by having models show selected styles informally in the store's tearoom, or by showing the line on models at a special breakfast or luncheon show for the benefit of a local charity. Interviews with the visiting vendor or representative may be arranged with print and broadcast media if the vendor is considered an authority on some special aspect of fashion or is otherwise newsworthy.

Maximum publicity benefits result from such vendor visits if the buyer or merchant who is handling the visit discusses the possibilities at an early date with the store's publicity staff. The publicity executive needs to know why the visitor is newsworthy and whether he or she can participate productively in press conferences, television interviews, and other promotional activities. Arrangements for such supplementary appearances have to be made well in advance, not only with the press but also with the visitor. A vendor who knows, for example, that he or she will have five or ten minutes on television may bring along a special group of unusually photogenic style numbers to show, and possibly one or two highly photogenic models.

VENDOR PUBLICITY. The fashion publicity efforts of stores are frequently supplemented by the work of the vendors' own publicity staffs. Sometimes the latter channel their publicity efforts through the stores, by making available suggested press releases and glossy photos of the styles they consider important. Sometimes they issue the publicity material directly to the news media, as described above. On occasion, producers may circulate reproductions of magazine pages on which appear either their advertising or editorial mention of their styles. At the same time they point out the local stores that have received advertising or editorial credits.

When such publicity is channeled through the store, the store's fashion coordinator and publicity staff have the opportunity to evaluate it in terms of their own scheduled promotional efforts.

TRADE GROUPS
AND ASSOCIATIONS.

Buyers and merchants who keep in close touch with the industries from which they purchase fashion goods are in a good position to coordinate their own store publicity efforts with those of trade associations serving those markets. Such associations frequently release publicity to print and broadcast media on new developments in their particular areas of fashion and relate these developments to current trends. Some of the fashion industry trade associations have fashion publicists on their staffs or retain the services of public relations firms, such as the one headed by Eleanor Lambert, originator of the New York market's press week.

When an industry trade association launches a drive to publicize its fashion message or its merchandise, or both, the buyer or merchant usually receives in the mail suggestions for tying in with such publicity efforts. These include ideas for press releases, photographs, and recommendations for fashion events. If such material is passed along to the store's publicity staff and discussed with them, it is often possible to work out ways to benefit locally from the national publicity efforts of these associations.

FASHION SELLING

Advertising, display, and publicity, as we have seen, are designed to bring a customer to the store ready to make a fashion purchase. It is at this point that a valuable sales promotion aid—the salesperson—makes the final selling contact between the store and the customer.

Many people have tried to define good retail salesmanship. It has been described by some as "the business of helping people to understand their needs and of showing them how those needs can be satisfied through the purchase of merchandise and service."[1] Retailers are more succinct in their definition of good sales ability: selling goods that won't come back to customers who will.

Fashion selling requires a more sophisticated type of sales ability than is required in the selling of most other consumer goods. This is because customer decisions about fashion often center around the intangibles of personal taste rather than the more tangible qualities such as durability and practicality. Fashion salespeople must be able to point out the fashion features of the merchandise and assure customers of the personal satisfaction they will have in owning the item. By displaying knowledge, awareness, and concern, fashion salespeople help each customer make purchases that are fashion-right, becoming, and appropriate. As the final link between designer and customer, the fashion salesperson performs an invaluable role in the process of fashion sales promotion.

Techniques of Fashion Selling

Modern retailers have a wide range of selling techniques at their command. The choice of the techniques or methods used is made by store management, depending upon the type of goods, the degree of fashion leadership the store or department wishes to assume, the price lines of the merchandise, the shopping preferences of the store's customers, and any other relevant factors.

Among the techniques most commonly used are personal selling, simplified selling, and mail and telephone selling.

PERSONAL SELLING.

In this selling method, a salesperson actively assists customers in choosing articles suited to their individual taste and needs. The salesperson seeks to do this in such a way that the customers will return to the store or department for future purchases. The goodwill engendered by pleasing customers and serving their interests through helping them identify and satisfy their wants is the foundation upon which fashion stores or departments build continued patronage.

Salon Selling. The most exacting type of personal selling is **salon selling.** It is most frequently used in stores or departments that offer higher-priced styles in the introductory or early rise stages of their fashion cycles. In salon selling, little or no stock is exposed to customers' view except that which is brought out by the salesperson for inspection. Close rapport is needed between customer and salesperson if this type of selling is to be successful. An advantage of this method is that once a mutual understanding has been developed, the customer usually comes back to the store to be served by the same salesperson, who understands the customer's wants and how to satisfy them.

Since salon salespeople are likely to develop a personal following of customers who return to them repeatedly and trust their suggestions, many maintain card files on their regular customers. On each customer's card is noted merchandise previously purchased, style and color preferences, sizes worn, price lines preferred, and other pertinent personal information. Salespeople then use these files to inform customers about new styles as they arrive in stock and about other fashion developments. Many specialty stores employ salon selling and encourage salespeople to keep records on their personal followings. Department stores, on the other hand, rarely employ salon selling except in their high-fashion departments.

Over-the-Counter Selling. A less exacting type of personal selling is employed in many fashion departments in both department and specialty stores, as well as occasionally in chain and discount organizations. For **over-the-counter selling,** selected portions of the stock are kept in glass display cases, often with some merchandise displayed on top of the cases. Most of the stock, however, is kept on shelves or in drawers below and behind the display cases. Sometimes a free-standing "island" or "square" is formed by three or four glass display cases, with the center of the island or square being occupied by departmental stock and a cash register.

In over-the-counter selling, some merchandise may be available for customers to personally examine. However, salespeople are needed to take other merchandise out of the display cases, off the shelves, or out of the drawers so that a customer can inspect it. This type of selling requires that a salesperson be thoroughly familiar with the departmental stock, well aware of the fashion points and importance of each item, and able to speak tactfully but with authority about differences in quality that exist between similar items at different prices.

Over-the-counter selling is the personal selling method most stores prefer for merchandise that is high-priced (such as fine jewelry), easily soiled (gloves or better lingerie), or fragile (fragrances and some types of costume jewelry). It is also used for merchandise requiring specialized knowledge on the part of the salesperson (cosmetics and shoes).

SIMPLIFIED SELLING. There has been a significant trend in recent years among mass distributors of fashion goods to employ simplified, less costly selling methods in preference to highly personalized selling service. The trend has its origins in rising costs of labor and other operating expenses, greatly increased competition, and decreasing store loyalty among customers. The trend is also a result of the growing preference among large segments of the shopping public for methods less formal than the traditional types.

Self-Selection Selling. In **self-selection selling,** merchandise is displayed and arranged so that customers can make at least a preliminary selection without the aid of a salesperson. Open wall racks, T-stands, display shelves, bins, and tables are among the fixtures most commonly used in self-selection departments. Salespeople are available to answer customers' questions about the merchandise, to check for styles, sizes, and colors not on the selling floor, to assist in the fitting room if requested, and to complete the sale once the customer has made a buying decision. This is the most

Selling lingerie over the years. The selling techniques have changed as dramatically as the lingerie. In the 1920s, nothing was available for the customer without the aid of a salesperson. In the 1950s, some self-service was beginning to appear and much more merchandise was displayed. By the 1980s, the salesperson had vanished and self-service fixtures had taken over.

prevalent fashion selling technique today. It is found in stores and departments handling all types of fashion merchandise except those in higher price lines, where personal selling usually prevails.

Self-service. In **self-service selling,** customers not only make their selection from the goods on display but also bring their purchases to a check-out counter where they make payment and where their purchases are prepared for takeout. Most self-service operations have stock personnel on the floor to keep the merchandise in order and to check, when requested by customers, for sizes and colors not on display. There are no salespeople as such, however, to give the customer fashion information and advice.

Self-service is the selling method most favored by discount operations and others whose low prices require that services be held to a minimum. Self-service techniques, however, may be employed by stores of the traditional type in some of their fashion departments, particularly those handling prepackaged, brand-name goods, such as pantyhose and brassieres.

Although self-service is usually equated with savings and bargain opportunities, this method of selling fashion is by no means used exclusively for low-priced merchandise, closeouts, and ''distress'' merchandise. Both medium-priced and high fashion goods have also been sold successfully by this method.

MAIL AND
TELEPHONE SELLING. A store can sell fashion products successfully by mail or telephone only when customers have confidence in the store's assortments, in its fashion position, and in its understanding of customer wants and tastes. Readiness on the part of the store to accept returns is essential in this method of selling, and returns of goods purchased by mail or telephone are much higher than on goods selected by the customer in person. Since customer returns reduce net sales and indirectly reduce profit, mail and telephone selling is usually restricted to merchandise on which the markup is large enough to

offset the cost of a high rate of returns. In addition, mail and telephone selling is usually restricted to classic styles and to merchandise that does not involve fit. Hosiery, some classifications of intimate apparel, and leisure apparel are typical of the kinds of fashion goods that may be profitably sold by mail or telephone.

Requirements for Success in Personal Selling of Fashion

To most customers, the salespeople *are* the store. It is rare that customers deal with a buyer or owner, with an advertising manager or display director, or with the president of the store, but they certainly see and deal with the salespeople. And just as customers prefer to buy their fashion merchandise from stores which reflect their own fashion and taste levels, so do they prefer to buy from salespeople who represent these same levels in their appearance and performance.

It is vital to the success of fashion merchandising that salespeople, the ultimate and most personal contact between the store and the customer, have the appearance, manners, speech, grounding in fashion information, and approach to their work that will enhance the store's relationship with its customers.

PERSONAL QUALIFICATIONS. There are certain essential attributes that a buyer or merchant seeks in fashion salespeople. Selling is greatly aided when salespeople have developed such personal qualities as:

- Attractive appearance, scrupulous cleanliness, businesslike dress, and careful grooming
- Good manners and good business etiquette
- Animation, alertness, and promptness in attention to customers
- Ability to form a quick estimate of customers and their preferences, as well as a sympathetic appreciation of their problems
- Ability to speak well, a pleasing voice, a lively and intelligent expression, clarity of speech, and a knowledge of when to talk and when to listen

- Orderliness in thinking, talking, working; accuracy in handling records, reports, and other paperwork
- A good memory for faces and names
- A friendly, tactful manner and, above all, sincerity[2]

FASHION AND
MERCHANDISE KNOWLEDGE.   Fashion salespeople need to know all of the fashion points of the merchandise they have been assigned to sell. They also need to know what fashion really is, how it works, and what the current fashion trends are and the direction in which they are going. Those who sell apparel need to be knowledgeable about the fitting of garments and the characteristics of the materials used. Whatever is being sold, salespeople should be able to guide customers in selecting related apparel and accessories, both in their own and in other departments, that will achieve the desired look. Above all, fashion salespeople need an appreciation of the fashion values of merchandise, so that they can state the price of the merchandise with confidence and respect.

Success in fashion selling often depends upon the ability of a salesperson to convey to customers the various intangible values of fashion goods. Equally important is the ability to understand and sympathize with the problems of individual customers. The salesperson must exercise patience and diplomacy in aiding a faltering customer to overcome objections and obstacles in making a favorable buying decision.

It is taken for granted that successful fashion salespeople are thoroughly familiar with all the pertinent facts about the merchandise they are selling: its quality, materials, and so on. A thorough knowledge of merchandise is basic to successful retail selling. Selling fashion goods, with all the intangibles that go to make up their value, presents by far the greatest challenge.

THE INDIVIDUAL APPROACH.   One of the most important points in selling fashion merchandise is the necessity of individualizing each sale. Handling either the merchandise or the customer in an impersonal or routine way must be avoided. Treating someone as one of the masses rather than as an individual creates animosity and ill will and, when that person is a customer, such treatment can mean a lost sale.

Where fashion is concerned, personal taste is an all-important factor in making a buying decision. Success in selling fashion merchandise, therefore, depends upon a salesperson's ability to cater to that personal taste and treat each customer as an individual.

Meeting this need to treat fashion customers individually is among the major problems confronting retailers of fashion merchandise today. Mass production and mass merchandising have made low prices possible, but often at the expense of both individualized merchandise and services offered to customers. The retailer's problem, for which there appears to be no easy solution, is to continue to give customers the attention and service that fashion selling requires, and yet to cope with rising costs of operation and with profit margins continually narrowed by competition. This is not exclusively a problem of large stores. Even in a tiny shop, it is often difficult for the proprietor to provide individual services to customers and at the same time to perform the many chores involved in running the business. Nor is it always possible to achieve the profit margin required to pay others to perform these chores.

Training of Fashion Salespeople

While some retailers believe that the best fashion salespeople are born with the talent, the fact is that most sales personnel develop their expert abilities through training and perseverance. To sell any type of merchandise, a salesperson must be well acquainted with the qualities, values, and uses of the goods. Selling fashion merchandise requires that the salesperson know the fashion picture as a whole and the significance of those elements that directly concern the specific merchandise he or she is selling. Some of the most knowledgeable fashion selling today takes place in boutiques, where each new fashion style is seen as part of a total fashion look that appeals to each boutique's customers. Only when salespeople understand the total fashion look can they explain to customers how its various elements are related to one another and how they may be coordinated to create currently acceptable styles.

Not all salespeople can be expected to be expert fashion consultants. But it should be clearly recognized that lack of fashion and merchandise information on the part of salespeople causes considerable customer dissatisfaction. When salespeople acquire such fashion information from the buyer, from fashion publications, from employee fashion shows, and from fashion training bulletins, they are better equipped to serve as consultants to customers. When salespeople radiate certainty and fashion authority, customers buy with more confidence.

SMALL STORES. In small shops, informal training of salespeople goes on in the course of the day-to-day operation of the business. Fashion points of the merchandise are explained to the sales personnel by the buyer or store owner as the goods come into stock. In the relatively small store, that buyer or store owner often is on the selling floor for much of the day and can answer any questions posed by customers and salespeople alike.

Frequently, salespeople in small stores are invited to view lines shown by visiting representatives of the store's resources and to express opinions with respect to the salability of the merchandise. They may be encouraged, moreover, to ask questions and to discuss the merchandise with vendors or representatives. The latter, in turn, may be asked by a store owner or buyer to hold meetings with the sales staff to discuss fashion features of the line each represents. Such a presentation often is made to all salespeople in the store, not only those who sell in the department that handles that vendor's goods. Smaller stores are more likely than large ones to ignore departmental barriers and to train their salespeople to sell in all departments. Their salespeople are thus able to help the customer to assemble his or her entire outfit—ready-to-wear, inner wear,

furnishings, or accessories—to achieve a desired look.

MULTIUNIT
STORE ORGANIZATIONS. In large, departmentalized stores, fashion training is more formalized than it is in small stores. Seasonal fashion reports, in the form of illustrated leaflets or color slides or closed-circuit television shows, are prepared by the store's training department in conjunction with the fashion coordinator and are shown to salespeople in all of the firm's store units. Buyers, and sometimes merchandise managers, hold meetings for salespeople upon their return from market trips, to report on the fashion trends they observed and to describe the merchandise they have purchased. In each department, the buyer or assistant holds weekly meetings at which the sales staff is told about scheduled advertising for the upcoming week, the fashion points of the merchandise to be featured in these ads, and anything else that will help them be more informed and fashion-conscious in their selling.

In chain organizations, the fashion coordinator usually prepares a seasonal summary of fashion trends in both ready-to-wear and accessories. This summary is sent to all stores in the chain at the start of each season. In addition, the central buyers of fashion goods alert the appropriate fashion department managers in the various units of the chain to current fashion developments. The medium commonly used is a fashion bulletin, which features sketches of items, swatches of the materials in which they come, and detailed descriptions, including colors and sizes available. Still another form of fashion training takes place when new styles are sent by the central buying office of the chain into some or all units for testing purposes. Pertinent information about the fashion features and selling points of the merchandise is sent along with the merchandise.

EMPLOYEE FASHION SHOWS. One of the most effective devices for briefing a fashion sales staff is the presentation of a special fashion show. The employee fashion show may be as formal and elaborate as one staged for customers. It may instead be a show taped in the parent store for future viewing in the branches. Or, it may be casual, using salespeople as models and substituting give-and-take conversation for prepared commentary. In some cases, it may consist simply of fully dressed and accessorized mannequins, displayed with explanatory signs in employee lounges or cafeterias. The basic idea, however, remains the same: to show concretely what lines, colors, or combinations of the two are expected to prove acceptable to the store's customers and to call attention to points of difference between last year's or last season's styles and those of the new fashion season.

Employee fashion shows in a large store are likely to be planned and carried out by the fashion coordinator or any buyer whose fashion sense and knowledge have the respect of the store staff. Shows are also often carried out, on a less ambitious scale, by buyers of related departments for the benefit of their combined sales forces. For example, a group of accessories buyers might work with a dress or coat buyer to explain how the new season's scarfs, belts, or jewelry can be combined effectively with new styles and colors in apparel.

VENDOR AIDS. Obviously, it is to the interest of vendors of fashion merchandise to do what they can to maintain a high level of retail salesmanship on behalf of their merchandise. Among the steps they may take to assist stores in this area, vendors give talks, distribute promotional literature, and demonstrate products in use.

Talks to salespeople may be given by the vendors' sales representatives who call upon buyers. Often these talks are given in meetings held before the store opens, but sometimes a vendor may invite the entire sales staff, the buyer, and other store executives to dinner and an evening meeting outside the store. The vendors' presentations made at such evening meetings are often quite elaborate, with charts, slides, films, or modeling.

Sales literature in the form of brochures is often given to salespeople for study and refer-ence. Typical examples of such literature might be a coat manufacturer's booklet on how to care for a leather coat or jacket, a fiber or fabric producer's leaflet about a new textile development, a foundation maker's explanation of figure types and how to fit them, or a lingerie or hosiery producer's color chart.

Many vendors train representatives to instruct salespeople in the use and benefits of their products. Demonstrators visit stores to conduct customer clinics, to assist in the training of salespeople, or both. The representative of a wig firm or a new cosmetic line, a hairstylist, and the instructor sent from a fiber or fabric source to explain the use and care of new products are typical visiting demonstrators. Some demonstrators become regular members of a store's staff. These appear to be in the store's employ but are paid, at least in part, by the producer who trains them to sell and stock a firm's goods. In large stores, representatives of major, nationally advertised cosmetic brands are likely to be permanent demonstrators.

OTHER SOURCES
OF INFORMATION. Retail selling efforts are also of vital interest to others who may be several steps removed from direct contact with consumers. These include fiber sources, both natural and synthetic; leather and plastic processors; fabric finishers; associations dedicated to publicizing the merits of fibers, fabrics, leathers, or other fashion materials; and consumer periodicals. From these outside organizations may come a battery of aids for training salespeople. These might include talks and demonstrations, exhibits, leaflets, and film and slide presentations.

Everyone in the fashion business, from the producers of fibers to the makers of finished goods, has a vested interest in improving the quality of retail selling. The reason is plain: If goods move only sluggishly across retail counters, the supply lines all the way back from retailer to manufacturer to source of raw material become choked with unsold goods. Often, fashion salespeople seem to be the focus of all eyes in the trade. Unless they perform their function well, little is sold to cus-

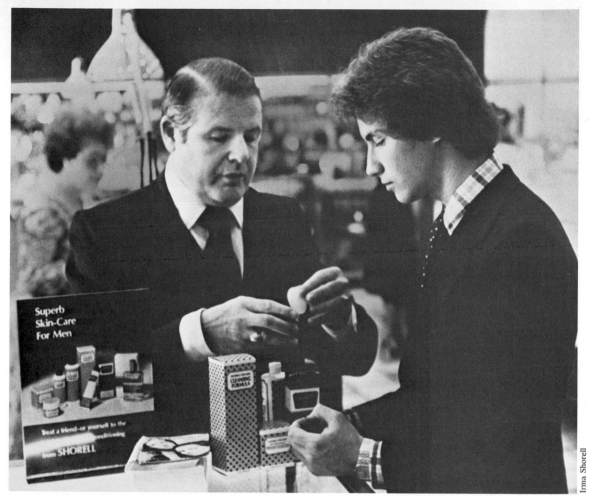

A company will often help a store to sell one of its products by holding clinics for the purpose of demonstrating to customers the uses and effectiveness of the product.

tomers. And nothing happens in the fashion business until something is sold.

In addition to all those who cooperate in the training of retail salespeople at no charge to the merchant, there are also professionals who sell their training services. Some come into stores where they hold rallies and workshops on the art of selling and generally try to stimulate people to sell more goods. Others offer film presentations to achieve the same ends. Although these services are usually concerned with retail salesmanship in general, their impact upon fashion salespeople is as important as upon those selling other types of merchandise.

The Buyer's Responsibility for Selling

The extent of a buyer's responsibility for the salesmanship in his or her department depends, to a large degree, upon the size and type of the store. In departmentalized stores, the buyer or department manager shares the responsibility for salesmanship with the training department. It is the duty of the training department to teach all new employees such things as store systems and procedures. These can range from dress code, to proper execution of a salescheck, to instruction in the store's security rules. Only when this training is complete is the new salesperson sent to the selling floor. From this point on, the training of the salesperson involves specific merchandise and is handled by the department head or buyer. The training department is no longer involved, unless some storewide effort is launched to accomplish a general aim—to curtail errors, to foster courtesy to customers, or to promote increased sales, for example.

In smaller stores, on-the-job supervision of salespeople is the responsibility of the buyer. But in major department stores and multiunit stores, supervision is generally handled by the department manager or group manager. The buyer sends merchandise information and fashion news on a daily basis to these intermediaries, who then share it with the salespeople. In these very large and complex retail stores, the buyer is involved with orders, projections, EDP printouts, and meetings—the many aspects of keeping goods moving through many departments in many branches. Thus it is necessary for the buyer to depend largely on written communications for contact with the salespeople.

MERCHANDISE INFORMATION. As the fashion authority for a department, the buyer is the primary source of information about merchandise carried in the department. The buyer is expected to alert the sales force to current and anticipated trends and to indicate how they will affect sales prospects.

The buyer is also expected to relay to the sales force information about the quality and value of the department's merchandise assortment. Specific selling points of an item should be pointed out, emphasizing to the salespeople the features that might make the merchandise more desirable to individual customers.

Sometimes buyers may also have to teach salespeople how to arrange the merchandise in stock: how to fold slips, how to place dresses on hangers, or how to replace shoes in boxes. Or, they may have to point out to salespeople

the most effective way to display merchandise to a customer. For example, they might show salespeople how to demonstrate the many ways in which a customer can wear a scarf.

SELLING TIPS. Because of their fashion expertise, buyers can also provide salespeople with effective selling tips. They should supply facts relating to the use and care of merchandise which the sales force can then pass on to customers. Or they may coach salespeople on proper size and fit.

Buyers may also tell salespeople what related items—even from other departments—to suggest in order to enhance customers' enjoyment of a purchase. For instance, they may show how a dress neckline may seem more flattering if just the right kind of jewelry or scarf is suggested for wear with it. By briefing salespeople on such suggestions, buyers make it easier for them to close the sale on a major item of apparel or on an important accessory. Moreover, it helps salespeople to impress upon customers the idea that the store is a headquarters for fashion advice.

Training Methods

The salesperson may be the ultimate link between the store and the customer, but it is the buyer's training and supervision that makes that salesperson a strong, productive, and profitable link for both store and customer. Today, more part-time salespeople are employed in fashion departments. More branches are being opened and store hours are being extended. Buyers have less and less time to devote to the selling floor. As a result of these changes, the proper training of salespeople has become an increasing problem. In order to convey needed merchandise information to salespeople, buyers or their assistants employ a variety of techniques.

DEPARTMENTAL MEETINGS. Each week, usually before the store opens, buyers, their assistants, the department managers, or the sales managers hold departmental meetings to review new or incoming merchandise and upcoming ads, to give pep talks, and to report any departmental problems or changes. Ideally these are discussion meetings, but often the pressure of time makes them a series of rapid-fire announcements. Some fashion stores, to dispense with formality or avoid the atmosphere of a stereotyped, dull session, use instead a daily five-minute "huddle" just before the opening bell.

FASHION SHOWS AND REPORTS.

In addition to what may be done on a storewide basis, buyers may present fashion shows for their own salespeople to bring out the fashion and selling points of the department's merchandise. They may also provide informal market reports, written or oral, telling their salespeople what they have seen and heard on their latest market trip, what fashion trends appear to be shaping up, and what they have purchased for future delivery.

MISCELLANEOUS.

Leaflets, clippings, and other matter related to the department's merchandise may be posted on conveniently located bulletin boards. Also commendation for special selling achievements, appropriate announcements, and bits of cartoon humor may find their way to such bulletin boards.

Other training media may include posted reprints of ads that have been run or preprints of ads that are to be run by the department, as well as posted or circulated printed material, such as fashion magazines and information received from vendors.

MERCHANDISING VOCABULARY

Define or briefly explain the following terms:

Advertising credits	**Release date**
Fashion coordinator	**Salon selling**
Over-the-counter selling	**Self-selection selling**
Press release	**Self-service selling**
Publicity	

MERCHANDISING REVIEW

1. Differentiate between advertising and publicity. What is the purpose of publicity?
2. Name and describe four methods of obtaining publicity, or ways of passing fashion news along to print or broadcast media.
3. What is the medium most favored by retail merchants for obtaining publicity? What other media may be used?
4. Differentiate between an advertising credit and an editorial credit. What are the advantages of these credits for a retail store?
5. What factors are considered by a store when deciding whether to accept or reject an editorial credit or an advertising credit?
6. Who is considered the main source of retail store publicity? Name at least three sources of fashion publicity ma-

terial and discuss the nature and importance of publicity emanating from each.

7. Differentiate between personal and simplified selling techniques. Name and describe the two major types of personal selling and the two types of simplified selling. For which types of merchandise is each best suited?

8. Discuss the importance of mail and telephone selling in relation to fashion merchandise.

9. Name at least 10 essential personal qualifications of a successful fashion salesperson.

10. Discuss employee fashion shows as a training device.

MERCHANDISING DIGEST

1. Discuss the following statement from the text: "Fashion selling requires a more sophisticated type of sales ability than is required in the selling of most other consumer goods," from the following standpoints: (a) fashion knowledge, (b) merchandise knowledge, and (c) customer approach.

2. Discuss the training of fashion salespeople in (a) large stores, (b) small stores, and (c) chain organizations.

3. Discuss the following statement from the text: "As the fashion authority for a department, the buyer is the primary source of information about merchandise carried in the department." Point out the various types of information buyers are responsible for providing to salespeople and the means they may employ to this end.

4. Discuss the pros and cons of using vendor aids. Name the different types of vendor aids available and discuss how each type of aid could be used by (a) large stores, (b) small stores, and (c) chain organizations.

REFERENCES

1 Robinson, Robinson, and Zeiss, *Successful Retail Salesmanship,* 3d ed., p. 2.

2 Nystrom, *Fashion Merchandising,* pp. 187-188.

20 FASHION COORDINATION

Fashion coordination is the function of analyzing fashion trends in order to ensure that the fashion merchandise offered is appropriate in terms of style, quality, and appeal to the target customer. Fashion coordination is not the concern of just one department or person in a store. It is the function of the entire store—of everyone involved in merchandising or its promotion. It is important, however, that one person or department have ultimate responsibility for the direction or coordination of fashion. A fashion coordinator is the person ultimately responsible for the overall presentation of fashion that a particular store offers its target customers.

Retail fashion coordination demands teamwork of the highest order. If the customer is to be able to find compatible apparel and accessories in a store's stock, the store must see to it that the assortments in each of its fashion departments are related to those in all others. Also important in fashion coordination is that merchandise offerings be properly timed to coincide with fashion demand.

Fashion coordination begins with the planning of the total fashion thrust, then with the selection of merchandise and the building of assortments. It extends to the training of sales personnel, the use of advertising and display, the staging of promotional events, and the placement of publicity.

THE FASHION COORDINATOR OR DIRECTOR

It was not until well into the 1920s that business executives began to understand fashion as a social force that could be defined and charted. Keeping one's products in line with the movements of this force made sales easier and more profitable. Once this concept was accepted, stylists were employed to study current consumer demand as well as to chart and anticipate fashion trends.

When women made their own clothes or had them made by dressmakers, "fashion dolls," fashion plates, and other types of illustrations provided the details of various fashion looks. But when women began buying ready-to-wear apparel in stores, retailers gradually realized that they needed help in determining customer needs as well as charting fashion trends and interpreting them in terms of the stores' assortments.

Development of the Coordinator Function

Tobé Coller Davis is credited with being the first **stylist** as fashion coordinators and directors were once called. It is said that Franklin Simon, impressed by her enthusiasm and energy, hired her in the period right after World War I and told her to find a way to make herself useful in his store. She found that what the store needed most was someone to chart and anticipate fashion trends and to help the store's buyers select and coordinate their assortments to reflect all the elements of each new fashion look as it became popular. This was an area in which she could be useful.

Other retailers soon added stylists to their staffs. These early stylists gradually began meeting together to share problems, ideas, and fashion information. These meetings were the beginning of The Fashion Group, which today has a membership of over 5,000 women executives representing all facets of the fashion business. The organization has chapters (called ''regional groups'') in 32 cities in this country and in a number of foreign countries, and additional chapters are in the process of being organized. The Fashion Group's meetings, fashion shows, and fashion ''spectaculars'' have become important events not only in the fashion apparel field but also in the accessories, home furnishings, and textile fields.

Today, in all but the smallest stores, a staff executive is usually assigned responsibility for fashion coordination. This executive is generally known as the fashion coordinator, but in some stores has the title of fashion director. Other titles include fashion administrator, fashion consultant, and stylist. The duties of this executive vary from store to store, depending on (1) the firm's fashion image, its management structure, and the responsibility allocated at each of its executive levels; (2) the amount of fashion authority and responsibility taken over by the store's top-level management; and (3) the amount of creativity, originality, and vision the fashion coordinator possesses.

Range of Responsibilities

Although the duties of a fashion coordinator or the store executive responsible for the coordination function are many and diverse, the major responsibility is to assist in promoting sales of fashion merchandise throughout the entire store. Therefore, the fashion coordinator must analyze and forecast trends, advise and assist merchandising executives in buying fashion merchandise that is coordinated and related throughout the store, and help develop the most effective presentation of fashion merchandise to the customer. All of these coordination functions ultimately help to build the fashion reputation of the store.

Although a fashion coordinator or director may be a man or a woman, in most retail organizations today this position is held by a woman. The coordinator functions in an advisory capacity as a staff aide to store management and achieves the goals of fashion coordination by being stimulating and persuasive in working with other store executives rather

Atlanta Apparel Mart

The fashion coordinator has a wide range of responsibilities—which may include giving the commentary at fashion shows.

than through any authority to approve or reject their merchandising decisions. The coordinator works with nearly everyone in the store, advising on buying, selling, advertising, publicity, and display activities, in order to coordinate the timing and emphasis of all fashion assortments so that a distinct fashion image is presented to the store's customers.

Briefly stated, the coordinator function involves three major areas of responsibility: merchandising, sales training, and sales promotion.

MERCHANDISING
RESPONSIBILITIES. The basic merchandising responsibilities of the fashion coordinator (or of any store executive who is responsible for the coordination function) are:

- To evaluate current fashion trends in terms of the store's clientele, image, and merchandising policies
- To alert management and buyers to incoming fashions, even before they become important to the store, so that appropriate action can be planned well in advance
- Conversely, to supply early warning about fashions currently in the store's stocks which appear likely to wane in customer interest soon
- To assist buyers, when requested, in selecting for their respective departments merchandise that reflects those fashion trends that the store has decided to promote
- To assist buyers, when requested, in coordinating their merchandise with that of other departments of the store
- To aid in developing merchandise or markets that are new to the store

When this job is well done, the store's fashion merchandise is well coordinated and its customers can select from its various departments apparel and accessories that go well together. Obviously, customers buy more readily under such circumstances than they do when each item under consideration poses a problem of what to wear with it or where to find suitable, related items.

The basic merchandising responsibilities of the fashion coordinator can be divided into three areas: market work, coordination within the store, and fashion forecasting.

Market Work. When a fashion coordinator shops or covers a market, she is interested in all markets collectively rather than each market individually. Only by seeing the entire fashion picture is she able to interpret the strength and direction of coming fashion trends.

Market work may take the fashion coordinator to showrooms not covered by the store's buyers. It may take her to fabric, fiber, and leather producers from whom opinions can be obtained about incoming trends. She may be in the market before the store's buyers, or with them, or both. She also regularly visits the offices of fashion and consumer magazines that are important to her store's customers. She assesses themes in upcoming issues and the value of the editorial and advertising credits offered to various departments of the store.

With this broad background of information, the coordinator is in a position to offer meaningful advice to individual buyers about offerings in their markets. Although she may not know any one market as thoroughly as does the buyer who covers it for the store, she will know, for example, what colors will be important in apparel during the forthcoming season. She can relate this information to the hosiery and shoe buyers so that they have appropriate colors available in their respective assortments. She may not know which producer has the best accessories, but she will know the ideal sizes and shapes to go with the new dresses and coats for the coming season. She advises, recommends, and informs; the rest is up to the buyers.

Developing Coordination. In order to achieve successful coordination among the various fashion departments of a store, top management first must make certain storewide decisions. The degree of fashion leadership for which the store wishes to be known must be determined, as well as the extent of the merchandising and promotional efforts to be undertaken.

The fashion coordinator consults first with

the store's management about what fashions should be promoted, to what extent, and when. Next, she works with store executives responsible for carrying out such decisions and assists each of them in implementing management's decisions.

For example, if management has decided that the romantic, feminine look is one of those that the store intends to promote, each buyer will select styles, colors, and silhouettes with that theme in mind. The dress buyer will include filmy chiffons and soft silks in her assortments. The sportswear buyer will be certain to have dainty, delicate, lace-trimmed blouses, as well as soft, print skirts. The fashion accessories buyer will include lace shawls, chiffon scarfs, flowers for the hair, and possibly neck ribbons.

In another season or in another store, the sporty, bulky look may affect assortments, fashion illustration, displays, store decor, advertising copy, and special events. The services of the fashion coordinator are always available to help any department effectively interpret whatever promotional themes the store has chosen.

Within the framework of the fashion themes the store has chosen to promote, there is often opportunity for a coordinated promotional effort within a single merchandising division. An accessories division may stage a promotion of its own with no direct tie-in with the apparel division. If neutrals are strong in apparel and highlights of bright color are to be introduced by accessories, these latter departments may join in promoting shoes, handbags, jewelry, scarfs, and blouses in a variety of colors. Or they may join in featuring accessories in a single, bright, accent color, such as royal blue or emerald green.

The prime objective of the fashion coordinator, whether she suggests ideas or merely assists in carrying them out, is to help make sure that the assortments and presentations of each department are in harmony with the fashion image that the store seeks to present. She also may be called upon to advise buyers on items to be featured in their department displays, in store windows, and in advertisements. She confers with display staff, adver-

tising people, and salespeople about how to show and what to say about the merchandise. She acts as liaison between apparel and accessories departments, furthering the store's efforts to give the consumer a clear, consistent picture of how to achieve the looks currently in fashion.

Fashion Forecasting. After the fashion coordinator has done her research and has collected all available fashion information, she makes an evaluation of all trends for the coming season. This is referred to as **fashion forecasting.** In both written and oral reports, she presents store management with complete information about coming trends and which of these she believes should be actively promoted during the coming season. From this fashion evaluation or forecast, management then selects the trends it wishes to promote. Management also determines, in broad terms, the extent of promotional effort to be expended.

The fashion coordinator's forecasts cover such points as trends in silhouette, details, colors, and textures—in short, the look or looks that are expected to be accepted by the store's customers in the coming season. Such a forecast may indicate, for example, that the longer, wider look in skirts requires higher, more slender heels on shoes. Or it may indicate that the heirloom look in jewelry goes well with certain nostalgic styles in dresses and blouses. The forecast may define whether favored colors in the coming season will be contrasts or monotones, bright or subdued, and whether or not some specific range of colors is featured above others. From such forecasts, knowledgeable buyers are able to proceed with more assurance, promotion executives can begin planning events, and display people can decide on the "props" to look for in their own markets. If, for example, the fashion trend is toward delicate colors and dainty fabrics, the fashion coordinator's forecast alerts the display department to the need for backgrounds that will be suitable.

Forecasts are supplied by the fashion coordinator as often and in as much detail as management specifies. Usually, however, they are

Feminine Apparel
June 5, 1980

CHRISTMAS CATALOGUE UPDATE

Hapsburg Era--the opulent feminine influence rises to the holiday occasion.

Richard Assatly	Winter White crepe faille blouse with stand band collar, passementerie and beading trim, $89 cost.
Leo Narducci	Reversible cape, satin to wool jersey, black only, $145 cost.
Lee Jordan	Long taffeta skirt, black velvet beaded trim top, $105 cost.
Anita Kantor	Brown velvet short bolero jacket with passementerie trim, over combination dress: skirt-black velvet, top-creme crepe, $48 cost.
Ellen Tracy	Holiday version of fall's trimmed velvet group
Bill Haire	Grey flannel group, with silver embroidery
Helene Sidel	Soutache trimmed velvet jacket, $125 cost
Ralph Lauren	Princess jacket with velvet collar, $160 cost
Mylesport	Trimmed velvet jackets

Accessories

Sylvia Beitscher and Franklin Wraps	Velvet jackets
Abbe Creations	Suede and passementerie belts from 1-4"
Lavis Purses	Evening bags--velvet, suede, kid with passementerie trim and tassels.
YSL	Fantasy jewelry--coins, tassels, medallions

TO: FASHION DIRECTORS
      UPSTAIRS GMMs-RTW

FROM: Sheila Bernstein
        Divisional Vice President
        Fashion Merchandising

Associated Merchandising Corporation; Sheila Bernstein, Divisional Vice President Fashion Merchandising

A resident buying office fashion director reaffirms the early forecasting of a particular fashion trend.

made on a six-month basis, just as merchandise plans are. In some cases, such as Easter or Back-to-School selling seasons, forecasts may be made for shorter periods of time.

SALES TRAINING RESPONSIBILITIES.

A fashion-educated selling staff is a major asset to any store that sells fashion goods. In each individual selling department, the buyer is the source of all merchandise information. However, for the overall fashion picture and for information on combining elements to achieve the currently fashionable look, the fashion coordinator may be called upon for training aid. Working with the store's training director, she often prepares seasonal fashion presentations for the salespeople.

Such presentations may take the form of fashion shows, sketch-and-copy pamphlets, talks illustrated by merchandise from stock, color slides, taped closed-circuit television shows, or any combination of these that is suitable to the store and its facilities. So important is this aspect of fashion coordination and promotion that some large, multiunit stores have a policy of preparing a fashion show each season for all employees, as noted in Chapter 19. Initially, the show may be presented to buyers and branch store managers who assemble at the main store for that purpose. Repeat performances then may be staged in the main store until all employees concerned—salespeople, display staff, advertising staff, and so on—have attended. Finally, either the show or a tape recording of the show "goes on the road" to the store's branches. At each showing, those who attend may be given a brochure to help them remember what they have seen. Selling phrases, suitable for the salespeople to use in talking to customers, are usually worked into the show's commentary and repeated in the booklets.

SALES PROMOTION RESPONSIBILITIES.

The advertising and display staffs look to the buyers for merchandise information about the specific goods to be featured in ads or windows. For background information on how the featured merchandise relates to fashion trends and how to present them, the fashion coordinator can be of great help.

Although the fashion coordinator may not write a line of advertising copy or sketch a fashion figure, she may be expected to see that the copy, merchandise illustration, and related items shown in an ad are all compatible with one another and in line with the store's fashion story. Similarly, she may never set up a display in a window or department of the store, but she may be called upon for advice by those who do the displays. She may suggest how to put the various elements of an outfit together, down to such fine points as the right spot for a pin or the right way to drape a scarf on a mannequin.

When stores stage promotional events featuring their fashion assortments, the fashion coordinator is very much in the picture. She may suggest the events, organize and supervise them, or simply stand by to see that the details of the fashion story are correctly presented.

Fashion shows for customers may be held in or out of the store, as direct sales builders or as public relations efforts to assist charitable and civic causes. They may be held in branch stores to enhance the fashion images of those stores. They may be formal, using models on a runway, or informal, with models strolling about a restaurant or departmental selling floor. Stage-managing such fashion shows, as well as coordinating the outfits and preparing the commentary, is usually the responsibility of the fashion coordinator.

Many other events also may be used to underline the importance of fashion coordination. There may be talks and discussion meetings for customers of a particular type, such as teenagers, home sewers, or expectant mothers. There may be occasions to talk to women's clubs and similar groups outside the store about current fashions and fashion trends that are of special interest to each particular group. In all such cases, the fashion coordinator is usually involved.

The coordinator also works with visiting

fashion experts in staging their presentations. For example, a producer of active sportswear may send a golf or tennis pro to a store to give a demonstration and to participate in a question-and-answer session with customers. Or a producer of patterns or sewing notions may send a representative to a store to hold one- or two-day clinics. Or a magazine may stage a fashion presentation on a theme it is currently sponsoring. The store's fashion coordinator, in such instances, makes sure that the presentation is in line with the store's fashion policy, assists in tying in all advertising, display, and personal selling, and helps secure as much publicity as the particular type of event warrants.

FASHION COORDINATION IN RETAIL ORGANIZATIONS

The primary objective of all retail fashion coordination, regardless of store size or type, is the projection of a specific fashion image through promotional and public relations activities and through the selection and presentation of merchandise. The fashion coordinator is responsible for seeing that the right fashion story is presented to the consumer and that the store has the right merchandise to support the fashion story.

The manner in which this objective is achieved however, as well as the personnel, skills, and responsibilities connected with the achievement of such coordination, varies widely with the size and type of store.

Large Multibranch Stores

The job of presenting coordinated fashion assortments in large, multibranch retail organizations is an awesome one indeed. Not only must the fashion assortments in the various branches meet the diverse needs of local customers, but they also must reflect the distinctive fashion image of the store organization as a whole. Dozens or even hundreds of fashion departments and their respective buyers must be considered and served; hundreds or even sometimes thousands of employees must be trained.

A major, multibranch retail organization usually maintains a fashion office that includes a complete staff of specialists. Each specialist is responsible for a special fashion area and reports to the fashion coordinator, or as they are known in many stores, the fashion director or fashion office head. For example, one specialist may be in charge of coordinating all special events. Another may be in charge of all fashion shows, and still another may be the coordinator for all branch stores. The newest trend in large stores is to have several fashion merchandise coordinators, each with specific responsibility; a coordinator for sportswear, one for menswear, and one for childrens' apparel, for example.

The fashion coordinator for a large store usually attends all market openings, both at home and abroad; maintains close contact with local newspaper and national magazine editors; whenever possible attends charity balls and opening nights of opera and theater; and frequents newly discovered and fashionable resorts and other "in" gathering places, all in order to observe firsthand what fashion leaders are wearing for such occasions. By means of these observations, the fashion coordinator seeks early indications of fashion trends that have or may in the future have meaning for her store's customers. For example, if at one of these events she sees a number of women wearing full-length evening gowns, she suggests to appropriate buyers in her store that full-length evening gowns should be shopped in the market and possibly promoted as part of the revival of the glamorous look. If the shortened hemline is the outstanding feature of the leading Paris couture collections, she can advise her store's dress buyers to look for this trend in the coming shows in the domestic dress market.

The fashion coordinator for a large retail organization is also responsible for suggesting seasonal fashion themes to be promoted throughout the store and for coordinating all sales promotion efforts to reflect these themes.

We'll dance at your wedding!

so you're getting married...
we'll help plan your honeymoon,
we'll bake the cake.
we'll engrave the napkins and
help you select the invitations,
we'll register your china, pottery
and silver patterns.
we'll show you sparkling rings, and
help with gifts for the wedding party
and dresses for the bridesmaids.
we'll make you a bride beautiful to behold!

come to our bridal fashion shows, saturday, february 2
You're invited to preview what beautiful brides of
the 80's will be wearing. Shows are at 11 am,
12:30 pm, 1:30 pm and 3 pm in our Downtown
store, on the ninth floor in Town Hall. Reservations
are a must, call 651-6975. There's a whole day of
events planned for you, too. Seminars and
demonstrations, refreshments, a wine tasting, and
dozens of prizes. The grand prize is a honeymoon
trip-- 6 nights and 7 days at Howard Hughes's
Xanadu Beach Hotel in Freeport on Grand
Bahama Island in the Bahamas, via Air Florida.
So, come join us, just for fun!
Shown from our show: v-neck organza dress with
venice lace trim; bishop sleeve; lace-flounced
skirt with chapel train, **225.00**
Two-tier crown veil with venice lace trim, **80.00**

foley*s

Courtesy of Foley's

**The fashion director often coordinates the offerings of several depart-
ments to make a major sales promotion event.**

Chain Store Organizations

The fashion coordinator of a national general merchandise or specialty store chain has many of the responsibilities of a coordinator in a multibranch organization, plus others that are unique to chain store operation.

Chain organizations largely restrict their fashion offerings to proven styles—those that have arrived at the culmination stage of their cycles. Fashion rightness, quality, promotional prices, and private labels are stressed in the advertisements, displays, and other sales promotion efforts related to these styles. In re-

424   Unit 3   **Retail Merchandising of Fashion**

cent years, major chains, such as Sears, Roebuck & Company, Montgomery Ward, and J. C. Penney Company, have made gigantic strides toward upgrading the quality and increasing the breadth of their fashion assortments. Catalogs of these chain organizations also reflect an increased awareness of the power of fashion to move huge quantities of apparel and accessories. This is evidenced by the increased number of pages devoted to illustrations of fashion apparel and accessories.

The fashion coordinator of a chain organization usually attends both domestic and European fashion market openings in order to keep abreast of fashion trends. She also visits other foreign markets for additional fashion inspiration. On such market trips, she may buy, for copying purposes, several original models that incorporate certain new details of design she believes should be featured in the fashion assortments offered by her firm in its stores, catalogs, or both. She also may arrange to have internationally famous designers create exclusive models, which, after consultation with the firm's merchandising executives, may be reproduced by domestic manufacturers to the specifications and under the private label of her firm.

After viewing the major collections, the coordinator prepares detailed market reports which go out to the manager of each store unit in the chain. Such reports serve to keep both store managers and their fashion sales staffs abreast of current trends in fashion apparel and accessories.

The fashion coordinator also carefully evaluates the fashion trends that she has observed. In close cooperation with her firm's merchandise managers, central and regional fashion buyers, as well as other merchandising executives, she attempts to pinpoint customer preferences and determine the best means of achieving coordinated fashion presentations throughout the chain.

The major responsibility of the chain organizations fashion coordinator is to expedite mass distribution of fashion goods on the basis of their wide appeal, good taste, quality, and moderate price. This responsibility is in direct contrast to that of the coordinator for a large specialty store, for example, who seeks to build and maintain her firm's reputation for fashion leadership.

Medium-Size Stores

The coordination of fashion assortments in medium-size retail organizations does not require as much experience or training as in larger volume firms. Former buyers frequently become fashion coordinators in medium-size stores, as do the young and ambitious former assistants to large store fashion coordinators.

In stores of medium size, with few branches or none, and with fewer fashion buyers, fewer departments, and fewer employees than in giant organizations, fashion coordinators may perform their function with only a small staff or, in some cases, even alone. If the store is at a distance from major fashion markets, she may attend openings in those markets only once a year, relying for her fashion knowledge on the observations of fashion editors, fashion reporting services, her store's buying office, and the observations of her own store buyers after they have completed a market trip.

Fashion coordination in medium-size stores is far less complicated than in larger stores for several reasons:

First, each fashion buyer in a medium-size store is responsible for merchandise in a larger number of classifications than is a buyer in a larger store. Thus buyers in the medium-size stores are already more alert to the coordination aspects of the many classifications for which they buy. For example, one buyer in a medium-size store may be responsible for all intimate apparel, whereas in a larger store that same merchandise may be segmented into several separate departments, such as foundations, sleepwear, daywear, and loungewear, each with its own buyer. One buyer in a medium-size store might be responsible for coats and suits in all size and price ranges, whereas in a larger store such merchandise may be segmented into several departments, each featuring separate types, sizes, and price ranges and each having its own buyer.

Second, effective training of salespeople is

more easily accomplished in medium-size stores than in large stores, because in the former, buyers are on the selling floor more frequently. Thus they are in a better position to motivate their sales personnel and, at the same time, provide them with pertinent fashion information about the various kinds of merchandise they have been hired to sell.

Third, coordination among the fashion assortments offered by related departments is easier to achieve in medium-size stores than in their larger counterparts, mainly because there are fewer buyers involved. With fewer buyers there are fewer personality conflicts, and the exchange of information about what is selling and what is not selling is easier.

Small Stores

Ideally, every store should have a fashion office or a fashion coordinator to assist it in building and maintaining a fashion reputation through better-coordinated assortments. There are many small retail firms, however, that either cannot afford to hire a full-time fashion specialist or for other reasons are obliged to achieve coordination without a full-time executive to take charge of this important store function. In such cases, responsibility for fashion coordination may be delegated to one of the store's buyers or to a merchandise manager, or it may be assumed by the store's manager or owner.

THE BUYER
AS COORDINATOR.

The fashion buyer in a relatively small, departmentalized store is usually responsible for merchandising a larger number of related classifications than is the buyer for a medium-size or large store. For instance, in a smaller store, one buyer may be responsible for buying all types of merchandise in the accessories group, whereas a medium-size store would have several accessories buyers, and in a large store there would be even more buyers, each highly specialized as to type of merchandise.

The same factors that aid buyers in the medium-size store in matters of coordination are even more influential for buyers in the smaller store. The buyer for a group of departments or classifications in a smaller store becomes responsible for coordinating several pieces of the fashion picture as a normal part of the job when planning purchases, promotions, and displays, and in the training of salespeople. In addition, not only is such a buyer in close daily contact with the salespeople, but salespeople in small stores often sell in more than one department and thus are more aware of coordination than if they were narrowly specialized.

Coordination in the small store is also easier to accomplish because very few buyers are involved. If only a few buyers cover all apparel and accessories fields, it is a simple matter to get them together either in the store or in the market to work out coordinated fashion themes for the store. In the market or at the store, it is easy for one buyer to exchange fashion ideas with another over lunch or on a coffee break. In a small organization, simple shoptalk often takes the place of much of the liaison work that a fashion coordinator does in a larger store.

Other coordinating procedures also are simpler in a small store than in a large one. Because the departments are usually physically close, displays of accessorized costumes benefit both apparel and accessories departments. Customers who like what they see on display can buy the entire outfit, if they choose to, right on the spot. Salespeople are more apt to keep one another informed in the same way that their buyers do; they chat about merchandise and fashion during breaks in their workday and while doing their personal shopping. Also, there is likely to be less regimentation in a smaller store and more of a feeling of belonging and of personal interest in the store and its merchandise.

THE MERCHANDISE
MANAGER AS COORDINATOR.

It often happens that the head of a fine specialty shop, or the apparel and accessories merchandise manager of a small department store, takes over many of the functions that a fashion coordinator might normally perform. Sometimes this is done because the store has no budget for a coordinator; sometimes the reason is that fashion is the merchant's first love, and the merchant refuses to be divorced from it.

Many merchandise managers who have worked their way up from a buying job refuse to lose contact with fashion resources. Like the fashion coordinators of other stores, they visit fiber, fabric, and leather firms. They talk to merchandising executives of fashion and consumer publications and maintain personal contact with the key resources of each of their principal fashion departments. Against this background, such executives can readily coordinate the merchandising and promotional efforts of their fashion departments. It is usually also part of the normal routine for such executives to counsel their buyers regarding sales training and other phases of fashion coordination.

THE OWNER
AS COORDINATOR. In the smallest stores, those run by the owner with perhaps a salesperson or two, the owner is buyer, coordinator, merchandise manager, and sometimes even housekeeper. In such stores, there is little need for liaison activities.

The demands on the time and energies of owners of small shops are enormous. As a result, many such shop owners concentrate on serving only one very narrow group of customers and seek out and remain faithful to those few resources whose merchandise has proved to be of exactly the right character for the selected clientele. Or sometimes a tiny store may divorce itself entirely from the coordination problem and specialize in dresses, sportswear, furs, or accessories. Such a shop will attempt to key its offerings to the tastes of the community it serves, suggesting in general terms other elements of the costume which customers will have to go elsewhere to buy.

Examples of Retail Fashion Coordination

One way a strong, coordinated store image can be achieved is by having all promotional and merchandising efforts during a certain period of time reflect an overall seasonal theme.

Imagine a large department store, for example. It is only early February, but daffodils and jonquils highlight the display of "Spring Yellow." Everywhere, fresh, new merchandise turns thoughts of the winter outside to the excitement of approaching spring. The store windows feature butterflies and buttercups, a combination also used in prints featured in the dresses and blouses. The new shade of "Spring Yellow" is available in dresses, sportswear, accessories, and lingerie, as well as in gift items. A ride up the escalator shows that on each floor the spring theme is consistent. Every mannequin, every display area, and every fashion department emphasizes the importance of this color in the coming season.

On one floor is a special "Spring Yellow" shop, a small, charming boutique decorated especially for a sunny spring day and for those who are especially fond of "Spring Yellow." The shop has everything from flower pots to yellow chiffon gowns. Once inside the shop, customers are surrounded with the theme and mood of "Spring Yellow."

On the furniture floor, the theme of spring is expressed again. Furniture designed for young marrieds is upholstered in the yellow butterfly and buttercup print. In the domestics and linen department, "Spring Yellow" towels and tablecloths brighten the shelves and tables.

The theme is carried out in yet other ways. In the morning newspaper, a color ad invited readers to come see the store with the "Spring Yellow" story. Signs in the windows, in every fashion department, beneath each interior display, and on every appropriate counter remind the customer of "Spring Yellow."

In addition to all this, customers soon discover that all of the new spring fashion items —from intimate apparel, to shoes, to hats— are already available to compliment the new "Spring Yellow." The customer has no difficulty in coordinating an entire wardrobe or home.

Without total coordination, the continuity and effectiveness of the campaign theme and look are weakened or completely lost. If the advertising director calls the new color "Spring Daffodil," the display director decides it is "Exciting Ecru," and the copy-writer for the color ad in the paper names it "Spring Taffy," then the customer might come into the store looking for three or four different colors, when there is actually only one. If the sportswear buyers decide they will display red merchandise that week and the dress department has not been informed about the "Spring Yellow" promotion and has no yellow merchandise in stock, much is lost. A coordinator must make certain that everyone knows and responds to what has been planned.

Because fashion trends are moving faster than ever and because fashion cycles are becoming shorter, coordination is increasingly difficult. Careful analysis, planning, and coordination are vital to the success of a fashion image.

SHOP MERCHANDISING

Bringing together all the various items of apparel and the accessories necessary to achieve a desired fashion look can require consider-able time and fashion know-how on the part of the customer. A customer may have to go from store to store or from department to department within a large store, making perhaps a dozen different purchases, each from a different salesperson, to assemble all the elements of the outfit wanted.

A relatively new approach to fashion merchandising recognizes this problem and attempts to solve it by offering the fashion customer a special kind of one-stop shopping: the shop. A shop offers the very essence of fashion coordination. Here are assembled all the elements of a particular fashion look or costume or special-purpose outfit. Because the assortment is so carefully coordinated, selection is simplified. Because the goods offered are grouped in one small area, customers, with the help of a single knowledgeable salesperson, can purchase all of the items for whatever outfit they are seeking in one single transaction.

Some of today's shops are separate enterprises— entire stores devoted to serving the fashion needs of a special type of customer.

the suede and leather shop

Hess's Department Store, Allentown, Pa.

Some of today's shops are set up as separate areas within a large store.

Others are set up as separate areas within a large store or as special areas within certain departments of a large store. These shops are distinguished from the rest of the department or store not only by their merchandise but also by their decor and atmosphere.

The Shop Concept

Special shops, either as independent operations or as departments within departmentalized stores, have existed for many years and continue to be established in increasing numbers as a means of presenting coordinated apparel and accessories to special groups of customers. For example, teen shops within department stores date back to the 1930s, and those set up as separate enterprises go back nearly as far. College, maternity, and bridal shops have also long been familiar.

Among fashion merchants, a **shop** refers to a small store or a small area within a large store that is stocked with merchandise for special end uses, intended for customers with specialized interests. These are the customers whose fashion requirements differ sufficiently from those of the general consumer to make it worthwhile for the merchant to assemble appropriate merchandise in a separate store or in a separately designated area of a large store.

TYPES OF SHOPS. Typical of such shops are those devoted to country clothes, ski or tennis or golf wear and equipment, maternity clothes, contemporary fashions, college clothes, and clothes for the career woman.

Temporary shops built on current fashion themes and trends, such as ''The Sweatery,'' ''Glitterings,'' ''The Long-Distance Runner,'' and ''Preppie-Perfect,'' have become more and more important for stores attempting to create or reinforce a fashion image. In such shops, the atmosphere, merchandise, selling techniques, and fashion coordination are all geared to the special interests of the particular customer to be served. What goes into a temporary shop built on a fashion theme differs with each store management. For some stores it is a category of merchandise which is seasonal and related by virtue of function. Exam-

ples are the ''Cold Weather Shop'' or the ''Swimwear Shop.'' Such categories are seasonal and are anticipated by the customer.

Another approach is also based on categories of merchandise, but on categories that are new or newly important. Examples might be the ''Denim Shop,'' ''Top Shop,'' or ''Shirting Shop.'' In a third approach, the temporary shop stimulates the customers' appetite for something they did not know they might want to buy. The ''Art Deco Shop,'' or the ''Jersey Turnpike'' for jersey dresses, pants, and tops, might be examples of this approach.

One of the special shops most frequently encountered in retail stores today is that devoted to the bride. A skilled bridal consultant assists the bride in the selection of her gown and those for the members of her wedding party. Services offered usually include answers to questions on etiquette and dress, and a visit by the bridal consultant to the bride's home just before the wedding to make any necessary last-minute adjustments in her costume. In addition, if the bride wishes to be photographed in her wedding gown before the day of the ceremony, the bridal shop usually can make arrangements for this as well.

The bridal shop in department and large specialty stores is capable of bringing added business to other departments of the store. Because the customer comes into the store for fittings, advice, and reassurance, she tends to purchase much of her trousseau there as well. Moreover, the bridal shop is usually located so that the bride and members of her wedding party, on their way to and from the salon, pass through departments featuring other fashion merchandise and are exposed to the appeal of their displays.

ASSORTMENT SELECTION
AND COORDINATION. Buying for shops is done in one of two ways, depending upon the nature of the shop. Shops that are permanent in nature and feature apparel and accessories of year-round interest usually are assigned their own buyer. This buyer covers many different kinds of markets to gather the particular types of apparel and accessories needed. Be-

cause a single person can do just so much work, a buyer relies heavily on information from other buyers, from the store's resident buying office, and from the store's fashion co-ordinator. Yet it is often the items that a buyer finds through out-of-the-way and unusual re-sources that give the assortment its special appeal.

On the other hand, shops featuring mer-chandise of a seasonal nature, such as swim shops, may present merchandise contributed by buyers of several different departments in the same store and coordinated by the fashion office staff. For instance, a swim shop might offer swim suits in every style from the cov-ered-up look to the "string." It may also offer beach cover-ups, beach hats, beach bags, san-dals, sand chairs, beach towels, sun um-brellas, casual jewelry, sunglasses, picnic bas-kets, and drink containers. In such shops, the display props that create the special-depart-ment atmosphere are removed when the peak of demand has passed. The merchandise is distributed among the departments whose buyers purchased it and the salespeople are reassigned to other areas.

Almost as important as the selection of the merchandise is the selection and training of the salespeople who staff the shops. These salespeople need to have a thorough knowledge of both the merchandise in the shop and its co-ordination possibilities, as well as an under-standing of the type of customer for whom the merchandise is intended.

The Boutique Concept

"Boutique" is the French word for "shop." In the fashion business today, **boutique** has come to mean a shop associated with few-of-a-kind merchandise, generally in very new or extreme styling, and an imaginative presenta-tion of goods.

Boutiques got their start in France. They originally were small shops operated by fa-mous designers to sell the often specially de-signed accessories to be worn with the design-ers' apparel creations. Like the more common kind of shop, they offered a kind of one-stop shopping. Their merchandise was limited in

Ken Karp

Boutiques offer customers newness, exclusiv-ity, and one-of-a-kind designs.

terms of categories but highly coordinated. The boutique bearing a designer's name was (and still is) the place where that designer's clientele could find the appropriate acces-sories needed to achieve the total fashion look created by the designer.

THE
BOUTIQUE IMAGE. Today, there are many shops called boutiques simply because they follow this tradition of newness, exclusivity, and few-of-a-kind designs. Occasionally a style that gets its start in a boutique later be-comes a popular best seller. When this hap-pens, boutiques usually lose interest in the style. This emphasis on newness and exclusiv-ity, as well as the lack of depth of assortments, is what usually distinguishes a boutique from a shop.

Boutiques are not new, but they are far more numerous and important in today's more affluent, fashion-alert society than they were a generation or two ago. There have always been some shops in which well-to-do women could find distinctive, well-coordinated apparel and accessories. And in large department and specialty stores in major cities, there have been corners, galleries, or alcoves set off from the general flow of traffic and devoted to merchandise more expensive and of higher fashion appeal than that offered elsewhere in the store.

What is new about today's boutiques is that many of them are dedicated to people whose tastes run to extremes in styling. Such boutiques are generally strikingly different from other departments on the selling floors of their stores; even their decor is dramatically keyed to the individualized merchandise they carry.

SELECTING AND COORDINATING BOUTIQUE ASSORTMENTS.

Buying for a store's boutique may be done by one buyer who covers several markets in search of appropriate merchandise or, as is more often the case in departmentalized stores, the responsibility may be shared by buyers for several of the store's regular departments. In the latter case, each participating buyer selects for the boutique such unusual styles as seem suitable for it, reserving for the regular department other styles that have wider, less individualized appeal. The salespeople in a boutique are carefully chosen and trained to understand its target customers, its merchandise, and its coordination possibilities.

The prosperity of a boutique does not depend entirely upon the ability of the merchant to judge correctly the needs and tastes of special groups of customers, but this ability is a key factor. Some boutiques, although skillfully operated, have a relatively brief life, simply because interest in the special fashions to which they are devoted is not yet strong enough, is declining, or has ceased to exist.

The era of boutiques within stores is beginning to fade. The concept now is for shops. What boutiques there are essentially small shops that continue to be called boutiques.

MERCHANDISING VOCABULARY

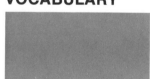

Define or briefly explain the following terms:

Boutique	**Shop**
Fashion forecasting	**Stylist**
Fashion coordination	

MERCHANDISING REVIEW

1. Discuss the historical development of the coordination function in retail stores from its beginning up to the present time.
2. What is the major responsibility of a fashion coordinator or director? Into what three major areas of responsibility are a coordinator's duties divided?
3. What are the five basic merchandising responsibilities of a fashion coordinator? Into what three general areas do these merchandising responsibilities fall?
4. Describe what is involved in a fashion coordinator's "market work."

5. Describe how a fashion coordinator goes about developing coordination within a retail organization.
6. Describe the activities of a fashion coordinator in carrying out fashion forecasting activities.
7. Name and briefly describe three methods commonly employed by large stores for fashion training its employees. Discuss the coordinator's responsibility with respect to each.
8. Name several retail promotional activities with which a fashion coordinator may be directly concerned, indicating the extent of responsibility with regard to each.
9. Give three reasons why fashion coordination in medium-size stores is less complicated than in large stores.
10. Differentiate between a shop and a boutique, and cite specific examples of each.

MERCHANDISING DIGEST

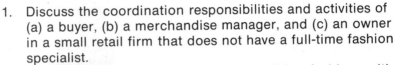

1. Discuss the coordination responsibilities and activities of (a) a buyer, (b) a merchandise manager, and (c) an owner in a small retail firm that does not have a full-time fashion specialist.
2. Discuss the shop concept of merchandising fashions with regard to:
   a) its advantages for customers,
   b) the selection and coordination of assortments,
   c) atmosphere and decor, and
   d) the selling techniques employed.
3. Discuss the chain store fashion coordinator's role, addressing the following:
   a) major responsibilities,
   b) unique responsibilities,
   c) types of markets worked,
   d) activities in the market, especially foreign markets, and
   e) information dissemination.
   Then discuss how her/his job is different from that of a coordinator in large and medium department stores, small stores, and specialty stores.

21
DEVELOPING A FASHION IMAGE

Practically from the moment that we are born, the word "image" becomes a part of our lives. As babies we are declared to be the "image" of our father or mother. As we grow up, we enhance our "image" by the way we dress, talk, act. And sometimes we discover that we need to "change our image." This means we need to change the way we are perceived by others in order to win or recapture their approval. Our "image" is made up of the various characteristics and facets of our personality that we present to the world.

A **store image** is the character or personality that the store presents to consumers. It is not something created by store management and presented to the public for admiration. Rather, it is the opinion which the public has formed of the store from the store's policies and activities. Perhaps Stanley Marcus, famous fashion merchant and former head of Neiman-Marcus in Dallas, best defined a store image as "an honest reflection of what the store actually is. It should accurately mirror what the store stands for in service, values, quality, assortments, taste, aggressiveness, and citizenship."[1]

A store's **fashion image** reflects the degree of fashion leadership the store seeks to project, the stage of the fashion cycle (as discussed in Chapter 3) that its assortments represent, and the customer it chooses to attract. A fashion image is one aspect of a store image.

Since fashion retailing is a very competitive business, one of the most effective ways a retailer can meet competition is by developing a distinctive fashion image.

By using fashion as a major attraction, retailers compete in their abilities to understand consumer preferences, to shop hundreds of markets to find the goods that will satisfy

those preferences, and to present those goods to the consumers in ways that encourage continued patronage.

In doing so, each fashion merchant attempts to project a fashion image within the store image that will attract the types of customers each wants to serve.

PROFILING TARGET CUSTOMERS

The first step in creating a fashion image is to define the store's target customers—those people for whom the merchandise assortments, the services, and the whole atmosphere of the store are planned. Only when a store has a clear-cut and definite profile of the customers who make up its target group can it create a successful fashion image.

A store relates its merchandising, promotion, decor, selling techniques, services, participation in community affairs, and even its housekeeping to that target customer it seeks to serve. Elegant fashion merchandise cannot be offered against a background of dusty displays and untidy fitting rooms, nor do customers expect to find bargain-priced shirts or skirts in departments with thick carpets and highly attentive salespeople.

Stores serving areas in which the preferences of potential customers are fairly similar tend to adopt somewhat similar fashion images, but stores with a variety of target groups to choose from have a variety of fashion image possibilities open to them. For instance, a small town in which a university is located probably would have two basic customer groups—the younger university students and the more adult faculty and townspeople.

A small city serving as the only metropolitan center in a large geographic area, and with limited business and industrial interests, would likely be dominated by people who have fairly similar general interests and thus form a homogenous target group of customers.

In large metropolitan areas, however, the diversity of business and industrial interests and of lifestyle creates a variety of different customer groups to be served, each with distinct and separate needs and wants. A sampling of some of the fashion images projected by stores in the New York City area shows how diverse that variety can be.

Macy's, New York, has made a tremendous change in its image in recent years. What was once the budget basement, for example, is now The Cellar, stocked with exciting, innovative merchandise for kitchen and bath. Macy's has changed its image to attract a new target customer—the young, working, married or single New Yorker who finds the merchandise in The Cellar tailored to his or her wants and needs. Macy's has also changed its assortments of fashion ready-to-wear, which now project an image of youth and excitement and are moderately priced. The scope and size of the store and the merchandise assortments presented to the customer are large and var-

ied, but always tailored to the new target customer.

Henri Bendel's is a very different kind of store, devoted to the concept of "small is beautiful." Bendel's has built its image around small, unique shops and boutiques as stores within a store. The store's target customers are small-sized, unique, and eager for fashions in the early stages of their cycles. Bendel's has been the leader in introducing sizes 1 and 2 into fashion apparel. It has been the first to present certain unique and intriguing designs from such designers as Zandra Rhodes and Jean Muir of London and Stephen Burrows of the United States.

The Lane Bryant stores serve women of all ages who have fuller figures. The store assures these target customers that whatever the fashion, Lane Bryant will have it in their sizes.

Bloomingdale's, or "Bloomie's" as it is affectionately known by its customers, has been an outstanding example of a store that has determined who its target customer will be and has successfully tailored its fashion image to this customer. Young, trendy, upper-income customers consider Bloomingdale's an innovator for all types of fashion-influenced merchandise. Furniture, home furnishings, and gourmet foods are areas other than fashion ready-to-wear in which Bloomingdale's projects a fashion leadership image to its target customer.

The Lerner chain has determined that its target customers want fashions at their peak, and this is the image conveyed to customers by Lerner stores across the country. When print fabric skirts are popular, Lerner's offers its customers print skirts in every available print, color, and size. When classic blouses are wanted, Lerner's stocks them in every possible color and size. Lerner's is never an innovator but always provides the right merchandise at the right time for its target customer. The chain's fashion image is clearly understood by these customers.

Each store or group of stores in these examples develops its own character through its merchandise assortments, decor, advertising, and display. It would not be difficult, given the

THAT AYRES LOOK

NIPON
A navy geometric
georgette is
romanced with Venise
lace and that tailored
Nipon touch, tucking
285.00. Crystal
Room, Third Floor,
Downtown and
Glendale

KASPER
The day-to-dark chemise
in navy and white crepe
changes form with its
own wrap of belt 185.00.
Crystal Room, Third
Floor, Downtown,
Glendale and Lafayette
Indiana

ADELE SIMPSON
A black and white taffeta
bow dramatizes a lean
streak of black matte
jersey. 300.00. Crystal
Room, Third Floor,
Downtown and Glendale

That Ayres Look began in 1936.
We have been featured
in Vogue magazine
for forty-four fabulous years.
Even before that,
we were recognized as
the fashion leader in Indiana.
On this, the forty-fourth
anniversary of That Ayres Look,
we celebrate our
continuing friendship
with Vogue,
the world's finest designers
and you.

DESIGNER ROSTER 1980
Harve Benard
Stanley Blacker
Bill Blass
Blassport
Oscar de la Renta
Charlotte Ford
Halston
Halston Sportswear
Betty Hanson
Kasper for Joan Leslie
Anne Klein
Calvin Klein
Leal
Frank Massandrea
Jack Mulgueen
Marita
Albert Nipon
Mollie Parnis
Don Sayres for Gamut
Jerry Silverman
Adele Simpson
St. John
Ernst Strauss
Charles Suppon for Gare
Koos van den Akker

Look for us in the February
issue of Vogue magazine

Don't miss our "Date" shows
highlighting That Ayres Look,
Keys to a Workable Life
Wednesday on Designer Lane,
Third Floor, Downtown
or Friday in the Ivy Room,
Glendale at 12:00 and 2:00.
Vogue editor Liz Groves
will be our guest at
the Wednesday shows.

L.S. Ayres & co.

L.S. Ayres & co.

Shop Ayres Suburban Stores today, 12:00 to 5:30

In Indianapolis the "Ayres look" means fashion leadership.

descriptions above and a time in which to inspect these stores and review their assortments and advertising, for someone completely new to the city to identify the image of each by its merchandise, its ads, its windows, and the behavior of its sales staff. Not only is the merchandise different in each store, but the atmosphere of each store is different. Each store has developed the atmosphere most natural and most comfortable to the target group of customers that the store wants to attract.

ELEMENTS OF FASHION MERCHANDISING POLICY

Once a store has defined and studied its target group or groups of customers, it then develops and maintains, through its fashion merchandising policies, the fashion image it hopes will attract those customer groups. A **policy** is ''a settled, clearly defined course of action or method of doing business deemed necessary, expedient, or advantageous. Policies are to business what sailing charts are to a seaman.''[2] A **fashion merchandising policy** is a long-range guide for the fashion merchandising staff, spelling out the store's fashion aims, standards of quality, price ranges, attitudes toward competition, and any other elements that may be considered pertinent.

Store policies are determined by top management, and it is the responsibility of all divisions of the store to adhere to these policies. Fashion merchandising policies are usually directed to the merchandising divisions, where buyers respond to them in their various buying and merchandising activities. Merchandising policies are also directed to other divisions, however, such as advertising and promotion, finance and control, operations and service, and personnel and labor relations. All of these have a part in successfully carrying out store policies. For example, if it is a policy to carry goods of superlative quality, the store's wrapping and packing materials must also be of excellent quality and its adjustment department would be expected to take a liberal attitude toward customer complaints. On the other hand, if the policy is to

have quality that is merely adequate, wrapping and packing may be of minimum quality, and the adjustment office may take a tougher line with customers who have complaints. If a store policy emphasizes newness, there may be a company rule against running ads featuring clearance merchandise, except for discreet, twice-a-year announcements. If the policy is to emphasize bargains, however, there may be numerous price promotions, mention of comparative prices in advertising, and general assurances that the store will not be undersold.

Fashion merchandising policies, therefore, affect almost every activity of the store, so that the image presented to the public is consistent throughout.

The Merchandise Assortment

The degree of fashion leadership established by a store's merchandising policy is most visible in the store's merchandise assortments. These assortments are characterized not only by the newness or uniqueness of the styles chosen but also by the length of time the styles are permitted to remain in stock.

For example, if the store chooses as its target customers those who want to be first with the newest, store buyers will be instructed to assemble assortments that consist primarily of prophetic styles—those that incorporate one or more incoming trends. Buyers probably will be required to apply a high initial markup to their merchandise in order to compensate for the risks involved when fashions are at the early experimental stages of their cycles. They will also be allowed quite liberal markdowns, because these are almost unavoidable in such an operation. They will be expected to promptly mark down nonstarting styles and to clear out any styles that have been copied into lower price lines or that show signs of being already well on the rise in their demand cycles.

By way of comparison, a store that caters to women who want to be in fashion but not necessarily among the experimenters will offer an assortment made up primarily of securely established styles. Such assortments may contain several versions of any particularly good style, or they may contain mainly classics with a sprinkling of forward-looking styles. Policy may specify that a few pieces may be purchased above the normal price range of the store or department and ahead of the store's normal position with relation to the fashion cycle. This procedure lends prestige to the regular assortment and provides exposure to styles probably too new for the firm's clientele but likely to prove acceptable somewhat later. "Getting the eye used to it" is one way to prepare customers for incoming fashions.

A store of this type will not require initial markups as high as those in a store carrying more experimental styles, since risks are not so great at this stage of the fashion cycle. Its policy on markdowns may not be especially liberal unless the store has a policy of refusing to be undersold and therefore requires its buyers to price everything as low as (or lower than) similar merchandise in competing stores.

Large stores often offer customers a choice in degree of fashion leadership by having two or more departments, each of which features styles for identical end uses but at different stages in their fashion acceptance and therefore at different price levels. In such cases, each department may have a different merchandising policy. The prestige department may have a policy of immediately clearing out any styles that have been copied down into lower price lines. The medium-priced department may have a policy of doing the same with any of their styles that have found their way into the stock of the store's basement or budget departments. When an individual style, a total look, a color, or a detail moves into a lower price level, the fashion merchandising policy of these stores usually requires its higher-priced departments to clear their stocks of similar merchandise.

Sales Promotion and Selling Techniques

To insure the smooth flow of merchandise from store to customer, sales promotion and selling techniques are usually geared to the degree of fashion leadership evidenced in the store's merchandise assortments. An overall fashion image must be coordinated so that the target group of consumers can be turned into customers.

Stores known for their fashion leadership are usually the first to introduce new trends, either in styling or in color. The ads that these stores run emphasize new themes and looks, and both window and interior displays reinforce these themes and looks. When possible, designer names are featured, exclusives are introduced, and fashion newness is underlined. It is very rare that price becomes a focal point in any of these ads or displays.

Stores whose target customers seek fashions at the peak of their cycles avoid extremes in styles or themes in their advertising. In general, their advertising and display stress the fashion rightness of the promoted styles rather than their newness. Price is given prominence only to the degree that it is important to the particular group of customers.

Stores in the mass-merchandising category give strong prominence to price in their advertising. Since the fashion leaders and the middle group have already proved the importance of the fashions concerned, these stores concentrate on promoting their availability at budget prices. Their assortments usually contain large quantities of nearly identical merchandise, thus reinforcing the idea that a particular fashion has made its mark.

Selling techniques are keyed to the fashion image the store wants to project in much the same way. In prestige stores, salespeople are coached to speak with authority about fashion, to present new ideas with confidence, and to give full service to the customer. Stores catering to the middle group of customers usually display their merchandise on open racks, but salespeople are present to answer customer questions and assist them in finding the desired styles in the right colors and sizes. Self-service fixtures dominate the mass merchandisers' selling floors, with store personnel limited primarily to stock clerks and cashiers.

Many experts believe it is at the point-of-sale that a store either succeeds or fails in its attempt to establish a particular fashion image —and that the salespeople are the key to that success or failure. Herbert Wittkin, former head of Stern Brothers, New York, explained it this way:

We can spend literally millions of dollars in merchandise investments; we can spend many millions more on display and merchandise presentation and advertising; we can spend unlimited energy and time in trying to influence people to think well of us—only to have it all go down the drain because of a surly sales clerk. . . . Our salespeople talk to our customers and convey a feeling with everything they do—in the way they look—the way they smile—the way they shrug their shoulders—in short, they project our image more forcefully than any other element in the store. If they are warm, friendly, alert, fashionable, efficient people, our customers make the equation that our store is all of those things. If they are brusque, short-tempered, curt, unpleasant, their impact is deadly and frequently permanently damaging . . . [3]

Other Essential Elements

Top management must consider many other essential elements in establishing the fashion merchandising policies of a store. Standards for the quality of merchandise to be carried must be defined. The pricing policies of the store and the depth and breadth of assortments must be determined. Management must also determine whether private or national brand goods will be featured and whether exclusivity of merchandise is important. Each of these elements must be in harmony with the overall fashion image the store wishes to create and maintain.

QUALITY STANDARDS. A store sets its quality standards in terms of those of its customers. In prestige stores, durability of merchandise may be of minor importance, but fineness of material and care in workmanship are usually of major importance. Among stores catering to the middle group of customers, both durability and good fit in merchandise may be important, the latter because of the high cost of alterations in relation to the price of the garment. Customers of mass merchandisers may evaluate each piece of merchandise in terms of the price asked for it, and stores of this type may have no set standards of quality other than that the goods be represented honestly.

GRADES. Some types of fashion merchandise, such as hosiery and shoes, are graded by the producer as "perfect," "irregulars," or "seconds." Less-than-perfect goods are graded **irregular** if they have defects that may affect appearance but not wear. **Seconds** are factory rejects that have faults that may affect wear. Depending upon its clientele, store policy may exclude anything except perfect goods or it may permit irregulars and seconds to be offered in special promotions or by basement departments. It is what customers want and expect that determines policy, in this as in the many other phases of fashion merchandising. If customers demand perfect goods, the store offers them; if they accept slight irregularities at concessions in price, the store follows the lead and makes such goods available when possible.

PRICES. Another policy that management must define involves the pricing of its fashion merchandise. In determining the price policy, management must consider price ranges, price lines, and selling prices of the merchandise.

The price range is the breadth of prices between the highest and lowest price at which merchandise is offered for sale. A price line is the price at which large assortments of merchandise are offered for sale. Top management specifies whether the selling price should be rounded off at or set a few cents below an even-dollar figure.

DEPTH VERSUS
BREADTH ASSORTMENTS. The degree of fashion leadership the store has chosen to project usually determines how deep and how

"Select. Don't Settle." Barney's advertising slogan gives the store's philosophy on depth and breadth of assortment.

wide its assortments will be. Broad, shallow assortments, presenting a large variety of styles, colors, and sizes, but not a large stock of any of these, are characteristic of prestige stores and departments. In stores catering to the middle group of customers, assortments are usually broad and shallow early in the season, when new styles are still being tested for acceptance, but relatively narrow and deep later in the season, once the trend of demand has become clear. Mass merchandisers concentrate on narrow, deep assortments of proven popular styles. Some large stores, with the space to carry wider assortments, may have broad, shallow stocks on the outer fringes of demand and narrow, deep stocks where demand is clearly defined.

EXCLUSIVITY.   **Exclusivity** is an important selling point for stores that cater to fashion leaders. It means allowing a store sole use of a style or styles. Stores serving the middle group of customers also welcome exclusivity as a competitive weapon. Exclusive styles may come from several sources: foreign markets; small factories; new, young designers; and some large manufacturers who prefer exclusive distribution and sell to only one store in an area. Some stores consider exclusives so important that their buyers are expected to work with producers toward having special styles made up for the store.

BRANDS.   A private or store brand, meeting standards specified by the retailer, belongs exclusively to that store and is used to ensure consistent quality of product or to meet price competition, among many other purposes. A **national brand,** sold by many stores across the country, can give stores and customers alike a consistent guarantee of quality and fashion correctness. Prestige stores tend to feature their own store labels and designer names. National brands are the backbone of assortments found in department stores. Chain and mail-order companies consistently feature private brands. National brands are sometimes offered by mass merchandisers, but as a rule these stores tend to feature unbranded merchandise.

CHANGING A FASHION IMAGE

Stores sometimes find it either necessary or advantageous to shift their sights and to aim for a different target group of customers than the one for which their fashion image was originally created. Such a change may be necessary if the character of the community the store serves undergoes a marked change. Such a change may be advantageous if the store wants to reach out for additional groups of customers not previously served, or to fill a merchandising need temporarily left unfilled by competing stores, or even to retreat from a merchandising area in which the competition has become too fierce.

The classic case of the necessity to change an image is that of the neighborhood store whose original customers have moved out of the area and have been replaced by people of other income or ethnic groups. If the store is to continue to do business at its old location, it must adjust its fashion image to attract the new potential clientele flowing into the area. If, on the other hand, the store wants to retain its original image, it must move to a different area where it can find enough customers of the original type to support it.

Changing an image, once it has been established, is not easy and should be a gradual process. In fact, it is more difficult to change an image than to build one from the start. Building an image can sometimes be done in a relatively short period of time, while some stores that have successfully changed their image have taken a decade or more to complete the process. Changes in fashion merchandise assortments, in promotion and advertising techniques, in quality standards, and in pricing all help to gradually change an image and permit a store to replace customers it has lost or no longer wishes to serve with new customers. The trick is to retain enough of the old customers while courting new ones to maintain volume and avoid losses.

One of the most sweeping image turnabouts in recent years occurred when discounters added fashion apparel to operations that formerly had been concerned only with hard goods. Starting with what might be called a negative image as nonfashion retailers, these merchants used assortments, displays, and advertising in their attempts to get people to consider them as apparel and accessories outlets. Some fumbled and ruined their businesses, but there have also been some spectacular successes.

TYPES OF FASHION IMAGES

Every activity and every feature of a store contributes to that store's image in the eyes of target customers. To create its own distinctive fashion image, management uses any and all elements that can help to build it.

In general, a store's fashion image is determined by its customers, degree of fashion leadership, store size, and type of operation.

Degree of Fashion Leadership

Although the degree of fashion leadership a store chooses to assume represents one among many possibilities, stores can be divided generally into three categories: those that project a high-fashion image, those that project a middle-of-the-road fashion image, and the mass marketers of widely accepted fashions.

FASHION LEADERS. Those merchants who elect to deal in high fashion and to cater to customers who want to be in the forefront of fashion have a relatively straightforward course in creating a fashion image. The styles they feature must be new and prophetic; every assortment in the store must be coordinated with all others; and customers must have their wants understood perfectly. This is easily said, but it involves a superlative job of coordinating the market work, the merchandise selections, the emphasis, and the promotion of every element of every new look in fashion that the store chooses to offer. Dresses must relate to coats, and slips must relate to dresses; loungewear must relate to ready-to-wear; all accessories, from bedroom slippers to cosmetics, must be in tune with the current fashion trend.

Stores that achieve a high degree of fashion leadership in their merchandise assortments have such distinctive advertising that their ads can be easily recognized even without the store name. Their promotions are usually developed around a theme rather than specific items of merchandise. They describe looks and themes rather than individual styles of dresses, shoes, or handbags. When they do advertise a specific item, it is promoted not as an item alone but as a necessary element of a currently acceptable fashion theme. Prices are mentioned almost as an afterthought and never prominently.

Salespeople in such stores are extremely well trained in fashion and coached in how and when to advise customers. Alterations to improve the fit of garments are carefully made and returns are accepted no matter what the reason. Physical surroundings are compatible with what customers are accustomed to at home: rich carpets; beautifully upholstered chairs and sofas; expensive draperies, wall treatments, and lighting fixtures.

Public relations activities of such stores are likely to be of the more subtle type. The head of the store may give parties for select groups of customers and friends that rate society-page mention. Fashion shows may be small and intimate, run by a store executive who knows everyone in the audience by name and who probably has a good idea of which designer's clothes are in the closet of each one there. Publicity on behalf of the store is likely to result from well-known people having patronized it, or from the store owner's personal participation in community projects.

MASS MARKETERS. At the lower end of the price and fashion scale, the method of creating a fashion image for a retail store is equally as direct as that of the fashion leaders. The image that mass merchandisers strive for is one associated with bargains in fashions that have become widely accepted. Target customers of such a store do not expect individual service; they are satisfied to wait on themselves, try on garments in crowded fitting rooms, and stand in line at a cashier's desk to pay for their purchases. Crowds do not bother them; instead, a crowd implies that the bargains must be good to draw so many shoppers. Little or no luxury is evident in the surroundings; only the simplest and most functional of furnishings and lighting are used.

Coordination of an outfit in mass-merchandising stores is strictly a customer's job. Although the store may have provided the related accessories to go with its clothes, it is up to the customer to collect them unaided from the assortments and to put the right pieces of the fashion look together. This task is not difficult, however, since the fashion looks with which he or she is concerned are familiar by the time they reach the mass level of acceptance and price. Coordination of apparel and accessories has been extensively displayed and advertised as well as widely worn before the fashion has reached that peak or waning stage at which the customers of such stores usually make purchases.

THE MIDDLE MARKETERS. Retailers who operate between the two extremes in fashion leadership have the advantage of serving the largest customer group. They have the problem, however, of marking out the particular segment of that total group they plan to serve and then developing their merchandising, services, and promotion policies accordingly.

Timing of merchandise presentation is a major challenge to stores that wish to project a middle-of-the-road fashion image. It is not as easy for them to judge the precise stage of the fashion cycle in which their customers are interested as it is for those retailers whose customers are always fashion leaders or those whose customers are always content with fashion in its late stages. Instead, their customers are the ones who are neither first nor last to adopt the new. They are the customers who looked with interest at displays of colored bed sheets for a long period before they actually bought anything other than white. To judge the precise moment when such customers are ready to test the new, and to judge how much emphasis to place upon the new in assortments, promotion, and personal selling, is a challenge to the merchandising skill and fashion knowledge of the retailer.

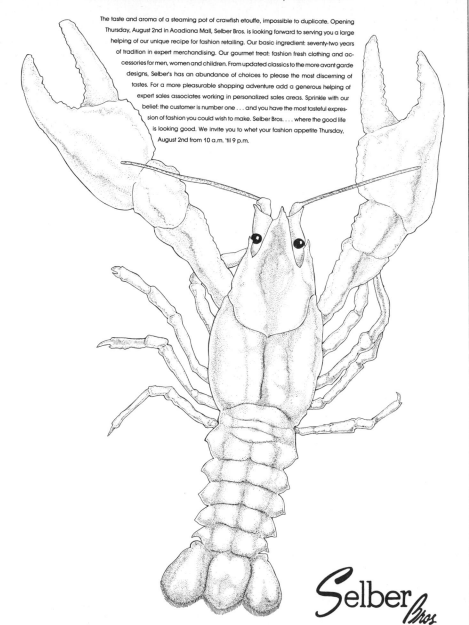

La Bonne Vie

WE'LL SOON BE A PART OF IT, LAFAYETTE!
SELBER BROS. GRAND OPENING IS THURSDAY, AUGUST 2ND.

The taste and aroma of a steaming pot of crawfish etouffe, impossible to duplicate. Opening Thursday, August 2nd in Acadiana Mall, Selber Bros. is looking forward to serving you a large helping of our unique recipe for fashion retailing. Our basic ingredient: seventy-two years of tradition in expert merchandising. Our gourmet treat: fashion fresh clothing and accessories for men, women and children. From updated classics to the more avant garde designs, Selber's has an abundance of choices to please the most discerning of tastes. For a more pleasurable shopping adventure add a generous helping of expert sales associates working in personalized sales areas. Sprinkle with our belief: the customer is number one . . . and you have the most tasteful expression of fashion you could wish to make. Selber Bros. . . . where the good life is looking good. We invite you to whet your fashion appetite Thursday, August 2nd from 10 a.m. 'til 9 p.m.

Selber Bros.

Selber Bros., Lafayette, La. store opening, 1979

Selber Bros. projects an image of fashion leadership and identifies with the community that is the site of their new store.

Another challenge to the middle marketers involves devising ways to suggest the appropriate combinations of apparel and accessories to their customers. These customers do not buy with the sure touch of fashion leaders, nor have the fashions they are buying become so familiar that coordination is almost automatic. Since selling techniques cannot be as personalized as they are in prestige stores, and since the customers resist being pushed into spending more than they planned, there is a limit to what can be done by the salespeople. Advertising and display usually do an important job in this respect, showing how, for example, the right scarf, necklace, or pin will set off the neckline of a coat or dress.

These are the stores, too, that face the most plentiful competition, and they function in a trading area in which one store's merchandise tends to look much like that of another. In their quest for distinction, some stores of this type make a point of managing their stocks to keep them complete at all times. Their image then becomes that of the store that "always has something for me."

Service and atmosphere that have no direct connection with fashion also help build a distinctive image for an individual store. Some stores lend luster to their image by using distinctive wrappings and boxes that customers are proud to be seen carrying. (The implication is that the smart wrap encloses equally smart merchandise.)

Some stores do things with such finesse that people automatically link their names with fashion excitement. Neiman-Marcus, the well-known Dallas-based specialty store, indulges in such delightful irrelevancies as offering "his and her" airplanes in one of their Christmas catalogs. The natural reaction of the public is to assume that a store whose customers can afford such spectacular gifts is a good place to shop—not only for a $50,000 fur coat but for a $25 fashion gift as well.

Size and Type of Organization

Different types of stores have different types of fashion images. The very large store has various problems and opportunities in estab-lishing a fashion image that a very small store may not have. The medium-volume store may maintain an image unlike that of either the larger or smaller store. Unlike the single-unit store, the multiunit retail organization has unique challenges to meet in creating and maintaining a distinctive fashion image throughout all of its many units.

THE GIANTS. Giant retailers have special image considerations because of their size. Some of them sell to such a broad range of the public that they need to segment their overall image, presenting one face to those customers who are fashion leaders and another to those who are fashion followers. They often handle this through special departments or shops, each one establishing an image for a specific group of customers: teens, tall girls, expectant mothers, sports enthusiasts, wearers of country clothes, and career or college people. The huge size of such stores permits them to engage in shop merchandising, whereas smaller stores, with more limited floor space and assortments, cannot set up such shops quite so freely.

Large stores often capitalize on their bigness. They stage promotions on a spectacular scale. Instead of devoting one or two windows to a new fashion, they devote block-long batteries of windows to an idea. They hire display executives who are highly creative and whose windows and interior displays are remembered for years. They turn their main floors into flower shows, as Macy's in New York City, and Hess Brothers in Allentown, Pennsylvania, do each spring. Or they regularly run ads that stress the vastness of their assortments.

Many large stores have special facilities, such as auditoriums, that they lend to civic groups for community events. Often the auditorium is used by the store for a fashion show or demonstration that is expected to draw large crowds.

THE SMALL INDEPENDENT. At the opposite end of the size scale is the small, independently owned shop in which the proprietor is likely to be the merchandiser, policymaker,

Large stores may feature lavish interior displays that are remembered for years. This is Saks Fifth Avenue's Christmas decor.

and promotion expert. Such stores, even though they may employ several salespeople, cannot afford and may not need the amount of advertising space that large stores use to enhance their image.

Small operations have their own special tools for image building, based on the personal approach. Salespeople and proprietors know customers by name; they suggest apparel to coordinate with what is already owned; and they send personal notes to customers when new merchandise of suitable type has arrived. They have coins readily available for parking meters; they gift wrap beautifully and individually; and they provide innumerable friendly, person-to-person services that cannot be offered practically by large stores.

In their merchandising, some small stores even capitalize on their smallness. They buy only a few pieces, or even single pieces, of a style. The customer who purchases a dress or coat from such a store can be certain that she will not meet herself on the street, at the bus stop, or at the club luncheon.

CHAIN ORGANIZATIONS. Units of apparel chains and general merchandising chains often use the image-building tools of both large and small stores. Among the large-store techniques a general merchandise chain could use, for example, might be the establishment of special shops within its stores to feature a particular look, such as country casuals. Or an apparel chain may create a series of ads and promotions devoted to the special needs of its customers, no matter in what part of the country they are located.

Other chains find ways to offer some of the personalized service characteristic of small stores. Salespeople may be encouraged to obtain customers' names for notification of special sales or new merchandise. Although the merchandise in one unit of a chain may not differ markedly from what is offered by another unit of the same organization, it is possible for the staff of each unit to develop warm, friendly relations with customers. In this way, all customers feel they are receiving personal attention and advice when making fashion purchases.

MERCHANDISING VOCABULARY

Define or briefly explain the following terms:

Exclusivity	**National brand**
Fashion image	**Policy**
Fashion merchandising policy	**Seconds**
Irregulars	**Store image**

MERCHANDISING REVIEW

1. Clearly distinguish between the terms "store image" and "fashion image." Do you think it is possible for a store to have a favorable store image and an unfavorable fashion image, or vice versa? Defend your answer.
2. Why is it important for a store to clearly define or have a clear-cut profile of its target group of customers before attempting to establish and implement its fashion philosophy?
3. Name and briefly discuss the elements of a store's fashion merchandising policy.
4. What are the implications of each for the store's fashion image?
5. For what specific reasons might a store seek to change its fashion image?
6. What are some of the things a store can do to achieve a distinctive fashion image if it is neither a fashion leader nor a mass merchandiser?
7. Describe the merchandise, selling, and promotional characteristics you might expect to find in a store whose image is one of fashion leadership.
8. Describe the merchandise assortments, selling techniques, and promotional characteristics you might expect to find in a mass-merchandising store.
9. Describe the merchandise assortments, selling techniques, and promotional characteristics you might expect to find in a store with a middle-of-the-road fashion image.
10. What are some of the image-building devices available to an independent store that may be too small to do much advertising?

MERCHANDISING DIGEST

1. It is stated in the text that "stores serving areas in which the preferences of potential customers are fairly similar tend to adopt somewhat similar fashion images, but stores with a variety of target groups to choose from have a variety of fashion image possibilities open to them." Discuss this statement and its implications, citing examples to illustrate your opinions on the subject.

2. Discuss the following statement from the text: "Changing an image, once it has been established, is not easy and is usually a slow and gradual process." What factors are involved? Why should change be slow rather than abrupt? Do you know of any store that has undertaken to change its previous image? If so, explain how such change was brought about.

REFERENCES
1 *Stores,* January 1960, p. 17.
2 Nystrom, *Fashion Merchandising,* p. 195.
3 Wittkin, "An Image Is a Multi-Faceted Thing," p. 230.

RETAIL
MERCHANDISING OF FASHION

Position Statement.

Management has decided to add a junior sportswear department to its ladies ready-to-wear store in your city. The fashion emphasis of this new department is to be on merchanidse at the late rise/early culmination point of the fashion cycle. You are to be the buyer.

A. Write an essay indicating:
1. What factors must be considered in choosing a location in the store for your sportswear department? How would these factors affect the target customer?
2. What planning must be done before you can go to the apparel market to purchase goods for your department?
3. What sources of fashion and merchandise information or aids are available to you as the buyer?
4. How would you define the fashion image you wish to convey to your customer?
5. What methods and media would you choose to promote the opening of your department?
6. What specific duties would a fashion coordinator perform in helping you with your new department?

B. Prepare an opening day newspaper advertisement for your new department, and write a short (30-second) commercial for the local radio/television station about the opening of your department.

C. Prepare a six month merchandising plan for your junior sportswear department based upon a planned sales volume for this department of $650,000 in the six month period (Feb/July) being planned.

D. Prepare a buying plan for the planned opening stock of the new department. Indicate the specific number of items you intend to buy by price lines and classifications. The total dollar limit set by management is $80,000.

The changing, challenging, and fascinating fashion industries include those concerned with fibers, textiles, manufacturing, retailing, the full range of communications media, publicity, and promotion. All of these industries offer career opportunities. Fashion offers an endless variety of opportunities for those who are career-oriented and are willing to spend time preparing for these careers. Because the fashion field is an enormous one, beginners often need a guide to the various paths that may lead them to their goals in the fashion field.

This appendix offers such a guide. Brief descriptions of the areas open to those interested in fashion may save beginners some initial uncertainty and may help direct them to that part of the fashion field to which they will be most suited.

There are opportunities in the fashion field for people of many different capabilities. Dedication, imagination, willingness to persevere, and sound business judgment are the important ingredients for success in this field.

SCOPE OF THE FASHION BUSINESS

The size and influence of the field of fashion cannot be measured in dollars alone. But out of every dollar spent on consumer goods in the United States each year, about 10 cents is used for apparel, accessories, and personal adornment.

The fashion field, in terms of all that it includes, cannot be readily defined. Fashion in the broadest sense is a reflection of the consumer's way of life. It manifests itself in cars as well as clothing, in houses as well as hats—in any commodity or service in which the consumer exercises personal choice.

In the earlier part of this century, some fashion industries went along for years with little regard for consumer preferences and saw little consumer demand for style change. But as preferences and demands became more diverse, as a result of fast-changing lifestyles, most fashion industries came to accept the fact that consumers alone make fashions by their acceptance or rejection of offered styles. To the career seeker, the growing influence of fashion on industries unrelated to apparel and accessories means this: Experience gained in the primary fashion industries can be applied to other industries serving consumers.

The person who embarks on a fashion career today enters a field that is far flung and many faceted. In this field there is freedom to grow, freedom to change jobs or direction, and freedom to move to different cities or even to different countries without having to begin anew in an unrelated type of work.

International Character of American Fashion

The American fashion business today is international. Raw materials, such as furs, hides, and fibers, are imported from remote areas of the world. Manufactured goods, too, including both apparel and accessories items, are imported from all over the world. Also imported are ideas and inspiration, not only from the couture houses of Europe but from any part of the world where general news or fashion news is being made. Even outer space is within fashion's territory, as evidenced by jumpsuits and other apparel that have been inspired by astronaut gear.

American goods and ideas are exported. Many American manufacturers contract to have their lines produced abroad under franchise agreements. American fashions are produced in foreign countries to the specifications of American firms. Producers in other countries send their young people to Seventh Avenue and to the fashion industries' technical schools in the United States to prepare them for fashion production careers. Sometimes the producers themselves seek United States know-how to help them establish or improve their fashion business in their home countries. In addition, the United States exports its know-how in fashion retailing. Stores from all over the world are members of the National Retail Merchants Association. Foreign delegates attend NRMA conventions as special guests, and the NRMA has sent delegations of domestic retailers to visit foreign stores and participate in workshops with executives of those foreign firms.

Within the borders of the United States, fashion activity is everywhere. Seventh Avenue in New York City remains the heart of the apparel-producing industries, but there are also creative centers in Los Angeles, Dallas, Miami, and cities of the Midwest, West Coast, East Coast, and Southeast. Even in some seemingly unlikely small towns, there are mills and factories that need people to guide their output along current fashion lines. And there are retailers of fashion in every major city, in every suburb, and in every small town.

Thus, geography is not a limiting factor in a fashion career. Almost any location in this country and throughout the world is one in which fashion work of some sort can be found or created.

Facets of Fashion Activity

The fashion field is many faceted, and the positions open to people starting a career are numerous and diverse. Some fields, such as designing, advertising, and display, usually demand a high degree of creativity and origi-

nality. Others, such as fiber and fabric research and development, require an interest and education in scientific subjects. Still others, such as plant management and retailing management, call for business acumen and administrative skills.

A pleasing personality, a genuine interest in people, and a willingness to work and learn are indispensable in the fashion field. A strong constitution and healthy feet will also be helpful in the market work of retail buyers, buying office representatives, magazine editors, fashion coordinators, and their assistants. Skills in writing, sketching, typing, and photography are much in demand in the fashion field. Sewing and draping skills, even without a designer's creativity, can lead to such interesting work as sample making. In personnel, supervisory, and training work, an ability to teach is very helpful. This ability can also lead to a position as a teacher in one of the many schools devoted to fashion training.

Another way to enter the fashion field is to begin as a model. In this part of the business, a person's natural qualities, such as a certain type of face and figure, can make this an easy area in which to begin a career in fashion. Some theatrical training can also be very helpful, especially when the goal is a position as fashion coordinator. Theatrical training can help to develop the poise and sophistication needed for success in this field.

Good work habits, a willingness to please, and an interest in fashion can be all that is needed to start as a receptionist or secretary to an executive in one of the many branches of the fashion industry. Such jobs often offer the opportunity to discover and develop interest and talents useful to a career in fashion.

CAREERS IN MANUFACTURING

The principal manufacturing industries in the fashion field require fashion-oriented and fashion-trained people to guide their production, reinforce their selling efforts, and disseminate fashion information to their customers and to the consuming public. In addition, these industries also require technical experts of many kinds, skilled and unskilled factory labor, and office workers of various types.

Fashion-related careers to be found in manufacturing include those in the raw materials fields, the apparel trade, suppliers to the apparel trade, the accessories trades, and the home sewing industry.

Raw Materials Industries

The greatest number and variety of fashion careers in the raw materials field are found among the producers of fiber and fabrics. This is not only a big field but also a field that is always in close contact with all phases of the fashion business. Similar positions, but in smaller number, are also to be found with other raw materials producers, such as leather and furs, and their respective industry associations.

FASHION EXPERT. Fiber producers and fabric firms have fashion departments headed by individuals with a variety of titles who attend worldwide fashion openings, keep in close touch with all sources of fashion information, and disseminate the fashion story throughout their respective organizations. Candidates for such positions either may have already acquired fashion expertise in other areas of the fashion business or are employees of the firm who have demonstrated an ability to handle such responsibilities.

The fashion department's activities usually require personnel with the ability to coordinate apparel and accessories, to stage fashion shows, to work with the press, to assist individual producers and retailers with fashion-related problems or projects, and to set up fashion exhibits for the trade or for the public. These extremely varied demands made upon all who work in such departments constitute an excellent training school. Even at the clerical level, the beginners in such a department learn much about fashion and, if sufficiently motivated, are in the position to train themselves for promotion.

FABRIC DESIGNER. While it takes technical skills to produce a fiber, it takes both technical and artistic skills to produce a fabric. Fabric companies employ designers who have both technical knowledge of the processes involved in producing a fabric as well as artistic ability and the ability to successfully anticipate fashion trends. The fabric designer, who works far in advance of the apparel trades, needs fashion radar of superlative quality. Some designers are allowed to concentrate on their own ideas, while others are expected to work out special fabric designs for certain customers. In either case, the chief designer for a fabric mill makes fashion decisions that can involve vast capital investments every time a new season's line is prepared.

FABRIC STYLIST. Many fabric companies employ a fabric stylist to revise existing fabric designs for a new seasonal line or adapt them for specific markets. Some people find this job a career in itself; others use it as a stepping-stone to the more creative job of fabric designer.

FABRIC LIBRARIAN. Most major synthetic fiber sources maintain libraries of fabrics that are made from their fibers. These libraries consist of fabric swatches clipped to cards on which detailed descriptions and sources of supply are recorded. The librarian in charge is expected to be thoroughly capable of discussing fashion trends and fabric matters with interested designers and manufacturers. The librarian must also be knowledgeable not only about the firm's products but also about the market in general.

EDUCATIONAL CONSULTANT. Most of the fiber producers and some of the fabric houses maintain departments to convey technical information about their products to apparel producers, retailers, and consumers. Educational departments answer inquiries, prepare exhibits, address groups of retail salespeople or consumers, and stage demonstrations. In addition to a knowledge of both the technology and the fashion influence involved, graciousness is a must in this work, along with an ability to talk to people at all educational and social levels.

Exciting careers as a fabric designer or stylist are available in the fashion manufacturing industries.

INDUSTRY CONSULTANT.   Most of the fiber companies and some of the fabric houses assign executives to study the needs of the individual industries in which their products are used. These executives act as a liaison between their firms and the industries in which they specialize. If a company is about to introduce a new fiber, fabric, finish, or treatment, its industry consultants work closely with consumer goods producers, encouraging them to try the new product and helping them to solve any problems related to its use. The help these consultants give may also extend to the retail level, where retailers may be assisted in launching fashions that employ the new product.

PUBLICITY EXECUTIVE.   In both fiber and fabric companies, the publicity staff keeps in close touch with technical as well as fashion matters and makes information about company products readily available to the trade and consumer press. Usually product stories can be tied to fashion information, enhancing their appeal to editors and readers alike.

The publicity executive in charge of the de-partment generally has a thorough understanding of fashion and journalism, along with a pleasing personality and a good memory for names and faces. These attributes are essential in preparing press releases, working with photographers who provide illustrative material for those releases, and working with members of the press who seek help on feature stories or who want background information. Skill in subtle selling is useful in placing unsolicited publicity, when an editor has to be convinced of the value and interest of the story to the publication's audience.

In the major fiber-producing companies, there may be a corps of publicity executives, each specializing in one or two closely related industries. One may concentrate on the use of specific fibers in apparel fabrics, for instance, while another may specialize in the use of the company's fibers in rugs and carpeting. In smaller organizations, there may be only one such executive. In any case, there are usually typists, secretaries, and assistants, and a beginner who starts in any such capacity is in an excellent position to learn fashion publicity.

OTHER AREAS. Both fiber and fabric industries offer career opportunities in sales, market research, and promotion. These are not always fashion jobs, however, and rarely are they open to beginners. Some experience within the company and some specialized skill in the field are likely to be more important than a knowledge of fashion alone in getting such jobs. Advertising, including its more exciting aspects such as the production of television shows, is often handled by advertising agencies rather than by the company's own advertising department.

Apparel Trades

For creative people, the plum of the fashion apparel trades is the designer's job. But the climb to this top job is often laborious and uncertain, and the footing at the top may be slippery. New talent is always elbowing its way in, and even the most successful couture designers are haunted by the prospect of a season when their ideas do not have customer appeal.

DESIGNING. Because so much of an apparel firm's success depends upon the styling of its line, the designing responsibility is rarely entrusted to a beginner, even a highly talented one. There are matters of cost and mass-production techniques involved, for example, and unless one is working in a couture house, there is also the business of judging accurately the point in the fashion cycle at which the firm's customers will buy.

For moderate-priced and mass-market producers, the designer's job may be one of adapting rather than creating. Immense skill may be required, nevertheless, to take a daringly original couture idea and modify it so that it appears bright and new but not terrifyingly unfamiliar to a mass-market or middle-income customer.

The beginner, aside from offering designs on a free-lance basis, can seek a number of jobs below the designer level in hopes of working up to that top level. Entry-level design jobs are:

- *Assistant Designer* As a member of a large designing team, the assistant works under a head designer. Designing talent, indicated by submitted samples and good technical knowledge, are expected so that the assistant can help the designer in every aspect of the latter's job. Also highly desirable are a good disposition and the ability to accept and learn from criticism. In the tensions and frustrations that surround a head designer's job, corrections and suggestions may not always be made with utmost tact.
- *Patternmaker* From the designer's sketch or sample, a pattern is made from which a sample garment is cut. The sample is tested for fit and appearance, and adjustments or even a new pattern may be required. Once acceptable results have been achieved and production of the new style decided upon, the patternmaker grades the pattern, that is, makes up a separate pattern for each of the sizes in which the style will be produced. The need for patience and technical skill is obvious, and these should be coupled with an understanding of sketching, draping, construction, and good workmanship.
- *Sketcher* From the designer's rough drawings, working sketches may be made for the information of the sample maker and also for illustrations to be used in the showroom book. The showroom book includes fashion sketches of each style in a line, together with swatches of the materials used for each style illustrated.
- *Sample Maker* An all-around sewer is expected to construct a garment from a sketch or pattern. If it is to be modeled, the sample maker adjusts it to fit the designated model perfectly. The job of a sample maker is a particularly instructive one for future designers, since it provides training in the fundamentals of design, sketching, pattern making, and construction.[1]

ADVERTISING
AND PUBLICITY. An advertising manager, with possibly an assistant or two, may handle the advertising and publicity for an apparel manufacturer. Whether or not the firm is large

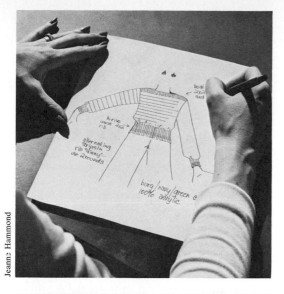

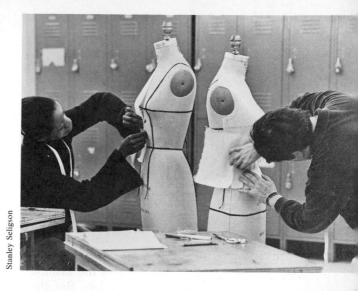

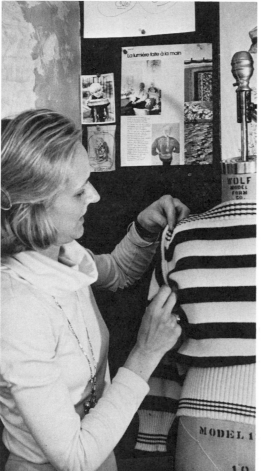

The apparel trades offer interesting careers in sketching, designing, patternmaking, and sample making.

enough to hire the services of an advertising agency (and most are not), there may be occasions on which ads are placed in cooperation with retailers or in cooperation with fiber and fabric sources. Publicity, usually a part of the advertising job, involves sending out press releases to interest consumer publications in some of the firm's new styles, and so on. Promotion kits for retailers are prepared under the direction of the advertising manager, as are statement enclosures and other direct-mail pieces offered for retail use. Aspiring assistants in this job have a distinct advantage if they have had enough retail advertising experience to be able to draw up rough layouts and suggest copy for store use.

SALES OPPORTUNITIES. The sales representatives who call upon retail stores should know the fashion points as well as the value points of their merchandise. Today, sales representatives are expected to be able to address retail salespeople, if invited to do so, or even to take part in consumer forums and clinics.

Showroom sales are sometimes handled by a junior sales representative who is awaiting the opportunity to cover a territory alone. At other times, a showroom assistant, with good disposition, good feet, and a good memory, is hired. The assistant is expected to greet customers, understand their requirements, show the line, and help them place orders.

An understanding of retail merchandising, promotion, and fashion coordination is extremely helpful in all sales jobs in the apparel field. When selling to retailers, it is important to understand their needs, problems, and methods of operation, as well as what stage of the fashion cycle is of major interest to their customers. With such a background, sales representatives can present a line more effectively and can also gather and develop sound retail merchandising and promotion ideas for their accounts.

Suppliers to the Apparel Trades

Belts, buttons, zippers, and other minor but necessary components of garments are produced and sold by companies that range in size from one-person operations to large national firms. A great deal of business with apparel producers is done by tiny firms that offer little opportunity to the outsider. Some of the larger producers, however, offer job opportunities in selling to the apparel trades or to retailers, working either for one firm or as a commission representative for several firms.

Fashion trends cause ups and downs for producers in this field, with consequent changes in selling opportunities. When fashion favors the industrial zipper, for example, no amount of sales ability is likely to create a market for delicate buttons or ruffling. When shifts are in, the most persuasive salespeople fail in their efforts to sell belts. In this field, a knowledge of fashion is important if producers are to know what products to offer and when to resign themselves to temporarily diminished sales prospects.

Sales representatives calling on the apparel trades should know, in addition to the fashion significance of what they offer, something about garment production, for the mechanics of production play an equally important part in a line's profitability as fashion does. Representatives calling on the retail trade usually find themselves selling to the notions department, whose buyer may not be strongly fashion-oriented. They must be especially skilled in presenting the fashion story of their wares, not only to the buyer but also to the salespeople. A notions department carries such a miscellaneous assortment of goods, from shoe polish to swim caps, that the fashion aspects of some of its assortment are often overlooked in sales training programs. The representative who can help the department on this point becomes doubly welcome.

Some of the larger producers of such items as buttons and zippers keep close track of fashion's impact on their business. It is not unusual for these firms to employ fashion experts who analyze trends to guide production toward the most salable types, sizes, and colors. The same expert also may have responsibilities in other areas such as publicity and promotion. In a large button firm, for example, the fashion expert may work out new and acceptable ways to use buttons to highlight the current fashion features of garments. These uses may then be publicized to apparel producers, notions departments, and to the press. Displays may be worked out that help retailers sell the company's buttons to the home-dressmaking customer. Such fashion specialist jobs are few in number, but they are fascinating for those who like widely varied activities. Entry is through the position of understudy or through acquiring sufficient fashion experience in other fields to be hired from the outside as a full-fledged expert or consultant.

Accessories Trades

For the artistic person, the designing of accessories is a huge field in which a talented beginner or an experienced free-lancer can find exciting creative opportunities. Many of the firms in the field are small; they depend upon free-lance designers to style their lines and upon their industry trade associations to promote and publicize their products.

A background in apparel fashions is necessary to design accessories that coordinate with the related garments. A knowledge of production procedures and problems is also essential, as designing for commercial purposes has to result in a practical as well as a fashionable style.

The larger firms and the large industries in the accessories field offer some positions that combine fashion coordination and publicity functions. Similar jobs also exist in some of the trade associations serving these industries. Those firms that do national advertising, such as the better-known makers of shoes, handbags, and hosiery, have advertising departments that work with agencies, and suggest or develop tie-ins for retailers.

Selling jobs require fashion knowledge. The sales representative or the showroom assistant who can give the retail buyer the fashion background of the merchandise has a natural advantage over the one who knows only quality and workmanship points.

A particularly interesting field of work is that associated with millinery syndicates, which are so close to their industry that they are almost a part of production. In these syndicates, the fashion staff works closely with both producers and retail stores, not only on millinery trends but on overall fashion trends and fashion coordination as well. Entry to these fashion staffs is usually gained as an assistant or as an already established expert from an allied field.

Jobs in the accessories field can lead to other fashion fields, too. One of the country's most successful fashion coordinators, who headed the coordination work at a major buying office for years, got her start as a stylist for a millinery syndicate. She won the syndicate job because she looked better in hats than other aspirants, but she succeeded because she brought to the job an excellent mind and sound training in fashion fundamentals.

Home Sewing Industry

The 40 million girls and women in this country who make clothes[2] are quite as fashion-conscious as those who buy ready-to-wear—and often more so. Some sew for the pleasure of it. Others sew in order to have garments of better quality than they could otherwise afford. Still others make their own clothes because their fashion ideas are a jump ahead of what they can find in the stores.

The industries that serve these home sewers include sewing machine companies, notions producers, pattern companies, and the over-the-counter divisions of fabric companies. All of these industries have learned—some of them the hard way—that fashion provides a stronger motivation for home dressmaking than either the economy or figure problems. All of these industries use stylists who can interpret fashion trends in terms of what the home sewer wants and can accomplish. Designers for the pattern companies are as much in step with fashion as those for apparel producers, but with an emphasis on finding ways to achieve currently important effects without taxing the skills of the average sewer or demanding too much time in the production of the garment.

The fashion staffs of industries serving women who make their own and their children's clothes have to learn the art of making instructions simple and clear. They work with photographers and sketchers to achieve illustrations that will show both how to make the garment and how the finished garment will look. Particularly in the fabric and pattern fields, members of fashion staffs have to be able to stage fashion shows for stores and give talks to consumers describing and illustrating how easily fashion can be created at home.

Working with schools and with schoolchildren is also vitally important, for if this effort is allowed to lapse, the industry may lose a generation of home sewers. Sewing was once learned at home, but many families have relinquished this training to the schools.

For those with designing ability, pattern companies offer jobs as assistants with the opportunity to work up. For those with a flair for fashion coordination, publicity, sales, or a combination of these, excellent career opportunities are offered by pattern companies, sewing machine companies, and some of the larger firms in the sewing notions field. Entry can be gained as an assistant or as an established expert in a related field.

CAREERS IN RETAILING

One of the best ways to begin a career in fashion is as a salesperson in a retail organization. Experience in selling to a customer is a must for all people interested in any career in the fashion field. For it is the salesperson who has direct contact with the customer, and in the fashion field it is the customer who is always right.

Every phase of retailing demands the ability to deal pleasantly with people—with customers, suppliers, and fellow workers alike. One of the earmarks of the successful buyer, merchandiser, or fashion coordinator is the ability to win the cooperation of subordinates as well as superiors. A much-admired and successful department store buyer was fond of saying that she was so fortunate in the cooperation she received from salespeople, publicity director, her fellow buyers, and others who worked with her, that she would do nothing to complicate their jobs. Her subordinates and her colleagues told the story differently: She was so thoughtful and considerate that there was nothing they would not do to help her.

Merchandising Careers

The starting place for most merchandising careers is in selling. Here one experiences face-to-face encounters with customers and the problem of anticipating what they will want.

From a selling job, the next move up the promotion ladder may be to head of stock. This is a position in which one may do some selling, but it mainly involves replenishing stock in the selling area from the stock room, reporting "outs," noticing and reporting slow sellers, and advising the buyer on unfilled customer wants. In branch stores, this position is usually handled by a department manager who acts as liaison between salespeople and buyer and who may be responsible for more than one related department. Both the head of stock in a large store and the department manager at a branch may do some of the more routine reordering, subject to the buyer's approval.

The assistant buyer's job is the next step upward. As an understudy to the buyer, the assistant buyer may be called in to view the line of a visiting sales representative and may be taken occasionally to the market on a buying trip. Usually, however, the assistant relieves the buyer of floor supervision, helps to train and supervise salespeople, processes branch questions and requests, and writes up reorders for basic stocks subject to the buyer's approval. The assistant buyer may verify prices on incoming merchandise, telephone resources in another city to expedite merchandise on order, verify advertising proofs, and post advertising tear sheets in the parent store department and dispatch other copies to the branches. The assistant buyer may also run meetings with salespeople on new merchandise or fashion or sales ability and schedule hours for sales and stock help.

Buyers are virtually in business for themselves, in the sense that they have to budget and plan their expenditures, select the actual merchandise for resale, and decide what is to be advertised or displayed and why. The job

Retailing offers absorbing careers in merchandising. The buyer "shops" the market, places orders in a manufacturer's showroom, and then sells the merchandise to a retail customer.

Jeanne Hammond

usually involves from two to a dozen or more market trips a year. The buyer must have the ability to teach and train subordinates and the ability to work well with advertising, display, personnel, and other divisions of the store.

In large stores, buyers of departments handling related merchandise are supervised by a divisional merchandise manager. Examples of related departments are: infants and children's wear, women's ready-to-wear, men's and boy's wear, and home furnishings. In smaller stores, the supervisor of all the store's buyers is usually called the general merchandise manager. In either case, this person is often either a former buyer or a graduate of a school of retailing or business administration, or both. He or she has sufficient knowledge of budgetary controls and principles of management to supervise buyers. The merchandise manager coordinates the efforts of a group of departments, with or without the aid of a fashion coordinator, so that the fashion picture each department presents to the public is related in theme, timing, and emphasis to those presented by the others.

The final rung on the merchandising career ladder is general merchandise manager, a top management position which demands, in addition to fashion and merchandising know-how, an understanding of every phase of store operation, from housekeeping to finances. To work from a selling position to a position responsible for policymaking is not impossible, but neither is it easy. A store may have hundreds or thousands of employees, but it has only a few people on its top management team.

For those interested in retailing as a career, well-qualified beginners may be recruited on college campuses or selected from among store employees who have demonstrated executive potential. For such people, large stores conduct formalized junior executive training programs. Total store orientation is provided through rotating job assignments in all phases of store operation and through regularly scheduled classes, usually conducted by heads of the various activities of the store. Those who successfully complete the training program qualify for junior executive positions, and they are assigned according to the talents and abilities they have shown during the training period.

The other way into large department and specialty stores is through their personnel departments, which interview, screen, and train desirable applicants 52 weeks of the year. A personal visit, with a preliminary mail contact if the store is in a distant city, is advisable. First, however, anyone interested in a retail merchandising career should examine a store's advertising, display, and merchandise before making an application; unless one feels at ease in a particular store, it might be wise to look to other retail establishments for employment opportunities.

Smaller stores are necessarily less formal in their interviewing, hiring, training, and promotion procedures. Openings are fewer, and advancement may come more slowly than in a larger store. In a small organization, however, there is little chance of being overlooked for promotion, and there is ample opportunity to learn every phase of store operation as part of each day's work.

As a general rule, those who enjoy administrative work and prefer to function within the framework of clearly defined responsibilities are well advised to investigate the larger retail organizations for the start of their careers. Those who enjoy a shirt-sleeves atmosphere, who are versatile, and who enjoy dealing with all kinds of challenges (from digging out after a snowstorm to working up a spectacular fashion display) will probably enjoy the variety of work in a smaller store.

Sales Promotion Careers

The career opportunities in sales promotion include jobs on the advertising staff, the publicity and public relations staff, and the display staff.

Copywriters and artists who begin in retailing usually enjoy a tremendous advantage ever afterward. If they leave the field and go into advertising agencies or go to work for producers, they carry with them an understanding of consumer reaction that can be learned in no better school than the retail store. There is something exciting about a

A fashion coordinator or fashion director often visits fabric resources to evaluate trends in colors and textures.

lineup of customers waiting for the store to open, telling a copywriter by their presence that the ad in last night's paper was good. Even if the merchandise offered was a real "doorbuster" special, the size and temper of the waiting crowd tell the copywriter just how effective the words were.

Publicity assignments usually grow out of copywriting jobs, although outsiders are sometimes hired for this work. Involved are such diverse activities as alerting the local press to newsworthy happenings, arranging for television interviews of visiting celebrities, and working up elaborate events—whether in the name of fashion, community, or charity— that will brighten the store image. Writing ability and the ability to handle contacts are important, but in a large store the ability to keep track of details is even more important. If a department store undertakes to stage a fashion show, the publicity person assigned to the event may be responsible for checking on invitations, press and broadcast coverage, notices posted outside the store, notification of all store personnel, and so on.

Display executives usually start as assistants with a willingness to work hard. They advance in position if they demonstrate artistic sense, a knowledge of fashion, the ability to speak in visual terms to the store's customers, and the ability to pick up important selling points about merchandise. Because there is a great deal of heavy physical work and after-hours work involved, many women have not entered this field in the past, although some have become display directors in smaller stores or have done excellent display work in jobs selling in or managing small shops.

Fashion Coordination Careers

Partly merchandising and partly promotion, the fashion coordination job is ideal for people who are extremely interested in fashion, know how to work with others, and are tireless. The job involves working with a great many people, from merchandise or fashion information resources to store staff to customers, and its goals are accomplished through recommendations and advice rather than direct orders. A store's fashion coordinator may have worked up through the merchandising or promotion staffs, or may have come into the store with sufficient outside experience in fashion to qualify as a store's top fashion authority.

The fashion coordinator's evaluation of a fashion trend or any aspect of it must be right, for he or she is making recommendations to experienced merchandisers who know their particular markets best. Each buyer is staking part of the budget on the coordinator's judgment when the recommendations are followed. Every ad that is written in line with these suggestions and every sales training session that is staged with the coordinator's help is done on the assumption that she or he knows how to read fashion's future. A beginner who has a chance to work as an assistant to such a fashion coordinator soon learns that intuition is no match for systematic checking and rechecking. A considered opinion arrived at by one fashion expert alone is not always as safe as a base for merchandising and promotion operations as the combined thinking of a store and a market full of expert watchers.

Sales-Supporting Careers

Retail stores have openings in fields not directly related to the buying, selling, and promoting of merchandise. These activities, which may involve more than half the employees of a store, include personnel, employment and training, accounting, customer services, and adjustments, among many others. Even in the rapidly growing area of data processing jobs, fashion knowledge can be a valuable asset. For instance, add a knowledge of fashion merchandising to an understanding of computer programming, and the result is the kind of background that can lead to a career in computer program design for fashion-oriented companies.

Of the many sales-supporting job opportunities, training is the field in which a fashion background is most likely to be of direct use. Large stores with well-staffed training departments sometimes assign one training executive to each merchandise division to assist buyers in training salespeople. A training ex-

ecutive assigned to a group of fashion departments, for instance, might compile a reference library of basic information on fashion merchandise and also collect and route current information on fashions. Another assignment might be setting up courses to teach salespeople and prospective buyers the basic elements of fashion, or devising contests and quizzes to keep salespeople alert or to encourage them to sell related items.

A background in fashion is extremely useful in this work, not only in the apparel and accessories departments but in any others that are part of the fashion business.

Chain and Mail-Order Careers

Chain and catalog firms offer careers that are similar to those offered by independent stores, with this important exception: Buying, merchandising, publicity, and fashion coordination are handled by the headquarters staff rather than by the individual stores.

Career advancement up the retail management ladder, if one starts in a unit of a chain or in a catalog organization, begins with selling and moves to department manager, merchandise manager, store manager, and finally to district, regional, or central management. Those interested in such fields as buying, fashion coordination, promotion, catalog preparation, merchandising, and quality control start as assistants in regional or central headquarters, where central buyers and merchandise managers are located.

Many highly specialized jobs in the chain and catalog companies call for intimate knowledge of the fashion business. For instance, the quality control department of one chain was called upon by the merchandising division to devise a size range for girls who fell between two size ranges currently offered by the children's market. The chain then made its new size range measurements available to any producers who wished to adopt them, whether or not they were resources of that chain.

Whatever special assets the beginner presents—apparel production techniques, laboratory know-how, or experience in copywriting, art, selling, buying, or coordination—the chain and the catalog companies can use them, but not always in the city or region where the applicant lives.

Resident Buying Office Careers

Fashion careers in resident buying offices center around market work. Market representatives "live" in their markets, see every line that is important (and many that are not), and know supply and delivery conditions in those markets as well as they know the fashion aspects of the merchandise. Market representatives also learn to work with any number of bosses: their own supervisors, the heads of the client stores, and the buyers in the stores they serve.

Entry into the market representative's job is through the position of apprentice. Beginners work as assistants, literally running errands in the market all day. If the smile, the ability to remember, or the arches are weak, the career may never develop. The major job of an assistant is to follow up on details, to check with resources on deliveries and other questions that may arise, and to spare the time of the market representative. In the process, the beginner gets to know the markets, the buying office routines, and the needs of the client stores. If the work is done against a background of fashion training, it is more easily mastered and promotion is apt to be more rapid.

Buying-office people demonstrate tremendous physical and mental stamina in attending showings, handling mail and telephone calls, and working with visiting buyers. But they have no selling departments to oversee, no branch stores to visit, no weekend or holiday work, and no sales goals to meet. Their responsibilities are limited to specific markets.

Fashion coordinators in buying offices must function with an especially sure touch. Any errors of judgment on their part can mean wrong advice given to a number of client stores. They tour the major market sources to collect information, check their findings with appropriate market representatives, and consider what fashion publications have to suggest.

A fashion coordinator for a resident buying office usually has a secretary and an assistant, at least one of whom is trained in fashion or sketching. In either job, a beginner with fashion training can quickly learn a great deal about fashion forecasting, markets, and coordination, knowledge of which is necessary in order to advance in the field.

Promotion staffs in resident buying offices are fairly small. In offices serving large stores, their function may be little more than reporting on what other stores are doing or what the New York stores are promoting. In offices serving small stores, they may draw up ads for the stores to use and send them out in the form of either rough layouts and copy suggestions or mats. The smaller the stores served by the office, the less likely it is that these stores will have full-fledged advertising departments and the more important it is for the buying office to supply them with such special assistance.

To find a place on the promotion staff of such an office, it is necessary for an applicant to have retail advertising experience or to show examples of how to prepare a retail ad. Sketching and a flair for layout are helpful; writing ability is essential.

It is possible eventually to establish one's own buying office, provided one starts small, with a few client specialty shops and a versatile staff. Specialty shops have fewer departments, and they need fewer—but very capable—market representatives than department stores need. The outlay in capital, office space, and staff is relatively small if one starts with only the fashion departments.

CAREERS IN FASHION SERVICE ORGANIZATIONS

A wide variety of job opportunities is available in the service organizations that aid and assist the wholesale and retail fashion industries. These service organizations, such as advertising and publicity agencies, consumer and trade publications, trade associations, and consulting firms, perform functions that have a show business quality about them. Work in these fields is hectic and, for those suited to it, fun. Each area has its own requirements, but

Ken Karp

Courtesy John Senger/Fashion Institute of Technology

A career in fashion advertising calls for a professional knowledge of the graphic arts as well as fashion flair.

in all of them there are important jobs in which an understanding of fashion is vital.

Advertising Agencies

Beginners, even those with special skills, often have a hard time entering the agency field. College graduates complain that they go to dozens of agencies and are offered nothing more exciting than a mail room or receptionist job. A solution to the beginner's problem may be to avoid the biggest and best-known agencies and seek a starting job in those of modest or small size. There the pay is likely to be small, the office tiny, and the future problematic, but the opportunities to work and learn are good and provide the experience necessary to qualify later for a good job in a major agency.

Among the careers in advertising agencies in which a fashion background can be useful are:

ACCOUNT EXECUTIVE. The man or woman who solicits accounts, who acts as liaison be-

tween client and agency staff, and who plans campaigns and calls upon the technical skills of the agency staff to develop them is known as an account executive.

COPYWRITER. These creative people are idea people, capable of originating campaign copy. Starting spot: copy cub. Top spot: copy chief.

ARTIST. Artists not only have creative talent and artistic ability but also understand the graphic arts, can specify type faces and sizes, and know the problems of reproducing material in various media. One starts with a skill and learns on the job.

FASHION COORDINATOR. Agencies handling fashion accounts need personnel to guide campaigns, assist in client contacts, and provide the fashion background that other specialized agency executives may lack. Even an agency that does not handle fashion accounts may have a fashion consultant on the staff to make sure that the figures in illustrations and television commercials are wearing currently acceptable apparel, accessories, and hairstyles.

OTHER POSSIBILITIES. Clerical, secretarial, and various technical jobs abound in large agencies and can offer the beginner a foothold. For example, the media department is a haven for those who understand statistics, since this department is responsible for measuring the worth of a publication's readership or broadcast station's audience in terms of cost and increased exposure of the client's product. The research department investigates available information to guide the client's marketing and advertising efforts and often does some related studies on its own. The traffic department follows up on production schedules and makes sure that deadlines for advertising insertions are met.

Essential for any agency job is the ability to work well under pressure. Agency people do not acknowledge the word "impossible" in meeting deadlines.

Consumer Publications

Nearly all consumer publications carry some sort of fashion material, and some are devoted exclusively to fashion. Career opportunities with such publications are immensely varied, ranging from editorial work to those numerous, behind-the-scenes activities that go into the publishing of a magazine or newspaper.

EDITORIAL. When fashion is presented in a publication, that publication's fashion judgment must be authoritative. Whether the publication is devoted entirely to fashion or whether it simply runs a fashion section, the editor's job is to discover what the reader responds to, locate those fashions in the market, and illustrate examples of them at the right time. The editorial job can be all the more complicated because of pressures from publicity-hungry producers. An editor may cover the entire fashion market or just one segment of it, depending on the type of publication and the size of the publication's staff.

Large fashion staffs generally can absorb a few inexperienced assistants. For small pay,

these people perform the necessary legwork in the market and do a thousand other chores. They learn how to select and how to work with models, photographers, and an art department. They learn how to cut down a lengthy description of a new style to a dozen words, if that is all the space allowed for a caption. Fashion know-how, the ability to meet deadlines, and the ability to work with people are vitally important—at times even more important than writing or sketching skills.

Small fashion staffs, such as those on newspapers in small cities, do no market work but depend on press releases that come from the wire services and from producers and local retailers of fashion merchandise. Spending time as a general assistant in such a fashion department, which may also cover society news and garden-club activities, is useful preparation for big-city, big-publication jobs.

MERCHANDISING. Behind the scenes, the merchandising editors of national publications and their staffs work to make sure that readers anywhere in the country can buy the merchandise that is featured editorially. They do this by reporting to retailers in advance of publication the details of what is to be run, why it is important, and from what resources it is available. With their formidable knowledge of markets, merchandise, and retailing, these editors are also well equipped to offer retailers practical suggestions about how to successfully merchandise, promote, and display the items featured in their publications.

Developing a following among retailers is good sales strategy for a magazine that sells advertising to producers. Therefore, the merchandising staffs must be extremely knowledgeable and often quite creative about retail promotion. Some work up storewide or divisional promotional ideas that stores—even large stores with their own capable promotional staffs—can use. A typical "package" for a store may begin with a theme that ties in with a forthcoming issue of the magazine. To promote the theme, the publication's staff suggests merchandise and resources for it, as well as advertising copy for various types of media. If the merchandise lends itself well to fashion shows or displays, the retailer may receive scripts, posters, display diagrams, and even the offer of an editor's services as a commentator. Many of the awards given by NRMA for outstanding retail fashion promotions are captured each year by just such packages developed by publications.

Merchandising staffs of consumer publications are usually large enough to absorb a beginner. Tirelessness and willingness to learn are essential; so is versatility. The beginner may be combing markets for weeks; then acting as host in a temporary showroom where future styles to be featured editorially are being shown to store buyers; then drafting copy for a suggested retail ad; then acting as liaison with outside experts hired to work up displays or the design of boutiques that have been suggested as part of a special promotion.

ADVERTISING SALES. Selling advertising space is the major source of revenue for a publication. The many aspects of selling accommodate various talents. Those who like selling deal with producers and their advertising agencies. People with a flair for research help the sales representatives to sell advertising space in the publication by supplying facts that indicate the ability of that publication to enlist retail cooperation or that measure the buying power of the publication's readers. Those with a flair for persuasive writing may find a place on the advertising promotion staffs, where presentations are developed to help the sales representatives conduct meetings with prospective advertisers.

Fashion background, sketching ability, and writing ability are aids to the beginner. Personality and contacts are vital in selling jobs, after one has become familiar enough with the publication to be entrusted with such assignments.

Trade Publications

Some trade publications are very narrowly specialized, such as *Handbags and Accessories* and *Hosiery and Underwear Review,* and are likely to be published monthly. Some are less specialized, such as *Retail Week*

and *Men's Wear,* and tend to be published semimonthly. A few, such as *Women's Wear Daily* (covering the women's apparel field) and *Daily News Record* (covering the menswear and textiles fields), provide in-depth coverage of a specific field and are published five days a week, Monday through Friday, except for holidays. All may offer opportunities for beginners with an interest in fashion.

Editors of trade publications spend part of their time in the market or investigating other sources of information and part of their time preparing material for publication. Assistants and secretaries to editors may be beginners learning how to make market calls, to select new products for illustration, and to write up what they have learned.

Trade publications hire beginners who are trained in publication procedures or journalism. Typing is indispensable, as is a durable smile for contacts with the trade and a good memory for names, places, and people. Knowing a particular industry is helpful, and knowing retailing even more so, because there is a regular need for articles for and about retailers. A good deal of rewriting is done from correspondents' reports and publicity releases.

Consulting Services

The most glamorous of the consulting services involved in the fashion field is, of course, the fashion consultant. Of these, the oldest and best known is the Tobé service, founded in 1927 by the late Tobé Coller Davis. As a young woman, she was hired to advise a retail store on its fashion merchandise by bringing the customers' point of view to bear on merchandise selections and promotions. From this start, she developed a syndicated service to which stores all over the country subscribed. With what is now a large staff, the firm continues to cover and interpret fashion news in such a way that buying, merchandising, and coordination executives can be guided by the views of skilled observers in every important fashion center. Reports, bulletins, clinics, and individual advice are the subscribers' diet.

Some of the other services, like Amos Parrish & Company, combine general advice on store operation with some fashion advice. Others exist primarily to make the skill of an expert in fashion promotion, such as Estelle Hamburger or Mildred Custin, available to interested stores. Still others, such as the Retail News Bureau, offer a wide range of consultant services that may involve any subject from merchandise resources to advertising results.

In approaching any enterprise of this kind, the beginner is wise to offer other qualifications in addition to a background in fashion: typing, writing or sketching ability, or some retail experience. Some of the "graduates" of these services have gone on to become fashion coordinators for major retailers, buying offices, or producers. The opportunities to learn are great if one has the stamina, ambition, and ability to work under pressure.

Some public relations and publicity consultants perform free-lance services in manufacturing and retailing. Writing skills, resourcefulness, and a knowledge of how to handle contacts of many kinds are basic requirements for job applicants to such firms. The beginner can enter as a secretary or copywriter to learn the techniques of getting product publicity and favorable mentions for client firms.

Television

Fashion-oriented specialists are beginning to find exciting careers in television. Many advertising agencies today engage outside companies to create fashion commercials for client producers or retailers.[3] The high cost of television time and production limits its appeal to retailers, but some make good use of television to present fashion. A fashion background alone is not sufficient to provide a beginner with an entry into this field. Some understanding of the technical aspects of the medium is vital.

Trade Associations

One of the more interesting areas of employment in the fashion field is trade association work. Industries, retailers, and professionals of all types form associations and hire executive staffs to do research, publicity, and public relations work. These associations also handle legislative contacts, run conventions, publish periodicals, run trade shows, or perform any other services members may require. Small or large, a trade association provides a great variety of work to its staff. Versatility is thus a paramount requirement. An assistant entering trade association work will find a background in the specific field served helpful, but the ability to communicate well is just as important.

The National Handbag Authority, EMBA (organized as the Eastern Mink Breeders Association and now nationwide), NAMSB (National Association of Men's Sportswear Buyers) and NRMA (National Retail Merchants Association) are only some of the many trade associations active in fashion or retailing fields. Other trade associations include local chambers of commerce, local and regional industry and merchants groups, and many others. Shopping centers have merchants' associations that employ promotion executives to keep the centers in the public eye. Producers in regional markets, like those in the New York and Los Angeles fashion markets, as well as traveling salespeople, sometimes form associations to establish and publicize seasonal market dates.

Each year, tens of thousands of people seek fashion-related jobs. Those who win those jobs and turn them into satisfying careers are those who have that very important asset: fashion know-how.

REFERENCES
[1] Brockman, *The Theory of Fashion Design,* p. 7.
[2] Brenner, *Careers and Opportunities in Fashion,* p. 25.
[3] Brenner, op. cit., p. 125.

CAREER OPPORTUNITIES

As a future graduate of a fashion merchandising curriculum, you should become aware of the many starting points in the field. You should be able to recognize and follow the career development opportunities and know their movement either horizontally or vertically within one industry, or within the fashion business since all merchandising activities are related and interdependent.

A. List the possible starting job opportunities that you will have upon graduation:
   1. in the fiber or fabric industry
   2. in fashion apparel or accessory manufacturing
   3. in retail stores (all types)
   4. in buying offices (all types)
   5. in advertising, promotion, or display

B. For each position listed, state what experience can be gained and then applied to another type and level of job in fashion merchandising.

C. List the possible advanced career opportunities in each of the areas listed above in A.

D. As a fashion buyer for the appropriate organizations considered, what greater opportunities are open to you?

E. Prepare a flow chart showing the possible jobs that would or could prepare an individual to advance from the beginning entry-level job to the position of a fashion buyer of a department in a large prestigious department store.

GLOSSARY

Adaptations   Designs that have all the dominant features of the style that inspired them but do not claim to be exact copies.

Advertising   The paid use of space or time in any medium. This includes newspapers, magazines, direct-mail pieces, shopping news bulletins, theatre programs, catalogs, bus cards, billboards, radio, and television.

Advertising credit   A mention of one or more store names in connection with the advertisement of a vendor, as being the retail source(s) for the merchandise advertised.

Advertising mat, matrix   A paperboard mold on which picture and/or copy are impressed and from which a plate can be made for reproduction in printed form.

Advertising plan   A projection of the advertising that a store intends to use during a specific period of time (such as a season, quarter, month, or week) in order to attract business.

Advertising request   A form prepared by a buyer stating when and where an ad is to appear and how much space is to be used. The form also requires a brief factual description of the style(s) selected for advertising and of what is important and exciting about the goods from the customer's standpoint.

Anticipation   An extra discount granted by some manufacturers for the prepayment of their invoices before the end of the cash discount period.

Apparel contractor   A firm whose sole function is to supply sewing services to the apparel industry.

Apparel jobber (manufacturing)   A firm that handles the designing, planning, and purchasing of materials, and usually the cutting, selling, and shipping of apparel, but does not handle the actual garment sewing.

Apparel manufacturer   A firm that performs all the operations required to produce a garment.

Assortment   See **Merchandise assortment**

Assortment display   A display created by showing, identifying, and pricing one of each of the styles currently in a section of the stock.

Assortment plan   A comprehensive and detailed listing of all items making up an assortment by type and price line.

Average gross sale   Net sales of a department divided by the number of sales transactions during the same period.

Balanced assortment   An assortment which types, quantities, and price lines of merchandise included in inventory during a given period of time are closely matched to the demand of target customers.

Basic stock   An item of merchandise that should always be kept in stock throughout a season or year because of consistent demand.

Best-selling price lines   Those limited number of price lines within an assortment that account for the greater share of the department's dollar and unit sales volume.

Boarding (hosiery)   A heat-setting process through which hosiery acquires permanent shape.

Book inventory   The dollar value of inventory that should be in stock at any given time, as indicated by the store's accounting records.

Boutique   A shop associated with few-of-a-kind merchandise, generally of very new or extreme styling, with an imaginative presentation of goods. French word for ''shop.''

Brand-line representative (cosmetics)   A trained cosmetician who advises customers in the selection and use of a specific brand of cosmetics, and handles the sales of that brand in a retail store.

Bridge jewelry department   A selling department handling merchandise ranging from costume to fine jewelry in price, materials, and newness of styling.

Buying motivation   Why people buy what they buy.

Buying on consignment   Placement of an order with the privilege of returning unsold goods by a specific date.

Buying plan   A general description of the types and quantities of merchandise a buyer expects to purchase for delivery within a specific period of time. Sets a limit on the amount of money to be spent.

Cash discount   The percentage or premium allowed by a manufacturer off an ivoice if payment is made within a certain specified period of time.

Caution   A fee charged for viewing a couture collection.

Caveat emptor   (pronounced ''ka ve at EMP tor'') Latin phrase meaning ''Let the buyer beware.''

Caveat venditor   (pronounced ''ka ve at VEN dee tor'') Latin phrase meaning ''Let the seller beware.''

Chain organization   A group of 12 or more centrally owned stores, each handling somewhat similar goods, which are merchandised and controlled from a central headquarters office (as defined by the Bureau of the Census).

Chambre syndicale (pronounced ''shahmb seen-dee-kahl'') A French elite couture trade association providing many services for the entire French fashion industry.

Charge-back A store's invoice for claims against and allowances made by a vendor.

Claim See **Charge-back**

Classic A style or design that satisfies a basic need and remains in general fashion acceptance for an extended period of time.

Classification An assortment of units or items of merchandise which are all reasonably substitutable for each other, regardless of who made the item, the material of which it is made, or the part of the store in which it is offered for sale.

Commissionaire (pronounced ''ko-me-see-ohn-air'') An independent retailers' service organization usually located in a major city of a foreign market area. It is roughly the foreign equivalent of an American resident buying office.

Confined style(s) Styles that a vendor agrees to sell to only one store in a given trading area. See **Exclusivity.**

Conglomerate A group of companies that may or may not be related in terms of product or marketing level but which are owned by a single parent organization.

Consignment selling An arrangement whereby a manufacturer places merchandise in a retail store for resale but permits any unused portion, together with payment for those garments that have been sold, to be returned to the wholesale source by a specified date.

Consumerism The efforts of consumers to promote their own interests.

Contemporary menswear A special type of styling that is often also referred to as ''updated,'' ''better,'' or ''young men's.'' Applies to all categories of male apparel and furnishings.

Contract or specification buying A ''development sample'' of an item is made up so that it can be copied or adapted for sale at a price more advantageous to producer and customer. This type of buying is commonly used by chain organizations and mail order firms and often in foreign buying, as well.

Contract tanneries Business firms that process hides and skins to the specifications of converters but are not involved in the sale of the finished product.

Contractors See **Apparel contractor**

Converter, leather Firms that buy hides and skins, farm out their processing to contract tanneries, and sell the finished product.

Converter, textiles A producer who buys fabrics in the greige, contracts to have them finished (dyed, bleached, printed, or subjected to other treatments) in plants specializing in each operation, and sells the finished goods.

Cooperative advertising Retail advertising, the costs of which are shared by a store and one or more producers on terms mutually agreed to.

Cosmetics Articles other than soap that are intended to be rubbed, poured, sprinkled, or sprayed on the person for purposes of cleansing, beautifying, promoting attractiveness, or altering the appearance (as defined by the Federal Trade Commission).

Costume jewelry Mass-produced jewelry made of plastic, wood, glass, brass, or other base metals, and set with simulated or nonprecious stones. Also called fashion jewelry.

Cotton A vegetable fiber from the boll (seed) of the cotton plant.

Couture house (pronounced ''ko-tour'') An apparel firm for which the designer creates original styles.

Couturier (male) or **couturiere** (female) (pronounced ''ko-tour-ee-ay'' and ''ko-tour-ee-air'') The proprietor or designer of a French couture house.

Coverage The maximum quantities to which each item's stock should be built after each regular stock count. Expressed either in terms of a certain number of weeks' supply, a specific number of units, or both.

Culmination (stage) See **Fashion cycle**

Customer demand Customer needs and wants for consumer goods.

Decline (stage) See **Fashion cycle**

Department store A store, as defined by the Bureau of the Census, that employs 25 or more people and sells general lines of merchandise in each of three categories: home furnishings, household linens, and dry goods (an old trade term meaning piece goods and sewing notions), and apparel and accessories for the entire family.

Design A specific version or variation of a style. In everyday usage, however, fashion producers and retailers refer to a design as a ''style,'' a ''style number,'' or simply a ''number.''

Details The individual elements that give a silhouette its form or shape. These include trimmings, skirt and pant length and width, and shoulder, waist, and sleeve treatment.

Direct expenses Those expenses incurred as a direct result of the operation of a specific department and that would cease if that department ceased to exist. Examples include costs of buying trips, advertising, and salaries of salespeople.

Discount store A departmentalized retail store using many self-service techniques to sell its goods. It operates usually at low profit margins, has a minimum annual volume of $500,000, and is at least 10,000 sq. ft. in size.

Discretionary income The money that an individual or family has to spend or save after buying such necessities as food, clothing, shelter, and basic transportation.

Display The impersonal, visual presentation of merchandise.

Disposable personal income The amount of money a person has left to spend or save after paying taxes. It is roughly equivalent to what an employee calls ''take-home pay'' and provides an approximation of the purchasing power of each consumer during any given year.

Dollar merchandise plan A budget or projection, in dollars, of the sales goals of a merchandise classification, a department, or an entire store for a specific future period of time, and the amount of stock required to achieve those sales.

Dollar open-to-buy See **Open-to-buy, dollar**

Downward-flow theory The theory of fashion adoption which maintains that to be identified as a true fashion, a style must first be adopted by people at the top of the social pyramid. The style then gradually wins acceptance at progressively lower social levels. Also called the ''trickle-down theory.''

Drop (menswear) Refers to the difference between the waist and chest measurements of a man's jacket. Designer suits are sized on a 7-inch drop; traditional suits are styled with a 6-inch drop.

Dual distribution A manufacturer's policy of selling goods at both wholesale and retail.

Economic ordering quantity (EOQ) When the stock for an item reaches a predetermined level, a reorder is automatically triggered.

Editorial credit The mention, in a magazine or newspaper, of a store name as a retail source for merchandise that is being editorially featured by the publication.

Environment The conditions under which we live that affect our lives and influence our actions.

Erogenous Sexually stimulating or newly exposed.

European look, menswear Features more fitted jackets that hug the body and have extremely square shoulders.

Exclusivity Allowing a store sole use within a given trading area of a style or styles. An important competitive retail weapon.

Eyeball control See **Visual control**

Fad A short-lived fashion that affects relatively few people within the total population.

Fashion A style that is accepted and used by the majority of a group at any one time.

Fashion coordination The function of analyzing fashion trends in order to insure that the fashion merchandise offered is appropriate in terms of style, quality, and appeal to the target customer.

Fashion coordinator A store's ranking fashion authority. Sometimes referred to as a fashion director.

Fashion cycle The rise, widespread popularity, and then decline in acceptance of a style. **Rise:** The acceptance of either a newly introduced design or its adaptations by an increasing number of consumers. **Culmination:** That period when a fashion is at the height of its popularity and use. The fashion then is in such demand that it can be mass-produced, mass-distributed, and sold at prices within the reach of most consumers. **Decline:** The decrease in consumer demand because of boredom resulting from widespread use of a fashion. **Obsolescence:** When disinterest has set in and a style can no longer be sold at any price.

Fashion forecasting A prediction of the trend of fashion as determined by the prevailing elements in all the fashion industries. Supplied by fashion coordinators as often and in as much detail as management requires—usually on a 6-month or seasonal basis.

Fashion image That aspect of a store's image that reflects the degree of fashion leadership the store strives to exercise and the stage of the fashion cycle that its assortments represent.

Fashion influential A person whose advice is sought by associates. An influential's adoption of a new style gives it prestige among a group.

Fashion innovator A person quicker than his or her associates to try out a new style.

Fashion jewelry See **Costume jewelry**

Fashion merchandising Refers to the planning required to have the right fashion-oriented merchandise at the right time, in the right quantities, and at the right prices for the target group(s) of customers.

Fashion merchandising policy A long-range guide for the fashion merchandising staff of a store, spelling out the store's fashion aims, standards of quality, price ranges, attitudes toward competition, and any other elements that may be considered pertinent.

Fashion retailing The business of buying fashion-oriented merchandise from a variety of resources and assembling it in convenient locations for resale to ultimate consumers.

Fashion theme The central subject chosen for a coordinated approach by specified fashion departments in their merchandise assortments.

Fashion trend The direction in which fashion is moving.

Fiber A hairlike unit of raw material from which yarn and, eventually, textile fabric is made.

Fine jewelry Jewelry made of such precious metals as gold and all members of the platinum family (palladium, rhodium, and iridium), which may be set with precious or semiprecious stones.

First cost The wholesale price of merchandise in the country of origin.

Flash sales reports Daily reports of sales, by department, developed from the unaudited sales checks and cash-register tapes for the previous business day.

Fords Styles that are widely copied at a variety of price lines.

Foundations The trade term for such women's undergarments as brassieres, girdles, panty-girdles, garter belts, and corselettes.

Franchise operation A contractual agreement in which a firm or individual buys the exclusive right to conduct a retail business within a specified trading area under a franchisor's registered or trademarked name.

Fur farming The breeding and raising of fur-bearing animals under controlled conditions.

Fusing A process in which various parts of a garment can be melded together under heat and pressure rather than stitched.

Gemstones Natural stones used in making jewelry. Precious stones include the diamond, emerald, ruby, sapphire, and real pearl. Semiprecious stones include the amethyst, garnet, opal, jade, cultured pearl.

General merchandise stores Retail stores which sell a number of lines of merchandise—apparel and accessories, furniture and home furnishings, household lines and drygoods, hardware, appliances, and smallwares, for example, under one roof. Stores included in this group are commonly known as mass-merchandisers, department stores, variety stores, general merchandise stores, or general stores.

General store An early form of retail store which carried a wide variety of mainly utilitarian consumer goods.

Going public Turning a privately-owned company into a public corporation and issuing stock for sale.

Graded Developed from a style's sample pattern; adjusted to meet the dimensional requirements of each size in which the style is to be made. Also referred to as "sloped."

Grade 6+ suit Man's suit that requires between 120 and 150 separate handtailoring operations and up to 15 hours of an experienced tailor's time for its production. Considered finest quality available.

Grade X suit Man's suit that can be produced in 90 minutes with only 90 stitching and pressing operations. An acceptable but lower-quality, high-volume suit made possible by recent technological advances.

Greige goods (pronounced "gray goods") Unfinished fabrics.

Gross margin The dollar difference between net sales for a period and the net cost of merchandise sold during that period.

Group purchase The purchasing from a given resource of identical merchandise by several stores at one time so that all participants may share in the advantages of a large-volume purchase.

Haute Couture (pronounced "oat-ko-tour") The French term literally meaning "fine sewing" but actually having much the same sense as our own term "high fashion."

Hides Animal skins that weigh over 25 pounds when shipped to a tannery.

High fashion Those styles or designs accepted by a limited group of fashion leaders—the elite among consumers—who are first to accept fashion change.

Horizontal-flow theory The theory of fashion adoption that holds that fashions move horizontally between groups on similar social levels rather than vertically from one level to another. Also called the "mass-market theory."

Horizontal integration Merging with or acquiring other firms that function at the same marketing level, such as the merger of two fabric producers or one retail store with another store or store group.

Hot items Items, new or otherwise, that have demonstrated greater customer acceptance than was anticipated.

Impulse items Items a customer buys on an impulse rather than as a result of planning.

Indirect expenses Those expenses that do not directly result from the operation of an individual department but are shared by all departments of a store, such as compensation of top management executives, utilities, maintenance, insurance, and receiving and marking expenses.

Inflation A substantial and continuing rise in the general price level.

Initial markup The difference between the delivered cost of merchandise and the retail price placed on it when it is first brought into stock.

Inside shops Garment factories owned and operated by menswear manufacturers who perform all the operations required to produce finished garments.

Institutional advertisement See **Prestige advertisement**

Intimate apparel The trade term for women's foundations, lingerie, and loungewear. Also called inner fashions, body fashions, or innerwear.

Irregulars Goods having defects that may affect appearance but not wear.

Item display A display featuring a single item or several versions of a single style.

Jobber A middleman who buys from manufacturers and sells to retailers. See also **Apparel jobber**.

Kips Animal skins weighing from 15 to 25 pounds when shipped to a tannery.

Knocked-off A trade term referring to the copying, at a lower price, of an item that has had good acceptance at higher prices.

Last (shoe) A wooden form in the shape of a foot over which shoes are built.

Leased department A department ostensibly operated by the store in which it is found but actually run by an outsider who pays a percentage of sales to the store as rent.

Let-out (furs) A cutting and re-sewing operation to make short skins into longer-length skins adequate for garment purposes.

Licensed trademark (fibers) A fiber's registered trademark used under a licensing agreement whereby use of the trademark is permitted only to those manufacturers whose end products pass established tests for their specific end use or application.

Licensing An arrangement whereby firms are given permission to produce and market merchandise in the name of a licensor, who is paid a percentage of sales for permitting his or her name to be used.

Licensing agreement A contract whereby the licensor usually agrees to pay the licensee a royalty for use of the licensee's name.

Line An assortment of new designs offered by manufacturers to their customers, usually on a seasonal basis.

Line-for-line copies These are exactly like the original designs except that they have been mass-produced in less expensive fabrics to standard size measurements.

Linen A vegetable fiber from the woody stalk of the flax plant.

Lingerie A general undergarment category that includes slips, petticoats, camisoles, panties of all types, nightgowns, and pajamas. Slips, petticoats, and panties are considered ''daywear,'' while nightgowns and pajamas are classified as ''sleepwear.''

Linters Very short fibers that remain on the seed of the cotton boll after ginning. Used mainly in the manufacture of rayon and for such non-fashion products as paper and absorbent cotton.

Long-run fashion A fashion that takes more seasons to complete its cycle than what might be considered its average life expectancy.

Loungewear The trade term for the intimate apparel category that includes robes, bed jackets, and housecoats.

Man-made fibers Fibers produced in chemical plants.

Manufacturer See **Apparel manufacturer**

Markdown The dollar difference between the previous price and the reduced price to which merchandise is marked.

Markdown percentage The dollar value of the net retail markdowns taken during a given period, divided by the dollar value of net sales for the same period.

Marker (apparel manufacturing) A long piece of paper upon which the pieces of the pattern of a garment in all its sizes are outlined and which is placed on top of many layers of material for cutting purposes.

Market (1) A group of potential customers. (2) The place or area in which buyers and sellers congregate.

Market representative A specialist who covers a narrow segment of the total market and makes information about it available to client stores.

Marketing The performance of business activities that directs the flow of goods from producers to consumers.

Marketing process The series of activities involved in converting raw materials into a form that can be used by ultimate consumers without further commercial processing.

Markup The difference between the wholesale cost and the retail price of merchandise (sometimes called ''markon'' by large retail stores).

Mass fashion Refers to those styles or designs that are widely accepted. Also called ''volume fashion.''

Mat See **Advertising mat, matrix**

Merchandise advertisement See **Promotional advertisement**

Merchandise assortment A collection of varied types of related merchandise, essentially intended for the same general end-use and usually grouped together in one selling area of a retail store. **Broad:** A merchandise assortment that includes many styles. **Deep:** A merchandise assortment that includes a comprehensive range of colors and sizes in each style. **Narrow:** A merchandise assortment that includes relatively few styles. **Shallow:** A merchandise assortment that contains only a few sizes and colors in each style.

Merchandising The planning required to have the right merchandise at the right time, in the right place, in the right quantities, and at the right price for specified target group(s) of consumers.

Merchandising policies Guidelines established by store management for merchandising executives to follow in order that the store organization may win the patronage of the specific target group(s) of customers it has chosen to serve.

Mom-and-Pop store A small store run by the proprietor with few or no hired assistants.

National brand A nationally advertised and distributed brand owned by a manufacturer or processor. Offers consistent guarantee of quality and fashion correctness.

Natural fibers Fibers derived from plant and/or animal sources.

Number, style number See **Design**

Obsolescence (stage) When distaste has set in and a style can no longer be sold at any price. See **Fashion cycle**

Off-shore production Domestic apparel producers who import goods either from their own plants operating in cheap, labor-rich foreign areas or through their long-term supply arrangements with foreign producers.

Open-to-buy, dollar The dollar value of planned purchases for a given period minus the dollar value of all orders scheduled for delivery during the same period but not yet received.

Open-to-buy, units The units of planned purchase for a given period minus the units on order for delivery during the same period but not yet received.

Operational satisfactions (customer) Those satisfactions derived from the physical performance of a product.

Organization chart A visual presentation of the manner in which a firm delegates responsibility and authority within its organization.

Outside shops See **Apparel contractor**

Over-the-counter selling Selected portions of stock are kept in display cases, shelves, or drawers, and salespeople are needed to take this merchandise out for customer inspection and to complete a sale.

Patronage motives (consumer) The reasons that induce consumers to patronize one store rather than another; why people buy where they do.

Pelt The skin of a fur-bearing animal.

Periodic stock count control A unit control system in which stock is counted and recorded at regular intervals and the results are used to compute sales for the intervening period.

Perpetual control A unit control system in which purchase orders, receipts of merchandise, and sales are recorded for individual style numbers as they occur, and stock on hand is computed.

Personal income The total or gross amount of income received from all sources by the population as a whole. It consists of wages, salaries, interest, and all other income for everyone in the country. (See also **Disposable personal income** and **Discretionary income.**)

Planned purchases The term used to indicate the amount of merchandise that can be brought into stock during a given period without exceeding the planned inventory for the end of that period.

Policy A settled, clearly defined course of action or method of doing business deemed necessary, expedient, or advantageous.

Precious stones Include the diamond, emerald, ruby, sapphire, and real, or oriental, pearl.

Pre-retail The practice of indicating on each purchase order the intended retail prices of all items being ordered.

Press release A written statement of news that has occurred or is about to occur, specifying the source of the information and the date after which its use is permissible.

Prestige advertisement An advertisement that ''sells'' the store as a good place to shop, rather than its specific merchandise. Also called ''institutional advertisement.''

Prêt-à-porter pronounced (''pret-ah-por-tay'') French term meaning ready-to-wear.

Price change form A special form required for reporting all upward or downward revisions in retail prices of merchandise in stock.

Price line A specific price point at which an assortment of merchandise is regularly offered for sale.

Price lining The practice of determining the various but limited number of retail prices at which a department's or store's assortments will be offered.

Price range The spread between the lowest and the highest price line at which merchandise is offered for sale.

Price zone A series of somewhat contiguous price lines that are likely to have major appeal to one particular segment of a store's or department's customers.

Prime resources Those producers from whom a department has consistently bought a substantial portion of its merchandise in past seasons.

Primary suppliers Producers of fibers, textile fabrics, finished leathers, and furs.

Prior stock report Reports that summarize information about the amount of stock still on hand in each of a number of prior seasons.

Private label or store brand Merchandise that meets standards specified by a retail organization and which belongs exclusively to it. Primarily used to insure consistent quality of product as well as to meet price competition.

Promotional or merchandise advertisement An advertisement that endeavors to create sales of specific items.

Prophetic styles Particularly interesting new styles that are still in the introductory phase of their fashion cycles.

Psychological satisfactions (consumer) Those derived from the consumer's social and psychological interpretation of the product and its performance.

Publicity The free and voluntary mention of a firm, brand, product, or person in some form of media.

Purchase or merchandise journal A monthly or semimonthly report listing all invoices for merchandise received, transfers of merchandise in and out, and returns to or claims against vendors that have been entered in a department's book inventory during a given period.

Purchase order A contract between a store and a vendor to purchase certain specified merchandise under certain specified conditions.

Purchasing power The value of a dollar as it relates to the amount of goods or services it will buy. A decline in purchasing power is caused by inflation.

Ready-to-wear (RTW) Apparel made in factories to standard size measurements.

Receiving apron A sequentially numbered form on which complete information about each shipment of merchandise received is recorded.

Regular tanneries Those companies that purchase and process hides and skins to the specifications of converters but are not involved in the sales of the finished product.

Release date The earliest date on which a publicity announcement can be made.

Reserve requisition control A form of periodic stock count control in which stock on the selling floor is considered sold and only the reserve stock is counted.

Resident buying office A service organization located in a major market area that provides market information and representation to its noncompeting client stores. **Associated:** One that is jointly owned and operated by a group of independently-owned stores. **Private:** One that is owned and operated by a single, out-of-town store organization and which performs market work exclusively for that store organization. **Salaried or Fee:** One that is independently owned and operated and charges the stores it represents for the work it does for them. **Syndicate:** One that is maintained by a parent organization which owns a group of stores and performs market work exclusively for those stores.

Resource Vendor, source of supply.

Retail method of inventory A method of inventory evaluation in which all transactions affecting the value of a store's or department's inventory (such as sales, purchases, markdowns, transfers, and returns-to-vendor) are recorded at retail values.

Retail reductions All reductions that occur in the retail value of the inventory, including merchandise markdowns, discounts allowed to employees and other special customers, and stock shortages.

Retailing The business of buying goods from a variety of resources and assembling these goods in convenient locations for resale to ultimate consumers.

Reticule A small drawstring bag introduced in the eighteenth century for carrying money and other small objects; forerunner of the modern handbag.

Return-to-vendor A store's invoice covering merchandise returned for cause to its vendor.

Rise (stage) The acceptance of either the original design or its adaptations by an increasng number of consumers. See **Fashion cycle**

Rubber-banding Cosmetic products that can be returned to the manufacturer and replaced with other products, if not sold within a specified period of time.

Sales promotion The coordination of advertising, display, publicity, and personal salesmanship in order to promote profitable sales.

Salon selling The most exacting type of personal selling: Little or no stock is exposed to the customer's view except that brought out for the customer's inspection by the salesperson.

Sample hand A designer's assistant who is an all-around sewer.

Season code A code indicating the month and season of receipt of merchandise. The code appears on the price ticket of an item and is used to determine how long the item has been in stock.

Seconds These are factory rejects having defects that may affect wear.

Section work The division of labor in apparel manufacturing whereby each sewing-machine operator sews only a certain section of the garment, such as a sleeve or hem.

Selection factors The various characteristics or components of an item of merchandise that influence a customer's decision to purchase.

Self-selection selling The method of selling in which merchandise is displayed and arranged so that customers can make at least a preliminary selection without the aid of a salesperson.

Self-service The method of selling in which customers make their selections from the goods on display and bring their purchases to a check-out counter where they make payment and their purchases are prepared for take-out.

Semi-precious stones Include the amethyst, garnet, opal, jade and other natural stones that are less rare and costly than precious stones.

Shop A small store or area within a large store that is stocked with merchandise for special end-use purposes; intended for customers with specialized interests.

Short run (apparel production) The production of a limited number of units of a particular item, fewer than would normally be considered an average number to produce.

Short-run fashion A fashion that takes fewer seasons to complete its cycle than what might be considered its average life expectancy.

Silhouette The overall outline or contour of a costume. Also frequently referred to as "shape" or "form."

Silk An animal fiber from the cocoons spun by silkworms.

Skins Animal skins that weigh 15 pounds or less when shipped to a tannery.

Sloped See **Graded**

Slop shops A name associated with the first shops offering men's ready-to-wear in this country. Garments lacked careful fit and detail work found in custom-tailored clothing of the period.

Specialty store A store that carries limited lines of apparel, accessories, or home furnishings (as defined by the Bureau of the Census). In the trade, retailers use the term to describe any apparel and/or accessories store that exhibits a degree of fashion awareness and carries goods for men, women, and/or children.

Specification buying See **Contract buying**

Spinerette A mechanical device through which a thick liquid base is forced to produce fibers of varying lengths.

Stock overage The condition existing when the physical inventory is greater than the book inventory.

Stock-sales ratio (monthly) The number of months that would be required to dispose of a beginning-of-the-month inventory at the rate at which sales are made in (or planned for) that month.

Stock shortage The condition existing when the book inventory is greater than the physical inventory.

Stock turnover The number of times that an average stock of merchandise (inventory) has been turned into sales during a given period.

Stockkeeping unit (SKU) A single or group of items of merchandise within a classification to which an identifying number is assigned and for which separate sales and stock records are kept.

Store image The character or personality that a store presents to the public.

Structured apparel Menswear garments whose construction involves many different hand-tailoring operations that give them a shape of their own when not being worn.

Style A characteristic or distinctive mode of presentation or conceptualization in a particular field. In apparel, style is the characteristic or distinctive appearance of a garment, the combination of features that makes it different from other garments.

Stylist Title given to persons employed to study consumer demand, who help buyers select and coordinate their assortment in line with this demand. Early title of fashion coordinator.

Sumptuary laws Laws regulating extravagance in dress, etc., on religious or moral grounds.

Sweatshop A garment manufacturing plant employing workers under unfair, unsanitary, and sometimes dangerous conditions.

Tailored clothing firms Those menswear firms that produce structured or semistructured suits, overcoats, topcoats, sport coats, and/or separate trousers in which a specific number of hand-tailoring operations are required.

Taking numbers Writing an adequate description of each style the buyer is considering for purchase, including style number, size range, available colors, fabric, wholesale price, and any other relevant details.

Tanning The process of transforming animal skins into leather.

Taste The recognition of what is and is not attractive and appropriate. Good taste in fashion means sensitivity not only to what is artistic but to these considerations as well.

Terms of sale The combination of allowable discounts on purchases and the time allowed for taking such discounts.

Textile fabric Cloth or material made from fibers by weaving, knitting, braiding, felting, crocheting, knotting, laminating, or bonding.

Textile converter See **Converter, textiles**

Texture The look and feel of material, woven or unwoven.

Trunk show A form of pre-testing that involves a producer's sending a representative to a store with samples of the current line, and exhibiting those samples to customers at scheduled, announced showings.

Unit control Systems for recording the number of units of merchandise bought, sold, in stock, and on order, and from which a variety of reports can be drawn.

Unit open-to-buy See **Open-to-buy, unit**

Unstructured apparel Menswear garments whose construction involves few if any hand-tailoring operations. A sports jacket, for example, often lacks padding, binding, and lining; it takes its shape in part from the person who wears it.

Upward-flow theory The theory of fashion adoption that holds that the young—particularly those of low-income families as well as those of higher income who adopt low-income lifestyles—are quicker than any other social group to create or adopt new and different fashions.

Variety store A store carrying a wide range of merchandise in a limited number of low or relatively low price lines.

Vendor One who sells goods to others; source of supply, resource.

Vertical integration The acquisition or merger of firms at different marketing levels, for example, a fiber mill with a fabric mill or a garment producer with a fabric producer.

Vignette A display showing a product or group of products in use.

Visual control A form of periodic stock count in which a rack or bin is assigned to each style, size, or classification, and a periodic visual check is made to see whether one of these bins or racks looks too empty or too full. Involves no use of records. Sometimes called "eyeball control."

Visual merchandising Everything visual that is done to, with, or for a product and its surroundings to encourage its sale. This includes display; print, broadcast, or film advertising; publicity; store layout; and store decor.

Volume fashion See **Mass fashion**

Want slip A form on which a salesperson reports a customer's request for something that is not in stock.

Wool An animal fiber from the hair of sheep.

Yarn A continuous thread formed by spinning or twisting fibers together.

BIBLIOGRAPHY

Alexander, Ron: "Shirt Makers: What's up Their Sleeves?" *New York Times*, January 8, 1980, p. B5.

American Marketing Association: "Report of the Definitions Committee," *Journal of Marketing*, October 1948.

"Apparel's Last Stand," *Business Week*, May 14, 1979, pp. 60–70

Arnold, Pauline, and Percival White: *Clothes and Cloth: America's Apparel Business*, Holiday House, Inc., New York, 1961.

Baccari, Michael: "Kids Wear Report Card," *Stores*, August 1979, pp. 11 ff.

Barmash, Isadore: *For the Good of the Company*, Grosset & Dunlap, New York, 1976.

Beaton, Cecil: *The Glass of Fashion*, Doubleday & Company, Inc., New York, 1954.

Bell, Quentin: *On Human Finery*, The Hogarth Press, Ltd., London, 1947.

Bender, Marilyn: *The Beautiful People*, Coward-McCann, New York, 1967.

Bennett-England, Rodney: *Dress Optional: The Revolution in Menswear*, Dufour Publishing Co., Chester Springs, Pa., 1968.

Binder, Pearl: *Muffs and Morals*, George G. Harrap & Co., Ltd., London, 1953.

Brenner, Barbara: *Careers and Opportunities in Fashion*, E. P. Dutton & Co., Inc., New York, 1964.

Brockman, Helen L.: *The Theory of Fashion Design*, John Wiley & Sons, Inc., New York, 1965.

Burke, John: *Advertising in the Marketplace*, 2d ed., McGraw-Hill Book Company, New York, 1980.

The Buyer's Manual, rev. ed., Merchandising Division, National Retail Merchants Association, New York, 1965.

Cash, Patrick R., ed.: *The Buyer's Manual*, rev. ed., Merchandising Division, National Retail Merchants Association, New York, 1979.

Calasibetta, Charlotte: *Fairchild's Dictionary of Fashion*, Fairchild Publications, Inc., New York, 1979.

Chaney, William: "Perspective and Position: A View of the Cosmetic Industry's Contribution," *Beauty/Fashion*, January 1979, pp. 48–51.

Cobrin, Harry A.: *The Men's Clothing Industry*, Fairchild Publications, Inc., New York, 1970.

Copeland, Melvin T.: *Principles of Merchandising*, A. W. Shaw Company, New York, 1924.

Corbman, Bernard P.: *Textiles: Fiber to Fabric*, 5th ed., McGraw-Hill Book Company, New York, 1975.

Cuccio, Angela: "Children's Budget Leaves the Basement," *Women's Wear Daily*, February 19, 1980, pp. 1, 24.

Cudliff, Edythe: *Furs*, Hawthorne Books, New York, 1978.

Cundiff, Edward W., and Richard R. Still: *Basic Marketing*, 2d ed., Prentice-Hall, Inc., Englewood Cliffs, N.J., 1971.

Dardis, Rachel: "The Power of Fashion," *Proceedings of the Twentieth Annual Conference, College Teachers of Textiles and Clothing, Eastern Region*, New York, 1966.

Daves, Jessica: *Ready-Made Miracle*, G. P. Putnam's Sons, New York, 1967.

Departmental Merchandising and Operating Results of 1978, Controllers' Congress, National Retail Merchants Association, New York, 1979.

"The Designer Syndrome," *Men's Wear*, January 28, 1980, p. 48.

"The Designer Licensing Phenomenon," *Earnshaw's*, September 1979, pp. 48–77.

Diamond, Jay, and Gerald Pintel: *Retail Buying*, 2d ed., Prentice-Hall, Englewood Cliffs, N. J. 1977.

Donovan, Carrie: "The Twenty-Two Top Talents," *The New York Times Magazine*, January 6, 1980. pp. 48–57.

Dorland, Wayne E.: *Fragrance and Flavor Industry*, MacNair-Dorland Co., New York, 1979.

Dorner, Jane: *Fashion in the Forties and Fifties*, Arlington House, New Rochelle, N.Y., 1975

Drew-Bear, Robert: *Mass Merchandising*, Fairchild Publications, Inc., New York, 1970.

Duncan, Delbert J., et al.: *Modern Retailing Management*, 9th ed., Richard D. Irwin, Homewood, Ill., 1977.

Dubbs, Edward S.: "NRMA's New MOR," *Stores*, October 1979, pp. 24–30.

Escobosa, Hector: "The Heartbeat of Retailing," *Readings in Modern Retailing*, National Retail Merchants Association, New York, 1969.

Ettorre, Barbara: "Businessmen and Buttonholes," *The New York Times*, October 28, 1979, pp. F1–F13.

_____: "The Dean of the Prep Look." *The New York Times*, April 27, 1980, p. F9.

_____: "Does 7th Avenue Need a Mart?" *The New York Times*, November 12, 1979, pp. D1–D3.

_____: "Stores Try Theatrical Selling Techniques," *The New York Times*, January 25, 1979, pp. D1–D4.

"Expanding Apparel Marts," *Ready-to-Wear*, Vol. 3, No. 10 (October 1979), p. 11.

"Eye" Column, *Women's Wear Daily*, September 9, 1973, p. 8.

Farnsworth, Clyde H. "Import Aid for Shoe Industry Weighed," *The New York Times*, January 26, 1980. pp. 27–34.

Fashion Group: *Your Future in the Beauty Business*, Rosen Press, New York, 1979.

"Fashion's New Regional Look," *Business Week*, November 6, 1978, pp. 187–188.

Feinberg, Samuel: "Imports Have Come a Long Way in a Half Century," *Women's Wear Daily*, October 3, 1978, p. 31.

Ferry, J. W.: *A History of the Department Store*, Macmillan & Co., New York, 1960.

Flügel, J. C.: *The Psychology of Clothes*, International Universities Press, New York, 1966.

Foley, Caroline: "Fashion," *Economic Journal* (London) 3:458, 1893.

Garland, Madge: *The Changing Form of Fashion*, Praeger Publishers, New York, 1971.

_____: *Fashion*, Penguin Books, Inc., Baltimore, Md., 1962.

Genders, Roy: *A History of Scent*. H. Hamilton, London, 1972.

Gillespie, Karen R.: "The Status of Women in Department and Specialty Stores: A Survey," *Journal of Retailing*, Vol 53, No. 4, Winter 1977–1978.

Gillespie, Karen R., and Joseph C. Hecht: *Retail Business Management*, 2d ed., McGraw-Hill Book Company, New York, 1977.

Gluck, Linda: "What's Happening to the Maternity Market," *Stores*, August 1978, pp. 33–36.

Gold, Annalee: *How to Sell Fashion*, 2d ed., Fairchild Publications, Inc., New York, 1978.

_____: *75 Years of Fashion*, Fairchild Publications, Inc., New York, 1975.

Golden, Jane: "Designer Brands: Phenoms Enter the '80s," *Men's Wear*, August 24, 1979, pp. 81–83.

_____: "Kid Status: Like Father/Like Son," *Children's Wear*, June 29, 1979, pp. 51–53.

Gore, Bud: *How to Sell the Whole Store as Fashion*, National Retail Merchants Association, New York, 1970

Greenwood, Kathryn Moore and Mary Fox Murphy: *Fashion Innovation and Marketing*, Macmillan Publishing Co, Inc., New York, 1978.

Hamburger, Estelle: *Fashion Business: It's All Yours*, Canfield Press, San Francisco, 1976.

Hanson, Kitty: "Special Seventh Avenue Report," *The Daily News*, May 4, 1980, pp. 1–8

Hayde, Jack: "Dual Distribution: Same Name-New Game," *Men's Wear*, April 13, 1979, pp. 56–58.

Herndon, Booton: *Satisfaction Guaranteed*, McGraw-Hill Book Company, 1972.

Hodden, John R.: "The Textile Economy—Another Drumbeat?" *Textile World*, January 1980, pp. 58–70.

Hollie, Pamela G.: "Los Angeles Luring Gem Trade," *The New York Times*, April 2, 1980, pp. D1–11.

Horn, Marilyn J.: *The Second Skin*, Houghton-Mifflin Co., Boston, 1968.

Hurlock, Elizabeth B.: *The Psychology of Dress*, Reprint of 1929 ed., Benjamin Bloom, New York.

Innes, Charlotte: "Apparel Exports: The Time is Ripe," *Knitting Times*, January 22, 1979, pp. 14–17.

Jabenis, Elaine: *The Fashion Director: What She Does and How to Be One*, John Wiley & Sons, Inc., New York, 1972.

Jarnow, Jeannette, and Beatrice Judelle: *Inside the Fashion Business*, 2d ed., John Wiley & Sons, Inc., New York, 1974.

Kelly, Katie: *The Wonderful World of Women's Wear Daily*, Saturday Review Press, New York, 1972.

King, Charles W.: "Fashion Adoption: A Rebuttal to the Trickle-Down Theory," *Proceedings of the Winter Conference,* American Marketing Association, New York, December 1963, pp. 108–125.

_____: "The Innovator in the Fashion Adoption Process," *Proceedings of the Winter Conference,* American Marketing Association, New York, December 1964, pp. 324–339.

King, Charles W., and Lawrence J. Ring: "Market Positioning Across Retail Fashion Institutions: A Comparative Analysis of Store Types," *Journal of Retailing, 56, No. 1,* Spring 1980, pp. 37–55.

King, Seth S.: "The Restoration of King Cotton," *The New York Times,* March 2, 1980, pp. C1–19.

Kleinfield, N. R.: "Jeffrey Banks Suits the Mood," *The New York Times Magazine,* March 2, 1980.

Kleppner, Otto, and Norman Govini: *Advertising Procedure,* 7th ed. Prentice-Hall, Inc., Englewood Cliffs, N.J., 1979.

Kornbluth, Jesse: "The Department Store as Theatre," *The New York Times Magazine,* April 29, 1979, pp. 30–48.

Kroeber, A. L.: "On the Principles of Order in Civilization as Exemplified by Change in Fashion," *American Anthropologist,* 21:235–263, July-September, 1919.

Kopkind, Andrew: "Dressing Up—Mysteries of Fashion Revealed," *Village Voice,* April 30, 1979, pp. 34–36.

Kybalová, Ludmila, et al.: *The Pictorial Encyclopedia of Fashion,* Crown Publishers, Inc., New York, 1968.

Laver, James: *The Concise History of Costume and Fashion,* Harry N. Abrams, Inc., New York, 1969.

_____: *Dandies,* Weidenfeld and Nicholson, Ltd., London, 1968.

_____: *Dress,* John Murray, Ltd., London, 1966.

_____: *Modesty in Dress,* Houghton Mifflin Co., Boston, 1969.

_____: *Taste and Fashion,* rev. ed., George G. Harrap & Co., Ltd., 1946.

Little, Co., Arthur D.: *Product Marketing,* January 1978.

MacSwiggen, Amelia E.: "Early Textile Mills," *The Town Crier,* Weed Publishers, Inc., Marblehead, Mass., April 14, 1965.

Mahoney, Tom, and Leonard Sloane: *The Great Merchants,* Harper, New York, 1974.

Mangan, Doreen: "Fur Is In!" *Stores,* March 1979, pp. 13–19.

_____: "Focus on Petites," *Stores,* April 1979, pp. 7–12.

_____: "Billion Dollar Baby? Furs!" *Stores,* March 1980, pp. 17–19.

Marcus, Stanley: *Quest for the Best,* Viking Press, New York, 1979.

Mason, J. Barry, and Morris L. Mayer: "Retail Merchandise Information Systems for the 1980s," *Journal of Retailing,* 56, No. 1, Spring 1980, pp. 56–76.

Mathisen, Marilyn: *Apparel and Accessories,* McGraw-Hill Book Company, New York, 1979.

McCarthy, Patrick: "YSL to Pay $7 Million for Rive Gauche," *Women's Wear Daily,* January 30, 1980, p. 27.

McClellan, Elisabeth: *History of American Costume,* Tudor Publishing Company, New York, 1969.

McGriff, Sylvia: "Fashion Seen Key Element for Success in the 80s," *Daily News Record,* November 11, 1979, pp. 10–12.

Morgan, Janet F.: "MW Consumer Poll: Boys' Wear," *Men's Wear,* May 1, 1979, pp. 9–10.

Morris, Bernadine: "Fashion Report," *The New York Times,* April 3, 1979, p. 8.

NRMA: *The Management of Fashion Merchandising —A Symposium,* Merchandising Division, National Retail Merchants Association, New York, 1977.

NRMA's Standard Classifications of Merchandise, 2d ed., Merchandising Division, National Retail Merchants Association, New York, 1969.

Nystrom, Paul H.: *Economics of Fashion,* The Ronald Press, New York, 1928.

_____: *Fashion Merchandising,* The Ronald Press, New York, 1932.

Ocko, Judy, and M. C. Rosenblum: *The Specialty Store and its Advertising,* National Retail Merchants Association, New York, 1976.

Packard, Sidney, Arthur Winter, and Nathan Axelrod: *Fashion Buying and Merchandising,* Fairchild Publications, Inc., New York, 1976.

Picken, Mary Brooks: *Fashion Dictionary,* Funk & Wagnalls, Inc., New York, 1973

Pierre, Clara: *Looking Good: The Liberation of Fashion,* Readers Digest Press, New York, 1976.

Readings in Modern Retailing, National Retail Merchants Association, New York, 1969.

Richardson, Jane, and A. L. Kroeber: "Three Centuries of Women's Dress Fashions: A Quantitative Analysis." *Anthropological Record,* 5(2), 1940.

Richert, G. Henry, et al.: *Retailing: Principles and Practices*, 6th ed., McGraw-Hill Book Company, 1974.

Robinson, Dwight E.: "The Economics of Fashion Demand," *The Quarterly Journal of Economics*, 75:376–398, August, 1961.

_____: "Fashion Theory and Product Design," *Harvard Business Review*, 36(6):126–138, November-December, 1958.

_____: "The Importance of Fashions in Taste to Business History: An Introductory Essay," *Business History Review*, 37(1,2):5–36, Spring/Summer, 1963.

_____: "The Rules of Fashion Cycles," *Harvard Business Review*, November-December, 1938, pp. 62–67, 113–117.

Robinson, O. Preston, Christine H. Robinson, and George H. Zeiss: *Successful Retail Salesmanship*, 3d ed., Prentice-Hall, Inc., Englewood Cliffs, N.J., 1961.

Rothman, Lynn: "Separates—New Tailored Separates Sales Spell Success," *F.I.R.E.*, February/March 1980.

Rubin, Leonard: *The World of Fashion: An Introduction*, Canfield Press, San Francisco, 1976.

Rudolfsky, Bernard: *The Unfashionable Human Body*. Doubleday & Company, Inc., New York, 1971.

Safire, William: "Words in Fashion," *The New York Times Magazine*, March 4, 1979, p. 9.

Sapir, Edward: "Fashion," *Encyclopedia of the Social Sciences*, Vol. VI, 1931, pp. 139–144.

Seidel, Leon E.: *Applied Textile Marketing*, W. R. C. Smith Publishing Co., Atlanta, Ga., 1971.

Seventy-five Years of Menswear Fashion: 1890–1965, Fairchild Publications, Inc., New York, 1965.

Sherman, Jerry, and Eric Hertz: *Woman Power in Textile and Apparel Sales*, Fairchild Publications, Inc., New York, 1979.

Simmel, George: "Fashion," *American Journal of Sociology*, 62:541–558, May 1957.

Smith, Liz: "Why We Wear What We Do," *New Woman*, March-April 1976, pp. 60–62.

Spaulding, Lewis A.: "In a Hot Streak?: Men's Wear," *Stores*, October 1979, pp. 48–52.

_____: "It's a Small World," *Stores*, June 1978, pp. 13–18.

Survey of Current Business, Office of Business Economics, U. S. Department of Commerce, Washington, D. C. Annual.

Tarde, Gabriel: *The Laws of Imitation*, Henry Holt and Company, New York, 1903.

Taylor, Charles G.: *Merchandise Assortment Planning*, Merchandising Division, National Retail Merchants Association, New York, 1970.

Taylor, John: *It's a Small, Medium, and Outsize World*, Hugh Evelyn, London, 1966.

Tokyo Women's and Children's Wear Manufacturer's Association: "Tokyo and Fashion," *Women's Wear Daily*, June 17, 1980, pp. 22–23.

"A Total Wardrobe for Petites," *Fashionnews*, February/March 1980, pp. 14–17.

Trachenberg, J. A.: "NY Petites Market to Offer Mixed Fare," *Women's Wear Daily*, April 2, 1980, p. 48.

Udell, Jon G.: "A New Approach to Consumer Motivation," *Journal of Retailing*, 40:6–10, Winter, 1964–65.

U. S. Industrial Outlook, Business and Defense Services Administration, U. S. Department of Commerce, Washington, D. C. Annual.

Veblen, Thorstein: *The Theory of the Leisure Class*, New American Library of World Literature, Inc., New York, 1963.

Wax, Judith: "Hold The Dressing," *The New York Times*, April 21, 1978, p. A27.

Webster's Seventh New Collegiate Dictionary, G. & C. Merriam Company, Springfield, Mass., 1963.

Weitz, John: *The Value of Nothing*, Stein and Day, Inc., New York, 1970.

Wingate, Isabel B.: *Fairchild's Dictionary of Textiles*, 6th ed., Fairchild Publications, New York, 1979.

Wingate, Isabel B., Karen R. Gillespie, and Betty G. Milgrom: *Know Your Merchandise*, 4th ed., McGraw-Hill Book Company, New York, 1975.

Wingate, John W.: "What's Wrong With the Planning of Stock Assortments," *New York Retailer*, October, 1959.

Wingate, John W., and Joseph S. Frielander: *The Management of Retail Buying*, 2d ed., Prentice-Hall, Inc., Englewood Cliffs, N.J., 1978.

Wingate, John W., Elmer O. Schaller, and F. Leonard Miller: *Retail Merchandise Management*, Prentice-Hall, Inc., Englewood Cliffs, N.J., 1972.

Winters, Arthur, and Stanley Goodman: *Fashion Sales Promotion*, 5th ed., Fairchild Publications, Inc., New York, 1980.

Wittkin, Herbert: "An Image Is a Multi-Faceted Thing," *Readings in Modern Retailing*, National Retail Merchants Association, New York, 1969.

Young, Agnes Brooke: *Recurring Cycles of Fashion: 1760–1937*, Harper & Brothers, New York, 1937. Reprinted by Cooper Square Publishers, Inc., New York, 1966.

INDEX